West's Law School Advisory Board

SCIENCE IN THE LAW

STANDARDS, STATISTICS AND RESEARCH ISSUES

By

David L. Faigman
University of California
Hastings College of the Law

David H. Kaye
Arizona State University
College of Law

Michael J. Saks
Arizona State University
College of Law

Joseph Sanders
University of Houston
Law Center

AMERICAN CASEBOOK SERIES®

WEST
GROUP

A THOMSON COMPANY

ST. PAUL, MINN., 2002

American Casebook Series, and the West Group symbol are registered trademarks used herein under license.

COPYRIGHT © 2002 By WEST GROUP
        610 Opperman Drive
        P.O. Box 64526
        St. Paul, MN 55164–0526
        1–800–328–9352

All Rights Reserved
Printed in the United States of America

ISBN 0–314–26287–3

TEXT IS PRINTED ON 10% POST CONSUMER RECYCLED PAPER

Preface

For the rational study of the law the black
letter man may be the man of the present, but
the man of the future is the man of statistics
and the master of economics.

— Oliver Wendell Holmes[1]

The intellectual life of the whole of western
society is increasingly being split into two
polar groups. . . . Literary intellectuals at one
pole — at the other scientists. . . . Between
the two a gulf of mutual incomprehension.

— C.P. Snow[2]

Judges and lawyers, in general, are not known for expertise in science and mathematics. Nor is science a subject given significant attention in American law schools. The reasons are manifold. Despite Justice Holmes' prescient and often-quoted statement, the legal profession has perceived little need for lawyers to have a grounding in the scientific method. Indeed, law students, as a group, seem peculiarly averse to math and science. The American educational system is partly at fault, for students routinely divide, or are divided, into two separate cultures early in their training. Students who display a talent in math and science typically pursue careers in medicine, engineering, biology, chemistry, computer science, and similar subjects. Students with less inclination toward quantitative analysis very often go to law school. It is perhaps not surprising that the student who excels in the humanities soon learns that the best job opportunities for a graduate in Nineteenth Century Russian Literature can be found through law school. Whatever its origins, the legal profession today is a particularly salient example of a literary culture that remains largely ignorant of scientific culture.

Increasingly, however, there are signs that a "third culture" is emerging in the law.[3] This third culture would be one that integrates a sophisticated understanding of science into legal decisionmaking. Perhaps the most visible sign of this emerging integration is the United States Supreme Court's decision

---

1. Oliver Wendell Holmes, Jr., *The Path of the Law,* 10 HARV. L. REV. 457, 469 (1897).
2. C.P. Snow, *The Two Cultures and the Scientific Revolution* 3 (Rede Lecture 1959).
3. Cf. JOHN BROCKMAN, THE THIRD CULTURE (1995) (chronicling the emergence of a "third culture" in society generally, through the increasing numbers of scientists writing for a general audience); STEVEN GOLDBERG, CULTURE CLASH: LAW AND SCIENCE IN AMERICA (1994) (exploring the many contexts in which law and science overlap in practice).

in *Daubert v. Merrell Dow Pharmaceuticals, Inc.*[4] The Court, for the first time in its history, considered the standard for evaluating the admissibility of scientific expert testimony. Briefly, the *Daubert* Court held that under the Federal Rules of Evidence, trial court judges must act as "gatekeepers," and evaluate the validity of the basis for proffered scientific expertise before permitting the expert to testify. In two subsequent cases – *General Electric Co. v. Joiner*[5] and *Kumho Tire Ltd. v. Carmichael*[6] – the Court further explicated the obligations that this gatekeeping role demands. These obligations were codified in the Federal Rules of Evidence in 2000. Moreover, states have increasingly followed the Supreme Court's lead, with many adopting *Daubert* outright, and still others incorporating the insights of *Daubert's* validity standard into their preexisting tests for admission of expert testimony.

Application of the *Daubert* standard requires an understanding of scientific research. Whether the Court intended to change the way the law responds to scientific evidence, or had more modest expectations, is impossible to know. Without doubt, however, the many judges, lawyers and scholars who have written on the decision have discovered a revolution of sorts. This revolution is one of perspective, and it affects profoundly not only the judges who guard the gate, but also the lawyers who seek to enter through it.

Until *Daubert,* courts had applied a variety of tests, with most courts being deferential to the scientists in their respective fields of expertise. This role was most closely associated with the general acceptance test articulated in *Frye v. United States.*[7] *Frye* instructed judges to admit scientific evidence only after it had achieved general acceptance in its field. The *Daubert* Court, in contrast, found that the Federal Rules of Evidence require judges themselves to determine the scientific validity of the basis for expert testimony. The shift in perspective is subtle yet profound. Whereas *Frye* required judges to survey the pertinent field to assess the validity of the proffered scientific evidence, *Daubert* calls upon judges to assess the merits of the scientific research supporting an expert's opinion. Implicitly, as well, the *Daubert* standard contemplates that lawyers will have sufficient expertise to explain the science to judges when they make admissibility arguments. The *Daubert* perspective immediately raised the spectre, as Chief Justice Rehnquist decried it, of judges assuming the role of "amateur scientists."[8] The gatekeeping role, he feared, was one most judges were ill-suited to fill.

Daubert has not come to mean that judges must be trained as scientists to carry out admissibility decisions. No one expects judges to join physicists soon in the search for grand unified theories.[9] But there is considerable space between being a trained scientist and being ignorant of science. Although *Daubert* does not expect judges and lawyers to be scientists, it does expect them to be sophisticated consumers of science. This book was formulated with that goal in mind. It is intended to introduce students to the rigors and details

---

4. 509 U.S. 579, 113 S.Ct. 2786, 125 L.Ed.2d 469 (1993).

5. 522 U.S. 136, 118 S.Ct. 512, 139 L.Ed.2d 508 (1997).

6. 526 U.S. 137, 119 S.Ct. 1167, 143 L.Ed.2d 238 (1999).

7. 293 F. 1013 (D.C. Cir. 1923).

8. 113 S.Ct. at 2800 (Rehnquist, C.J., concurring in part and dissenting in part).

9. See generally STEVEN WEINBERG, DREAMS OF A FINAL THEORY: THE SEARCH FOR THE FUNDAMENTAL LAWS OF NATURE (1992).

underlying scientific expert testimony. This book offers an entry point to a host of scientific fields that are highly relevant to the law. It is not intended to provide simple "answers" or final "conclusions." Instead, it is designed and organized to acquaint aspiring lawyers with scientific fields that will be crucial to their practices.

This volume is part of a special student edition of a much larger work intended for a professional audience, our four volume treatise, MODERN SCIENTIFIC EVIDENCE: THE LAW AND SCIENCE OF EXPERT TESTIMONY (2d ed. 2002). There are three volumes in the student edition. The first volume, *Standards, Statistics and Research Issues*, concentrates on the background issues in both law and science that lie behind the sundry contexts in which experts are employed. The second volume, *Social and Behavioral Science Issues*, is organized around substantive topics in the social and behavioral sciences. The third volume, *Forensic Science Issues*, concentrates on an array of important forensic subjects. We hope that the three volumes will be of service either standing alone or as companions to regular texts in a variety of classes, ranging from social science in law to forensic science classes. More fundamentally, we hope that the process of educating lawyers and judges regarding the scientific method will begin in law school. If *Daubert* stands for the proposition that judges and lawyers must henceforth understand science well enough to integrate it successfully into the law, then the educational process that will allow this to occur must begin in law school.

The chapters follow one of two formats. Several chapters provide general overviews of the subject. Most chapters, however, are divided into two sections, one dedicated to the legal relevance of the particular field and the second concerned with the state of the art of the research in that field. The first section is authored by the editors and the second is authored by one or more eminent scientists. The sections on the state of the science are all written largely following a similar organizational scheme. We asked the contributors to discuss the scientific questions or hypotheses posited by the researchers, the methods brought to bear to study these hypotheses, the areas of scientific agreement, the areas of scientific disagreement, and the likely future directions for scientific research in the area. Some scientific topics lend themselves to this scheme better than others. Nonetheless, our guiding objective was to make the science accessible to the non-scientifically trained generalist.

Daubert, perhaps, represents nothing more, *or less,* than that the legal culture must assimilate the scientific culture. As compared to the sciences, the law obviously has different objectives, values, and time tables in which to work. The law should not, nor could it, adopt the scientific perspective wholly and without qualifications. Science is merely a tool that the law can and must use to achieve its own objectives. Science cannot dictate what is fair and just. We can confidently conclude, however, that science has become, and will forever more be, a tool upon which the law must sometimes rely to do justice.

David L. Faigman
David H. Kaye
Michael J. Saks
Joseph Sanders

February, 2002.

*

Acknowledgments

At the conclusion of THE ADVENTURES OF HUCKLEBERRY FINN, Huck states, ". . . and so there ain't nothing more to write about, and I am rotten glad of it, because if I'd a knowed what a trouble it was to make a book I wouldn't a tackled it and ain't agoing to no more."[1] We, perhaps, suffer Huck's lament more than he, for he never knew the pain of periodic supplements, as are planned for these volumes. However, we have had the immeasurable assistance of a score of colleagues and students who have made our task less trouble. We wish to thank all of the people who contributed so much to both the first and second editions.

At the University of California, Hastings College of the Law, we wish to thank our colleagues Mary Kay Kane, William Schwarzer, Roger Park, and Eileen Scallen for their support, encouragement and comments on various parts of this book. In addition, much is owed the student research assistants who spent innumerable hours on the project, including Tamara Costa, Kathryn Davis, Jamie Tenero, Paula Quintiliani, Amy Wright, Ali Graham, Cliff Hong, Lucia Sciaraffa, Faith Wolinsky and Sara Zalkin. Finally, we owe a considerable debt to Ted Jang and, especially, Barbara Topchov for secretarial support.

At Arizona State University, College of Law, we thank Gail Geer, Sonja Quinones and Rosalind Pearlman for secretarial support and Vivian Chang and James Pack for research assistance.

At the University of Iowa, College of Law, we thank research assistants "Max" Wilkinson, Alec Hillbo, and Patricia Fowler.

At the University of Houston Law Center, we wish to thank the students in the Spring 1996 Scientific Evidence seminar who did much in assisting on the toxic tort sections of the of the first edition: Angela Beavers, Chris Blanton, Armi Easterby, Nellie Fisher, Stephanie Hall, Jim Hildebrandt, Lynn Huston, Preston Hutson, Dino Ioannides, Candice Kaiser, Bill Long, Helen O'Conor, Ruth Piller, Larry Pinsky, John Powell, Jane Starnes, Donna Woodruff, and Kirk Worley. On the second edition, we extend our grateful appreciation to the research assistance of William Campbell, Mary Chapman, Alison Chein, Cynthia DeLaughter, Linda Garza, Linda Glover, Jamie Liner, Laura Moore, Jason Pinkall, Scott Provinse, Amanda Snowden and Angela Williams. Special thanks goes to Bethany Fitch who helped to cite check and proof read the manuscript.

Outside of our respective home institutions, we have had the generous assistance of many colleagues and institutions. At the Federal Judicial Center, we wish to thank Joe Cecil for his support and encouragement of this project. We are also indebted to Bert Black, for both his assistance in identifying authors and his generous sharing of ideas on a variety of topics.

*

---

[1] MARK TWAIN, ADVENTURES OF HUCKLEBERRY FINN 363 (Random House 1996).

List of Contributors

Edith D. Balbach is a postdoctoral fellow at the Institute for Health Policy Studies, University of California at San Francisco, where she studies issues related to youth and tobacco.

Alfred A. Biasotti (1926–1997), M.S. in Criminalistics, U.C. Berkeley, was a criminalist, supervising criminalist, and administrator from 1951 to 1990, retiring as Assistant Chief of the Bureau of Forensic Sciences, California Department of Justice. He helped establish the California Criminalistics Institute; authored numerous articles on firearms and toolmark identification; was a Fellow of the American Academy of Forensic Sciences; and a distinguished member of the Association of Firearm and Toolmark Examiners. He passed away on June 24, 1997, from complications associated with Parkinson's Disease.

Stuart Bondurant received his B.S. in Medicine and his M.D. from Duke University. He interned and completed his residency in Internal Medicine at Duke University Medical Center and the Peter Bent Brigham Hospital in Boston. He served in the United States Air Force as a research internist and chief medical officer in the Acceleration Section of the Aeromedical Laboratory at Wright–Patterson Air Force Base. Dr. Bondurant was a member of the faculty of the School of Medicine at Indiana University Medical Center and was Chief of the Medical Branch of the Artificial Heart–Myocardial Infarction Program at the National Heart Institute. Dr. Bondurant was also Professor and Chair of the Department of Medicine prior to serving as President and Dean of Albany Medical College in Albany, New York. In 1979 he became Professor of Medicine and Dean of the School of Medicine of the University of North Carolina at Chapel Hill. In July 1994 he retired as Dean and on leave of absence from UNC-CH served as Director of the Center for Urban Epidemiologic Studies of the New York Academy of Medicine. He is currently Professor of Medicine and Dean Emeritus at the School of Medicine of the University of North Carolina at Chapel Hill. During his career, Dr. Bondurant has served as an officer of many organizations and societies including President of the American College of Physicians, the Association of American Physicians, and the American Clinical and Climatological Association, Acting President of the Institute of Medicine of the National Academy of Sciences, Vice President of the American Heart Association and of the American Society for Clinical Investigation, Chairman of the Board of the North Carolina Biotechnology Center, Chair of the Council of Deans of the Association of American Medical Colleges, and Chair of the Association of American Medical Colleges. From 1989 to 1995 he served as Chair of the North Carolina Governors Commission on the Reduction of Infant Mortality.

Dr. Bondurant has also served as advisor to the National Institutes of Health, the Veterans Administration, the Department of Defense, and the Department of Health and Human Services. He is a Master of the American College of Physicians, and a Fellow of the Royal College of Physicians of Edinburgh and of the Royal College of Physicians of London. He holds an Honorary Doctor of Science Degree from Indiana University, the Citizen Laureate Award of the Albany (New York) Foundation, and the 1998 Thomas Jefferson Award of the Faculty of the University of North Carolina. He received the David P. Rall Award of the Institute of Medicine of the National Academy of Sciences in 2000.

Eugene Borgida, Ph.D. is Professor of Psychology and Law at the University of Minnesota, Twin Cities. He is also a Morse–Alumni Distinguished Teaching Professor of Psychology. In addition, Borgida is Adjunct Professor of Political Science and serves as Co–Director of the University's Center for the Study of Political Psychology. He has served as Associate Dean of the College of Liberal Arts and as chair of the Psychology Department. Borgida is a Fellow of the APA and APS, and on the Board of Directors for APS and the Social Science Research Council. He has published on a variety of research issues in psychology and law and in social psychology, and his work has been funded by NIMH, NIH, and NSF.

Dr. C. Michael Bowers practices dentistry and law in Ventura, CA. He has been a Deputy Medical Examiner for the Ventura County Coroner's Office since 1988. He is a diplomate of the American Board of Forensic Odontology.

Robert M. Bray is the director of the Substance Abuse Epidemiology, Prevention, and Risk Assessment Program at Research Triangle Institute in Research Triangle Park, North Carolina, where he has been since 1980. Previously, he was a faculty member at the University of Kentucky. He holds B.S. and M.S. degrees in psychology from Brigham Young University and a Ph.D. in social psychology from the University of Illinois, Urbana–Champaign. He is a member of the American Psychological Association and the American Public Health Association. He served on the Committee on Drug Use in the Workplace for the National Research Council, Institute of Medicine. His recent work has focused on substance use epidemiology and related problems in military and civilian populations. He has directed the 1982, 1985, 1988, 1992, 1995, and 1998 Worldwide Surveys of Substance Use and Health Behaviors Among Military Personnel and is currently conducting the 2001 survey in the series. He also was coordinator of analytic reports for the 1988 and 1990 National Household Surveys on Drug Abuse (NHSDAs) and is currently directing the National Analytic Center, a project focused on analyzing data from the NHSDA and other substance abuse datasets. Dr. Bray directed the Washington, DC, Metropolitan Area Drug Study (DC*MADS), a 6-year comprehensive project of the prevalence, correlates, and consequences of drug abuse in household and nonhousehold populations (including people who are homeless or institutionalized, adult and juvenile offenders, clients entering treatment programs, and new mothers). He is the principal editor of a book, published by Sage Publications, based on findings from DC*MADS and titled DRUG USE IN METROPOLITAN AMERICA. Dr. Bray is co-editor of THE PSYCHOLOGY OF THE COURTROOM.

Diana Burgess, Ph.D. is a senior research associate in Strategic Growth Initiatives in the Consumer Insights division of General Mills. She has conducted research on sexual harassment, gender stereotyping and political participation. Currently, she is conducting organizational research on knowledge sharing and knowledge seeking within General Mills. She also is conducting pro bono research for the National Campaign to Prevent Teen Pregnancy.

Stephen J. Ceci, Ph.D., holds a lifetime endowed chair in developmental psychology at Cornell University. He studies the accuracy of children's courtroom testimony, and is the author of over 300 articles, books, and chapters. Ceci's honors include a Senior Fulbright–Hayes fellowship and a Research Career Scientist Award. In 1993 Ceci was named a Master Lecturer of the American Psychological Association. He is currently a member of seven editorial boards and a fellow of six divisions of the APA, and of the American Association of Applied and Preventive Psychology, British Psychological Society, and American Psychological Society. His book (co-written with Maggie Bruck) JEOPARDY IN THE COURTROOM: A SCIENTIFIC ANALYSIS OF CHILDREN'S TESTIMONY (1995) is an American Psychological Association bestseller and winner of the William James Book Award by APA. He is a senior scientific advisor to the Canadian Institute for Advanced Research. Ceci is a member of the National Academy of Sciences Committee on Behavioral, Cognitive, and Sensory Sciences, and a member of the American Psychological Society's Board of Directors. He is past president of Division 1 (General Psychology) of APA. In 2000 Ceci received the Lifetime Distinguished Contribution Award from the American Academy of Forensic Psychology.

Michael R. Chial is Professor of Audiology in the Department of Communicative Disorders at the University of Wisconsin–Madison. His doctorate is from the University of Wisconsin–Madison. For 20 years he has worked with the American National Standards Institute and is currently working with the Audio Engineering Society to develop technical standards for forensic applications of audio recordings. He is past associate editor of the JOURNAL OF SPEECH AND HEARING RESEARCH, and Fellow of the American Speech–Language–Hearing Association and the American Academy of Audiology.

Dennis J. Crouch is the interim director at the Center for Human Toxicology, University of Utah, where he has been employed since 1977. He is also a research assistant professor at the University of Utah's College of Pharmacy, Department of Pharmacology and Toxicology. He received a B.S. degree from Western Illinois University, Macomb, Illinois, in 1971; received graduate training at the University of Utah, 1980–1981 in biochemistry and pharmacology; and received a M.B.A. degree from Utah State University, Logan, Utah in 1989. From May 1990 through November 1991, he was at the National Institute on Drug Abuse. He was responsible for administrative aspects of the National Laboratory Certification Program for forensic laboratories and research on the impact of occupational drug testing on drug use patterns, transportation safety, and business. He is a member of the California Association of Toxicologists, Society of Forensic Toxicologists, and the International Association of Forensic Toxicologists, as well as a fellow of the American Academy of Forensic Sciences. Mr. Crouch has published over 50 peer-reviewed scientific articles on therapeutic drug monitoring, analytical toxicology, forensic toxicology, drugs and driving, and workplace drug testing. Current research interests include alcohol and other drug use in transportation safety, evaluating the impact of workplace testing programs on businesses, monitoring of laboratories performing workplace testing, GC/MS, LC/MS, and MS/MS analyses of drugs of abuse.

Russellyn S. Carruth is an Adjunct Professor of Law at the University of Pittsburgh School of Law, where she teaches in the environmental law clinic.

She practiced law with the firm of Burr, Pease & Kurtz in Anchorage, Alaska from 1974–1995. Her practice included toxic torts litigation, which involved issues of admissibility of scientific evidence. Since retiring from private practice, she has taught environmental law at the University of Medicine and Dentistry of New Jersey, School of Public Health, where she is an Adjunct Assistant Professor. She has written and spoken on legal/scientific issues, including the admissibility of scientific evidence in litigation. She serves on the Board of the Society of Risk Analysis Section on Risk Law. She received her B.A. degree from University of California at Berkeley in 1966 and J.D. from University of California at Davis in 1974.

Shari Diamond, a social psychologist and attorney, is a Professor of Law and Psychology at the Northwestern University School of Law and a Senior Research Fellow at the American Bar Foundation. She has practiced intellectual property law at Sidley & Austin. She was a member of the Panel on Evaluation of DNA Forensic Evidence and the Panel on Sentencing Research for the National Academy of Sciences. Professor Diamond was President of the American Psychological Association's Division of Psychology and Law, received the APA's Distinguished Contributions to Research in Public Policy Award, and was Editor of the LAW & SOCIETY REVIEW.

Patricia L. Dill completed her Master of Science degree in Social Psychology at Mississippi State University in 1997 and currently is a doctoral student in Health Psychology at University of Missouri–Kansas City. She also is currently a Health Communication Intern at the National Cancer Institute. Her research interests include prevention and intervention of alcohol use (particularly DUI offenders) and tobacco use, treatment of obesity, and health behavior, with a focus on community and public health interventions.

John P. Foreyt, Ph.D., received his Ph.D. in clinical psychology in 1969 from Florida State University and completed his clinical internship at the University of Southern California Medical School. He served on the faculty at Florida State University until 1974 when he moved to Baylor College of Medicine, Houston, Texas. He is currently Professor there in the Department of Medicine and Department of Psychiatry. He is the Director of the DeBakey Heart Center's Behavioral Medicine Research Center, Department of Medicine. He is a member of the Medical Scientist Staff, Internal Medicine Service, The Methodist Hospital, Houston, Texas. Dr. Foreyt is a Fellow of the Society of Behavioral Medicine, a Fellow of the Behavioral Therapy and Research Society, and a Fellow of the Academy of Behavioral Medicine Research and other professional organizations. He also is an honorary member of the American Dietetic Association. Dr. Foreyt is currently a member of the editorial boards of: *Eating Disorders, Obesity Research, Journal of Cardiopulmonary Rehabilitation, American Journal of Health Promotion, Journal of Behavioral Medicine, American Journal of Health Promotion,* and *Diabetes, Obesity and Metabolism*. Dr. Foreyt has published extensively in the areas of diet modification, cardiovascular risk reduction, eating disorders, and obesity. He has published 15 books and more than 230 articles in these areas.

Professor Patricia Frazier received her Ph.D. in Social Psychology and Counseling Psychology in 1988 from the University of Minnesota. She currently is an Associate Professor in the Counseling Psychology and Social Psychology programs at the University of Minnesota. Dr. Frazier is past Associate Editor of LAW AND HUMAN BEHAVIOR and past chair of the Courtwatch Committee of the Society for the Psychological Study of Social Issues. Her research interests include sexual victimization and the interface between psychology and the law, particularly the use of expert testimony in rape trials.

David A. Freedman is Professor of Statistics, University of California, Berkeley, California. He is the author of many works on probability theory and statistics, including a widely used elementary textbook. He is a member of the American Academy of Arts and Sciences.

Gary L. French is Senior Vice President and Director of Litigation and Regulation Practice with Nathan Associates Inc., Arlington, Virginia. He earned his Ph.D. in economics from the University of Houston and then taught economics, finance, and statistics as a member of the faculties at three universities.

James C. Garriott is a toxicology consultant in San Antonio, Texas. He holds a Ph.D. in Toxicology and Pharmacology, and is a diplomat of the American Board of Forensic Toxicology, Inc. He served as the chief toxicologist for Dallas County, Texas from 1970 to 1982, and then held the same position at Bexar County, Texas until retiring in 1997. He was also professor at the University of Texas Health Science Centers of Dallas and San Antonio. Dr. Garriott is the author of over 100 articles and book chapters in the toxicology literature, as well as co-author and editor of two toxicology reference books and is on the editorial review board of four toxicology and forensic journals. He is recognized for his knowledge and expertise in the forensic toxicology of ethyl alcohol, and he edited the text Medicolegal Aspects of Alcohol, now in its third edition. Dr. Garriott was the 1993 recipient of the Alexander O. Gettler award for outstanding achievements in analytical toxicology by the American Academy of Forensic Sciences.

David W. Gjertson, Ph.D., is Associate Professor of Biostatistics and Pathology, UCLA, and chair of the Parentage Testing Unit of the Standards Program Committee of the American Association of Blood Banks.

Stanton A. Glantz, a professor of medicine at the University of California at San Francisco and a member of the Institute faculty. He also served as a consultant to OSHA.

Bernard D. Goldstein is the Dean of the University of Pittsburgh's Graduate School of Public Health. He served as the Director of the Environmental and Occupational Health Sciences Institute, a joint program of Rutgers, The State University of New Jersey and the University of Medicine and Dentistry of New Jersey (UMDNJ)–Robert Wood Johnson Medical School from 1986–2001. He was the Chair of the Department of Environmental and Community Medicine, UMDNJ–Robert Wood Johnson Medical School from 1980–2001. He was the first Principal Investigator of the Consortium of Risk Evaluation with Stakeholder Participation (CRESP). Dr. Goldstein earned his B.S. degree at the University of Wisconsin in 1958 and his M.D. degree at New York University School of Medicine in 1962. He is a physician, board certified in Internal Medicine and Hematology; board certified in Toxicology. Dr. Goldstein's past activities include Member and Chairman of the NIH Toxicology Study Section and EPA's Clean Air Scientific Advisory Committee; Chair of the Institute of Medicine Committee on the Role of the Physician in Occupational and Environmental Medicine, the National Research Council Committees on Biomarkers in Environmental Health Research and Risk Assessment Methodology and the Industry Panel of the World Health Organization Commission on Health and Environment. He is a Member of the Institute of Medicine where he has chaired the Section on Public Health, Biostatistics, and Epidemiology and he has been a Member of the Institute of Medicine Committee on Environmental Justice: Research, Education, and Health Policy Needs. He is the author of over two hundred articles and book chapters related to environmental health sciences and to public policy.

Dr. Grant Harris is a Research Psychologist at the Mental Health Centre, Penetanguishene, Ontario, Canada. He is also an adjunct Associate Professor of Psychology at Queen's University, Kingston. He obtained a B.Sc. from the University of Toronto, and his Ph.D. in Experimental Psychology from McMaster University. He first worked at the Penetanguishene Mental Health Centre in 1974 and rejoined the staff in 1980. He was, for several years, responsible for the development and supervision of behavioral programs on maximum security units for dangerous and assaultive men. Since joining the Research Department in 1988, he has been awarded several research grants and has conducted extensive scientific research on violent and criminal behavior, psychopathy, and sexual aggression and deviance. He is (together with Vernon Quinsey, Marnie Rice and Catherine Cormier) an author of the recent book, *Violent Offenders: Appraising and Managing Risk* published by the American Psychological Association. In 1997, with colleagues from MHCP's Research Department, Dr. Harris received the Amethyst Award for Outstanding Achievement in the Ontario Public Service.

Patricia A. Hastings, Ph.D., York University, is currently on staff at DecisonQuest in Washington, D.C.

Kirk Heilbrun is Professor and Chair, Department of Clinical and Health Psychology, MCP Hahnemann University, and Lecturer in Law, Villanova Law School. He received his A.B. from Brown University in 1975 and his Ph.D. from the University of Texas at Austin in 1980. He is past-president of both the American Psychology–Law Society and the American Board of Forensic Psychology. He is the author of PRINCIPLES OF FORENSIC MENTAL HEALTH ASSESSMENT (forthcoming, Klumer/Plenum) as well as a number of articles in related areas.

Roger C. Herdman, born in Boston, MA, September 22, 1933; Phillips Exeter Academy, 1951; Yale University, Magna Cum Laude, Phi Beta Kappa, BS, 1955; Yale University School of Medicine, MD, 1958. Interned at the University of Minnesota. Medical Officer, US Navy, 1959–1961. Thereafter, completed a residency in pediatrics and continued with a medical fellowship in immunology/nephrology at Minnesota. Held positions of Assistant Professor and Professor of Pediatrics at the University of Minnesota and the Albany Medical College between 1966–1979. In 1969, appointed Director of the New York State Kidney Disease Institute in Albany. During 1969–1977 served as Deputy Commissioner of the New York State Department of Health responsible for research, departmental health care facilities and the Medicaid program at various times. In 1977, named New York State's Director of Public Health. From 1979 until joining the US Congress's Office of Technology Assessment (OTA) was a Vice President of the Memorial Sloan–Kettering Cancer Center in New York City. In 1983, named Assistant Director of OTA and then Acting Director and Director from January 1993–February 1996. After the closure of OTA, joined the National Academy of Sciences' Institute of Medicine as a Senior Scholar, directed studies on a national trust fund for graduate medical education, medical and ethical issues in organ transplantation, the safety of silicone breast implants, and the VA National Formulary. After completing those studies was appointed Director of the IOM's National Cancer Policy Board in August 2000. He also works on Institute relations with the U.S. Congress and chairs the National Academies' Institutional Review Board.

Professor Charles R. Honts is the Department Head and a Professor of Psychology at Boise State University and Editor of The Journal of Credibility Assessment and Witness Psychology. He is the recipient of grants from the U.S. Office of Naval Research and from the Royal Canadian Mounted Police to conduct research on the psychophysiological detection of deception. He is a Forensic Psychological Consultant to numerous public agencies in the United States in Canada. He has been a licensed polygraph examiner for 25 years.

Herbert Hovenkamp is the Ben V. & Dorothy Willie Professor of Law at the University of Iowa. He is the author of Federal Antitrust Policy: the Law of Competition and its Practice (1994), co-author of Antitrust Law (rev. ed.1995–1999), and many other works on anti-trust law, the law of property, legal history, and the history of law and science and law and economics.

James I. Hudson, M.D. is an Associate Professor of Psychiatry at Harvard Medical School and an Associate Psychiatrist at McLean Hospital, Belmont, Massachusetts. He is an author of more than 150 articles in the areas of eating disorders, fibromyalgia, psychopharmacology, the neurophysiology of sleep, and the issues of trauma and memory. He is currently engaged in studies of the genetic epidemiology of affective spectrum disorder, and of new medications for mood, anxiety and eating disorders.

Jennifer S. Hunt, Ph.D. is an Assistant Professor of Psychology at the University of Nebraska–Lincoln. Her research investigates the ways that preexisting expectations, including stereotypes, influence people's thoughts and behavior. Her current work is examining the effects of stereotypes on health judgments, as well as the influence of individuating information on stereotype activation. In addition, she is investigating how cultural variations in beliefs about the justice system affect legal participation.

Melissa L. Hyder is currently a doctoral student in the Interdisciplinary Ph.D. program in Clinical Health Psychology at the University of Missouri–Kansas City. She received her B.A. in Psychology from Rockhurst University in 1999. Her research interests include physical activity, sports medicine, and childrens' obesity and nutrition.

William G. Iacono, is Distinguished McKnight University Professor, Professor of Psychology, University of Minnesota, Director, Clinical Science and

Psychopathology Research Training Program, recipient of the American Psychological Association's Distinguished Scientific Award for an Early Career Contribution to Psychology, the Society for Psychophysiological Research's Distinguished Scientific Award for an Early Career Contribution to Psychophysiology, Past–President of the Society for Psychophysiological Research (1996–97) and former Member, Department of Defense Polygraph Institute's Curriculum and Research Guidance Committee.

Kristina Kelly is a doctoral candidate at the University of Minnesota, Twin Cities. Her research interests include the psychology of gender and the study of health judgment and decision-making. She is currently investigating how social and cultural factors affect women's behaviors and cognitions, and in particular, how these factors influence the ways that women explain their own behavior in health and non-health domains.

Raymond D. Kent is Professor of Speech Science in the Department of Communicative Disorders, University of Wisconsin–Madison. His doctorate is from University of Iowa and he did postdoctoral work in speech analysis and synthesis at the Massachusetts Institute of Technology. He has edited or written eleven books, including THE ACOUSTICAL ANALYSIS OF SPEECH (with Charles Read, 1992), and is past editor of the JOURNAL OF SPEECH AND HEARING RESEARCH. He holds an honorary doctorate from the University of Montreal Faculty of Medicine, is a Fellow of the Acoustical Society of America, the International Society of Phonetic Sciences, and the American Speech–Language–Hearing Association, and has earned Honors of the American Speech–Language–Hearing Association.

Professor John C. Kircher is an Associate Professor of Educational Psychology, University of Utah. He specializes in the use of computer, psychometric, and decision theoretic methods for assessing truth and deception from physiological recordings. He pioneered the development of the first computerized polygraph system and has collaborated with David C. Raskin and Charles R. Honts since 1977 on research and development of methods for the physiological detection of deception.

John J. Lentini is a fire investigator and chemist who manages the fire investigation division of Applied Technical Services of Marietta, Georgia. He is a fellow of the American Academy of Forensic Sciences and the American Board of Criminalistics, holds certificates from the National Association of Fire Investigators and the International Association of Arson Investigators. He chairs the ASTM Committee Responsible for developing forensic science standards, and is a principal member of the National Fire Protection Association's Technical Committee on Fire Investigations. Mr. Lentini has investigated more than 1500 fires, and analyzed more than 20,000 samples of fire debris.

Paul S. Lowengrub is a consulting economist and financial expert with Nathan Associates, Arlington, Virginia. He earned his Ph.D. in economics and finance from Arizona State University, and taught economic and finance courses for a year at The American Graduate School of International Management.

David T. Lykken is Professor of Psychology, University of Minnesota, author of A TREMOR IN THE BLOOD: USES AND ABUSES OF THE LIE DETECTOR, (2d ed. 1998), recipient of the American Psychological Association's Award for a *Distinguished Contribution to Psychology in the Public Interest* (1991) and for *Distinguished Scientific Contributions for Applications of Psychology* (2001), Past-President of the Society for Psychophysiological Research (1980–81), and recipient of that Society's *Award for Distinguished Scientific Contributions to Psychophysiology* (1998).

John Monahan, a clinical psychologist, holds the Doherty Chair in law at the University of Virginia, where he is also a Professor of Psychology and of Legal Medicine. He has been a Guggenheim Fellow, a Fellow at Harvard Law School and at the Center for Advanced Study in the Behavioral Sciences, and a Visiting Fellow at All Souls College, Oxford. He was the founding President of the American Psychological Association's Division of Psychology and Law and received an honorary doctorate in law from the City University of New York. Monahan has won the Isaac Ray Award of the American Psychiatric Association, has been elected to membership in the Institute of Medicine of the National Academy of Sciences, has been appointed to the Committee on Law and Justice of the National Research Council, and has directed the MacArthur Research Network on Mental Health and the Law. His work has been cited frequently by courts, including the California Supreme Court in *Tarasoff v. Regents* and the United States Supreme Court in *Barefoot v. Estelle*, in which he was referred to as "the leading thinker on the issue" of violence risk assessment.

Jeffrey W. Morris, M.D., Ph.D., is the former Director, Long Beach Genetics and Clinical Associate Professor of Pathology, University of California, Irvine. He serves as a member of the Parentage Testing Ancillary Committee, College of American Pathologists and is a past Chairman, Committee on Parentage Testing of the American Association of Blood Banks.

John E. Murdock, M.C. in Criminalistics, U.C. Berkeley, is a Senior Firearms and Toolmark Examiner with the Bureau of Alcohol, Tobacco, and Firearms, San Francisco Laboratory Center. Author of a number of articles on firearms and toolmark examination, he is past president of the California Association of Criminalists, an emeritus member of the American Society of Crime Laboratory Directors, and a distinguished member of the Association of Firearm and Toolmark Examiners.

Robert Nadon, Ph.D., is Associate Professor of Psychology at Brock University in St. Catharines, Ontario, Canada. Actively engaged in both research and teaching, Dr. Nadon has published extensively on hypnosis, with particular interest in personality and methodological issues. He is a Fellow of the Society for Clinical and Experimental Hypnosis, a past Research Fellow of the Canadian Social Sciences and Humanities Research Council, an Advisory Editor for the INTERNATIONAL JOURNAL OF CLINICAL AND EXPERIMENTAL HYPNOSIS, and a Consultant Editor, for CONTEMPORARY HYPNOSIS.

Michael Nash, Ph.D., is Associate Professor at the University of Tennessee and is actively engaged in clinical training, research, and teaching. He is Editor in Chief of the INTERNATIONAL JOURNAL OF CLINICAL AND EXPERIMENTAL HYPNOSIS, Past President of Division 30 of the American Psychological Association, Fellow of both the Society for Clinical and Experimental Hypnosis and the

American Psychological Association, and is a Diplomate of the American Board of Professional Psychology. Dr. Nash has published extensively on the effects of sexual abuse, short-term psychotherapy, and hypnosis. Dr. Nash is Co–Editor with Dr. Fromm of the classic text on experimental hypnosis, Contemporary Hypnosis Research, and his research and writing have earned him numerous awards.

Paul Oliva, B.A., M.A. is a former senior clinical research technician in the Biological Psychiatry Laboratory at McLean Hospital, Belmont, Massachusetts.

Joseph L. Peterson, D.Crim., is Professor of Criminal Justice at the University of Illinois at Chicago. His research has tracked the evolution of the forensic sciences over the past thirty years, focusing on the quality of results emanating from crime laboratories, ethical dilemmas facing scientists, and the impact of science on legal decision making. Previously, he served as Executive Director of the Forensic Sciences Foundation and directed the criminal justice research center at John Jay College of Criminal Justice in New York.

Henry Petroski, Ph.D., P.E., is Aleksandar S. Vesic Professor of Civil Engineering and Professor of History, Duke University, Durham, North Carolina.

Harrison G. Pope, Jr., M.D. is a Professor of Psychiatry at Harvard Medical School and Chief of the Biological Psychiatry Laboratory at the McLean Hospital Alcohol and Drug Abuse Research Center in Belmont, Massachusetts. He is an author of more than 300 published papers on a range of topics in psychiatry, including eating disorders, mood disorders, psychiatric diagnosis, substance abuse, psychopharmacology, and the current debate about trauma and memory. Dr. Pope currently devotes most of his time to research and teaching.

Walker S. Carlos Poston II, M.P.H., Ph.D. received his Ph.D. from the University of California-Santa Barbara and an M.P.H. from the University of Texas Houston Health Sciences Center. He is Co–Director of Behavioral Cardiology Research at the Mid America Heart Institute and Assistant Professor in the Clinical Health Psychology Interdisciplinary Ph.D. program at the University of Missouri–Kansas City. His research focuses on understanding genetic and environmental contributions to cardiovascular disease and obesity, particularly in minority populations. Dr. Poston has been the principal or co-investigator on several funded studies examining health outcomes in obesity treatment and the epidemiology of hypertension and obesity in African Americans. He has published nearly 80 articles and book chapters focusing on obesity and cardiovascular disease and has presented his work in national and international scientific forums. Dr. Poston is a fellow of the North American Association for the Study of Obesity and a member of the American Heart Association's Council on Epidemiology and Prevention and the Society of Behavioral Medicine.

Martine Powell, Ph.D. is a Senior Lecturer in the School of Psychology, Deakin University, Melbourne Australia. She has been conducting research in the area of child eyewitness memory, as well as training programs in investigative interviewing, for the past ten years. She has also trained and worked as a clinical psychologist, specializing in the treatment of child abuse and neglect.

Norman Poythress is a Professor in the Department of Mental Health Law & Policy, Florida Mental Health Institute, University of South Florida. He received his A.B. from Indiana University in 1969 and his Ph.D. from the University of Texas at Austin in 1977. He is past-president of the American Psychology–Law Society (Division 41 of the American Psychological Association). In 1990, he received the American Academy of Forensic Psychology's Award for Distinguished Contributions to Forensic Psychology. He is a coauthor of PSYCHOLOGICAL EVALUATIONS FOR THE COURTS: A HANDBOOK FOR MENTAL HEALTH PROFESSIONALS AND LAWYERS, as well as numerous articles on the interaction of mental illness and the criminal justice system.

Gabrielle F. Principe is a National Institute of Mental Health Postdoctoral Fellow at Cornell University. She was educated at Temple University and the University of North Carolina at Chapel Hill, where she received her doctorate in developmental psychology. Her research examines factors affecting the accuracy and retention of young children's memories for salient personal experiences.

Professor David C. Raskin is Professor Emeritus, University of Utah and Editor of Psychological Methods in Criminal Investigation and Evidence and Co–Editor of Electrodermal Activity in Psychological Research. He has been the recipient of numerous grants and contracts from the National Institute of Justice, U.S. Department of Defense, U.S. Secret Service, and U.S. Army Research and Development Command to conduct research and development on psychophysiological detection of deception. He was the Co–Developer of the first computerized polygraph system. He was Past President Rocky Mountain Psychological Association and is an Elected Fellow in the American Psychological Association, American Psychological Society, American Association for Applied and Preventive Psychology. He has served as a Forensic Psychological Consultant to numerous federal and local agencies and legislative bodies in the United States, Canada, Israel, United Kingdom, and Norway. He has been a licensed polygraph examiner for 27 years.

Dr. Marnie Rice is Director of Research of the Mental Health Centre, Penetanguishene, Ontario, Canada. She is Professor of Psychiatry and Behavioural Neurosciences at McMaster University, Associate Professor of Psychology at Queen's University, and Scientific Director of the Centre for the Study of Aggression and Mental Disorder. She has been awarded several research grants and has over eighty publications including three coauthored books on the topics of violent and criminal behavior, sex offenders, psychopaths and arson. Dr. Rice obtained her honours B.A. in Psychology from McMaster University; a Master's Degree from the University of Toronto; and a Ph.D. in Clinical Psychology from York University. She was the 1995 recipient of the American Psychological Association's award for Distinguished Contribution to Research in Public Policy, and the 1997 recipient of a Government of Ontario Amethyst Award for Outstanding Contribution by an Ontario Public Servant.

D. Michael Risinger is a Professor of Law at Seton Hall University School of Law; B.A. Magna Cum Laude, Yale University, 1966, J.D. Cum Laude, Harvard Law School, 1969.

Dr. Victor L. Roggli received a B.A. degree in Biochemistry and Environmental Engineering from Rice University in Houston Texas in 1973, and doctor of medicine degree from Baylor College of Medicine in 1976. He completed residency training in pathology at Baylor Affiliated Hospitals in 1980, and is board certified in Anatomic and Clinical Pathology. Dr. Roggli has published more than 120 articles in peer reviewed journals, approximately half of which deal with asbestos or asbestos-related diseases. He has also published 21 chapters in textbooks and is the author/editor of three books, including Pathology of Asbestos–Associated Diseases.

Daniel L. Rubinfeld is Robert L. Bridges Professor of Law and Professor of Economics at the University of California, Berkeley. He has been a fellow of the National Bureau of Economic Research, the Center for the Advanced Study in the Behavioral Sciences, and the Simon Guggenheim Foundation.

Sara Rzepa is a graduate student in the Psychology Department at York University in Toronto, Ontario, Canada. Her research interests include jury decision making and she is currently involved in research on jury decision making in trials involving battered women who have killed their abusers.

Regina A. Schuller, Ph.D. is Associate Professor of Psychology at York University in Toronto, Ontario, Canada. She is actively engaged in both research and teaching and in 1995 received York's President's Prize for Promising Scholars. Her research interests focus on the impact of social science framework testimony, in particular, expert testimony pertaining to battered women and on juror/jury decision processes. She also serves on the editorial board of LAW & HUMAN BEHAVIOR AND PSYCHOLOGY, PUBLIC POLICY, AND LAW.

George F. Sensabaugh, Jr., is Professor, School of Public Health, University of California at Berkeley. He was a member of the National Academy of Sciences' Committee on DNA Technology in Forensic Science and its subsequent Committee on DNA Forensic Science: An Update.

Christopher Slobogin is Stephen C. O'Connell Professor of Law at the University of Florida Levin College of Law, an affiliate professor with the Department of Psychiatry at the University of Florida, and an adjunct professor at the Florida Mental Health Institute, a department of the University of South Florida. Professor Slobogin received an A.B. from Princeton University, and a J.D. and LL.M. from the University of Virginia. He has served as chair of the American Association of Law Schools Section on Mental Disability and Law, Reporter for the American Bar Association's Standards on Criminal Responsibility, editor or reviewer for Behavioral Science & the Law, Law & Human Behavior, the American Journal of Psychiatry, and Psychology, Public Policy & Law, and as the Director of the University of Virginia's Forensic Psychiatry Clinic. He has authored a casebook and a treatise on mental health law, as well as numerous articles in the area.

John L. Solow is Associate Professor of Economics at The University of Iowa, where he has been a member of the faculty for over twenty years. He received his B.A. in economics from Yale University, and his M.A. and Ph.D. in economics from Stanford University.

Tomika N. Stevens is currently an advanced student in the Law–Psychology Program at Villanova Law School and MCP Hahnemann University, where she is a candidate for Juris Doctorate (2003) and Doctor of Philosophy, Clinical Psychology (2004). She received her A.B. from Princeton University in 1997.

David A. Stoney has a Ph.D. in Forensic Science from the University of California, Berkeley, where he worked on the statistical modeling of fingerprint identifications. He worked for six years at the Institute of Forensic Sciences, Criminalistics Laboratory, in California before joining the faculty of the University of Illinois at Chicago. After serving as Director of Forensic Sciences for eight years he left to become Director of the McCrone Research Institute in Chicago, a not-for-profit corporation dedicated to teaching and research in microscopy and microscopic analysis.

John Thornton, D.Crim., is an Emeritus Professor of Forensic Science at the University of California at Berkeley. He worked in an operational crime laboratory for 15 years and taught at Berkeley for 24 years. He also has taught forensic science in Colombia, Israel, Mexico, India, and the People's Republic of China. He is a past president of the California Association of Criminalists and past chairman of the Criminalistics Section of the American Academy of Forensic Sciences.

Dr. Lawrence M. Tierney, Jr. is a professor of medicine at the University of California at San Francisco. He received his M.D. From the University of Maryland in 1967, and did his residency in internal medicine at Emory University and the University of California at San Francisco. After two years in the U.S. Navy, he joined the faculty at the latter institution, where he is Professor of Medicine. He served as director of the residency training program as well of the third and fourth year medical student clerkships, and is also Associate Chief of the Medical Service at the San Francisco Veterans Affairs Medical Center. He has won over twenty major teaching awards, and has been invited on five separate occasions to address the UCSF medical school's graduating class. He is the senior editor of Current Medical Diagnosis and Treatment, a textbook in its 42nd edition, and has published numerous articles in medical journals, his principal interests being clinical decision-making, medical education, and evidence-based medicine.

Dr. Wartenberg received a Ph.D. degree in Ecology and Evolution from the State University of New York at Stony Brook in 1984 and then was a Fellow in the Interdisciplinary Programs in Public Health at the Harvard School of Public Health. He joined the faculty of the Robert Wood Johnson Medical School of the University of Medicine and Dentistry of New Jersey (UMDNJ) in Piscataway, New Jersey in 1986 where he is currently Professor and Chair of the Doctoral Committee for the UMDNJ School of Public Health. He serves on the New Jersey Commission on Radiation Protection, is a member of the National Council on Radiation Protection and Measurement, and served on both the National Academy of Sciences Committee and the National Institute of Health's Working Group addressing the possible health effects of electric and magnetic fields. Dr. Wartenberg has investigated a variety of methodological issues related to the study of magnetic fields and cancer, and has conducted two meta-analyses of the magnetic field and childhood cancer studies. Currently, he is completing a study of children with unusually high magnetic field exposures that he has identified using geographic information system (GIS) technology. In addition to his work on magnetic fields, he also conducts research on risk assessment, the effects of exposure to toxic chemicals and the investigation of disease clusters.

Noel S. Weiss received an M.D. degree from Stanford University School of Medicine and an M.P.H. and Dr. P.H. from the Harvard School of Public Health. In 1973, after two years at the National Center for Health Statistics, he joined the faculties of the University of Washington School of Public Health and Community Medicine and the Fred Hutchinson Cancer Research Center. He served as Chairman of the Department of Epidemiology at the University of Washington from 1984–1993. While the majority of his research has been in the area of cancer (he was awarded an Outstanding Investigator grant from the National Cancer Institute for the period 1985–1999), he has maintained an interest in and written extensively on epidemiologic methods and clinical epidemiology.

Gary Wells is Professor of Psychology and Distinguished Professor of Liberal Arts and Sciences at Iowa State University, Ames, Iowa. His experiments and papers on eyewitness testimony have appeared in scientific psychology's premiere journals.

Summary of Contents

———————

*

Table of Contents

―――――――

Table of Cases

References are to section and note.

SCIENCE IN THE LAW

STANDARDS, STATISTICS AND
RESEARCH ISSUES

*

CHAPTER 1

ADMISSIBILITY OF SCIENTIFIC EVIDENCE

Table of Sections

Westlaw Electronic Research

See Westlaw Electronic Research Guide preceding the Summary of Contents.

———————

§ 1–1.0 INTRODUCTION

The problem of defining standards for admitting scientific expert testimony is one with a venerable history[1] and, in all likelihood, an enduring future. Although modern science's roots lie in the eighteenth century,[2] only in the twentieth did it spread and bloom across virtually the entire human landscape. Science and technology will only grow in importance in the twenty-first century. The courtroom, never an isolated corner of the societal landscape, has similarly felt science's impact.[3] Over the years, courts have tried various methods to respond to the increasing influx of science.

Under virtually all evidence codes, trial courts must evaluate the admissibility of proffered expert testimony. The manner in which they accomplish this task, however, varies greatly among jurisdictions. This variability revolves around two basic aspects of the admissibility determination. The first concerns the nature and rigor of the legal test to be applied. Courts differ substantially in the ways they define the judge's role concerning scientific evidence, with some adopting an active role in screening the evidence and others taking little or no responsibility to check the evidence. The second concerns the criteria used to assess the expertise under whatever legal test is adopted. Some courts use criteria that call for deference to the professional opinion of experts from the respective field, whereas others assume the responsibility themselves to evaluate the scientific basis of the proffered opinion.

Legal standards vary from rigorous to permissive. The more permissive the legal standard, the greater the quantum of expert testimony that will be heard by the trier of fact. A jurisdiction's decision regarding how high the bar should be set for experts typically depends on its resolution of the classic problem of defining the proper roles for judges and juries in the trial process. A high threshold indicates a relatively active judicial role in screening expert opinion for the jury. A low threshold leaves the weighing functions to jurors— a task that might include, of course, according some expert evidence a weight of zero.

The second basic matter involves the manner by which a jurisdiction evaluates the probative value of proffered expertise. Some jurisdictions, for example, are highly deferential to the proffered expert and rely principally on

§ 1–1.0

1. For a general historical overview of the use of expert testimony, see Stephan Landsman, *Of Witches, Madmen, and Products Liability: An Historical Survey of the Use of Expert Testimony,* 13 Behav. Sci. & L. 131 (1995); David L. Faigman et al., *Check Your Crystal Ball at the Courthouse Door, Please: Exploring the Past, Understanding the Present, and Worrying About the Future of Scientific Evidence,* 15 Cardozo L. Rev. 1799, 1803–1809. (1994) (examining the modern rule in light of the standards that prevailed in the nineteenth and early twentieth centuries). The classic exploration of this historical question is Learned Hand, *Historical and Practical Considerations Regarding Expert Testimony,* 15 Harv. L. Rev. 40 (1901).

2. *See generally* Toby E. Huff, The Rise of Early Modern Science (1995).

3. *See generally* David L. Faigman, Legal Alchemy: The Use and Misuse of Science in the Law (1999); Sheila Jasanoff, Science at the Bar: Law, Science and Technology in America (1995).

qualifications or credentials. Other jurisdictions also consult the particular field from which the expert comes, requiring it to achieve some consensus regarding the proffered opinion. Finally, some jurisdictions, while considering the expert's qualifications and the field's acceptance of the basis for the opinion, also consider directly the theoretical principles, research methods, and accumulated data behind the expert's opinion.

In this chapter we consider the various approaches courts have taken to evaluating expert testimony. We have structured our analysis around the two principal tests employed by courts today. The first is the general acceptance test originally formulated in *Frye v. United States*[4] in 1923. The second, and our primary focus, is the rule set forth in *Daubert v. Merrell Dow Pharmaceuticals, Inc.*,[5] a standard further developed in two subsequent cases,[6] and finally codified in the Federal Rules of Evidence in 2000. Both tests answer in varying ways the basic issue presented by scientific evidence: what threshold showing should be required for the admission of scientific evidence.

§ 1–2.0 THE GENERAL ACCEPTANCE STANDARD OF *FRYE*

§ 1–2.1 Before *Frye*

Courts in the nineteenth and early twentieth centuries queried only whether the expert was "qualified" before the expert's testimony could be admitted.[1] If the expert was an expert, then opinion testimony was "entitled" to be admitted as evidence (given, of course, its apparent relevance to the issues to be determined at trial).[2] A more sophisticated version of this pre-*Frye* test focused, first, on the nature of the subject matter in issue and whether that subject matter was beyond the range of knowledge of the average juror. If so, a qualified expert's opinion was considered to be helpful,[3] if not essential, to the jury's determination of facts at issue.[4]

---

4. 293 F. 1013 (D.C.Cir.1923).

5. 509 U.S. 579, 113 S.Ct. 2786, 125 L.Ed.2d 469 (1993).

6. Often referred to as parts of the *Daubert* trilogy, the two cases that complete the triad are *General Electric Co. v. Joiner*, 522 U.S. 136, 118 S.Ct. 512, 139 L.Ed.2d 508 (1997) and *Kumho Tire, Ltd. v. Carmichael*, 526 U.S. 137, 119 S.Ct. 1167, 143 L.Ed.2d 238 (1999).

§ 1–2.0

1. For an examination of the modern application of the qualifications requirement, *see infra* § 1–3.3.

2. Albert S. Osborn, *Reasons and Reasoning in Expert Testimony*, 2 Law & Contemp. Probs., 488, 489 (1935). Conditioning the admission of expert testimony on nothing more than the expert's "qualifications" went on before *Frye*, after *Frye*, after the Federal Rules, and perhaps will after *Daubert*. *See generally*, Paul C. Giannelli, *The Admissibility of Novel Scientific Evidence: Frye v. United States, a Half Century Later*, 80 Colum. L. Rev. 1197, 1210 (1980). However, this approach is erroneous under either *Frye* or *Daubert*.

3. The "helpfulness" element of admissibility is still present today in the Federal Rules of Evidence. *See, e.g.,* Fed. R. Evid. 702 (expert can testify if it "will *assist* the trier of fact") (emphasis added). Today, this helpfulness element is also referred to as a "relevancy" requirement. *See infra* § 1–3.2.

4. *See* John B. Chapin, *Experts and Expert Testimony*, 22 Alb. L. J. 365 (1880).

The assurance of expertise was implied by the expert's success in an occupation or profession that embraced that knowledge. If a person could make a living selling his knowledge in the marketplace, then presumably expertise existed.[5] Although courts sometimes spoke of an expert's "greater study respecting certain subjects" or having "made the subject upon which he gives his opinion a matter of particular study,"[6] it seems clear that a modicum of prosperity in the practice of the occupation or profession possessing that knowledge almost always accompanied the expertise. In effect, the marketplace determined whether valid knowledge existed by endowing it with commercial value. This is not a point that courts made explicitly, but it seems to be implicit in the courts' determinations of who was "qualified."[7]

On the one hand, this seems practical enough. What better crucible for testing expertise than the everyday world of life's activities, with stakes as great or greater than those at issue in trials, and decisions reflected in consumers' hard earned dollars? Knowledge that proved valuable in the marketplace could hardly be without worth in a courtroom. But though it might be a practical and easily administered test, the test of commercial value is a poor one. Its major weaknesses are perhaps more obvious today than they were a century or two ago. The market not only selects for validity, it selects also for entertainment, desire, wishful thinking, hope, sometimes even desperation. These are not without their value, but they are not good proxies for what courts are looking for in expert testimony. If the marketplace approves, as it does, of astrologers, sellers of phony cancer cures, and guides to new age

---

The practice of the courts is to admit the testimony of a class of witnesses who are not supposed to have personal knowledge of any facts or circumstances bearing upon a pending case, but on the assumption that they are able from their special training and experience to apply scientific tests and present to the court and jury the import and value of such evidence as may appear, which laymen could not be expected to comprehend and properly estimate.

Id. at 365.

5. We, therefore, refer to this as the "commercial marketplace test."

6. *Jones v. Tucker*, 41 N.H. 546, 548 (1860).

7. Consider three examples from the middle of the 19th century.

Chief Justice Lemuel Shaw, writing in *New England Glass Co. v. Lovell*, 61 Mass. (7 Cush.) 319 (1851):

It is not because a man has a reputation for superior sagacity, and judgment, and power of reasoning, that his opinion is admissible; if so, such men might be called in all cases, to advise the jury, and it would change the mode of trial. But it is because a man's professional pursuits, his peculiar skill and knowledge in some department of science, not common to men in general, enable him to draw an inference, where men of common experience, after all the facts proved, would be left in doubt.

Id. at 321.

Chief Justice Ames writing in *Buffum v. Harris*, 5 R.I. 243 (1858), affirming a lower court decision to admit the opinions of two civil engineers, a well-digger, a farmer, and a gardener in an action on the case to recover damages for interference with the flow of water from a natural spring on plaintiff's property:

Indeed, knowledge of any kind, gained for and in the course of one's business as pertaining thereto, is precisely that which entitles one to be considered an expert, so as to render his opinion, founded on such knowledge, admissible in evidence.

Id. at 251.

Or the Supreme Court of Maine in *Clark v. Rockland Water Power Co.*, 52 Me. 68 (1860):

The foundation on which expert testimony rests, is the supposed superior knowledge or experience of the expert in relation to the subject matter upon which he is permitted to give an opinion as evidence. This knowledge must be such as is peculiar to persons of skill and experience in some particular branch of business, or department of science, which is the subject of investigation, and not of such a character as to be open and common to all persons.

Id. at 77.

vortices, are those therefore good enough to provide guidance in a courtroom? The marketplace test is incapable of distinguishing astrology from astronomy.[8]

A second problem is that some fields exist that have little or no life in any commercial marketplace. Indeed, some fields have come into being in the past century that have no function outside of their possible courtroom utility.[9] The courtroom *is* their marketplace.

Finally, the marketplace test conflates the expert and the expertise.[10] Before the twentieth century courts apparently never considered the question of expertise disentangled from the professionals and trades-people who carried the knowledge at issue. That is, they never asked whether a body of asserted knowledge existed, and could be validated, separate from the "qualified expert" who "possessed" it. The people and the knowledge were treated as one. If experts were "qualified," then expertise existed.[11] But being a "qualified expert" presupposes that an expertise exists.

§ 1–2.2 The *Frye* Extension

The defendant in *Frye* proffered an early form of polygraph testing, the "systolic blood pressure deception test," the results of which supported James Alphonso Frye's plea of innocence to a charge of murder.[12] This was an unfamiliar problem for a court. There were as yet no polygraphers and no developed market for their services. There might never be, if the only place that had any use for them was the courtroom, and if the only way to get into the courtroom was to gain prior marketplace acceptance.[13] A novel scientific question presented itself and the conventional test offered no ready solution.[14] The asserted expertise offered in *Frye* demanded a different test than the one that had served the law for so long.

8. The *Frye* test also cannot distinguish between science and pseudoscience; after all, astrological forecasts are "generally accepted" in the "particular field" of astrology. *See infra* notes 35–42 and accompanying text.

9. Some of these have been appropriately gathered under the heading of forensic sciences, and they include the identification of firearms, handwriting, tire marks, fibers, toolmarks, and so on.

10. The problem of conflating the expert and the expertise continues right up to the present time. *See, e.g.*, Giannelli, *supra* note 2.

11. Osborn, *supra* note 2, at 489.

12. *See generally* James E. Starrs, *A Still Life Watercolor: Frye v. United States*, 27 J. Forensic Sci. 684 (1982) (discussing the facts presented in the case and refuting the assertion that *Frye* might have been innocent).

13. *See Science in the Law: Social and Behavioral Science Issues* (Chapter 12) or *Science in the Law: Forensic Science Issues* (Chapter 10) for a review of the admissibility of polygraph tests. Today, the polygraph has a highly developed market outside the courtroom. This market, however, as the chapter from Professors Iacono and Lykken argues, *infra*, is not necessarily based on the utility of the technique in the courtroom. Polygraphs might serve a useful practical function—such as promoting confessions—that is substantially unrelated to their validity.

14. The court in *Frye* may have had a second problem. Suppose it wanted to exclude the lie detection results, then and thereafter, even if some day such examiners did attain a commercial market and qualified polygraphers became plentiful. The most obvious reason a court might feel this way is that polygraph testing could become a major vehicle by which at least some defendants could make a jury feel there is reasonable doubt about guilt. This would not be easy in a legal world which, despite "constant complaining and mistrust" of experts, routinely admitted them—so long as they were "qualified." And William Marston, Frye's expert witness, was well qualified by conventional standards (if he actually had an expertise in the subject at issue). Marston was an attorney and research psychologist who had done a considerable amount of empirical research on the physiological correlates of lying. *See* William M. Marston, *Systolic Blood Pressure Symptoms of Description*, 2 J. Exper. Psych. 117 (1917).

Judge Van Orsdel found a solution that departed as little as possible from prior law. The entire *Frye* opinion occupied only two pages. The critical words are these:

> Just when a scientific principle or discovery crosses the line between the experimental and demonstrable stages is difficult to define. Somewhere in this twilight zone the evidential force of the principle must be recognized, and while the courts will go a long way in admitting expert testimony deduced from a well-recognized scientific principle or discovery, the thing from which the deduction is made must be sufficiently established to have gained general acceptance in the particular field in which it belongs.[15]

In one sense, this is nothing more than the familiar market test relocated into a different marketplace. Where there is no commercial market, and may never be one, the evaluation of the asserted expertise can be performed in the "field's" marketplace by those who trade there.[16] The intellectual or professional marketplace was simply a proxy for the commercial marketplace. The test is still a marketplace test; the real evaluation still is conducted outside of the court or the law, and it still is incapable of distinguishing astrology from astronomy.

Yet, the *Frye* extrapolation did some new things. First, it separated the expertise from the expert, thereby creating legal accommodation to the notion that a body of asserted knowledge has an existence separate from any individual, no matter how brilliant, well-educated, or experienced that person might be, and that the body of asserted knowledge had to be evaluated apart from the individual who brings it to court. Second, of course, the alternative marketplace, the intellectual marketplace, allows more knowledge to be assessed, even if the knowledge is too new to be marketed commercially or if there is no hope of ever marketing it commercially.

Third—and most remarkable—as assessors of the value of what was being offered, *Frye* replaced buyers with sellers.[17] The commercial marketplace test, even with its serious weaknesses, had the virtue of allowing buyers in the marketplace to be the authority on whether something was valuable and therefore "valid." Under the *Frye* variation, that control was passed to the people who produced the knowledge and offered it, and themselves, to the courts.[18]

---

15. *Frye*, 293 F. at 1014.

16. *See, e.g.*, People v. Barbara, 400 Mich. 352, 255 N.W.2d 171, 194 (Mich. 1977) ("It therefore is best to adhere to [the *Frye*] standard which in effect permits the experts who know most about a procedure to experiment and to study it. In effect, they form a kind of technical jury, which must first pass on the scientific status of a procedure before the lay jury utilizes it in making its findings of fact.").

17. The practical result is that courts adopt the standards of the field that is the subject of the admissibility decision. Rigorous scientific fields result in rigorous admissibility standards, whereas fields lacking a rigorous tradition result in low admissibility standards. Even tea leaf reading is generally accepted if the field surveyed is practicing tea-leaf readers.

18. While this might seem an odd or even dangerous relocation of the power to make important judgments, it was entirely consistent with one of the defining notions of professionalism that was alive in that period and for some time thereafter: to be a profession is to hold a monopoly of judgment over what constitutes your field's expertise, and in many respects the courts have been deferential to claims of other professions. The latter part of the twentieth century has seen a weakening of the status of professions, and the most recent shifts in the rules of evidence may be seen to parallel the loss of autonomy of professions. *See generally* SAMUEL HABER, THE QUEST FOR AUTHORITY AND HONOR IN THE AMERICAN PROFESSIONS 1750–1900 (1991); RONALD M. PAVALKO, SOCIOLOGY OF OCCUPATIONS AND PROFESSIONS (2d ed. 1988).

Primarily, the *"Frye* test" was a minor adaptation of a major theme. For most kinds of expertise in most circumstances, the larger doctrine and the special situation would lead to the same result. So unimportant was the *Frye* extrapolation that it went unnoticed for decades. No contemporaneous law review articles were written about it and other courts did not cite it.[19] In fact, *Frye* only became fashionable in the 1970s as an argument arose over the admissibility of scientific evidence, perhaps in anticipation of the new Federal Rules of Evidence.[20]

§ 1–2.3   *Frye's* Ascendance

Although barely noticed for decades, the *"Frye* Test" eventually became the icon for one of the dominant notions of the proper criterion for the admissibility of scientific evidence—general acceptance within its field.[21] *Frye* may have become the standard of choice for several reasons. Foremost, perhaps, it was easy to apply and required little scientific sophistication on the part of judges. Moreover, the controversial cases were of the subset of scientific evidence cases that *Frye* was designed to deal with: asserted new knowledge that lacked an established clientele. To established fields of endeavor, to old "knowledge," the courts implicitly applied the old marketplace notions: if one were a card carrying member of a recognized occupation or profession, one's proffered expert testimony was admitted and the validity of the underlying knowledge was assumed.[22] Finally, by the middle of the twentieth century, the distinction between experts and expertise had grown more apparent. Not only did new fields or new specializations arise, but old fields acquired and offered distinct new knowledge. New knowledge was sometimes put before courts in a form more abstracted and isolated from the people who presented it. *Frye* had been designed to fit just these kinds of situations.[23]

§ 1–2.4   The Decline of *Frye*

Over time, courts and commentators found the general acceptance test to

---

19. *Frye* was not cited by a single court for a decade. During the first quarter century after its publication, *Frye* was cited in eight federal cases and five state cases. During its second quarter century, it was cited fifty-four times in federal cases and twenty-nine times in state cases. By the 1980s, it was being cited as much each year as it had been in its first fifty years. These numbers suggest that judicial interest in the *Frye* test did not pick up until a few years before the promulgation of the Federal Rules of Evidence.

20. *See* Paul C. Giannelli, Frye v. United States—*Background Paper Prepared for the National Conference of Lawyers and Scientists,* 99 F.R.D. 188, 191 (1983); J.E. Starrs, *"A Still–Life Watercolor"*: Frye v. United States, 27 FORENSIC SCI. 684, 685 (1982).

21. *See, e.g.,* United States v. Skeens, 494 F.2d 1050, 1053 (D.C.Cir.1974) (*Frye* "has been followed uniformly in this and other circuits."); Reed v. State, 283 Md. 374, 391 A.2d 364, 368 (Md. 1978) ("This criterion of 'general accep-

tance' in the scientific community has come to be the standard in almost all the courts in the country which have considered the question of the admissibility of scientific evidence."); Steven M. Egesdel, Note, *The* Frye *Doctrine and Relevancy Approach Controversy: An Empirical Evaluation,* 74 GEO. L.J. 1769, 1769–70 (1986).

22. Yet, some portion of the "knowledge" of established fields is invalid. For example, many accepted medical techniques have been found after finally being subjected to rigorous empirical testing to be no better or worse than less well accepted treatments or no treatment at all. *See* John P. Gilbert et al., *Progress in Surgery and Anesthesia: Benefits and Risks of Innovative Therapy, in* COSTS, RISKS, AND BENEFITS OF SURGERY 124 (John P. Bunker et al. eds., 1977).

23. For further discussion of the strengths and weaknesses of the *Frye* Test, *see infra* § 1–3.4.4 and accompanying text (discussing the general acceptance standard as a factor in the *Daubert* validity test).

have significant limitations.[24] In particular, the vagueness of the general acceptance test renders it susceptible to manipulation and tends to obscure the relevant inquiry.[25] Indeed, virtually every component of the test has sustained severe criticism.

Frye is often criticized as overly conservative, for it imposes a protracted waiting period that valid scientific evidence and techniques must endure before gaining legal acceptance.[26] This criticism highlights the fact that all significant scientific findings gestate before they are accepted by the general scientific community.[27] During this time period courts and the parties before them are deprived of this work. Moreover, many critics also note the "nature" of the scientific enterprise which sometimes responds negatively to revolutionary findings, because they might threaten entrenched "paradigms" and thus entrenched scientists.[28] Proponents of this view observe that the opinions of a scientist heralded today as brilliant, but dismissed in his day as misguided or worse, would be excluded under a general acceptance test. Galileo, for example, or Einstein early in his physics career, would not have been allowed to testify because of the radical nature of their views.[29]

Commentators responding to this criticism of *Frye* argue that for every Galileo or Einstein there are hundreds of Lysenkos with "revolutionary" theories that are eventually proven false by empirical research. They maintain further that judges (and jurors) should not be expected to distinguish "true" scientific revolutions from "false" ones. If scientists are unable to recognize an Einstein when they see one, laypersons are unlikely to have this ability.

Another asserted weakness of the *Frye* approach concerns the difficulty of ascertaining when a scientific proposition has been generally accepted.[30] The test does not specify what proportion of experts constitute general acceptance.[31] Courts have never required unanimity, and anything less than full consensus in science can quickly resemble substantial disagreement.[32] In fact, the most rigorous fields with the healthiest scientific discourse might fail the

24. *See* MCCORMICK ON EVIDENCE, § 203, at 871–77 (4th ed. 1992); JAMES R. RICHARDSON, MODERN SCIENTIFIC EVIDENCE: CIVIL AND CRIMINAL § 9.2, at 290 n.8 (2d ed. 1974); *see generally* United States v. Downing, 753 F.2d 1224, 1235–37 (3d Cir.1985).

25. *Downing,* 753 F.2d at 1236.

26. *See* 1 DAVID LOUISELL & CHRISTOPHER B. MUELLER, FEDERAL EVIDENCE § 703.2 at 821–22 (3d ed. 1991); Giannelli (1980), *supra* note 2, at 1223; *see also* United States v. Addison, 498 F.2d 741, 743 (D.C.Cir.1974).

27. Constantine J. Maletskos & Stephen J. Spielman, *Introduction of New Scientific Methods in Court, in* LAW ENFORCEMENT, SCIENCE & TECHNOLOGY, 957, 958 (S.A. Yefsky ed. 1967) ("A literal reading of *Frye v. United States* would require that the court always await the passing of a 'cultural lag' during which period the new method will have had sufficient time to diffuse through scientific discipline and create the requisite body of scientific opinion needed for acceptability.").

28. *See* David F. Horrobin, *The Philosophical Basis of Peer Review and the Suppression of Innovation,* 263 J. AM. MED. ASSN. 1438

(1990). The classic treatment of "paradigms" in science is THOMAS KUHN, THE STRUCTURE OF SCIENTIFIC REVOLUTIONS (1970).

29. *See, e.g.,* Brief Amici of Physicians, Scientists, and Historians of Science in Support of Petitioners, at 14, submitted in Daubert v. Merrell Dow Pharmaceuticals, Inc., 509 U.S. 579, 113 S.Ct. 2786, 125 L.Ed.2d 469 (1993) (No. 92–102) (The Brief noted Galileo's persecution by the inquisition and quoted Thomas Huxley's remark that "[e]xtinguished theologians lie about the cradle of every science as the strangled snakes beside that of Hercules.") (*citing and quoting* Darwiniana, THE ORIGIN OF SPECIES (1860)).

30. *See generally* Bert Black, *A Unified Theory of Scientific Evidence,* 56 FORDHAM L. REV. 595, 627–28 & n.156 (1988).

31. *See, e.g.,* United States v. Williams, 583 F.2d 1194, 1198 (2d Cir.1978).

32. John W. Strong, *Questions Affecting the Admissibility of Scientific Evidence,* 1970 U.ILL. L.F. 1, 10–11.

Frye test with the greatest frequency. In light of the skeptical perspective of good scientific investigation, judges should be cautious when they approach a field in which there is too much agreement.[33]

Moreover, the *Frye* test requires general acceptance in the *particular field*. But there are no standards defining which field to consult. Courts have had considerable difficulty assessing scientific information under this standard because it often extends into more than one academic or professional discipline.[34] Furthermore, each field may contain subspecialties.[35] This difficulty leads to paradoxical results. General acceptance, often criticized for being the most conservative test of admissibility, in practice can produce the most liberal standards of admission.[36] The more narrowly a court defines the pertinent field, the more agreement it is likely to find.[37] The general acceptance test thus degenerates into a process of deciding whose noses to count.[38] The definition of the pertinent field can be over-inclusive or under-inclusive.[39] Because the pertinent field can be so readily manipulated,[40] the test by itself provides courts with little protection against shoddy science.

Even more critically, the particular field of inquiry leaves the law at the mercy of the practitioners of the respective fields. Different fields have widely varying standards. Some fields have a tradition of vigorous debate, data gathering, and hypothesis testing, an ethos consistent with the scientific enterprise. In these fields, an idea does not become generally accepted until it passes a rigorous gauntlet of testing. Other fields lack these traditions and accept ideas with far less scrutiny.[41] The courts have difficulty telling one of

33. To be sure, although science does not prove things "true," the scientific library is filled with volumes that are not seriously disputed. But even though this library contains some legally relevant knowledge that is located in the dusty rooms of near-certain science (so that judicial notice can be taken of it), most legal questions raise matters in the uncertain corridors of science. *See* United States v. Jakobetz, 955 F.2d 786 (2d Cir.1992) (The court took judicial notice of the general theory and application of DNA profiling technology, but held that particular applications of that technology were a matter for the trier of fact to assess.). For example, few seriously dispute the carcinogenic properties of cigarettes; but science remains some distance from permitting doctors to conclude that particular lung cancers are attributable to smoking. *See* Chapter 37.

34. *See, e.g.,* Cornett v. State, 450 N.E.2d 498 (Ind.1983) (The court defined the relevant scientific fields for spectrographic voice identification as linguistics, psychology, engineering and voice spectography.). *See generally* Giannelli, *supra* note 2, at 1208.

35. *See* Giannelli, *supra* note 2, at 1209.

36. In addition to what follows, see the discussion at *infra* § 1–3.4.4.

37. *See Williams,* 583 F.2d at 1198 (noting that "[s]election of the 'relevant scientific community,' appears to influence the result"); *see also* National Academy of Sciences, *On the*

Theory and Practice of Voice Identification (1979) (in which a group composed of acoustical engineers, physiologists, statisticians, and others gave a less favorable assessment of the technique than the narrower range of developers of the technique).

38. DeLuca v. Merrell Dow Pharmaceuticals, Inc., 911 F.2d 941, 955 (3d Cir.1990).

39. *See* Reed v. State, 283 Md. 374, 391 A.2d 364, 377 (Md. 1978) ("The purpose of the *Frye* test is defeated by an approach which allows a court to ignore the informed opinions of a substantial segment of the scientific community which stands in opposition to the process in question."); *see also* Giannelli, *supra* note 2, at 1210.

40. *See, e.g.,* Commonwealth v. Lykus, 367 Mass. 191, 327 N.E.2d 671, 678 (Mass. 1975) (*Frye* test is met when the technique is "generally accepted by those who would be expected to be familiar with its use."); People v. Williams, 331 P.2d 251, 253–54 (Cal.Super.1958) (Court admitted a technique that was "generally accepted by those who would be expected to be familiar with its use" *even though* "it cannot truthfully be said that the ... test has met with general acceptance by the medical profession as a whole.").

41. Important examples of the latter fields are many of the forensic identification sciences. *See, e.g.,* D. Michael Risinger et al., *Exorcism of Ignorance as a Proxy for Rational Knowl-*

these fields from another. Indeed, and especially ironically for courts, they may mistake vigorous research and debate over the meaning of the findings for lack of agreement (rather than the process of reaching trustworthy findings) and the lack of research and debate as a sign of consensus (rather than a sign of an immature or retarded science).[42] Under the *Frye* variant, because the courts have to rely on the standards set within each field, they find themselves accepting more readily the offerings of less rigorous fields and less readily the offerings of more rigorous fields. Fields that set higher thresholds will place a smaller proportion of their knowledge over the threshold.

Despite *Frye's* limitations, it remains the standard by which science is evaluated for courtroom use in many jurisdictions.[43] Increasingly, however, jurisdictions are using the alternative perspective articulated by the United States Supreme Court in *Daubert* and now the standard codified in the Federal Rules of Evidence. Yet the *Daubert* Court did not abandon *Frye* because of its real or perceived defects.[44] Indeed, the general acceptance core of *Frye* was borrowed as one of the four principal factors that might be consulted when applying the *Daubert* standard. The Court did not wholly follow *Frye* for the more simple reason that it did not find it to have been incorporated into the Federal Rules.[45]

§ 1–3.0 THE FEDERAL RULES OF EVIDENCE AND THE VALIDITY TEST OF *DAUBERT*

Consistent with its recent practice of applying the plain meaning rule to the Federal Rules of Evidence, the Supreme Court stated in *Daubert* that it was simply interpreting the Rules as written.[1] A reading of even a small

---

edge: *The Lessons of Handwriting Identification "Expertise,"* 137 Pa. L. Rev. 731 (1989); Michael J. Saks & Jonathan J. Koehler, *What DNA "Fingerprinting" Can Teach the Law About the Rest of Forensic Science,* 13 Cardozo L. Rev. 361 (1991); I.W. Evett, *Criminalistics: The Future of Expertise,* 33 J. Forensic Sci. Soc'y 173 (1993).

42. *See United States v. Christophe,* 833 F.2d 1296, 1299 (9th Cir.1987), in which the Ninth Circuit concluded that proffered expert testimony on eyewitness identification "does not conform to a generally accepted explanatory theory [because] psychologists do not generally accept the claimed dangers of eyewitness identification in a trial setting." *Id.* To support this conclusion, the court cited a single article: Michael McCloskey & Howard Egeth, *Eyewitness Identification: What Can a Psychologist Tell a Jury?,* 38 Am. Psychologist 550, 551 (May 1983). For a contrasting viewpoint, see the California Supreme Court's decision in *People v. McDonald,* 37 Cal.3d 351, 208 Cal. Rptr. 236, 690 P.2d 709, 721 (Cal.1984), in which the court dismissed these same scientists as a minority viewpoint whose theories were "vigorously disputed by their peers." *Id.*

43. *See* Joseph R. Meaney, *From* Frye *to* Daubert: *Is a Pattern Unfolding,* 35 Jurimetrics 191 (1995).

44. The Court did make note of the controversy surrounding the merits of *Frye:* "The merits of the *Frye* test have been much debated, and scholarship on its proper scope and application is legion." *Daubert,* 509 U.S. at 586.

45. *See id.* at 586–587.

§ 1–3.0

1. *See* Daubert v. Merrell Dow Pharmaceuticals, Inc., 509 U.S. 579, 587, 113 S.Ct. 2786, 125 L.Ed.2d 469 (1993) ("We interpret the legislatively-enacted Federal Rules of Evidence as we would any statute."). Professor Andrew Taslitz, *Daubert's Guide to the Federal Rules of Evidence: A Not–So–Plain–Meaning Jurisprudence,* 32 Harvard J. on Legisl. 3 (1995), argued, persuasively, that the *Daubert* Court did not faithfully adhere to a plain-meaning test. For general discussion and criticism of the Court's method of interpreting the Rules, *see* Randolph N. Jonakait, *The Supreme Court, Plain Meaning, and the Changed Rules of Evidence,* 68 Tex. L. Rev. 745 (1990) (warning that

sample of the voluminous literature dedicated to explaining *Daubert*,[2] however, suggests that the meaning of Rule 702 in 1993 was not so plain.[3] Indeed, the variety of views in the lower courts before *Daubert*, and especially the then prevailing reliance on the general acceptance test of *Frye*,[4] indicate a certain lack of clarity in Rule 702. Ironically, perhaps, the Court's interpretive style betrayed no break with the past,[5] yet most courts and commentators found *Daubert* to herald a substantial change from past practice.[6] The sense that *Daubert* had changed the rules was confirmed when Federal Rules 701, 702 and 703 were amended in 2000 to set forth the new practice.[7] Thus, the

application of the plain meaning standard will have a negative impact on evidence law and will fail to satisfy policy goals); Eileen A. Scallen, *Classical Rhetoric, Practical Reasoning and the Law of Evidence*, 44 Am. U. L. Rev. 1717 (1995) (arguing that the best approach to construction of the Evidence Rules is practical reasoning); Glen Weissenberger, *The Supreme Court and the Interpretation of the Federal Rules of Evidence*, 53 Ohio St. L.J. 1307 (1992) (arguing that application of the doctrine of legislative intent is misplaced in the interpretation of the Federal Rules of Evidence).

2. Hundreds of articles have been published in response to the *Daubert* decision. For a representative sample, *see*, Michael J. Saks, *The Aftermath of* Daubert: *An Evolving Jurisprudence of Expert Evidence*, 40 Jurimetrics J. 229 (2000); Adam J. Siegel, Note, *Setting Limits on Judicial Scientific, Technical, and Other Specialized Fact–Finding in the New Millenium*, 86 Cornell L. Rev. 167 (2000); Michael H. Graham, *The Expert Witness Predicament: Determining "Reliable" Under the Gatekeeping Test of* Daubert, Kumho, *and Proposed Amended Rule 702 of the Federal Rules of Evidence*, 54 U. Minn. L. Rev. 317 (2000); Note, *Navigating Uncertainty: Gatekeeping in the Absence of Hard Science*, 113 Harv. L. Rev. 1467 (2000); Harvey Brown, *Procedural Issues Under* Daubert, 36 Houston L. Rev. 1133 (1999); *Symposium, At the Daubert Gate: Managing and Measuring Expertise in an Age of Science, Specialization, and Speculation*, 57 Wash. & Lee L. Rev. 661 (2000); *Symposium, Truth and Its Rivals: Evidence Reform and the Goals of Evidence Law*, 49 Hastings L.J. 289 (1997); Margaret A. Berger, *Procedural Paradigms for Applying the* Daubert *Test*, 78 Minn. L. Rev. 1345 (1994); Bert Black et al., *Science and the Law in the Wake of* Daubert: *A New Search for Scientific Knowledge*, 72 Tex. L. Rev. 715 (1994); David L. Faigman, *Mapping the Labyrinth of Scientific Evidence*, 46 Hastings L.J. 555 (1995); Richard D. Friedman, *The Death and Transfiguration of* Frye, 34 Jurimetrics J. 133 (1994); Paul C. Giannelli, Daubert *and Forensic Science*, 1 Shepard's Expert & Sci. Evid. Q. 457 (1994); Paul S. Miller et al., Daubert *and the Need of Judicial Scientific Literacy*, 77 Judicature 254 (1994); Linda Sandstrom Sinnard, Daubert's *Gatekeeper: The Role of the District Court Judge in Admitting Expert Testimony*, 68 Tul. L. Rev. 1457 (1994);

Symposium, *Evidence After the Death of* Frye, 15 Cardozo L. Rev. 1745 (1994). *See generally* 3 Christopher B. Mueller & Laird C. Kirkpatrick, Federal Evidence § 353, at 665–67 (2d ed. 1994).

In addition to the multitude of articles published on *Daubert*, the profession has responded with books (including this one) and programs to improve judges' proficiency with scientific methods. For instance, the Federal Judicial Center (FJC) has held programs on scientific evidence for judges throughout the country. In addition, although not prompted by *Daubert* and its progeny, but certainly magnified by it, the FJC published the second edition of the Scientific Evidence Reference Manual in 2000.

3. *See* Taslitz (1995), *supra* note 1, at 4–5 (arguing that the Court did not use a plain-meaning standard in *Daubert*—and it's a good thing too).

4. Without commenting on its pertinence to the Court's "plain-meaning" approach to interpreting the Rules, the Court noted *Frye's* ascendance: "In the 70 years since its formulation in the *Frye* case, the 'general acceptance' test has been the dominant standard for determining the admissibility of novel scientific evidence at trial." *Daubert*, 509 U.S. at 585.

5. Paul C. Giannelli, Daubert: *Interpreting the Federal Rules of Evidence*, 15 Cardozo L.Rev. 1999 (1994).

6. *See* Polaino v. Bayer Corp., 122 F.Supp.2d 63, 66 (D.Mass.2000) (The *Daubert* trilogy "radically altered the approach of the federal trial court to expert testimony."); *see also* Lennon v. Norfolk & Western Rwy. Co., 123 F. Supp. 2d 1143 (N.D.Ind.2000) (*Daubert* "profoundly changed" admissibility standards).

7. The 2000 amendments follow (italicized material is new):

Rule 701. Opinion Testimony by Lay Witness

If the witness is not testifying as an expert, the witness' testimony in the form of opinions or inferences is limited to those opinions or inferences which are (a) rationally based on the perception of the witness, (b) helpful to a clear understanding of the witness' tes-

Federal Rules were amended in 2000 to state more plainly the plain meaning the Court had ascribed to them in 1993. Federal courts, of course, are bound to follow this new course, and states, in increasing numbers, have followed suit.[8]

timony or the determination of a fact in issue *and (c) not based on scientific, technical or other specialized knowledge.*

Rule 702. Testimony by Experts

If scientific, technical, or other specialized knowledge will assist the trier of fact to understand the evidence or to determine a fact in issue, a witness qualified as an expert by knowledge, skill, experience, training, or education, may testify thereto in the form of an opinion or otherwise, *provided that (1) the testimony is sufficiently based upon reliable facts or data, (2) the testimony is the product of reliable principles and methods, and (3) the witness has applied the principles and methods reliably to the facts of the case.*

Rule 703. Bases of Opinion Testimony by Experts

The facts or data in the particular case upon which an expert bases an opinion or inference may be those perceived by or made known to the expert at or before the hearing. If of a type reasonably relied upon by experts in the particular field in forming opinions or inferences upon the subject, the facts or data need not be admissible in evidence *in order for the opinion or inference to be admitted. If the facts or data are otherwise inadmissible, they shall not be disclosed to the jury by the proponent of the opinion or inference unless their probative value substantially outweighs their prejudicial effect.*

8. The states divide roughly into five categories concerning their response to *Daubert.*

First, twenty-one states have accepted the essential principles of *Daubert,* either because they were persuaded by the Supreme Court's reasoning or they already adhered to a substantially similar test. *See* State v. Porter, 241 Conn. 57, 694 A.2d 1262 (Conn. 1997); Nelson v. State, 628 A.2d 69 (Del.1993); Jordan v. Georgia Power Company, 219 Ga.App. 690, 466 S.E.2d 601 (Ga.App.1995); State v. Parkinson, 128 Idaho 29, 909 P.2d 647 (Idaho App.1996); Steward v. State, 652 N.E.2d 490 (Ind.1995); Hutchison v. American Family Mutual Insurance Co., 514 N.W.2d 882 (Iowa 1994); Mitchell v. Commonwealth, 908 S.W.2d 100 (Ky.1995); State v. Foret, 628 So.2d 1116 (La.1993); Green v. Cessna Aircraft Co., 673 A.2d 216 (Me.1996); Commonwealth v. Lanigan, 419 Mass. 15, 641 N.E.2d 1342 (Mass. 1994); State v. Weeks, 270 Mont. 63, 891 P.2d 477 (Mont. 1995); Schafersman v. Agland Coop, 262 Neb. 215, 631 N.W.2d 862 (2001); State v. Cavaliere, 140 N.H. 108, 663 A.2d 96 (N.H. 1995); State v. Goode, 341 N.C. 513, 461 S.E.2d 631 (N.C.

1995); Taylor v. State, 889 P.2d 319 (Okla. Crim.App.1995); State v. O'Key, 321 Or. 285, 899 P.2d 663 (Or. 1995); State v. Schweitzer, 533 N.W.2d 156 (S.D.1995); E.I. du Pont de Nemours & Co., Inc. v. Robinson, 923 S.W.2d 549 (Tex.1995); State v. Streich, 163 Vt. 331, 658 A.2d 38 (Vt. 1995); Wilt v. Buracker, 191 W.Va. 39, 443 S.E.2d 196 (W.Va.1993); Springfield v. State, 860 P.2d 435 (Wyo.1993).

Second, seven states have stated their openness to reconsidering the rule they apply to scientific evidence. *See* Mattox v. State Dept. of Revenue, Child Support Enforcement Div., 875 P.2d 763 (Alaska 1994); Lindsey v. People, 892 P.2d 281 (Colo.1995); Dotto v. Okan, 269 Ill. App.3d 808, 207 Ill.Dec. 190, 646 N.E.2d 1277 (Ill.App.1995); Fairview Hospital and Health Care Services v. St. Paul Fire & Marine Insurance Co., 535 N.W.2d 337 (Minn.1995); Ripa v. Owens–Corning Fiberglas Corp., 282 N.J.Super. 373, 660 A.2d 521 (1995); Commonwealth v. Crews, 536 Pa. 508, 640 A.2d 395 (Pa. 1994); State v. Russell, 125 Wash.2d 24, 882 P.2d 747 (Wash. 1994).

Third, ten states have rejected the *Daubert* standard, at least for the time-being, preferring to remain with the *Frye* test or an alternative state formulation of general acceptance and relevancy. *See* State v. Bible, 175 Ariz. 549, 858 P.2d 1152 (Ariz. 1993); People v. Leahy, 8 Cal.4th 587, 34 Cal.Rptr.2d 663, 882 P.2d 321 (Cal. 1994); Flanagan v. State, 625 So.2d 827 (Fla.1993); State v. Haddock, 257 Kan. 964, 897 P.2d 152 (Kan. 1995); Schultz v. State, 106 Md.App. 145, 664 A.2d 60 (Md.App.1995); People v. Peterson, 450 Mich. 349, 537 N.W.2d 857 (Mich. 1995) *amended* 450 Mich. 1212, 548 N.W.2d 625 (Mich. 1995); Kansas City Southern Railway Co. v. J.C. Johnson, 798 So.2d 374, 381, 2001 WL 107864 *7 (Miss.2001); Callahan v. Cardinal Glennon Hospital, 863 S.W.2d 852 (Mo.1993); People v. Wesley, 83 N.Y.2d 417, 611 N.Y.S.2d 97, 633 N.E.2d 451 (N.Y. 1994); City of Fargo v. McLaughlin, 512 N.W.2d 700 (N.D.1994).

Fourth, seven states and the District of Columbia follow their own state version of a relevance/reliability determination, usually based on the respective state code of evidence. *See* Moore v. State, 323 Ark. 529, 915 S.W.2d 284 (Ark. 1996); Taylor v. United States, 661 A.2d 636 (D.C.1995); State v. Maelega, 80 Hawai'i 172, 907 P.2d 758 (Hawaii 1995); State v. Anderson, 118 N.M. 284, 881 P.2d 29 (N.M. 1994); State v. Clark, 101 Ohio App.3d 389, 655 N.E.2d 795 (Ohio App.1995); State v. Council, 335 S.C. 1, 515 S.E.2d 508 (S.C. 1999); State v. Crosby, 927 P.2d 638 (Utah 1996);

Although *Frye* was not the only alternative to *Daubert's* validity test, it does represent the basic alternative perspective to it. In fact, if *Daubert* is a significant break from the past, the departure lies in the changed focus of the admissibility determination. *Frye* asks judges to decide the admissibility of scientific expert testimony by deferring to the opinions of scientists in the "particular field." Thus, under *Frye,* judges seemingly do not need to have any facility with scientific methods to make the admissibility decision. They must merely have some basis for knowing what most scientists believe. Under *Daubert*, judges have the specific responsibility of evaluating the scientific validity of the basis for expert testimony. The "revolution" of *Daubert* lies therein.[9] Judges and lawyers, long insulated from the scientific revolution, are now obligated to become familiar with the methods and culture of science.

§ 1–3.1 Applying *Daubert*

§ 1–3.1.1 Preliminary Considerations Regarding the Management of Expert Testimony

Under *Daubert*, the trial court itself is initially responsible for determining the admissibility of scientific expert testimony by determining that the science supporting that opinion is valid.[10] Although courts and commentators initially debated the point, it now appears clear that *Daubert* deepened and expanded the trial judge's responsibilities over scientific evidence.[11] That new obligation was captured colorfully in the Court's use of the gatekeeper metaphor to describe the judge's task. The practical necessities of these new duties have been the subject of substantial debate.

An important component of the *Daubert* trilogy concerns the court's management of the expert testimony before trial. In particular, courts have divided somewhat on just when they should hold preliminary hearings under

State v. Peters, 192 Wis.2d 674, 534 N.W.2d 867 (Wis.App.1995).

Fifth, five states remain undecided, remaining on the fence for now. These states apply some combination of *Frye* or *Daubert*, without clearly specifying one or the other. *See* Courtaulds Fibers, Inc. v. Long, 779 So.2d 198 (Ala. 2000); Dow Chemical Co. v. Mahlum, 114 Nev. 1468, 970 P.2d 98 (Nev. 1998); Soares v. Vestal, M.D., 632 A.2d 647 (R.I.1993); State v. Smith, 1994 WL 361851 (Tenn.Crim.App. 1994); Cotton v. Commonwealth, 19 Va.App. 306, 451 S.E.2d 673 (Va.App.1994).

See generally Heather G. Hamilton, Note, *The Movement From Frye to Daubert: Where Do the States Stand?*, 38 Jurimetrics J. 201 (1998).

9. *See* David L. Faigman, *The Law's Scientific Revolution: Reflections and Ruminations on the Law's Use of Experts in Year Seven of the Revolution*, 57 Wash. & Lee L. Rev. 661 (2000).

10. *See* Cavallo v. Star Enterprise, 892 F.Supp. 756, 774 (E.D.Va.1995), *aff'd in part, rev'd in part*, 100 F.3d 1150 (4th Cir.1996) ("*Daubert* assigned district courts a more vigorous role to play in ferreting out expert opin-

ion not based on the scientific method."). *See, e.g.*, Wilson v. City of Chicago, 6 F.3d 1233, 1238–39 (7th Cir.1993) ("The elimination of formal barriers to expert testimony has merely shifted to the trial judge the responsibility for keeping 'junk science' out of the courtroom.... It is a responsibility to be taken seriously."); Daubert v. Merrell Dow Pharmaceuticals, Inc., 43 F.3d 1311, 1315 (9th Cir. 1995) (*Daubert II*) ("Federal judges face a far more complex and daunting task in a post-*Daubert* world than before."); Casey v. Ohio Medical Products, 877 F.Supp. 1380, 1383 (N.D.Cal.1995) ("The responsibilities of district courts under *Daubert* are indeed heavy ones."). *See also In re* Joint Eastern & Southern District Asbestos Litigation, 52 F.3d 1124, 1132 (2d Cir.1995) ("The *Daubert* Court significantly changed the standards governing the admissibility of scientific evidence by expanding district court's discretion to evaluate the reliability and relevance of contested evidence.").

11. *See also infra* § 1–3.5 and § 1–3.6 and the discussion of *Weisgram v. Marley, Co.*, 528 U.S. 440, 455, 120 S.Ct. 1011, 145 L.Ed.2d 958 (2000) (Court observed that "[s]ince *Daubert* ... parties relying on expert testimony have

Rule 104(a) to fulfill their gatekeeping obligations. Although this determination appears to be largely within the district judge's discretion, failure to hold a 104(a) hearing might constitute an abuse of discretion under certain circumstances.[12] In general, most courts considering the matter hold that a separate hearing to determine the validity of the basis for scientific evidence is not required.[13] Very often, however, courts do hold *"Daubert* hearings" or "Rule 104(a) hearings" in order to assess the validity of the science. Indeed, *Daubert* apparently permits judges to exclude expert testimony as invalid even in the absence of an objection by the opponent of the evidence.[14] At the same time, as many courts have emphasized, a key aspect of the *Daubert* standard is its flexibility. While in one case proper application of *Daubert* might call for a separate hearing, in another no separate hearing might be needed.[15]

had notice of the exacting standards of reliability [scientific] evidence must meet.").

12. In an excellent opinion, the Sixth Circuit in *United States v. Smithers*, 212 F.3d 306 (6th Cir.2000), reversed the district court for failure to hold a *Daubert* hearing to consider the relevance and validity of expert testimony on the reliability of eyewitness identifications. The district court found that jurors could understand the weaknesses of eyewitness testimony and remarked, further, that "I'm also interested in seeing what a jury will do absent that expert testimony. It makes it a more interesting case. I recognize it's the defendant's fate that's at stake, but you can always argue for a new trial if he's convicted." *Id.* at 310. The Sixth Circuit explained that *Daubert* places an affirmative obligation on trial courts to evaluate the relevance and the scientific basis for proffered expert testimony. *Id.* at 312–15. The lower court had abused its discretion in not conducting this evaluation. *Id.* at 314–15. The court noted that this does not mean that eyewitness expert testimony is always admissible, or even that it is always necessary to provide a *Daubert* hearing to consider it. Here, however, there was no other evidence linking the defendant to the crime. Moreover, the court found the attitude and comments made by the district court especially troubling. The comment that excluding the expert testimony will make the case more interesting, the Sixth Circuit said, was "gamesmanship at its worst and reveals a troubling disregard for this Defendant's rights, relegating those rights to mere abstractions." *Id.* The court noted finally that the district court's conclusion that juries understand the limitations of eyewitness identifications was not correct: "Today, there is no question that many aspects of perception and memory are not within the common experience of most jurors, and in fact, many factors that affect memory are counter-intuitive." *Id.* at 315–16. *See also* Jahn v. Equine Services, PSC, 233 F.3d 382, 393 (6th Cir.2000) (criticizing district court for failing to provide a full record by which "a proper *Daubert* determination" could be done.).

13. United States v. Johnson, 28 F.3d 1487, 1496 (8th Cir.1994) (not error for trial court to make preliminary assessment "based upon [the expert's] foundational testimony before the jury"); United States v. Quinn, 18 F.3d 1461, 1465 (9th Cir.1994) (Same). *But see* Hoult v. Hoult, 57 F.3d 1, 4 (1st Cir.1995) (holding that a preliminary assessment of validity is necessary before admission of expert testimony).

14. *See Hoult*, 57 F.3d at 4 ("We think *Daubert* does instruct district courts to conduct a preliminary assessment of the reliability of expert testimony, even in the absence of an objection.").

15. In *United States v. Alatorre*, 222 F.3d 1098 (9th Cir.2000), the court upheld the lower court's admission of expert testimony following its denial of the defendant's request for a separate *Daubert* hearing. The district court permitted the defendant to *voir dire* the expert during the trial in front of the jury. *Id.* at 1099. The Ninth Circuit stated that flexibility was the watchword of *Daubert*, and requiring a preliminary hearing to be held in all cases would undermine that principle. However, the court did stress that it might be appropriate in many cases for district courts to hold separate hearings—outside of the presence of the jury— to evaluate the reliability of proffered expert testimony:

Having held that neither the Supreme Court's trilogy nor any of our own compels trial courts to conduct separate, pretrial hearings to discharge their gatekeeping duties, we note that holding such hearings— or at least ensuring an opportunity for voir dire outside the presence of the jury—may be appropriate in certain cases. Trial courts should be mindful of the difficulties posed when counsel must explore an expert's qualifications and the basis for the expert's opinion in the presence of the jury and, depending on the circumstances of the case, should give due consideration to requests that questioning occur unconstrained by that presence.

Id. at 1105.

In *Padillas v. Stork–Gamco, Inc.*,[16] for example, the Third Circuit held that the district court had committed reversible error in not holding a 104(a) hearing in order to assess the basis for the expert's testimony.[17] In the underlying action, the plaintiff had been injured while he was washing down the blade of a drum and thigh cutter which is used in the processing of chickens. The district court granted summary judgment after ruling that the plaintiff's expert would not be allowed to testify. The court explained that the expert had offered no basis for his conclusions, and had not indicated what tests, if any, he had employed.[18] In an important opinion, written by Judge William Schwarzer (sitting by designation), the appellate court reversed, finding that the lower court erred in not holding a 104(a) hearing. "We have long stressed the importance of *in limine* hearings under Rule 104(a) in making the reliability determination required under Rule 702 and *Daubert*."[19] Indeed, the court found that the lower court had erred despite the fact that the plaintiff had not asked for an *in limine* hearing.[20] The appellate court explained that this failure was irrelevant, since the district court's gatekeeping responsibility requires it to manage complex scientific issues. Moreover, the court noted, the proponent of expert testimony has the burden to demonstrate reliability, a burden that he should be allowed to meet in an *in limine* hearing.

Appellate courts increasingly insist that even when no *Daubert* hearing is held, the district court must create a sufficient record so that the basis for the admissibility decision can be reviewed. The Tenth Circuit, in *Goebel v. Denver and Rio Grade Western Railroad Co.*,[21] emphasized the importance of a detailed record for purposes of appellate review. In *Goebel*, the district court admitted plaintiff's medical doctor who testified that the plaintiff's brain damage was caused by exposure to diesel fumes.[22] The lower court denied the defendant's request for a *Daubert* hearing, but allowed a *voir dire* of the witness at trial. Thereafter, the court overturned the defendant's objection, stating simply that "I believe there is sufficient foundation here for the jury to hear this testimony."[23]

The Tenth Circuit reversed, holding that the district court had failed its gatekeeping duties. The court observed that "[t]his gatekeeper function requires the judge to assess the reasoning and methodology underlying the expert's opinion, and determine whether it is scientifically valid and applicable to a particular set of facts."[24] Whether this gatekeeping function was fulfilled, the court explained, is reviewed on appeal *de novo*.[25] "While the district court has discretion in the manner in which it conducts its *Daubert* analysis, there is no discretion regarding the actual performance of the gatekeeper function."[26] Here, the district court never stated its reason for admitting the expert opinion and, thus, it could not be evaluated on appeal.[27]

---

16. 186 F.3d 412 (3d Cir.1999); *see also* Alcan Intl. v. S.A. Day Mfg. Co., 1999 WL 605702 *4 (W.D.N.Y.1999).

17. *Id*. at *4.

18. *Id*.

19. *Id*.

20. *See id*. at *5.

21. 215 F.3d 1083 (10th Cir.2000).

22. *Id*. at 1086.

23. *Id*. at 1087.

24. *See id*.

25. *Id*.

26. *Id*.

27. The court explained that "[w]ithout specific findings or discussion on the record, it is impossible on appeal to determine whether the district court 'carefully and meticulously' review[ed] the proffered scientific evidence or

The court then stated that "we specifically hold that a district court, when faced with a party's objection, must adequately demonstrate by specific findings on the record that it has performed its duty as gatekeeper."[28] Under *Daubert*, therefore, judges must have—and demonstrate on the record—a sufficient appreciation of the scientific method to make this preliminary assessment.[29]

§ 1–3.1.2   The Burden of Proof Regarding Admissibility

At one level the answer to the question of who should have the burden of proof to show that proffered expert testimony is relevant and reliable is obvious: the proponent of evidence always bears the burden of persuading the court that the conditions for its admission are met. But the question has nevertheless led to confusion in *Daubert* hearings on a variety of expert areas, and one particularly confusing instance arose in the context of a proffer of expert evidence on fire causation.

Maryland Casualty Co. v. Therm–O–Disc, Inc.[30] involved a fire that began in a clothes dryer, allegedly due to a malfunctioning part. The district court initially placed the burden on the opponent of the expert witness to show that the testimony could not meet the requirements of *Daubert*. Here is the Fourth Circuit's recitation of what happened:

simply made an off-the-cuff decision to admit the expert testimony." *Id.* at 1088 (*quoting* United States v. Call, 129 F.3d 1402, 1405 (10th Cir.1997)). *See also* United States v. Velarde, 214 F.3d 1204, 1209 (10th Cir.2000) ("*Kumho* and *Daubert* make it clear that the [district] court must, on the record, make some kind of reliability determination.").

28.   *Goebel*, 215 F.3d at 1088.

29.   The Court explained this responsibility as follows:

> Faced with a proffer of expert scientific testimony, then, the trial judge must determine . . . whether the reasoning or methodology underlying the testimony is scientifically valid.... We are confident that federal judges possess the capacity to undertake this review.

Daubert, 509 U.S. at 592–93. Scientific expert testimony is admissible only after the judge has determined by a preponderance of the evidence, pursuant to Rule 104(a), that the supporting science is valid. *See id.* at 593, 593 n. 10. (*citing* Bourjaily v. United States, 483 U.S. 171, 107 S.Ct. 2775, 97 L.Ed.2d 144 (1987)). *See infra* § 1–3.4.1 for a fuller discussion of the application of the 104(a) standard to Rule 702.

See also Recent Developments in the Law: Confronting the New Challenges of Scientific Evidence, 108 Harv. L. Rev. 1481 (1995):

> In 1897 Justice Holmes observed that "[f]or the rational study of the law the black-letter man may be the man of the present, but the man of the future is the man of statistics and the master of economics." Now, almost a

century later, the Supreme Court in Daubert v. Merrell Dow Pharmaceuticals, Inc. has directed federal judges to take a scientific approach to the admissibility of scientific evidence.

Id. at 1532 (*quoting* Oliver W. Holmes, Jr., *The Path of the Law*, 10 Harv. L. Rev. 457, 469 (1920) (citation omitted)). In a recent decision, Judge Ellis drew a distinction between the judge ensuring that the experts relied on tests that adhered to the scientific method and the judge knowing the science produced by that method:

> In granting the . . . summary judgment, the Court scrupulously attempted to walk this fine line: analyzing the experts' adherence to the scientific methodology, while declining to weigh the evidence before it. Significantly, nothing in the Court's review and analysis of this issue required any scientific training. Rather, the Court did nothing more than use the customary legal tools of logical reasoning to carry out its gatekeeping function.

Cavallo v. Star Enterprise, 892 F.Supp. 756, 774–75 (E.D.Va.1995), *aff'd in part, rev'd in part*, 100 F.3d 1150 (4th Cir.1996); *see also* Bradley v. Brown, 42 F.3d 434, 438 (7th Cir. 1994) ("The district court took its gatekeeping function conscientiously while at the same time refusing to 'don the amateur scientist's cap in ruling on scientific validity.'") (*quoting* Bradley v. Brown, 852 F.Supp. 690, 698 (N.D.Ind.1994)).

30.   137 F.3d 780 (4th Cir.1998).

Neither party disputes that, at the beginning of the *Daubert* hearing, the district court told Jim Rothschild, counsel for Therm–O–Disc, "[y]ou have the burden of proof" with regard to Rodems's testimony. However, counsel immediately corrected the district court on this point, and from then forward it appears that the district court understood both the demands of *Daubert* and its own role as "gatekeeper," and conducted the hearing accordingly. Immediately after the objection, the district court withdrew its call for Mr. Rothschild to come forward and show that Rodems's testimony was not admissible, and called Rodems himself to the stand to explain the basis for that testimony. This Rodems did under both direct and cross-examination. After several hours of testimony, the district court determined that, although it had some reservations about the proffered basis for Rodems's opinion, "the defendant has failed to establish ... [that] Mr. Rodems relied upon a scientific principle that was not valid."[31]

Although the Court of Appeals goes to considerable (and confusing) lengths to try to establish both that there is no burden of persuasion in a 104(a) hearing and that the district court did not err because it placed the burden where it was supposed to be, the final sentence in the quotation above—offered in support of the correctness of the district court's hearing process—should leave readers wondering if, at the end of the day, the district judge did understand who bore the burden of persuasion.

The confusion in *Daubert* hearings is perhaps understandable, because the first voice heard is that of the opponent of proffered expert testimony. This has given some lawyers and judges the impression that the opponent has the burden of convincing the court that the witness does not meet *Daubert's* requirements. This impression may be all the more compelling when the expertise being challenged is a type that has become familiar to the courts. But the correct procedure is the opposite of that.

The opponent of expert evidence need only make a showing sufficient to convince a trial court that the objection to the evidence is not frivolous; this triggers a *Daubert* hearing under Rule 104(a). In a Rule 104(a) hearing on the question of admissibility of expert evidence, "These matters should be established by a preponderance of proof."[32] This statement of a standard of proof implies that the hearing is analogous to a civil bench trial. The proponent has the initial burden of production and the ultimate burden of persuading the court that the proffered expert evidence satisfies Rule 702, as interpreted by *Daubert* and *Kumho Tire*. The trial judge serves as the factfinder.[33] And the judge must believe the expert's opinion by a preponderance of the evidence.[34] Thus, if both parties sat mute, the court would have to rule against the party with the burden of persuasion, namely, the proponent of the evidence. If at

31. *Id.* at 784.

32. *Daubert*, 509 U.S. at 593 n.20.

33. Note that Rule 104(a) also provides, "In making its determination [the court] is not bound by the rules of evidence except those with respect to privileges." FED. R. EVID. 104(a).

34. This still does not answer the question of how much error is too much error to be admissible. For example, would expert predictions that are shown by all of the available evidence to be correct only 51% of the time be sufficiently "reliable" to be admissible? Would expert predictions that are wrong more often than they are right be admissible? Rule 403 might also guide judges in making these determinations. *See infra* § 1–3.8.

the end of the hearing, the evidence on the evidence were in equipoise, again the court would have to rule against the proponent of the evidence.

§ 1–3.2 The Requirement of Relevancy

Rule 702 provides as follows:

If scientific, technical, or other specialized knowledge will assist the trier of fact to understand the evidence or to determine a fact in issue, a witness qualified as an expert by knowledge, skill, experience, training, or education, may testify thereto in the form of an opinion or otherwise, provided that (1) the testimony is sufficiently based upon reliable facts or data, (2) the testimony is the product of reliable principles and methods, and (3) the witness has applied the principles and methods reliably to the facts of the case.[35]

Focusing on the language "assist the trier of fact," many courts and commentators characterized this rule as a "relevancy test."[36] In the area of scientific evidence, the *Daubert* Court explained, relevance foremost is a question of fit. Specifically, whatever the validity of the science, it must pertain to some disputed issue in the case.[37] As the *Daubert* Court stated succinctly, Rule 702 "requires a valid scientific connection to the pertinent inquiry as a precondition to admissibility."[38] Only when the science pertains to a factual question in the case can expert testimony be helpful to the trier of fact.[39] This helpfulness component is at the core of Rule 702.[40]

The "helpfulness" standard departs from the more stringent standard that was prevalent before the Federal Rules and is still in use in some jurisdictions today. This more stringent standard requires that the expert testimony provide knowledge that is "beyond the ken" of an ordinary per-

---

35. Fed. R. Evid. 702.

36. *See Daubert*, 509 U.S. at 591 (stating that the language " 'assist the trier of fact' . . . goes primarily to relevance").

37. *See Daubert*, 509 U.S. at 592; *see also* 3 Jack B. Weinstein & Margaret A. Berger, Weinstein's Evidence ¶ 702[02], at 702–18 (1994) ("Expert testimony which does not relate to any issue in the case is not relevant and, ergo, non-helpful."); Fusco v. General Motors Corp., 11 F.3d 259, 264 (1st Cir.1993) (excluding re-enactment offered to illustrate "scientific principles," because it "did not adequately replicate the conditions of the accident"); United States v. Libutti, 1994 WL 774646 (D.N.J. 1994) (concluding that expert testimony regarding "pathological gambler's lifestyle" did not "fit" and was irrelevant to the defendant's mens rea in a prosecution for multiple tax offenses); United States v. Powers, 59 F.3d 1460 (4th Cir.1995) (evidence indicating the defendant was not a "fixated pedophile" held irrelevant where the charge was "incest abuse"); Gier v. Educational Service Unit No. 16, 66 F.3d 940 (8th Cir.1995) (concluding that psychological evaluations are "not reliable enough to make factual or 'investigative conclusions' in legal proceedings"); United States

v. Downing, 753 F.2d 1224, 1242 (3d Cir.1985) ("[E]xpert testimony proffered in the case [must be] sufficiently tied to the facts of the case that it will aid the jury in resolving a factual dispute.").

38. *Daubert*, 509 U.S. at 591–92; *see also* In re Paoli R.R. Yard PCB Litig. (Paoli II), 35 F.3d 717, 745 n. 13 (3d Cir.1994)("[fit] is higher than bare relevance").

39. *See, e.g.*, Christophersen v. Allied–Signal Corp., 939 F.2d 1106, 1113–14 (5th Cir. 1991) (*en banc*); *see also* Viterbo v. Dow Chem. Co., 826 F.2d 420, 424 (5th Cir.1987); Peterson v. Sealed Air Corp., 1991 WL 66370, at *7 (N.D.Ill.1991) (excluding testimony that Cytoxan causes transitional cell carcinoma when the plaintiff suffered from basaloid cell type cancer); Novak v. United States, 865 F.2d 718, 723–24 (6th Cir.1989); Bailiff v. Manville Forest Prods. Corp., 772 F.Supp. 1578, 1583–84 (S.D.Miss.1991); Marder v. G.D. Searle & Co., 630 F.Supp. 1087, 1089–90, 1093 (D.Md.1986).

40. *See* Walker v. Yellow Freight Systems, Inc., 1999 WL 955364 *9 (E.D.La.1999) (Court excluded proffered "human factors expert" because his testimony amounted to little more than what the jurors, "expending a minimum of brain power," could do on their own.).

son.[41] Although some jurisdictions continue to adhere to this more stringent standard, sometimes implicitly,[42] most follow the Rule 702 mandate that permits expert testimony when it will merely assist the trier of fact.[43] In this way, the helpfulness standard incorporates the idea of "probative value" to be found in Rule 401's definition of relevance.[44]

Arguably, of course, the notions of "fit" and "helpfulness" already exist in Rule 402's relevancy requirement.[45] Thus, if relevancy were the sole meaning of Rule 702, its existence would either be redundant or solely for emphasis. The Court, however, held that Rule 702 contains two other requirements. The first, explicitly stated in the Rule, is the qualifications test. This is the subject of the next section. The second, scientific validity, is now an explicit component of Rule 702 and is the central operating tenet of the *Daubert* trilogy. The validity test is considered in detail in the section following the discussion of qualifications.

§ 1–3.3   The Qualifications Test

Courts have always required experts to be "qualified" in order to testify.[46] The more controversial issue is whether qualifications are not only a necessary, but also a sufficient condition for expert testimony. Although no modern court has held that qualifications alone suffice, many commentators suspect that, in practice, some courts adhere to this view.[47] In addition, this seemingly straightforward criterion turns out to contain considerable ambiguity. In particular, two issues arise. The first concerns what sorts of qualifications are

41. *See* McCormick on Evidence, § 13, at 54 (4th ed. 1992); 7 John H. Wigmore, Evidence in Trials at Common Law § 1923, at 29–32 (Chadbourn rev. 1978). *See, e.g.*, Pena v. Leombruni, 200 F.3d 1031, 1034 (7th Cir.1999) (Court upheld exclusion of plaintiff's police expert, who was to testify regarding excessive force, because "the jury needed no help in deciding whether [the defendant-officer] was acting reasonably."); Wal–Mart Stores, Inc. v. White, 476 So.2d 614 (Ala.1985) (holding inadmissible expert testimony on the effect of rainwater on a store's floor).

42. *See, e.g.*, State v. Poland, 144 Ariz. 388, 698 P.2d 183, 194 (Ariz. 1985) (concluding that there was "nothing that an [eyewitness expert] witness would testify to that was not within the juror's common experience"); State v. Porraro, 121 R.I. 882, 404 A.2d 465, 471 (R.I. 1979) (ruling that eyewitness expert testimony was inadmissible because the subject matter was "not beyond the ken of the jurors").

43. Weinstein & Berger, *supra* note 37, ¶ 702[02].

44. Rule 401 provides as follows:

"Relevant evidence" means evidence having any tendency to make the existence of any fact that is of consequence to the determination of the action more probable or less probable than it would be without the evidence.

Fed. R. Evid. 401.

45. Rule 402 provides as follows:

All relevant evidence is admissible, except as otherwise provided by the Constitution of the United States, by Act of Congress, by these rules, or by other rules prescribed by the Supreme Court pursuant to statutory authority. Evidence which is not relevant is not admissible.

Fed. R. Evid. 402.

46. *See generally* Poust v. Huntleigh Healthcare, 998 F.Supp. 478, 490 (D.N.J.1998) ("[A] proponent of expert testimony must establish that his expert is qualified and his testimony is admissible by a preponderance of the evidence."); Hand v. Norfolk Southern Railway Co., 1998 WL 281946 at *4 (Tenn.App. 1998) ("the trial court must analyze the science and not merely the qualifications, demeanor or conclusions of experts"). For an excellent overview of the qualifications requirement, *see* Margaret A. Berger, *Evidentiary Framework,* in Reference Manual on Scientific Evidence 37, 55–67 (Federal Judicial Ctr. ed. 1994).

47. *See, e.g.*, Paul C. Giannelli, *The Admissibility of Novel Scientific Evidence: Frye v. United States, a Half Century Later,* 80 Colum. L. Rev. 1197, 1210 (1980). *Cf.* Hopkins v. Dow Corning, 33 F.3d 1116, 1124 (9th Cir.1994) ("The district court is not required to hold a Rule 104(a) hearing, but rather must merely make a determination as to the proposed expert's qualifications.").

necessary; for instance, must the expert have an advanced degree? The second concerns whether the expert's credentials must be in the specialty area in which the expert is to testify.

§ 1–3.3.1 Necessary Qualifications

Rule 702 defines expertise broadly. Not just Ph.D.s and M.D.s are contemplated by the Rule, but a wide assortment of specialists, ranging from nuclear physicists to real estate agents.[48] Because the range is wide, so are the standards for qualifications.[49] Rule 702 requires only that the expert be qualified "by knowledge, skill, experience, training, or education."[50] By necessity, therefore, courts approach the issue of what background qualifications are necessary in a flexible manner.

In general, courts interpret the main qualifications requirement in relation to the expert's claimed expertise and the demands of the testimony.[51] Hence, experts on medical matters are expected to have medical degrees, appropriate certifications, and experience,[52] but auto mechanics might only need years of experience and demonstrable skills.[53] In many contexts, experience alone will be sufficient to qualify a witness,[54] while in others, the lack of

48. *See, e.g.,* Cayuga Indian Nation of N.Y. v. Pataki, 79 F. Supp. 2d 78, 90 (N.D.N.Y.1999) (upholding qualifications of "ethno-historian"); *see* 2 J. Wigmore, Evidence § 556, at 751 (Chadbourn rev. 1979) (The witness' expertise "may have been attained, so far as legal rules go, in any way whatever; all the law requires is that it should have been attained.").

49. The Advisory Committee's Note to Fed. R. Evid. 702 states as follows:

[Rule 702] is broadly phrased. The fields of knowledge which may be drawn upon are not limited merely to the "scientific" and "technical" but extend to all "specialized" knowledge. Similarly, the expert is viewed, not in a narrow sense, but as a person qualified by "knowledge, skill, experience, training or education." Thus within the scope of the rule are not only experts in the strictest sense of the word, e.g., physicians, physicists, and architects, but also the large group sometimes called "skilled" witnesses, such as bankers or landowners testifying to land values.

50. Fed. R. Evid. 702.

51. *See, e.g.,* Seatrax v. Sonbeck Int'l, Inc., 200 F.3d 358, 372 (5th Cir.2000) ("In a complex case involving trademark infringement, [the expert's] lack of formal training or education in accounting, and his failure to conduct an independent analysis of [defendant's] sales figures were insurmountable obstacles for [plaintiff] in its attempt to qualify him as an expert.").

52. *See, e.g.,* Gebhardt v. Mentor Corp., 191 F.R.D. 180 (D.Ariz.1999) (excluding expert who offered to testify on medical causation who did not have a medical degree); Edmonds v. Illinois Central Gulf Railroad, 910 F.2d 1284, 1287 (5th Cir.1990) (clinical psychologist

not qualified to testify on plaintiff's heart condition); *see also* Stull v. Fuqua Industries, Inc., 906 F.2d 1271, 1275 (8th Cir.1990).

53. *See, e.g.,* Fox v. Dannenberg, 906 F.2d 1253, 1256–57 (8th Cir.1990).

54. *See* United States v. Corey, 207 F.3d 84, 88–90 (1st Cir.2000) (allowing firearms expert to testify regarding provenance of a gun based on experience); United States v. Withorn, 204 F.3d 790, 793 (8th Cir.2000) (Court upheld admission of certified nurse midwife who testified that the complainant "had been struck, choked, and raped by" the defendant, based on the expert's experience as a rape counselor.); United States v. Majors, 196 F.3d 1206 (11th Cir.1999) (allowing proffered government expert regarding financial practices who only had an associates degree, but who had extensive experience working for the FBI on such matters); Davis v. United States, 865 F.2d 164, 168 (8th Cir.1988) ("Rule 702 does not state a preference for academic training over demonstrated practical experience."); Circle J. Dairy, Inc. v. A.O. Smith Harvestore Products, Inc., 790 F.2d 694, 700 (8th Cir. 1986) ("Rule 702 . . . does not rank academic training over demonstrated practical experience."); American Computer Innovators, Inc. v. Electronic Data Systems Corp., 74 F.Supp.2d 64, 69 (D.Mass.1999) (allowing experience-based expert and noting that he was "not analogous to the all-purpose engineer who offers testimony on everything from refrigerators to diapers to airplane engines"). Courts' reliance on experience as a mark of expertise is especially frequent when police officers testify to the modus operandi of various crimes. *See, e.g.,* United States v. Sparks, 949 F.2d 1023, 1026 (8th Cir.1991) (use of street gangs to

experience will disqualify an expert.[55] As a practical matter, this means courts consult the experts' respective fields for guidance regarding what constitutes a "qualified" expert. Not all fields, however, have well-articulated standards and many subjects of interest to the law are studied by fields with widely varying professional requirements.[56]

§ 1–3.3.2   Specificity of the Necessary Qualifications

The hallmark of late twentieth century science (and all expertise) is specialization. This trend leaves courts somewhat uncertain as to whether generalists should be permitted to testify about matters that are highly specialized.[57] Once again, courts approach this matter flexibly.[58] Some courts require experts to have demonstrated expertise in the specific areas and topics on which they are to testify.[59] Other courts provide that generalists may testify on specialty areas and that their lack of expertise in those areas is a matter of weight for the trier of fact.[60] Too often, however, expedience leads

distribute drugs); United States v. Solis, 923 F.2d 548, 550 (7th Cir.1991) (use of beepers in drug trafficking); United States v. Hoffman, 832 F.2d 1299, 1309–10 (1st Cir.1987) (code words used in drug trafficking). *See generally* Annot., *Admissibility of Expert Evidence Concerning the Meaning of Narcotics Language in Federal Prosecution for Narcotics Dealing— Modern Cases*, 104 A.L.R. Fed. 230 (1991); Gail Sweeney Stephenson, Note, *Police Expert Witnesses and the Ultimate Issue Rule*, 44 LA. L. REV. 211 (1983). *See* discussion *infra* § 1–3.5.1[1].

55. *See, e.g.,* O'Conner v. Commonwealth Edison Co., 13 F.3d 1090, 1107 & n. 19 (7th Cir.1994) ("We do not believe that this limited experience [five cases of radiation-induced cataracts in twenty years] qualifies as a basis for a scientifically sound opinion.").

56. Perhaps the best example of the difficulty with setting uniform standards comes from the study of human behavior, a topic of obvious and frequent legal relevance. Qualifications requirements vary widely between the fields which focus on this topic, including psychiatry, psychology, social work, counseling and others. Qualifications also vary widely within each of these fields. For instance, in psychology, some practitioners have the Ph.D., some the Ed.D., some the M.S.W., and some the M.A. or M.S. *See* Jenkins v. United States, 307 F.2d 637, 644 (D.C.Cir.1962) ("[W]e must examine the reality behind the title 'psychologist.' ").

57. *See* United States v. Roldan–Zapata, 916 F.2d 795, 805 (2d Cir.1990) ("A witness may be qualified as an expert on certain matters and not others.").

58. *See generally* Berger, *Evidentiary Framework, supra* note 46, at 59 ("The governing principle should be whether the expert can assist the trier of fact.").

59. *See, e.g.,* Gates v. The City of Memphis, 210 F.3d 371 (6th Cir.2000) (requiring forensic

expert to have expertise in sub-area of "trajectory analysis"); Robertson v. Norton Co., 148 F.3d 905 (8th Cir.1998) (holding that an expert qualified to testify about a manufacturing defect was not qualified to testify about the adequacy of warnings); Alexander v. Smith & Nephew, 90 F. Supp. 2d 1225, 1229 (N.D.Okla. 2000) ("The simple possession of a medical degree is insufficient to qualify a physician to testify as to the advantages of an (sic) spinal fixation device, the medical causation of spine-related ailments, or the mechanical functioning of an orthopedic implantation device."); Kirstein v. W.M. Barr & Co., 983 F.Supp. 753, 759 (N.D.Ill.1997) (Same); Watkins v. Schriver, 52 F.3d 769, 771 (8th Cir.1995) (holding that neurologist could not testify to cause of injury since he was not "an expert in either accident reconstruction or forensic medicine"); Chikovsky v. Ortho Pharmaceutical Corp., 832 F.Supp. 341, 344–46 (S.D.Fla.1993) (The court excluded the testimony of an obstetrician/gynecologist that the topical application of Retin–A causes birth defects, because the doctor had no demonstrated expertise in embryology, teratology or genetics.); Christophersen v. Allied–Signal Corp., 939 F.2d 1106, 1112–13 (5th Cir. 1991) (*en banc*) ("The questions … do not stop if the expert has an M.D. degree. That alone is not enough to qualify him to give an opinion on every conceivable medical question."); People v. Kelly, 17 Cal.3d 24, 130 Cal. Rptr. 144, 549 P.2d 1240, 1250 (Cal. 1976) ("[The expert] has an impressive list of credentials in the field of voice print analysis. However, these qualifications are those of a technician and law enforcement officer, not a scientist."); State v. Priester, 301 S.C. 165, 391 S.E.2d 227 (S.C. 1990) (technologist cannot testify to the intoxicating effects of blood alcohol level).

60. *See, e.g.,* Tuf Racing Products, Inc. v. American Suzuki Motor Corp., 223 F.3d 585, 591 (7th Cir.2000) ("The notion that [*Daubert*]

courts to allow experts to venture into areas outside of their true expertise.[61]

The evaluation of qualifications is a fact-based preliminary inquiry that will be overturned on appeal only for an abuse of discretion.[62] There seems to be a small trend toward greater scrutiny of expert credentials and qualifications in post-*Daubert* admissibility hearings. A number of recent cases have rejected expert testimony on the basis of a lack of qualifications. Representative of these is *Mancuso v. Consolidated Edison Co. of New York*.[63] There, the court concluded that an internist did not have the requisite qualifications to testify that the plaintiff's ailments were caused by exposure to polychlorinated biphenyls (PCB). The internist lacked formal training and credentials in PCB toxicology or in environmental or occupational medicine. The internist was unable to answer basic questions about PCB toxicology and relied upon the plaintiffs' attorney to provide him with the scientific literature with which he formed his opinion.[64]

requires particular credentials for an expert witness is radically unsound."); Carroll v. Morgan, 17 F.3d 787, 790 (5th Cir.1994) (holding that *Daubert* does not require a pathologist to testify to cause of death and the fact that three testifying pathologists disagreed with the cardiologist's conclusion is "grist for the jury"); Payton v. Abbott Labs, 780 F.2d 147, 155 (1st Cir.1985) ("The fact that the physician is not a specialist in the field in which he is giving his opinion affects not the admissibility of his opinion but the weight the jury may place on it.") (*citing* Alvarado v. Weinberger, 511 F.2d 1046, 1049 (1st Cir.1975)); Quinton v. Farmland Indus., Inc., 928 F.2d 335, 337 (10th Cir. 1991) ("This assumption about the insufficiency of general medical study, which reflects the implausible view that such training qualifies a doctor to diagnose and treat a wide range of physical disorders in the real world but not to render expert opinions about particular examples in the courtroom, has been expressly rejected in the case of physicians."); Zemaitatis v. Innovasive Devices, Inc., 90 F.Supp.2d 631, 633 (E.D.Pa.2000) (allowing a physician who was a "jack-of-all-trades" to testify). *See generally* McCormick, *supra* note 41, § 203, at 875 n.40 ("Even a scientist eminently qualified in one area may not be knowledgeable in another. For example, an immunogeneticist may have a detailed understanding of the chemistry of blood types and typing procedures, but only a superficial acquaintance with the statistical method for computing a probability of paternity. Generally, cross-examination should expose such deficiencies.").

61. *See* ANDRE A. MOENSSENS, FRED E. INBAU & JAMES E. STARRS, SCIENTIFIC EVIDENCE IN CRIMINAL CASES (3d ed. 1986) ("[E]xperts, in their sworn testimony, frequently transgress into fields that are beyond their expertise.")

62. *Poust*, 998 F. Supp. at 491; *see also* United States v. Velasquez, 64 F.3d 844, 849 (3d Cir.1995); United States v. Kelley, 6 F. Supp. 2d 1168 (D.Kan.1998) (excluding expert whose "qualifications [were] largely a matter

provable only through his own opinion of himself").

63. 967 F.Supp. 1437 (S.D.N.Y.1997). *See also* United States v. Cunningham, 194 F.3d 1186 (11th Cir.1999) (excluding proffered expert who only had an undergraduate degree in chemistry).

64. For example, the expert in *Mancuso* was unable to state what levels of PCB contamination would be dangerous to humans. 967 F. Supp. at 1443–45. *See also* Cooper v. Laboratory Corp. of America Holdings, Inc., 150 F.3d 376 (4th Cir.1998); Jesionowski v. Beck, 955 F.Supp. 149, 150 (D.Mass.1997) ("I find that Dr. Johnson, ' ... although able to discuss the reliability of polygraph examinations in general terms, was unable to articulate with sufficient precision the reasons for its reliability.' ") (*quoting* Miller v. Heaven, 922 F.Supp. 495, 502 (D.Kan.1996)); Sutera v. The Perrier Group of America, Inc., 986 F.Supp. 655, 667 (D.Mass.1997) (plaintiff's expert, an oncologist and hematologist with no expertise in epidemiology, toxicology, biostatistics or risk-assessment, lacks the specific knowledge, education, training and experience to render an opinion as to whether the exposures to low levels of benzene in Perrier for a short time period caused the plaintiff's leukemia); Wintz v. Northrop Corporation, 110 F.3d 508, 512 (7th Cir.1997) (expert, a toxicologist, was not a licensed physician and lacked sufficient expertise in birth defects bromide exposure, or the specific birth defect from which the plaintiff suffered to testify that bromide exposure to the mother during her pregnancy caused the plaintiff's injury); Everett v. Georgia–Pacific Corp., 949 F.Supp. 856, 857 (S.D.Ga.1996) (expert, practicing family medicine and surgery, possesses no specialized knowledge or training in the field of toxicology); Muzzey v. Kerr–McGee Chemical Corp., 921 F.Supp. 511 (N.D.Ill.1996) (witnesses without expertise in hematology not qualified to testify whether plaintiff's exposure to radiation from refining byproduct caused her to contract the disease polycythemia vera).

It is worth noting that the issue of qualifications is intrinsically bound to the Court's holding in *Kumho Tire* that *Daubert's* gatekeeping requirement extends to non-scientific expert testimony.[65] Of course, if an asserted expertise cannot be shown to be sound, then even the most eminent (most highly qualified) practitioner of that asserted expertise still would not be permitted to testify as an expert. In fact, courts are likely to find that the issues of qualifications, reliability and fit are inextricably entwined and, in practice, cannot easily be disentangled. Qualifications are relative, being more or less useful depending on the expert's familiarity with the subject that fits, or is relevant to, the matter to be decided by the trier of fact. Qualifications, therefore, cannot be evaluated in the abstract. At some point, certainly, the question of qualifications becomes a matter of weight rather than admissibility.[66] And this is true of all Rule 702 matters. But just as with Rule 702 validity assessments, the judge's gatekeeping obligation should extend not merely to qualifications in the abstract, but qualifications to testify about the subject that is relevant to the issues in controversy.[67]

§ 1–3.4   Applying *Daubert*: The Standards for Determining Validity

The *Daubert* Court articulated four *non-exclusive* factors that courts should consider when evaluating the validity of the basis for proffered expert opinion:[68] (1) testability (or falsifiability), (2) error rate, (3) peer review and

The *Mancuso* saga, the subject of four published decisions, finally came to an end in 1999. In *Mancuso v. Consolidated Edison Co.*, 56 F. Supp. 2d 391 (S.D.N.Y.1999), the court once again found the proffered expert's credentials inadequate. The expert was a medical doctor but that was where her expertise ended. She had no specialized training in toxicology, had failed to evaluate exposure levels, did not evaluate the literature to determine if PCBs produced the illnesses complained of, and did not do a differential diagnosis to ascertain specific causation. *See id.* The court concluded that "with [the expert's] mantle of academic credentials and her dazzling, even if inappropriate, incantation of medical jargon, she has the troubling potential of misleading a jury of laypersons naturally inclined to be sympathetic to a likable family punished by cruel circumstances and to give them economic relief at the expense of a deep-pocket defendant." *Id.* at 410.

65. *See* Alexander v. Smith & Nephew, 98 F. Supp. 2d 1310, 1315 (N.D.Okla.2000) ("A blanket qualification for all physicians to testify to anything medically-related would contravene the Court's gate-keeping responsibilities.").

66. Many courts provide little or no gatekeeping to an expert's qualifications. *See, e.g.*, Rushing v. Kansas City Southern Ry. Co., 185 F.3d 496, 507 (5th Cir.1999) (The court held that, under *Daubert*, "as long as some reasonable indication of qualifications is adduced, the court may admit the evidence without abdicating its gate-keeping function."); In re Tasch,

Inc. v. Sabine Offshore Service, Inc., 1999 WL 596261 *3 (E.D.La.1999) (same); Lillis v. Lehigh Valley Hospital Inc., 1999 WL 718231 *5 (E.D.Pa.1999) ("The 'specific expertise' requirement . . . does not demand a perfect fit.").

67. *See, e.g.*, Walker v. Yellow Freight Systems, Inc., 1999 WL 955364 *9 (E.D.La.1999) ("[B]ecause of [the expert's] admitted lack of familiarity with the relevant standards and regulations, the Court agrees with [the defendant's] argument that [the expert] 'has no basis to describe the proper standard of care . . . .' In other words, the Court finds [the expert] to be unqualified to testify in the instant case and finds that his testimony would not 'fit' the relevant issues."); United States v. Cunningham, 194 F.3d 1186 (11th Cir.1999) (finding expert with only an undergraduate degree in chemistry to be unqualified to testify whether certain waste was hazardous.); Schmerling v. Danek Medical, Inc., 1999 WL 712591 (E.D.Pa.1999) (Expert, a professor of orthopedic surgery at Harvard Medical School, did not have the credentials that would permit him to opine on the alleged deleterious consequences of defendant's pedicle bone screws.).

68. Although the Court emphasized that these four factors did not represent "a definitive checklist or test," many courts have applied them this way. *Daubert*, 509 U.S. at 593; *see, e.g.*, Roback v. V.I.P. Transport, Inc., 1994 WL 548197, at *4–*5 (N.D.Ill.1994); Stanczyk v. Black & Decker, Inc. 836 F.Supp. 565, 567–68 (N.D.Ill.1993).

publication and (4) general acceptance. Other courts and commentators offer additional factors that might be of assistance to the gatekeeping court.[69] This section examines the four *Daubert* factors together with several of the additional factors that might contribute to a judge's evaluation of scientific validity.

At the outset, certain general observations can be made about the approach to validity[70] assessment encompassed by these four factors. Despite the substantial concern raised by many that *Daubert* demands a level of scientific sophistication among judges that would make them "amateur scientists,"[71] only two of the *Daubert* factors focus on the scientific merit directly. Of the remaining two, one—general acceptance—is very deferential to the field from which the evidence comes. The other, peer review and publication, is somewhat deferential to the opinion of the field, though as we explain below, should operate as an aid to courts needing to evaluate the methodology employed by the experts. The Court thus indicated that although judges must become sophisticated consumers of science,[72] and must understand the philo-

---

69. Professor Mark McCormick, *Scientific Evidence: Defining a New Approach to Admissibility*, 67 IOWA L. REV. 879, 911–12 (1982), a former state supreme court justice, lists 11 factors for determining admissibility:

(1) the potential error rate in using the technique; (2) the existence and maintenance of standards governing its use, (3) presence of safeguards in the characteristics of the technique, (4) analogy to other scientific techniques whose results are admissible, (5) the extent to which the technique has been accepted by scientists in the field involved, (6) the nature and breadth of the inference adduced, (7) the clarity and simplicity with which the technique can be described and its results explained, (8) the extent to which the basic data are verifiable by the court and jury, (9) the availability of other experts to test and evaluate the technique, (10) the probative significance of the evidence in the circumstances of the case, and (11) the care with which the technique was employed in the case.

See also, United States v. Downing, 753 F.2d 1224, 1239–41 (3d Cir.1985) (adding to the *Daubert* four, body of professional literature, nonjudicial uses of the science, novelty of the technique and the qualifications of the witness); Wade–Greaux v. Whitehall Laboratories, 874 F.Supp. 1441, 1478 (D.Vi.1994) (same); Daubert v. Merrell Dow Pharmaceuticals, Inc., 43 F.3d 1311, 1317 (9th Cir.1995) (*Daubert II*) (discussed *infra* note 73, re discounting testing specifically designed to support litigations).

70. For some time, courts and commentators have confused the terms reliability and validity. *See, e.g.*, United States v. Distler, 671 F.2d 954, 962 (6th Cir.1981) (confusing estimates of reliability with assertions of validity); Bert Black, *A Unified Theory of Scientific Evidence*, 56 FORDHAM L. REV. 595 (1988) (conflating validity and reliability).

The *Daubert* Court noted this confusion and stated its support for the scientific meaning of those terms: "[S]cientists typically distinguish between 'validity' (does the principle support what it purports to show?) and 'reliability' (does the application of the principle produce consistent results?)." *Daubert*, 509 U.S. at 590n.9. The Court stated clearly that "validity" is the germane inquiry: "In a case involving scientific evidence, evidentiary reliability will be based upon scientific validity." *Id.*

71. *See, e.g., Daubert*, 509 U.S. at 600–01. (Rehnquist, C.J., concurring) ("I do not think [Rule 702] imposes on [district court judges] either the obligation or the authority to become amateur scientists."). It is worth noting that Chief Justice Rehnquist authored *General Electric Co. v. Joiner*, 522 U.S. 136, 118 S.Ct. 512, 139 L.Ed.2d 508 (1997), in which he closely evaluated the research offered to support the expert's opinion before concluding that the district court did not abuse its discretion in excluding the expert. *See also* Zuchowicz v. United States, 870 F.Supp. 15 (D.Conn.1994) ("judges may not always have the 'special competence' to resolve complex issues which stand at the frontier of current medical and epidemiological inquiry").

72. The debate about judges' competence to evaluate scientific research is likely to continue for some time. *See generally Developments— Scientific Evidence, supra* note 29, at 1538–39 ("[E]ven before *Daubert,* many courts had successfully evaluated legal reliability according to principles of scientific validity and scientific reliability.").

Just how severe the burden is on federal judges, and whether this burden is too great for them to bear, remains a matter of some dispute. Judge Legge offered the following ruminations on the topic:

The responsibilities of district courts under *Daubert* are indeed heavy ones. The training

sophical and practical considerations raised by the scientific method, they can sometimes employ proxies to help them decide the issue. Of course, scientists themselves do the same when they evaluate scientific fields that are not their areas of specialty or when time prohibits a more thorough evaluation.

No single list of factors, however, can capture the sundry considerations that go into determining the validity of research results. Indeed, it is somewhat misleading to suggest one, for, as every scientist knows, validity is not a categorical conclusion. Scientists tend to speak of validity in terms of the strength of the evidence and reasoning supporting a conclusion, not in terms of its "truth." Similarly, although judges must assess validity in order to make a categorical decision—admitting or excluding the testimony—judges need not have a categorical view of the science. Judges are expected to use the *Daubert* factors (and others) to determine if it is more likely than not that the methods and reasoning validly support the proffered expert testimony.[73]

Many courts assumed that *Daubert* set a lower threshold for admissibility than had *Frye*.[74] At the same time, various courts have discovered that the

of a judge is of course in law and not in medicine. . . . A court's analysis of medical causation necessarily forces a court to become as familiar as it can, with little or no scientific training, to understand the medical and scientific concepts. The vocabulary alone is daunting; and the danger of merely grabbing at words, and attaching too much significance to them, is very real. . . . Armed with a degree of intellectual curiosity inherent in district court judges, and guided by two centuries of reviewing the wisdom of other occupations, federal courts will perform the assigned task. Whether the *Daubert* analysis is ultimately viewed as "wise" law, or whether it promotes "good" science, must be answered at some time in the future. Casey v. Ohio Medical Products, 877 F.Supp. 1380, 1383 (N.D.Cal.1995).

73. In addition to the sundry factors beyond the *Daubert* four suggested by courts and commentators, *see supra* note 69, Judge Kozinski, in *Daubert v. Merrell Dow Pharmaceuticals, Inc.*, 43 F.3d 1311 (9th Cir.1995) (*Daubert II*), offered the following practical observation:

One very significant fact to be considered is whether the experts are proposing to testify about matters growing naturally and directly out of research that they have conducted independent of the litigation, or whether they have developed their opinions expressly for purposes of testifying. That an expert testifies for money does not necessarily cast doubt on the reliability of his testimony, as few experts appear in court merely as an eleemosynary gesture. But in determining whether proposed expert testimony amounts to good science, we may not ignore the fact that a scientist's normal workplace is in the lab or the field, not the courtroom or the lawyer's office.

Id. at 1317. For applications of Judge Kozinski's insight, *see* In re Hanford Nuclear Reser-

vation Litigation, 894 F.Supp. 1436, 1446–47 (E.D.Wash.1995); Marbled Murrelet v. Pacific Lumber Co., 880 F.Supp. 1343, 1364–65 (N.D.Cal.1995).

74. The assumption that *Daubert* is more permissive than *Frye* is reflected in the following cases: General Elec. Co. v. Joiner, 522 U.S. 136, 118 S.Ct. 512, 139 L.Ed.2d 508 (1997) (". . . . the FRE allow district courts to admit a somewhat broader range of scientific testimony than would have been admissible under *Frye*. . . ." (concerning possible carcinogenic effect of certain chemicals)); United States v. Bonds, 12 F.3d 540 (6th Cir.1993) ("easily meets the more liberal test set out . . . in *Daubert*" (concerning DNA typing)); United States v. Kwong, 69 F.3d 663 (2d Cir.1995) ("The FRE, although concededly more liberal than the *Frye* test. . . ." (concerning polygraph evidence)); Borawick v. Shay, 68 F.3d 597 (2d Cir.1995) ("[B]y loosening the strictures on scientific evidence set by *Frye*, *Daubert* reinforces the idea that there should be a presumption of admissibility." (concerning repressed memory, hypno-therapy)); United States v. Jones, 107 F.3d 1147 (6th Cir.1997) ("Such a result[, that is, excluding asserted 'science' that had for a century been admitted,] truly would turn *Daubert*, a case intended to relax the admissibility requirements for expert scientific evidence, on its head." (concerning handwriting identification)). Indeed, the point is made in *Daubert* itself:

such a rigid standard [as *Frye*] would be at odds with the Rules' liberal thrust and their general approach of relaxing the traditional barriers to "opinion" testimony.

509 U.S. at 588. But in *Daubert* there is significant tension attached to the assumption that a test of scientific soundness is necessarily a lower threshold than a test of "acceptance" within a particular community. The *Daubert*

conscientious application of *Daubert* leads them at least to the brink of excluding asserted areas of expertise that under *Frye* had gained admission easily.[75] To unravel this seeming paradox, we need only to compare the two tests and should not be misled by the dicta of *Daubert* itself or the mantra repeated in so many other cases.[76]

The two tests look at different attributes of asserted knowledge. *Frye* inquires into the general acceptance of a proposition among a community thought to understand the matter; *Daubert* inquires directly into a proposition's scientific foundation. As Table 1 helps to illustrate, these two questions usually will lead to the same result. That which has a strong scientific foundation usually will be generally accepted; that which has a weak scientific foundation usually will not be widely accepted. In those situations, both standards will admit or both will exclude.

But sometimes the two will diverge. When asserted knowledge is sound but not generally accepted, *Daubert* permits its admission while *Frye* does not.[77] This is the category of cases that most commentators and courts have in mind when they think that *Daubert* is more liberal than *Frye*. When asserted knowledge has not been shown to be sound, but nevertheless has gained general acceptance in its field, then *Daubert* excludes even though *Frye* would admit.[78] This category contains the asserted areas of expertise that have surprised judges who did not expect to find *Daubert* leading toward exclusion. Put most simply, *Daubert* sets a higher threshold for admissibility under some circumstances and a lower threshold under other circumstances. *Frye* and *Daubert* diverge because of widely varying practices among different scientific communities. Some fields are very rigorous in their evaluation of hypotheses, while others are rather less so.[79] Courts have been surprised at *Daubert's*

court apparently realized that scientific assertions that had long been accepted could still be found to be unsound science:

> [W]e do not read the requirements of Rule 702 to apply specially or exclusively to unconventional evidence. Of course, well-established propositions are less likely to be challenged than those that are novel, and they are more handily defended.

Id. at 593 n.11.

75. We say "to the brink of excluding" because in such cases it has not been unusual for judges to create ways of avoiding the implications of *Daubert*, and admitting the expertise at issue. *See, e.g.*, United States v. Starzecpyzel, 880 F.Supp. 1027, 1036 (S.D.N.Y.1995) ("Were the court to apply *Daubert* to the proffered [handwriting identification] testimony, it would have to be excluded.").

Since *Kumho Tire*, in the handwriting area, several federal courts have excluded expert testimony purporting to identify the author of a questioned document. *See* United States v. Santillan, 1999 WL 1201765 (N.D.Cal.1999); *See also* United States v. Hines, 55 F. Supp. 2d 62 (D.Mass.1999); *see also* United States v. McVeigh, 1997 WL 47724 (D. Colo. Trans. Feb. 5, 1997). *Cf.* United States v. Van Wyk, 83 F. Supp. 2d 515 (D.N.J.2000) ("forensic stylistics").

76. One court described the tension within *Daubert* thusly:

> In *Daubert*, the Supreme Court acknowledged the "liberal thrust" of rule 702 but nevertheless refused to jettison the requirement of a threshold showing of reliability for expert scientific testimony, stating that "the trial judge must ensure that any and all scientific testimony or evidence admitted is not only relevant, but reliable."

State v. Crosby, 927 P.2d 638, 641 (Utah 1996).

77. *E.g.*, United States v. Galbreth, 908 F.Supp. 877 (D.N.M.1995) (concerning the polygraph).

78. *E.g.*, Williamson v. Reynolds, 904 F.Supp. 1529 (E.D.Okla.1995) (concerning hair and fiber identification).

79. In *Falise v. American Tobacco Co.*, 107 F.Supp.2d 200 (E.D.N.Y.2000), Judge Weinstein, in refusing to overanalyze proffered expert testimony, commented as follows:

> Too nitpicking an approach to find reasons to exclude expert testimony from distinguished scientists will tend to drive the best of them out of the courtroom. The greatest danger to the courts is not the incompetent who will testify for pay, but our failure to encourage sound scientists to assist the law.

tendency to bar evidence when applied to fields that for too long rested on uncritical consensus rather than uncompromising empirical investigation.

Table 1. Comparison of the *Frye* and *Daubert* Tests
and their Consequences

FRYE: General Acceptance	*DAUBERT*: Scientific Foundation	
	Strong	Weak
High	Both Admit	*Frye* admits *Daubert* excludes
Low	*Frye* excludes *Daubert* admits	Both Exclude

§ 1–3.4.1   Testability (Falsifiability)

The problem of identifying uniquely scientific knowledge has occupied countless volumes in the philosophy of science. Of the sundry philosophical choices the Supreme Court could have made, it chose the criterion of falsifiability, which is most closely associated with Sir Karl Popper. Although the Court cited Popper in only a passing reference, it chose as its first factor his falsifiability criterion for distinguishing scientific from nonscientific and, especially, pseudoscientific statements. In short, the criterion of falsifiability provides that "a statement or theory is ... falsifiable if and only if there exists at least one potential falsifier—at least one possible basic statement that conflicts with it logically."[80] As the Court quoted Popper, " 'the criterion of the scientific status of a theory is its falsifiability, or refutability, or testability.' "[81] The hallmark of scientific statements is that they are vulnerable to refutation.

Contrary to Popper's original formulation of falsifiability, the Court selected this factor as one of four possible indices of validity. For Popper, however, falsifiability was *the* criterion of scientific status.[82] In fact, courts will find application of *Daubert* difficult if they treat testability as an optional factor. The other three factors all presuppose testability; in science, a nontestable hypothesis cannot have an error rate and is exceedingly unlikely to be published in a peer-reviewed journal and achieve general acceptance.[83] And indeed, since *Daubert*, courts generally appear to treat testability as a prerequisite rather than just another factor.[84] In practice, therefore, the *Daubert* testability criterion is entirely consistent with Popper's philosophy.

Id. at 205.

80. K. Popper, Realism, and the Aim of Science x [From the Postscript to the Logic of Scientific Discovery] (W. Bartley, III ed. 1983).

81. *See Daubert*, 509 U.S. at 593 (*citing and quoting* K. Popper, Conjectures and Refutations: The Growth of Scientific Knowledge 37 (5th ed. 1989)).

82. Whereas the Court stated that testability was "a key question," Popper would have said it was "the" key question. *See Daubert*, 509 U.S. at 592–93.

83. *See* David L. Faigman, *To Have and Have Not: Assessing the Value of Social Science to the Law as Science and Policy*, 38 Emory L.J.

1005, 1016–18 (1989); Bert Black, Francisco J. Ayala & Carol Saffran, *Brinks, Science and the Law in the Wake of* Daubert: *A New Search for Scientific Knowledge*, 72 Tex.L.Rev. 715, 754–62 (1994).

84. *See generally* Claar v. Burlington Northern Railroad Co., 29 F.3d 499, 503 (9th Cir.1994) ("'[S]cientists whose conviction about the ultimate conclusion of their research is so firm that they are willing to aver under oath that it is correct prior to performing the necessary validating tests could properly be viewed ... as lacking the objectivity that is the hallmark of the scientific method.'"); Bradley v. Brown, 852 F.Supp. 690, 698 (N.D.Ind.1994) ("The first of these considerations, which asks

The concept of falsifiability is separate from the question of when a scientific theory has been corroborated or falsified by observations.[85] The *status* of a statement as scientific depends on its amenability to test; the *merit* of a scientific statement depends on the degree to which it has survived attempts at falsification.[86] Both the status and the merit of purportedly scientific statements are subjects to be assessed by judges under *Daubert*.[87] Therefore, although *Daubert* added the necessary step that the basis for an expert's testimony must be both testable and have been tested, it did not articulate the manner in which this should be done. Lower courts must establish those standards.

[1] *Evaluating Empirical Tests of Falsifiability*

Not all empirical tests of a theory are equally valuable. Research methods vary considerably, and some tests amount to no test at all.[88] If *Daubert* is not to become a dead letter, judges must develop sufficient scientific literacy to recognize research designed to truly test a hypothesis as compared to research designed merely to supply impressive looking graphs and imposing numbers to a researcher's theory.[89] In other words, judges (and lawyers) must be able to distinguish the methods of science from those methods that merely imitate science.[90]

whether the theory or methodology has been subjected to the scientific method, is the most weighty."); Rosen v. Ciba–Geigy Corp., 892 F.Supp. 208, 212 (N.D.Ill.1995) ("[The expert's] opinion that the nicotine patch caused the heart attack has not been tested and is purely his own speculation. His testimony is not the type of scientific knowledge the Supreme Court contemplated in *Daubert* and would be inadmissible at trial.").

85. POPPER (1983), *supra* note 80, at x ("[Falsifiability] has to do only with the logical structure of statements and classes of statements. And it has *nothing* to do with the question whether or not certain possible experimental results would be accepted as falsifications.") (emphasis in original).

86. *See, e.g.*, Buckman v. Bombardier Corp., 893 F.Supp. 547, 556 (E.D.N.C.1995) (noting and applying principle that testable propositions must be adequately tested). *See also* Sean O'Connor, *The Supreme Court's Philosophy of Science: Will the Real Karl Popper Please Stand Up?* 35 JURIMETRICS 263 (1995).

87. *Daubert*, 509 U.S. at 593 ("[A] key question to be answered in determining whether a theory or technique is scientific knowledge that will assist the trier of fact will be whether it can be (*and has been*) tested.") (emphasis added). *See* Brumley v. Pfizer, Inc., 200 F.R.D. 596 (S.D.Tex.2001) (rejecting plaintiff's contention that *Daubert* requires merely that an expert's opinion be testable, not that it have been tested).

The testability criterion also has what could be termed an affirmative component. Specifically, expert testimony that is testable should

be tested. A complication of *Daubert's* interpretation of Rule 702 was that on its face the opinion only applied to "scientific" expert testimony. It was silent regarding other forms of expert testimony encompassed by the Rule based on "technical or other specialized knowledge." FED. R. EVID. 702. The Supreme Court resolved this matter in *Kumho Tire, Ltd. v. Carmichael*, 526 U.S. 137, 119 S.Ct. 1167, 143 L.Ed.2d 238 (1999), holding that *Daubert's* gatekeeping duties extend to all expert testimony. *See infra* § 1–3.5.

88. *See, e.g.*, Schmaltz v. Norfolk & Western Railway Co., 878 F.Supp. 1119, 1122 (N.D.Ill.1995) ("[T]he record before me fails to make clear why the incidence of eye irritation in rabbits exposed to high doses of [the chemical] could reasonably lead a doctor to conclude that an indirect exposure to [it] could cause pulmonary or respiratory conditions in humans."); Williamson v. General Motors Corp., 1994 WL 660649 *5–*6 (N.D.Ga.1994) (noting that *Daubert* requires not simply that "some" tests be carried out, but that "adequate tests" be conducted).

89. *See* Glastetter v. Novartis Pharm. Corp., 252 F.3d 986 (8th Cir.2001) (District courts are expected to "separate[] expert opinion evidence based on 'good grounds' from subjective speculation that masquerades as scientific knowledge."). *See generally* Paul S. Miller et al., *Daubert and the Need of Judicial Scientific Literacy*, 77 JUDICATURE 254 (1994).

90. Professor Richard Feynman, the Nobel Prize-winning physicist, referred to the latter kinds of research as "cargo cult science." Ac-

Some methods, such as gazing into a crystal ball, obviously have little scientific merit. But judges must also recognize those methods that, in reality, fail to progress significantly beyond crystal ball gazing or, as in many instances, beyond a researcher's creativity.[91] Moreover, judges must appreciate that assessing scientific research methods is a difficult and complex matter. There is no single way to conduct research to answer a particular question and research programs rarely answer factual questions definitively. Thus, there are no "perfect" studies or "final" answers in science.

In large measure, the highly sophisticated and subtle subject of scientific methods is the principal subject of this book. Several chapters are devoted specifically to research methods[92] and statistical analysis[93] and every substantive chapter revolves around the issue of the methods brought to bear on certain legally relevant factual questions.

[2]   What, Exactly, Must Be Tested?

[a]   The Methodology–Conclusion Paradox: A Proposed Solution

When applied to scientific research offered in the trial setting, the falsification criterion contains an added complexity. It is not entirely clear which aspects of the science must have been tested to cross the threshold of admissibility, and which aspects are a matter of weight for the trier of fact to determine. The *Daubert* Court wrote that the "focus, of course, must be solely on principles and methodology, not on the conclusions that they generate."[94]

This statement caused some confusion among courts and in the scholarly literature, because it does not provide as clear a demarcation between the issues for judges and the issues for triers of fact as it implies.[95] When scientists conduct research, although they clearly demarcate the methods employed from the conclusions they reach, they also well understand that the two are mutually dependent. Some conclusions are permitted by a particular methodology and some are not. Thus, when studying the toxic effects of drugs, using animals rather than humans as subjects restricts the conclusions that might be drawn from the work. The decision to use multiple regression analysis rather than analysis of variance affects what conclusions might be drawn from the data. Failure to include a comparison group in a study of

---

cording to Professor Feynman, after World War II certain Pacific Islanders wanted the cargo planes to keep returning. These Islanders made runways, stationed a man with wooden headphones and bamboo for antennas, lighted some fires and waited for the planes to land. Cargo cult scientists act in the same way. "They follow all the apparent precepts and forms of scientific investigation, but they're missing something essential because the planes don't land." N.Y. TIMES, Feb. 17, 1988, at D27, col. 1. *See generally* PETER WORSLEY, THE TRUMPET SHALL SOUND: A STUDY OF "CARGO" CULTS IN MELANESIA (1957).

91. In *Thomas v. FAG Bearings Corp.*, 846 F.Supp. 1382 (W.D.Mo.1994), the court excluded expert "opinions . . . concocted of impermissible bootstrapping of speculation upon conjecture." *Id.* at 1394. *See also* Reynard v. NEC

Corp., 887 F.Supp. 1500, 1504–08 (M.D.Fla. 1995) (finding that expert's conclusion that electromagnetic radiation from a cellular phone caused a brain tumor was "worse than speculation" and "not supported by any objective source").

92. *See* Chapter 4.

93. *See* Chapter 5.

94. *Daubert*, 509 U.S. at 595 (emphasis added).

95. Kenneth J. Chesebro, *Taking Daubert's "Focus" Seriously: The Methodology/Conclusion Distinction*, 15 CARDOZO L. REV. 1745, 1745–53 (1994); *see also* David E. Bernstein, *The Admissibility of Scientific Evidence After Daubert v. Merrell Dow Pharmaceuticals, Inc.*, 15 CARDOZO L. REV. 2139, 2164–66 (1994).

leukemia rates in a particular neighborhood would obviously affect what conclusions could be reached. Research on the carcinogenic character of second-hand smoke conducted on white rats, by subjecting them to the equivalent of ten packs-a-day, might employ exactly the right methodology and reasoning for concluding that such smoke causes cancer in white rats; but if the researcher is interested in generalizing the study to humans, then we must evaluate the methodology and reasoning in light of that purpose. Scientific conclusions are inextricably connected to the methodologies used to reach them.

Thus, in *Joiner*, the Court rejected the suggestion that *Daubert* created a sharp distinction between the validity of scientific methodology and the plausibility of conclusions:

> [C]onclusions and methodology are not entirely distinct from one another. Trained experts commonly extrapolate from existing data. But nothing in either *Daubert* or the Federal Rules of Evidence requires a district court to admit opinion evidence which is connected to existing data only by the *ipse dixit* of the expert. A court may conclude that there is simply too great an analytical gap between the data and the opinion proffered.[96]

Courts have begun to suggest another way to understand Justice Blackmun's distinction between methodology and conclusions, an interpretation that conforms to both the realities of scientific research and the needs of the law. The primary purpose of the methodology-conclusion distinction was to draw a line between the judge's task as gatekeeper and the jury's role as finder and weigher of fact. The line between methodology and conclusions was ill-suited for this purpose, because it did not describe the reality of scientific practice. However, courts have increasingly noted the different levels of abstraction at which science comes to the law. Science comes to courts as an amalgam of general principles or theories and specific applications of those principles. These two basic levels of abstraction offer a solution to the judge/jury problem inherent in all admissibility determinations.

Courts have recognized these two levels of abstraction most clearly in medical causation cases in which they routinely distinguish between "general causation" and "specific causation." General and specific causation are merely sub-instances of the inherent division between the general and the specific in applied science, but they nicely illustrate the distinction. General causation refers to the proposition that one factor (or more) can produce certain results, and thus the finding transcends any one case. Specific causation considers whether those factors had those results in the specific case at bar. Consider, for example, the complaint in *Daubert* itself. The plaintiffs claimed that Jason Daubert's mother's ingestion of Bendectin during pregnancy caused or contributed to his birth defects. This claim has both general and specific compo-

---

96. *Joiner*, 522 U.S. at 519. *See also* Pride v. BIC Corp., 218 F.3d 566, 578 (6th Cir.2000) (evaluating methodology of experts and finding that it cannot sustain their conclusions); Heller v. Shaw Ind., Inc., 167 F.3d 146, 153 (3d Cir. 1999) (Courts "must examine the expert's conclusions in order to determine whether they could reliably flow from the facts known to the expert and the methodology used.").

The *ipse dixit* language of *Joiner* has proved popular with lower courts. *See, e.g.,* Freeport–McMoran Resource Partners v. B–B Paint Corp., 56 F.Supp.2d 823 (E.D.Mich.1999) (The court found that the expert's opinions are nothing more than his own "experience" and are tied to each defendant through nothing more than his "*ipse dixit*.").

nents. As a matter of general causation, the plaintiffs were obligated to show that Bendectin sometimes causes birth defects. This hypothesis transcends the particular dispute, and is as true in California as it is in New York. In addition, the plaintiffs had to show that Jason's birth defects were attributable to his mother's ingestion of Bendectin. This proof might involve showing that she took the drug during the relevant period and that other factors probably did not cause the defects. This is specific causation.

Virtually all scientific evidence shares this basic dichotomy between the general and the specific. The general premises of fingerprinting, for instance, are that every person's fingerprint is unique, and that a known print can be compared to a latent print. The conclusion regarding the identity of the person who left a particular print at a particular place is specific. Litigation involving asbestos, agent orange, trichlorethelyne, phen-fen, cellular phones, and so on, all have both general premises and specific conclusions. Engineering and the forensic and social sciences also fit this description. Science provides a method by which relationships or associations can be identified and, typically, quantified. Scientific theories often involve induction from the particular to the general. The law, however, is interested in applying these general lessons to specific cases. It may be said that scientists tend to focus on general propositions, whereas judges and lawyers concentrate primarily on specific applications.

Although not without ambiguities, the distinction between the general and the specific helps to distinguish the admissibility decision for the judge from the weight determination for the jury. The rule of thumb we suggest is as follows. Under Rules 702 and 104(a), a judge must find that the general principles and theories underlying an expert's opinion are reliable and valid. This responsibility includes an evaluation of the methodology used to make a specific inference, since the validity of such methodologies (such as clinical assessments, differential diagnosis, polygraph machines, DNA technologies (PCR or RFLP) and so on) depend on general principles and theories. If a body of data supports both valid generalizations and the methods employed to determine specific propositions, the jury should evaluate what weight to accord the testimony.

This reading of Justice Blackmun's distinction between methodology and conclusions is consistent with the traditional roles of these two decision makers. Judges, by virtue of their education and experience, are well situated to assess the features of science and technology that are general and do not change from case to case. Moreover, courts should be reluctant to allow different juries to decide common issues differently. The effects of second-hand smoke are the same in Iowa and Florida. Giving judges a strong initial role in evaluating scientific findings that transcend particular cases will go a long way toward achieving consistency. In contrast, whether a particular plaintiff's lung cancer is due to second-hand smoke, or possibly has a genetic cause, is unique to the case. If doctors have the theory and technology to make these determinations, then the accuracy of the conclusion that the plaintiff's cancer was caused by the defendant's cigarettes should be for the trier of fact to decide.

In short, judges should evaluate under Rule 104(a) the general principles or methods by which experts derive their opinions about specific causation.

Once the court has determined that such methods exist and that they were applied in the particular case, the trier of fact must assess the weight the result receives. For instance, if research indicates that a method of characterizing DNA is accurate and the expert used that technology in the particular case, it should be for the trier of fact to determine whether the test was employed correctly.[97]

Not all scientific expert testimony, of course, will be able to meet validity requirements, especially at the start. In the usual case, general relationships will be validated before they can be extended to individuals in a reliable fashion. This does not mean juries will be left without guidance, for the general science itself often provides substantial assistance. Moreover, allowing experts to take the next step and apply the science to the case without research supporting their ability to do so invites unfounded speculation. In fact, many scientists refuse to take this step, because of the lack of competence to offer an opinion better than triers of fact could do on their own. For example, experts on the reliability of eyewitness identifications do not testify on case-specific facts. Researchers looking at factors associated with unreliable identifications are able to specify factors that interfere with identifications, such as "weapons focus," but they cannot state with any confidence whether a particular witness is accurate. Their testimony might still be of use to triers of fact, but the science simply does not permit an opinion on case-specific facts.[98] Such humility should be appreciated by the courts. Sometimes, the law asks factual questions that scientists, or any expert, cannot answer any better than laypersons.

Ordinarily, experts should not be allowed to testify to specific conclusions when there is a lack of data on the general proposition sought to be generalized to the specific case. Courts considering the issue have agreed with this proposition. Yet, this proposition has proved difficult to enforce in practice. Many experts reason backward from their conclusions to their premises. For example, a doctor's statement that plaintiff's exposure to chemical Y caused her respiratory ailment might be premised on both the specifics of the case (e.g., temporal proximity between exposure and onset of illness) and more general experience with this or similar chemicals. The question, then, is what value "experience" should be accorded in demonstrating general causation. This is an important subject that we return to *infra* in our discussion of *Kumho Tire*.[99] It is safe to say here that with no proof of general causation, an expert should not be permitted to testify about specific causation.

97. *See* Edward J. Imwinkelried, *The Debate in The DNA Cases over the Foundation for the Admission of Scientific Evidence: The Importance of Human Error as a Cause of Forensic Misanalysis*, 69 WASH. U.L.Q. 19 (1991). Of course, all such determinations are subject to Rule 104(b). If no reasonable jury could find that the fact is true, then the evidence must be excluded. FED. R. EVID. 104(b).

98. Some courts find departure from this limitation on expert testimony fatal. *See e.g.*, United States v. Serna, 799 F.2d 842 (2d Cir. 1986) (Expert's inability to testify about the reliability of a particular eyewitness' testimony indicated lack of probative value.). *But see* Advisory Committee's Note for Fed. R. Evid. 702 ("Most of the literature assumes that experts testify only in the form of opinions. The assumption is logically unfounded. [Rule 702] accordingly recognizes that an expert on the stand may give a dissertation or exposition of scientific or other principles relevant to the case, leaving the trier of fact to apply them to the facts.").

99. *See infra* § 1–3.5.

[b]   The Question Studied in the Field vs. the Legally Relevant Inquiry

An extremely important issue on which post-*Daubert* courts have stumbled is the matter of translating the "answers" that respective fields offer into the questions that the law asks. This is a problem of vocabulary and general lack of understanding among lawyers and judges regarding what, exactly, a particular field's interest is in the subject. There are numerous examples. We will discuss two in particular here, but the issue is fundamental and deserves substantial attention.[100] Probably the best two examples of the sometimes lack of understanding between law and science come from the fields of medicine and psychology, professions that occupy a disproportionate amount of courts' attention.

Medical doctors and lawyers both use the term "differential diagnosis," but the two professions often mean different things by it.[101] The Eighth Circuit's decision in *Turner v. Iowa Fire Equipment Co.*,[102] illustrates the different meanings the two professions attribute to the term. In *Turner*, the plaintiff brought suit after the automatic fire extinguisher system at her workplace was accidently activated. It dumped a white powdery substance—mainly baking powder—on her grill. Soon after, plaintiff developed a host of symptoms, including shortness of breath and headaches. At trial, her treating physician testified in support of her claim. He stated, however, that as the treating physician, his task was to determine what the plaintiff suffered from, not what had caused her condition. The district court excluded the expert and the Eighth Circuit affirmed.

The Eighth Circuit explained that there were two meanings of the term "differential diagnosis." The medical community defines it as the attempt to identify the ailment in order to determine treatment.[103] This has to be contrasted with the legal community's definition of "differential diagnosis," which is concerned with the identification of the *cause(s)* of the ailment.[104] In *Turner*, the court explained, the treating physician had conducted a medical differential diagnosis, but had failed to conduct a legal one. The relevant legal query might better be termed "differential etiology."

In psychology, the phenomenon is even more salient. Lawyers and judges routinely consider psychological diagnoses for forensic purposes when, to the extent they have been tested at all, they are deemed valid only for therapeutic purposes. Thus, for example, a lawyer asking a clinical psychologist whether post-traumatic stress disorder (PTSD) is "generally accepted" or "has been

100. The problem of departures in understanding between the law and science is also discussed in the substantive chapters of this treatise.

101. *Compare* Mattis v. Carlon Elec. Prod., 114 F. Supp. 2d 888, 893 (D.S.D.2000) (allowing differential diagnosis because of "widespread acceptance in the medical community") *with* Moore v. Ashland Chemical, Inc., 151 F.3d 269 (5th Cir.1998) (*en banc*) (excluding expert opinion relying on differential diagnosis on very similar facts). *Cf.* Cooper v. Carl A. Nelson & Co., 211 F.3d 1008, 1019 (7th Cir.2000)

(reversing district court's "overly aggressive role as 'gatekeeper,'" finding that the medical doctor "employed the accepted diagnostic tool of examination accompanied by physical history as related by the patient"); Campbell v. Chiles, 2000 WL 730423 *3–*5 (N.D.Tex.2000) (despite expert's failure to even do a differential diagnosis, the court found the opinion to be sufficiently supported by "objective evidence").

102. 229 F.3d 1202 (8th Cir.2000).

103. *Id.* at 1208.

104. *Id.*

tested" is likely to get an affirmative response. However, psychologists mean that it has been tested for therapy, not necessarily that it has been tested for forensic use.[105] For example, when PTSD is used by a prosecutor in a rape trial, typically as a component of Rape Trauma Syndrome, the rape itself serves as the traumatic stressor that a psychologist relies on to make the diagnosis. Psychologists, however, do not challenge their patients' claims to have been raped. In court, of course, that is the controverted issue. In effect, then, a PTSD diagnosis, which partly rests on the alleged victim's statements that she was raped, is introduced to prove that very contention. Other examples abound. Most syndromes and diagnoses have not been evaluated for forensic use. Lawyers and judges, therefore, must consider not only whether the basis for the expertise is valid for some purpose, but whether it is valid for its intended use by courts. This is a matter of "fit."[106]

§ 1–3.4.2   Error Rate

At first glance, Justice Blackmun's inclusion of error rates as a principal factor for courts to consider would seem obvious. Yet, on closer inspection, employing this important concept might seem perplexing. It appears that "error" occurs in science in a multitude of ways, not all of which are quantifiable. It is useful once again to distinguish between the general levels of science and the application of that general work to an individual situation.

[1]   Error Rates in Stating Features of an Individual

The typical use of the term "error rate" refers to the number of "mistakes" a particular technique or method will make in some specific number of trials. In this sense, error rate corresponds primarily to the "general technology" level of science outlined above. There are two types of mistakes that might be made. A polygraph examiner, for instance, might mistakenly conclude that the subject is telling the truth when he is lying (a "false negative"), or the examiner might mistakenly conclude that the subject is lying when he is telling the truth (a "false positive"). A scientist's judgment of the value of a technique will depend on both the amount and kind of error.

Importantly, the Court did not specify what error rates are tolerable. There are good reasons for this omission. The costs of making an error are different in different contexts. For example, the error rate associated with predictions of violence is fairly high.[107] Yet, psychiatric predictions appear to be better than chance and, for some populations, substantially better. The costs of making a mistake, therefore, should guide a court's evaluation of the proffered evidence. Thus, a judge might require a relatively low error rate before admitting predictions of violence in a capital case, but permit higher error rates in a probation matter.[108] This determination, however, cannot

105. *See, e.g.,* United States v. Barnette, 211 F.3d 803, 815–16 (4th Cir.2000) (allowing psychologist's reliance on "Psychopathy Checklist Revised," because experts in the field rely on that type of testing).

106. *See supra* § 1–3.2 (discussing "fit" and relevance under Rule 702).

107. *See Science in the Law: Social and Behavioral Science Issues* (Chapter 2) (Clinical and Actuarial Predictions of Violence).

108. The Supreme Court has decided that in the capital sentencing context, the Constitution allows a high error rate, because juries should be able to distinguish accurate predictions from inaccurate ones. The Court reached this conclusion despite statements from psychologists and psychiatrists that they could not make this distinction. Barefoot v. Estelle, 463 U.S. 880, 103 S.Ct. 3383, 77 L.Ed.2d 1090 (1983). Of course, the Constitution provides the minimum protection guaranteed to crimi-

simply be an application of Rule 702. Rule 702 queries whether the scientific evidence will "assist the trier of fact." Subject to the other qualifications discussed in this section, any science that is even slightly better than flipping a coin is likely to meet this test. The Rule 702 error rate factor thus embodies, at least in part, a Rule 403 analysis.[109] But in practice, it would be virtually impossible to disentangle the Rule 702 probative value component of scientific evidence from the matter of error rate. Because scientific knowledge is almost never known with complete certainty, its value (i.e., relevance) depends substantially on the costs associated with being wrong.

[2] Error Rates Attributable to the Research Methods Used in Studying Population Features

In scientific investigation, a multitude of limitations affect the methods that are chosen and thus the knowledge that they generate. The sources of error (or limitations) include such matters as sample size, sample studied (college students, registered voters, or white rats?), choice of comparison group (random assignment, self-selection, or none?), and apparatus or materials used (live, video, or written?).[110]

Errors can be random or systematic. Random sampling, for example, entails random error. A random sample of 20 is less likely to represent an underlying population than a random sample of 2000. Unreliable coding of data could produce essentially random error. Researchers might accidently code some people who are exposed to a substance as not exposed and vice versa.

Systematic errors, unlike random errors, tend to work in a single direction and, therefore, introduce bias into the data. For example, if researchers rely on self reports of exposure to some substance, and if some of the people asked have already become ill, "recall bias" can arise. Those who are sick will be more likely to have searched through their past and recalled more exposures than those who are well. As a consequence, there will be an artificially high correlation between exposure and illness.[111] Inferential statistics cannot quantify systematic errors. A basic advantage of experimental research is its ability to control for many systematic errors.

Because of the limitations inherent in scientific studies, few scientists would be confident in stating conclusions from one or even a few studies. Only through replications, using various designs and methods, do scientists gain confidence that a hypothesis has been sufficiently corroborated. No magic number or moment determines this point, however; like many areas of the law, science presents a broad spectrum of grays that only over time sharpens into black and white.

nal defendants. The Federal Rules of Evidence require a higher threshold of scientific validity than the *Barefoot* Court contemplated.

109. Although the opinion does not tie the error rate factor to Rule 403, Justice Blackmun emphasized the important role this rule plays in admitting scientific evidence. *See Daubert,* 509 U.S. at 597; *see infra* § 1–3.8.

110. *See* Chapter 4, for discussion of these and other issues as possible sources of error.

111. *See* Chapter 7.

§ 1–3.4.3   Peer Review and Publication

For the average scientist, publication in a peer reviewed journal is the mark of successful completion of a research project. But not all peer-reviewed journals are equal in status. Since scientists view the quality of scholarship, in part, through the lens of the journal name in which it is situated, it should be no surprise that judges too notice this criterion.[112] At the same time, even the highest quality journals sometimes publish work that is later found to be wrong. In addition, mainstream peer-reviewed journals, by definition, are more likely to publish conventional scholarship and might be slow to recognize revolutionary findings or methods. The *Daubert* Court considered these costs and benefits and concluded that peer review and publication is a factor to be considered in assessing admissibility, but it is not a prerequisite.[113]

The limitations of peer review and publication are akin to those of using general acceptance, discussed below, as a factor. Both criteria are mere proxies for the determinative factor. The value of peer review depends on the quality of those reviewers. If scientists publish in journals with lax standards, this criterion is not likely to lead to the exclusion of bad science. Thus, judges must consider carefully the range of journals that qualify under this standard. Judges would be well-advised to return to the first two factors the Court identified, falsifiability and error rate. These two criteria clearly indicate the Court's choice of a conventional ("scientific realist") view of the scientific method. Publication in journals that do not share the values reflected in these first two factors, therefore, should warn judges that the studies need to be scrutinized with particular care. To be sure, just as the Court did not establish publication as a prerequisite to admissibility, so too publication in non-rigorous journals should not mean *per se* exclusion. But in both cases, when studies lack placement in mainstream journals or when they have not been published at all, judges should use caution before admitting testimony relying on them.

Many courts and commentators take "peer review and publication" in isolation, as merely one of the four *Daubert* "factors" for assessing the reliability of scientific evidence. This common interpretation reflects the organization and emphasis within the paragraph that seeks to explain the factor,[114] rather than the logic of the point being made. "Peer review and publication" are features of a larger project, a synecdoche for a more important and more fundamental activity of scientific communities, for which the phrase stands. The more important point is found in the middle of the paragraph: "submission to the scrutiny of the scientific community is a component of 'good science' ... because it increases the likelihood that

---

112. For better or worse, using journal placement as the criterion of quality is a phenomenon well known in law. Of course, most law journals are edited by students, while scientific journals are edited by scientists.

113. *Daubert,* 509 U.S. at 594 ("The fact of publication (or lack thereof) in a peer-reviewed journal thus will be a relevant, though not dispositive, consideration in assessing the scientific validity of a particular technique or methodology on which an opinion is premised."). *See, e.g.,* Smith v. Ford Motor Co., 215

F.3d 713 (7th Cir.2000) (finding that district court abused its discretion in excluding plaintiff's experts on the sole basis that the research they relied on had not appeared in peer reviewed journals).

114. The first sentence of *Daubert's* discussion of this point seems to direct the reader's attention to "peer review and publication" with a seeming simplicity that has misled many a reader.

substantive flaws in methodology will be detected."[115] That is the real concern of scientific communities—detecting serious flaws in the design of studies. A substantive finding is no better than the methods used to find it. Peer review and publication facilitate that effort. They are not the beginning and the end of the effort.

A scientific community is interested in critically evaluating the research products of its members, as part of the process of deciding whether any given set of findings is good enough to be added to the field's corpus of knowledge. "Peer review and publication" are a part of, and contribute to, that larger process of critical evaluation. "Peer review" is not limited to deciding what gets published. Peer review takes place before research is conducted (such as when a funding agency evaluates research proposals). And it takes place after publication. Indeed, most of the "scrutiny of the scientific community" takes place after publication. Work that is too weak or flawed or unimportant even to be published, it is hoped, does not survive the first, small phase of peer review,[116] is not published, and is thus not set before the relevant scientific community for its larger[117] and ultimately more thorough scrutiny. *Daubert's* discussion of "peer review and publication" takes pains to alert the reader to the fact that publication in a peer reviewed journal is no assurance of soundness of a finding,[118] and the lack of publication is no assurance that a study and its findings are not sound.[119] These are merely aids to assessing the soundness of a study's methodology and execution.

The larger purpose of such scrutiny in all its forms is to assess the quality of a study's (or a line of studies') research methodology and, in light of that assessment, the meaning and value of the data generated by the research. The courts, no less than the scientific community, should be concerned not with the mere formal act of submission to the scrutiny of the scientific community, but with what the community concluded following such scrutiny. What weaknesses were discovered in the research methods? How do those affect the meaning or weight of the findings? Were there erroneous interpretations of the findings? Or did the study's design and its findings withstand the critical evaluation of a discerning community?

In short,"peer review and publication" do not themselves establish the "reliability" of the proffered knowledge. The more sensible reading of this "*Daubert* factor"—if the *Daubert* Court was tracking the common sense of most scientific communities—is that it stands for critical evaluation, with the help of the scientific community, of the research on which the asserted expertise is based.

§ 1–3.4.4 General Acceptance

Like peer review and publication, general acceptance is only as good as the field that is surveyed. Under *Frye,* of course, general acceptance was the

---

115. *Daubert*, 509 U.S. at 593.

116. The peer review process of scientific journals usually involves between a few and half a dozen peer reviewers.

117. Open to the hundreds or thousands or tens of thousands of members of a given field.

118. "Publication (which is but one element of peer review) is not a sine qua non of admissibility; it does not necessarily correlate with reliability." *Daubert*, 509 U.S. at 593.

119. "Some propositions, moreover, are too particular, too new, or of too limited interest to be published." *Id.*

standard by which expert testimony was judged. But general acceptance operates differently under *Daubert,* where it is used in conjunction with other factors and is no longer a necessary or sufficient condition for admission.

Shortly after *Daubert* was decided, a major debate arose over whether the new test would be more liberal (i.e., allow more expert testimony) or would be more conservative (i.e., allow less expert testimony). This question cannot be answered simply. Although the Court cited the principle embraced by the Federal Rules of Evidence to liberalize admissibility standards,[120] it adopted the most demanding test contained in the Rules for preliminary assessments of fact. As noted above, Rule 104(a) mandates that judges determine the validity of the science underlying an expert's testimony rather than submit the question to the jury.

As for the answer to the persistent question whether *Daubert* should lead to more or less expert testimony, the correct answer is "yes and no." In those areas of science with a tradition of rigorous research, *Daubert* can be expected to be more liberal, but in those areas without such a tradition, it should be more conservative. The first question *Daubert* requires judges to ask is, "where are the data?," and failure to produce them should result in exclusion of the expert opinion.[121] As judges become familiar with the scientific method and the fields that employ it, they will become more skeptical of those fields that use it poorly.[122] In general, trial courts can be expected to admit expert opinion in fields in which rigorous testing is part of the culture. In those fields, substantial testing of hypotheses that have not yet achieved general acceptance will likely be permitted as support for an expert's opinion.

§ 1–3.5 *Daubert's* Application to "Technical, or Other Specialized Knowledge": *Kumho Tire, Ltd. v. Carmichael*

In *Kumho Tire, Ltd. v. Carmichael,*[123] the Court considered a question that had bedeviled the lower courts, whether *Daubert's* gatekeeping obligation extended to so-called non-scientific expert testimony. The Court declared that it did: "We conclude that *Daubert's* general holding—setting forth the trial judge's general 'gatekeeping' obligation—applies not only to testimony based on 'scientific' knowledge, but also to testimony based on 'technical' and 'other specialized' knowledge."[124] The plaintiffs had brought suit after their tire blew out causing an accident in which one person was killed and several others were severely injured. Their claim rested largely on the testimony of their expert witness who testified in a deposition that the blowout was caused by a defect in the manufacture or design of the tire. His testimony was based exclusively on his experience in the tire industry. He had conducted no tests on the tire in question or on similarly situated tires. He provided no statistical information linking the factors he identified as being indicative of tire failures

---

120. This policy is reflected in Rule 402. FED R. EVID. 402. Those who cite this Rule to argue for liberal admission standards of expert testimony overlook that, by its own terms, this rule is subject to the other rules. Rule 402, therefore, provides little assistance with the construction of Rule 702.

121. This statement might be qualified by the possibility that Courts will fail to apply

Daubert to testable, but not yet scientifically tested, evidence. *See infra* § 1–3.5.1.

122. *See* Michael J. Saks & Jonathan J. Koehler, *What DNA "Fingerprinting" Can Teach the Law About the Rest of Forensic Science,* 13 CARDOZO L. REV. 363 (1991).

123. 526 U.S. 137, 119 S.Ct. 1167, 143 L.Ed.2d 238 (1999).

124. *Id.* at 141.

to a manufacturing defect.[125] The defendant moved to exclude the expert's testimony and for summary judgment. It claimed that the plaintiff's expert's testimony failed the *Daubert* standard, for it was not based on tested research, had no known error rate, had not been published in peer reviewed journals, and was not generally accepted among engineers. The court agreed that the plaintiff's engineer failed the *Daubert* test. Plaintiffs asked for reconsideration, arguing that the court had applied the *Daubert* factors too inflexibly. The court concluded that, however flexibly it applied the *Daubert* test, the plaintiffs' expert's testimony was not sufficiently reliable to allow.

On appeal, the Eleventh Circuit reversed.[126] The Circuit Court applied a *de novo* standard to "the district court's legal decision to apply *Daubert*."[127] It then went on to find that the *Daubert* test was limited to "scientific knowledge," and that since the plaintiffs' expert based his testimony on his "experience" and not the scientific method, it had to remand for a different admissibility analysis.[128]

The Supreme Court reversed. Justice Breyer, writing for the Court, stated that the *Daubert* gatekeeping function applies to all expert testimony. The Court explained that Rule 702 "makes no relevant distinction between 'scientific' knowledge and 'technical' or 'other specialized' knowledge."[129] The limitation of *Daubert* to "scientific knowledge" occurred merely because "that [was] the nature of the expertise at issue" there.[130] The plain meaning of Rule 702, therefore, supports extending the gatekeeping function to all experts. Moreover, the policy underlying Rule 702 supports this result. First, experts are granted great leeway in testifying to opinions, a fact that is true for nonscientist experts as well. Second, "it would prove difficult, if not impossible, for judges to administer evidentiary rules under which a gatekeeping obligation depended upon a distinction between 'scientific' knowledge and 'technical' or 'other specialized' knowledge. There is no clear line that divides the

---

125. The plaintiff's expert reasoned from the premise that if user misuse had not occurred, the cause of the tire failure must be a manufacturing defect. User misuse—described as "overdeflection" resulting from underinflation of the tire or carrying too heavy loads on the tire—could be identified, according to the expert, by the presence of at least two of four possible symptoms. The Court summarized his testimony:

> These symptoms include (a) tread wear on the tire's shoulder that is greater than the tread wear along the tire's center; (b) signs of a "bead groove," where the beads have been pushed too hard against the bead set on the inside of the tire's rim; (c) sidewalls of the tire with physical signs of deterioration, such as discoloration; and/or (d) marks on the tire's rim flange.... [The expert] said that where he does not find at least two of the four physical signs just mentioned (and presumably where there is no reason to suspect a less common cause of separation), he concludes that a manufacturing or design defect caused the separation.

Id. at 144. Presumably, the four factors identified could be empirically tested. Indeed, if these are factors commonly associated with tire failures, it would be surprising if statistics were not available on their frequency under different failure scenarios. Quite simply, a tire expert ought to be able to say what percentage of "over-deflected" tires show shoulder tread wear, bead groove, sidewall marks or discoloration and flange marks. *See generally* Moisenko v. Volkswagenwerk, 198 F.3d 246 (6th Cir. 1999) (finding that the plaintiff utterly failed to establish any of the *Daubert* factors for his engineering expert, thus failing to show that the expert's "findings were based on 'sound science' and of showing 'some objective, independent validation of the expert's methodology.' ").

126. Carmichael v. Samyang Tire, Inc., 131 F.3d 1433 (11th Cir.1997).

127. *Kumho Tire*, 526 U.S. at 147.

128. *Id.*

129. *Id.* at 147.

130. *Id.* at 148.

one from the others."[131] The Court concluded "that *Daubert's* general principles apply to the expert matters described in Rule 702."[132] This means that, as regards all expert testimony, trial court judges "must determine whether the testimony has a reliable basis in the knowledge and experience of [the relevant] discipline."[133]

On the more specific question whether a trial court "may" consider the *Daubert* factors in assessing so-called non-scientific evidence, the Court said it could. Initially, the Court observed, engineering is itself a discipline that relies on scientific principles.[134] It might even be the quintessential "applied science." Hence, some of the *Daubert* factors could be helpful in assessing the reliability of an engineering expert.[135] More to the point, however, the Court stated that "[a]s the Solicitor General points out, there are many different kinds of experts, and many different kinds of expertise."[136] The form of the expertise will dictate what factors might be of assistance in assessing its evidentiary reliability. The Court explained:

> The conclusion, in our view, is that we can neither rule out, nor rule in, for all cases and for all time the applicability of the factors mentioned in *Daubert*, nor can we now do so for subsets of cases categorized by category of expert or by kind of evidence. Too much depends upon the particular circumstances of the particular case at issue. . . . [A] trial court should consider the specific factors identified in *Daubert* where they are reasonable measures of the reliability of the expert testimony.[137]

Whether or not the specific *Daubert* factors apply, the trial court still has gatekeeping responsibilities.[138]

The *Kumho Tire* Court next turned to an issue that is likely to create some difficulty in the years ahead. In *Joiner*, the Court had held that the abuse of discretion standard applied to appellate review of Rule 702 admissibility determinations.[139] In *Kumho Tire*, the Court extended this very deferential standard to the matter of the district court's selection of factors by which it evaluates reliability. "[W]hether *Daubert's* specific factors are, or are not, reasonable measures of reliability in a particular case is a matter that the law grants the trial judge broad latitude to determine."[140] The Court continued, "[t]he trial court must have the same latitude in deciding how to test an expert's reliability, and to decide whether or when special briefing or other

---

131. *Id.*

132. *Id.* at 149.

133. *Id.*

134. *Id.* at 149–50.

135. For an excellent illustration of how *Kumho Tire* should be applied to engineering testimony, *see* Samuel v. Ford Motor Co., 96 F. Supp. 2d 491 (D.Md.2000).

136. *Kumho Tire*, 526 U.S. at 150.

137. *Id.* at 150–52.

138. In *In re Husting Land & Development*, 255 B.R. 772 (Bankr.D.Utah 2000), the court stressed that whatever factors might be considered, the proponent of the evidence must demonstrate reliability:

Some of these non-exclusive factors may be inapplicable to non-scientific testimony, or an expert witness relying solely or primarily on experience. However, under these circumstances, "the witness must explain how that experience leads to the conclusion reached, why that experience is a sufficient basis for the opinion, and how that experience is reliably applied to the facts."

Id. at 781 (*quoting* Advisory Committee Notes, Amendments to FED.R.EVID. 702 (effective December 1, 2000)).

139. *See infra* § 1–3.6 for extensive discussion of the *Joiner* decision.

140. *Kumho Tire*, 526 U.S. at 153.

proceedings are needed to investigate reliability, as it enjoys when it decides whether or not that expert's relevant testimony is reliable."[141]

This appellate deference to the factors used to assess the different categories of expertise is a possible Achilles' heel in an otherwise solidly reasoned opinion. If taken literally, it would allow different judges in the same district to apply different factors to similar kinds of expert testimony. It might allow the same judge to apply different factors to similar kinds of experts. For instance, in one case, forensic document examination might be evaluated harshly because it has yet to be tested adequately, and, in another case in the same district, it might be permitted because it is thought to be reliable based on the practitioner's experience with the subject. If trial courts fail to craft consistent guidelines for these cases, parties will engage in forum shopping to obtain judges most sympathetic to their point of view.

We do not expect that this sort of inconsistency will be too great a problem among trial courts.[142] District court judges are interested in maintaining some consistency and are likely to look to prevailing practices in their circuits as regards particular forms of expert testimony. Moreover, despite the Court's injunction that appellate courts should defer to trial courts about the factors chosen to assess reliability, we expect that appellate judges will still provide some oversight to maintain consistency. In a concurring opinion, for example, Justice Scalia emphasized that "[t]hough, as the Court makes clear today, the *Daubert* factors are not holy writ, in a particular case the failure to apply one or another of them may be unreasonable, and hence an abuse of discretion."[143] Appellate courts are likely to continue to play an important role in these cases.[144] Although some within circuit variation will inevitably occur, we believe the more likely danger is that differences will emerge between circuits. The Supreme Court might yet find the need to revisit this issue.

The task for judges after *Kumho Tire*, therefore, is to select factors that are useful in assessing the evidentiary reliability of the many types of expertise that enters their courtrooms. Trial courts, of course, consistently see specific types of expert testimony, from firearms identification experts to clinical medical doctors. Given the press of time, they are likely to seek factor-lists or tests, such as the one *Daubert* offered for traditional scientific evidence, for the myriad of "subsets of cases categorized by category of expert."[145]

As courts engage in this task they will be wise to heed the underlying premise of *Kumho Tire*. In asking whether the expertise is "science" or "non-science," courts have asked the wrong question. Rather, in all cases where expert testimony is proffered courts should be inquiring into the methods experts are using, whether expert judgments are based on experimental research, clinical evaluation, or other types of experience. Consider the

---

141. *Id.* at 152.

142. Although it remains too early to be sure, lower courts do not appear to be acting inconsistently as regards similar kinds of expert evidence. The greater problem seems to be courts acting inconsistently regarding the degree of rigor they bring to *different* kinds of testimony.

143. *Id.* at 159 (Scalia, J., concurring).

144. *See, e.g.*, Walker v. Soo Line Railroad Co., 208 F.3d 581, 584–91(7th Cir.2000) (Circuit court reversed all of lower court's expert testimony holdings, finding that the lower court applied an overly aggressive *Daubert* standard.).

145. *Kumho Tire*, 526 U.S. at 150.

example of clinical medical opinion, surely one of the more vexing issues that will confront the courts after *Kumho Tire*. Presumably, medical doctors' experience gives them insights not shared by the average trier of fact or judge. Should the courts admit this experience in the form of expert testimony? The answer is, it depends. In science, experience usually is where the process begins, not ends. Judges would be wise to recall that centuries of experience with bloodletting indicated that it was an effective therapy for a variety of ailments. Clinical trials eventually demonstrated the futility of this brutal form of therapy.[146] Experience provides insights useful for generating hypotheses that can be tested more systematically and more rigorously. It might be, for instance, that clinical experience indicates a relationship between silicone implants and autoimmune disorders. But the scientific arsenal contains a battery of weapons that can be brought to bear on this question, methods that have far greater power than the relatively myopic perspective of casual observation. Whether the courts should expect, or should demand, that these methods be brought to bear to answer particular legally relevant issues is a matter of policy. Therein lies the challenge. Courts must develop an understanding of the appropriate ways to ensure the reliability of different types of expertise.[147]

As scientists well know, different empirical questions require different methods of inquiry. This is true both between and within subject areas. Whether it is physics, biology, engineering, psychology, economics, sociology or anthropology, some questions can be approached experimentally, others require more indirect means, and most require an assortment of research strategies in order to approach an answer. This is why the so-called *Daubert* factors could never have been the test for all expert testimony. Under *Daubert* and *Kumho Tire*, judges are gatekeepers who are responsible for checking the bases for all expert testimony. The tools used to conduct this test might differ depending on the identity of the proposed entrant, but the basic responsibility remains the same. As judges and lawyers become more proficient in the scientific method, this responsibility will increasingly appear less daunting.

Finally, the opinion in *Kumho Tire* is suffused with the recognition that a court should not focus on the dependability of the expertise in some global sense, but its dependability in its application to the "task at hand."[148] The question is whether the practitioners of the expertise can be shown to be able to do what they are claiming to do in the particular case. Thus, the existence of data showing that engineers, or physicians, or psychologists, or forensic scientists, can measure or diagnose or predict or correct certain conditions does little if anything to support an inference that they possess the requisite expertise for another task or condition for which there are no data. Put simply, evidence with regard to dependability for one task does not establish dependability for a different task. *Kumho Tire* expects courts to identify the nature of the particular problem that an expert is being asked to solve, and

---

146. JAMES LE FANU, THE RISE AND FALL OF MODERN MEDICINE 33 (1999) (discussing Pierre Charles Louis' clinical trials evaluating the benefits of bleeding in pneumonia patients—and finding none).

147. *See* Chapter 2, in which Professor Michael Risinger discusses a taxonomy of expertises in an effort to bring some order to the challenge of the many "subsets of cases categorized by category of expert."

148. *Kumho Tire*, 525 U.S. at 141.

then to assess whether the available data support a conclusion that the necessary expertise exists to offer a dependable opinion on that problem.

§ 1–3.5.1 When Must a Fact Be a Matter of Scientific Inquiry?

Now that the Supreme Court has held that the trial court's gatekeeping obligation extends to all expert testimony, the real work begins. In particular, the question arises, when should substantial research be required? "How much research, and what kinds of research, should we expect?" For instance, a particular cause and effect relationship might be supported by anecdotal experience or case studies, toxicological animal studies (using animals ranging from rats to monkeys) and human epidemiological research. The problem is that the *Daubert* standard is not static. Whether the basis for a proffered expert opinion is valid depends on what that opinion is, and what consequences follow from it. This is a matter of policy, not science.

Implicit in *Daubert*, therefore, is a sufficiency analysis. It is not sufficiency in the classic civil procedure sense, but rather a judgment about how much evidence it takes before we believe a certain proposition. For instance, we might be mildly skeptical if told it would rain today because the day dawned with a red sky (i.e., "red sky at night, sailor's delight; red sky in the morning, sailor take warning"), but typically little turns on this prediction and we might simply accept the opinion and carry an umbrella. However, if the dire predictions of global warming were premised on similar evidence, presumably few would be willing to spend billions of dollars to avoid this predicted fate. We demand opinion premised on sounder grounds. It appears that courts have made similar judgments, albeit implicitly. In civil cases, the more expensive and numerous the litigation, the more science that is expected.[149] In criminal cases, the more likely the jury is to be overwhelmed by the expert opinion, the better the research is expected to be.[150]

[1] Police Officer Experts and Other Specialists by Experience

Somewhat disappointing has been courts' willingness to admit prosecution experts who have little research or data to support their opinions. While there is some evidence that this is changing in some areas, such as the forensic sciences, courts continue to permit many prosecution experts with hardly a glance at the methods underlying their testimony. Perhaps the best example is the testimony of police officers regarding the intent of defendants caught with drugs. Courts almost invariably admit this sort of testimony.[151]

---

149. *See, e.g.*, Glastetter v. Novartis Pharm. Corp., 252 F.3d 986 (8th Cir.2001) (re: Parlodel); Schmerling v. Danek Medical, Inc., 1999 WL 712591 (E.D.Pa.1999) (re: pedicle bone screws).

150. This appears to be the explanation for the courts' almost uniform exclusion of polygraph evidence. In fact, in the polygraph context this conclusion is buttressed by the courts' particular reliance on Rule 403 to exclude the evidence.

151. *See, e.g.*, United States v. Brown, 230 F.3d 1360 (6th Cir.2000) ("[The expert's] thirteen years of experience in drug investigation

together with his involvement in classes in which the issue was discussed is enough grounding to avoid the testimony being labeled 'speculative.' "); United States v. Lua, 230 F.3d 1368 (9th Cir.2000) ("[The expert] testified that he has directed or participated in over 500 drug investigations with over 300 involving drug couriers.... Given his broad experience in such cases, there was no abuse of discretion in admitting his testimony under Rule 702."); United States v. Brumley, 217 F.3d 905 (7th Cir.2000) (finding "extensive investigative experience" to be sufficient basis to meet *Daubert* and *Kumho Tire* and allow officer to testi-

For instance, in *United States v. Harris*,[152] the defendant had been convicted of possession of cocaine with intent to distribute. On appeal, he argued that the trial court had erred in admitting the expert testimony of a police officer concerning the methods and operations of street dealers. The trial and appellate courts hardly paused before permitting the officer to testify. The Sixth Circuit offered no ground whatsoever for believing that the officer's testimony had a valid basis. The court simply offered this conclusory observation: " 'Courts have overwhelmingly found police officers' expert testimony admissible where it will aid the jury's understanding of an area, such as drug dealing, not within the experience of the average juror.' "[153]

We do not mean to advocate the wholesale exclusion of police officers' experience-based testimony. We do believe, however, that courts ought to provide a more discriminating analysis of the methods underlying this testimony.[154] It may be that experience lends itself particularly well to learning certain relevant facts, but not others. For instance, in *United States v. Tocco*,[155] in the prosecution of the reputed "boss" of the Detroit "mafia," the expert was permitted to testify, based on "experience" alone, to "the structure, the organization, the rules, the interpretation of phrases and jargon that's been used in [the] trial [and] on the tapes, the hierarchy and the roles

fy that the amount of drugs the defendant was caught with was consistent with distribution and not mere personal use); United States v. Hankey, 203 F.3d 1160 (9th Cir.2000) (relying on "street intelligence" of police officer regarding defendant's intent to distribute PCP); United States v. Potts, 2000 WL 943219 *3 (E.D.La.2000) (holding that experience-based police testimony meets the *Daubert/Kumho* test); United States v. Belin, 2000 WL 679138 *7 (S.D.N.Y.2000) (allowing police testimony without a *Daubert–Kumho* hearing concerning the meaning of a "coded conversation," "because the admission of such expert testimony is a settled question of law in this Circuit"— and citing pre-*Kumho* precedent).

Courts are less permissive when criminal defendants offer experience-based experts to refute the inference that they possessed the drugs for purposes of distribution. *See, e.g.,* United States v. Allerheiligen, 221 F.3d 1353 (10th Cir.2000) (Court excluded author of books on marijuana and two police officers who sought to testify that the defendant's possession was inconsistent with an intention to sell.); *cf.* Kerman v. Dilucia, 2000 WL 1056315 *2 (S.D.N.Y.2000), affirmed in part, reversed in part 261 F.3d 229 (2d Cir.2001) (excluding officer with over 40 years of experience who was proffered by the plaintiff in a lawsuit against nine New York City police officers for excessive force).

However, in a good example of critical evaluation of an officer's proffered testimony, the D.C. Circuit, in *United States v. Williams*, 212 F.3d 1305 (D.C.Cir.2000), excluded the government's expert. The defendant fled after a routine traffic stop. After he was apprehended, the police found a gun along the route of the chase. The gun had no fingerprints on it. In its case

in chief, the prosecutor asked the officer whether, in his experience, "as a patrol officer, is it common for people who use drugs or sell drugs to carry weapons for protection." *Id.* at 1308. The witness answered "yes." The D.C. Circuit held that the officer's experience was not sufficient to allow him to form such an opinion: "The foundation of [the officer's] opinion linking drug users and possession of weapons is anything but firm. Fewer than one dozen arrests involving possession of a firearm is not sufficient grounding to qualify him as an expert under Rule 702 of the Federal Rules of Evidence (FRE), particularly without evidence establishing that any of those arrests involved a drug user." *Id.* at 1309. The court, however, upheld the conviction, finding the error in admitting the testimony to be harmless. *Id.* at 1310.

152. 192 F.3d 580 (6th Cir.1999).

153. *Id.* at 588 (*quoting* United States v. Thomas, 74 F.3d 676, 682 (6th Cir.1996)). *See also* United States v. Carroll, 2000 WL 45870 *8 (E.D.La.2000) (relying on "general acceptance" among courts to validate police officer's expertise, and conducting no other *Daubert* analysis).

154. At the very least, courts should inquire into the nature and extent of the asserted experience. Did the knowledge come from direct observation or through informants? If direct, how much opportunity did the witness have to observe, of this particular organization or others, one or many such organizations? If indirect, courts should employ hearsay-like considerations in determining how reliable the hearsay is which constitutes the "experience."

155. 200 F.3d 401 (6th Cir.2000).

of individuals."[156] These facts might be termed "descriptive facts" and are analogous to the kinds of facts an expert such as a translator might provide.

Well founded experience-based testimony as to such descriptive facts generally should be allowed, but further inferences may not be sufficiently helpful to be admissible. Consider, for example, the police officer as drug expert. As noted, courts routinely allow police officers to testify that the quantity or packaging of drugs found on the defendant indicate an intention to distribute them, not simply possess them for personal use.[157] How do these witnesses know this? Presumably, their thought process goes something like the following. The defendant was arrested with twenty ounces of high-grade marijuana, and scales for weighing the drug; materials commonly used to package the drug for sale were found in the defendant's house. An average user consumes about an ounce of this high grade-marijuana every month and has no more than a three month supply on hand at any given time; also, most personal users do not have their own scales to weigh the drugs and do not possess an excess supply of packaging materials. These factors, and possibly others, indicated to the experienced police officer that a similarly situated person would intend to sell the drugs and not merely possess them for personal use.

Are courts correct in admitting this testimony? We think only in part. The officer undoubtedly has knowledge from experience that the average fact finder does not share. The descriptive elements of this experience might be valuable. How much marijuana does the average user consume in a month? Do those who smoke marijuana typically own scales? The expert should ordinarily be permitted to testify to these observations, provided that he gives good reasons for believing that his experience with the drug business would produce such knowledge.[158] Courts should be more critical, however, when the expert seeks to provide the inferences the jurors should draw from these facts. There is no reason to believe that a police officer is better able to draw these inferences than the average layperson.[159]

---

156. *Id.* at 418.

157. *See supra* note 151.

158. It must be emphasized that these kinds of "descriptive facts" are amenable to scientific measurement. For instance, a police officer might testify that "most" marijuana smokers consume about an ounce a month. The officer is unlikely to have any data or records to support this observation. Social scientists, of course, could design a study to answer this question more scientifically.

159. Courts' uncritical acceptance of experience is not limited to police officers or government experts. In *Sullivan v. Ford Motor Co.*, 2000 WL 343777 (S.D.N.Y.2000), for example, the plaintiff proffered a safety engineer's expert testimony after her nephew was partially decapitated when the air bag deployed following a severe car accident. Based on the expert's experience, the court found both that he was qualified to testify and that the basis for his testimony was reliable. The court explained as follows:

The fact that [the expert] did not know all of the precise details about the accident at issue in this case does not indicate that his expertise based on his experiences investigating approximately 15,000 road accidents, preparing approximately 10,000 reports based on these investigations, witnessing approximately 100 test crashes, authoring studies based on his observations, as well as his education in the area of physics, mechanical engineering and law, would not be helpful to the jury in determining this factual issue.

Id. at *5.

Brief reflection on the expert's claimed experience suggests that it is somewhat incredible. To have investigated 15,000 accidents, he would have had to visit approximately 2 accident scenes every working day for 30 years. This leaves little time to write 10,000 accident reports.

[a]   *The "Same Intellectual Rigor that Characterizes ... the Relevant Field" Test*

Another trend that is beginning to develop after *Kumho Tire* is for courts to take a shortcut around application of the four *Daubert* factors, or other factors that might be used, by asking simply whether the expert "employs in the courtroom the same level of intellectual rigor that characterizes the practice of an expert in the relevant field."[160] The quoted language comes from *Kumho Tire.*[161] This is a dangerous trend and one certainly not endorsed by the *Kumho Tire* Court, much less the operating premises of *Daubert*. As the *Kumho Tire* Court stated in the very same paragraph in which this language appears, "the objective of [the gatekeeping] requirement is to ensure the reliability and relevancy of expert testimony."[162] Bringing the same intellectual rigor to the courtroom that is used in the respective field is, like the other *Daubert* factors, merely a factor to consider on the way to making the ultimate determination: "the reliability and relevancy of expert testimony." It should not substitute for that determination.[163]

The same intellectual rigor requirement is not a sufficient condition for an obvious reason. If the field itself brings little intellectual rigor to the subject, this factor will provide scant gatekeeping protection against bad science or flimsy expertise. In this way it is similar to the general acceptance standard. If the field is occupied by those who uncritically accept the "science" or technique, surveying their opinion will provide almost no information about the reliability of the evidence. The *Kumho Tire* Court itself stressed this danger: "Nor ... does the presence of *Daubert's* general acceptance factor help show that an expert's testimony is reliable where the discipline itself lacks reliability."[164] In the same way, where the discipline lacks intellectual rigor, finding that an expert has applied the same intellectual rigor will not demonstrate the reliability of that testimony.

160. *Kumho Tire*, 526 U.S. at 152. *See, e.g.*, Bryant v. City of Chicago, 200 F.3d 1092 (7th Cir.2000) (allowing expert who had brought same intellectual rigor to courtroom, despite the fact that none of the *Daubert* factors, or any other factor, had been met); Skidmore v. Precision Printing & Packaging, Inc., 188 F.3d 606, 618 (5th Cir.1999) (In a case involving psychiatric diagnosis, the court stated, "Dr. House testified to his experience, to the criteria by which he diagnosed Skidmore, and to standard methods of diagnosis in his field. Absent any indication that Dr. House's testimony amounted to the sort of 'junk science' *Daubert* blocks, we see no abuse of discretion in the district court's admitting the testimony."); Benjamin v. Kerik, 2000 WL 278085 (S.D.N.Y. 2000) (finding *Daubert* factors "unhelpful" but concluding that expert used same intellectual rigor as relevant field—but without describing what that rigor was).

161. Judge Kozinski, in his opinion in *Daubert* on remand, asked an analogous question:

One very significant fact to be considered is whether the experts are proposing to testify about matters growing naturally and directly out of research they have conducted independent of the litigation, or whether they have developed their opinions expressly for purposes of testifying. That an expert testifies for money does not necessarily cast doubt on the reliability of his testimony, as few experts appear in court merely as an eleemosynary gesture. But in determining whether proposed expert testimony amounts to good science, we may not ignore the fact that a scientist's normal workplace is the lab or the field, not the courtroom or the lawyer's office.

Daubert v. Merrell Dow Pharmaceuticals, Inc. (*Daubert II*), 43 F.3d 1311, 1317 (9th Cir.1995).

162. *Kumho Tire*, 526 U.S. at 152.

163. It is certainly true, however, that the same intellectual rigor requirement can be very helpful if the evidence comes from a field that critically assesses its findings. *See, e.g.*, Munoz v. Orr, 200 F.3d 291 (5th Cir.2000) (upholding exclusion of statistician's testimony where "his methods were not in accord with those of experts in his field.").

164. *Kumho Tire*, 526 U.S. at 151.

[b]   The Parameters of "Science"

Although the *Daubert* Court spoke of the importance of "scientific" knowledge, the key to Rule 702 lies in the search for "facts" that are, without expert assistance, beyond a jury's ability to appreciate fully.[165] The purpose of expert testimony under Rule 702 is to "assist the trier of fact;" and the trier of fact's task is to arrive at the best possible conclusions in light of the evidence before it. Rule 702 contemplates that sometimes nonscientific disciplines will have access to facts that might assist jurors. Perhaps the best way to approach Rule 702, then, is to understand its task as regulating the supply of facts to the jury in a manner that states a preference for science as the preeminent method for discovering facts.[166]

Although the scientific method continues to attract its share of detractors and skeptics, the significant advances in science and technology since the seventeenth century illustrate the power of that method. In explaining, predicting, and controlling the world around us, science is by far the most powerful intellectual technique known. The recognition of the power of science, however, should not lead to blind allegiance to its dictates. Science provides no assistance over broad and profoundly important areas of human concern, most particularly that of values. Moreover, science is slow, even plodding. Often, it requires ideal conditions that rarely exist, or it studies only small numbers of variables, limiting its ability to generalize any findings. Finally, researchers' values guide the questions they ask and can affect the conclusions they reach.[167]

These limitations on science are implicit in Rule 702's recognition that "technical or other specialized knowledge" should sometimes be permitted to form the foundation for expert opinion.[168] But given the power of the scientific method, these alternatives should suffice only where science provides too little assistance or so much assistance that it amounts to overkill. In general, two situations limit science's usefulness to the law. The first involves factual questions that do not lend themselves to scientific analysis because they are either inherently not amenable to it or they are so complex that scientists do not have the tools to study them; the second concerns matters so elementary that nonscientists' extensive experience with them should be sufficient for the law's purposes.

Some facts are simply not amenable to the methods of science. Science, as the Supreme Court recognized, operates in the realm of testable hypotheses. For example, an expert might be called upon to validate the authenticity of a painting. The expert's conclusion that the painting was painted by, say, Cezanne, on the basis of the character of the brush strokes, cannot be tested,

165. *See* John W. Strong, *Language and Logic in Expert Testimony: Limiting Expert Testimony by Restrictions of Function, Reliability and Form,* 71 Or. L. Rev. 349, 355–56 (1992).

166. *See* David L. Faigman, *The Evidentiary Status of Social Science Under* Daubert*: Is It "Scientific," "Technical" or "Other" Knowledge?*, 1 Psychol. Pub. Pol'y & Law 960 (1995).

167. For a general discussion of the limitations of science and a criticism of the overly "positivistic" approach taken by some commentators (including the *Daubert* Court itself), see Andrew E. Taslitz, *Interpretive Method and the Federal Rules of Evidence: A Call for a Politically Realistic Hermeneutics*, 32 Harv. J. on Legis. 331, 367–71 (1995).

168. Fed. R. Evid. 702.

since it defies replication and does not generate testable hypotheses. This is not to say that the law should not demand the best methods that art experts and other nonscientists have in their arsenal, only that those methods are not "scientific."[169] Indeed, *Daubert* might be read to impose a responsibility on judges to apply standards of good art evaluation just as it requires them to apply good science to scientific evidence. Thus, just as there are a number of factors by which scientists evaluate the validity of science (four of which the Court specifically articulated), there are factors that art historians bring to their work for ensuring the best results possible given the inherent limitations of the subject.

Some facts of relevance to the law involve matters so complex that scientists have not, and perhaps can never, isolate the phenomena sufficiently to study them in depth. Indeed, many of the factual questions the law raises about human behavior are examples of complex phenomena not easily studied. For example, the psychological effects of extreme stress present formidable difficulties for psychologists. To recognize that many reputedly scientific matters remain on the margins of scientific skill, however, should not lead to scientific nihilism.[170] The appropriate response to complexity should not be to call in the witch doctor for a magic spell, but rather to demand the best science available and remain aware of its limitations. For instance, although meteorologists remain some distance from being able to predict accurately as complex a phenomenon as the weather,[171] they far out-perform their witch doctor competitors. Similarly, the difficulty inherent in studying, for instance, the Battered Woman Syndrome, should not excuse researchers' failure to use sound research methods. Under Rule 702, judges must be sophisticated enough to appreciate the differences in the methodological tools used by meteorologists and those wielded by the authors of the Farmers Almanac.

At the other extreme, the law depends on facts that are readily known through extensive study or experience, but with which triers of fact are likely to have little familiarity. A common example of specialized knowledge contemplated by Rule 702 is that possessed by auto mechanics.[172] The law permits auto mechanics to testify, so long as they spent enough time studying the matter, because their knowledge is thought to be readily obtainable.[173] But recognizing that some facts can be known without the elaborate methods of science does not refute the relevance of the scientific method; it only indicates that sometimes that level of expertise is not necessary. The workings of a carburetor are no less susceptible to scientific understanding than the work-

---

169. Some aspects of an art expert's evaluation of a painting purported to be a Cezanne might very well be testable and thus scientific. For example, radio carbon dating of the paint to determine whether Cezanne *could* have painted it is amenable to systematic and rigorous testing.

170. The so-called "hard sciences" also raise questions that might never be amenable to testing, *see, e.g.,* STEPHEN W. HAWKING, A BRIEF HISTORY OF TIME: FROM THE BIG BANG TO BLACK HOLES 74–75 (1988) (discussing the physical impossibility of building a particle accelerator large enough to test grand unified theories of the universe directly.).

171. *See generally* JAMES GLEICK, CHAOS: MAKING A NEW SCIENCE 7 (1987) ("Predictability is one thing in a cloud chamber where two particles collide at the end of a race around an accelerator. It is something else altogether in the simplest tub of roiling fluid, or in the earth's weather, or in the human brain.").

172. *See* MICHAEL H. GRAHAM, FEDERAL PRACTICE AND PROCEDURE § 6641, 244 (1992) ("The local carpenter and auto mechanic are illustrative of admissible skilled witness testimony.").

173. *See generally* MCCORMICK ON EVIDENCE, *supra* note 41, at 21–22.

ings of an atom. The law merely assumes that an experienced mechanic can accurately describe the former, but only a scientist can accurately describe the latter. In short, Rule 702 implicitly relaxes the requirement for a scientific demonstration when a less rigorous, less time consuming, and less expensive alternative would provide sufficiently accurate information. When the subject of expert testimony is straightforward, the law dispenses with the requirement of scientific proof because it is excessive, not because it is unavailable.

[2] Is Forensic Science *Science?*

It remains too early to determine whether courts will closely scrutinize the wide range of techniques that fall within forensic science. The principal difficulty, it appears, is that many of these techniques have been relied on for so long that courts might be reluctant to rethink their role in the trial process. Topics like handwriting identification analysis, firearms identification, bite marks, and fiber analysis are the staples of expert testimony. Yet, even from a distance, it appears that some forensic techniques could not pass the most minimal *Daubert* scrutiny.[174] At the very least, *Daubert* requires judges to ask where are the data.[175] In many forensic areas, effectively no research exists to support the practice.

Kumho Tire increasingly appears to be a wake-up call for defense counsel in criminal cases. Like most lawyers and judges, the defense bar is not well trained in scientific and statistical methods. It appears that historically these lawyers brought few challenges to the basic validity of a wide range of techniques routinely relied on by prosecutors. From arson investigators to toolmark identifiers, the lawyers mainly assumed that these experts could do what they claimed they did. With *Daubert*, however, the subject of scientific evidence was moved to the forefront of trial considerations across a broad spectrum of legal disputes. It was just a matter of time before this heightened consciousness reached the criminal courts. *Kumho Tire* was the spark that ignited the defense bar. It raised the issue of what bases *all* experts have to support their testimony. Even a cursory glance at many forensic fields revealed a striking paucity of research support. Even fingerprinting, the supposed gold standard of the forensic sciences, has come under attack. And if fingerprinting is susceptible to evidentiary challenge, then what forensic technique is not?

Some courts, however, have expressed great trepidation about excluding forensic scientists, even when it is abundantly clear that those experts cannot meet the requirements of *Daubert*. In fact, courts' fear of defanging prosecutors by excluding their experts poses the danger of distorting the very standards of *Daubert*.

An excellent, albeit deeply troubling, example of a court straining scientific credulity for the sake of a venerable forensic science comes from the area

---

174. *See* Randolph N. Jonakait, *Real Science and Forensic Science,* 1 SHEPARD'S EXPERT & SCI. EVIDENCE Q. 435, 441 (1994); Randolph N. Jonakait, *Forensic Science: The Need for Regulation,* 4 HARV. J.L. & TECH. 109 (1991); Michael J. Saks, *Implications of the* Daubert *Test for Forensic Identification Science,* 1 SHEPARD'S EXPERT & SCI. EVIDENCE Q. 427 (1994).

175. Of course, *Daubert* requires not only that scientist-experts supply some data, but that they demonstrate the validity of that data. *See supra* § 1–3.4.1[1].

of fingerprinting. In *United States v. Havvard*,[176] the defendant filed a motion *in limine* seeking to exclude the government's fingerprint expert under *Daubert* and *Kumho Tire*. The defense argued that "there is no reliable statistical foundation for fingerprint comparisons and no reliable measure of error rates in latent print identification, especially in the absence of a specific standard about the number of points of identity needed to support an opinion as to identification."[177] The government, in response, suggested that "fingerprint identification is so well-established that the court should not even hold a hearing on the issue."[178] The court, however, ruled that a hearing was necessary, because "it is clear that the court has no discretion as to whether to evaluate reliability."[179]

The court then applied the *Daubert* factors in a way that approaches a caricature of the scientific culture. The court observed first that "the methods of latent print identification can be and have been tested." The court explained:

> They have been tested for roughly 100 years. They have been tested in adversarial proceedings with the highest possible stakes—liberty and sometimes life. The defense has offered no evidence in this case undermining the reliability of the methods in general. The government points out correctly that if anyone were to come across a case in which two different fingers had identical fingerprints, that news would flash around the legal world at the speed of light. It has not happened in 100 years.[180]

Obviously, *Daubert's* reference to testing involves studies by scientists, not cross-examination by lawyers in the courtroom. If the court's definition of testing were correct, then no previously admitted scientific evidence could be subsequently challenged, at least until the opponents of the evidence produced research refuting it.[181] In addition, the court confuses two testable hypotheses pertinent in these cases. Even if, as the court believes, every person's fingerprints are unique, this does not mean that forensic scientists have the ability to make reliable identifications. The court cited no validity or proficiency tests whatsoever on this more important issue.[182]

176. 117 F. Supp. 2d 848 (S.D.Ind.2000). *See also* United States v. Malveaux, 208 F.3d 223 (9th Cir.2000) (Without conducting a *Daubert* analysis of the challenged fingerprint evidence, the court stated that "we conclude that [the defendant's] contention is without merit because the record reflects that the expert's testimony was based on scientific techniques and advanced a material aspect of the government's case."). The Seventh Circuit affirmed *Havvard* in *United States v. Havvard*, 260 F.3d 597 (7th Cir.2001). The appellate decision nearly matches the district court's opinion for missing the point. The Seventh Circuit observed that "The standards of *Daubert*, however, are not limited in application to 'scientific' testimony alone. Therefore, the idea that fingerprinting comparison is not sufficiently 'scientific' cannot be the basis for exclusion under *Daubert*." Of course, this is the very reason why proffered scientific opinion might be excluded under *Daubert*.

177. *Havvard*, 117 F. Supp. 2d at 850–51.

178. *Id.* at 851.

179. *Id.* The court further noted that a hearing was necessary despite the fact that its "decision may strike some as comparable to a breathless announcement that the sky is blue and the sun rose in the east yesterday." *Id.* at 849. Of course, unlike finding that the sky is blue, the ability of fingerprint experts to reliably identify the person who left a latent fingerprint is not merely a product of casual observation.

180. *Id.* at 854.

181. The *Havvard* court appears to place the burden of proof on the defendant when *Daubert* places it squarely on the proponent of the evidence.

182. The *Havvard* court also assumed that the finding of two "identical fingerprints" would become public knowledge immediately. There are good reasons for doubting this to be true. First of all, since the research has not

The court next found that the peer review and publication requirements were met for fingerprint identification.[183] The peer review comes from the fact that it is routine practice in government laboratories to have a second examiner compare the prints. However, as the court acknowledged, this is not done blind,[184] and it is not the type of "peer review" mentioned in *Daubert*. For the court, the publication requirement is met by the same one-hundred years of "adversarial testing" that satisfied the first *Daubert* prong. Needless to say, this is not what the *Daubert* Court had in mind.

As regards the third *Daubert* factor, error rates, the government claimed that the "error rate for the method is zero."[185] The court was disinclined to believe this "breathtaking" claim, pointing out that individual examiners could make mistakes. The court found that "[e]ven allowing for the possibility of individual error, the error rate with latent print identification is vanishingly small when it is subject to fair adversarial testing and challenge."[186] The court never explained how it knew this to be so.[187]

It might very well turn out that fingerprint identification easily meets *Daubert* because research will show that error rates associated with the practice are "vanishingly small." But the basic orientation of the scientific culture is to be skeptical until the research is done. There are significant costs, as well as lost opportunities, from simply rubber stamping fingerprint identification because we all believe it to be valid.

On the costs side, even if fingerprinting turns out to be valid, not requiring empirical testing for one type of forensic science sets a bad precedent. There are a score of forensic techniques, such as handwriting identification, hair comparison analysis, and bitemarks, that might not survive empirical test. If the adversarial process has been such an effective test for fingerprinting, why has it not been so effective for these other specialties. Handwriting identification, for instance, has been used in court for over one-hundred years too.[188]

On the lost opportunities side, research has a tendency to uncover fruitful avenues of further research, and often suggests improvements in current

---

been done, it appears that no one has checked the possibility. It is like the belief that no two snowflakes are identical. If no one has investigated the hypothesis, then how do we know? Second, since fingerprint matching is not done publicly, errors or mismatches are not likely to be brought to the public's attention. For example, if a fingerprint expert initially concluded that a latent print belonged to the suspect when it turns out to belong to the supervising investigator, the expert is unlikely to inform the defense that he thought the suspect and the investigator had "identical" prints. It must be remembered that fingerprint experts do not compare latent prints *directly* to known prints. They take points of comparison and then estimate the [subjective] likelihood that the two prints came from the same person. *See* Chapter 27.

183. *Havvard*, 117 F. Supp. 2d at 854.

184. *Id.*

185. *Id.*

186. *Id.*

187. The court concluded that "after going through this analysis, [it] believes that latent print identification is the very archetype of reliable expert testimony under [*Daubert* and *Kumho Tire*]." *Id.* at 855. It stated, finally, that "[a]t the request of the government, the court has prepared this written opinion so that other courts might avoid unnecessarily replicating the process of establishing these points as they try to ensure they comply with the Supreme Court's directive to ensure that all types of expert testimony are subject to screening for reliability." *Id.* The court did not evaluate general acceptance of fingerprint identification.

188. *See* DAVID L. FAIGMAN, LEGAL ALCHEMY: THE USE AND MISUSE OF SCIENCE IN THE LAW 1–5 (1999) (discussing People v. Molineux, 168 N.Y. 264, 61 N.E. 286 (1901)).

practices. Failure to research forensic techniques systematically tends to leave them static and moribund.[189] Handwriting identification, for instance, is practiced today much the way it was practiced at the end of the nineteenth century. Research not only evaluates the current state of the art, but it can also illuminate paths to an improved state of the art. Courts should insist on knowing the former. Forensic scientists should strive for the latter.

[3]   Is Social Science *Science?*

In principle, the character of social science does not differ substantially from forensic science in regard to its "scientific" status under Rule 702. Yet, in terms of complexity and difficulty in testing the phenomena of interest, social scientists might have a better excuse than forensic scientists for having little data to support their opinions.[190] Moreover, despite the free use of the science label, the general perception is that social science is soft[191] and non-threatening.[192] With *Kumho Tire*, however, social scientists will be called upon to demonstrate the validity of the premises that lie behind their testimony. The question now for lower courts concerns how to carry out their gatekeeping duties in this difficult area.[193]

189.   *Cf.* State v. Kunze, 97 Wash.App. 832, 988 P.2d 977, 983 (Wash.Ct.App.1999) (law enforcement consultant professed "personal belief was that human ears are sufficiently unique to support a positive identification in an appropriate case, and that the latent print on [a] door 'matche[d] exactly' the exemplars taken from" defendant).

190.   *See generally* David McCord, *Syndromes, Profiles and Other Mental Exotica: A New Approach to the Admissibility of Nontraditional Psychological Evidence in Criminal Cases,* 66 OR. L. REV. 19 (1989).

191.   The basis for this view is perhaps exemplified by the testimony of a psychiatrist in a 1954 Louisiana case: "In response to the question: 'Is that your conclusion that this man is a malingerer?' Dr. Unsworth responded: 'I wouldn't be testifying if I didn't think so, unless I was on the other side, then it would be a post traumatic condition.'" Ladner v. Higgins, 71 So.2d 242, 244 (La.Ct.App. 1954).

Many courts have been reluctant to apply *Frye's* general acceptance standard to social science. *See* G. JOSEPH & S. SALTZBURG, EVIDENCE IN AMERICA: THE FEDERAL RULES IN THE STATES § 51.5, at 24 (1987) ("All of this underscores the point that *Frye's* utility in determining the admissibility of testimony regarding psychology is questionable at best.").

192.   McCord, *supra* note 190, at 86 ("[T]he jury most likely has the ability to fairly and intelligently weigh the strengths and weaknesses of psychological evidence without being overwhelmed or overawed by it.").

193.   *See* United States v. Hall, 93 F.3d 1337 (7th Cir.1996) (concluding that Rule 702 and *Daubert* apply fully to social science expert

testimony). *See, e.g.,* State v. Foret, 628 So.2d 1116 (La.1993) (adopting *Daubert's* validity test and excluding expert testimony on child abuse accommodation syndrome.); Gier v. Educational Serv. Unit No. 16, 845 F.Supp. 1342, 1344–45 (D.Neb.1994), *aff'd,* 66 F.3d 940 (8th Cir.1995) (same). There are several possible explanations for why courts automatically applied *Daubert* to social science before *Kumho Tire* but hesitated in applying it to forensic science. First, social scientists have for some time insisted they were scientists; and, indeed, some social science research is very rigorous. Perhaps courts ask themselves why some social scientists do good research while others do not. The forensic sciences have been more uniform in their eschewing rigorous testing. This might change, however, in light of the example of DNA profiling, a technique that survived the sort of rigorous testing envisioned by *Daubert,* but which most forensic techniques never experience. *See* Saks & Koehler, *supra* note 122, at 363–64. Alternatively, or in addition, the social sciences have been perceived for some time as a problem child for the law. Although judges regularly turn to social science research, too much reliance on it is perceived as muddled thinking or worse. *See e.g.,* Ballew v. Georgia, 435 U.S. 223, 246, 98 S.Ct. 1029, 55 L.Ed.2d 234 (1978) (Justice Powell characterized Justice Blackmun's use of social science to set a constitutional floor for jury size as "heavy reliance on numerology derived from statistical studies."). Also, the social sciences tend to be associated with criminal defendants, whereas forensic work typically supports prosecutors. Finally, forensic science often appears obvious, whereas social science often appears creative. *See generally* Daniel W. Shuman & Bruce D. Sales, *The Impact of* Daubert *and Its Progeny*

Just as with forensic science, social science is, in principle, testable, though it is often advanced before any significant testing has been done. The previous section's discussion concerning forensic science, therefore, applies to the social sciences. The social sciences differ, however, in two significant respects. The first might support treating it differently than traditional science,[194] while the second counsels against such a move. On the one hand, whereas most forensic science is eminently testable, much social science that is legally relevant is very difficult to test. On the other hand, social science, more than forensic science, is likely to convey normative considerations that are outside the jury's charge to decide.

Because social science's subject matter is the human animal, many hypotheses prove quite difficult to test. In particular, experiments on, and direct observations of, certain phenomena can be complicated, both by the complexity of the subject and, often, by ethical considerations. For instance, researchers studying the Battered Woman Syndrome cannot simply record the psychological manifestations of violence between family members without proffering assistance from mental health professionals or reporting the situation to the appropriate authorities.[195] But these limitations on the social sciences should not change the essential legal analysis significantly. In every scientific field, from physics to psychology, there are hypotheses that defy direct observation or straightforward testing. Our inability to "see" an electron, for example, does not foreclose a rigorous examination of its existence and nature. Similarly, our inability to lace drinking water with PCBs does not foreclose our examination of the effect of the chemical on human health. Difficult and complex theories sometimes require more imaginative research designs, but certainly the difficulty of studying certain social phenomena does not excuse sloppy research.[196] One of the basic lessons of *Daubert* should not be lost: *Daubert* exhorts scientists to do good science and expects them to be scientists first and expert witnesses (and advocates) second.[197]

To the extent that social science is not tested, it contains the potential for a large advocacy component. To be sure, the forensic sciences, too, pose this danger, but they tend to be fairly blunt in specifically favoring the side paying the fees (typically the prosecution). The social science normative component is more complex. In a wide range of contexts, permitting social science expert

on the *Admissibility of Behavioral and Social Science Evidence*, 5 PSYCHOL. PUB. POL'Y & L. 3 (1999); David L. Faigman, *The Evidentiary Status of Social Science Under* Daubert*: Is It "Scientific," "Technical" or "Other" Knowledge?* 1 PSYCHOL., PUB. POL'Y AND L. 960 (1995).

194. *See, e.g.,* Officer v. Teledyne Republic/Sprague, 870 F.Supp. 408, 410 (D.Mass. 1994) (remarking that the *Daubert* standard has "less use in fields like design engineering where 'general acceptance' is the norm, not the exception").

195. *See Science in the Law: Social and Behavioral Science Issues* (Chapter 4).

196. In fact, the problem cases in social science tend not to suffer from the complexity of the subject, but instead simply fail to apply even the most basic principles of research methodology.

197. For an example of a critical evaluation of social science expert testimony, see *Collier v. Bradley University*, 113 F.Supp.2d 1235 (C.D.Ill.2000); for an example of the reverse, see *Bachir v. Transoceanic Cable Ship Co.*, 2000 WL 1738409 (S.D.N.Y.2000). *Cf.* Thomas J. Kline, Inc. v. Lorillard, Inc., 878 F.2d 791, 800 (4th Cir.1989) ("Although it would be incorrect to conclude that Gordon's occupation as a professional expert alone requires exclusion of her testimony, it would be absurd to conclude that one can become an expert simply by accumulating experience in testifying."); In re Air Crash Disaster at New Orleans, 795 F.2d 1230, 1234 (5th Cir.1986) ("[E]xperts whose opinions are available to the highest bidder have no place testifying in a court of law, before a jury, and with the imprimatur of the trial judge's decision that he is an 'expert.'").

testimony leads to the admission of information that the jury would not otherwise hear.[198] There are numerous examples. In battered woman self-defense cases, admission of the Battered Woman Syndrome means the jury hears evidence of the abuse the woman endured before the fatal act. In rape trauma syndrome cases, use by defendants can lead to character evidence of the alleged victim that is ordinarily protected by rape shield statutes.[199] Moreover, it might be presented through an eloquent and highly experienced witness. In effect, this form of testimony appears to call upon the jury to nullify the law, either because the defendant is particularly sympathetic or the victim is not.

§ 1–3.6 *Daubert* and Appellate Review

In *Joiner*, the Supreme Court would appear to have settled the issue of what standard of appellate review applies to district court decisions regarding the admissibility of expert testimony. The Court followed the great majority of circuit courts in holding that the proper standard is "abuse of discretion."[200] This standard of review, commonly applied to evidentiary rulings, is deferential.[201] But whether this issue is truly settled remains to be seen. The *Joiner* opinion does not take account of a similarly long standing practice, especially among state supreme courts, which have had considerable historical experience in this realm, of treating decisions about the fundamental admissibility of scientific evidence as a matter of law—to be evaluated *de novo*.[202]

The trial court in *Joiner* applied *Daubert's* four criteria and excluded the plaintiff's proffer of medical testimony in a suit for damages allegedly arising out of Robert Joiner's exposure to PCBs that had been manufactured by the

198. *See, e.g.*, State v. Kelly, 97 N.J. 178, 478 A.2d 364, 377–78 (N.J. 1984) (discussing the prior acts of abuse committed by the decedent against the defendant).

199. *See Science in the Law: Social and Behavioral Science Issues* (Chapter 6, § 6–1.5).

200. *Joiner*, 522 U.S. at 145.

201. The Court could cite cases following this practice as far back as *Congress & Empire Spring Co. v. Edgar*, 99 U.S. (9 Otto) 645, 658, 25 L.Ed. 487 (1879).

202. *See, e.g.*, State v. Hungerford, 142 N.H. 110, 697 A.2d 916, 920 (N.H. 1997) ("[W]e review the reliability or general acceptance of novel scientific evidence independently when the determination is not likely to vary according to the circumstances of a particular case."); State v. O'Key, 321 Or. 285, 899 P.2d 663, 688 (Or. 1995) ("When the preliminary facts are not case-specific, little or no deference to the trial court's findings is appropriate."). Indeed, the U.S. Supreme Court has treated social scientific evidence exactly the same way, though in a somewhat different legal situation. For instance, in *Lockhart v. McCree*, 476 U.S. 162, 106 S.Ct. 1758, 90 L.Ed.2d 137 (1986), the Court was asked to consider the constitutional significance of the social science research that indicated that capital juries might be biased in favor of the prosecution because jurors who

could not impose the death penalty are systematically removed from these panels. The Court noted that an inherent difficulty arises when appellate courts must review identical facts that reoccur in different cases:

> [Petitioner] argues that the "factual" findings of the District Court and the Eighth Circuit on the effects of "death qualification" may be reviewed by this Court only under the "clearly erroneous" standard of Federal Rule of Civil Procedure 52(a). Because we do not ultimately base our decision today on the invalidity of the lower courts' "factual" findings, we need not decide the "standards of review" issue. We are far from persuaded, however, that the "clearly erroneous" standard of Rule 52(a) applies to the kind of "legislative" facts at issue here. The difficulty with applying such a standard to "legislative" facts is evidenced here by the fact that at least one other Court of Appeals, reviewing the same social science studies . . . has reached a conclusion contrary to that of the Eighth Circuit.

Id. at 169 n.3 (citations omitted).

See John Monahan & Laurens Walker, *Social Authority: Obtaining, Evaluating, and Establishing Social Science in Law*, 134 U. Pa. L. Rev. 477 (1986).

defendants.[203] The plaintiff, a longtime cigarette smoker, suffered from lung cancer and claimed that his exposure to PCBs hastened the onset of the disease. The court reviewed the basis for the expert opinion underlying the plaintiff's claim and concluded that there was insufficient scientific support to allow it. Consequently, the trial court granted the defendants' motion for summary judgment.

In reversing the trial court, the Eleventh Circuit applied a *"de novo"* standard to the grant of summary judgment, an "abuse of discretion" standard to the exclusion of scientific evidence, and a "plenary review" standard to the lower court's interpretation of Rule 702.[204] Pursuant to this "particularly stringent" form of review, the circuit court concluded that the district court had erred in excluding the plaintiff's expert testimony. Because the exclusion of the expert's testimony had led the court to grant the defendant's motion for summary judgment, the decision was "outcome determinative." This aspect of the admissibility ruling had figured prominently in the Eleventh Circuit's reasoning and assiduous review. But the Supreme Court rejected any resort to "a more searching standard of review" when admissibility rulings are "outcome determinative." The Court stated simply that "the question of admissibility of expert testimony . . . is reviewable under the abuse of discretion standard."

The Court then went on to find "that a proper application of the current standard of review here indicates that the District Court did not abuse its discretion."[205] The Court reviewed in some detail the several studies plaintiff's experts offered to show causation. The Court found "that the studies upon which [the] experts relied were not sufficient, whether individually or in combination, to support"[206] Joiner's claim, and that the district court had not abused its discretion in so holding.

The *Joiner* Court laid the foundation for its holding by observing that, in general, "abuse of discretion is the proper standard of review of a district court's evidentiary rulings."[207] Underlying the Court's holding is the judgment that scientific evidence is just like any other kind of evidence. But this assumption is questionable and might yet need to be further refined. In the balance of this section, we discuss whether further refinement of this issue may be compelled by the nature of scientific evidence.

One of the most coherent explanations of whether a trial court ruling is reviewed on a deferential or a plenary basis is whether the matter being decided is specific to the case at bar or whether it has trans-case implications.[208] Thus, matters of fact, which typically affect only the case before the

---

203. Joiner v. General Elec. Co., 864 F.Supp. 1310, 1326–27 (N.D.Ga.1994), *rev'd*, 78 F.3d 524 (11th Cir.1996). The other plaintiff in the case was Karen Joiner, Robert's wife.

204. Joiner v. General Elec. Co., 78 F.3d 524, 529 (11th Cir.1996), *rev'd*, 522 U.S. 136, 118 S.Ct. 512, 139 L.Ed.2d 508 (1997).

205. *Joiner*, 522 U.S. at 141–43. Justice Stevens dissented from this part of the decision. As he explained, he would have remanded "the case to [the circuit] court for application of the proper standard of review." According to Justice Stevens, a proper review of the studies

relied on by the experts "requires a study of the record that can be performed more efficiently by the Court of Appeals than by the nine members of [the Supreme] Court." *Id.* at 149 (Stevens, J., concurring in part and dissenting in part).

206. *Joiner*, 522 U.S. at 145.

207. *Id.*

208. *O'Key*, 899 P.2d at 688; *see also* discussions of this in Monahan & Walker, *supra* note 202; Laurens Walker & John Monahan, *Social Frameworks: A New Use of Social Sci-*

court and do not have meaning for future cases, generally stand except when clear error is found. And matters of law, which by definition are trans-case, are reviewed *de novo*. Among other things, this leads to more coherent and more consistent decision-making. To have different rules on different days in different cases on the same issue within the same jurisdiction would be contrary to any concept of the rule of law. But the details of a particular incident, which may, for example, determine whether a hearsay exception applies, are specific to the case at hand. Accordingly, appellate courts play a more active role in reviewing "law" and are more deferential when reviewing "fact." Moreover, this analysis suggests that a distinction between issues that are case-specific and those that transcend the individual case is more coherent than a distinction between fact and law. Some facts have a trans-case nature. Some of the "facts" of science fall into this category, and it may make sense to decide those as matters of law.[209]

Scientific knowledge, and therefore scientific evidence, exists at different levels of abstraction.[210] For instance, "general causation" involves aspects of scientific research that transcend individual cases.[211] Is Bendectin a teratogen? Do silicone implants cause autoimmune disorder? Specific causation, in contrast, refers to the application of scientific research to the particular case. Were *this* plaintiff's birth defects caused by Bendectin? Was *this* plaintiff's autoimmune disorder caused by her silicone implants?

More generally, whether a scientific theory is sound, or whether a sound theory has produced sound general applications or general technology, are conclusions that cannot rationally vary with the details of a case.[212] To allow those matters to be decided one way in one case in one trial court, and differently in another case in another trial court in the same jurisdiction would strike most observers as patently irrational.[213] Moreover, to require the appellate courts, in the absence of clear error, to declare that such contradictory decisions below are "both right," only underscores the problem.[214]

On the other hand, applications of valid scientific theories to the case at bar are case-specific facts: they depend on the details of one case, affect no other cases, and credibility of witnesses may play a role. For example, an expert opinion based on a generally admissible expertise may be barred

---

ence in Law, 73 Va. L. Rev. 559 (1987); Laurens Walker & John Monahan, *Social Facts: Scientific Methodology as Legal Precedent,* 76 Calif. L. Rev. 877 (1988); David L. Faigman, *Mapping the Labyrinth of Scientific Evidence,* 46 Hastings L. J. 555, 573 (1995).

209. This analysis has been worked out with great care by Professors Monahan & Walker, in their articles cited in *supra* notes 202 and 208. Also see the multitude of cases illustrating the analysis, presented in John Monahan & Laurens Walker, Social Science in Law: Cases and Materials (5th ed. 2002).

210. *See supra* § 1–3.4.1[2][a].

211. *See, e.g.,* Raynor v. Merrell Pharmaceuticals, Inc., 104 F.3d 1371, 1375–77 (D.C.Cir.1997); In re Joint Eastern & Southern District Asbestos Litigation, 52 F.3d 1124, 1130 (2d Cir.1995).

212. These are the bases of knowledge that make a scientific expert a scientific expert.

213. Examples of such issues abound and these volumes are replete with them: Does smoking cause lung cancer? Does Bendectin cause birth defects? Can memories be lost for decades and then be recovered intact with the help of psychotherapy? Are forensic identification techniques, such as toolmarks, shoeprints, hair, fingerprints, DNA profiling, and handwriting identification analysis valid and reliable? Are polygraphs valid?

214. *See* Dunagin v. City of Oxford, 718 F.2d 738 (5th Cir.1983) (for an example of one appellate court which refused to uphold two contradictory findings of legislative fact below).

because too great a gap exists between the content of the opinion and the studies or other data on which a scientific opinion must rest.[215]

It is not contradictory, therefore, to find case-specific evidence rulings being reviewed deferentially alongside trans-case scientific issues treated as matters of law, with courts below deferring to those latter decisions as they would to holdings of law.[216] This is not to say that some of the appellate courts writing these opinions did not sense the tension, and felt obliged to say that the admission decision was "within the sound discretion of the trial judge," even as they were reviewing the trial court on a ruling (especially if it was deemed an error) that was anything but "clear," seeking information outside of the trial record, and making a decision that had, and was intended to have, precedential impact on courts below. Sometimes one must look at what an opinion does, rather than what it says.

Additional reasons exist for such a doctrine. First, while there is no judicial inefficiency in deferring to a trial court's rulings on matters of fact (because the same pattern of facts rarely if ever will re-appear), it is inefficient to allow parties to relitigate the same *general* question over and over. Once a higher court determines, on the scientific merits, that a substance is not capable of causing a certain effect, or that a certain forensic identification technique can do what it purports to do (unless there is a change in the state of scientific knowledge), there is not much sense in allowing the same question to be revisited by the trial courts in case after case.[217] But that is what a broad reading of *Joiner* would permit, if not require.

Second, trial judges are in no better position, and may be in a worse position, to decide scientific matters that exist at a general level of abstraction. Such issues are better understood from an examination of a field's theoretical and empirical literature, and with the aid of briefs and arguments of counsel, than from any particular witnesses, and do not depend at all on the "credibility" of specific witnesses.

With more experience, courts may conclude that it makes sense for them to decide the soundness of scientific theories and general applications *de novo,*

---

215. This is the flaw in the expert opinion proffered in *Joiner*: "[N]othing in either *Daubert* or the Federal Rules of Evidence requires a district court to admit opinion evidence which is connected to existing data only by the ipse dixit of the expert. A court may conclude that there is simply too great an analytical gap between the data and the opinion proffered." *Joiner*, 522 U.S. at 145. Moreover, the Court perceived a lack of fit between the research data and the facts of the case at bar: "The studies were so dissimilar to the facts presented in this litigation that it was not an abuse of discretion for the District Court to have rejected the experts' reliance on them." *Id.*

216. Numerous such cases can be found throughout these volumes. For examples, see the following chapters: *Science in the Law: Social and Behavioral Science Issues:* 2—Clinical and Actuarial Predictions of Violence; 4—The Battered Woman Syndrome; 6—Rape Trauma Syndrome; 8—Eyewitness Identifica-

tions; 12—Polygraph Tests; and *Science in the Law: Forensic Science Issues:* 2—Fingerprint Identification; 4—Firearms and Toolmark Identification; 5—Bitemarks and Dental Identification; 6—Talker Identification.

217. In *People v. Venegas*, 18 Cal.4th 47, 74 Cal.Rptr.2d 262, 954 P.2d 525 (Cal. 1998), the court observed that "[t]he first ground for reversal stated by the Court of Appeal was based on the correct premise that the admissibility of evidence produced by a new scientific technique requires a preliminary showing of the technique's general acceptance in the relevant scientific community. An important corollary of that rule, however, is that if a published appellate decision in a prior case has already upheld the admission of evidence based on such a showing, that decision becomes precedent for subsequent trials in the absence of evidence that the prevailing scientific opinion has materially changed." *Id.* at 527 (citations omitted).

and to decide the soundness of specific applications as matters of fact. *Joiner* itself should be read less as a sweeping call for deferential review of all scientific evidence admissibility decisions at all levels of abstraction, and instead as speaking only about scientific issues at low levels of abstraction, where the admissibility issue is case-specific.[218]

Somewhat supporting this expectation of future active involvement of appellate courts in scientific evidence matters is the Supreme Court's decision in *Weisgram v. Marley Co.*[219] The Eighth Circuit found that the trial court abused its discretion in admitting the plaintiffs' experts.[220] The district court had admitted the testimony of a fire captain, a fire investigator and a metallurgist in a civil action involving whether a home heater had been defective and had caused the fire. The Court of Appeals reversed, but instead of remanding for a new trial it held, as a matter of law, that the expert opinion was inadmissible and then remanded and ordered the district court to enter judgment for defendant. The plaintiffs appealed, arguing that the appellate court erred when it granted judgment as a matter of law to the defendant after excising portions of the plaintiffs' experts' testimony. The Supreme Court disagreed. The Court held "that the authority of courts of appeals to direct the entry of judgment as a matter of law extends to cases in which, on excision of testimony erroneously admitted, there remains insufficient evidence to support a jury's verdict."[221]

In a revealing discussion of the Court's own understanding of *Daubert*, the Court rejected plaintiffs' complaint that it was "unfair" to direct a verdict against them without giving them a chance to procure admissible expert testimony.[222] Justice Ginsburg, writing for the Court, held that the plaintiffs were not entitled to a second bite at the apple:

> Since *Daubert*, ... parties relying on expert evidence have had notice of the exacting standards of reliability such evidence must meet. It is implausible to suggest, post-*Daubert*, that parties will initially present less than their best expert evidence in the expectation of a second chance should their first try fail. We therefore find unconvincing [the plaintiffs'] fears that allowing courts of appeals to direct the entry of judgment for defendants will punish plaintiffs who could have shored up their cases by other means had they known their expert testimony would be found inadmissible.[223]

§ 1–3.7 Application of *Daubert* to Criminal Cases

Although created in a civil case within the swirl of controversy surrounding fears of exploding litigation, federal courts apply *Daubert* with equal force

---

218. *Joiner* can easily be read to be just such a case. The Court could have concluded that while the basic principles of epidemiology and toxicology were sound, and the empirical studies were sound, the proffered expert's proposed application to the facts of the case at bar did not follow from those studies. This would have been a more straightforward analysis, and would have enabled the Court to avoid muddying the distinction between methods and results.

219. 528 U.S. 440, 120 S.Ct. 1011, 145 L.Ed.2d 958 (2000).

220. Weisgram v. Marley Co., 169 F.3d 514, 522 (8th Cir.1999).

221. *Weisgram*, 528 U.S. at 457.

222. *See id.* at 454–55.

223. *Id.* at 456–57.

to their criminal docket.[224] Rule 702 does not distinguish between the civil and criminal contexts in regard to expert testimony and courts quickly assumed *Daubert's* applicability to criminal cases. In fact, much of *Daubert's* early evolution occurred through court responses to DNA evidence offered in criminal prosecutions.[225]

An important issue pertinent to *Daubert's* application to criminal cases concerns the rigor with which courts will assess forensic evidence. Prosecutors rely heavily on empirical techniques that remain largely untested; techniques, such as handwriting identification and bitemarks, that have a long tradition of admission, but whose continuing vitality under *Daubert* remains in doubt. Indeed, the vitality of *Daubert* itself might be assessed on whether courts embrace the gatekeeping function seriously enough to challenge forensic scientists to live up to the title "scientist."

§ 1–3.8   Expert Testimony and Rule 403

The *Daubert* Court devoted relatively little attention to the balance of probative value and unfair prejudice encapsulated in Rule 403.[226] In time, however, this Rule might prove to be one of the most important tools lower courts have for managing scientific evidence.[227] Because of the typically blunt nature of the concept of scientific validity, courts are likely to use Rule 403 to sharpen their gatekeeping function.[228] Under Rules 702 and 104(a), judges must decide whether the proponent of scientific evidence has demonstrated the validity of the scientific basis for the testimony by a preponderance of the evidence. In many cases, however, while judges might find scientific evidence to be "valid,"[229] they might believe that it is not valid enough, in light of the

---

224. *See* United States v. Bahena, 223 F.3d 797, 808 (8th Cir.2000) ("*Daubert* does apply to criminal cases.").

225. *See, e.g.,* United States v. Bonds, 12 F.3d 540 (6th Cir.1993); United States v. Martinez, 3 F.3d 1191 (8th Cir.1993); Government of the Virgin Islands v. Penn, 838 F.Supp. 1054 (D.Vi.1993).

226. In fact, the Court's brevity allows us to quote its full Rule 403 discussion here:

Finally, Rule 403 permits the exclusion of relevant evidence "if its probative value is substantially outweighed by the danger of unfair prejudice, confusion of the issues, or misleading the jury...." Judge Weinstein has explained: "Expert evidence can be powerful and misleading because of the difficulty in evaluating it. Because of this risk, the judge in weighing possible prejudice against probative force under Rule 403 of the present rules exercises more control over experts than over lay witnesses."

Daubert, 509 U.S. at 595 (quoting Judge Jack B. Weinstein, 138 F.R.D. 631, 632 (1991)).

227. *See* United States v. Dorsey, 45 F.3d 809, 813–14 (4th Cir.1995).

228. *See* United States v. Posado, 57 F.3d 428, 435 (5th Cir.1995) ("While not discussed at length in *Daubert,* the presumption in favor of admissibility established by Rules 401 and

402, together with *Daubert's* 'flexible' approach, may well mandate an enhanced role for 403 in the context of the *Daubert* analysis, particularly when the scientific or technical knowledge proffered is novel or controversial."); *see also* United States v. Cordoba, 194 F.3d 1053 (9th Cir.1999) (upholding exclusion of polygraph on both 702 and 403 grounds); United States v. Waters, 194 F.3d 926, 932 (8th Cir.1999) (upholding exclusion of polygraph under Rule 403 without ever considering Rule 702).

229. Although it has taken substantial time for courts to adopt "validity" as the operative construct, as courts begin to work with this term they will find that it is not a simple or straightforward synonym for "accuracy." Validity, in scientific usage, is complex and subtle. One classic text cautions readers as follows:

We shall use the concepts validity and invalidity to refer to the best available approximation to the truth or falsity of propositions, including propositions about cause.... [W]e should always use the modifier "approximately" when referring to validity, since one can never know what is true. At best, one can know what has not yet been ruled out as false. Hence, when we use the terms valid and invalid ... , they should always be un-

dangers associated with its use.[230]

Consider the example of expert testimony reporting the results of a polygraph examination. Polygraphy might be offered for a wide variety of purposes and admitted in a wide variety of ways. It is typically offered to attack or support the veracity of witnesses, ranging from criminal defendants to non-party witnesses in civil cases. Courts respond to these proffers using rules ranging from *per se* exclusion to case-by-case evaluation. But in all of these contexts, Rule 403 provides the blueprint.[231]

Although the research supporting the validity of polygraphy remains controversial, significant research has been conducted on the validity and reliability of polygraph tests.[232] Despite the flaws associated with this research, a court could reasonably conclude that some form of polygraphy was more likely than not valid. But few courts, if any, would complete their scrutiny there.

Polygraphy is a potentially awesome technique that might displace jurors' traditional task of evaluating credibility. A large percentage of courts and observers fear the overwhelming impact polygraphy might have, causing jurors to overlook the significant errors associated with even the best application of the technology.[233] The regulation of this technology is largely accomplished through the balancing mechanism provided by Rule 403.

Virtually all other forms of scientific evidence present similar difficulties and opportunities. Therefore, for instance, some courts permit hypnotically refreshed recall so long as the witness' statements are recorded before hypnosis and any testimony at trial is limited to those facts recalled prior to hypnosis;[234] some courts view psychiatric predictions of violence as more problematic at the capital sentencing stage of trials than in ordinary civil

derstood to be prefaced by the modifiers "approximately" or "tentatively."

THOMAS D. COOK & DONALD T. CAMPBELL, QUASI-EXPERIMENTATION: DESIGN & ANALYSIS ISSUES FOR FIELD SETTINGS 37 (1979). The authors then devote 57 pages specifically to the issue of "validity," examining such variants as "statistical conclusion validity," "internal and external validity," and "construct validity." *Id.* at 37–94. *See generally* Joseph Sanders, *Scientific Validity, Admissibility, and Mass Torts After Daubert*, 78 MINN. L. REV. 1387, 1399–1405 (1994).

230. Rule 403 only comes into play if the court finds that the evidence is "sufficiently reliable" under Rule 702. Thus, Rule 403 provides additional power to keep evidence out after Rule 702 gatekeeping is done. Yet, if the Rule 702 threshold is substantially higher than mere relevancy, then the courts' ability to adjust the showing of validity to the use and context of the evidence is limited.

231. *See, e.g.,* Ulmer v. State Farm Fire & Casualty Co., 897 F.Supp. 299 (W.D.La.1995); United States v. Crumby, 895 F.Supp. 1354 (D.Ariz.1995).

232. *See Science in the Law: Social and Behavioral Science Issues* (Chapter 12), or *Sci-*

ence in the Law: Forensic Science Issues (Chapter 10).

233. *See, e.g.,* United States v. Alexander, 526 F.2d 161, 168 (8th Cir.1975) ("When polygraph evidence is offered . . . , it is likely to be shrouded with an aura of near infallibility, akin to the ancient oracle of Delphi"); State v. Catanese, 368 So.2d 975, 981 (La.1979) ("trier of fact is apt to give almost conclusive weight to the polygraph expert's opinion").

For empirical research concerning the impact of polygraphs, see Ann Cavoukian & Ronald J. Heslegrave, *The Admissibility of Polygraph Evidence in Court: Some Empirical Findings*, 4 LAW & HUM. BEHAV. 117 (1980); Stephen C. Carlson, et al., *The Effect of Lie Detector Evidence on Jury Deliberations: An Empirical Study*, 5 J. POLICE SCI. & ADMIN. 148 (1977); Alan Markwart & Brian E. Lynch, *The Effect of Polygraph Evidence on Mock Jury Decision–Making*, 7 J. POLICE SCI. & ADMIN. 324 (1979). *cf.* J. Widacki & F. Horvath, *An Experimental Investigation of the Relative Validity and Utility of the Polygraph Technique and Three Other Methods of Criminal Investigation*, 23 J. OF FORENSIC SCIENCES 596 (1978).

234. *See Science in the Law: Social and Behavioral Science Issues* (Chapter 9).

commitment proceedings;[235] courts overwhelmingly find that the little proba-tive value they consider expert testimony on the unreliability of eyewitness identification to have is easily outweighed by unfair prejudice or undue consumption of time.[236] Whether explicit or, more often, implicit, Rule 403 is an integral part of admissibility decisions surrounding scientific expert testi-mony.

§ 1–3.9   Court–Appointed Experts

The most striking difference between judges' pre-*Daubert* job responsibili-ties and those post-*Daubert* is the greater sophistication in science expected from them. Not surprisingly, for judges with little background in the many technical subjects that enter the courtroom today, this new responsibility can be daunting. With increasing frequency, though still a relatively rare occur-rence, courts are turning to independent court appointed experts for assis-tance. For the judge who wants to employ his own expert, two basic models are available to choose from. The first is the traditional one of appointing an independent expert under the rules of evidence who would assist the court—judge and jury—fulfill its obligations. Under the Federal Rules, Rule 706 provides the blueprint by which this model is governed. A second model, and one that has emerged largely in response to *Daubert*, is the appointment of technical advisors. Unlike traditional court-appointed experts, who primarily assist the jury, technical advisors provide exclusive assistance to the judge. Although Rule 706 experts sometimes help judges make admissibility deci-sions, their principal role is to help triers of fact understand the weight expert evidence should be given. Technical advisors, in contrast, serve the more limited function of helping judges decide admissibility. We begin our discus-sion with the more traditional court-appointed expert, and then examine the recent innovation of the appointment of a technical advisor.

§ 1–3.9.1   Rule 706 Experts

Although rules of evidence have long provided for court-appointed ex-perts, judges are reluctant to embrace this option.[237] However, the chorus of voices calling for judges to exercise Rule 706 has grown nearly deafening.[238]

235. *See id.* Chapter 2.

236. *See id.* Chapter 8.

237. *See* WEINSTEIN'S EVIDENCE, *supra* note 37, ¶ 706(1), at 706–13; Joe S. Cecil & Thomas E. Willging, *Accepting Daubert's Invitation: De-fining a Role for Court–Appointed Experts in Assessing Scientific Validity*, 43 EMORY L. J. 995, 1004 (1994).

238. *See, e.g.*, Sorensen v. Shaklee Corp., 31 F.3d 638, 649 (8th Cir.1994); United States v. Shonubi, 895 F.Supp. 460 (E.D.N.Y.1995). *See also* WEINSTEIN'S EVIDENCE, *supra* note 37, at ¶ 706[01]; AAAS–ABA NAT'L CONFERENCE OF LAWYERS & SCIENTISTS TASK FORCE ON SCIENCE & TECHNOLOGY IN THE COURTS, ENHANCING THE AVAIL-ABILITY OF RELIABLE AND IMPARTIAL SCIENTIFIC AND TECHNICAL EXPERTISE TO THE FEDERAL COURTS: A REPORT TO THE CARNEGIE COMMISSION ON SCIENCE, TECHNOLOGY, AND GOVERNMENT (1991); AMERICAN ASSOCIATION FOR THE ADVANCEMENT OF SCIENCE, EXECUTIVE SUMMARY, SCIENCE, TECHNOLOGY AND THE COURTS: THE USE OF COURT APPOINTED EXPERTS (Jan. 1994); Margaret A. Berger, *Novel Foren-sic Evidence: The Need for Court–Appointed Experts after* Daubert, 1 SHEPARD'S EXPERT & SCI. EVIDENCE Q. 487 (1994); Samuel R. Gross, *Ex-pert Evidence*, 1991 WIS. L. REV. 1113, 1211; Rebecca J. Klemm, *A Court–Appointed Expert as the Sole Source of Statistical Analysis*, 34 JURIMETRICS J. 149 (1994); Tahirih V. Lee, *Court Appointed Experts and Judicial Reluctance: A Proposal to Amend Rule 706 of the Federal Rules of Evidence*, 6 YALE L. & POL'Y REV. 480 (1988); Ellen Relkin, *Some Implications of* Daubert *and Its Potential for Misuse: Misappli-cation to Environmental Tort Cases and Abuse of Rule 706(a) Court Appointed Experts*, 15 CARDOZO L. REV. 2255 (1994); Joseph Sanders, *From Science to Evidence: The Testimony on Causation in the Bendectin Cases*, 46 STAN. L. REV. 1 (1993). *But see* Richard O. Lempert,

The impetus is obviously *Daubert's* mandate to judges to act as gatekeepers to keep out invalid science and the concomitant concern that they will have difficulty accomplishing this task.[239] This chorus has now been joined by an influential voice. Concurring in *Joiner*, Justice Breyer wrote specially to emphasize the availability of court appointed experts and other procedural devices that would assist courts to parse difficult scientific and technical subjects.[240]

Justice Breyer wrote separately to underline the importance of the gatekeeping function and the necessity that judges develop an understanding of the methods of science. The gatekeeping requirement, he explained, "will sometimes ask judges to make subtle and sophisticated determinations about scientific methodology and its relation to the conclusions an expert witness seeks to offer."[241] Recognizing that "judges are not scientists," he asserted that, nonetheless, "neither the difficulty of the task nor any comparative lack of expertise can excuse the judge from exercising the 'gatekeeper' duties that the Federal Rules impose."[242] Accordingly, he urged, to do the assigned task trial judges should be encouraged to seek assistance. He cited the *amicus* brief filed by the *New England Journal of Medicine* which called upon courts to employ non-affiliated experts to assist them when navigating the complex pathways of science:

> "[A] judge could better fulfill this gatekeeper function if he or she had help from scientists. Judges should be strongly encouraged to make greater use of their inherent authority ... to appoint experts.... Reputable experts could be recommended to courts by established scientific organizations, such as the National Academy of Sciences or the American Association for the Advancement of Science."[243]

Justice Breyer noted that with the cooperative effort of the scientific community, the gatekeeping task of *Daubert* would "not prove inordinately difficult to implement."[244] Faithful accomplishment of this function, Breyer concluded, would "help secure the basic objectives of the Federal Rules of Evidence; which are ... the ascertainment of truth and the just determination of proceedings."[245]

Researchers at the Federal Judicial Center conducted a survey of federal judges examining the use of court-appointed experts.[246] In general, they found

Civil Jurors and Complex Cases; Let's Not Rush to Judgment, 80 MICH. L. REV. 68, 124 (1981).

239. Chief Justice Rehnquist, concurring in the main holding of the opinion, nonetheless wrote separately to question whether Rule 702 should be interpreted to require judges to become "amateur scientists." *Daubert,* 509 U.S. at 597; *see also* E.I. du Pont de Nemours & Co. v. Robinson, 923 S.W.2d 549 (Tex.1995) (dissenters echoed Chief Justice Rehnquist's concern in response to Texas' adoption of *Daubert*).

240. Summarizing the range of tools available to district judges to "help them overcome the inherent difficulty of making determinations about complicated scientific or otherwise technical evidence," Justice Breyer suggested

the following: "Among these techniques are an increased use of Rule 16's pretrial conference authority to narrow the scientific issues in dispute, pretrial hearings where potential experts are subject to examination by the court, and the appointment of special masters and specially trained law clerks." *Joiner,* 522 U.S. at 147 (Breyer, J., concurring).

241. *Id.* at 146 (Breyer, J., concurring).

242. *Id.*

243. *Id.* at 149 (Breyer, J., concurring) (*quoting* Brief for NEW ENGLAND JOURNAL OF MEDICINE, 18–19).

244. *Id.*

245. *Id.*

246. Cecil & Willging, *supra* note 237.

that judges relied little on this mechanism. Two factors, in particular, explain judges' failure to seek expert assistance. First, many judges view the appointment of experts as a highly unusual act, only to be done under extraordinary circumstances.[247] Second, a significant number of judges expressed their belief that the adversarial process should be relied upon, and that court-appointed experts would take the matter away from the able hands of the parties.[248]

The second factor leading judges not to seek expert assistance, the adversarial process, is not very compelling under close scrutiny. Two aspects of this complaint must be evaluated. First, Rule 706 experts often play a significant role assisting the judge in making the admissibility decision. On this matter, although the adversarial process remains part of the equation, the adversarial principle contains less force when the fact-finding is part of the gatekeeping responsibility. Judges regularly raise, research, and resolve legal matters *sua sponte*. The "factfinding" judges do under Rule 104(a) resembles such legal issues, in that these facts are found by judges as a necessary prerequisite to the application of legal rules. Moreover, the task for court-appointed experts will often be to educate the judge on technical matters, so that the judge can make a better informed decision.[249] In fact, over time, the use of court-appointed experts should decline as judges' sophistication with scientific methods increases. Second, even in their role as experts for the jury, Rule 706 experts do not entirely undermine the basic elements of the adversarial process. In most cases, the court-appointed expert will not displace parties' own experts, but will merely add an additional view to the jury's deliberations. Moreover, the court's expert will often pay dividends by helping move the parties to resolve issues not seriously disputed and allow them to concentrate on those that are. The court's expert is likely to influence the parties' experts' testimony, leading them to curtail more extreme statements and have them focus on the more important differences separating the sides.

§ 1–3.9.2   Technical Advisors Appointed Under the Inherent Authority of the Court

Under *Daubert*, judges must determine whether the basis for proffered expert testimony is valid, or has evidentiary reliability. Under the *Frye* test, this determination depended mainly on the court's surveying a group of experts to find out what they thought about the subject. This task, at least the way most courts practiced it, required little knowledge of the scientific method. *Daubert* demands more. Yet most judges have had little advanced training in science and statistics, subjects central to carrying out their new

---

247. *Id.* at 1015–18 (Cecil and Willging report that of the eighty-one judges asked "why they thought the authority had been exercised so infrequently," fifty judges expressed the opinion that "appointment of an expert [is] an extraordinary action.").

248. *Id.* at 1018–19.

249. For example, Cecil and Willging quote several judges in their survey on judicial use of court-appointed experts who expressed the view that these experts should educate them to be better judges; the experts were not hired to decide the merits. One judge commented as follows:

I instructed [the expert] that his role was to help me and that he was not to decide the case. His main role was to interpret the language to me, give me background on computer technology, tell me how the various systems work.

Cecil & Willging, *supra* note 237, at 1026. Other judges shared this perspective. One said, " '[I] emphasized that I did not want him to give his opinion on the substance of the dispute, but to explain and guide me through the testimony.' " *Id.* And another "defined the expert's role as that of 'interpreter.' " *Id.*

gatekeeping obligations. Therefore, judges have increasingly sought technical assistance to aid them in making the admissibility decision. In effect, technical advisors sit at judges' sides, like law clerks, assisting them to maneuver through the labyrinth of scientific evidence.

District courts appoint technical advisors pursuant to their inherent authority under the rules of evidence. This authority is sometimes located in Rule 104(a).[250] Unlike Rule 706 experts, technical advisors are not strictly subject to the adversarial process. They are not subject to cross-examination or the discovery process more generally. Depending on one's point of view, this is either the virtue or the vice of using technical advisors.

In *The Assoc. of Mexican–American Educators v. California*,[251] the Ninth Circuit considered the use of technical advisors for the first time. In the underlying case, plaintiffs were a class of Mexican–American, Asian–American and African–American educators who challenged the district court's ruling that the California Basic Education Skills Test (CBEST), which was given to teachers for continuing certification purposes, did not violate Titles VI or VII of the Civil Rights Act of 1964. In reaching this conclusion, the trial court was aided by a technical advisor who assisted it parse the difficult technical and statistical validation methods used by the State. The plaintiffs complained both about the appointment of the advisor and their inability to cross-examine him. The Ninth Circuit, however, dismissed these complaints, noting that "Rule 706 applies to court-appointed *expert witnesses*, but not to technical advisors."[252] Only if the court had called him to testify, or if he was a "source of evidence," would he be subject to the provisions of Rule 706 and thus be subject to cross-examination.[253] The court held, therefore, that "[i]n those rare cases in which outside technical expertise would be helpful to a district court, the court may appoint a technical advisor."[254]

The role of a technical advisor is, to be sure, a delicate one. For a process based in fact, and even more so in romantic theory, on the adversarial process, the use of technical advisors might appear inconsonant. However, courts regularly rely on law clerks for substantial assistance, and technical advisors could be seen as merely part-time, specially trained, law clerks.[255] Of course, advisors must refrain from impermissibly influencing court decisions,[256] and the parties should have ample opportunity to object on grounds of lack of neutrality or qualifications. Ultimately, of course, the decision regarding admissibility is the judge's. Technical advisors, like law clerks, can better

---

250. *See* Hall v. Baxter Healthcare Corp., 947 F.Supp. 1387, 1392 n. 8 (D.Or.1996).

251. 231 F.3d 572 (9th Cir.2000).

252. *Id.* at 591 (emphasis in original).

253. *Id.*

254. *Id.* at 590.

255. *See* General Elec. Co. v. Joiner, 522 U.S. 136, 149, 118 S.Ct. 512, 139 L.Ed.2d 508 (1997) (Breyer, J., concurring) (endorsing the appointment of special masters and specially trained law clerks to assist judges with complex scientific evidence).

256. In *Mexican–American Educators*, Judge Tashima, in dissent, agreed that district courts have the inherent authority to appoint technical advisors, and must be granted "wide latitude" in choosing their experts. At the same time, Judge Tashima would

> hold that a district court minimally must: (1) utilize a fair and open procedure for appointing a neutral technical advisor; (2) address any allegations of bias, partiality, or lack of qualification; (3) clearly define and limit the technical advisor's duties; (4) make clear to the technical advisor that any advice he gives to the court cannot be based on any extra-record information; and (5) make explicit, either through an expert's report or a record of ex parte communications, the nature and content of the technical advisor's advice.

Id. at 611 (footnote omitted).

enable a court to render an informed decision, but they cannot substitute their judgment for that of the court.

Court-appointed experts are no panacea. They will not free judges from making difficult decisions regarding scientific evidence. Also, scientists, though perhaps not identified with the parties to a matter, possess biases of their own. Inevitably, scientists are more or less conservative concerning their willingness to draw certain inferences or make certain conclusions based on the available data. While these biases cannot be avoided, court-appointed experts should make them explicit so that judges can take them into account to the extent possible in making their decisions.

§ 1–3.10 Conclusion

Virtually all courts and commentators agree that some line must be drawn between the judge's responsibility to evaluate the admissibility of expert testimony and the jury's role to assess its weight. It would be radical, indeed, to suggest that the parties decide what evidence to bring to the jury. Thus, astrology, tea leaf reading and alchemy are considered obviously unfit for jury consideration. The issue, then, is relatively easy to define. What principle should determine when expert proof can be admitted and when it must be turned away? In *Daubert*, the Court articulated a validity test, which premises admissibility of expert opinion on the merit of the principles, methods and reasoning behind it.

In effect, *Daubert's* test of evidentiary reliability is nothing more—or less—than the scientific method itself. Thomas Huxley said that science is nothing more than "organized common sense." *Daubert* has brought scientific common sense to the law. This fact, of course, hardly settles the many difficult debates over the admissibility of the wide assortment of experts and expertises courts see every day. Indeed, it has unsettled matters considerably. But this is a very good thing. The law's embrace of the scientific method, and its adoption in principle of the basic premises of the scientific revolution, were largely inevitable. In fact, it came very late in the day. Now the questions confronting courts are much more interesting, though admittedly of enormous complexity. Courts must now get down to the business of examining the many experts and the myriad of types of expertise before them. It is to that subject that this multi-volume work is ultimately aimed.

CHAPTER 2

PRELIMINARY THOUGHTS ON A FUNCTIONAL TAXONOMY OF EXPERTISE FOR THE POST-*KUMHO* WORLD

by

D. Michael Risinger*

Table of Sections

Westlaw Electronic Research

See Westlaw Electronic Research Guide Preceding the Summary of Contents.

---

§ 2–1.0 INTRODUCTION

Everyone is familiar with the tale of the elephant and the three blind men, each of whom touched a separate part of the animal, and each of whom therefore came to a dramatically different conclusion on the fundamental nature of elephants. Less familiar is a corollary tale. In a certain kingdom was a cave containing a treasure, guarded by a beast of fierce repute. The king wished to know the nature of the beast, and dispatched three of his subjects to invade the pitch darkness of the cave and report. The first returned and declared that he had felt the head of the beast, and it was toothed and maned

---

* B.A., Yale University, 1966, J.D., Harvard Law School, 1969; Professor of Law, Seton Hall University School of Law.

like a lion. The second reported that he had felt the sides of the beast, and that it was winged and feathered like an eagle. The third reported that the legs of the beast were long and hoofed like a horse. A fearsome portrait of the beast was drawn up, and all were thereafter afraid to approach the cave. Of course, in reality, the cave contained a lion, an eagle, and a horse.

The notion of "expertise" as currently conceived by the courts is in much the same state as the idea of judicial notice was before Kenneth Culp Davis.[1] There are more beasts in that cave than we have come to understand, and we have handled them poorly by applying rules to each beast that are appropriate only to the proper handling of another. We cannot really develop a system of satisfactory principles of control until we gain a better idea of how many beasts are in the cave, and how they are similar to and different from each other. This essay hopes to begin that quest.

A less allegorical way of saying this is that many of the problems that the law has had in handling expertise in the courtroom have sprung from a failure to examine the concept of expertise in appropriate taxonomic detail. Witnesses perform many functions which might be described as expert witness functions. There has been surprisingly little effort to examine this variety of functions in any organized way.[2] The only classification commonly attempted is to distinguish between scientific and non-scientific expertise, and that attempt has not been wholly coherent or successful.[3]

§ 2–1.0

1. *See* Kenneth Culp Davis, *An Approach to the Problems of Evidence in the Administrative Process*, 55 HARV. L. REV. 364 (1942); Kenneth Culp Davis, *Judicial Notice*, 55 COLUM. L. REV. 945 (1955). Davis examined phenomena where casual use of "judicial notice" as an umbrella term by courts obscured important functional subcategories. It is almost unnecessary to observe that these works have been very influential. *See, e.g.*, Fed. R. Evid. 201, Advisory Committee's Note.

2. Perhaps Professor Wigmore bears some responsibility for this. He was clearly a believer in the maxim, *cuicunque in arte sua perito credendum est* ("every man is to be trusted in his own art"), and was generally willing to uncritically accept most claims of expertise by apparently respectable people. *See* D. Michael Risinger, Mark P. Denbeaux & Michael J. Saks, *Exorcism of Ignorance as a Proxy for Rational Knowledge: The Lessons of Handwriting Identification "Expertise,"* 137 U. PA. L. REV. 731, 767–69 n.172 (1989). He further believed that any doubtful cases would be dependably disposed of properly by the average judge in the exercise of a discretion he thought should be unreviewable. 2 JOHN HENRY WIGMORE, WIGMORE ON EVIDENCE § 561 (3d ed. 1940). Wigmore treats "expertise" (a term which he himself avoided, without explanation, in the text of his great treatise) as a subheading in the general discussion of the requirement that all witnesses have "experiential capacity" which he defined as "the skill to acquire accurate conceptions." *Id.* § 555, at 749. This he

further breaks down into two types: that possessed by "every person of ordinary fortunes in life" and that "special and peculiar experience." *Id.* He then asserts that this "special and peculiar experience" can be derived from two sources or a combination thereof: "occupational experience" and "systematic training," which he generally terms "*scientific* experience." *Id.* (emphasis in original). Beyond this he simply does not go, saying only that "the question in each instance is whether the particular witness is fitted as to the matter at hand." *Id.* The latter phrase is in some ways an ironic prefiguration of the holding in Kumho Tire v. Carmichael, 526 U.S. 137, 119 S.Ct. 1167, 143 L.Ed.2d 238 (1999), ironic because *Kumho Tire* prescribes extensive particularized reliability analysis and Wigmore prescribed virtually none. *See generally* D. Michael Risinger, *Defining the "Task at Hand": Non–Science Forensic Science after* Kumho Tire v. Carmichael, 57 WASH. & LEE L. REV. 767 (2000). Some cogent observations on varieties of expertise may be found in John William Strong, *Language and Logic in Expert Testimony: Limiting Expert Testimony by Restrictions of Function, Reliability and Form*, 71 OR. L. REV. 349 (1992).

3. Some attempt to distinguish between "scientific" and "nonscientific" expertise became necessary with the rise of the "Frye test" for the admissibility of novel *scientific* evidence, see Frye v. United States, 293 F. 1013 (D.C.Cir.1923), and of course has come even more to the fore as the result of the decision in Daubert v. Merrell Dow Pharmaceuticals, Inc.,

At the outset, we must keep clearly in mind that expertise, whatever it is, is important in the courtroom only as it is manifested in particular testimony. While a witness may in common parlance be declared an "expert," this does not render everything the witness utters from the witness stand a product of expertise. Any specific statement by the witness may be no more than "fact" testimony, which might be given by any human who had perceived the conditions being testified to. In addition, two different assertions by a single "expert" witness may manifest different functional categories of expert testimony, while a third may be beyond the expert competence of the particular witness for any number of reasons.[4] While a variety of expert competencies may inhere in the mind of a given witness, they are made functionally available only through particular testimonial assertions. Any taxonomy must therefore concentrate on examining the function of specific kinds of testimonial assertions claimed to reflect expertise. Only then can the problem of what ought to establish witness competency to perform a particular function be helpfully addressed.

§ 2–2.0   A TAXONOMY OF EXPERTISE

§ 2–2.1   Non-expert Testimony—The Fact Witness Function

To begin our examination of expertise, we may profitably examine what is generally conceded *not* to involve expertise: the "fact witness" function. When one human takes the witness stand and testifies to another group of humans in the jury box concerning his or her particular perceptions in the past which are relevant to some material fact issue under the substantive law applicable to the case, that person is performing the fact witness function. We assume that the only general difference between the witness and a juror is not a difference in the capacity to process and derive meaning from information, but merely a space-time difference: the witness was someplace the juror was not, and therefore perceived things directly that the juror could not perceive because the juror was not there. It is the fact witness function to recount perceptions as concretely as is practical. It is the function of the jury to evaluate the dependability and meaning of those asserted perceptions, when viewed with other available competing information.

Fact testimony occurs whenever the only assumed advantage of the witness over the juror is this space-time advantage. However, the addition of certain other advantages to the witness does not seem to change the nature of the testimony to something usefully called an exercise of expertise. For

---

509 U.S. 579, 113 S.Ct. 2786, 125 L.Ed.2d 469 (1993). Professor Imwinkelried perceptively noted early on that the real problem might be fashioning dependability criteria for *non*scientific expertise, but without any detailed analysis of its characteristics. *See generally* Edward J. Imwinkelried, *The Next Step after* Daubert: *Developing a Similar Epistemological Approach to Ensuring the Reliability of Nonscientific Expert Testimony*, 15 Cardozo L. Rev. 2271 (1994). Much recent scholarship attempts to contrast scientific expertise with expertise based largely on experience. The contrast is generally drawn in ways that are less than satisfactory both analytically, *see infra* § 2.3.1,

and in regard to recommended tests of admissibility, which often have little to do with the actual reliability of asserted "experiential" expertise. *See* Risinger, *Defining the "Task at Hand," supra* note 2, at nn.14 & 15.

4. This circumstance also makes the practical control of expert witnesses sometimes quite difficult, as each individual sentence may shift with the facility of Proteus from a statement within the scope of both an acceptable expertise (and one actually possessed by the witness) to a statement beyond the witness's capacities or, indeed, beyond the bounds of any existing expertise.

example, suppose the witness can be proven to have abnormally keen hearing, so that her assertion that she heard some relevant conversation from a surprising distance moves from absurd to credible. Now the witness has a basic perceptual capacity advantage over the juror, but that would not seem to make her testimony expert testimony in any sense either common or useful. The testimony is still testimony that the juror can understand by reference to the juror's own basic capacities of perception: "The witness heard the statement from fifty feet away in the same way I would have from five feet away." It seems expertise must involve something beyond this.

§ 2–2.2   Summarizational Expertise—The Expert as Educator[1]

§ 2–2.2.1   Basis in Direct Experience

The simplest variety of testimony commonly referred to as involving expertise appears functionally to be very close to ordinary fact testimony. To illustrate, consider a case under the Uniform Commercial Code in which the proper construction of a contract turns on industry practice in the wholesale shoe business. A witness is called who has been in the wholesale shoe business for thirty-five years. He will universally be declared an expert, and his testimony will generally be characterized as "expert testimony." However, to the extent he merely recounts the contours of practice in the shoe industry as he knows them to be from his experience, how does his testimony differ from that of the ordinary fact witness? He is not necessarily possessed of any relevant skills or talents beyond the members of the jury. There is no reason to believe that if any of them had been where he has been and perceived what he has perceived, that they would not in the ordinary course know what he knows. He seems to have nothing more than a space-time advantage over the jurors, no different than a fact witness.

There is one important difference, however, between the desired testimonial function of the ordinary fact witness and that of the shoe man. We want the ordinary fact witness to traffic in empirical specifics. In addition, we want those specifics expressed in the most concrete fashion practicable. When the fact witness begins to express herself in more inferential terms, summarizing a number of specific percepts with an umbrella inference such as the word "drunk" or the word "angry," fights start to break out in the courtroom over the propriety of the terms in which the witness is testifying. We need not tarry at length over the unhelpful terms in which those battles are often waged.[2] Suffice it to say that the general principles which should guide the

---

§ 2–2.0

1. I have generally used the term "summarizational" to emphasize the information processing function of such testimony. On the uncommon occasions when such testimony is explicitly dealt with in the literature, however, the witnesses are usually referred to as "educational" experts, and that is likely to remain the common term. *See generally*, Ronald J. Allen & Joseph S. Miller, *The Common Law Theory of Experts: Deference or Education?* 87 Nw.U.L.Rev. 1131 (1993); Ronald J. Allen & Joseph S. Miller, *The Expert as Educator: Enhancing the Rationality of Verdicts in Child* *Sex Abuse Prosecutions*, *in* 1 Psychology, Public Policy & Law 323 (1995).

2. These fights generally are said to concern "lay opinion." *See* Fed. R. Evid. 701. Few terms in the law of proof are so common and so indeterminate and unhelpful as the term "opinion." I have endeavored to use the term sparingly, and then only within explicit or implied quotation marks. For one problematical case appearing to declare (almost) globally that investigating police officers may always testify conclusionally as *lay witnesses* about the point of impact at an automobile collision scene, even when they might appear to be able to

judge in controlling the manner of expression of fact witnesses are reasonably agreed upon: (1) No inferences beyond the capacity of the witness; (2) Even if inferentially conclusory testimony is within ordinary capacity to accurately render, require more concrete testimony and leave the inference to the jury unless: (a) the inference is based upon subliminal percepts not fairly reproduced in testimony, or (b) trying to explain to the witness what is desired will confuse the witness and result in a net loss of dependable relevant information.[3]

In the case of the shoe man, such an approach would defeat the whole purpose of his testimony. He is there to give precisely the kind of summary we would *not* want from the ordinary fact witness, in order to educate the jury about the practices of the shoe industry as efficiently as possible consistent with giving accurate information. This summary is derived from a data base of many particular and concrete observations over a long period of time. Much of this is now beyond specific recall, but we assume that, as a person who remained long in business,[4] his resultant impressions and conclusions are in general accurately weighted conclusions based on the totality of his experience. If we were to require him to testify in more concrete terms, his testimony would become a series of anecdotes which would not necessarily represent a proper sample of his whole experience.[5] We want him to perform what can profitably be labeled the "summarizational function," and because ordinary fact witnesses are debarred from it, the price of admission for the shoe man is to label him something other than a fact witness. Traditionally, there is only one other label available, so he is declared an expert, which is taken to authorize the summarizational form of his testimony.

§ 2–2.2.2 Basis in Direct Experience Plus Secondary Sources

To this point, our model of the summarizational expert has been our shoe man, and there has been an assumption that most or all of the knowledge which goes into his summary testimony is knowledge derived from his direct personal experience. This may be the case in a given situation, and it is this direct personal experience summarizational expert function which is conceptually closest to the fact witness function. But, in reality, a real shoe man might derive much of his information about the workings of the industry from secondary sources, such as industry meetings, networks of friends, and so forth. He may also have read industry publications of various sorts. In this case the shoe man's testimony will be a summary result not only of his direct personal experience, but of these secondary hearsay sources as well. We could hardly do otherwise and allow him to testify at all, because he himself could not say with confidence which parts of his knowledge were based on personal experience and which on secondary information. But we assume that his first-hand experience has enabled him in various ways to evaluate and internalize

reproduce concretely all the information that went into such conclusion, see State v. LaBrutto, 114 N.J. 187, 553 A.2d 335 (1989).

3. *See generally* MICHAEL H. GRAHAM, FEDERAL PRACTICE AND PROCEDURE § 6637, at 228–34 (1992).

4. His ability to remain long in business in this competitive field is the main circumstance that warrants a belief in the general accuracy

of his summary of the relevant contours and usages of the shoe business. For a few further observations on the necessity of developing a legal theory of warrants, *see infra* § 4.0.

5. Though of course we might properly allow him to illustrate a general point with an anecdote which he asserts is in fact typical.

the secondary information, with reasonable reliability inhering in the resultant summary. Our tolerance for this hearsay element, and our reliance on the witness as filter of it, is a second way in which a summarizational expert differs from the ordinary fact witness.

§ 2–2.2.3 Basis in Secondary Sources

So far we have dealt with direct experience summarizational experts and direct and secondary experience summarizational experts.[6] Do we allow summarizational experts whose testimony summarizes secondary sources exclusively? We do, sometimes. Such persons are most commonly academics whose function is to educate the jury to the relevant results of academic research. The belief is that so educating the jury may provide them with information to support conclusions about the *other* evidence in the case that one would not expect the jury to have derived from common experience, or indeed might even be counter-intuitive from common experience. A good example would be the testimony of a cognitive psychologist such as Elizabeth Loftus on the weaknesses of eyewitness identification as shown by the published research in that area.[7] Note that when such an expert testifies, she is not normally asked about her own evaluation of the accuracy of the identification in the case *sub judice*. If she were, and if that were allowed, it would represent another expert function. For now, we limit ourselves to a consideration of the summarizational function.

§ 2–2.2.4 Basis in Supplemental Secondary Sources

Up to this point we have considered only witnesses who were in possession of all their relevant knowledge prior to any involvement in the litigation in which they are called to testify. Do we allow summarizational witnesses to supplement their pre-existing knowledge with new information which they seek out only for the purposes of giving testimony? The answer to this would seem to be yes, although the dangers of such specially developed information seem obvious. Notionally, the summarizational expert is not supposed to be involved in an adversarial exercise, but merely recounting knowledge for the side that it coincidentally helps in the litigation. While there is nothing

---

6. We are verging on the "autoptic proference" problem. When Wigmore was attempting to classify various offers of physical evidence, he labeled the offering of a physical object which was a relic of the event under investigation an "autoptic proference" (autoptic from a Greek word actually meaning "with his own eye," emphasizing that the jury would actually be able to see the object rather than hear testimony concerning it, and proference, a longer and less common synonym for "proffer"). *See* 1 John Henry Wigmore, Wigmore on Evidence § 24 (3d ed. 1940). The concept was ill defined, the words obscure and the phrase awkward and ugly. Needless to say, it was not incorporated into the working vocabulary either of lawyers or scholars, and worse, became something of a joke, as the gleeful observations of the court in Morse v. State, 10 Ga.App. 61, 72 S.E. 534 (Ga.Ct.App.1911), demonstrate. I have racked my brain for alternatives to such cumbersome phrases as "direct experience summarizational witness" and others in the text, but I have failed. And since I believe each of these cleavages may bear importantly on the proper construction of dependability standards, I have done the best I could and then left them as they stand.

7. Loftus's qualifications and activities in this regard are well known. *See, e.g.,* Elizabeth F. Loftus, Eyewitness Testimony (1979); Chapter 15, §§ 2.0–2.4 (discussing, *inter alia*, the contributions of Professor Loftus). Some of her courtroom experiences are recounted in Elizabeth F. Loftus, Witness for the Defense (1991). Of course, Loftus is not in fact always summarizing secondary sources alone, since she herself may have personally undertaken some of the relevant studies, but nevertheless, there may be cases where none of her personal studies are directly relevant, and only enter in as experiences qualifying here to summarize the relevant literature with sufficient accuracy.

logically dictating that, for example, issue-directed research into the literature by an academic will be skewed in its results by identification with the side employing the expert, human beings might commonly be expected to so respond. Suffice it to say for now that some summarizational experts testify to present knowledge specially acquired for the purposes of litigation.[8]

§ 2–2.2.5 Basis in Supplemental Direct Experience and Original Research

While a witness might undertake supplementary direct personal experience after involvement in litigation, the practicalities of arranging for such life experiences during the pendency of the litigation practically rule this out in many classes of cases. However, the long delays of modern litigation sometimes allow a technical witness to add to the corpus of research being summarized in ways specifically designed to meet the needs of the individual case, and this has become quite common in some areas such as obscenity and trademark infringement cases.[9] In addition, while in theory a secondary source summarizational expert might acquire all secondary source information to be summarized after litigation begins, practical considerations rule out the employment of a person as an expert who is not at least partially qualified by education or experience to find and evaluate such information prior to their involvement in the litigation.[10]

As a result of the foregoing, we can identify two sources of knowledge for summarizational expert testimony: direct personal experience and secondary source information. In addition, we can identify two important time variables for when secondary source information might be acquired: pre involvement in the litigation and post involvement.

§ 2–2.2.6 Everyday vs. Academic Summarization Expertise

At this point it is necessary to expand on a distinction inchoate in the above discussion, the difference between the shoe man and Elizabeth Loftus.

---

8. There have been judicial warnings concerning the caution required in evaluating expertise developed especially for the case at bar. *See* the Advisory Committee's Note to the recently revised Fed. R. Evid. 702 and cases there cited.

9. *See generally* the materials collected in Chapter 3 of John Monahan & Laurens Walker, eds., SOCIAL SCIENCE IN LAW: CASES AND MATERIALS (4th ed. 1998). Courts are increasingly sensitive to the dangers of litigation-driven research, and whether research relied upon by an expert was "conducted independent of litigation" is one consideration in evaluating its dependability. Daubert v. Merrell Dow Pharm., Inc., 43 F.3d 1311, 1317 (9th Cir. 1995) (on remand from the Supreme Court decision in Daubert v. Merrell Dow Pharm., Inc., 509 U.S. 579, 113 S.Ct. 2786, 125 L.Ed.2d 469 (1993)). This caution is understandable in regard to tort causation issues, perhaps, but it must be kept in mind that empirical issues such as the likelihood of specific product confusion are unlikely to be addressed in any context except litigation.

10. An exception to this, which explicitly involves the summarizational function but does not necessarily involve anything comfortably called expertise, is the summarization of voluminous materials pursuant to such rules as Federal Rule of Evidence 1006. Virtually every witness called to perform this function will have obtained the information summarized only after the controversy being tried has arisen. Many such witnesses will require special skills, such as accounting skills, to produce the summary, and thus they will be exercising an expert function. But other such witnesses may require no capacities beyond those assumed to be present in the ordinary juror, and their testimony is merely a way of sparing each juror the tedium of generating the information themselves. It requires no special knowledge or skill to take voluminous phone records and count the number of times the defendant called a particular phone number, and to enter the total on a chart.

The shoe man is summarizing the salient aspects of professional experiences which, even if not necessarily within the talents and inclinations of the average juror to accomplish, are certainly relatively easy to understand, and therefore to evaluate, in ways closely related to the evaluation of normal fact testimony. However, Professor Loftus is summarizing the net conclusions resulting from evaluation of many empirical studies of varying quality which add to the corpus of knowledge in uneven ways. Her testimony is in essence a social science literature review and requires not only much specialized learning, but in all likelihood, analytical and mathematical talents and skills greater than those of the average juror. Her testimony is therefore more difficult for the average juror to evaluate dependably. We may think of the shoe man and Professor Loftus as defining two poles on a continuum of ease of juror evaluation; however, as summarizational witnesses tend to cluster toward the ends of the continuum, we may profitably speak of "everyday" summarizational experts and "academic" or "technical" summarizational experts.

We should have no quarrel with labeling the everyday summarizational witness an expert, at least in part because the term, both in law and ordinary understanding, is so broad and so ill defined that it is difficult to criticize its application to almost anything beyond rendition of concrete percepts. However, it should be recognized that such summarizational witnesses are the lowest order of expertise. This is especially true when what is being summarized is experience and information of a type requiring little unusual learning to understand. In the case of every-day summarizational expertise, it seems there is little the law ought to require beyond the facial relevance of their claimed experience. The main danger with such a witness is only that once they have obtained the imprimatur of the label "expert," they will be allowed to go beyond their summarizational competence, or that the low standards of scrutiny appropriate to them will be generalized to other, less appropriate, contexts.[11]

---

11. Sometimes allowing the everyday witness to go from summarization to specific conclusion (translation) is perfectly justified. In the civil case involving our shoe man, it might be reasonable to conclude that he is better able than the jury, not only to give information about the workings of the industry, but also to accurately apply that information to the particular circumstances of the case at hand, and that the jury would be rationally aided in its own decision by hearing what he had to say, especially since they are likely to hear a contrary conclusion from an expert for the other side. However, in a criminal trial, with liberty at stake, different standards of proof, and a different trial dynamic, it behooves the system to take greater precautions against the jury too easily surrendering responsibility for the conclusion by merely adopting the conclusory testimony of the witness. This has been something of a problem in the case of law enforcement officers called to testify from their experience and study concerning the general way criminal schemes and enterprises operate, and/or the usual meaning of criminal slang and code words. Such "M.O./argot" witnesses are often investigators in the case being tried, which creates a significant problem of jury confusion, and may easily cross the line from "users generally can't afford to hold more than a few grams for personal use, so amounts above that are generally intended for sale" to "ounces are intended for sale" to "this was a sale amount." *See* United States v. Bruck, 152 F.3d 40 (1st Cir.1998) (finding no error in permitting conclusory testimony of federal agent that based on "certain indicators," a fire was deliberately set for economic reasons); United States v. Sepulveda, 15 F.3d 1161 (1st Cir.1993) (affirming district court's decision to strike police officer's particularized statements as to the structure and operation of a drug ring where officer could not specify source of his knowledge regarding drug ring at issue). *See generally* D. Michael Risinger, *Navigating Expert Reliability: Are Criminal Standards of Certainty Being Left on the Dock*, 64 ALB. L. REV. 99, 133–37 (2000).

Technical summarizational expertise presents more difficult problems of control. Indeed, witnesses who frankly perform this function, and this function alone, are a relatively recent development,[12] and have been met with some skepticism and resistance by courts, generally for all the wrong reasons. Because these witnesses are frankly educational, and because they do not perform this function in the context of defending "opinions," or conclusions about particular adjudicative facts in the case *sub judice*, courts have often been perplexed on whether such a novelty should be allowed at all.[13] However,

---

12. *See generally* Laurens Walker & John Monahan, *Social Frameworks: A New Use of Social Science in Law*, 73 U. Va. L. Rev. 483 (1987). Walker and Monahan's "Social Framework" facts are generally synonymous with what in many situations might be called "jury notice facts," generalized notions about the way the world works derived from life experience, without which a jury could not reason from the formal evidence to conclusions about the more particularized "adjudicative facts," properly so called. *See also* John H. Mansfield, *Jury Notice*, 74 Geo. L. J. 395 (1985). *See also* John William Strong, *Language and Logic in Expert Testimony: Limiting Expert Testimony by Restrictions of Function, Reliability and Form*, 71 Or. L. Rev. 349, 350–53 (1992). Walker and Monahan would attempt to end-run any problems concerning the presentation of evidence about such facts through experts, by requiring that the judge present such "social-framework" facts to the jury by instruction after reviewing the relevant information, an approach which seems unworkable to me in all but the clearest and most recurrent contexts. For an example of such an analysis, *see* State v. Cromedy, 158 N.J. 112, 727 A.2d 457 (N.J. 1999), where, after extensive discussion of the risks and benefits of such a course, it was found to be error to fail to give a cautionary instruction on the dangers of cross-racial identification in the particular circumstances of that case, though it was not error to refuse to allow expert testimony.

13. *See, e.g.,* Lewis v. State, 572 So.2d 908, 911 (Fla.1990) (criticizing the proposed expert's intention to offer only "general comments" about eyewitness identification, rather than testifying about the "reliability of any specific witness"). Decisions disallowing such testimony are often based, not on the dependability of the testimony, but on its "usurping the function of the jury" or "not being helpful to the jury," as if what we mean by due process of law is the right to be tried by twelve ordinary people who not only believe some important "major premise" general social facts which are contrary to the implications of substantial research, but who are required to be kept ignorant of that research, at least unless it is presented by someone who is willing to go beyond the bounds of their expertise and hazard an opinion about the particular details of the individual case. For more on the "usurpation" argument, *see generally* the materials on

Florida v. Zamora, set out in John Monahan & Laurens Walker, Social Science in Law: Cases and Materials (4th ed. 1998), at 485–494. Also, compare United States v. Holloway, 971 F.2d 675 (11th Cir.1992) (adopting *per se* rejection of such testimony) with United States v. Hines, 55 F.Supp.2d 62 (D.Mass., 1999) (admitting such evidence). In addition, *see* State v. Cromedy, 158 N.J. 112, 727 A.2d 457 (N.J.1999), where the court held it error not to have given a cautionary instruction on the dangers of cross-racial identification, but at the same time held that expert testimony on the same subject was not admissible because, as the result of a " 'widely held commonsense view that members of one race have greater difficulty in accurately identifying members of a different race,' expert testimony on this issue would not assist a jury." *Cromedy*, 727 A.2d at 167–68 (quoting United States v. Telfaire, 469 F.2d 552, 559). *See generally* Chapter 15, § 1.6. General resistance to such "educational" testimony in the federal courts would be especially hard to account for, since the second paragraph of the Advisory Committee's Note to both the original and revised Fed. R. Evid. 702 generally embraces it. However, it is important to note that judicial hostility to "educational" testimony is neither uniform nor even-handed, since prosecution "syndrome" witnesses are routinely allowed to testify on that basis. *See* Risinger, *Navigating Expert Reliability*, *supra* note 11, at 123. This has prompted one commentator to observe:

Witnesses on the weaknesses of eyewitness identification are testifying to educate the jury on why the jurors' everyday assumptions about the strengths and weaknesses of eyewitness identification may be wrong, and are generally testifying concerning the findings of a substantial body of controlled research including a large number of experimental studies. Witnesses on the existence and characteristics of "syndromes" are offered to educate the jury on why their everyday assumptions on the strengths and weaknesses of sex crime complainants' testimony may be wrong, and they are generally testifying to the results of studies that are heavily rooted in anecdotal data and non-reproducible clinical judgements. Yet the proffer by criminal defendants of the epistemically stronger "education" is often rejected, but the proffer by the prosecution of the weaker

in theory, the jury-education function should actually be *preferred* to the "opinion" giving function, because it empowers the jury to draw their own conclusions more accurately instead of relying on the conclusions of others. Therefore, the frankly limited function of such a witness should be no impediment to testimony. However, because such witnesses traffic in providing information—often unexpected or counterintuitive information—which is relevant to the jury's ultimate fact reconstruction function, and moreover, because they claim to be summarizing valid, empirically based knowledge from an established discipline, it seems reasonable that the same standards of threshold control properly applicable to such testimony in the more traditional "opinion" function should be applied to such academic summarizational witnesses.

§ 2–2.3 Translational Expertise

At further remove from the fact witness is the "translational" expert, represented most clearly by the language translator.[14] In order to understand what is going on in the case of such expertise, one must adjust one's notion of relevance to take into account a common, but all-too-often overlooked, phenomenon: Sources of information can be brought before the trier-of-fact that undoubtedly contain information relevant to material issues in the case, but the information is encoded in the source in a way that we cannot assume it is intelligibly or usefully available to the average person on the jury. Is such information relevant? In one sense it is, but in the most important sense it is not. Here we may profit by an analogy to the distinction between potential and kinetic energy. It seems appropriate to say that the source being offered has potential relevance, but does not possess kinetic (or working or useable) relevance.[15] Once the distinction is drawn, it is clear that the only kind of relevance which is of use to a rational fact finding process is such working or useable relevance. Even when a source undoubtedly contains information of extremely important potential relevance, if that information cannot be rendered rationally available to the trier-of-fact, its potential relevance ought not to justify its presentation to the trier-of-fact.

Suppose a woman of intelligence and perspicacity was standing on a street corner when a murder occurred in front of her. She saw it, she heard it, and she can remember what she saw and heard. Unfortunately she speaks only Urdu. She comes before the trier-of-fact and, inferring what is desired of her, she tells in Urdu all that she remembers of the event. The sounds in the air of the courtroom contain a great deal of precisely encoded information of great potential relevance to an accurate determination of the material facts of the case. The sounds are potentially relevant. However, we must assume that

---

"education" rarely, if ever, is rejected. Something is wrong with this picture.

Id. at 134–5 (footnotes omitted).

14. The fact that language translators are mentioned explicitly only in the general section on witnesses, Article 6 of the Federal Rules of Evidence (specifically Rule 604), that procedurally they appear unusual because their testimony is interspersed with that of another witness, and that the term "expert" is not universally applied to them as a matter of routine, should not obscure the fact that they not only perform an expert function, but are in many ways the ideal example of the most central expert function, the translation function which lies behind most so-called expert "opinion."

15. This notion is explored at length in D. Michael Risinger, *Johnny Lynn Old Chief, John Henry Wigmore and "Legitimate Moral Force": Keeping the Courtroom Safe for Heartstrings and Gore*, 49 HASTINGS L.J. 403, 431–40 (1998).

none of the jurors can speak Urdu. Thus they cannot derive accurately (or at all) the meaning encoded in the sounds. Without some mechanism to allow the jurors to reach a dependable conclusion about the information encoded in the sounds, it would seem to make little sense to allow the woman to testify. What is needed is at least one person bilingual in both Urdu and English. Such a person knows a system whereby the meaning of the sounds in the courtroom may be dependably converted to a form understandable by the jury.

There are two ways such a person might put the jurors in a position to understand the message encoded in the sounds in the courtroom: She could translate directly, or she could teach the jurors Urdu and allow them to translate for themselves. As previously indicated, the latter course ought to be viewed as preferable, all things being equal. Then the jurors would be in the same position relative to the evidence and to each other as they are in relation to evidence in English. Of course, all things are rarely equal. In the case of a language skill, it is obvious that the translational system cannot be taught to jurors within the time constraints of any process that must be time efficient enough for dispute resolution. In addition, language is subject to a great range of aptitudes, at least in adults, and even were time available, the newly taught language would be learned by jurors in wildly different degrees. Hence, in the case of a language translator, the expert will normally testify to the expert's own inferences concerning the correspondence in meaning between the Urdu sounds and the English sounds. That is, the expert will give her translation, and the potential system-teaching, or educational, function will rarely play a role (such an educational function may emerge as much more important in other translational expert contexts, however, as the reasons for the "opinion" of the witness emerge on direct or cross examination).

What should we call the translator's direct translation testimony? It is common to speak of experts testifying in terms of opinions. Yet it sounds odd to refer to the language translator's testimony as an "opinion" in any but the most general and unhelpful sense, a sense so broad that a fact witness's testimony could be equally characterized as the fact witness's "opinion." The language translator's testimony viewed in this way looks very like fact testimony in some ways. In a sense we all translate our perceptions into language. However, the translator from Urdu to English is applying a translational system unknown to the jurors, and therein lies the expertise, whether or not its expression can constructively be called "opinion."[16]

The language translator is merely the most archetypal and easily understood model of the translational function. A large variety of asserted translational systems and skills exist in the world which may be at least facially relevant in legal proceedings. Indeed, the bulk of expert witnesses are called upon to perform some form of translational function, and such testimony is best examined and classified by the characteristics of the translation process involved in each. First, however, it is necessary to consider the general characteristics of what I have called a translational system.

---

16. For a case that treats a language translator *both* ways, *see* United States v. Gomez, 67   F.3d 1515, 1525 (10th Cir.1995).

In its most general sense, a translational system exists when there is an assertion that *A* means or indicates *B*. In this most general sense there is no necessary requirement that either *A* or *B* be factual. Interpreting dreams or animal entrails to determine whether the gods love someone is a kind of translational system, in the general sense. However, it is not the kind which the law allows into the courtroom (at least not knowingly). The kind of translational system which yields the sort of conclusions we might consider in litigation must normally[17] traffic in facts both as raw material and as results. Generally, there is some sort of taxonomic system which defines and organizes the factual conditions asserted to have meaning, and there is a set of process rules or principles which yield a resultant translation from the factual conditions found to exist. This resultant must also be factual. Hereafter we will generally restrict our discussion to translational systems having these characteristics, either formally or by implication.

§ 2–2.3.1 Subjective v. Objective Translational Systems

The first great distinction in examining such translational systems is the distinction between subjective systems and objective systems. Subjective translational systems depend in large part on human judgment calls. In addition, such asserted translational systems may not be empirically available to any but the asserted translator, though in principle their results may be empirically checkable. Subjective translational systems are "clinical,"[18] depending upon the experience and often the claimed inherent special talent of practitioners for their accuracy. Identification of wine by taste is perhaps the best example.[19] Objective systems do not depend upon human judgment calls in their operation, and are empirically available to all, or at least a substantial proportion, of humans after appropriate study. Note that this does not mean that such a system necessarily yields perfectly exact results. What is usually derived from such a system is a probability statement, though sometimes the probability is so high that it is practically certain. Blood group analysis translates the potentially relevant information of blood bearing on its source, such that *exclusion* of a source may be near perfect in probability terms, but *establishment* of a source may be merely somewhat more probable than not, or even less. DNA analysis properly done may raise the probability of the establishment of source so high as to be more dependable than virtually any other information we count as "fact" in most aspects of life, including litigation. Most highly objective translational systems are also highly instrumented, that is, they depend on instruments of various kinds to perform the perception and classification of the stimulus data and the translation of the data into its non-obvious meanings.[20]

17. The "normally" is used here as a hedge against the observations made below concerning "normative" expertise. *See infra* § 2.4.

18. The word "clinical" is much more apposite than the terms "experiential" or "experience-based" for describing expertise of this sort, since even the hardest of scientific expertise is based on experience. "Clinical" alerts one both to the kinds of experience, and the kinds of interpretive or "translational" claims, that are involved.

19. Other well-known images include Judge McKenna's harbor pilots, *see* United States v. Starzecpyzel, 880 F.Supp. 1027 (S.D.N.Y.1995); Judge Guy's beekeepers, *see* Berry v. City of Detroit, 25 F.3d 1342, 1349–50 (6th Cir.1994); and Justice Breyer's "perfume testers," *see* Kumho Tire Co. v. Carmichael, 526 U.S. 137, 151, 119 S.Ct. 1167, 143 L.Ed.2d 238 (1999).

20. Notice that little has been said in the text about the concept of "science." This is not because the notion of science is irrelevant to

Pure objectivity and pure subjectivity of translational systems are polar extremes on a continuum. In the real world many asserted systems have elements of both, though one or the other is often so predominant that appropriate classification can be made on that basis, as long as the implications of the other element are kept firmly in mind. For the present, we will begin by examining subjective, or largely clinical, translational systems.

§ 2–2.3.2 Subjective Translational Systems

Subjective translational systems range from personal to highly normed[21] group systems. In personal systems the only guarantee of dependability is "black-box" testing of the individual translator. In highly normed group systems, black-box testing of a sample of the group may suffice, when coupled with sufficient evidence of the success of the norming process. Therein lies the rub.

The hallmark of a purely personal subjective translational system is the assertion that a person can observe a stimulus, and that the stimulus assertedly means something, but the translator cannot describe how the conclusion of meaning is reached, and cannot demonstrate that the same translational system is shared with anyone else, even if others claim to have the same skill. Water dowsing might be an example. In principle, we might devise proficiency tests for the asserted skill which would have to be administered to each practitioner to determine if the asserted skill was in fact present for that person. In practice, we seem to be so skeptical of any such purely personal claims that most traffickers in subjective translation claim to be members of a group of practitioners who share a common and therefore more or less teachable and learnable approach. The desirable endpoint of such a process would be a group of people who had: (1) A sufficiently empirically unmistakable common taxonomy that they would always perceive and classify in the same way the stimulus to be translated; and (2) A set of translational rules that they would be able to define and would always agree on, and which would yield results which were definite. This would result in a perfectly normed group translational system. Were such an endpoint actually achieved, it would be questionable whether the result would properly be referred to as a subjective process. The human agent would have become as dependable and understandable as a thermometer is in translating heat energy to a visual and quantified analogue.[22] In practice, of course, this is rarely approached very

---

the taxonomy of expertise. To the contrary, *see* D. Michael Risinger, Mark P. Denbeaux, & Michael J. Saks, *Brave New Post* Daubert *World: A Reply to Professor Moenssens*, 29 SE-TON HALL L. REV. 405, 433–40 (1998). However, the text deals with ideas which cut across the science/non-science border (although any scientific enterprise aspires to well defined and objective or highly normed translational systems). In addition, it is here an advantage to clear exposition not to get involved in the "science/non-science" debate.

21. In this article the word "norm" appears in two different contexts, with two different meanings—an unfortunate byproduct of combining observations concerning two different contexts in which the word is used. At this

point the word "norm" is used as a verb to indicate the process of inducing predictability of agreement, or reduction in predicted disagreement, between two persons making the same clinical judgment about the same phenomenon. The process of "norming" is attempted in many contexts, from clinical medicine to getting graduate assistants to respond to an essay with the same grade. It is tied therefore to the notion of "reliability" in testing theory, which denotes consistency of result, not necessarily accuracy of result.

22. This is not to say that thermometers have perfect reliability or validity. Mechanical and electronic measuring devices have their own error rates and failure rates, which engineers and industrial statisticians customarily

closely, and how far away from this ideal a system falls is a good indicator of its general likely dependability.

As already noted, most translational expertise offered for admission in court is assertedly the product of a normed group translational process. This is true whether or not the process claims (rightly or wrongly) to be "scientific," as virtually all sciences relevant to legal issues retain an identifiable element of subjective judgement somewhere in their application to the circumstances of a particular case, to a greater or lesser degree.

Most normed group subjective translational systems, whether they claim to be scientific or not, are distinctly imperfect. This does not mean simply that they fail to generate translated meaning of perfect accuracy, but that they are systemically imperfect in a relatively small number of definable ways. The first problem typically encountered is an imperfection in their underlying descriptive or taxonomic system, such that the categories in the system are not based on data empirically unmistakable by all properly trained (and therefore normed) practitioners. Instead, individual classifications are the product of judgement calls by each individual practitioner, or worse, the resultant product of a number of such judgement calls weighed together by an unquantified and subjective combinative rule, a "weighing" or a "balancing," with no empirically unmistakable weights available. The success of the norming process at the descriptive level is measured by how much agreement there is among practitioners in giving the same classification to the same observed phenomenon. High levels of agreement result in "reliable"[23] taxonomies. The less agreement among practitioners, the less reliable the system.

Three instructive examples might be drawn from the biological taxonomic system for animals, the DIAGNOSTIC AND STATISTICAL MANUAL OF MENTAL DISORDERS (DSM),[24] and the criteria for sufficiency of comparable real property sales for valuation purposes. The biological taxonomy tends to be highly (though not perfectly) reliable among properly trained and credentialed practitioners; The DSM less so, perhaps much less so in regard to some conditions. Finally, as to land valuation, formal studies on taxonomic reliability do not exist, but anecdotally, it seems to be quite uncommon for two practitioners to agree on a common set of most comparable recent sales.

---

measure. Indeed, one of the paradoxes of the popular response to human and machine devices is that we assume humans make mistakes but often do not measure the extent of those errors, while on the other hand we often treat machines as error-free even though we routinely measure their error rates.

23. At some point someone took two everyday synonyms, "reliability" and "validity," and turned them into terms of art in the area of measurement in science, using them to define an important distinction. "Reliability" refers to consistency of measurement or result (and might better have been *called* consistency, but it appears to be too late now), while "validity" refers to the actual output accuracy of a process. *See generally* Chapter 4, § 2.3 and Chapter 5, §§ 2.1.1 & 2.1.2. To make matters worse, in *Daubert*, the Court rather perversely (and intentionally) used the term "evidentiary

reliability" to mean "scientific validity." Daubert v. Merrell Dow Pharm., Inc., 509 U.S. 579, 590 n. 9, 113 S.Ct. 2786, 125 L.Ed.2d 469 (1993). This virtually guarantees confusion and miscommunication. In this chapter the terms "reliability" and "validity" have generally been used in their technical sense, and when a broader term of legal standard seemed appropriate, the word "dependability" is used.

24. Published by the American Psychiatric Association and now in its fourth incarnation (or fifth, depending on how one counts an intermediate revision known as "III–R") generally referred to as the "DSM–IV." Its problems are well known, if controversial. *See generally* PAULA J. CAPLAN, THEY SAY YOU'RE CRAZY (1995); STUART A. KIRK & HERB KUTCHINS, SELLING THE DSM: THE RHETORIC OF SCIENCE IN PSYCHIATRY (1992).

It would be tempting to say that low taxonomic reliability necessarily results in undependable and invalid translation, and that high reliability results in highly valid translation. However, things are not quite so simple. Low taxonomic reliability merely moves the practitioner back to the status of an individual subjective translator. Any given individual *might,* unaccountably, be a good translator, but it would take some sort of individually administered proficiency test to establish that. Nor, as should be obvious, does the highly reliable norming of a taxonomy even begin to guarantee accurate translation. Many astrology systems are both detailed and highly normed descriptively.[25]

Which brings us to our next point of imperfection, the translational system itself. A translational system is a system of formulas, rules, algorithms, or principles (or simply subjective responses) whose purpose and effect is to begin with the taxonomic data of a given situation and convert that to a statement concerning some other non-obvious, assertedly factual, state. Like the underlying taxonomy, a translational system may be implicit, explicit, or partially explicit. To the extent it is explicit, a translational system may be highly objective and determinate, utilizing quantifiable aspects of the data present and mathematically describable relationships, or it may be more subjective and indeterminate, ranging from attempts to formally describe and combine parameters of incommensurate factors through such tools as "fuzzy logic,"[26] to the use of human beings as instruments to the same end. In cases of the latter type, which are very common, the translational process reiterates the "more or less normed group" problems already discussed in relation to taxonomies. What this mean is that the translation is dependant on subjective judgments of unquantified and often incommensurate variables.[27] The claim is usually that some process of common education results in the properly trained practitioner coming to more or less the same translation that any other properly trained practitioner would arrive at. This claim is testable (though often not tested), and to the extent that testing reveals it to be true, the translational system may be said to be reliable. If an asserted normed group translational expertise is not reliable, then once again, the only way to discover reliable (not yet to mention *accurate)* individual practitioners (if any) would be some regime of individual proficiency testing.

---

25. Astrology is a subject matter which the Supreme Court in *Kumho Tire* held up as an archetype of asserted expertise which "lacks reliability." 526 U.S. at 151. At least one commentator has, (in passing, but with apparent seriousness), taken the Supreme Court to task for this exercise in judicial notice of legislative fact. *See* Stuart Minor Benjamin, *Stepping in the Same River Twice: Rapidly Changing Facts and the Appellate Process,* 78 TEX. L. REV. 269, 373 (1999). However, the predictive validity of astrology is hardly a subject that has not been examined by the methods of normal science. For example, Eysenck and Nias reviewed hundreds of studies of the accuracy of astrological predictions, and concluded that there is no replicated and statistically significant evidence that astrologers can predict the future. *See*

HANS J. EYSENCK & DAVID K. B. NIAS, ASTROLOGY: SCIENCE OR SUPERSTITION (1982).

26. The term "fuzzy logic" was coined by American computer scientist Lofti Zadeh, to describe "a type of logic used in computers and other electronic devices for processing imprecise or variable data; in place of the traditional binary values, fuzzy logic employs a range of values for greater flexibility." WEBSTER'S NEW WORLD DICTIONARY 549 (3d ed. 1988). "Fuzzy logic deals in degrees of truth, instead of an absolute distinction between true and false." CONCISE OXFORD DICTIONARY OF LINGUISTICS 140 (P.H. Matthews ed., 1997); *see also* DANIEL MCNEILL & PAUL FREIBERGER, FUZZY LOGIC (1993).

27. That is, variables with no common system of comparative values.

Finally, reliability does not establish accuracy, but merely highly objective or highly normed agreement. A highly normed group of numerologists might be very reliable in their predictions but yet be only randomly accurate. An unreliable process cannot be accurate in any but a subset of cases, but a highly reliable process may be wrong most of the time in all cases.

Thus, some reason to believe that a translational process is not only reliable but accurate[28] is necessary before we should consider evidence based on it.[29] This becomes a special problem in regard to any claimed expertise that does not have common, non-courtroom real world applications, coupled with unambiguous feedback in practice on the accuracy of conclusions. Plumbers, auto mechanics and harbor pilots have frequent opportunities to learn whether their judgments are correct in practice. Other fields, such as clinical psychology or practitioners of purely forensic specialties (like handwriting identification, for example), could obtain such feedback only from systematic empirical studies undertaken for that purpose—as has been done for some or much of clinical psychology but for little or none of forensic science.[30]

§ 2–2.4 Normative[31] Expertise

At first blush this might seem an empty set, if we accept an unsophisticated version of the standard model of functions in the litigation system: Juries decide facts; the judge rules on the law; the value judgments appropriate to the outcome are contained in the law. Witnesses testify only to things relevant to the jury's function.[32] Thus, no expert should be allowed to testify on issues of right or wrong, good or bad. If a witness should happen to testify in such terms, it merely represents an isolated failure of control in a particular case.

However, such a model hardly reflects the reality of practice, and hardly accounts for many common aspects of the jury function and the distribution of authority between the judge and jury. In particular, it fails to recognize the official delegation of a normative, or value-judgment function to the jury in many contexts, often under the unhelpful (and inaccurate) label "mixed questions of law and fact" (which would better be called "mixed questions of fact and value").

As to many issues in many contexts, the law delegates to the jury as representatives of the community the authority to make particularized value judgements subject only to the most general constraining principles. The jury becomes, in effect, a legislature for the particular case. Some of these issues are utterly common and centrally important. Take for example, negligence. Even if all the factual issues of a case are removed from doubt, even if we had a full sense hologram of the entire episode which gave rise to the controversy,

---

28. Or "validity," to use the measurement scientist's term of art.

29. How much and what kind of information might provide a warrant for the conclusion of sufficient dependability to be admitted in various circumstances is tentatively addressed *infra* § 4.0.

30. *See* Randolph N. Jonakait, *The Assessment of Expertise: Transcending Construction*, 37 Santa Clara L. Rev. 301, 344–45 (1997); D. Michael Risinger & Michael J. Saks, *Science*

and Nonscience in the Courts: Daubert *Meets Handwriting Identification Expertise*, 82 Iowa L. Rev. 21, 33–34 (1996).

31. The term "normative" is used here in the sense of something reflecting a value judgment. *See supra* note 21.

32. For a good summary of the "standard model," *see* William Twining, Theories of Evidence: Bentham & Wigmore (1985) at 12–18.

coupled with a special helmet which would allow us to follow the changing states of mind of all the actors from second to second, there would still be a critically important function for the jury: to say whether the behavior of the defendant was or was not "careful enough."

In general, we do not allow testimony by persons claiming to be experts on the normative aspects of such questions, at least not explicitly. The function of such an expert would be to say, "I have thought a lot about how much risk it is right for one person to impose upon another under such circumstances, and in my judgement, this defendant did (or did not) act properly." It is not that such arguments should never be heard by the jury. On the contrary, one of the functions of counsel in closing is to make such arguments (though not in so personalized a manner). Rather, it is that in general we recognize no one whose opinions on such matters is entitled to be considered more "expert" than anyone else's, including most especially the jurors. In general. But sometimes there are exceptions.

Occasionally these anomalies are explicit: For decades some obscenity trials have featured the spectacle of "experts" being called on the issue of "serious literary, artistic, political or scientific value" under the third prong of the test for obscenity created in *Miller v. California*.[33] In these cases the jury is regularly treated to academics with literature credentials testifying to aesthetic merit or artistic worth. The results have not necessarily been bad for the First Amendment, but they have been corrosive to the maintenance of any tenable categorical limitation excluding "normative experts." A similar circumstance obtains in regard to expert testimony on applicable conduct standards for professional malpractice in many jurisdictions—the danger arises when the witness strays from testifying about the empirical question of what professionals do to the normative question of what the witness *should* do.

Examples of explicit authorization for normative expertise are uncommon. Examples of normative expert testimony being given by witnesses called arguably for some other more factual function are not uncommon. One familiar example is testimony by members of various psychological disciplines offered as relevant to insanity, diminished capacity, child custody, or similar issues. For instance, it is widely accepted that the term "insane" as a legal term is a normative label dealing with responsibility and blameworthiness. Yet various practitioners of the psychological disciplines are regularly called to give expert testimony in regard to the issue of insanity.

The normal account for this is that these disciplines can give factual knowledge which the jury would reasonably want to take into account in making the normative decision. If it were an empirical fact, for example, that 999 out of a thousand persons with one blue eye and one brown eye reported such an overwhelming drive to possess chocolate that they would seize it whenever it was physically within reach, that might arguably be something properly considered in determining the criminal responsibility of such a person charged with stealing chocolate. While the exact relation between the "is" and the "ought" is by no means conclusively established, some connection is generally conceded *ex necessitate*, and providing accurate factual

33. 413 U.S. 15, 24, 93 S.Ct. 2607, 37 L.Ed.2d 419 (1973).

information to inform the normative judgement is not a violation of any prohibition on normative expertise.

The problem with this position is twofold. First, such experts are generally not very carefully restricted to this role.[34] Second, on a more fundamental level, the entire enterprise of abnormal psychology and the "disease model" of abnormal behavior is profoundly normative at its root. Albert Einstein and Jeffrey Dahmer were equally abnormal in an empirical or statistical sense, but only one is counted as having a "disease." "Disease" is a profoundly normative word, a circumstance which can be perhaps ignored in regard to physical conditions which cause death, pain or impairment of physical function, but which becomes more important to recognize in regard to behavioral categorizations.

All of this is widely appreciated. The purpose in raising here is to make the following point: Whatever justifications may exist for a relaxed threshold of admissibility concerning asserted expertise on issues where there is a normative component in the "factfinder's" official function, it would be wrong to carry over any such casual attitude to elemental issues of concrete empirical fact, properly so called. This would seem to be especially true when such expertise is offered by the prosecution in a criminal case, given the high standard of proof involved. That is to say, to give one blunt example, forensic pathology ought properly to be held to higher standards of dependability than forensic psychology. Forensic psychology generally has relevance only to such normatively charged issues as criminal responsibility and *mens rea* (broadly defined), but forensic pathology deals with the most concrete kind of "who, what, when, and where" *actus reus*/identity fact issues. As to the latter, if the promise of proof beyond a reasonable doubt has any core application, it is to those kinds of specific brute fact details of the crime and the identity of the defendant as its perpetrator. Hence, the necessity of especially careful evaluation of dependability in regard to forensic pathology, and the inappropriateness of importing and applying to it loose standards appropriate, perhaps, in the normative issue context.

But perhaps the distinction between the realms of forensic pathology and forensic psychology is simply no longer true. Part of the growing concern for dependability in expertise can be traced to the mutation of forensic psychology beginning several decades ago from a beast that confined itself to ultimately normative issues such as sanity and capacity, to one that also attacked important "real fact" criminal guilt-or-innocence issues such as identity or the existence of the *actus reus*, generally through the medium of so called "syndrome" evidence.[35] In their new area of operation, the old standards of dependability just aren't good enough.[36]

---

34. On how far the normative component of such testimony normally reaches, *see* John Monahan & David Wexler, *A Definite Maybe: Proof and Probability in Civil Commitment*, 2 LAW & HUM. BEHAV. 37, 40 (1978).

35. A history of the development of "syndrome evidence" and its shift from state-of-mind to brute fact uses in criminal prosecu-

tions is given in Risinger, *Navigating Expert Reliability supra* note 11, at 113–119.

36. For an analysis of the cases dealing with syndrome evidence, *see id.* at 119–123; for more on the cases, and the dependability problems of this kind of evidence in general, *see* Chapters 9 through 13.

§ 2–2.5 Expertise on the Law, and on Inference

It is beyond the need for citation that, in American jurisprudence, the determination of the content of the domestic law applicable to a case is a solely judicial function.[37] No respectable taxonomy of expertise generated on theoretical principles would include a category for anything like an expert witness on "what the law is."[38] That said, the line between "law" and "fact" is not always clear to judges,[39] and it is not unheard of for people to be sworn as witnesses whose testimony is, in whole or in part, testimony concerning the proper construction of the law.[40] The appropriate role for such a "witness" is at most as an *amicus curiae*, and if the judge feels colloquy would be helpful to the judge's decision, this could as well be accomplished by oral argument. Perhaps in a bench trial this confusion of roles is of minor import, since the judge in the process of decision can treat such a witness as functionally an *amicus*, but this confusion sometimes leads to such persons being allowed to testify before juries.[41] For example, experts on "legal ethics" regularly testify in professional malpractice cases.[42] If there is a danger, already noted, that a normal "professional standard of care" witness in a malpractice case may stray from testifying about the empirical question of what lawyers do, to the normative question of what the witness believes lawyers should do, the problem of an "expert on legal ethics" is even worse. *Ex neccessitate*, the role of such a witness must frankly be either to testify to the legal obligations created by ethical codes and precedents, or to the witness's own notions of what those obligations ought to be. Either form of testimony in front of a jury improperly presents legal constructions as the subjects of expertise equal or superior to that of the judge, and often judges, having allowed such testimony, may be tempted to leave the choice of construction to the jury.[43]

A related and compounded problem is presented by the "law content expert" who is not only allowed to function as an expert on the content of the law in front of the jury, but also to give the appearance of a translational expert by opining on why, in the particular case, this or that party was or was not in compliance with the law. For instance, the author knows someone who regularly is called upon to testify in front of juries about the fiduciary duties of corporate boards, and then to opine about whether this particular board did, or did not, violate such duties. He is aware of the theoretical problems of this testimony, but he believes it proper for him to give such testimony as

---

37. *See generally* Benjamin J. Vernia, Annotation, *Admissibility of Expert Testimony Regarding Questions of Domestic Law*, 66 A.L.R.5th 135 (1999). *But see*, Note, *Expert Legal Testimony*, 97 HARV. L. REV. 797 (1984) (arguing against a blanket prohibition of such testimony).

38. The sole exception might be the *sui generis* situation of a choice of law issue where the rule of decision is dependant on the construction of foreign law for which no normal authoritative sources of determination exist. *See, e.g.,* RUSSELL J. WEINTRAUB, COMMENTARY ON THE CONFLICT OF LAWS § 3.7 (4th ed. 2001).

39. *See* Charles M. Liebson, *Legal Malpractice Cases: Special Problems in Identifying Issues of Law and Fact and in the Use of Expert Testimony*, 75 KY. L.J. 1, 20 (1986–87).

40. *See* Vernia, *supra* note 37. (attempting a complete collection of all cases of admissibility and inadmissibility that might be characterized as testimony on the content of the law in all contexts, including jury trials).

41. *See id.*

42. *See, e.g.,* Cohen v. Radio–Electronics Officers Union, 146 N.J. 140, 679 A.2d 1188 (N.J. 1996).

43. *See* People v. Lyons, 93 Mich.App. 35, 285 N.W.2d 788, 794 (Mich.App. 1979) ("Allowing witnesses to testify as to questions of law invites jury confusion and the possibility that the jury will accept as law the witness's conclusion rather than the trial judge's instructions.").

long as judges allow it (we all like to be philosopher kings if allowed), and he likes the fees. The conclusory part of his testimony is nothing more than a closing argument from the witness stand (though in his case always a sincerely believed closing argument) and as such grossly compounds the role confusion already identified, and simply ought not to be allowed.[44]

§ 2–3.0   THE TAXONOMY APPLIED

§ 2–3.1   An Instructive Special Case

Lest the reader form the impression that "more dependability, more dependability" is always and everywhere the irreducible solution to problems of expert testimony, consider the following situation, in which expertise of quite low dependability functions quite satisfactorily to accomplish the proper purposes of the law. Earlier, land valuation was given as an example of an imperfectly normed subjective translational system. There are many legal contexts, mainly in civil controversies, where the market value of land, or some similar non-fungible good, is an important element of a remedial formula. The very nature of the concept "market value" in such a case is fraught with conceptual problems. With its notional "willing buyer" and "willing seller" operating under conditions often not existing in the real world, it is a purely abstract concept not theoretically determined by any particular actual sale, even of the very land in question, since the exact amount of a particular sale might have been influenced by idiosyncratic factors not reflected in the abstract notion of market value. Thus, market value is not a "fact," even a predictive fact, in the same sense that, say, the result of a future election is a fact. Nevertheless, market value is constructed from empirically factual knowledge. No one believes that the notion of market value is totally unrelated to sales that have been made in markets. Rather, the assumption is that comparable sales fairly close in time to the relevant time suggest a probable range of likely sale prices for a particular item in question. However, no one can say with any confidence what the exact market value of a non-fungible item like land is, and, as previously noted, those who study the process of predicting likely future sale value do not dependably agree on what constitutes comparable sales. As a result, the law finds itself in a quandary. If the existence of a remedy is made to turn on market value, and if this inherent imprecision and indeterminacy is unacceptably vague, then the plaintiff (and the discussion here is restricted to civil cases) will suffer a failure of proof in every case. What to do? Allow each side to call its own "expert," knowing that each side's experts will cheat as far in favor of their own employer as they judge the "straight-face" test will allow.[1] The penalty for cheating too far is that the jury is likely to swing toward the number offered by the other expert. Each expert's number, then, will define the limits of a range. Any number within the range is an acceptable remedy—truly, this is a case without a determinate single right answer.[2] Where in the range the

---

44. As Judge Learned Hand observed in Nichols v. Universal Pictures Corp., "[a]rgument is argument whether in the box or at the bar, and its proper place is the last." 45 F.2d 119, 123 (2d Cir.1930).

§ 2–3.0

1. For a recent recognition of the litigation realities in the preparation of expert witnesses

for trial, *see* TV–3, Inc. v. Royal Ins. Co. of Amer., 193 F.R.D. 490 (S.D.Miss.2000).

2. This arrangement has much in common with "final offer" arbitration, also known as

damages are fixed is left to the jury's judgement, based on its own evaluation of the persuasiveness of each expert. In this case, very undependable expertise is used to forge a satisfactory result.[3]

§ 2–3.2 A Less Instructive Special Case

Another difficult special issue is causation in tort. Expert testimony concerning causation in products liability and toxic tort cases has become a subject of particular controversy and, indeed, was the issue that precipitated *Daubert* itself, and *Daubert's* enhanced concern for dependability of expertise, at least "scientific" expertise.[4] Undoubtedly, "causality expertise" presents a special problem resulting from a number of factors: On the one hand, there is no shortage of credentialed scientists in the world who will confuse hypothesis with confirmed fact, and testify (sincerely), to the actual existence of causal relations or substantially enhanced risks on weak or no evidence.[5] On the other hand, these cases are civil cases subject to a "preponderance of the evidence" standard of proof, a standard lower than would usually be required to establish the validity of a relationship in normal science practice. Finally, as every first-year law student learns, legal causation entails normative risk allocation judgments which are part of the jury function. What to do in the face of these colliding considerations? Perhaps the best thing would be to allow the experts to testify on a dependability standard more consistent with the civil standard of proof than one might otherwise think was necessary,[6] but

---

"baseball arbitration," except that in that case the decision maker is not allowed to pick an intermediate number. *See, e.g.,* Southern Pac. Transp. Co. v. ICC, 69 F.3d 583, 585–86 (D.C.Cir.1995); In re Hopewell Int'l Ins. Ltd., 238 B.R. 25, 40–41 (Bankr.S.D.N.Y.1999).

3. It is clear that, even after *Daubert,* valuation experts have been subject to very weak reliability scrutiny. *See* Alan Ratliff, *Kicking the Tires after Kumho: The Bottom Line on Admitting Financial Expert Testimony*, 37 Hous. L. Rev. 432, 434 (2000). While *Kumho Tire* could change this in some areas, especially those involving high levels of complexity, such as the valuation of large going concerns, at least as to real estate valuation in breach of sale contract and condemnation cases, the traditional laxity is probably a good thing, as the text suggests. This is not to say that there are not, or should not be, limits to the threshold tolerance of a particular expert's ability to suppress his giggle response. For instance, in Blue Dane Simmental Corp. v. American Simmental Ass'n, 178 F.3d 1035 (8th Cir.1999), somebody named Risinger (no relation), with the approval of the defendant registry association, had introduced nineteen cattle which could not be affirmatively established as genetically pure, including two that were shown to be "3%" genetically impure, into the American Simmental cattle breeding population, which numbered in excess of 138,000 animals. *Id.* at 1039. Plaintiffs claimed that this injured the value of their own cattle. *Id.* They showed that, after the registry of the Risinger cattle, the average price of such cattle dropped on both the Ameri-

can market, and on the Canadian market, but the price dropped substantially more on the American market. *Id.* at 1040. Without considering a number of variables normally considered in livestock valuation, plaintiff's damages expert attributed the entire difference in price between the two markets to the impurity of the American herd resulting from the Risinger cattle. *Id.* at 1041. Not surprisingly, the court found that this went too far, and refused to let the expert testify pursuant to Federal Rule of Evidence 702, and the Eighth Circuit affirmed. *Id.* at 1040–41.

4. *See* Daubert v. Merrill Dow Pharm., Inc., 509 U.S. at 579, 582–84. There are those who see a special irony in this, since it took a threat to the pocketbook of corporate America to finally focus the Court's attention on dependability issues which the Court showed little interest in when what was at stake was the execution of a criminal defendant in Barefoot v. Estelle, 463 U.S. 880, 103 S.Ct. 3383, 77 L.Ed.2d 1090 (1983).

5. This is not only not shocking, it may in fact be a byproduct of the normal practice of healthy science as a community enterprise, which may require a certain admixture of individuals irrationally committed to their own hypotheses. *See* D. Michael Risinger, Mark P. Denbeaux, & Michael J. Saks, *Brave New Post* Daubert *World: A Reply to Professor Moenssens*, 29 Seton Hall L. Rev. 405, 438 (1998).

6. Tying the level of certainty required for admission to the standard of proof applicable to the material issues to which the expert's

treat the expert as a summarizational expert. This would foreclose the expert from testifying to the conclusion of causation, thus requiring the presentation to be more in terms of educating the jury through a review of the affirmative evidence in the research literature, and less a matter of the witness's assertion of a conclusory "opinion."

§ 2–4.0 LEGAL STANDARDS OF DEPENDABILITY—SOME RECOMMENDATIONS

The Supreme Court's decision in *Daubert v. Merrell Dow* was revolutionary—perhaps more revolutionary than the Justices who fashioned it perceived. Like many revolutionary writings, the *Daubert* opinion was in some ways naïve and incoherent, but it is becoming clear from this remove that it has set in motion a process which is transforming the rules of the expert game in litigation. That process is still working itself out, and, as in most periods of profound change, there have been both counter-revolutionary currents[1] and excesses of misplaced zeal.[2] But the decision in *Kumho Tire v. Carmichael* has reinforced the trans-substantive and systematic nature of the process, and fashioned an approach to threshold dependability which will insure that the process of change continues, hopefully in fruitful directions.

Kumho Tire stands for two important principles: First, that the gatekeeping requirement of minimum threshold dependability pursuant to Federal Rule of Evidence 702 applies to *all* proffered expert testimony, not only to the explicit products of science. And second, that this threshold judgement must

---

testimony is directed will strike some as inappropriate. They will argue that admissibility should be judged by the same standard in every case, leaving differences in standard of proof to be protected by a sufficiency of evidence decision once the record is closed. The problem with that approach in regard to expert testimony is substantial, however. It forces us to select a unitary standard of dependability which either lets in too much of dubious dependability on behalf of the prosecution in criminal cases, or which excludes too much of adequate dependability for the purposes of tort law. The result of the latter situation would be too many failures of proof in tort, based on the easiest insufficiency judgment to make, a record without evidence on some essential issue like causation. On the other hand, the result of a lower uniform standard would be the admission of too much of low dependability in criminal cases, under circumstances where the sufficiency check is likely to prove largely illusory. If such expert testimony provides all or most of the evidence on a particular issue such as identity of the perpetrator or existence of the *actus reus* (a not uncommon situation where forensic expertise is offered by the prosecution), how likely is a judge to rule that the evidence he just said was dependable enough to be admitted is not dependable enough to support a finding? Not likely enough to depend on sufficiency alone to control the ill effects of such expertise on accuracy of result in criminal cases. This would seem an especial concern in

a world where the current reality appears to be that civil plaintiffs are often held to a *higher* standard of expert dependability than prosecutors in criminal cases. *See generally,* D. Michael Risinger, *Navigating Expert Reliability: Are Criminal Standards of Certainty Being Left on the Dock*, 64 ALB. L. REV. 99.

§ 2–4.0

1. The most obvious ploy was the widespread attempt to claim that *Daubert* applied only to "scientific" evidence, and therefore to maintain the pre-*Daubert* status quo as to everything else. Clearly *Kumho Tire* has explicitly made this approach impossible. Kumho Tire v. Carmichael, 526 U.S. 137, 141, 119 S.Ct. 1167, 143 L.Ed.2d 238 (1999). Another instinct may be seen in the almost mystical nostalgia for the days when virtually anything was admissible.

2. Perhaps best represented by the impossibly high standards of dependability imposed by some courts in some tort cases. *See generally* Lucinda M. Finley, *Guarding the Gate to the Courthouse: How Trial Judges Are Using Their Evidentiary Screening Role to Remake Tort Causation Rules*, 49 DEPAUL L. REV. 335 (1999). Civil defendants challenging such plaintiff proffered expertise have been the most successful class of litigants under *Daubert*. D. Michael Risinger, *Navigating Expert Reliability: Are Criminal Standards of Certainty Being Left on the Dock*, 64 ALB. L. REV. 99 (2000), at 108, 110–12, 147.

be made in regard to the particular "task at hand," not globally in regard to the average dependability of a broadly defined discipline or area of expertise, which might be dependable when applied in other contexts, but not to the "task at hand." This process of particularized "task at hand" analysis regarding the dependability of all proffered expertise will characterize the next stage in the development of the new expert control jurisprudence. But it must be remembered that while *Kumho Tire* requires the judge to apply a proper standard of threshold dependability to all proffered expertise, at least upon an appropriately serious objection,[3] it does not say that exactly the same threshold standard is applicable to every kind of expert evidence in every kind of case. Rather, it appears more consistent with the opinion's emphasis on flexibility to conclude that proffered evidence must be shown to be sufficiently reliable for the task at hand, given the jury's role and capacities, and the nature of the case.

Thus, it is not only consistent with *Kumho Tire*, but implied by it, that evidence reliable enough in one legal context pursuant to rule 702 may not be reliable enough in another. Consider the land valuation issue previously discussed. In the normal civil case, as previously argued, a fairly lax threshold standard of dependability would appear to be appropriate, given the jury's presumed ability to understand the issues involved, and the balance of the opposing parties and their experts in the "baseball arbitration" dynamic of the case. However, were the same issue of the value of the same land to arise in a criminal fraud prosecution, where, let us say, the difference between a felony and a misdemeanor turned on the value of the property being above or below a certain exact amount, the judge is obliged to apply a more stringent threshold standard to the methodology of the prosecution's valuation expert. While the jury might be warranted in relying on, or being influenced by, the expert's testimony in the circumstances of the civil case, it might not be so warranted in the criminal case.

What we are likely to see over the next decade is the working out of a task-at-hand warrant analysis, which asks the question "what indices of dependability ought to be present to render this asserted expertise sufficiently dependable on this particular issue, in this kind of case, so that a jury would be warranted in relying on, or being influenced by it?" It is in the working out of this task-at-hand warrant analysis for which a new taxonomy of expertise will not only be helpful, but essential. Some recent scholarship has already looked in that general direction.[4]

---

3. *Kumho Tire* leaves open the issue of the "price of admission" burden on the opponent of expertise, distinguishing between "ordinary" cases, where sufficient dependability "is properly taken for granted," and "less usual [and] more complex cases where cause for questioning the expert's reliability arises." 526 U.S. at 152–53. Clearly what is envisioned is something more weighty than a conclusory or *pro-forma* objection, and one criticism that might be leveled at the criminal defense bar as a group may be that in the press of time, they have not properly come to grips with what is necessary for an effective *Daubert/Kumho* challenge. *See supra* note 2, at 137–145.

4. *See, e.g.*, Scott Brewer, *Scientific Expert Testimony and Intellectual Due Process*, 107 YALE L.J. 1535 (1998), Note, *Navigating Uncertainty: Gatekeeping in the Absence of Hard Science*, 113 HARV. L. REV. 1467 (2000). The theory of warrants for assertion or belief is associated with the Pragmatists, most particularly, John Dewey (though Prof. Brewer displays a partiality for C.S. Peirce). *See* H. S. Thayer, *Pragmatism, in* 6 ENCYCLOPEDIA OF PHILOSOPHY (Paul Edwards ed., 1967). The conclusion of Prof. Brewer's article, that ordinarily non-scientist judges and juries can never be warranted in evaluating (choosing between) the claims of disagreeing scientists seems a bit extreme. The Harvard note bites off a smaller

What variables, then, have we seen from our preliminary taxonomic exercise that affect the dependability we should demand of tendered expertise, and what statements does it seem tentatively appropriate to make about them?[5] The following is a non-exclusive and incomplete list:

1. "Everyday" summarizational expertise is easily understood by the jury and its dependability can be left to their evaluation, though care must be taken so that such a witness is not allowed to wander into translational expertise.

2. Dependability of technical summarizational expertise should be judged by standards applicable to translational expertise in the same context.

3. Translational expertise with a high clinical subjectivity component should be approached cautiously, especially where real world practice does not provide unambiguous feedback concerning the correctness of the conclusions reached. Generally there ought to be strong external evidence of dependability in such cases, through well designed tests showing individual proficiency, or at least group error rates, in regard to the particular task at hand.

4. Translational expertise offered on normative issues can perhaps be safely allowed on a lower standard of certifiable dependability than should be required of "brute fact" or "pure fact" issues such as *actus reus* and identity, in the same litigation context. The same is true in regard to magnitude judgment or theoretical "no one right answer" issues such as market value.

5. All things being equal, the higher the standard of proof applicable to the issue upon which the expertise is offered, the higher the required threshold dependability should be.

6. High standards should apply to pure fact issues, and extremely high standards to prosecution expertise bearing on pure fact issues in criminal cases, such as identity or the existence of the *actus reus*.

7. Courts should be careful, especially in jury cases, to prevent an expert from testifying to a construction of the law. Further, the court should

piece, but persuasively argues that in at least a class of cases involving issues of "strong scientific uncertainty" (where many experimental scientists claim no answer to a legally pertinent question has been dependably derived, and clinicians claim an answer can be properly inferred), there are warrant guidelines for choosing between "generic toxic tort" rules and "slip and fall" rules. Note, *supra* at 1470–71. Another useful approach to the warrant problem, *sub nom* the "better evidence principle" is found in David L. Faigman, David H. Kaye, Michael J. Saks & Joseph Sanders, *How Good is Good Enough?: Expert Evidence Under* Daubert *and* Kumho, 50 CASE W. RES. L. REV. 645 (2000).

5. Lists of "factors" for judges to consider abound. *Daubert* itself had one, and so does the

Advisory Committee's Note to revised Fed. R. Evid. 702. I have endeavored to include only observations that have grown out of the taxonomic exercise in this article, not every important consideration in the evaluation of threshold dependability. For instance, one of the most pervasive phenomena undermining dependability of forensic expertise is the presence of expectancy effects, and these must be taken into consideration in any approach to threshold dependability. *See generally*, D. Michael Risinger et al., *The Daubert/Kumho Implications of Observer Effects in Forensic Science: Hidden Problems of Expectation and Suggestion*, CAL. L. REV. (forthcoming). However, this important issue did not arise in the body of the essay, and is therefore not on the list, and is held for another day.

prevent expert "opinion" which might be fair forensic argument, but should clearly be presented only as such by counsel in closing.

8. Courts should be careful not to apply to expertise in general, standards of dependability appropriate only to a limited context.

No claim is made that this list is complete, nor indeed that any given statement may not properly be subject to substantial qualification on further reflection and analysis. Nor is it suggested that the taxonomic exercise upon which it is based is yet close to being completely worked out. We cannot, however, finally come to grips with the problems of expert testimony and its control in the courtroom except in the light of some such attempt to identify the varying functions and contexts of what we globally label "expertise."

CHAPTER 3

ETHICAL STANDARDS OF AND CONCERNING EXPERT WITNESSES*

Table of Sections

Westlaw Electronic Research

See Westlaw Electronic Research Guide preceding the Summary of Contents.

---

§ 3–1.0   INTRODUCTION

The ethical and effective use of scientific expert witnesses presents special challenges to the law and to experts. The two cultures and their respective norms do not fit together neatly. The general goal of providing fact finders in a legal forum with information relevant to, perhaps even necessary for, making an informed and rational decision is entirely and obviously sensible. And, viewed from the separate vantage points of the law or the experts' fields, no problem is immediately apparent. Experts' fields would be happy to have some of their members come to court and share what the field knows about some topic. The law would like to have available to it whatever knowledge

---

* Portions of this chapter are adapted from Michael J. Saks, *Normative and Empirical Issues About the Role of Expert Witnesses, in* Handbook of Psychology and Law (D.K. Kagehiro & W.S. Laufer eds., 1992).

91

may be relevant to making the decisions it has to make. It is when the two actually meet that problems emerge and seem to resist solution.[1]

Although the experts themselves largely control the flow of their fields' knowledge to the legal system, lawyers and judges control the case, including exactly what, from the corpus of available information and techniques, is to be brought to bear and how. The operating paradigms of the legal process and virtually any field of knowledge are almost assured to be in conflict with each other. Any field of knowledge tends to emphasize its shared understanding of its subject matter and has its own methods of identifying issues and working toward resolution or tolerance of these differences. By contrast, the adversary process tends to focus on those parts of a body of knowledge that are relevant to the case at bar and then tends powerfully to find and emphasize differences and disagreements within a body of information, or between the experts presenting different parts in different ways for different parties[2]—rather than to work toward their resolution. Often, it is those differences on which a case turns, and good lawyers with the time to do their work properly do not let information that can usefully be disputed go unchallenged.

This chapter is concerned largely with the paradigm clashes, role conflicts, and other tensions that erupt when members of various fields are invited into lawsuits as experts, and what the formal and informal legal process does to create and manage those problems.[3] The chapter also addresses ethical constraints to the litigator's role that specially arise when scientific evidence is at issue. These concerns raise the larger question of whether the law's methods of obtaining expert evidence facilitate or interfere with achieving some of the most important purposes of the trial process.[4]

---

§ 3–1.0

1. At least under the regime of the adversary system. Prior to the civil war, experts were more likely to be called by judges than by the parties. Stephan Landsman, *One Hundred Years of Rectitude: Medical Witnesses at the Old Bailey, 1717–1817*, 16 L. & HIST. REV. 445 (1998); Stephan Landsman, *Of Witches, Madmen, and Products Liability: An Historical Survey of the Use of Expert Testimony*, 13 BEHAV. SCIENCE & L. 131 (1995). Dissatisfaction with the role of experts rose later, along with the rise of the adversary process. Even today, when judges call their own experts under Fed. R.Evid 706, they are overwhelmingly pleased with the experts and the work they do. JOE CECIL & THOMAS WILLGING, COURT-APPOINTED EXPERTS: DEFINING THE ROLE OF EXPERTS APPOINTED UNDER FEDERAL RULE OF EVIDENCE 706 (1993).

2. Sheila Jasanoff, *What Judges Should Know about the Sociology of Science*, 32 JURIMETRICS J. 345 (1992). Also, compare provisions of the Model Expert Witness Act, aimed at reducing conflict over expert testimony but never adopted. Reprinted in WIGMORE ON EVIDENCE § 563 (Chadbourne Rev., 1979).

3. Complaints and concerns about the use of expert witnesses has a long history. L.M. Friedman, *Expert Testimony, its Abuse and Reformation*, 19 YALE L. J. 247 (1910), provides one example:

> The position of an expert on the witness stand, who does not testify either to what he has observed or known as fact but expresses merely his opinion as to a situation or on facts which have been established by other witnesses, is anomalous in Anglo–Saxon law. It was to be expected that former generations of judges and lawyers, trained in older precedents and practices who recognized the appearance in the courts of an expert witness as an innovation would look with suspicion and doubt on such testimony. While the principles on which such evidence is introduced have come to be well recognized and while the [legal] profession no longer has any reservations in approving theoretically of the use of expert testimony, yet, on the other hand, there is a constant complaining and mistrust on the part of judges, juries and lawyers of the expert witness.

4. For example, legal policymakers should be concerned with whether the legal process delivers reasonably accurate information to factfinders or whether the process systematically and habitually distorts the knowledge of the fields it calls on for expertise.

§ 3–2.0 THE EXTERNAL ENVIRONMENT FROM WHICH EXPERTS AND THEIR KNOWLEDGE COME

The greatest amount of knowledge and discussion about expert witnesses concerns the subject matter that they have to offer to trial courts. Most of this treatise is concerned with that information, how it comes into being, what it consists of, its strengths and weaknesses, and whether it meets the law's admissibility requirements. Also of interest are the differences among fields and how they and their knowledge relate to the legal process. One important dimension of difference is how different fields bring their knowledge into being, including how—or whether—they test the validity of their hypotheses.[1] Another important dimension of difference is the base from which the experts operate—ranging from those fields whose members are employed totally apart from the law and typically live out their careers without ever being asked to serve as an expert, to those who are similarly independent but who are called upon with some regularity (e.g., some physicians, accountants, economists, epidemiologists, statisticians, psychologists), to those whose field exists for little reason other than to provide expert evidence for litigation (the clearest example being forensic scientists). No doubt other dividing lines between groups of experts exist, and the nature and extent of ethical tensions between legal actors and experts is likely to depend in part on these differences among different expert fields and their work settings.[2]

The most serious dividing line is between those fields that are more sound and dependable and those that are less sound and less dependable. *Daubert* obviously raises the concern that some fields are pseudo-sciences or not-yet-sciences, or that some knowledge within otherwise sound disciplines is not valid or not yet validated. What ethical concerns does this often gray dividing line create?

Where a proffered expert knows himself or herself to be a quack or is engaged in charlatanry, the situation is like any other witness who is perpetrating a fraud on the court. Their act would be illegal as well as unethical. A more ambiguous version of this is the proffered expert who comes from a field that has valid knowledge and is capable of doing sound work, but in the case at bar the expert has failed to perform up to the usual standards (with "the same intellectual rigor," as some courts and commentators have put it) and that looseness has produced less reliable results (and presumably

---

§ 3–2.0

1. Those asserted sciences which fail to test the validity of their ideas, or do so in unsystematic ways are in essence asking courts to share their own faith in their assumptions and conclusions. Such trust is the foundation of *Frye*-type tests, Frye v. United States, 293 F. 1013 (D.C.Cir.1923). For *Daubert*-type tests, Daubert v. Merrell Dow Pharmaceuticals, Inc., 509 U.S. 579, 113 S.Ct. 2786, 125 L.Ed.2d 469 (1993), which require a demonstration of validity, trust is not enough, and testing is required. "In scientific inquiry it becomes a matter of duty to expose a supposed law to every possible kind of verification, and to take care, moreover, that this is done intentionally, and not left to a mere accident" T. H. Huxley, *The Method of Scientific Investigation, in* SCIENCE: METHOD AND MEANING (Samuel Rapport & Helen Wright eds., 1974) at 6.

2. This is not to suggest that the tensions are necessarily bad. The best use of expert evidence in trials might come from a productive tension between lawyers who have a particular goal for the knowledge being used and experts whose goal is to protect the integrity of their field's knowledge.

the lack of reliability results in conclusions that lean closer to the proponent's preferred position).[3]

The interesting questions have to do with the responsibilities of the lawyer calling such witnesses to the stand. If the lawyer knows the testimony is invalid or fraudulent, the lawyer's obligation is to prevent the witness's testimony from entering the court.[4] But to what extent does the lawyer have an obligation to investigate the expert or the expertise? Is it sufficient for the lawyer to accept the asserted expert's claims about himself, the field, and the conclusions resulting from the application of the field's supposed principles? Is it enough for the lawyer to accept the popular culture's belief about the existence and nature of the expertise? Is it enough for the lawyer to not *know* that the expert is no expert or that the expertise is invalid? Or, in the realm of expert evidence does the sponsoring attorney have a duty to the court to find out?[5]

The ethical rules governing the offering of witnesses at trial are generally written to prohibit the knowing perpetration of a fraud on the court. For ordinary fact witnesses this makes considerable sense. It generally would be difficult or impossible for an attorney to develop sufficient independent knowledge of the facts of a case to be in a position to decide which witnesses are telling the truth and which are not. After all, the witnesses often are the source of whatever knowledge there is about a disputed event. But with scientific expert witnesses the situation is quite different. Any attorney, like any intelligent citizen, who takes the time and effort to research a purported scientific subject can, at least in principle, come to her own conclusion about

---

3. Some courts and commentators, apparently in search of an easier test of junk science than *Daubert* articulates, have focused on the notion that if the expert at bar performs at the same level that people in his field operate at in matters outside of court, then all will be well. *E.g.*, J. Brook Lathram, *The "Same Intellectual Rigor" Test Provides an Effective Method for Determining the Reliability of All Expert Testimony, Without Regard to Whether the Testimony Comprises "Scientific Knowledge" or "Technical or Other Specialized Knowledge,"* 28 U. MEMPHIS L. REV. 1053 (1998). The failure to perform up to par certainly can be one reason for undependable expert testimony, but, as many of the chapters of this treatise make evident, and as will become clear shortly in the discussion below, that is far from the only reason expert evidence can lack validity. The flaw in the reasoning of those cases and commentators who have become enamored of "the same intellectual rigor" test can be explained with one word: astrology.

4. There are several complex and debatable exceptions to the prohibition on false or misleading testimony, but need not delay us since they are mostly or completely inapplicable to expert witnesses.

5. An infamous forensic dentist from Mississippi invented techniques that were never tested, which he could not document, which he alone could perform, and which went beyond the domain of bitemark impressions. More than this, in his opinions he exaggerated the

certainty of the conclusions that his techniques could produce ("indeed and without doubt"). As a result, several of the professional associations he belonged to denounced him and suspended or terminated his membership, though not before his testimony led to convictions of the innocent. Did the prosecutors who put him on the stand have no independent professional obligation to ascertain that his investigative inventions and his testimony were valid? (After he was exposed, he continued to be used as an expert witness. Did those prosecutors have an additional burden to insure that he was not offering junk science to the courts, or could they take his word for it that he was not?) Another infamous forensic scientist, from West Virginia, was renowned for coming up with the answers that investigators and prosecutors wanted for their cases, mostly by making up the results of tests never performed. Did the prosecutors who used his work have any obligation to insure the validity of what he was offering beyond taking him at his word? His "work" was so valued that after he was exposed and fired and moved his practice to another state, West Virginia law enforcement officials continued to send cases to him for his reports and opinions. For details on these and many other instances of fraud by expert witnesses, *see* Paul Giannelli, *The Abuse of Scientific Evidence in Criminal Cases*, 4 VA. J. Soc. POL'Y & L. 439 (1997).

whether or not its beliefs rest on a foundation of data and logic that is solid, soft, mushy, or non-existent. It is hard to think of principled reasons why an attorney should not be obligated to acquire a good faith basis for believing the proffered expertise is valid, or that the specific facts or skills to be brought to bear on the task-at-hand in the trial are valid, as a precondition for ethically offering such expert evidence to a court.[6] Reasons of practicality and efficiency rather than principle might justify exempting the proponent of scientific evidence from the obligation to know whether the evidence is valid. The argument would be that it is inefficient and burdensome for the proponent of expert evidence to have to engage in research for every kind of expertise she wishes to offer and that it would be more efficient if it is left to the potential opponent of admission to raise initial doubts and ask for a *Daubert* hearing for those experts and expertises about which there are doubts. From the court's viewpoint, of course, this is anything but practical and efficient.

A similar but more challenging situation arises where the proposed expert believes sincerely in the validity of the expertise, or at least in the validity of his conclusion, but the expert has no sound basis for those beliefs. For example, consider the situation of a treating physician who believes sincerely that her patient's cancer is caused by a chemical made by the defendant, but no research has ever been conducted showing general causation between the chemical and the disease. The physician ought to know enough about science, and about the literature on this condition, to know the basis is not there. But her belief is nevertheless sincere.[7] Or, to take another example, suppose the asserted expert is performing a task that is said to be based on sound science, but the expert is only a technician who follows the field's cookbook procedures and has no knowledge or understanding of the underlying science. And suppose that any relevant scientist, and any properly informed court, would quickly come to the conclusion that there is no valid basis to what the expert is doing, or at least no valid basis that is yet known. But the expert does not know that. Can the attorney offer the testimony of such an asserted expert to a court? Or does the attorney have an obligation to first find out enough about the underlying science claims to have a good faith belief that what is being offered to the court is valid?[8] If the attorney is prohibited only from offering false expertise when he knows it to be false, then ignorance is bliss for both the proffered expert and the attorney. Indeed, the attorney would be rewarded for avoiding learning about the expertise. Then the burden of

6. The argument that it is too time consuming or difficult for the attorney to become conversant with the subject matter fails because, once in court, especially in a *Daubert* hearing, the attorney will have the burden of rationally educating and persuading the judge that the expertise is valid, and that can only be done competently if the attorney has taken the time and effort to learn about the asserted expertise. Also, because the attorney as proponent of the expert evidence has the burden of persuading the court that it meets the admissibility requirements, she cannot say that the obligation to figure out what is valid and what is not rests entirely on the court.

7. The witness might think: "The necessary research may not have been done yet to prove it, but if and when it is conducted I am sure it will bear out my hunches."

8. The prosecutor must scrupulously avoid misleading the court or the jury as to the evidence, and may be disciplined for knowingly offering false evidence, failing to withdraw it upon discovering its falsity, or bringing evidence before the court without a good faith belief in its admissibility. *See* Amer. Bar Ass'n, Model Rules of Professional Conduct 3.3(a)(1) and DR 7–102(A)(4), (5); Rules of Professional Responsibility 3.4(e) and DR 7–106(C)(1); and ABA Standards Relating to the Administration of Criminal Justice, Prosecution Function, Standards 5.6 and 5.8.

screening out junk science falls on the opponent of admission and the court. If the proponent of the expert evidence is a prosecutor, a greater burden may attach, given the special obligations of prosecutors to find truth and not merely engage in a fair fight. If such a good faith belief is ethically required, what would constitute sufficient grounds for a good faith belief? Clearly something more would be required than reliance on nothing more than the assertions of the asserted expert about his field and himself. Otherwise, an attorney could properly offer astrologers to courts. Would it be a sufficient basis that the expertise is regarded as valid by a substantial segment of the popular culture? Astrology is still in. If a reasonable good faith belief is ethically required, it seems inescapable that the attorney could not use a shortcut or proxy test, but would have to at least ask himself: Do I know enough about this subject so that if it were challenged under *Daubert* I could make a well grounded showing that, at least on current knowledge, it satisfies the relevant validity criteria?

Handwriting identification evidence probably fits the problematic pattern of the above paragraph. Its practitioners are said to be technicians who cannot be expected to know much about the underlying science. There is a severe lack of underlying science. There is no case in which *Daubert* challenges to asserting handwriting expertise did not result in judicial declarations that the field was not a valid science, along with rulings that often placed limits of one kind or another on the testimony of asserted handwriting experts.[9] Yet it can safely be assumed that the examiners' personal faith in the validity of what they do was, and remains, heartfelt—even after its weaknesses have been exposed and judged. Did the attorneys[10] who offered handwriting expert evidence have any ethical obligation to look below the surface, to make sure they were not offering false evidence to the court, or was it permissible to keep offering such experts until the courts slowed them down or stopped them?[11] Once challenges were made, it seems appropriate that the proponents offered the courts the best case they could for continued admission. But what happens after some number of cases have considered the challenges and routinely rejected handwriting expertise at some level; what then is the obligation of subsequent proponents? Do attorneys, especially prosecutors, now have an ethical duty to independently evaluate the validity of handwriting expertise, and continue to offer it only if they reach a considered conclusion that it is valid and that they can make a sound case to a court that it ought to be admitted?[12]

9. *See Science in the Law: Forensic Science Issues* (Chapter 3).

10. Presumably, if there is such a duty to offer only valid evidence to the court, the duty falls more heavily on prosecutors than on lawyers offering such expertise in civil cases. It is, however, hard to see why it would make a difference in what is an implicit motion to admit an expertise on the grounds that it satisfies the requirements of *Daubert*.

11. This becomes relevant with respect to other forensic sciences that share similar weaknesses with asserted handwriting identification expertise. What, if any, independent ob-

ligation do the proponents of such evidence have following *Daubert* and *Kumho Tire Co. v. Carmichael*, 526 U.S. 137, 119 S.Ct. 1167, 143 L.Ed.2d 238 (1999)? Or is it ethically proper for them to continue offering the evidence whether or not they have satisfied themselves about its validity?

12. One Assistant U.S. Attorney of 25 years' experience volunteered to one of the editors of this treatise that he now believes there is no valid handwriting identification expertise and, accordingly, he no longer offers courts their testimony.

If an attorney does, for whatever reason, offer such expertise to a court, what are the proponent's obligations to counsel on the other side and to the court? Is there any obligation to make known the weaknesses of the science or the cases that have considered and, at varying levels, rejected the claims of the proffered field?

The answer probably depends upon whether the scientific material in question constitutes adjudicative facts or legislative facts. This requires a few sentences on the nature of scientific knowledge. Scientific knowledge exists at several levels of abstraction, but it will suffice to consider two. At a high level of abstraction are the trans-situational principles, relationships, theories, hypotheses, and so on of the field. These constitute the general facts of the field; they are the science of the science. They will be true across cases and across jurisdictions. (These are the sorts of facts that sometimes become legislative facts.) At a low level of abstraction are the case-specific facts to which the principles of the science are applied and the case-specific conclusions that emerge from that application. They are true for the case at bar but not for other cases involving other parties and other case facts. (These are adjudicative facts.)[13]

There is no debate about facts that occupy the lower level of abstraction. They are facts like any other, and there is no reason why the usual rules of procedure, professional responsibility, and due process should not apply to the circumstances under which they must be made known to opposing counsel or to the court and when they may be withheld.[14]

If the facts at the higher level of abstraction also are thought of as adjudicative facts,[15] then the above answer is the same for them. For criminal prosecutors, this probably means that the weaknesses of the proffered science need to be disclosed to the defense and perhaps to the court. If the facts (of the shakiness of the science) are material to the issue of the identification of the defendant as the perpetrator and they tend to weaken the identification and negate guilt, then they are adjudicative facts which tend to exculpate and must be disclosed.[16]

But the more coherent analysis is that these trans-case facts, if adopted by a court as part of a ruling on the admission or exclusion of a specie of evidence and having precedential effect, constitute legislative facts. And if they are legislative facts, then they usually are treated as law is treated.[17] And if they are treated as law, then they probably must be disclosed on the same terms that other adverse legal authority must be made known to a court.[18]

---

13. For a more detailed discussion, *see* the comments on *General Electric Co. v. Joiner*, 522 U.S. 136, 118 S.Ct. 512, 139 L.Ed.2d 508 (1997) in Michael J. Saks, *The Aftermath of Daubert: An Evolving Jurisprudence of Expert Evidence*, 40 JURIMETRICS J. 229 (2000).

14. This is reflected in ABA Model Rules of Professional Conduct 3.8 and DR 7–103, which prohibit the prosecutor from instituting charges known to be not supported by probable cause, and which require the disclosure of evidence to the defense that negates guilt or mitigates the offense. *See also* Brady v. Maryland, 373 U.S. 83, 83 S.Ct. 1194, 10 L.Ed.2d 215

(1963); United States v. Bagley, 473 U.S. 667, 105 S.Ct. 3375, 87 L.Ed.2d 481 (1985).

15. Which seems to be at least the tentative inference to be drawn from the *Joiner* decision.

16. *See supra* note 14.

17. John Monahan & Laurens Walker, *Social Authority: Obtaining, Evaluating, and Establishing Social Science in Law*, 134 U. PA. L. REV. 477 (1986).

18. The Code of Professional Responsibility and the Rules of Professional Conduct require a lawyer to disclose legal authority ''in the

While the duty of disclosure of adjudicative facts falls most heavily on prosecutors, the duty to disclose adverse legal authority falls on both sides of both civil and criminal cases.

§ 3–3.0 DEFINING THE ROLE OF EXPERT WITNESSES

The central normative aspiration of the rule of law is to have its decisions conducted according to a set of principles, rather than according to the caprice or systematic bias of particular decision makers. Although this ideal, like all ideals, is never fully achieved, the hope is that juries will apply the law as it is given to them by judges and that judges will give juries the law as it is understood to be and not as the judge wishes it were.

Fields of expertise have a parallel ideal. They hope that when called upon to share the field's knowledge with a court, the field's members will present the field's knowledge and not some idiosyncratic version of it or one distorted to serve some narrow partisan purpose. Just as judges and jurors and lawyers might stray from the law's ideal, experts sometimes stray from the aspirations that their field, as well as the law, has for them.

Suppose an unusually candid expert witness turns to the audience after testifying, and says:

> Perhaps you noticed that I withheld some information from the court, stretched other information, and offered an opinion that sounded more certain than our field's knowledge really permits. I did that because I am committed to making the world a better place, and I think it will be better if the court reaches the outcome I want to see in this case. That is why I gave the particular testimony that I did and withheld other evidence.

One need not look too far to find examples of less explicit but no less imperialistic conduct by real experts.[1] However well intentioned they are, such experts display a willingness, first, to disregard what knowledge has been developed by the field from which they claim to derive their expertise and to substitute for that their own guesses. Or to fill gaps in the field's knowledge with their own guesses. And, second, where the assertion of idiosyncratic expertise is chosen strategically to bring about a certain result desired by the expert, then the expert is trying to substitute the expert's own preferences for a societal preference expressed through the law.[2]

---

controlling jurisdiction" known to be "directly adverse" to the position of the client and which is not disclosed by opposing counsel. CPR 106(B)(1) and RPC 3.3(a) (3). Whether legislative facts that are integral to a holding are disclosable in the same way that the holding is has not, to our knowledge, been considered yet by any court.

§ 3–3.0

1. "The temptation to fabricate or to exaggerate certainly exists. All experts are tempted, many times during their careers, to report positive results when their inquiries come up inconclusive, or indeed to report a negative result as a positive when all other investigative leads seem to point to the same individual. Experts can feel secure in the belief that their indiscretions will probably never come to light." Andre Moenssens, *Novel Scientific Evidence in Civil and Criminal Cases: Some Words of Caution*, 84 J. Crim. L. & Criminology 1, 17 (1993).

2. Surely, the legal process is an imperfect instrument. But not as imperfect as a single judge or a single expert installing himself or herself as temporary monarch.

Complaints about expert witnesses and from expert witnesses are widespread, across various fields and across the decades if not centuries.[3] The extent to which these observers echo each other suggests that they are describing a shared experience that is profoundly and persistently confusing.

§ 3–3.1 Alternative Visions of the Expert Role

There are a number of possibilities discussed, more among experts than among lawyers, for what the expert witness role could or should be.

§ 3–3.1.1 Expert as Pure Educator

If the role of an expert is essentially that of conduit from the corpus of knowledge of a field to the court, the "pure educator" role, its occupant would describe it much like this:

> My first duty is to share the most faithful picture of my field's knowledge with those who have been assigned the responsibility to make the decisions. To do this may be to offer myself as a mere technocrat, rather than a complete human being concerned with the moral implications of what I say and with the greater good of society. But in doing that I recognize that the responsibility to set normative policies, and to make the decision in this particular case, have been assigned to others, not to me. The central difficulty of this role is whether it is all right for me to share hard-won knowledge in the service of causes I do not personally support.

Valerie Hans sums up this role:

> [Some] experts embraced a social science normative stance, in which they qualified statements made on the witness stand and discussed evidence against their side: "Adherence to professional standards is the only thing that justifies you being in court...."[4]

This type of witness is saying, in essence: They don't want to hear *me*; they want to hear my field, of which I am only a representative.

§ 3–3.1.2 Expert as Assistant Advocate

This role's occupant sees the world of litigation something like this:

> There is a greater good at stake in this case, and that is (fill in the blank: creating safe schools, seeing to it that this child goes to the right home, saving people from being executed, seeing to it that people are executed, etc., etc.). I must advocate for those outcomes, and that obviously means giving testimony that involves a certain amount of editing, selecting, shading, exaggerating, or glossing over.

3. *See* the complaints from judges and lawyers, and the generally confused or pained descriptions from experts. C. Herschel, *Services of Experts in the Conduct of Judicial Inquiries*, 21 Am. L. Rev. 571 (1887); Tracy Peerage, 10 Clark & F. 154 (1839, 1843); L.M. Friedman, *Expert Testimony, its Abuse and Reformation*, 19 Yale L. J. 247 (1910); Michael J. Saks & Richard Van Duizend, The Use of Scientific Evidence in Litigation (1983).

4. Valerie Hans, *Expert Witnessing*, 245 Science 312 (1989) (reviewing M.A. Chesler, J. Sanders & D.S. Kalmuss, Social Science in Court (1989)).

This role raises the question whether it is all right to mislead on behalf of a cause in which one believes.[5] Hans nicely sums up this role as well:

> Some experts chose a legal-adversary stance, in which they volunteered only research evidence that supported their side, de-emphasized or omitted the flaws in the data, or refrained from discussing opposing evidence. In the words of one expert,
>
>> I understood the partisan nature of the courtroom and I realized that I would be on the stand arguing for a position without also presenting evidence that might be contrary to my . . . side. But, you see, that didn't bother me, because I knew that the other side was also doing that.[6]

§ 3–3.1.3   "Hired Gun"

The role of the "hired gun" is much like the role immediately preceding, except that the hired gun works in the service of someone else's values rather than trying to advance his or her own. This role occupant sees the job this way: "I must do what I can to help the people who hired me." This style of expert witnessing raises the question of whether it is morally correct to mislead in the service of a cause for which one is indifferent.

§ 3–3.1.4   Provider of Good Data for a Favored Cause

Each of the three roles presented thus far focuses on the central dilemma the expert must confront in relating his or her field's knowledge to the cause at stake in the litigation. Each requires resolving a conflict between loyalty to one's field of expertise and the outcome of a legal case.[7] The educator makes the field the first priority and resists the claims of the cause on whose behalf it is employed. The assistant advocate focuses on the cause and is relatively indifferent to the contents of the field. The hired gun is indifferent to both field and cause, perhaps motivated only by an altogether too obvious third force. The fourth alternative, in its pure form, is an expert witness's heaven on earth: Everything is in harmony, no dilemmas, one can have one's cake and eat it too. The data are so helpful to a cause the experts believe in that they can be entirely forthcoming about them. An expert who would testify only under the harmonious conditions of this cell raises a different ethical problem. As a practical matter, however, this cell does not exist. No matter how good the data are, they almost never are good enough for an advocate's

---

5. Another problem here is that the expert witness is giving the court something less than "the whole truth" that was promised when the expert mounted the witness stand. Even if the expert can justify misleading a judge or jury in the service of a worthy cause, then why promise to provide the whole truth? Tactically, of course, it would seem to be the effective stratagem. Promising to tell only "the truth" enhances the impact of the witness's fibs. The trouble with that, however, is that over time judges and lawyers and perhaps jurors come to view expert witnesses with skepticism. As indeed, they have.

6. Hans, *supra* note 4, at 312. A statistician who served as an expert in a discrimination case studied by SAKS & VAN DUIZEND, *supra* note 3, put the matter somewhat differently. He likened the fact-finding task of the judge to trying to see as much of a matrix as possible, when each side was going to fill in only those cells favorable to it. The court's ability to see the whole picture depended on how completely and how well each side filled in its share of the cells.

7. This may represent commitment to a larger ideology or may amount only to commitment to a single case.

purposes. Pressures develop to stretch or to overstate, or to make clear and unambiguous data that are never altogether clear and unambiguous.

Resolving these problems—by removing the role conflict or by designating one conflicted role to be the one appropriate role or by some other innovation—requires first that we try to understand the intentions of the role senders: the expert's field, the law and the courts, and counsel for the parties to a dispute.

§ 3–3.2 How Do Professional and Scientific Fields View the Expert Witness's Role?

Various fields have thought about the part their members play when serving as expert witnesses and in related capacities. Through their codes of ethics, they have expressed their notion of what members are expected to do.[8] Not surprisingly, they emphasize fidelity to the discipline and resistance to the partisan pressures of the legal world. Following are excerpts from the ethical codes of several such disciplines.

> The forensic scientist should render technically correct statements in all written or oral reports, testimony, public addresses, or publications, and should avoid any misleading or inaccurate claims. The forensic scientist should act in an impartial manner and do nothing which would imply partisanship or any interest in a case except the proof of the facts and their correct interpretation.[9]

> Engineers shall issue public statements only in an objective and truthful manner. Engineers shall be objective and truthful in professional reports, statements, or testimony. They shall include all relevant and pertinent information.[10]

> Psychologists do not make public statements that are false, deceptive, misleading, or fraudulent, either because of what they state, convey, or suggest or because of what they omit.... In forensic testimony and reports, psychologists testify truthfully, honestly, and candidly and, consistent with applicable legal procedures, describe fairly the bases for their testimony and conclusions. Whenever necessary to avoid misleading, psychologists acknowledge the limits of their data or conclusions.[11]

§ 3–3.3 How Does the Law Conceive the Role of the Expert Witness?

§ 3–3.3.1 The Archetype: Testimonial Experts at Trial

In terms of the formal rules of the legal system, the greatest clarity is to be found in the law governing trials. The law[12] expects expert witnesses to be unbiased educators and not advocates. Authority for this conclusion is plentiful.

8. Symposium, *Ethical Conflicts in the Forensic Sciences*, 34 J. FORENSIC SCIENCES 717 (1989).

9. American Academy of Forensic Science, CODE OF ETHICS (1989).

10. National Society of Professional Engineers, CODE OF ETHICS FOR ENGINEERS (1990).

11. American Psychological Association, ETHICAL PRINCIPLES OF PSYCHOLOGISTS AND CODE OF CONDUCT (1992).

12. And here we mean the black-letter law—the law on the books rather than the patterned behavior of actors in the legal system. The latter will be discussed shortly.

First and most obvious, an expert witness at trial is cast in the role of a witness, not as one of the advocates and not as the decision maker. As with other witnesses, before being allowed to testify, the expert is required to promise to "tell the truth, the whole truth, and nothing but the truth."[13] For the purpose of trying to figure out what the law wants expert witnesses to be, the typical oath reveals several things. First, the law seems to know not only about lying but about half truths and withheld truths, and it wants expert witnesses, like all witnesses, to refrain from such manipulations. Second, experts are required to take the oath but advocates are not.[14] That is because experts are there to give evidence and lawyers are not.

One test of how well an expert has adopted the honest educator role is to ask how the witness would answer a question such as this: "Is there anything else you know about this case that you think the court might want to know about?" Would the witness openly share the information with the court or hide it for the benefit of one side? Experienced experts were interviewed and asked if this question had ever been put to them and if so how they responded, or if it had not been put to them how they think they would respond.[15] Of two especially strong and independent experts, one said he had once been asked that question and had replied that he had nothing to add. The other seemed surprised at such an unorthodox question, but said that if it ever did happen she would refer the judge to her written report. Thus, it appears that even the most independent expert has a sense that there is a line that separates the "whole" truth from the realm of the traitor, a line that one crosses at some social, if not financial, peril. Of course, expert witnesses will rarely, if ever, be put to such a test, because few lawyers would risk asking such an open-ended question, especially of witnesses of whom they are as suspicious as they are of expert witnesses.

To be sure, there are circumstances for which the law protects the right of people to withhold information, sometimes even to the point of misleading others. These include a wide array of situations, among them negotiations in business and in litigation, privacy, trade secrets, and privileged communications. But an expert witness at trial is not in one of those situations. To the contrary, the witness is present for the very purpose of supplying the factfinder with information, has just sworn to do so truthfully and fully, and faces perjury charges for lying to the court.[16] Moreover, any information that a party thinks a witness ought not to divulge can become the subject of explicit objections, such as to protect against intrusions into areas of privileged communications. The power to decide whether or not such information may be shielded is assigned not to the witness but to the judge. An additional and telling point is that almost all privileges to suppress information belong to the

---

13. "[E]very witness shall be required to declare that the witness will testify truthfully." Fed.R.Evid. 603.

14. The statements of lawyers to the jury at the opening and close of trial are not evidence. And the questions put to witnesses are regarded as eliciting evidence, not providing it. However, no one doubts that lawyers have persuasive effect and do supply the jurors with information through these routes.

15. SAKS & VAN DUIZEND, *supra* note 3.

16. Fortunately, for the partisan expert, perjury charges generally cannot be based on giving incomplete or unresponsive answers, even if that is done with the intention of misleading. The cross-examiner is expected to ask a sufficiently refined question that a perjurious witness will answer with a false statement.

parties, not to their witnesses.[17] In the trial context, it would be bizarre for a witness to possess a "right" to mislead a court. And, indeed, no one ever tries to defend such deceptions by saying the law authorizes them.

Surely, in such an explicit forum for arguing and ruling on what a witness must or need not testify about, it is not the job of a witness or one party to decide what to reveal and what to conceal. In short, the law's formal view of the expert witness is summed up by the legal aphorism that "a witness is not an advocate and an advocate is not a witness."

§ 3–3.4 The Role Defined by the Law Is Rarely Enforced

The clarity of the formal expectations about the proper role and behavior of expert witnesses at trial must not conceal the fact that experts are highly unlikely to be sanctioned for their misdeeds. Few complaints are brought to the attention of legal or professional authorities, and fewer still result in consequences to the allegedly offending experts. Perhaps this massive inaction conveys the "real" expectations of the law and the professions. Consider the following.

During an eight-year period, the American Academy of Forensic Sciences (AAFS) received only 18 complaints against members, with the following results.[18]

1. A document examiner who gave an insupportable opinion received a formal censure.

2. A medical examiner who submitted to court reports of autopsies that never were performed was expelled from the AAFS.

3. A forensic scientist accused of misrepresentation of case facts in a paper presented at a professional meeting was adjudged not guilty; the ethics committee concluded that a reasonable difference of opinion accounted for the conflict.

A review of the case law involving civil suits and perjury prosecutions against experts revealed that the most common complaints against experts were for giving false educational credentials.[19] Unless the expert witness is also a fact witness, and except for credentials, most of the important statements are either "opinion" testimony or the basis of that opinion, which insulates most expert testimony from sanction, regardless of how great the "analytical gap between the data and the opinion proffered."[20] Opinions are neither true nor false and therefore cannot be "lies."[21]

---

17. Indeed, none of the privileges enacted or even contemplated would give an expert witness a privilege against disclosing anything. The rules that were proposed would have created privileges for these relationships: lawyer-client, physician and psychotherapist-patient, husband-wife, and for information concerning religious beliefs, political votes, and several other categories. The rule adopted is a flexible and open one that allows courts to add or delete privileges "in the light of reason and experience."

18. Michael J. Saks, *Prevalence and Impact of Ethical Problems in Forensic Science*, 34 J. FORENSIC SCIENCES 772 (1989).

19. *Id.* (which was also true of complaints filed with the AAFS ethics committee). For much more on false credentials by expert witnesses, *see* James E. Starrs, *Mountebanks Among Forensic Scientists*, in 2 FORENSIC SCIENCE HANDBOOK (R. Saferstein ed., 1987).

20. *Joiner*, 522 U.S. at 146.

21. It may be possible, however, to show that an expert has offered a contrary opinion elsewhere, such as in another trial or in a public lecture. In such a circumstance, it might be possible to show that the expert "lied" concerning what his or her opinion actually was. Although these situations are possible, no

Concerning the basis of the experts' opinions, most experts apparently are wise enough not to stray too far from the bounds of disciplinary knowledge. That by itself might be regarded as an achievement by the law or the expert's field. But by subscribing to the core knowledge of one's field and by offering an opinion based on one's "professional" or "scientific" judgment or experience—even an opinion shared by only a small minority of one's peers—an expert witness who overlooks important contrary data or theory or commits errors still is almost certain to remain safe from any formal penalty.

In short, as the Illinois Supreme Court observed, "It is virtually impossible to prosecute an expert witness for perjury."[22]

Expert witnesses are protected even more fully from civil liability. When civil suits for damages have been brought against expert witnesses for errors or lies presented on the witness stand, those suits have failed because testimony given in court is privileged. A witness may say whatever he or she likes under oath, and no private remedies are available to persons who may be harmed as a result.[23]

One case that illustrates the expert witness's near invincibility involved fingerprint evidence.[24] An object was offered as evidence linking the defendant to a crime. The object had three fingerprints on it, but the fingerprint expert reported only the two belonging to the defendant. The third one, which helped save the defendant from a death sentence, was not revealed until much later. Was the expert witness dishonest or merely incompetent? Unless one has evidence of dishonesty, a court must conclude the expert witness was merely incompetent. Incompetence provides no basis for a perjury conviction. And because no civil remedy is available for harm done to a person by testifying in a legal proceeding, both civil and criminal action against this expert witness failed.

To sum up, the formal message of both the law and the professions to testifying experts is to tell the complete truth and not to become a junior advocate. But no price is exacted from those experts who violate the role that the law and their profession have defined for them.

The one price the law does seem prepared to charge for being untrustworthy is to be deeply suspicious about what experts have to say. This was evident in a series of interviews with lawyers and judges,[25] few of whom had anything good to say about experts, as well as in much of the legal literature on expert witnesses.[26]

---

examples of them were found in the cases. The greatest damage such lies may do to the witness who offers them is to open the way for the cross-examiner to discredit the witness. But finding an expert witness's past contradictions requires a level of diligence practiced by few attorneys.

22. Sears v. Rutishauser, 102 Ill.2d 402, 80 Ill.Dec. 758, 466 N.E.2d 210, 212 (Ill. 1984).

23. Compare this to the rule that would apply if the harmful deliberate misrepresentation occurred off the witness stand: "One who fraudulently makes a misrepresentation of fact, opinion, intention, or law for the purpose of inducing another to act or to refrain from action in reliance upon it, is subject to liability to the other in deceit for pecuniary loss caused him by his unjustifiable reliance upon the misrepresentation." AMERICAN LAW INSTITUTE, RESTATEMENT (SECOND) OF TORTS 55 (1965).

24. In re Imbler, 60 Cal.2d 554, 35 Cal. Rptr. 293, 387 P.2d 6 (Cal.1963); Imbler v. Craven, 298 F.Supp. 795 (C.D.Cal.1969); Imbler v. Pachtman, 424 U.S. 409, 96 S.Ct. 984, 47 L.Ed.2d 128 (1976).

25. SAKS & VAN DUIZEND, *supra* note 3.

26. E.g., Friedman, *supra* note 3; Herschel, *supra* note 3; F.S. Rice, *the Medical Expert as a Witness*, 10 THE GREEN BAG 464 (1898); and

One case in which the judicial attitude is made explicit is *Tagatz v. Marquette University.*[27] Like other cases alleging employment discrimination, this one involved the presentation of statistical evidence. But in this case, the plaintiff, who himself was a "specialist in statistical evidence in employment discrimination cases, prepared the statistical evidence on which his case rides,"[28] and he wanted to serve as his own expert witness at trial. According to the appellate court, "The case is remarkable because, for the first time ever so far as we know, the plaintiff testified as his own expert witness."[29] For our purposes, this case presents the curious situation of the most partisan person in the courtroom (the plaintiff) and what formally would be regarded as one of the most objective and disinterested persons in the courtroom (the expert witness) being merged into one. The defense objected to this odd arrangement, but the court of appeals saw no problem:

> As Dr. Tagatz's counsel pointed out at argument, the fact that a party testifying as his own expert is not disinterested does not distinguish him from any other party who testifies in his own behalf; and hired experts, who generally are highly compensated—and by the party on whose behalf they are testifying—are not notably disinterested.[30]

Jurors have their own views of the trustworthiness and competence of expert witnesses. A survey of jurors in Massachusetts found that the higher the educational level of a juror, the less competent and the less honest expert witnesses of all kinds were thought to be.[31]

Consider the circular ironies in all of this: Lawyers seeking advantage select favorable experts and prepare them to be even more favorable. Experts seeking undue influence cooperate, sometimes by exaggerating favorable testimony, understating unfavorable testimony, and otherwise distorting their field's knowledge. Judges (and at least the better-educated jurors) steeply discount what the expert has to say. The end result may be courts that overprotect themselves from being fooled, by undervaluing expert testimony, thereby depriving themselves of some knowledge they might have used to improve their decisions. In short, the collective cost of reaching for more influence than the system has allotted is to be accorded less weight than is due—all to the long-term detriment of experts, litigants, legal professionals, and society.

§ 3–3.5   Challenging and Countering Expert Witnesses

As a practical matter, for actual trials, much of the above discussion may be of limited relevance. Opposing counsel has little choice but to assume the worst and prepare for the worst. That means to assume the expert is a slippery advocate of doubtful competence, and to prepare for cross examination accordingly. With expert witnesses the examination and cross examination can be of a high degree of substance, because the scientific expert

more modern commentaries discussed in SAKS & VAN DUIZEND, *supra* note 3.

27. 861 F.2d 1040 (7th Cir.1988).

28. *Id.* at 1042.

29. *Id.*

30. *Id.* The judge who wrote this opinion was Richard Posner, whose experience before judging included being a law professor who sometimes served as an expert witness.

31. Michael J. Saks & Roselle L. Wissler, *Legal and Psychological Bases of Expert Testimony*, 2 BEHAVIORAL SCIENCES & L. 435 (1984).

witness's testimony is by its nature about scientific substance, not credibility or opportunity to observe.

The ethical questions for the lawyers are also about substance. If there is scientific evidence that would help a party's claim or defense, counsel ought to find out about it and offer it. Failure to do so is a failure to provide competent representation.

Does counsel adverse to expert testimony which is offered have an ethical duty to challenge the admission of the evidence and (if it is admitted) the weight of the evidence? Surely zealous and competent representation mean that the weaknesses in evidence offered against your client should be brought to light (unless there is some tactical reason for letting them go). Those who fail most often in this regard appear to be criminal defense lawyers. In a recent extensive review of published cases for several years preceding and following *Daubert*, Risinger found, for example, that out of 90 state court opinions in which handwriting identification evidence was proffered, there was not a single challenge to the admissibility of the forensic handwriting examiners.[32] Risinger concluded:

> We have seen that, on their face, the numbers seem to indicate that civil defendants have benefitted greatly from *Daubert* but that criminal defendants have not. This seems especially true in regard to what might be called non-science forensic science, and it appears to be attributable partly to the inertia of courts, but at least as much to the criminal defense bar's failure to construct sophisticated challenges and develop the evidence to support them.[33]

§ 3–4.0 THE WORKING RELATIONSHIP OF LAWYERS AND EXPERTS

§ 3–4.1 Finding and Establishing a Relationship With the Expert

What goes on outside the courtroom, before the trial, is another source of insights into the role the law has created for expert witnesses. Most of the contact between experts and legal actors goes on outside of the purview of the court, and the great majority of cases never reach trial. What goes on in the pretrial phase is controlled far less by rules than the trial is and more by informal practices. The pretrial phase may tell us something about the structure of the legal process and may reveal its underlying norms in ways that a look at the trial does not. As we shall see, in terms of the messages sent to experts about what is expected of them, the black-letter rules of trial and the informal processes of pre-trial are at war with each other, sometimes trapping expert witnesses in the crossfire.

The first thing to notice is that the selection and preparation of experts is by the parties. Whereas fact witnesses are limited to those who have observed the events at issue in a case, expert witnesses come from a pool that is

32. D. Michael Risinger, *Navigating Expert Reliability: Are Criminal Standards of Certainty Being Left on the Dock?*, 64 ALBANY L. REV. 99 (2000).

33. *Id.*

virtually unlimited. Lawyers quite properly (from the viewpoint of the adversary system) seek experts whose testimony will be favorable to their clients. If they think a preliminary choice unwise, they can dismiss that expert and hire a new one or several new ones. On the other hand, shopping for experts is given as one of the reasons for counter-measures such as Fed. R. Evid. 706.[1] Does it create an ethical problem if counsel searches for an expert who agrees with the client's position? At one extreme, it would be ethically troubling if counsel selected expert witnesses at random. At the other extreme, it seems ethically dubious if counsel searched diligently, discarding dozens of experts until the rare one is found who happens to agree with the lawyer's theory of the case. Should a line be drawn? How can a line be drawn?

Once suitable experts are selected, a competent lawyer will set about to secure their loyalty and cooperation. Experts learn much of what they know of the law and of the trial from this teacher with a very particular agenda.[2] Lawyers are, after all, professional persuaders and negotiators; they do not reserve those skills for the courtroom. Experts are introduced to the facts of the case and informed of what is at issue by the lawyer who is obtaining their services. From this lawyer, in a less or more subtle way, the experts will learn of the righteousness of the case for which they have been recruited. What the expert is or is not comfortable testifying to at trial is tested out and, if necessary, is negotiated between expert and attorney. On the one hand, it seems reasonable and perhaps necessary for the attorney to test out the extent to which the expert's knowledge and opinions will support the attorney's theory of the case. It is necessary for the expert to draw the line and not go where reasonable inferences from the field's principles will not allow. If the positions presented later are too far out on a limb, is it the fault of the attorney who invited the expert there, or the expert who agreed to go? Sometimes the "negotiation" between counsel and the expert gets down to what language is to be used to describe the expert's opinion. The attorney is looking for language that will be most helpful to the closing argument he wishes to be able to make, while the cooperative, yet not dishonest, expert is looking for language that will allow him to feel that he did not lie or misrepresent his opinion.[3]

In a world of powerful subtleties, why even consider money? But the law does. The law prohibits the payment of expert witnesses to be contingent upon what they say or the outcome of the case. Yet in civil cases experts may understand that unless the outcome is favorable, there may be no money to pay the expert (if she is called on behalf of the plaintiff), or that future

---

§ 3–4.0

1. "The practice of shopping for experts" is listed as being among "matters of deep concern." Advisory Committee's Comments to Fed.R.Evid. 706.

2. Imagine how different the expert's education would be if it were provided by a judge or a law teacher or a lawyer hired by experts for experts.

3. One example of such language negotiation is provided by the prosecutor and the ballistics expert in the case of Sacco and Vanzetti. The firearms expert initially concluded that because his tests were inconclusive, they did not confirm that the defendant's weapon was the murder weapon. But the prosecutor negotiated the expert's testimony into an equivalent yet very different-sounding version: that the ballistics findings were not inconsistent with a theory that the murder bullets came from the defendant's gun. The defense was afraid to try to dissect this testimony, thinking that to do so unsuccessfully would put the defense in an even worse position. L. JOUGHIN & E.M. MORGAN, THE LEGACY OF SACCO AND VANZETTI. (1976).

employment of the expert may depend on helping with a successful outcome in the present case. What would we think if a law firm that specialized in representing tort plaintiffs had at its disposal a firm of varied experts who worked exclusively for tort plaintiffs; made their incomes exclusively from the work they did for plaintiff's lawyers; and their salaries, vacation schedules, working conditions, and careers depended on the evaluations they received on the work they did for these attorneys. And imagine that this firm of varied experts was the exclusive employer of some kinds of experts, so that the defendants in these tort cases had no experts available to them. Does this scenario raise any ethical issues about either the experts or the attorneys' use of the experts? With a few small adjustments to the scenario, this fairly well describes our system of scientific expert witnesses in the criminal justice system.[4]

By the time the expert arrives in court the morning of trial, who is allied with whom could not be more apparent. From that point, the court has a limited opportunity to transform the witness from being an honorary member of the advocacy team to being a "witness" whose loyalty is to the factfinder, whom the witness promises to inform fully and honestly.

§ 3–4.2 Discovery

In a well-prepared case, lawyers and experts learn much from each other during consultations before trial. Scheppele suggests that "The social distribution of knowledge permeates social relations from the most intimate to the most impersonal, and much of what we think of as social structure grows out of the patterns of hidden and revealed knowledge."[5] If so, then how much knowledge different players typically have of the knowledge about a case, and the access one side has to the knowledge possessed by the other side's experts, should provide clues to the social structure of the legal process.

With respect to the first issue, expert witnesses often are given more detailed information about a case than ordinary fact witnesses are. That is partly because experts can help a lawyer to think about the factual issues within the expert's purview, and perhaps also because the nature of opinion and interpretation is that they are more moldable than the observations of a fact witness. This can be helpful to the lawyer, but it also places more information in the vessel of the expert, potentially accessible to the other side.

The Federal Rules of Civil Procedure reflect a dual concern about trials. On the one hand, the more each side knows about the evidence the other side is going to present, the more a trial will be a contest over the meaning of that evidence and the less it will be a "trial by ambush." On the other hand, the system is adversarial, and the parties are encouraged to seek out information and views beneficial to themselves, to prepare their cases independently, and not to free ride on the other side's efforts. The rules seek to protect both of these interests. That is accomplished by making witnesses and other evidence subject to disclosure but barring access by each side to the other side's

---

4. It might be noted that a few crime laboratories in the United States are deliberately organized so that they are not answerable to police or prosecutors, but their funding and governance have been arranged so as to keep them more independent.

5. Kim Lane Scheppele, Legal Secrets: Equality and Efficiency in the Common Law 23 (1988).

theories and strategy. Thus, the rules of discovery are expansive, generally limited only by whether the information sought is "relevant" to the subject matter of the lawsuit and whether the information is protected by a privilege.

In particular, discovery is limited by the attorney work-product doctrine. Protection from discovery of the knowledge of the advocate may serve as a benchmark for deciphering whether the expert is to be regarded as an advocate or an educator.

§ 3–4.2.1   The Work–Product Doctrine and Discovery From Experts

Lawyers often try to insulate their experts and their communications with their experts from discovery, asserting or implying that the expert is covered by the doctrine. The work-product doctrine has been stated in this language: "In ordering discovery . . . the court shall protect against disclosure of the mental impressions, conclusions, opinions, or legal theories of an attorney or other representative of a party concerning the litigation."[6] Examples of "other representatives" given by the drafters of the rule are private investigators and insurance claim agents.[7] There are at least two reasons to think that the phrase "other representative" does not include expert witnesses, and therefore what expert witnesses think or write is not attorney work product. First of all, it certainly does not include fact witnesses. Second, additional rules were developed specifically to regulate discovery from experts, to which we turn next.

Discovery from experts is divided into two parts. The first pertains to expert witnesses and the second to nonwitness experts.

[1]   Testifying Expert Witnesses

Concerning testifying expert witnesses, Fed.R.Civ.P. 26(b)(4)(A) states: "A party may depose any person who has been identified as an expert whose opinions may be presented at trial. If a report from the expert is required . . . the deposition shall not be conducted until after the report is provided."[8]

That seems to leave little to secrecy. The reasoning behind the rule removes all doubt:[9]

> Many . . . cases present intricate and difficult issues as to which expert testimony is likely to be determinative. . . .
>
> [A] prohibition against discovery of information held by expert witnesses produces in acute form the very evils that discovery has been created to prevent. . . .
>
> Effective rebuttal requires advance knowledge of the line of testimony of the other side. If the latter is foreclosed by a rule against discovery, then

---

6.   Fed.R.Civ.P. 26(b)(3).

7.   *See also* Hickman v. Taylor, 329 U.S. 495, 67 S.Ct. 385, 91 L.Ed. 451 (1947).

8.   This is greater access than provided by the previous version of this rule:

A party may through interrogatories require any other party to identify each person whom the other party expects to call as an expert witness at trial, to state the subject matter on which the expert is expected to testify, and to state the substance of the facts and opinions to which the expert is expected to testify and a summary of the grounds for each opinion. Upon motion, the court may order further discovery by other means.

9.   Advisory Committee's Notes to Fed. R.Civ.P. Rule 26.

the narrowing of issues and elimination of surprise which discovery normally produces are frustrated....

These considerations appear to account for the broadening of discovery against experts in the cases cited.... In some instances, the opinions are explicit in relating expanded discovery to improved cross-examination and rebuttal at trial....

These new provisions ... repudiate the few decisions that have held an expert's information privileged simply because of his [or her] status as an expert....

They also reject as ill-considered the decisions which have sought to bring expert opinion within the work-product doctrine.

By the lights of the black-letter law, expert witnesses appear to be witnesses, and their knowledge, before trial as well as during, is not shielded in the way that the knowledge of the advocate is.

[2] Nonwitness Experts

An expert who is not expected to be called as a witness, who instead "has been retained or specially employed"[10] for such purposes as to educate or consult with an attorney about a case, is not subject to discovery unless the expert has conducted a physical or mental examination of a party or "upon a showing of special circumstances."[11] Thus, for a psychologist or physician asked to conduct an examination, the rule provides no shelter from discovery. Beyond that, whether or how much information may be discovered from non-witness experts is a subject on which courts are divided.

Clearly, the rule exists to serve the complex purposes of using knowledge effectively in an adversarial setting. But the exact contours of the rule are controversial and unclear.[12] In dealing with this rule, courts and commentators have wrestled with distinctions among multiple-status experts, twice-retained experts, second-tier experts, in-house experts, and nonwitness experts before versus after retention. When is an expert informally consulted versus retained? Complex mixtures of considerations are taken into account by courts called on to decide what category an expert is to be placed in. For experts who are deemed nonwitnesses, what, if anything, can be discovered about them—name? subject matter? opinions? basis of opinion? Even to reveal the witness's name might give one side a clue to a line of reasoning abandoned by the other side. If discovery is ordered, should it apply only to the expert's knowledge before consultation with the attorney or to opinions the expert has formed by combining case-specific facts with the expert's prior knowledge?

10. Fed.R.Civ.P. Rule 26(b)(4)(B).

11. Fed.R.Civ.P. Rule 26(b)(4)(B). An example of special circumstances is provided in Sanford Constr. Co. v. Kaiser Aluminum, 45 F.R.D. 465 (E.D.Ky.1968).

12. *See* David S. Day, *Expert Discovery in the Eighth Circuit: an Empirical Study.* 122 F.R.D. 35 (1988); David S. Day, *A Judicial Perspective on Expert Discovery under Federal Rule 26(b)(4): An Empirical Study of Trial Court Judges and a Proposed Amendment,* 20 JOHN MARSHALL L. REV. 377 (1987); Ager v. Jane C. Stormont Hospital & Training School for Nurses, 622 F.2d 496 (10th Cir.1980); Note, *Civil Procedure–Ager v. Jane C. Stormont Hospital: Discovery of a Non-testifying Expert,* 60 N. CAROLINA L. REV. 695 (1982).

The theory of the court in *Ager v. Jane C. Stormont Hospital & Training School for Nurses*[13] is illuminating. That theory is that access to experts should wax and wane across a series of stages. Before consultation by anyone, the expert is freely available to whomever the expert is willing to talk with. If an expert has been informally consulted, however, no discovery is permitted. Retained consulting experts are available for discovery only when unusual need is shown. Retained testimonial witnesses are fully subject to discovery. Testimonial experts in court are, of course, subject to complete examination and disclosure.

An alert witness who passes through each of these stages, and who is asked at each stage what expectations the law has of the expert—independent witness or adversarial teammate—will be led to different conclusions at different stages. A conclusion drawn from one stage will misinform the expert about what the law expects at another stage. Yet, the average expert witness has no notion of any of this. Clearly, the law is not concerned with defining a consistent and coherent role for the expert. The law is concerned with enabling each party to prepare its case without hiding and without free riding. The expert role must shift to meet the most compelling needs at the various stages of litigation.[14]

§ 3–4.2.2   Tactics for Shielding Information in Possession of Experts

As discussed above, to help the expert understand the case sufficiently to be of help, the attorney will have to share with the expert some information and ideas that the attorney would not have to reveal to the other side. What happens, then, if this expert is deposed by the other side? How is the information that belongs to an expert, and which is subject to discovery, to be disentangled from the information that belongs to the attorney, and is protected by the work-product doctrine? What happens to experts an attorney has dismissed as unhelpful or harmful to the case? Can those experts become witnesses for the other side?

From the viewpoint of an educator expert, little of this may appear to be a problem.[15] The educator expert will be pleased to share his or her knowledge with anyone who asks for it. And although such an expert has, from his or her own perspective, no ethical or legal worry even about sharing specific opinions on particular aspects of the case at hand (which the expert learned from the lawyer), in order to assist the law in carrying out its policies the expert ought

---

13.   622 F.2d 496 (10th Cir.1980).

14.   In light of the above discussion, would it be appropriate to ask a survey researcher to serve as an expert in both of the following two different functions in a trial. The researcher is asked to conduct a study of the venire to determine the prevalent attitudes toward the trial issues and participants. The researcher is told that if the findings support a motion for a change of venue, her first responsibility will be to testify as an expert witness in a hearing on the venue motion. If the motion is not granted, the researcher will next serve as the lawyer's trial consultant using the survey data to help the lawyer select a favorable jury. Note that

this is a more dramatic shift of roles, from witness presenting findings to a court for its decision to a trial consultant whose discussions with the attorney really would be work product. Note what that implies for discovery of the data and the expert's knowledge and opinions. Are these two roles incompatible for one person in one trial?

15.   This discussion is less relevant for the advocate-expert, who presumably already is withholding information that the law expects to be disgorged. That, of course, is the problem on the other side of this coin.

to be cautious enough so that any attorney work product that can and should be kept from the other side has the opportunity to be shielded. Thus, even the purest educator expert who is to be called as a witness, whose knowledge is discoverable under the applicable rule, still may have at least some adversary knowledge, which he or she must think about revealing to or concealing from the "other side." Even for such an expert, there is no escape from the adversary nature of the trial process.

From the viewpoint of the attorney, the process of working with experts presents a major problem, because the discovery of expert information risks the release of work-product information along with it. What some attorneys do to avoid this, and to strengthen their cases as well, is to have "clean" experts and "dirty" experts.[16] "Dirty" experts are retained as nonwitnesses, thereby reducing or eliminating their amenability to discovery. Once the attorney learns, with the expert's help, the strongest version of the case's technical facts, a "clean" expert is hired to serve as the trial witness. The clean expert is informed only of the best features of the case, told only what is necessary to produce the most favorable expert reading of the case. Such an expert is safe for both discovery and trial. Assuming it is ethical to use clean and dirty experts in order to insure that nondisclosable work product does not seep out during discovery, is it permissible to use multiple experts in order to learn in advance what aspects of the case will lead an expert to have the most favorable possible opinion of the issue on which the expert will testify? If it is improper to manipulate experts in this way, is it also impermissible for an attorney who understands the evidence and the expert field so well that the lawyer knows at the outset what to share and what not to share with the expert in order to elicit a highly favorable opinion? If that is improper, is it necessary for an attorney to share everything about the case with an expert, in case something has a significance that the attorney does not realize it has which would change the expert's opinion?

§ 3–4.2.3 Discovery Under the Rules of Criminal Procedure

The rules of criminal procedure reflect still other concerns and a different balance to accommodate those concerns. These include protection of a defendant's constitutional right against disclosing anything that might be incriminating and concern that criminal defendants who learn the details of the case against them will combat that evidence with false testimony or threaten witnesses with harm. One solution found in the federal rules is a process of defense-controlled, tit-for-tat, mutual exchange of information.[17] Whenever the defense seeks discovery of prosecution evidence, the prosecution is entitled to obtain comparable information from the defense. Information subject to discovery includes "reports of physical or mental examinations, and of scientific tests or experiments."[18] Thus, the rules of criminal procedure shield much

---

16. Discussed in Michael J. Saks & Richard Van Duizend, The Use of Scientific Evidence in Litigation (1983).

17. At least 40 states have statutes governing discovery in criminal cases, and most of these are modeled after the federal rule. But a considerable amount of variation exists as to whether any particular category of information is something the defendant is entitled to as a

matter of right, or whether it is controlled by judicial discretion, or whether discovery of the information is precluded.

18. Fed.R.Crim.P.   16(a)(1)(D)   and 16(b)(1)(B). The rule does not authorize discovery of reports, memoranda, or other internal government or defense documents made by the attorneys or the defendant or their agents, nor

more evidence from discovery than the civil rules do. And yet, they single out much of the information supplied by experts to be made the most accessible.

But, whether for reasons of overwork or to stymie the defense, government experts tend to produce reports that present minimal information about their conclusions and the bases for those conclusions. Thus, the law's goal of forcing the exchange of critical information to facilitate trial preparation is frustrated by experts producing reports that will afford little help in that trial preparation. In an investigation of questionable practices at the FBI Crime Laboratory, the Inspector General of the U.S. Department of Justice found that some forensic scientists would "spruce up" lab notes (enlarge, embellish and change them) as the case approached trial.[19] Some of the embellishment was calculated to make the expert's conclusions be more consistent with other evidence in the trial. In addition to frustrating the goals of the law, this is poor scientific practice.

§ 3–5.0 CONCLUDING COMMENTS

Unlike the limited historical information brought to a case by ordinary fact witnesses, the information brought by experts on some body of more general knowledge should, in principle, be resolvable, eventually, if nothing else at least into a consensus. But the adversary process, by its nature, tends to ensure that this does not happen. Reacting to these distorting effects of the adversary process, some commentators have suggested trying to reduce or eliminate them. Edward Cleary has suggested that, "It is not only essential to reduce the partisan element in the selection of experts, but it is equally important that the contentious character of the presentation of the results of the expert's investigation be modified."[1]

The adversary process, however, serves other important functions that few would want to dispense with, among them, party control of the presentation of their respective cases and other features of a system that is principally in the business of ensuring the perception of fair process ("procedural justice") and only secondarily with accurate findings of fact.[2] The institutional culture of the adversary process is well established and reforms that push in the direction of limiting control over expert evidence is going to be resisted and such reforms are probably doomed. For example, the Model Expert Witness Act, published in 1937,[3] would have improved the fit between fact-oriented experts and the normative tensions of the law. Under that act, for example, pretrial conferences between experts would have been held to resolve their factual disagreements. Such provisions of the Model Act have never been adopted into law.

of statements made by witnesses. Fed. R.Crim.P. 16(a)(2) and 16(b)(2).

19. U.S. Dep't of Justice, Office of the Inspector General, the FBI Laboratory: An Investigation into Laboratory Practices and Alleged Misconduct in Explosives-Related and Other Cases (U.S. Doc. J. 1.14/2:L 11/2) (April 1997), available at http://www.usdoj.gov/oig/fbi-lab1/fbil1toc.htm (last visited Feb. 16, 2001).

§ 3–5.0

1. Edward W. Cleary, McCormick on Evidence 44 (3rd ed. 1984).

2. E. Allen Lind & Tom R. Tyler, the Social Psychology of Procedural Justice (1988); John Thibaut & Laurens Walker, *A Theory of Procedure*, 66 Cal. L. Rev. 541 (1978).

3. Reprinted in Wigmore on Evidence § 563 (Chadbourne Rev., 1979).

Other suggestions have become part of the law of evidence and procedure, such as provisions for court-appointed experts and advisory juries composed of experts. Perhaps because these, too, run counter to the adversary culture, although they are on the books they rarely are put to use.[4]

Any solutions proposed to relieve the role conflict of experts or the distortion of expert information must take care to preserve essential elements of procedural justice built into the adversary system.

4. Joe Cecil & Thomas Willging, Court-Appointed Experts: Defining the Role of Experts Appointed Under Federal Rule of Evidence 706 (1993).

CHAPTER 4

SCIENTIFIC METHOD: THE LOGIC OF DRAWING INFERENCES FROM EMPIRICAL EVIDENCE

Table of Sections

Westlaw Electronic Research

See Westlaw Electronic Research Guide preceding the Summary of Contents.

———————

§ 4–1.0 INTRODUCTION

This chapter is a primer on scientific method. Its aim is to provide the non-scientist judge or lawyer an easily accessible understanding of how scientists learn about how the world works. At the root of scientific method is the application of logic to the problem of how to observe an empirical phenomenon in a way that will allow one to draw valid inferences about that phenomenon. In that sense, this chapter is really about a particular branch or application of logic.

The subject of scientific method is a necessary foundation of *every* discipline that seriously attempts to gain knowledge of the world through systematic empirical inquiry—the physical, biological, behavioral and social sciences alike—and as such it has been described innumerable times, in a multitude of works on manifold subjects, from elementary school textbooks to post-graduate treatises. And yet it remains a subject that is foreign to most lawyers and judges. This is a subject about which most lawyers and judges are, to put it bluntly, quite illiterate. For these reasons, this chapter will be presented in a simple and direct form, without footnotes, though it will conclude with a general bibliography of sources to which the reader can turn for more detailed learning about these concepts.

§ 4–1.1 How Science Finds Answers

How does a scientist learn the answer to a question? For examples: Which of several proposed treatments for cancer, inflation, or pilot error work best? Does Vitamin C prevent colds, does one surgical technique work better than another, which methods of teaching, giving judicial instructions, or farming work best? Or, to ask less "applied" and more "basic" questions: What is the nature of motion? What accounts for the inheritance of traits? How does memory work?

God does not whisper the answers into the ears of scientists, as though they were members of a modern priesthood. The only way a scientist can reach an answer to an empirical question is to conduct an empirical inquiry. This means observing the phenomenon of interest, though usually in an especially disciplined way. Mere observation is a part of the scientific method, but it usually is not nearly enough.

For example, how many teeth are in a horse's mouth? While Platonic philosophers believed that the answer was to be found by reasoning or debating what the proper number should be, a modern scientist's immediate instinct is that the answer is to be found in a horse's mouth. But one look into the mouth of one horse may be misleading. Any one horse might have a defective set of teeth, due perhaps to injury; or the number may change with age; or different breeds or sexes may have different numbers. So the modern scientist would systematically sample horses, and would most likely report the average and the range of variation for major subgroupings of horses. This illustrates how even the simplest of questions needs to be approached in a systematic and thoughtful way to avoid arriving at incorrect answers.

Many of the questions posed in the three paragraphs above can be answered only with a more specialized and more disciplined way of observing, which involves comparing things under different conditions. For example, for a century many surgeons believed that the best treatment for breast cancer was to remove the entire breast and considerable additional tissue along with it, so as to get downstream of any cancer cells and head them off (so the theory went). Suggestions that less destructive surgery might do as much good were met with defenses based on faith, rather than evidence, that it is only logical that radical mastectomies provided the greatest protection against spread of the cancer. In the 1970's experiments were performed which finally compared the efficacy of radical mastectomies to the far more conservative procedure of lumpectomy plus radiation. A sample of breast cancer patents was randomly divided so that some were given the traditional mastectomy while others were assigned to receive the more breast-conserving treatment. The latter proved to be at least as good as the former at stopping the cancer. This illustrates an experimental comparison, where the value of a treatment is discerned by comparing it to another treatment.

To real scientists a finding of fact is only as good as the methods used to find it. Scientific method is the logic by which the observations are made. Well designed methods permit observations that lead to valid, useful, informative answers to the questions that had been framed by the researcher. For scientists, the key word in the phrase "scientific method" is *method*. Methodology—the logic of research design, measures, and procedures—is the engine that generates knowledge that is scientific. While for lawyers and judges credibility is the key to figuring out which witnesses are speaking truth and which are not, for scientists the way to figure out which one of several contradictory studies is most likely correct is to scrutinize the methodology.

We conclude this introduction on a note of caution. Although this chapter is focused on the challenges of doing science well, the reader should be alert to the problem of assertions made on the basis of no science at all. Not all knowledge asserted by people who are commonly thought of as scientists is the product of the scientific method. It will help to think of science as a verb, not a noun. Science is what one does to build knowledge, not what someone is.

Some people or groups who call themselves scientists do not use the scientific method. That is, their beliefs have not been subjected to systematic empirical testing. Their own and their field's beliefs are based on casual observation, or intuition, or faith, or the authority of past generations of members of their field exercising *their* intuition. Masquerading as science, such claims are likely to be defended by statements that the truth of the assertion rests on "my many years of experience," or "generations of study by my field." Were the findings based on evidence produced by the scientific method, the expert should be able to present those studies to any audience, including a court, along with the methodology and the results of the studies.

By shifting the attention of federal judges from the consensus of opinion among the field's members to the underlying science of a field, *Daubert v. Merrell Dow Pharmaceuticals* has caused a number of fields to begin to re-examine themselves. At a panel discussion at a conference, defenders of one field responded to critics with such answers as these:

> We who practice in this field know that what we are doing is correct, though we have no way of demonstrating that truth to outsiders.

> You critics have focused your attack on our one weak spot, the lack of data about our claims.

To anyone with even a modest understanding of how scientific knowledge is generated and tested, these "defenses" will be recognized as admissions that science is absent from this field.

Sometimes there is a zone of genuine scientific knowledge possessed by a field, but some or many of its members step outside of that zone and make assertions that exceed their field's empirically tested knowledge. Or they are answering questions that are based in part on well tested knowledge and in part on speculation. Before research had been conducted on the relative efficacy of breast cancer surgical strategies, the cancer surgeons performing radical mastectomies were not applying scientific knowledge about which treatment was most effective, because such knowledge did not exist. With respect to other surgical techniques, they may have been applying knowledge tested by the scientific method. A review of experiments testing a number of the most popular surgical techniques found that about a third of them were indeed effective, about a third were worthless, and about a third were doing more harm than alternative techniques that were available. Thus, it is less helpful to ask whether a person making an assertion is "a scientist" (such as a research chemist or research psychologist) or is "applying science" (such as a physician or engineer or clinical psychologist), and more helpful to ask how well grounded the assertion is on well-designed and well-conducted empirical studies testing the propositions contained in the assertion.

§ 4–1.2 The Nature of Empirical Questions

Not all questions are "empirical questions." Empirical questions and the search for their answers are the special, and limited, contribution of scientific inquiry. Empirical questions can and should be tested empirically. Other kinds of questions do not call for empirical answers and are not subject to empirical testing.

Consider the following examples:

"Is the moon made of green cheese?" This is an empirical question that at one time had no answer and today the answer is known.

"Is there life on other planets?" This question remains unanswered. Note that we will never be able to say, "no, there is no life other than on Earth," unless and until we can examine every other planet in the universe. Some people may be content to examine several thousand planets without life and make the inferential leap that there won't be life on any of the other billions either. But the moment life is found elsewhere, if it ever is, we can say, "yes."

"Is astrology valid?" There is nothing unscientific about the question. Numerous empirical studies have been conducted to test the claims of astrology, and virtually all of them have found astrological predictions not to be correct and astrology therefore not to be valid. The results might have come out the other way. That is how the scientific method sorts out the valid from the invalid.

"Does God exist?" "Is the death penalty moral?" "Does the word 'vehicle' in the statute include tricycles?" These are three questions that are not empirical questions and can have no empirical answers. Science cannot help. The first question asks about the supernatural, while empirical questions are confined to the natural world. The second question is a normative judgment, a value judgement. Again, that is not something scientists can study directly. A social scientist could, however, conduct a survey to see how many people believe the death penalty is a proper punishment, or a study of whether it in fact deters, or whether it is applied disproportionately more to some groups of people convicted of capital crimes and less to others. Those are empirical questions. But they are very different from the question of whether the death penalty is or is not moral. The third question is one of interpretation, of the lawmaker's intentions, no doubt in the context of a court's application to a particular situation. Interpretation of such meanings is not the realm of empirical question asking and answering.

§ 4–1.3   Empirical Questions and Normative Questions

Empirical questions are questions of "is." Normative questions address issues of "ought." In one sense they exist in two different intellectual worlds and the responsibility for dealing with them is divided into different professions. Scientists, engineers, and therapists handle the former; philosophers, theologians, and literary scholars deal with the latter. But sometimes there are important connections among them.

Sometimes normative decision-makers make decisions based on empirical questions to which answers are assumed. A lawmaker may have a goal in mind, such as, "we want to save lives by closing the gap between the supply of and demand for transplantable organs." How to accomplish that is an empirical question. Methods may be chosen that cause the opposite to happen. In such a situation, an organ procurement organization might challenge the statute in court as one that fails the rational relationship test. Lawmakers may want to limit the availability of pornography because they believe it causes some harm. Whether it causes harm, has no effect on anything, or does some good is an empirical question. Thus, normative decision-making usually cannot be made entirely free of knowledge of the factual world.

The other side of the coin is that normative assumptions may guide, or mislead, empirical research. For example, in testing which of two medical treatments works "better," the researchers are likely to measure how long those receiving the different treatments live. The one that produces longer life is inferred to be the better treatment. But implicit in that empirical study is the value judgment that longer life, and not something else (such as freedom from pain, ability to function normally) is what matters. Patients might have made a different value choice and concluded that by their criteria the other treatment was "better."

§ 4–1.4 Purposes of Research

Research may be conducted for a variety of different purposes, among them curiosity and exploration, applied testing, description, formal theory development (basic research), and, occasionally, generating evidence relevant to resolving disputed factual questions in litigation.

Research may be conducted to answer a question that has piqued a researcher's curiosity. For examples: Benjamin Franklin wondered about the nature of those flashes in the sky during storms. Someone else wondered what might happen if one tried to combine one of the "noble" elements with some other element. An early astronomer may have wondered what would be seen if a telescope were aimed in a certain direction in the sky. To be human is to have questions about the world, and research can be conducted to answer many of those questions.

Closely related would be more systematic exploration in the pursuit of some phenomenon. For example, the early dentists who discovered pain killing drugs did so by trying one compound after another and observing their effects.

"Applied research" is aimed at answering immediate, practical questions. In developing a new jacket for sailors so as to increase their chances of survival if they fell into the sea, researchers wanted to know, first, from what parts of the human body was most heat lost (so extra insulation could be placed in those areas) and, second, what color is most easily perceived by people looking out into water from the angles at which rescuers tend to be looking (so the jackets would be made in that color). The search for anesthesia, mentioned above, fits this category as well. Or, does a certain drug cross the placental barrier? Which of several available paving compounds is stronger and lasts longer? Do analog or digital displays convey information more quickly and accurately to pilots and nuclear plant operators?

Some research is conducted to provide a thorough description of something. Thus, 19th century naturalists tried to collect every kind of specimen of plant or insect or bird that they could, in order to describe what they found. Later scientists would try to explain the patterns of similarity and variation that had been found.

"Basic research" is performed in order to develop theoretical understanding of a phenomenon of interest. In everyday parlance, theory often is taken to mean the opposite of fact. But in science it means an explanation for a set of observed facts. Theory is not contrary to fact, it is the abstract or conceptual account for why the observed facts exist as they do. These may or may not lead to practical applications. The goal of basic research is knowledge and understanding for its own sake. The steps in the process of theory development and testing—hypothetico-deductive research—is oft-repeated in textbooks, and runs along these lines:

1. Observations of some phenomenon are made. For example, the movements of planets (which move in more complex orbits than the stars).

2. Possible explanations (theories) are proposed for what is observed. (For the movement of planets, one such theory, radical at the time of its first suggestion, was that the movements of planets could be

explained by a theory that placed the Sun and not the Earth at the center of our solar system.)

3.   Hypotheses are logically derived from the theories. (If the Sun is the center of the solar system, then certain other observations should be true. If the Earth is the center of the solar system, that would lead to different predictions.)

4.   Studies are designed to test the hypotheses. In essence, the study makes new observations that might disconfirm the hypothesis and thereby falsify the theory. Different theories have different implications and lead to different hypotheses. (Ideally, a study can be devised whose outcome will disconfirm one theory's hypotheses and not the other's. This is called a "critical experiment" because it permits a head-to-head test of two or more theories, and helps to determine which has done the best job of accounting for the relevant phenomena. Sometimes scientific controversies persist for a very long time because no commonly agreed upon critical experiment can be conducted.)

5.   The results of such empirical tests lead to the revision or abandonment of older theories or the creation of still newer and hopefully better theories.

6.   The process repeats itself as more empirical tests are conducted and theories undergo continued re-evaluation.

Note that a hypothesis or a theory is never proven or confirmed to be true. Testing is capable only of disconfirming. But theories that withstand such attempts at falsification better and longer become accepted, at least until something better comes along. The opposite approach can readily be seen in non-scientific activities of numerous kinds, where investigators engage in a search for evidence that confirms their suspicions. This "confirmatory bias" is based on the erroneous assumption that a theory is confirmed by the accumulation of facts consistent with the theory. The logic of science is that innumerable consistencies can be found, all of which tell us little. It is the diligent search for inconsistencies, for falsification, that really puts a theory to the test. A theory that can withstand such scrutiny is one that deserves credence.

Finally, research sometimes is conducted to address disputed questions of fact "in anticipation of litigation." Such "tailor made" research affords the benefit of being focused more directly on the issues before the court than "off the shelf" research, which had been conducted for one of the other purposes discussed above. On the other hand, research conducted specifically to address litigated factual questions is more suspect for having been prompted by the litigation and designed and carried out in consultation with counsel for one party.

§ 4–1.5   Settings for Research

Research can take place in a number of different settings, for example, in the laboratory, in the field, or through a simulation or models of various kinds. There is no one best place to study the phenomena of interest. Each choice involves trade-offs. The question, as always, is whether the circumstances of the research are appropriate for the focus of the study, and whether the conclusions drawn are sensible in light of the data collected and every-thing about the manner in which the data were collected.

Research conducted in a *laboratory* has the advantage of allowing the researcher to exercise the utmost control over extraneous influences on the phenomenon being studied. It also is more convenient and less expensive. Laboratory research sometimes involves a simulation of the phenomenon of interest. The disadvantage is that studies conducted in laboratories may involve more artificial instances of the phenomenon of interest, and may therefore be less generalizable to the more natural situation in which the researcher (and the law) may be interested. Further, laboratory studies of biological phenomena can be conducted *in vitro* (that is, in glass, in a test tube) or *in vivo* (in a living organism, such as a laboratory animal). Though both occur in laboratories, the difference between in vitro and in vivo studies is obviously a considerable one.

Field research is one solution to the problem of wanting to make sure that the phenomenon studied behaves as much like the natural versions to which the researcher would like to generalize any findings. The problem with field research is that it is harder to keep the variation from extraneous influences from intruding and masking the effects of interest. A review of research comparing studies of attitude change in laboratory settings versus field settings found that in answer to the same research questions, the two settings did not so much produce contradictory results as that often a phenomenon that was detected in the laboratory setting (where control was high) was not able to be detected in the field setting (where control was low).

Simulations of the real thing can make research more efficient, but perhaps also more dubious, depending upon how well the simulation captures the essential features of the phenomenon of interest. Simulations can consist of computer models (mathematical representations of the phenomenon of interest), animal models (study something in animals before doing so in humans), building a physical model of a process or object to be studied (e.g., testing the characteristics of a new aircraft design), simulations of social situations (e.g., how people react to emergencies), games (as in political science, business, or economics studies of how people interact), and so on.

Finally, there is *survey research* conducted by live interviewers or written questionnaires asking people to answer questions about their own past behavior (e.g., how much they purchase of a particular product), or how much they will do something in the future (e.g., if we build it, will you come?), or their attitudes and beliefs (e.g., whether they think a defendant who is to be tried in a court in their community is guilty or not), or about their reactions to something presented to them at the time of the research (e.g., who they think manufactured a certain product shown to them).

Such studies give the researcher a great gain in efficiency. It is easier to ask someone how often they drive while intoxicated than it is to try to follow them around and directly observe the behavior. But, as the example makes apparent, the price of ease of inquiry may be decreased accuracy. People may give untrue answers in order to try to appear more socially acceptable. Or their sincere memories may be imperfect. Moving through the list in the preceding paragraph from the top to the bottom brings us from the sorts of questions that may produce the least accurate information (recall of past behavior and prediction of future behavior) to what probably are some of the most trustworthy responses (being shown something and asked relatively innocuous-sounding questions about it). Thus, the content of the question needs to be scrutinized.

Of course, as every lawyer and judge knows, the way a question is framed, the choice of words, and other features of it can skew the answers obtained. For example, people give different answers when asked about, say, rights of "the pre-born" versus of "the products of conception." For more discussion of the topic of self report survey research, see Chapter 5—Legal Applications of Survey Research.

§ 4–2.0 DEFINING AND MEASURING THINGS

The first step in the scientific method is to define what is to be observed. Though this may seem terribly basic, it is the first chance for the research to seriously misfire.

§ 4–2.1 Conceptual and Operational Definitions

Conceptual definitions are abstract statements of the phenomena of interest. *Operational definitions* are the concrete procedures one must undertake to observe the things being discussed. Talking about concepts in the abstract is one thing (e.g., aggressiveness, intelligence, reasonable decisions, disability). Defining precisely what observations are to count as an instance of the concept and what is not—that is, an operational definition—at least for the purposes of the research, is far more difficult. Moreover, one can make the world appear to be quite a different place merely by using different operational definitions of something. Consider several examples:

One study set out to find out how much intra-family violence occurred in a given locale and found it to be epidemic. A second study concluded, by contrast, that family violence was quite a rare occurrence. By their conceptual definitions, the studies were interested in the same thing. The discrepancy between their findings can be understood by examining their respective operational definitions. The first study defined family violence to include anything from a raised voice onward. The second study did not count as violence anything that did not require hospitalization.

The manufacturer of a headache remedy once tried to convince consumers that "all aspirin is not alike" by insisting that theirs was "better" than the competition and flashing an address on the screen where viewers could write for a report on the supporting details of that claim. That report revealed that the product was superior along such dimensions as: clarity of labeling, accuracy of the count of pills in a 100–count bottle, stick-to-it-ness of the glue on the label, number of broken tablets in the average bottle, and so on. While the advertiser's operational definition of "better aspirin" included those sorts of attributes, potential consumers no doubt assumed the manufacturer was informing them about the pharmacologic efficacy of the aspirin.

Years ago, a presidential administration was able to improve its civil rights record overnight by redefining "a desegregated school district" from being more than half of the schools in a district desegregated to being at least one school in a district. Similarly, indices of crime, cost of living, economic growth, educational achievement, and just about anything else can appear to change merely by changing the operational definition used, even though the world did not change a bit.

Changes in operational definitions sometimes can be quite subtle, as in the following example. Some researchers have concluded that apparent progress in cancer treatment is illusory, because increases in standard 5–year survival rates reflect nothing more than improvements in early detection. That is, by starting the clock sooner, more people reach the five year point, even though the natural history of their disease was unchanged and the same number of people died at the same time. This example involves an almost unnoticeable change in the operational definition of when the cancer "begins," which changes the definition of whether one "survived" it or not.

A consumer of research knowledge has to satisfy himself that the researcher's operational definitions adequately capture the concept that the research consumer is interested in knowing.

§ 4–2.2   Scales of Measurement

Once the operational definition is judged to be acceptable, the thing to be observed has to be measured. There are four basic "scales of measurement" that can be used. The importance of these scales is that the statistical procedures to be used to analyze the data depend upon what type of scale was used. A researcher who uses a statistical procedure that is not suited to the scale of measurement used can obtain results that are not valid.

Nominal scale measurement involves nothing more than "naming," often placing the thing to be measured into one category or another. Hair color, gender, disease diagnosis, numbers on athletes, or phone numbers all are examples of nominal scale data. With this kind of measurement, one can do no more than to count the number of objects in a category, use as a measure of central tendency the mode (that is, the most frequently occurring category), and employ statistical tools that work with categorical data, such as chi square tests.

Ordinal scale measurement adds order to naming, that is, notions of greater or lesser on some dimension. Ordinal scaling involves ranking. Runners finish first, second, third, and so on. We know that the one who finished first was faster than the one who finished second, but we cannot tell from the ranking how much faster the first place finisher was than the others. The gap between first and second may have been an hour, and between second and third only a minute. With ordinal measurement, one can calculate medians and use statistical tools such as rank correlations, in addition to those suited to nominal measurement.

Interval scale measurement adds quantity to order. Interval scaling involves rating rather than ranking. It tells us that the distances between scores consist of equal intervals. A person with an IQ score of 130 is as much smarter than a person with a 120 as the person with a 60 is compared to a person with a 50. Attitude scales, ratings of disease seriousness, and ratings of employee performance are other examples of interval scale measurement. But interval scales do not possess true zero points, so one cannot say that a person whose job rating is 100 performs twice as well as someone with a 50. Such a statement distorts what is possible with interval scale measurement. With interval measurement one can calculate means, standard deviations, Pearson correlations, and use statistical significance tests such as t-tests and F-tests. One can also use any of the statistical techniques permitted for nominal or ordinal data.

Ratio scale measurement adds a true zero origin to the above and permits ratio statements to be made. With ratio scales it becomes possible to say, for example, that a person who runs a mile in five minutes is twice as fast as someone who runs the mile in ten minutes. Quantities such as weight, cost, distance, and time are examples of ratio scale measurement.

The governor of a particular state once argued that it had improved its expenditures on education, and offered as evidence the fact that compared to the previous year, it had increased its expenditures by some considerable amount. An opponent said the state had, by contrast, slipped in its treatment of education, and offered as evidence the fact that its rank among all the states had not increased but fallen. Very likely both had their basic facts correct, but were using different scales of measurement. Accordingly, they can arrive at different conclusions. The ratio measure of absolute expenditures can go up at the same time that relative rank can go down.

At a committee meeting, the chair asked members to rank order the preferences for certain policy options before them. The chair then computed the mean rank of each option. But ranked data cannot validly be used to calculate means, because the mathematical process employed requires data that are at least interval. When properly analyzed, the median (the middle score) of the ranked data, revealed a different set of preferences among the committee members than the other, incorrect, technique for averaging the data had.

§ 4–2.3   Reliability and Validity

Scientists draw a sharp distinction between reliability and validity. In *Daubert*, Justice Blackmun took pains to reject that distinction for the law of evidence, and to combine both reliability and validity into what he and many lawyers and judges before him referred to as the reliability of evidence. This is more than a semantic distinction, and perhaps it could be made more apparent by using three different words to refer to the concepts. For example, we might say that measures need to be "trustworthy" before we can put much confidence in them, and the main components of such trustworthiness are repeatability (reliability) and accuracy (validity). Both have to do with how good a measure is, and they tell us different things about the measure.

To a scientist or statistician, *reliability* refers to the ability of a measure to produce the same result each time it is applied to the same thing. Reliability refers to consistency, or reproducibility. If each time a person steps on to a bathroom scale it gives a different reading (while the person's weight has not changed) then the scale is said to lack reliability. The reliability of a bathroom scale may be tested, for example, by having 50 people who weigh different amounts step on to it twice each, and then comparing the 50 pairs of readings. If the two sets of scores are highly correlated (that is, a person's first reading is highly predictive of the second reading), then the bathroom scale can be said to be a reliable measure. Reliability is a necessary but not sufficient condition for a good measure. A measure can be reliable without being valid. Suppose someone decided to use the bathroom scale to measure intelligence. Even a bathroom scale with perfect reliability would have no correlation with whatever we mean by intelligence. So as a measure of intelligence the bathroom scale would have perfect reliability but no validity. *Validity*, then, is the extent to which something measures what it purports to measure. A measure can have no more validity than it has reliability. Think about the bathroom scale: if the readings bounce around (low reliability), we cannot know which reading is correct (low validity).

The reliability and validity of measures generated by human subjective judgment, as well as by mechanical instruments, laboratory tests, and paper-and-pencil (these days, computer-assisted) tests can be assessed by appropriate studies of reliability and validity. For example, there have been studies of the reliability (and sometimes the validity) of the clinical judgment of psychologists, teachers, trial judges, juries, radiologists, sonar operators, and others. For an interesting example of the complete divergence of reliability and validity, see Chapter 28—Handwriting Identification (reporting a study in which all document examiners reached the same answer to a problem (perfect reliability) but they were all wrong (zero validity)).

§ 4–2.4 Roles Variables Play

Variables may play a number of different roles in a study, depending on the nature of the study and the questions posed by the research. Some studies are designed merely to measure and describe something, but not to explain or predict that something. Where the question posed by the research is one of cause and effect, the variable that is the cause will be termed the *independent variable* and the one that is the effect that responds to the cause is termed the *dependent variable*. Sometimes this relationship is a complex one, with other variables mediating between the cause and the effect, and these are called *intervening variables*. Extraneous variables which themselves systematically influence the dependent variable, and create the illusion of a cause-effect relationship between an independent and dependent variable, are called *confounding variable*s, or sometimes merely *confounds* or *confounders*. In a frankly predictive study, which has no aspiration to explaining cause and effect, the variables doing the predicting may be called *predictor variables* and the variables being predicted will be called either *criterion variables* or, again, *dependent variables*.

Nothing inherent in the variables leads to these designations. Rather, the roles they play in different kinds of studies lead to their being referred to by different designations that reflect those roles.

§ 4–2.5 Statistical Aspects

Once variables are operationally defined, reliable and valid measures of that variable have been chosen, and the objects of study have been measured, those data can be analyzed using statistical tools. Rather than a study resulting in a long list of numbers, descriptive statistics are computed to provide summaries of the distribution of those data. The central tendency (also known as the ''average'') of the distribution may be given by the mean, the median, or the mode, depending on the scale of measurement used and the shape of the distribution. The variability (the spread-out-ness) of the distribution can be expressed by the variance, the standard deviation, or the range, among other ways. (For further details about these descriptive statistics, see Chapter 3—Statistical Proof.)

§ 4–3.0 SAMPLING

Researchers rarely collect data on every single instance of the objects of study. That is called a *census*. They usually *sample* those objects. Agricultural researchers sample the corn in a field; they do not measure each and every ear. The same goes for every other kind of empirical researcher. Sampling not only is less expensive and less time-consuming, under most circumstances it is more accurate than a census. With a proper sampling design, resources can be directed at collecting the most accurate data on a smaller number of people, things, or events. Indeed, demographers evaluate how well the United States census is conducted by comparing the results of the census to samples.

§ 4–3.1 Units of Analysis

The first step in sampling is to decide what is to be sampled, that is, what is the unit of analysis, what is the level of aggregation. For example, does one collect data about individual people or about aggregations such as cities or nations? About workers, organizations, or industries? About rocks, planets or solar systems? Some things exist only at higher levels of aggregation. For example, the way a corporation is organized cannot be discerned by examining individuals, but only the structural relationships of groups of individuals to other groups.

These choices may have consequences for the statistical analyses that can be conducted and the conclusions that are drawn. Sometimes, when the phenomenon of interest can be studied by observing things at different levels of aggregation, different conclusions result from one using one unit of analysis rather than another.

§ 4–3.2 Types of Sampling

Typically, the goal of sampling is to learn about an entire population of things by looking at a subset of them. The key to accomplishing this is to select the sample in such a way that it is representative of the population. Then, what one learns about the sample is likely to be true also for the population.

The methods used to do this are known collectively as probability sampling. *Probability sampling* involves selecting cases from the population in such as way that there is a known probability of any case appearing in the sample. This permits the use of probability theory to draw inferences about the nature of the population. Following are some common kinds of probability sampling.

Simple random sampling involves drawing a sample from the relevant population so that every member of the population has an equal chance of being selected into the sample. For example, if one wanted to measure the incidence of a certain disease among students at a school, a sample of students could be chosen at random from a hat or a computer could generate a random subset of students. Then the sample could be contacted for whatever testing was needed. *Systematic sampling* is similar, but instead of choosing at random, a random starting point would be selected and then every, say, 10th student in the student directory would be chosen (providing a 10% sample of the student body). These methods work fine if every member of the population of interest is known and the population is homogeneous.

A *stratified sample* is one in which subgroups of the population have been specified in advance, and then sampling takes place from within each stratum. This is helpful when some groups within the population occur in small numbers, and a researcher wants to be sure that enough of them are drawn so that a large enough sample of them is obtained to draw trustworthy inferences about the subgroups in the population. One could draw samples proportionate to the size of each stratum. For example, 40% of the sample could be drawn from the stratum that contains 40% of the population and 60% of the sample from the stratum that contains 60% of the population. Alternatively, one might wish to draw a "disproportionate stratified sample." For example, a sample of 250 from the 10% minority and 250 from the 90% majority. Simple random sampling would have yielded only about 50 for the minority, and that might have been too few. The two subsamples from this stratified sampling would then be weighted (one receiving nine times the weight of the other) so that in the end the statements made about the population would be accurate.

The two preceding methods can be combined in various ways to deal with more complicated circumstances, such as where the population is far flung, heterogeneous, and the identities of elements (usually, names of people) are not known. An example of this is *multi-stage cluster sampling*. Imagine that we wanted to study the health of people within the U.S. We do not have a list of every individual to choose them at random, and even if we did it would be inefficient to try to visit those selected, dispersed all over the country. But we could obtain a list (a "sampling frame") of all counties in all states. We could draw a representative sample of counties from that list. The list might even be stratified in some way, such as by region of the country. (That provides the first stage of the sampling design.) From within the selected counties, we could draw a random sample of people to be tested, perhaps through random digit dialing of telephone numbers and inviting them to be tested. (Selecting those individuals is the second stage.) Thus, the people who become the sample are "clustered" in selected counties around the country.

Two lessons should be drawn from the sampling designs described. A particular sampling design can be devised to suit the nature of what is to be sampled by combining different sampling methods (random and stratified, in different stages). And each such design is, nevertheless, a probability sample because one would know the likelihood of selecting any element at any stage.

Various methods of *non-probability* sampling have been developed. One of these is *purposive sampling*, reflecting that the researcher has a particular purpose in mind for the way the sample is chosen. For example, in a study to discover how physicians learn about new drugs, researchers began with pharmacy records showing which physicians prescribed the drug in a given community. Then they interviewed the physicians, asking, among other things, which of their professional friends they also socialize with, and asked those friends who their professional friends were. The particular method described here is called "snowball sampling." As the sample grew, the researchers could track the diffusion of awareness of the new drug through the emerging friendship network. (It was found that doctors were more likely to learn about new medications from their friends than from medical journals.) It should be apparent that one of the more traditional probability sampling methods would not have been as useful to answering the research question.

More detailed discussion of several aspects of sampling can be found in Chapter 6—Survey Research.

§ 4–3.3 Selection Bias

The major defect of any sampling project would be that it fails to select representative elements from the population of interest. Most commonly this results from selection bias.

Selection bias refers to a sample being drawn in a way that makes it unrepresentative of the population to which inferences are to be made. The problem of selection bias is most easily understood by considering several examples. The reader might ponder why conclusions from each of the following samples are likely to be misleading. (Following in parentheses are likely answers.)

A criminologist set out to study criminals by conducting extensive interviews with a random sample of inmates in a state's prisons. (Whatever the study finds can tell us only about those criminals who were caught and incarcerated.)

Doctors learned about the nature of the disease histoplasmosis by studying patients who came to their hospitals with the disease, and concluded that it was a rare disease which was almost always fatal. (By contrast, public health researchers sampled the public at large and found the disease to be far more common and to lead only rarely to serious harm. Doctors in hospitals saw only the few patients who suffered from the disease seriously enough to require medical attention.)

During World War II a study was done to determine where additional armor might be placed on planes to protect them from anti-aircraft fire. To do the study, planes returning from missions were examined to see where they had taken the most hits from enemy fire. (The planes that were shot down but could have been saved with additional armor were the ones that would have been the most informative, but, of course, those never returned.)

A graduating class organizing committee sent an anonymous questionnaire to their members prior to their 25th reunion. It included the question of the classmate's income. When the responses that came back were averaged, the committee was surprised to learn how successful their graduating class members had been in life. (A "response rate" of less than 100%, even a low one, is not in itself a problem. The issue, as usual, is whether those who responded are representative of the population. In the present example, if the more successful alumni are more likely to send back their questionnaires, the average income for the class will appear higher than it actually is.)

§ 4–3.4 Statistical Aspects

§ 4–3.4.1 Sample Size

How large should a sample be to yield valid results? The answer is somewhat counter-intuitive. First of all, the absolute size of the sample is what is important, not the size of the sample relative to the size of the population. (The mathematics of this fact are presented in most textbooks on the statistics of sampling.) Second, the researcher usually has a better idea of what the needed sample size was after the data are collected than before. Third, the larger the sample size the better. The problem researchers face, however, is that while a real gain in accuracy can be achieved when going from n=10 to n=25 or to n=100, as larger numbers are added to the sample, the marginal gain in accuracy shrinks quite considerably. So a researcher has to ask whether the extra trouble and expense involved in adding another 100 or 500 is worth the gain in accuracy that will be achieved.

How large a sample needs to be depends upon three things:

1. The homogeneity of the variable to be measured in the population. For example, suppose a warehouse holding cans of soup had been flooded and all the labels washed off. But it was known that only a single flavor (that is the variable of interest) of soup was stored per warehouse. How many cans have to be opened to answer the question of what flavor soup was in all of the cans in the warehouse? The obvious answer is: one. (But if the warehouse held numerous different kinds of soup, a larger sample would have to be gathered.) The homogeneity of the variable often cannot be known until after the data are collected.

2. How narrowly the researcher needs to zero in on the answer. That is, how narrow the researcher wants the "confidence limits" to be around the statistical statements that can be made about the population. (Depending on the research question, sometimes plus or minus 10 or 20 percentage points will do well enough; other times it will not do at all.)

3. How confident the researcher needs to be that the obtained range around the population parameters is correct—logically, this depends upon the nature of the research questions, although typically researchers follow the convention of aiming for 99% or 95% confidence.

§ 4–3.4.2 Confidence Limits

Since samples are collected not for their own sake, but for the purpose of inferring back to the population from which the samples came, methods have been developed to allow researchers to perform that task of statistical inference. Suppose a regulator needed to determine the average amount of carbon monoxide being discharged per day per automobile in a given city. The researchers might sample cars and days. Suppose they found the mean amount in their sample to be "50 units." By knowing (a) the variation (heterogeneity) in their sample, (b) the sample size, and (c) the level of confidence the researcher wishes to have, the researchers can also calculate, for example, that the true population parameter falls within the range of, say,

50 units plus or minus 8 units, with 95% confidence. That is, there is a 95% probability that the true population mean falls somewhere between 42 and 58.

Further discussion about sample size and confidence limits can be found in Chapter 5—Statistical Proof and Chapter 6—Survey Research.

§ 4–4.0 RELATIONSHIPS AMONG VARIABLES

To this point we have discussed methodological issues related only to the question of measuring one variable at a time—from how many teeth are in a horse's mouth to incidence rates of a disease to consumer perceptions relevant to a possible trademark infringement to the amount of auto exhaust—without trying to relate one variable to another.

Quite often, however, people are interested in the relationship of variables to other variables: Which of several treatments is most likely to cure a disease? What variables predict who will do well in law school, astronaut training, etc.? What management techniques make workers more productive? What policies can cause the economy to grow? What programs are most likely to reduce crime? Which educational methods are most effective? What methods of communicating ideas makes them most persuasive? What causes tornadoes? Life is filled with such questions, and researchers of all kinds are at work searching for the answers.

§ 4–4.1 Minimum Conditions for Inferring a Relationship

In order to draw any inference about a relationship among variables, one must have data from at least two levels of at least two variables. Anything less makes it impossible to say anything about a relationship. Figure 1a illustrates these minimum conditions. Suppose the question is whether scores on an intelligence test are related to performance in a particular job. Suppose a study were done on 1000 workers doing that job. Suppose that by some valid and reliable measures their job performance was evaluated and their intelligence was measured. The data in Figure 1a show that people tended to cluster in the two cells where (a) intelligence was high and performance was good and (b) intelligence was low and performance was poor. So we would infer from this pattern of evidence that higher intelligence was associated with better job performance. But the differences between these two cells and the remaining two are small, so the relationship is a small one: intelligence does not have a great deal to do with performance on this job.

Consider Figure 1b. Here the relationship is the opposite: high intelligence is associated with poor job performance. Moreover, the relationship is stronger than the previous one: on this job, high intelligence is an impediment to good performance.

Examine the data in Figure 1c. These reveal no relationship whatsoever between intelligence and job performance. Among workers of high intelligence, the ratio of those who perform well to those who perform poorly is 4:1. Among workers of low intelligence the ratio is exactly the same.

Note that any less data than these two measures on two variables would not permit us to draw any inferences at all about the relationship between the two variables of intelligence and work performance. Nevertheless, people often can be led to believe an assertion that lacks data to support it. This point can be understood by considering missing data patterns.

Figure 1

Minimum conditions for finding a relationship

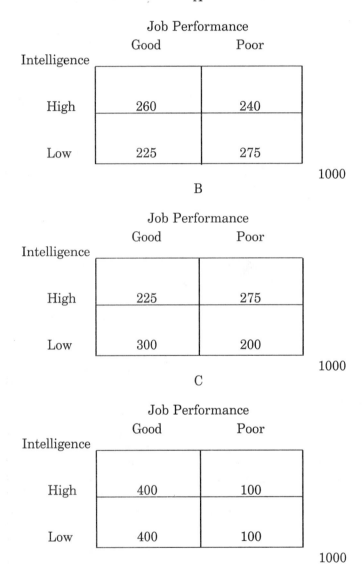

A

Job Performance

Intelligence	Good	Poor
High	260	240
Low	225	275

1000

B

Job Performance

Intelligence	Good	Poor
High	225	275
Low	300	200

1000

C

Job Performance

Intelligence	Good	Poor
High	400	100
Low	400	100

1000

§ 4–4.1.1 Single Cell Missing Data Pattern

Consider a situation where only one cell out of the minimum four cells is provided, and an inference is sought to be drawn from that evidence. Here is an example.

In a debate over the value of trying to form a strong trade relationship with one's enemies of long-standing, as a way of trying to reduce the chances that war would break out between them, one of the debaters offered as evidence against the proposition a list of eight pairs of nation-states that had been primary trade partners just prior to going to war against each other.

Figure 2

Single cell missing data pattern

Primary Trade Partners?

	Yes	No
War		
Yes	8	
No		

During the debate, this had a strong impact against the proposition that trade relationships reduce the chances of war. But an examination of Figure 2 shows us that, because we do not know what data exist in the remaining three cells, we do not actually know anything yet about the relationship between trade and armed conflict. The relationship could be discovered only by collecting representative data, filling those remaining cells, and examining the pattern revealed.

In short, the debater offered a single-cell missing data pattern, and managed to convince most of the audience that it told them something important about the relationship at issue, when it did not tell them anything about the relationship.

§ 4–4.1.2 Single Row (or Column) Missing Data Pattern

Sometimes the data that are offered in support of some proposition consist of only one row or column from the basic 2x2 matrix that is the minimum necessary for drawing inferences of a relationship.

For example, occasionally people have suggested that marijuana, even if not harmful in itself, is dangerous because it leads (by some pharmacological or psychological or sociological route) to the use of harder drugs. They have offered the suggestion that if a substantial number of heroin addicts were found to have used marijuana when they were younger, that would confirm the hypothesis. Figure 3 depicts the pattern of data such commentators have in mind. The hypothetical data in the figure show 60% of a sample of 500 heroin addicts to have used marijuana at an earlier time.

Figure 3

Single row (or column) missing data pattern

Heroin Addict at Time-2	Smoke Marijuana at Time-1 Yes	No
Yes	300	200
No		

Because these data constitute a single-row missing data pattern, they cannot reveal whether or not a relationship exists. More specifically, without comparison data we cannot know whether fewer than 60%, about the same 60%, or more than 60% of people who are not heroin addicts earlier smoked marijuana. And it is on that comparison that the existence or non-existence of a relationship depends.

Suppose, for example, that someone had proposed that drinking milk as a child led to heroin addiction as an adult. The same table with marijuana replaced by milk would reveal that more than 99% of heroin addicts drank milk as children. Would that reveal that milk was to blame? Filling in the data for the rest of the table would make clear that 99% of non-heroin addicts drank milk as children, and therefore no relationship between milk drinking and heroin addiction existed. Until the rest of the data were supplied for Figure 3, one could not tell whether a relationship existed between marijuana smoking and heroin addiction, other than by speculating on what the missing cells contained.

§ 4–4.1.3 Main Diagonal Missing Data Pattern

The final pattern of missing data is where the data supplied fill only the cells along the diagonal, usually the main diagonal. As an illustration, suppose an asserted expert in the prediction of dangerousness is asked to report his track record, and his reply is that on 50 occasions he predicted that individuals would be dangerous and that they did do something harmful, while on 200 occasions he predicted that individuals would not be dangerous and that they did not do anything harmful. Figure 4 displays these data. By now the reader should readily see that until we know what occurred in the remaining cells, it is impossible to know from the limited data given whether the expert is highly accurate or highly inaccurate. If the expert made 2000 other predictions, which wound up in the two remaining cells, then we would know that these data portray an expert who was wrong on nearly 90% of his predictions.

Figure 4

Main Diagonal Missing Data Pattern

Prediction of Dangerousness	Harmful Conduct	
	Yes	No
Yes	50	
No		200

§ 4–4.2 Predictive Relationships

When the minimum necessary data are available, as explained above, a predictive relationship, if one exists between the variables, can be discerned. Mere predictive relationships—also known as correlational relationships or findings that are the product of observational studies—tell us only whether one variable is associated with another, and how strong that association is. They do not tell us that changes in one of those variables *causes* changes in the other variable. Establishing causal relationships, a much more difficult task, is discussed in the sub-section following this one.

Here are some illustrations of predictive relationships. They are offered to illuminate the point that correlation does not prove causation, although often mere correlations are spoken of as if they established a causal relationship.

Bugs, beards, and spurious correlations: Researchers once found that the beards of some indigenous men of a third world venue tended to be inhabited by lice but not the beards of other men, and that the men with the lice tended to be healthier than those without the lice. Thus, a correlation was found such that lice and health went together. On these data alone, numerous explanations are possible: lice promote health, whatever these men are doing to remain healthy also promotes lice, whatever sickness has overcome the ill men also overcomes the lice, healthy men attract lice, and so on. Correlational relationships do not enable one to distinguish among a variety of different possibilities.

Marriage and crime, and the direction of the causal arrow: Observing that single men were more likely than married men to commit crimes, one commentator recommended that society try to marry off as many single men as possible so as to reduce crime and a whole array of other problems that these men presented to society. Single men also were more likely to have more illnesses, lower incomes, less education, and various other problems. But it is at least as likely that the causal arrow runs in the opposite direction. That is, men who are actively engaged in crime are more likely to suffer from health problems, poverty, and so on, and therefore are less likely to be found to be acceptable marriage partners and so have lower rates of marriage.

Smoking during pregnancy and children's intelligence, and the "third variable" problem: A study found that women who smoked during pregnancy bore children with lower IQ's, on average, than women who did not smoke. This finding allows the *prediction* that the offspring of women who smoked during pregnancy would have lower intelligence. But it does not by itself permit a conclusion that smoking *caused* the lowered intelligence. A plausible alternative explanation is that mothers with lower IQs are more likely to smoke (which is true) and also are more likely to produce children with lower IQs (also true). Thus, it is a third variable (mother's IQ) which causes both of the other variables (smoking and children's IQ).

Here are two additional, and more obvious examples of the third variable problem:

A study finds that states with higher levels of pickle sales also have students who attain higher scores on tests of educational achievement. The researchers conclude that pickles improve school performance, and recommend that school cafeterias serve more pickles to students. A more likely explanation is that the economic situation of the state is responsible for both the level of pickle sales (in good economies more of everything gets sold, including pickles) and the performance of students (good economic conditions allow stronger tax bases, more expenditures on education, and better schools).

An observer from Mars who is studying the earth notes that cars tend to turn left after a light on the car's left side begins to blink, and they tend to turn right when a light on the right side begins to blink. Using the same faulty logic that earthlings often use, the martian concludes that the light *causes* the cars to turn (rather than the "third variable" of the driver, who causes both of those other events). A good predictive relationship has been found, but the observer has the causation wrong.

In none of these illustrations can causation be ruled out (until information is collected on the third variable), but mere correlation does not establish the causation.

§ 4–4.2.1 Statistical Aspects

Predictive relationships can be examined graphically with the help of "scatterplots" and "crosstabulation" tables (Figure 1 provides examples of crosstabulations). They can be measured using a variety of correlational statistics (the Pearson Product Moment Correlation and Spearman's Rank Correlation being two of the more common). Correlation coefficients vary between 0 and 1. The greater the coefficient the stronger the association between the two variables. Correlations also have signs accompanying them: Positive correlations mean that as one variable increases in magnitude, so does the other. Negative correlations mean that as one variable increases in magnitude, the other decreases. Slightly different ways of calculating correlations are used depending upon the nature of the data: whether the data in one or both variables are measured using nominal, ordinal, or interval scales. (See discussion of these, supra.)

Following are several illustrative correlations from various areas of research, which cover a wide span of the range of strengths of relationships:

Aspirin and heart attacks	.033
Psychotherapy effectiveness	.320
First year law school grades predicted from the LSAT	.410
Polygraph accuracy	.670
Civil jury awards predicted from medical specials	.714
Distance from hole and putting success for pro golfers	-.940

The nature of a predictive relationship between two variables can be described more fully by the use of Regression Analysis. This kind of analysis enables one to describe the relationship between the two variables with the formula for a straight line. Of particular interest is the slope of that line: the steeper the slope, the more change is "produced" in one variable by a change in the other variable. Having such a formula allows a direct and literal prediction of a score on one variable by knowing the score on the other variable. For example, how well is a student likely to do in the first year of law school predicted from the student's LSAT score? Correlation and regression permit that prediction to be made with some accuracy.

Often, several predictor variables can be brought to bear on predicting some outcome variable. For example, how well can a law student's first year grades be predicted by knowing the student's undergraduate grade point average and age as well as LSAT score? The technique of multiple regression analysis permits several predictor variables to be combined in order to improve the accuracy of the prediction. One of the important additional statistics that accompanies a multiple regression analysis is the "multiple R squared," symbolized as R^2. This is the square of the correlation between the scores *predicted* using the several predictor variables and the actual *observed* scores. It tells us the proportion of variance in the criterion (or predicted) variable that is predicted (or accounted for) by the predictor variables.

Some researchers have come to believe that "proportion of variance accounted for" gives an impression of a relationship that understates the magnitude of relationships. They have suggested converting correlations and multiple correlations into a "binomial effect-size display," or "BESD," which is more intuitively meaningful. Figure 5 illustrates such a display. Take a correlation of r=.32 (which is the correlation between receiving or not receiving psychotherapy and showing at least substantial improvement in the patient's condition based on a large number of studies). From the correlation alone, researchers would tend to call this a modest or moderate relationship. Squaring the r, to find the proportion of the variation in symptoms ameliorated by the psychotherapy, the relationship appears even more modest: 10% of the variance in symptoms is associated with the treatment. Figure 5 shows, however, that this correlation (.32) is equivalent to a change in cure rates from 34% to 66%.

Figure 5

Illustration of Binomial Effect Size Display

r=0.320

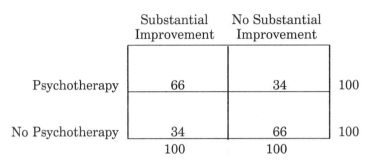

	Substantial Improvement	No Substantial Improvement	
Psychotherapy	66	34	100
No Psychotherapy	34	66	100
	100	100	

Some research, such as epidemiology, deals with relationships of more subtle magnitude. For example, look at the correlation between taking or not taking aspirin and having or not having a heart attack. Figure 6 shows the data on which this correlation is based. The vast majority of people in the study had no heart attacks whether they took aspirin or not. The correlation is .033 and the proportion of variance accounted for is .001 (or one-tenth of one percent). Even the BESD shows only a small change in survival rate (a change in heart attack occurrence from 52.6% to 47.4%). But in this area of research, one will find the relationship expressed neither in terms of correlations, variance accounted for, or BESD, but in terms of "relative risk," or RR, that is, the likelihood that a person in the exposed group will suffer from the condition compared to a member of the unexposed group. In this example, the RR=.55, which is a protective relationship (exposure reduces the likelihood of the condition). Using this way of describing the data, one can say that aspirin cuts the risk of having a heart attack in half. That sounds quite different from saying that one tenth of 1% of the variance in heart attacks is associated with aspirin taking. Yet both are accurate statements of the relationship.

Figure 6

The Effect of Aspirin on Heart Attacks

RR=0.5499

	Heart Attack	No Heart Attack	Attacks per 1000
Aspirin	104	10,993	9.42
Placebo	189	10,845	17.13

More detailed discussion of the statistical aspects of predictive relationships can be found in Chapter 5—Statistical Proof. More detailed discussion of the statistical aspects of epidemiological research can be found in Chapter 7—General Concepts of Epidemiology.

§ 4–4.3   Causal Relationships

Most of the time researchers are more interested in understanding causation than they are in discovering merely predictive relationships. (Though prediction is itself quite important, as testing for admissions in higher education, economic forecasting, and meteorology demonstrate.)

§ 4–4.3.1   Squeezing Causation From Correlational Data

If the reader takes nothing else away from the preceding section, it should be that "correlation does not prove causation." Nevertheless, the first step in trying to establish that a relationship is causal rather than merely correlational often is to try to extract causal inferences from correlational data.

The first temptation is to examine the correlation, and argue that particularly large correlations reflect underlying causation. This argument cannot succeed on its own. Many strong correlations have been found to be spurious, often due to "third variables." (See the discussion of spurious correlations, supra.) Conversely, truly causal relationships come in various strengths and therefore can have correlations of various sizes. The logic of establishing causation requires more.

Numerous statistical techniques have been developed to try to help researchers draw better causal inferences from correlational data. These involve "controlling for" potentially confounding variables. These techniques include partial correlations, certain applications of multiple regression analysis, path analysis, cross-lagged panel correlation, and others. Discussing these is beyond the scope of this chapter. Suffice it to say that each of these techniques requires relatively sophisticated quantitative analysis aimed at statistically removing the effects of possible confounding variables. They also entail the hope that all of the important extraneous variables have been measured so that their effects can be statistically controlled (removed from having any influence) so that the real effects, if any, of the independent variables of interest can be seen. At the end of the day, causal inferences from correlational data must always be received with a healthy respect for the possibility that the statistical adjustments have been incorrect or the true causal variables have been omitted from the model and therefore could not be adjusted for at all. (For more discussion of these issues, see Chapter 5— Statistical Proof.)

§ 4–4.3.2   Threats to Internal Validity

By far the simpler and more powerful solution to the problem of drawing causal inferences is to design a study in such a way that cause can be inferred more directly, without having to resort to a panoply of statistical fixes. In fact, research designs vary in the extent to which they allow unconfounded inferences to be drawn about what is causing the observed changes in the dependent variable. The logical structure of a research design is known as its "internal validity." Designs which minimize threats to internal validity allow the clearest inferences of causation. Designs with poor internal validity do not permit sound causal inferences to be drawn.

If designs high in internal validity exist, why don't researchers use them all of the time, and avoid the need for mathematical manipulations to try to clear up the confusion in their data? When circumstances permit, competent researchers are eager to use such designs. But for reasons of practicality or ethics, the best research designs may not be possible. The research designs that allow the strongest inferences are true experiments, which require that people or things be assigned at random to differing treatment conditions. (This and other designs will be discussed in more detail, in § 4–6.0, *infra*.) Astronomers, for example, simply have no ability to randomly assign different celestial bodies to experimental and control groups. They must take them as they find them. Researchers of the biological effects of toxic substances cannot instruct people to spend their lives exposed to certain substances and other people to remain unexposed. On the other hand, researchers in fields such as medicine, physics (though not astrophysics or geophysics), psychology, and agriculture, among others often can avail themselves of the most powerful research designs.

Where there is a threat to internal validity, plausible rival hypotheses exist which the research design is unable to rule out. The existence of plausible rival hypotheses that cannot be discounted means that inferences about causation are ambiguous. In order to understand the strengths and weaknesses of different research designs, in terms of their relative ability to permit unambiguous causal inferences, we must first acquire some appreciation for the various threats to internal validity, or confounds. To understand the following threats to internal validity, think of a simple study in which a group of patients is given a new treatment.

[1] History

History is the threat to internal validity that refers to events to which the people or things are differentially subjected in addition to the independent variable. Thus, if patients who receive the treatment also are placed on a special diet and are given physical therapy, one cannot unambiguously infer what is affecting the outcomes for the patients, the treatment or the confounds (in this example, diet and physical therapy).

[2] Maturation

Maturation refers to processes going on within the respondents, such as growing older, growing tired, growing hungry. Thus, for example, the body's natural healing processes are confounded with any treatments that are given (from which comes the old saying that a physician should make haste to treat a patient before the illness goes away on its own).

[3] Testing

The second time a person takes a test the scores will be different from what they would otherwise have been, merely because of changes in the person's experience of the test. Changes due to these effects should not be mistaken for changes from the first to the second testing due to the independent variable.

[4] Instrumentation

Instrumentation refers to changes that take place in the measuring instruments, including human observers, which can be mistaken for changes in the people or things being observed. For example, patients attended by nurses on one shift may be evaluated differently than by nurses on a different shift; the differences may be due not to changes in the patients but due to differences in the nurses. A whole area of social psychological research has developed that has illuminated these "subject-experimenter artifacts." For example, there are expectancy biases, in which observers, tend to see what they are given an expectation to see. In addition to affecting the perceptions of the observers, expectations change their behavior toward the persons or animals being studied and the person under study may himself change due to expectations about the effects of the treatment. A classic example of this problem (known as the "Hawthorne Effect") occurred in an industrial plant, where any and every change introduced by organizational effectiveness researchers raised the productivity and morale of the employees. What was happening was partly that the employees thrived on the attention and partly that they shared the expectations of the researchers that the changes being introduced would improve the circumstances and the work of the employees. Because of such expectancy effects many studies are conducted in a "blind" fashion, that is, where a person receiving an experimental treatment (for example, medications) is kept uninformed of whether what is being administered is the active substance or a placebo. Where circumstances permit, the studies are conducted in "double-blind" fashion: not only are the people being studied kept blind, but the researchers administering the treatment also are kept blind to which treatment they are giving and, when possible, blind as well to the hypotheses being tested.

[5] Statistical Regression

Statistical regression occurs when objects of study, including people, are selected because of their extreme scores on some measure. With no treatment at all, they tend to "regress" toward the mean of the distribution from which they came. Therefore, observed changes due to that regression effect can be mistaken for changes due to the treatment.

[6] Selection

Selection confounds occur where some of the people or objects placed into experimental and control conditions differ initially in some way. For example, suppose relatively healthier people are chosen for an experimental medical treatment (because it is thought that they can better withstand the rigors of the treatment) and less healthy people with the same illness are used as a comparison group. Distinguishing the effects of the treatment from the initial differences in health will be difficult or impossible.

[7] Experimental Mortality

Experimental mortality refers to the differential loss of participants from different experimental conditions. It introduces the same problem later in a study that selection artifacts introduce at the outset of a study.

[8] Selection–Maturation Interaction, Etc.

Some of the confounds defined above can work together and thereby further obscure the results. A likely one is the interaction of selection and maturation: the people selected to be in different conditions of a study differ between experimental and control conditions in that those in one group are "maturing" at a different rate or to a different degree than those in the other group. For examples: patients of different age or condition are likely to heal at different rates, children of different ages will learn at different rates, nations at different stages of economic development can react to new challenges with different degrees of success.

[9] Chance

Chance is an artifact that results from random fluctuations in sampling and measurement. Two groups can be identical in every respect, and yet at the end of the study their measured scores still will not be identical. A difference due to chance might be mistaken for a difference due to the independent variable. While all of the artifacts defined above can be protected against by proper research design, chance is the one that cannot be. It is to deal with the artifact of chance that significance testing was invented. For a very brief summary of statistical significance testing, see § 4–6.4 on statistical aspects of research designs, *infra*. For more detailed discussion, see Chapter 5—Statistical Proof.

[10] Distortions in Independent and Dependent Variables

In thinking about things that interfere with the capacity of research to permit valid inferences to be drawn about the possible effects of an independent variable on a dependent variable, problems with the independent and dependent variables themselves should not be overlooked. (The nine subsections immediately above define types of confounds, which are factors *other than an independent* variable that may be causing apparent changes in a dependent variable.)

Faulty operational definitions: Recall from our earlier discussion of operational definitions, in § 4–2.1, *supra*, that if a variable is not meaningfully operationalized, then the findings it produces would not answer the question a consumer of that research may have thought was being asked.

Failure to induce the experimental manipulation: Even a well operationalized variable may not reach the respondents or may not be presented to them or done to them or, having reached them, may not be perceived in the intended way. For examples: In a study of the effects of toxic substances, a group presumed to have been exposed may not in fact have been. A prisoner rehabilitation program may not actually have been carried out. A study might seek to examine how people react to "rich" corporate defendants, while the people in the study do not perceive the defendants as being any wealthier than average. In each of these instances, it would not be accurate to conclude that the independent variable had no effect if that independent variable was, in reality, not tested. Researchers concerned about these matters often perform "manipulation checks," that is, they test whether the independent variable was induced as intended.

Floor and ceiling effects: When a manipulation is so extreme in its strength or weakness that there is no variation possible between groups—that is, all people in all groups respond to it the same way—then it is impossible to test the effects of some other variable on it. For example, any study of the subtle effects on verdicts of innumerable variables that affect judge or jury decision making will be incapable of detecting differences if the basic case facts are so extreme that everyone viewing the case reaches the same verdict. What good researchers try to do is to pre-test their procedures to make sure that floor or ceiling effects do not occur and that adequate variability exists in the dependent variable.

§ 4–5.0 THREATS TO EXTERNAL VALIDITY

In the preceding section we discussed internal validity: the logic of the structure of a study that permits or impedes drawing causal inferences about the effect of independent variables on dependent variables. Once we are satisfied that a study is internally valid, the next issue is whether it is externally valid, that is, whether it can be generalized beyond itself. This order of appraising a study is not arbitrary. Without internal validity there is nothing to generalize.

External validity refers to the representativeness of a study. If a study is externally valid, its findings can be generalized to other populations (of people, objects, organizations, times, places, etc.). Usually one does research at a specific time and place on a particular population, but hopes to be able to generalize the findings beyond the immediate people and circumstances of the study.

For examples: Can the findings of a study done in Minnesota be generalized to people in Arizona? Does a study of the efficacy of information presented in written form generalize to the same information presented in verbal, video, or computerized form? Does a study of manufacturing organizations have application to financial services organizations? If people are exposed to a battery of treatments, will any one of them work on people who have not been exposed to the others? Can we generalize to humans the findings of a study of the effects of a drug tested on laboratory rats? Or tested on monkeys? Or from adults to children? Or males to females?

Particular kinds of threats to external validity have been defined more precisely. By way of illustration, we will examine more closely only one of them: Reactive effects of testing are the change-inducing effects of taking a test on the person being tested. For example, suppose a firm wants to test the effects of an advertising campaign on people's attitudes. If it begins by testing public attitudes and plans to call the respondents back after the advertisements have been airing for a period of time, the pre-testing itself may cause respondents to pay more attention to the ads than other members of the public, who had not been pre-tested. Thus, the findings can be generalized only to people who had been interviewed about the topic before the ads were aired.

While the logic of research design is a great help in evaluating the internal validity of research, concerns about external validity cannot be dealt with so easily. With respect to any of the questions posed two paragraphs above, readers could exercise their intuition: how similar do we feel that different settings or types or organisms are (with respect to the independent and dependent variables of interest)? But these are merely guesses. At the end of the day the only way to know with any rigor whether an effect observed in Minnesota will hold in Arizona, or whether an effect observed in rats will hold for humans, is replication. This is one reason that researchers rarely place much faith in any single study, or even any single type of study. For reasons of generality, among other reasons, they prefer to see findings replicated in other places, using other participants, under various other conditions. The more different circumstances a phenomenon can be replicated in, the greater its generality, and the more confidence researchers as well as consumers of research should have in the phenomenon.

§ 4–6.0 RESEARCH DESIGNS

Various research designs are more or less vulnerable to threats to internal and external validity. The following discussion is not an exhaustive review of research designs, but provides the reader with the ability to appreciate the power of some research designs to provide answers and the weakness of others.

Our discussion will proceed by way of an extended example. Let us take as our research project a study of the question whether Vitamin C cures colds or not. Following are a variety of approaches a researcher could take in attacking this empirical question. Through these we will be able to see the strengths and weaknesses of different research designs. The emphasis of our discussion will be on threats to internal validity.

§ 4–6.1 Pre-experimental Designs

First, suppose the researcher employs a *case study*. A person who is observed to have a cold is given Vitamin C, and soon thereafter the cold goes away. Is this convincing evidence of the curative powers of Vitamin C? Let's think about the confounding variables that may be operating in this study (see § 4–4.3.2). Some other factor may have cured the cold, such as the chicken soup or bed rest the cold sufferer also was taking (history). The patient's immune system may have cured the cold rather than the Vitamin C (maturation). To these let us add the lack of generality produced by a study with a sample size of n=1.

Suppose, then, that the researcher rounds up 100 people to conduct essentially the same study. This is a *one-group pre-test post-test design*. At the outset they all have colds, they are given vitamin C, and a week later, of those who could be examined, only 40% still have their colds. Is the decline from 100% ill to 40% attributable to the vitamin C? The confounds mentioned above have not gone away. In addition: Perhaps those rating the cold symptoms had become so insensitive to them from $time_1$ to $time_2$ that it took worse symptoms to register as still having a cold (instrumentation). Perhaps those whose colds turned to pneumonia and were now in the hospital or quit the study in frustration were the ones who could not be found, thus exaggerating the observed cure rate (mortality). As a result of the confounds in this design, this study also leaves us less than persuaded.

Our persistent researcher next tries a *static group comparison*. In this study people are found who either already take vitamin C regularly or who do not, and their colds are monitored over time. Suppose a relationship is found such that those who take vitamin C get fewer colds and the colds they get are milder and shorter. Can we now conclude that vitamin C cures (and prevents) colds? The reader may recognize this as a fairly primitive correlational (or observational) study (discussed earlier, in § 4–4.2). It still is vulnerable to a variety of threats to its internal validity. Those who take vitamin C regularly may systematically differ from those who do not in other things they do: nutrition, exercise, rest (history confounds). Those who regularly take vitamin C may, either constitutionally or because of their other health habits, be basically healthier to begin with than their counterparts (selection), or have more active immune systems that kill cold viruses more effectively (interaction of selection and maturation). Note that instrumentation is, in this design, not likely to be a problem, because both groups are being examined at approximately the same times, so any such problems would be equal for both groups.

§ 4–6.2 True Experiments

Let us now contrast the above designs to a true experiment. It is worth taking a moment to define the term "experiment." In common parlance an experiment simply means testing something out, trying something out. To scientists it refers to a specific type of research design through which such testing is done. It means a testing situation in which a basis for comparison is provided such that conditions are identical between two or more groups (such as an experimental group and a control group) except for the feature that is the focus of the study.

For social, behavioral, and biological scientists, accomplishing this requires *randomly assigning* the participants of the study to experimental and control conditions so as to maximize the probability that the two groups do not differ. True experiments are known by several synonyms. They may be called, simply, experiments. In medical research they often are termed "randomized controlled trials," or "controlled trials," or "clinical trials." Whatever the name, the meaning is that people are randomly assigned to be exposed to different conditions or treatments, so that confounds are eliminated and the groups do not differ except with respect to the independent variable. Cause and effect inferences will be unambiguous.

Let us see how this works with the vitamin C inquiry. Imagine that 200 cold sufferers are randomly assigned to two groups. One group receives vitamin C, the other receives nothing, or a placebo. (Ideally, the vitamin C and placebo are given in double blind fashion, so that neither the person administering nor the person receiving the drug can know which is the active drug and which the placebo. Identifying numbers will be decoded later by the researchers.) A week later the people are examined and it is found, let us say, that 50% of the control group still have their colds, but only 40% of the vitamin C group does. On the face of things, that difference of 10 percentage points suggests that the vitamin C did more good than the placebo.

Moreover, because of the use of a true experimental design, we will see that confounds have been eliminated. History: Because of random creation of the two groups, the proportion of those eating chicken soup or staying home in bed is highly likely to be equal between the two groups. Maturation: The immune system response will be the same, on average, in the two groups. We can see that although even the control group lost half of its colds due to spontaneous remission (something that, in the one-group pre-test post-test design could not be distinguished from an alleged vitamin C effect) the difference of 10 percentage points represents the effect of vitamin C over and above maturation. Instrumentation: If patients were sent for examinations at random before and after administration of the independent variable, any changes in the perceptions of the examiners will be evenly distributed between the experimental and control groups and could not have caused an artifactual difference. Selection: Had young adults been placed in the vitamin C group and older people in the control group, or if people had been allowed to select themselves into the vitamin C or control groups, then any observed difference might have been due to those differences between the people in the two groups. But random assignment of people to groups maximizes the likelihood that, on any dimension we could name, we would find the same proportion of such people in one group as the other, and those differences would not have been able to exert an effect on one group and not the other. Mortality: Similarly, people dropping out of the two groups would be expected to occur at the same rates and not differentially. This would be true with respect to any characteristic we could name.

If we had doubts about any of these things, we could check them and see if they were present differentially in one group compared to the other.

§ 4–6.3 Quasi-experiments

Quasi-experiments are research designs that are not as clean and straightforward as true experiments, but which provide enough control, or some randomization, or can be supplemented or corrected so as to eliminate many, and occasionally all, threats to validity. In short, partly by virtue of the design, partly by collecting additional data to address shortcomings, a quasi-experimental design can be made to approximate an experiment, and allow cause-effect inferences that may approach the clarity of experiments.

For example, in an *interrupted time series* design, data are collected on the dependent variable (e.g., highway death rates) over a period of time (e.g., five years), then the independent variable is induced (e.g., the introduction of seat belts) and then data are collected for a period of time following the introduction of the innovation (e.g., another five years). Suppose it is found that after the introduction of seat belts the accident death rate fell. The only confound that is not protected against in this design is history. Perhaps other changes occurred at the same time as the treatment. Suppose it is suspected that at the same time as seat belts were introduced: the price of gasoline rose so people drove less, speed limits were lowered and enforced better, the weather was less icy, and so on. What the researcher would do would be to collect data on those things, to see if any of the suspected history confounds really occurred. If they did not, the inference that it was the seat belts that lowered the death rate is strengthened. If they did, statistical adjustments might be possible to see if, after the effects of the confounds are statistically removed, a seat belt effect can still be discerned.

Sophisticated correlational (observational) studies, which include enough data to test or control statistically for possible confounds, can be thought of as members of the quasi-experimental class of research designs. Crude correlational studies are better regarded as members of the pre-experimental class.

Case-control studies, found in epidemiological research, may be thought of as quasi-experimental designs. For each case in the group exposed to the substance of interest, a comparison case is chosen which is similar on many characteristics, except that the control case has not been exposed to the substance. It should be obvious to the reader that this is an attempt to reduce the effects of possible confounding variables, and to try to approximate the power of a true experiment.

Research designs come in great variety. Both the researcher and the consumer of research knowledge have to think carefully and clearly about the strengths and weaknesses of the research design, and whether the inferences sought to be drawn from the study are possible in light of the design. When the findings of a number of studies are combined, either by old fashioned reading of the studies or by a formal, quantitative, meta-analysis, the various findings can be given more weight or less weight, depending upon the quality of the research design through which the findings were obtained.

§ 4–6.4 Statistical Aspects

As noted earlier, the confound of *chance* cannot be ruled out, even by the most ideal experimental design. In the example above, is the difference between 40% and 50% in the number of patients in the experimental and control groups who still have colds a real difference or is it the product of random fluctuation? This question is answered by statistical hypothesis testing. The data permit the researcher to calculate the probability that, were the starting assumption of no difference between the experimental and control groups (known as the null hypothesis) to be rejected, what is the likelihood that the researcher would be making a Type I error (erroneously rejecting a true null hypothesis). Conventionally, unless this probability falls below .05 (fewer than five chances in 100 of committing a Type I error), the researcher refrains from rejecting the null hypothesis. For more detailed discussion of inferential statistics and hypothesis testing, see Chapter 5— Statistical Proof.

§ 4–7.0 CONCLUSION

Science is neither mechanical nor magical. It is a process of drawing inferences from evidence. The evidence for those inferences is generated by research which necessarily employs a selection of research methods. A finding is only as good as the methods used to find it. There is no one best way to study a phenomenon of interest. Each methodological choice involves trade-offs. The issue, always, is whether the methodology of the research is appropriate for the questions posed by the study, and whether the conclusions drawn are justifiable in light of the data collected and everything about the methods by which those data were generated. The choices of methods require careful thought, both by researchers and consumers of the research. The purpose of this chapter has been to arm legal consumers of scientific research with concepts that will facilitate that critical and thoughtful appraisal.

Appendix 1

References on Research Methods and Philosophy of Science

ADVANCES IN QUASI-EXPERIMENTAL DESIGN AND ANALYSIS (William M.K. Trochim ed., 1986).

PETER ACHINSTEIN, CONCEPTS OF SCIENCE: A PHILOSOPHICAL ANALYSIS (1968).

DONALD T. CAMPBELL & JULIAN C. STANLEY, EXPERIMENTAL AND QUASI-EXPERIMENTAL DESIGNS FOR RESEARCH (1963).

THOMAS D. COOK & DONALD T. CAMPBELL, QUASI-EXPERIMENTATION: DESIGN AND ANALYSIS ISSUES FOR FIELD SETTINGS (1979).

SHARI S. DIAMOND, *Methods for the Empirical Study of Law in* LAW AND THE SOCIAL SCIENCES (Leon Lipson & Stanton Wheeler eds., 1986).

EVIDENCE AND INFERENCE: THE HAYDEN COLLOQUIUM ON SCIENTIFIC CONCEPT AND METHOD (Daniel Lerner ed., 1959).

ANTHONY M. GRAZIANO & MICHAEL L. RAULIN, RESEARCH METHODS: A PROCESS OF INQUIRY (1989).

JACQUES L. GOUPY, METHODS FOR EXPERIMENTAL DESIGN: PRINCIPLES AND APPLICATIONS FOR PHYSICISTS AND CHEMISTS (1993).

MARTIN GOLDSTEIN, HOW WE KNOW: AN EXPLORATION OF THE SCIENTIFIC PROCESS (1978).

HANDBOOK OF SURVEY RESEARCH (Peter H. Rossi et al. eds., 1983).

ROM HARRE, GREAT SCIENTIFIC EXPERIMENTS: 20 EXPERIMENTS THAT CHANGED OUR VIEW OF THE WORLD (1981).

KLAUS HINKELMANN & OSCAR KEMPTHORNE, DESIGN AND ANALYSIS OF EXPERIMENTS (1994).

SHELIA JASANOFF, SCIENCE AT THE BAR: LAW, SCIENCE, AND TECHNOLOGY IN AMERICA (1995).

GEORGE F. KNELLER, SCIENCE AS A HUMAN ENDEAVOR (1978).

THOMAS S. KUHN, THE STRUCTURE OF SCIENTIFIC REVOLUTIONS (2d ed., 1970).

GERHARD LANG & GEORGE D. HEISS, A PRACTICAL GUIDE TO RESEARCH METHODS (3d ed., 1984).

CHARLES LIPSON & NARENDRA J. SHETH, STATISTICAL DESIGN AND ANALYSIS OF ENGINEERING EXPERIMENTS (1973).

EMILE MEYERSON, EXPLANATION IN THE SCIENCES (Mary–Alice & David A. Sipfle transl., 1991).

JOHN STUART MILL, PHILOSOPHY OF SCIENTIFIC METHOD (Ernest Nagel ed., 1950).

OBSERVATION, EXPERIMENT, AND HYPOTHESIS IN MODERN PHYSICAL SCIENCE (Peter Achinstein & Owen Hannaway eds., 1985).

ANTHONY O'HEAR, INTRODUCTION TO THE PHILOSOPHY OF SCIENCE (1989).

KARL R. POPPER, CONJECTURES AND REFUTATIONS: THE GROWTH OF SCENTIFIC KNOWLEDGE (2d ed., 1965).

KARL R. POPPER, THE LOGIC OF SCIENTIFIC DISCOVERY (3d ed. rev., 1968).

QUALITATIVE AND QUANTITATIVE METHODS IN EVALUATION RESEARCH (Thomas D. Cook & Charles S. Reichardt eds., 1979).

ARTHUR NEWELL STRAHLER, UNDERSTANDING SCIENCE: AN INTRODUCTION TO CONCEPTS AND ISSUES (1992).

WILLIAM A. WALLACE, CAUSALITY AND SCIENTIFIC EXPLANATION (1985).

WALTER B. WEIMER, NOTES ON THE METHODOLOGY OF SCIENTIFIC RESEARCH (1979).

WILLIAM R. SHADISH, THOMAS D. COOK & DONALD T. CAMPBELL, EXPERIMENTAL AND QUASI-EXPERIMENTAL DESIGNS: FOR GENERALIZED CAUSAL INFERENCE (2002).

CHAPTER 5

STATISTICAL PROOF*

by

David H. Kaye** & David A. Freedman***

Table of Sections

A. LEGAL ISSUES

B. SCIENTIFIC STATUS

* This chapter is a revised version of David H. Kaye & David A. Freedman, *Reference on Statistics, in* REFERENCE MANUAL ON SCIENTIFIC EVIDENCE 83 (Federal Judicial Center, 2d ed. 2000).

** David H. Kaye is Regents' Professor, Arizona State University College of Law, Tempe, Arizona, and Fellow, ASU Center for the Study of Law, Science, and Technology. He has writ-

ten extensively on the application of probability and statistics to litigation and legal theory.

*** David A. Freedman is Professor of Statistics, University of California, Berkeley, California. He is the author of many works on probability theory and statistics, including a widely used elementary textbook. He is a member of the American Academy of Arts and Sciences.

Westlaw Electronic Research

See Westlaw Electronic Research Guide preceding the Summary of Contents.

A. LEGAL ISSUES

§ 5–1.0 THE LEGAL RELEVANCE OF STATISTICAL STUDIES

§ 5–1.1 Introduction

Statistical assessments are prominent in many kinds of cases, ranging from antitrust to voting rights. Statistical reasoning can be crucial to the interpretation of psychological tests, toxicological and epidemiological studies, disparate treatment of employees, and DNA fingerprinting; this list could easily be extended.[1]

---

§ 5–1.0

1. *See generally* STATISTICS AND THE LAW (Morris H. DeGroot et al. eds., 1986); PANEL ON STATISTICAL ASSESSMENTS AS EVIDENCE IN THE COURTS, NATIONAL RESEARCH COUNCIL, THE EVOLVING ROLE OF STATISTICAL ASSESSMENTS AS EVIDENCE IN THE COURTS (Stephen E. Fienberg ed., 1989) [hereinafter THE EVOLVING ROLE OF STATISTICAL

This chapter describes the elements of statistical thinking and the law governing the use of statistics in court. We hope that the explanations will permit judges and lawyers who deal with statistical evidence to understand the terminology, place the evidence in context, appreciate its strengths and weaknesses, and apply legal doctrine governing the use of such evidence. The chapter is organized as follows:

• This section 5–1.0 provides an overview of the field, discusses the admissibility of statistical studies, and offers some suggestions about procedures that encourage the best use of statistical expertise in litigation.

• Section 5–2.0 addresses data collection. The design of a study is the most important determinant of its quality. The section reviews controlled experiments, observational studies, and surveys, indicating when the various designs are likely to give useful results.

• Section 5–3.0 discusses the art of describing and summarizing data. The section considers the mean, median, and standard deviation. These are the basic descriptive statistics, and most statistical analyses seen in court use them as building blocks. Section 5–2.2 also discusses trends and associations in data, as summarized by graphs, percentages, and tables.

• Section 5–4.0 describes the logic of statistical inference, emphasizing its foundations and limitations. In particular, this section explains statistical estimation, standard errors, confidence intervals, p-values, and hypothesis tests.

• Section 5–5.0 shows how relationships between two variables can be described by scatter diagrams, correlation coefficients, and regression lines. Statisticians often use regression in an attempt to infer causation from association; § 5–5.4 briefly explains the techniques and some of their limitations.[2]

• An appendix presents certain technical details, and the glossary defines many statistical terms that might be encountered in litigation.

§ 5–1.2 Admissibility and Weight of Statistical Studies

To be admissible, statistical studies must use methods that meet the jurisdiction's special standard for the admissibility of scientific expert testimony[3]—typically, the "scientific knowledge" requirement articulated in *Daubert v. Merrell Dow Pharmaceuticals, Inc.*,[4] or the "general acceptance" requirement of *Frye v. United States*.[5] In addition, in many jurisdictions studies must be developed and implemented with the "intellectual rigor" required by *Kumho Tire Co., Ltd. v. Carmichael*[6] of all expert testimony.[7] Finally, the

ASSESSMENTS]; Michael O. Finkelstein & Bruce Levin, STATISTICS FOR LAWYERS (2d ed. 2001); 1 & 2 JOSEPH L. GASTWIRTH, STATISTICAL REASONING IN LAW AND PUBLIC POLICY (1988); HANS ZEISEL & DAVID KAYE, PROVE IT WITH FIGURES: EMPIRICAL METHODS IN LAW AND LITIGATION (1997).

2. For an in-depth review of multiple regression analysis, *see* DAVID L. FAIGMAN, DAVID H. KAYE, MICHAEL J. SAKS & JOSEPH SANDERS, MODERN SCIENTIFIC EVIDENCE: THE LAW AND SCIENCE OF EXPERT TESTIMONY, Chapter 6 (2d ed. 2002).

3. *See supra* Chapter 1.

4. 509 U.S. 579, 589–90, 113 S.Ct. 2786, 125 L.Ed.2d 469 (1993).

5. 293 F. 1013 (D.C.Cir.1923).

6. 526 U.S. 137, 119 S.Ct. 1167, 143 L.Ed.2d 238 (1999).

7. *Id.* at 152 (requiring trial courts "to make certain that an expert, whether basing testimony upon professional studies or personal experience, employs in the courtroom the same level of intellectual rigor that characterizes the practice of an expert in the relevant

study must possess sufficient probative value to warrant admission in light of the confusion that it could engender and the time that it could consume.[8] Thus, the fact that a statistical procedure is commonly used by statisticians or other experts is not sufficient.[9] A study might use a well-established method, but be so poorly executed that it should be inadmissible. The method, while suitable in some contexts, could be inappropriate for the problem at hand and thus lack the "fit" spoken of in *Daubert*.[10] The study might rest on data of the type not reasonably relied on by statisticians or substantive experts, and hence run afoul of Rule 703.[11]

For many years, however, statistical testimony was admitted solely under the broad principles of relevance applicable to expert testimony generally. That is, the evidence had to be relevant and not too prejudicial or time-consuming. In addition, it had to deal with matters comprehensible to ordinary jurors only with the assistance of an expert; or under a more liberal standard, it had to offer knowledge that would assist the jury in resolving factual questions.[12] Under this classical approach, some statistical assessments fared well, while others encountered more judicial resistance.[13]

Even when special demands came to be imposed on other scientific evidence, the courts generally continued to apply only the classical relevance-and-expertise standards to statistical testimony.[14] Traditionally, the general-acceptance requirement simply was not perceived as a barrier to statistical testimony.[15] Starting in the 1970s, parties in employment discrimination cases

field."); *cf.* Sheehan v. Daily Racing Form, Inc., 104 F.3d 940, 942 (7th Cir.1997) ("failure to exercise the degree of care that a statistician would use in his scientific work, outside of the context of litigation" renders analysis inadmissible under *Daubert*).

8. *See* FED. R. EVID. 403. The hearsay rule rarely is a serious barrier to the presentation of statistical studies, since such studies may be offered to explain the basis for an expert's opinion or may be admissible under the learned treatise exception to the hearsay rule. *See generally* 2 MCCORMICK ON EVIDENCE §§ 321, 324.3 (John Strong ed., 5th ed. 1999). Studies published by government agencies also may be admissible as public records. *Id.* § 296; United States v. Esquivel, 88 F.3d 722, 727 (9th Cir. 1996) (taking judicial notice of 1990 census data showing the number of Hispanics eligible for jury service). Opinion surveys raise additional hearsay issues. *See infra* note 30.

9. For example, courts have described regression analysis as "a mainstream tool in economic study." In re Industrial Silicon Antitrust Litig., 1998 WL 1031507, at *2 (W.D.Pa. 1998); *see also* City of Tuscaloosa v. Harcros Chemicals, 158 F.3d 548, 565 (11th Cir.1998) (noting that multiple regression analysis is a methodology that is well-established as reliable); In re Polypropylene Carpet Antitrust Litig., 93 F.Supp.2d 1348 (N.D.Ga.2000) ("[e]conomists frequently look to regression models to explain changes in prices"). These observations may be correct, but they do not imply that every use of regression is reliable and admissible.

10. 509 U.S. at 591; *cf.* People Who Care v. Rockford Bd. of Educ., 111 F.3d 528, 537–38 (7th Cir.1997) ("a statistical study that fails to correct for salient explanatory variables, or even to make the most elementary comparisons, has no value as causal explanation and is therefore inadmissible in a federal court"); *Sheehan*, 104 F.3d at 942 (holding that expert's "failure to correct for any potential explanatory variables other than age" made the analyst's finding that "there was a significant correlation between age and retention" inadmissible).

11. Even if the study is admitted despite its flaws, similar criticisms can be used at trial to attack the weight or sufficiency of the statistical work.

12. *See, e.g.,* 1 MCCORMICK, *supra* note 8, § 13, at 38–39.

13. *Compare* Robinson v. Mandell, 20 F.Cas. 1027 (C.C.D.Mass.1868) (discussed in Paul Meier & Sandy Zabell, *Benjamin Pierce and the Howland Will*, 75 J. AM. STAT. ASS'N 497, 499 (1980)), *with* People v. Risley, 214 N.Y. 75, 108 N.E. 200 (N.Y. 1915).

14. This observation is developed more fully in D.H. Kaye, *The Dynamics of* Daubert: *Methodology, Conclusions, and Fit in Statistical and Econometric Studies*, VA. L. REV. (forthcoming).

15. *See, e.g.,* THE EVOLVING ROLE OF STATISTICAL ASSESSMENTS, *supra* note 1, at 220 (citing *Symposium on Science and the Rules of Evi-*

brought under Title VII of the Civil Rights Act of 1964 began to make extensive use of statistical expertise.[16] Early cases involved simple comparisons of proportions,[17] but as "the floodgates ... opened,"[18] more complicated studies were introduced.[19] Courts discussed standard deviations, correlation coefficients, significance levels, hypothesis tests, Mantel–Haenszel tests, scattergrams, nonlinear regressions, and reverse regressions. Judges decided issues such as whether a study that fails to show a disparity that is significant at the 5% level could create a prima facie case of disparate impact,[20] or whether a study that does show a significant difference in salaries but omits certain variables "must be considered unacceptable as evidence of discrimination."[21] However, the opinions and arguments in these cases almost never questioned the admissibility of the evidence.[22]

After criticism in the 1970s of "junk science" used to prove causation in toxic-tort cases, the courts began to apply the general acceptance and reliability standards to statistical and epidemiological testimony.[23] In parentage proceedings, courts initially questioned the general acceptance of serological methods,[24] and for many years blood group typing was admissible to exclude an alleged father but not to establish paternity.[25] As the number and power of genetic tests that could be applied to determine parentage grew, the traditional rule began to crumble under the weight of cases[26] and specialized statutes.[27]

dence, 99 F.R.D. 188 (William A. Thomas ed., 1983), for the view that "the *Frye* doctrine ... will almost never limit a statistical expert even if his or her particular statistical theories or methods of analysis are not generally accepted").

16. *See* THE EVOLVING ROLE OF STATISTICAL ASSESSMENTS, *supra* note 1, at 103.

17. *E.g.*, Washington v. Davis, 426 U.S. 229, 96 S.Ct. 2040, 48 L.Ed.2d 597 (1976) (disparate impact of civil service test on African–Americans seeking jobs as police officers); Griggs v. Duke Power Co., 401 U.S. 424, 91 S.Ct. 849, 28 L.Ed.2d 158 (1971) (disparate impact on African–Americans of high school diploma requirement and employment test).

18. THE EVOLVING ROLE OF STATISTICAL ASSESSMENTS, *supra* note 1, at 93.

19. *Id.* at 94–102 (describing cases involving and arguments over multiple and logistical regressions). Statistical studies played an important part in Title VII litigation (and in paving the way for the use of statistical expertise in other types of litigation) for a variety of reasons. *See id.* at 102.

20. *See, e.g.*, Segar v. Smith, 738 F.2d 1249 (D.C.Cir.1984).

21. Bazemore v. Friday, 751 F.2d 662, 672 (4th Cir.1984), *rev'd*, 478 U.S. 385, 106 S.Ct. 3000, 92 L.Ed.2d 315 (1986).

22. *Bazemore* is a rare case in which the Supreme Court spoke in terms of admissibility of a study said to omit important variables. But the Court did not ask whether the regression conformed to standard statistical practice. Instead, it remarked that a "plaintiff in a

Title VII suit need not prove discrimination with scientific certainty," 478 U.S. at 400, and it alluded to the broad principles of relevancy codified in Rules 401 and 403, explaining that "[n]ormally, failure to include variables will affect the analysis' probativeness, not its admissibility." *Id.* An accompanying footnote indicates that to be inadmissible for lack of probative value, a regression would have be grossly inadequate. *Id.* at 400 n.10 ("There may, of course, be some regressions so incomplete as to be inadmissible as irrelevant; but such was clearly not the case here.").

23. *See* David Bernstein, Frye, Frye, *Again: The Past, Present, and Future of the General Acceptance Test*, 41 JURIMETRICS J. 385 (2001). Cases involving the drug Bendectin were prominent in this development. *See* MICHAEL D. GREEN, BENDECTIN AND BIRTH DEFECTS: THE CHALLENGES OF MASS TOXIC SUBSTANCES LITIGATION (1996); JOSEPH SANDERS, BENDECTIN ON TRIAL: A STUDY OF MASS TORT LITIGATION (1998).

24. *See, e.g.*, Huntingdon v. Crowley, 64 Cal.2d 647, 51 Cal.Rptr. 254, 414 P.2d 382 (Cal. 1966) (lack of general acceptance justified exclusion); State v. Damm, 62 S.D. 123, 252 N.W. 7, 12 (S.D. 1933) (same).

25. *See infra* § 26–1.

26. *See* Ira Ellman & David Kaye, *Probabilities and Proof: Can HLA and Blood Group Testing Prove Paternity?*, 54 NYU L. REV. 1131 (1979).

27. *See* D.H. Kaye & Ronald Kanwischer, *Admissibility of Genetic Testing in Paternity Litigation: A Survey of State Statutes*, 22 FAM. L.Q. 109 (1988).

Laboratories usually accompanied their inclusionary findings with impressive "probabilities of paternity"—statistics that went largely unchallenged. Eventually, some courts restricted the practice,[28] but the basis was the normal balancing of probative value and prejudicial effect rather than general acceptance.

Similarly, "[n]ot so long ago, the courts refused to admit either survey or sampling evidence."[29] Public opinion was not established through systematic polls, but through the testimony of representatives of the public itself—what the law called "public witnesses."[30] In categorically rejecting survey and sampling evidence, courts rarely mentioned *Frye* or any other specialized standards for scientific evidence.[31]

In criminal cases, the courts have been skeptical of efforts to assign numerical probabilities to events, and often rightly so. Once again, the courts relied on the usual principles of relevance rather than the general-acceptance or other special standards for scientific evidence.[32] Recent DNA cases stand out as the only instance in which courts in *Frye* jurisdictions have responded to criminal "probability evidence" with a *Frye* analysis.[33]

With the advent of *Daubert v. Merrell Dow Pharmaceuticals, Inc.*,[34] the situation has changed. Litigators once concentrated on the weight that a judge

---

28. *See, e.g.*, Plemel v. Walter, 303 Or. 262, 735 P.2d 1209 (Or. 1987) (discussed in D.H. Kaye, Plemel *as a Primer on Proving Paternity*, 24 WILLAMETTE L.J. 867 (1988)); *see also* D.H. Kaye, *The Probability of an Ultimate Issue: The Strange Cases of Paternity Testing*, 75 IOWA L. REV. 75 (1989).

29. ZEISEL & KAYE, *supra* note 1, gives the following example:

> That attitude led to monstrosities such as *James S. Kirk & Co. v. Federal Trade Commission*[, 59 F.2d 179 (7th Cir.1932)], in which the manufacturer's claim that a soap was based on olive oil was challenged. This earth-shaking issue brought an administrative law judge to Seattle, Washington, where he heard, one by one, the testimony of 700 women as to their understanding of the manufacturer's message.

Id. at 101.

30. *Id.* Historically, hearsay has been the major objection to survey evidence. In most large surveys, many persons are employed to do the interviewing or other forms of data collection. Furthermore, when opinion polls are in issue, the individuals whose opinions were sampled are not testifying in court. Various arguments to circumvent or overcome the hearsay rule have been used by courts electing to receive the evidence. *See, e.g.*, Schering Corp. v. Pfizer Inc., 189 F.3d 218 (2d Cir.1999) (analyzing state-of-mind and residual exceptions); Texas Aeronautics Comm'n v. Braniff Airways, Inc., 454 S.W.2d 199, 203 (Tex.1970) ("admissible whether it is considered to be nonhearsay or within the state of mind exception to the hearsay rule"); Hans Zeisel, *The*

Uniqueness of Survey Evidence, 45 CORNELL L.Q. 322 (1960).

31. *See, e.g.*, Irvin v. State, 66 So.2d 288 (Fla.1953), *cert. denied*, 346 U.S. 927, 74 S.Ct. 316, 98 L.Ed. 419 (1954). Modern courts are more hospitable to survey evidence. *See, e.g.*, Schering Corp. v. Pfizer Inc., 189 F.3d 218; Susan J. Becker, *Public Opinion Polls and Surveys as Evidence: Suggestions for Resolving Confusing and Conflicting Standards Governing Weight and Admissibility*, 70 OR. L. REV. 463 (1991); 1 MCCORMICK ON EVIDENCE, *supra* note 8, § 208. However, the transformation has been traced to developments such as special statutes admitting Census Bureau reports based on sampling, Judge Wyzanski's *sua sponte* use of sampling in *United States v. United Shoe Machinery Corp.*, 110 F.Supp. 295 (D.Mass.1953), and an Advisory Committee Note to the Federal Rules of Evidence that (without mentioning *Frye*) speaks approvingly of expert opinions based on sampling. *See* ZEISEL & KAYE, *supra* note 1, at 101.

32. *See, e.g.*, People v. Collins, 68 Cal.2d 319, 66 Cal.Rptr. 497, 438 P.2d 33 (Cal. 1968) (speculative calculations of the probability of randomly finding a couple with unusual characteristics); State v. Garrison, 120 Ariz. 255, 585 P.2d 563 (Ariz. 1978) (bite marks); State v. Joon Kyu Kim, 398 N.W.2d 544 (Minn.1987) (ABO and PGM typing); 1 MCCORMICK, *supra* note 8, § 210.

33. *See, e.g.*, People v. Soto, 21 Cal.4th 512, 88 Cal.Rptr.2d 34, 981 P.2d 958 (Cal. 1999); People v. Venegas, 18 Cal.4th 47, 74 Cal. Rptr.2d 262, 954 P.2d 525 (Cal. 1998).

34. 509 U.S. 579, 113 S.Ct. 2786, 125 L.Ed.2d 469 (1993).

or jury might place on testimony about probability and statistics; now the admissibility of such testimony is often challenged. Pitched battles, in the form of *"Daubert* motions" to exclude statistical studies have become commonplace.[35]

§ 5–1.3 Varieties and Limits of Statistical Expertise

For convenience, the field of statistics may be divided into three subfields: probability, theoretical statistics, and applied statistics. Theoretical statistics is the study of the mathematical properties of statistical procedures, such as error rates; probability theory plays a key role in this endeavor. Results may be used by applied statisticians who specialize in particular types of data collection, such as survey research, or in particular types of analysis, such as multivariate methods.

Statistical expertise is not confined to those with degrees in statistics. Because statistical reasoning underlies all empirical research, researchers in many fields are exposed to statistical ideas. Experts with advanced degrees in the physical, medical, and social sciences—and some of the humanities—may receive formal training in statistics. Such specializations as biostatistics, epidemiology, econometrics, and psychometrics are primarily statistical, with an emphasis on methods and problems most important to the related substantive discipline.

Individuals who specialize in using statistical methods—and whose professional careers demonstrate this orientation—are more likely to apply appropriate procedures and correctly interpret the results. On the other hand, forensic scientists and technicians often testify to probabilities or statistics derived from studies or databases compiled by others, even though some of these testifying experts lack the training or knowledge required to understand and apply the information. *State v. Garrison*[36] illustrates the problem. In a murder prosecution involving bite mark evidence, a dentist was allowed to testify that "the probability factor of two sets of teeth being identical in a case similar to this is, approximately, eight in one million," even though "he was

35. *See, e.g.,* Munoz v. Orr, 200 F.3d 291 (5th Cir.2000) (plaintiffs' expert's statistical analysis properly excluded as unreliable under *Daubert* for problems ranging "from particular miscalculations to his general approach to the analysis" including tables that did not add to anywhere near 100%, failure to do regression and thereby account for pertinent variables); *In re* Polypropylene Carpet Antitrust Litig., 2000–2 Trade Cases ¶ 72,982 (N.D.Ga. Apr.27, 2000) (denying motion to permit interlocutory review of pretrial ruling to admit economist's testimony about prices based on regression said to omit an important variable); Johnson Elec. N.A., Inc. v. Mabuchi Motor America Corp., 103 F. Supp.2d 268 (S.D.N.Y.2000) (invoking *Daubert, Joiner,* and *Kumho* to exclude a "speculative" and "preposterous" econometric model for estimating demand in a patent infringement case "despite its dazzling sheen of erudition and meticulous methodology"); Allapattah Services, Inc. v. Exxon Corp., 61 F. Supp. 2d 1335 (S.D.Fla.1999) (admitting econo-

metric testimony under modified *Daubert* analysis); *In re* Industrial Silicon Antitrust Litig., 1998 WL 1031507 (W.D.Pa.1998) ("before-and-after" regression satisfies *Daubert* and *Bazemore*); Estate of Bud Hill v. ConAgra Poultry Co., 1997 WL 538887 (N.D.Ga.1997) (denying motion to exclude economist's regression study to determine whether chickens were misweighed); Diehl v. Xerox Corp., 933 F.Supp. 1157 (W.D.N.Y.1996) (denying motion to exclude simple comparisons rather than regressions to show disparate impact in layoffs of workers); Newport Ltd. v. Sears, Roebuck & Co, 1995 WL 328158 (E.D.La.1995) (denying *Daubert* motion to exclude calculations of lost profits involving "the absorption rate for industrial park property" based on multiple regression model because regression in general and as used to estimated lost profits in other contexts is accepted and valid).

36. 120 Ariz. 255, 585 P.2d 563 (Ariz. 1978).

unaware of the formula utilized to arrive at that figure other than that it was 'computerized.' "[37]

At the same time, the choice of which data to examine, or how best to model a particular process, could require subject matter expertise that a statistician might lack. Statisticians often advise experts in substantive fields on the procedures for collecting data and not infrequently analyze data collected by others. As a result, cases involving statistical evidence often are (or should be) "two-expert" cases of interlocking testimony.[38] A labor economist, for example, may supply a definition of the relevant labor market from which an employer draws its employees, and the statistical expert may contrast the racial makeup of those hired to the racial composition of the labor market. Naturally, the value of the statistical analysis depends on the substantive economic knowledge that informs it.[39]

§ 5–1.4   Procedures That Enhance Statistical Testimony

§ 5–1.4.1   Maintaining Professional Autonomy

Ideally, experts who conduct research in the context of litigation should proceed with the same objectivity that they would apply in other contexts. Thus, experts who testify (or who supply results that are used in testimony by others) should be free to do whatever analysis is required to address in a professionally responsible fashion the issues posed by the litigation.[40] Questions about the freedom of inquiry accorded to testifying experts, as well as the scope and depth of their investigations, may reveal some of the limitations to the analysis being presented.

§ 5–1.4.2   Disclosing Other Analyses

Statisticians analyze data using a variety of statistical models and methods. There is much to be said for looking at the data in a variety of ways. To permit a fair evaluation of the analysis that the statistician does settle on, however, the testifying expert may explain the history behind the development of the final statistical approach.[41] Indeed, some commentators have

---

37. *Id.* at 566 & 568.

38. Sometimes a single witness presents both the substantive underpinnings and the statistical analysis. Ideally, such a witness has extensive expertise in both fields, although less may suffice to qualify the witness under Fed. R. Evid. 702. In deciding whether a witness who clearly is qualified in one field may testify in a related area, courts should recognize that qualifications in one field do not necessarily imply qualifications in the other.

39. In *Vuyanich v. Republic National Bank*, 505 F.Supp. 224, 319 (N.D.Tex.1980), *vacated*, 723 F.2d 1195 (5th Cir.1984), defendant's statistical expert criticized the plaintiffs' statistical model for an implicit, but restrictive, assumption about male and female salaries. The district court trying the case accepted the model because the plaintiffs' expert had a "very strong guess" about the assumption, and her expertise included labor economics as well as statistics. *Id.* It is doubtful, however, that eco-

nomic knowledge sheds much light on the assumption, and it would have been simple to perform a less restrictive analysis. In this case, the court may have been overly impressed with a single expert who combined substantive and statistical expertise. Once the issue is defined by legal and substantive knowledge, some aspects of the statistical analysis will turn on statistical considerations alone, and expertise in another subject will not be pertinent.

40. *See* THE EVOLVING ROLE OF STATISTICAL ASSESSMENTS, *supra* note 1, at 164 (recommending that the expert be free to consult with colleagues who have not been retained by any party to the litigation and that the expert receive a letter of engagement providing for these and other safeguards).

41. *See, e.g.*, Mikel Aickin, *Issues and Methods in Discrimination Statistics, in* STATISTICAL METHODS IN DISCRIMINATION LITIGATION 159 (D. H. Kaye & Mikel Aickin eds., 1986).

urged that counsel who know of other data sets or analyses that do not support the client's position should reveal this fact to the court, rather than attempt to mislead the court by presenting only favorable results.[42]

§ 5–1.4.3 Disclosing Data and Analytical Methods Before Trial

The collection of data often is expensive, and data sets typically contain at least some minor errors or omissions. Careful exploration of alternative modes of analysis also can be expensive and time consuming. To minimize the occurrence of distracting debates at trial over the accuracy of data and the choice of analytical techniques, and to permit informed expert discussions of method, pretrial procedures should be used, particularly with respect to the accuracy and scope of the data, and to discover the methods of analysis. Suggested procedures along these lines are available elsewhere.[43]

§ 5–1.4.4 Presenting Expert Statistical Testimony

The most common format for the presentation of evidence at trial is sequential. The plaintiff's witnesses are called first, one by one, without interruption except for cross-examination, and testimony is in response to specific questions rather than by an extended narration. Although traditional, this structure is not compelled by the Federal Rules of Evidence.[44] Some alternatives have been proposed that might be more effective in cases involving substantial statistical testimony. For example, when the reports of witnesses go together, the judge might allow their presentations to be combined and the witnesses to be questioned as a panel rather than sequentially. More narrative testimony might be allowed, and the expert might be permitted to give a brief tutorial on statistics as a preliminary to some testimony. Instead of allowing the parties to present their experts in the midst of all the other evidence, the judge might call for the experts for opposing sides to testify at about the same time. Some courts, particularly in bench trials, may have both experts placed under oath and, in effect, permit them to engage in a dialogue. In such a format, experts are able to say whether they agree or disagree on specific issues. The judge and counsel can interject questions. Such practices may improve the judge's understanding and reduce the tensions associated with the experts' adversarial role.[45]

---

42. THE EVOLVING ROLE OF STATISTICAL ASSESSMENTS, *supra* note 1, at 167; *cf.* William W Schwarzer, *In Defense of "Automatic Disclosure in Discovery,"* 27 GA. L. REV. 655, 658–59 (1993) ("[T]he lawyer owes a duty to the court to make disclosure of core information."). The Panel on Statistical Assessments as Evidence in the Courts also recommends that "if a party gives statistical data to different experts for competing analyses, that fact be disclosed to the testifying expert, if any." THE EVOLVING ROLE OF STATISTICAL ASSESSMENTS, *supra*, at 167. Whether and under what circumstances a particular statistical analysis might be so imbued with counsel's thoughts and theories of the case that it should receive protection as the attorney's work product is an issue beyond the scope of this chapter.

43. *See* The Special Comm. on Empirical Data in Legal Decision Making, Recommendations on Pretrial Proceedings in Cases with Voluminous Data, *reprinted in* THE EVOLVING ROLE OF STATISTICAL ASSESSMENTS, *supra* note 1, app. F; *see also* David H. Kaye, *Improving Legal Statistics*, 24 LAW & SOC'Y REV. 1255 (1990).

44. *See* FED. R. EVID. 611.

45. THE EVOLVING ROLE OF STATISTICAL ASSESSMENTS, *supra* note 1, at 174.

B. SCIENTIFIC STATUS

§ 5–2.0 HOW HAVE THE DATA BEEN COLLECTED?

Statistics, broadly defined, is the art and science of gaining information from data. For statistical purposes, data mean observations or measurements, expressed as numbers. A statistic may refer to a particular numerical value, derived from the data. Baseball statistics, for example, is the study of data about the game; a player's batting average is a statistic. The field of statistics includes methods for (1) collecting data, (2) analyzing data, and (3) drawing inferences from data. To ascertain the probative value of a statistical study, each of these aspects must be considered.

An analysis is only as good as the data on which it rests.[1] To a large extent, the design of a study determines the quality of the data. Therefore, the proper interpretation of data and their implications begins with an understanding of study design. Different designs help answer different questions. In many cases, statistics are introduced to show causation. Would additional information in a securities prospectus disclosure have caused potential investors to behave in some other way? Does capital punishment deter crime? Do food additives cause cancer? The design of studies intended to prove causation is the first and perhaps the most important topic of this section.

Another issue is the use of sample data to characterize a population: the population is the whole class of units that are of interest; the sample is a set of units chosen for detailed study. Inferences from the part to the whole are justified only when the sample is representative, and that is the second topic of this section.

Finally, it is important to verify the accuracy of the data collection. Errors can arise in the process of making and recording measurements on individual units. This aspect of data quality is the third topic in this section.

§ 5–2.1 Is the Study Properly Designed to Investigate Causation?

§ 5–2.1.1 Types of Studies

When causation is at issue, advocates have relied on three major types of information: anecdotal evidence, observational studies, and controlled experiments.[2] As we shall see, anecdotal reports can provide some information, but

---

§ 5–2.0

1. For introductory treatments of data collection, see, *e.g.*, DAVID FREEDMAN ET AL., STATISTICS (3d ed. 1998); DARRELL HUFF, HOW TO LIE WITH STATISTICS (1954); DAVID S. MOORE, STATISTICS: CONCEPTS AND CONTROVERSIES (3d ed. 1991); HANS ZEISEL, SAY IT WITH FIGURES (6th ed. 1985); and HANS ZEISEL & DAVID KAYE, PROVE IT WITH FIGURES: EMPIRICAL METHODS IN LAW AND LITIGATION (1997).

2. When relevant studies exist before the commencement of the litigation, it becomes the task of the lawyer and appropriate experts to explain this research to the court. One example of such "off-the-shelf" research are experiments pinpointing conditions under which eyewitnesses tend to err in identifying criminals

and studies of how sex stereotyping affects perceptions of women in the workplace. *See, e.g.*, State v. Chapple, 135 Ariz. 281, 660 P.2d 1208, 1223–24 (Ariz. 1983) (reversing a conviction for excluding expert testimony about scientific research on eyewitness accuracy); Price Waterhouse v. Hopkins, 490 U.S. 228, 235, 109 S.Ct. 1775, 104 L.Ed.2d 268 (1989). Some psychologists have questioned the applicability of these experiments to litigation. *See, e.g.*, Gerald V. Barrett & Scott B. Morris, *The American Psychological Association's Amicus Curiae Brief in* Price Waterhouse v. Hopkins: *The Values of Science Versus the Values of the Law*, 17 Law & Hum. Behav. 201 (1993). For a rejoinder, see Susan T. Fiske et al., *What Constitutes a Scientific Review?: A Majority Retort*

they are more useful as a stimulus for further inquiry than as a basis for establishing association or causation. Observational studies can establish that one factor is associated with another,[3] but considerable analysis may be necessary to bridge the gap from association to causation. Controlled experiments are ideal for ascertaining causation, but they can be difficult to undertake.

"Anecdotal evidence" means reports of one kind of event following another. Typically, the reports are obtained haphazardly or selectively, and the logic of "post hoc, ergo propter hoc" does not suffice to demonstrate that the first event causes the second. Consequently, while anecdotal evidence can be suggestive,[4] it can also be quite misleading.[5] For instance, some children who live near power lines develop leukemia; but does exposure to electrical and magnetic fields cause this disease? The anecdotal evidence is not compelling because leukemia also occurs among children who have minimal exposure to such fields.[6] It is necessary to compare disease rates among those who are exposed and those who are not. If exposure causes the disease, the rate should be higher among the exposed, lower among the unexposed. Of course, the two groups may differ in crucial ways other than the exposure. For example, children who live near power lines could come from poorer families and be exposed to other environmental hazards. Such differences could create the

to Barrett and Morris, 17 LAW & HUM. BEHAV. 217 (1993).

If no preexisting studies are available, a case-specific one may be devised. E.g., United States v. Youritan Constr. Co., 370 F.Supp. 643, 647 (N.D.Cal.1973) (investigating racial discrimination in the rental-housing market by using "testers"—who should differ only in their race—to rent a property), aff'd in part, 509 F.2d 623 (9th Cir.1975). For a critical review of studies using testers, see James J. Heckman & Peter Siegelman, The Urban Institute Audit Studies: Their Methods and Findings, in CLEAR AND CONVINCING EVIDENCE: MEASUREMENT OF DISCRIMINATION IN AMERICA 187 (Michael Fix & Raymond J. Struyk eds., 1993) (including commentary).

3. For example, smokers have higher rates of lung cancer than nonsmokers; thus, smoking and lung cancer are associated.

4. In medicine, evidence from clinical practice is often the starting point for the demonstration of a causal effect. One famous example involves exposure of mothers to German measles during pregnancy, followed by blindness in their babies. N. McAlister Gregg, Congenital Cataract Following German Measles in the Mother, 3 TRANSACTIONS OPHTHALMOLOGICAL SOC'Y AUSTL. 35 (1941), reprinted in THE CHALLENGE OF EPIDEMIOLOGY 426 (Carol Buck et al. eds., 1988).

5. Indeed, some courts have suggested that attempts to infer causation from anecdotal reports are inadmissible as unsound methodology under Daubert v. Merrell Dow Pharmaceuticals, Inc., 509 U.S. 579, 113 S.Ct. 2786, 125 L.Ed.2d 469 (1993). See, e.g., Glastetter v. Novartis Pharms. Corp., 252 F.3d 986 (8th Cir. 2001) ("Though case reports demonstrate a

temporal association between Parlodel and stroke, or stroke-precursors, that association is not scientifically valid proof of causation."); Haggerty v. Upjohn Co., 950 F.Supp. 1160, 1163–64 (S.D.Fla.1996) (holding that reports to the Food and Drug Administration of "adverse medical events" involving the drug Halcion and "anecdotal case reports appearing in medical literature ... can be used to generate hypotheses about causation, but not causation conclusions" because "scientifically valid cause and effect determinations depend on controlled clinical trials and epidemiological studies"); Cartwright v. Home Depot U.S.A., Inc. 936 F.Supp. 900, 905 (M.D.Fla.1996) (excluding an expert's opinion that latex paint caused plaintiffs' asthma, in part because "case reports ... are no substitute for a scientifically designed and conducted inquiry").

6. See COMMITTEE ON THE POSSIBLE EFFECTS OF ELECTROMAGNETIC FIELDS ON BIOLOGIC SYSTEMS, NATIONAL RESEARCH COUNCIL, POSSIBLE HEALTH EFFECTS OF EXPOSURE TO RESIDENTIAL ELECTRIC AND MAGNETIC FIELDS (1997); ZEISEL & KAYE, supra note 1, at 66–67. There are serious problems in measuring exposure to electromagnetic fields, and results are somewhat inconsistent from one study to another. For such reasons, the epidemiologic evidence for an effect on health is quite inconclusive. Id.; Martha S. Linet et al., Residential Exposure to Magnetic Fields and Acute Lymphoblastic Leukemia in Children, 337 NEW ENG. J. MED. 1 (1997); Edward W. Campion, Power Lines, Cancer, and Fear, 337 NEW ENG. J. MED. 44 (1997) (editorial); Gary Taubes, Magnetic Field–Cancer Link: Will It Rest in Peace?, 277 SCIENCE 29 (1997) (quoting various epidemiologists).

appearance of a cause-and-effect relationship, or they can mask a real relationship. Cause-and-effect relationships often are quite subtle, and carefully designed studies are needed to draw valid conclusions.[7]

Typically, a well-designed study will compare outcomes for subjects who are exposed to some factor—the treatment group—and other subjects who are not so exposed—the control group. A distinction then must be made between controlled experiments and observational studies. In a controlled experiment, the investigators decide which subjects are exposed to the factor of interest and which subjects go into the control group. In most observational studies, the subjects themselves choose their exposures. Because of this self-selection, the treatment and control groups are likely differ with respect to important factors other than the one of primary interest.[8] (These other factors are called confounding variables or lurking variables.[9]) With studies on the health effects of power lines, family background is a possible confounder; so is exposure to other hazards.[10]

§ 5–2.1.2   Randomized Controlled Experiments

In randomized controlled experiments, investigators assign subjects to treatment or control groups at random. The groups are therefore likely to be quite comparable—except for the treatment. Choosing at random tends to balance the groups with respect to possible confounders, and the effect of

7. Here is a classic example from epidemiology. At one time, it was thought that lung cancer was caused by fumes from tarring the roads, because many lung cancer patients lived near roads that had recently been tarred. This is anecdotal evidence. But the logic is incomplete, because many people without lung cancer were exposed to tar fumes. A comparison of rates is needed. Careful study showed that lung cancer patients had similar rates of exposure to tar fumes as other people; the real difference was in exposure to cigarette smoke. Richard Doll & A. Bradford Hill, *A Study of the Aetiology of Carcinoma of the Lung*, 2 British Med. J. 1271 (1952).

8. For present purposes, a variable is a numerical characteristic of units in a study. For instance, in a survey of people, the unit of analysis is the person, and variables might include income (in dollars per year) and educational level (years of schooling completed). In a study of school districts, the unit of analysis is the district, and variables might include average family income of residents and average test scores of students. When investigating a possible cause-and-effect relationship, the variable that characterizes the effect is called the dependent variable, since it may depend on the causes; dependent variables also are called response variables. In contrast, the variables that represent the causes are called independent variables; independent variables also are called factors or explanatory variables.

9. A confounding variable is related to the independent variables and to the dependent variable. If the units being studied differ on

the independent variables, they are also likely to differ on the confounder. Therefore, the confounder—not the independent variables—could be responsible for differences seen on the dependent variable.

10. Confounding is a problem even in careful epidemiologic studies. For example, women with herpes are more likely to develop cervical cancer than women who have not been exposed to the virus. It was concluded that herpes caused cancer; in other words, the association was thought to be causal. Later research suggests that herpes is only a marker of sexual activity. Women who have had multiple sexual partners are more likely to be exposed not only to herpes but also to human papilloma virus. Certain strains of papilloma virus seem to cause cervical cancer, while herpes does not. Apparently, the association between herpes and cervical cancer is not causal but is due to the effect of other variables. *See* The Epidemiology of Cervical Cancer and Human Papillomavirus (N. Muñoz et al. eds., 1992); S.A. Cannistra & J.M. Niloff, *Cancer of the Uterine Cervix*, 334 New Eng. J. Med. 1030 (1996); A. Storey et al., *Role of a p53 Polymorphism in the Development of Human Papillomavirus–Associated Cancer*, 393 Nature 229 (1998). For additional examples and discussion, see Freedman et al., *supra* note 1, at 12–27, 150–52; David Freedman, *From Association to Causation: Some Remarks on the History of Statistics*, 14 Stat. Sci. 243 (1999).

remaining imbalances can be assessed by statistical techniques.[11] Consequently, inferences based on well-executed randomized experiments are more secure than inferences based on observational studies.[12]

The following illustration brings together the points made thus far. Many doctors think that taking aspirin helps prevent heart attacks, but there is some controversy. Most people who take aspirin do not have heart attacks; this is anecdotal evidence for the protective effect, but proves very little. After all, most people do not get heart attacks—whether or not they take aspirin regularly. A careful study must compare heart attack rates for two groups: persons who take aspirin (the treatment group) and persons who do not (the controls). An observational study would be easy to do, but then the aspirin-takers are likely to be different from the controls. If, for instance, the controls are healthier to begin with, the study would be biased against the drug. Randomized experiments with aspirin are harder to do, but they provide much better evidence. It is the experiments that demonstrate a protective effect.

To summarize: First, outcome figures from a treatment group without a control group generally reveal very little and can be misleading. Comparisons are essential. Second, if the control group was obtained through random assignment before treatment, a difference in the outcomes between treatment and control groups may be accepted, within the limits of statistical error, as the true measure of the treatment effect.[13] However, if the control group was created in any other way, differences in the groups that existed before treatment may contribute to differences in the outcomes or mask differences that otherwise would be observed. Thus, observational studies succeed to the extent that their treatment and control groups are comparable—apart from the treatment.

§ 5–2.1.3   Observational Studies

The bulk of the statistical studies seen in court are observational, not experimental. Take the question of whether capital punishment deters mur-

---

11. *See infra* § 5–4.0.

12. Experiments, however, are often impractical, as in the power line example. Even when controlled experiments are feasible, true randomization can be difficult to achieve. *See, e.g.*, Kenneth F. Schulz, *Subverting Randomization in Controlled Trials*, 274 JAMA 1456 (1995); Rachel Nowak, *Problems in Clinical Trials Go Far Beyond Misconduct*, 264 SCIENCE 1538 (1994). For statistical purposes, randomization should be accomplished using some definite, objective method (like a random number generator on a computer); haphazard assignment may not be sufficient.

13. Of course, the possibility that the two groups will not be comparable in some unrecognized way can never be eliminated. Random assignment, however, allows the researcher to compute the probability of seeing a large difference in the outcomes when the treatment actually has no effect. When this probability is small, the difference in the response is said to be "statistically significant." *See infra* § 5–

4.2.2. Randomization of subjects to treatment or control groups puts statistical tests of significance on a secure footing. FREEDMAN ET AL., *supra* note 1, at 503–24, 547–78.

Even more important, randomization also ensures that the assignment of subjects to treatment and control groups is free from conscious or unconscious manipulation by investigators or subjects. Randomization may not be the only way to ensure such protection, but "it is the simplest and best understood way to certify that one has done so." Philip W. Lavori et al., *Designs for Experiments—Parallel Comparisons of Treatment, in* MEDICAL USES OF STATISTICS 61, 66 (John C. Bailar III & Frederick Mosteller eds., 2d ed. 1992). To avoid ambiguity, the researcher should be explicit "about how the randomization was done (e.g., table of random numbers) and executed (e.g., by sealed envelopes prepared in advance)." *Id.; see also* Colin Begg et al., *Improving the Quality of Reporting of Randomized Controlled Trials: The CONSORT Statement*, 276 JAMA 637 (1996).

der. To do a randomized controlled experiment, people would have to be assigned randomly to a control group and a treatment group. The controls would know that they could not receive the death penalty for murder, while those in the treatment group would know they could be executed. The rate of subsequent murders by the subjects in these groups would be observed. Such an experiment is unacceptable—politically, ethically, and legally.[14]

Nevertheless, many studies of the deterrent effect of the death penalty have been conducted, all observational, and some have attracted judicial attention.[15] Researchers have catalogued differences in the incidence of murder in states with and without the death penalty, and they have analyzed changes in homicide rates and execution rates over the years. In such observational studies, investigators may speak of control groups (such as the states without capital punishment) and of controlling for potentially confounding variables (e.g., worsening economic conditions).[16] However, association is not causation, and the causal inferences that can be drawn from such analyses rest on a less secure foundation than that provided by a randomized controlled experiment.[17]

Of course, observational studies can be very useful. The evidence that smoking causes lung cancer in humans, although largely observational, is compelling. In general, observational studies provide powerful evidence in the following circumstances:

• The association is seen in studies of different types among different groups. This reduces the chance that the observed association is due to a defect in one type of study or a peculiarity in one group of subjects.

• The association holds when the effects of plausible confounding variables are taken into account by appropriate statistical techniques, such as comparing smaller groups that are relatively homogeneous with respect to the factor.[18]

---

14. *Cf.* EXPERIMENTATION IN THE LAW: REPORT OF THE FEDERAL JUDICIAL CENTER ADVISORY COMMITTEE ON EXPERIMENTATION IN THE LAW (Federal Judicial Center 1981) [hereinafter Experimentation in the Law] (study of ethical issues raised by controlled experimentation in the evaluation of innovations in the justice system).

15. *See generally* Hans Zeisel, *The Deterrent Effect of the Death Penalty: Facts v. Faith,* 1976 SUP. CT. REV. 317.

16. A procedure often used to control for confounding in observational studies is regression analysis. The early enthusiasm for using multiple regression analysis to study the death penalty was not shared by reviewers. *Compare* Isaac Ehrlich, *The Deterrent Effect of Capital Punishment: A Question of Life and Death,* 65 AM. ECON. REV. 397 (1975), and Isaac Ehrlich, *The Deterrent Effect of Capital Punishment: Reply,* 67 AM. ECON. REV. 452 (1977), *with, e.g.,* Lawrence R. Klein et al., *The Deterrent Effect of Capital Punishment: An Assessment of the Estimates, in* PANEL ON RESEARCH ON DETERRENT AND INCAPACITATIVE EFFECTS, NATIONAL RESEARCH COUNCIL, DETERRENCE AND INCAPACITATION: ESTIMAT-

ING THE EFFECTS OF CRIMINAL SANCTIONS ON CRIME RATES 336 (Alfred Blumstein et al. eds., 1978); Edward Leamer, *Let's Take the Con Out of Econometrics,* 73 AM. ECON. REV. 31 (1983).

17. *See, e.g.,* EXPERIMENTATION IN THE LAW, *supra* note 14, at 18:

[G]roups selected without randomization will [almost] always differ in some systematic way other than exposure to the experimental program. Statistical techniques can eliminate chance as a feasible explanation for the differences, ... [b]ut without randomization there are no certain methods for determining that observed differences between groups are not related to the preexisting, systematic difference.... [C]omparison between systematically different groups will yield ambiguous implications whenever the systematic difference affords a plausible explanation for apparent effects of the experimental program.

18. The idea is to control for the influence of a confounder by making comparisons separately within groups for which the confounding variable is nearly constant and therefore has

● There is a plausible explanation for the effect of the independent variables; thus, the causal link does not depend on the observed association alone. Other explanations linking the response to confounding variables should be less plausible.[19]

When these criteria are not fulfilled, observational studies may produce legitimate disagreement among experts, and there is no mechanical procedure for ascertaining who is correct. In the end, deciding whether associations are causal is not a matter of statistics, but a matter of good scientific judgment, and the questions that should be asked with respect to data offered on the question of causation can be summarized as follows:

● Was there a control group? If not, the study has little to say about causation.

● If there was a control group, how were subjects assigned to treatment or control: through a process under the control of the investigator (a controlled experiment) or a process outside the control of the investigator (an observational study)?

● If the study was a controlled experiment, was the assignment made using a chance mechanism (randomization), or did it depend on the judgment of the investigator?

● If the data came from an observational study or a nonrandomized controlled experiment, how did the subjects come to be in treatment or in control groups? Are the groups comparable? What factors are confounded with treatment? What adjustments were made to take care of confounding? Were they sensible?[20]

§ 5–2.1.4 Can the Results Be Generalized?

Any study must be conducted on a certain group of subjects, at certain times and places, using certain treatments. With respect to these subjects, the study may be persuasive. There may be adequate control over confounding variables, and there may be an unequivocally large difference between the treatment and control groups. If so, the study's internal validity will not be disputed: for the subjects in the study, the treatment had an effect. But an

---

little influence over the variables of primary interest. For example, smokers are more likely to get lung cancer than nonsmokers. Age, gender, social class, and region of residence are all confounders, but controlling for such variables does not really change the relationship between smoking and cancer rates. Furthermore, many different studies—of different types and on different populations—confirm the causal link. That is why most experts believe that smoking causes lung cancer and many other diseases. For a review of the literature, see 38 INTERNATIONAL AGENCY FOR RESEARCH ON CANCER (IARC), WORLD HEALTH ORG., IARC MONOGRAPHS ON THE EVALUATION OF THE CARCINOGENIC RISK OF CHEMICALS TO HUMANS: TOBACCO SMOKING (1986).

19. A. Bradford Hill, *The Environment and Disease: Association or Causation?*, 58 PROC. ROYAL SOC'Y MED. 295 (1965); ALFRED S. EVANS, CAUSATION AND DISEASE: A CHRONOLOGICAL JOURNEY 187 (1993).

20. These questions are adapted from FREEDMAN ET AL., *supra* note 1, at 28. For discussions of the admissibility or weight of studies that overlook obvious possible confounders, see *People Who Care v. Rockford Board of Education*, 111 F.3d 528, 537–38 (7th Cir.1997) ("The social scientific literature on educational achievement identifies a number of other variables besides poverty and discrimination that explain differences in scholastic achievement, such as the educational attainments of the student's parents and the extent of their involvement in their children's schooling.... These variables cannot be assumed to be either randomly distributed across the different racial and ethnic groups in Rockford or perfectly correlated with poverty...."); cases cited *supra* § 5–1.2 note 10 and *infra* § 5–4.3 note 52.

issue of external validity remains. To extrapolate from the conditions of a study to more general circumstances always raises questions. For example, studies suggest that definitions of insanity given to jurors influence decisions in cases of incest;[21] would the definitions have a similar effect in cases of murder? Other studies indicate that recidivism rates for ex-convicts are not affected by temporary financial support after release.[22] Would the same results be obtained with different conditions in the labor market?

Confidence in the appropriateness of an extrapolation cannot come from the experiment itself.[23] It must come from knowledge about which outside factors would or would not affect the outcome.[24] Sometimes, several experi-

21. *See* RITA JAMES SIMON, THE JURY AND THE DEFENSE OF INSANITY 58–59 (1967).

22. For an experiment on income support and recidivism, see PETER H. ROSSI ET AL., MONEY, WORK, AND CRIME: EXPERIMENTAL EVIDENCE (1980). The interpretation of the data has proved controversial. *See* Hans Zeisel, *Disagreement over the Evaluation of a Controlled Experiment*, 88 AM. J. SOC. 378 (1982) (with commentary).

23. Suppose an epidemiologic study is conducted on the relationship between a toxic substance and a disease. The rate of occurrence of the disease in a group of persons exposed to the substance is compared to the rate in a control group, and the rate in the exposed group turns out to be more than double the rate in the control group. (More technically, the relative risk exceeds two.) Do these data imply that a plaintiff who was exposed to the toxic substance and contracted the disease probably would not have contracted the disease but for the exposure? If we assume that the substance causes the disease and all confounding has been properly accounted for (a judgment that might not be easy to defend), then we can conclude that over half the cases of disease in the exposed group would not be there but for the exposure. Applying this arithmetic to a specific person, however, is problematic. For instance, the relative risk is an average over all the subjects included in the study. The exposures and susceptibilities almost certainly are not uniform, and the plaintiff's exposure and susceptibility cannot be known from the study. Nevertheless, several courts and commentators have stated that a relative risk of more than two demonstrates specific causation, or, conversely, that a relative risk of two or less precludes a finding of specific causation. *E.g.*, DeLuca v. Merrell Dow Pharms, Inc., 911 F.2d 941, 958–59 (3d Cir. 1990); Marder v. G.D. Searle & Co., 630 F.Supp. 1087, 1092 (D.Md.1986) ("a two-fold increased risk is ... the equivalent of the required legal burden of proof—a showing of causation by the preponderance of the evidence or, in other words, a probability of greater than 50%."), *aff'd sub nom.*, Wheelahan v. G.D. Searle & Co., 814 F.2d 655 (4th Cir.1987); Bert Black & David E. Lilienfeld, *Epidemiologic Proof in Toxic Tort Litigation*, 52 FORDHAM L. REV. 732, 769 (1984); Michael D. Green et al.,

Reference Guide on Epidemiology, *in* REFERENCE MANUAL ON SCIENTIFIC EVIDENCE (Federal Judicial Center 2d ed., 1999). A few commentators have sharply criticized this reasoning. Steven E. Fienberg et al., *Understanding and Evaluating Statistical Evidence in Litigation*, 36 JURIMETRICS J. 1, 9 (1995); Diana B. Petitti, *Reference Guide on Epidemiology*, 36 JURIMETRICS J. 159, 168 (1996) (review); David A. Freedman & Phillip B. Stark, *The Swine Flu Vaccine and Guillain–Barré Syndrome: A Case Study in Relative Risk and Specific Causation*, 64 LAW & CONTEMP. PROBS. 49 (2001); James Robins & Sander Greenland, *The Probability of Causation Under a Stochastic Model for Individual Risk*, 45 BIOMETRICS 1125, 1126 (1989); Melissa Moore Thompson, Comment, *Causal Inference in Epidemiology: Implications for Toxic Tort Litigation*, 71 N.C. L. REV. 247 (1992).

24. Such judgments are easiest in the physical and life sciences, but even here, there are problems. For example, it may be difficult to infer human reactions to substances that affect animals. First, there are often inconsistencies across test species: A chemical may be carcinogenic in mice but not in rats. Extrapolation from rodents to humans is even more problematic. Second, to get measurable effects in animal experiments, chemicals are administered at very high doses. Results are extrapolated—using mathematical models—to the very low doses of concern in humans. However, there are many dose-response models to use and few grounds for choosing among them. Generally, different models produce radically different estimates of the "virtually safe dose" in humans. David A. Freedman & Hans Zeisel, *From Mouse to Man: The Quantitative Assessment of Cancer Risks*, 3 STAT. SCI. 3 (1988). For these reasons, many experts—and some courts in toxic tort cases—have concluded that evidence from animal experiments is generally insufficient by itself to establish causation. *See generally* Bruce N. Ames et al., *The Causes and Prevention of Cancer*, 92 PROC. NAT'L ACAD. SCI. USA 5258 (1995); Michael D. Green, *Expert Witnesses and Sufficiency of Evidence in Toxic Substances Litigation: The Legacy of Agent Orange and Bendectin Litigation*, 86 NW. U. L. REV. 643 (1992); Susan R. Poulter, *Science and*

ments or other studies, each having different limitations, all point in the same direction. This is the case, for example, with eight studies indicating that jurors who approve of the death penalty are more likely to convict in a capital case.[25] Such convergent results strongly suggest the validity of the generalization.

§ 5–2.2   Descriptive Censuses and Surveys

Having discussed the statistical logic of studies to investigate causation, we turn to a second topic—sampling, that is, choosing units for study. A census tries to measure some characteristic of every unit in a population of individuals or objects. A survey, alternatively, measures characteristics only in part of a population. The accuracy of the information collected in a census or survey depends on how the units are selected, which units are actually measured, and how the measurements are made.[26]

§ 5–2.2.1   What Method Is Used to Select the Units?

By definition, a census tries to measure some characteristic of every unit in a whole population. It may fall short of this goal, in which case the question must be asked whether the missing data are likely to differ in some systematic way from the data that are collected. The U.S. Bureau of the Census estimates that the past six censuses failed to count everyone, and there is evidence that the undercount is greater in certain subgroups of the population.[27] Supplemental studies may enable statisticians to adjust for such omissions, but the adjustments may rest on uncertain assumptions.[28]

Toxic Torts: Is There a Rational Solution to the Problem of Causation?, 7 HIGH TECH. L.J. 189 (1993) (epidemiological evidence on humans is needed); *see also* STEPHEN BREYER, BREAKING THE VICIOUS CIRCLE: TOWARD EFFECTIVE REGULATION (1993); COMMITTEE ON COMPARATIVE TOXICITY OF NATURALLY OCCURRING CARCINOGENS, NATIONAL RESEARCH COUNCIL, CARCINOGENS AND ANTICARCINOGENS IN THE HUMAN DIET: A COMPARISON OF NATURALLY OCCURRING AND SYNTHETIC SUBSTANCES (1996); COMMITTEE ON RISK ASSESSMENT OF HAZARDOUS AIR POLLUTANTS, NATIONAL RESEARCH COUNCIL, SCIENCE AND JUDGMENT IN RISK ASSESSMENT 59 (1994) ("There are reasons based on both biologic principles and empirical observations to support the hypothesis that many forms of biologic responses, including toxic responses, can be extrapolated across mammalian species, including *Homo sapiens*, but the scientific basis of such extrapolation is not established with sufficient rigor to allow broad and definitive generalizations to be made."). *But see infra* Chapter 34.

25. Phoebe C. Ellsworth, *Some Steps Between Attitudes and Verdicts, in* Inside the Juror 42, 46 (Reid Hastie ed., 1993). Nevertheless, in *Lockhart v. McCree*, 476 U.S. 162, 106 S.Ct. 1758, 90 L.Ed.2d 137 (1986), the Supreme Court held that the exclusion of opponents of the death penalty in the guilt phase of a capital trial does not violate the constitutional requirement of an impartial jury.

26. For more extended treatment of these issues, see *infra* Chapter 6.

27. *See generally* PETER SKERRY, COUNTING ON THE CENSUS (2000).

28. For conflicting views on proposed adjustments to the 1990 census, see the exchanges of papers at 9 STAT. SCI. 458 (1994), 18 SURV. METHODOLOGY No. 1 (1992), 39 SOCIETY 3 (2001), and 34 JURIMETRICS J. 65 (1993). In *Wisconsin v. City of New York*, 517 U.S. 1, 116 S.Ct. 1091, 134 L.Ed.2d 167 (1996), the Supreme Court resolved the conflict among the circuits over the legal standard governing claims that adjustment is compelled by statute or the Constitution. The Court unanimously determined that the exacting requirements of the equal protection clause, as explicated in congressional redistricting and state reapportionment cases, do not "translate into a requirement that the Federal government conduct a census that is as accurate as possible" and do not provide any basis for "preferring numerical accuracy to distributive accuracy." *Id.* at 17, 18. The Court therefore applied a much less demanding standard to the Secretary's decision. Concluding that the government had shown "a reasonable relationship" between the decision not to make post hoc adjustments and "the accomplishment of an actual enumeration of the population, keeping in mind the constitutional purpose of the census ... to determine the apportionment of the

The methodological framework of a scientific survey is more complicated than that of a census. In surveys that use probability sampling methods, a sampling frame (that is, an explicit list of units in the population) is created. Individual units then are selected by a kind of lottery procedure, and measurements are made on the selected units, which constitute "the sample." The objective is to generalize from the sample to the population. For example, a defendant charged with a notorious crime who seeks a change of venue may commission an opinion poll to show that popular opinion is so adverse and deep-rooted that it will be difficult to impanel an unbiased jury. The population consists of all persons in the jurisdiction who might be called for jury duty. A sampling frame here could be the list of these persons as maintained by appropriate officials.[29] In this case, the fit between the sampling frame and the population would be excellent.[30]

In other situations, the sampling frame may cover less of the population. In an obscenity case, for example, the defendant's opinion poll about community standards[31] should identify the population as all adults in the legally relevant community, but obtaining a full list of all such people may not be possible. If names from a telephone directory are used, people with unlisted numbers are excluded from the sampling frame. If these people, as a group, hold different opinions from those included in the sampling frame, the poll will not reflect this difference, no matter how many individuals are polled and no matter how well their opinions are elicited.[32] The poll's measurement of

Representatives among the States," the Court held that the decision satisfied the Constitution. Indeed, having rejected the argument that the Constitution compelled statistical adjustment, the Court noted that the Constitution might prohibit such adjustment. *Id.* at 19 n.9, 20. The debate over adjustment continues for the 2000 census. *See* Lawrence D. Brown et al., *Statistical Controversies in Census 2000*, 39 JURIMETRICS J. 347 (1999).

29. If the jury list is not compiled properly from appropriate sources, it might be subject to challenge. *See* David Kairys et al., *Jury Representativeness: A Mandate for Multiple Source Lists*, 65 CAL. L. REV. 776 (1977).

30. Likewise, in drug investigations the sampling frame for testing the contents of vials, bags, or packets seized by police easily can be devised to match the population of all the items seized in a single case. Because testing each and every item can be quite time-consuming and expensive, chemists often draw a probability sample, analyze the material that is sampled, and use the percentage of illicit drugs found in the sample to determine the total quantity of illicit drugs in all the items seized. *E.g.*, United States v. Shonubi, 895 F.Supp. 460, 470 (E.D.N.Y.1995) (citing cases), *rev'd on other grounds*, 103 F.3d 1085 (2d Cir.1997). For discussions of statistical estimation in such cases, see C.G.G. Aitken et al., *Estimation of Quantities of Drugs Handled and the Burden of Proof*, 160 J. ROYAL STAT. SOC'Y 333 (1997); Dov Tzidony & Mark Ravreby, *A Statistical Approach to Drug Sampling: A Case Study*, 37 J. FORENSIC SCI. 1541 (1992); Johan Bring &

Colin Aitken, *Burden of Proof and Estimation of Drug Quantities Under the Federal Sentencing Guidelines*, 18 CARDOZO L. REV. 1987 (1997).

31. On the admissibility of such polls, compare *Saliba v. State*, 475 N.E.2d 1181, 1187 (Ind.Ct.App.1985) ("Although the poll did not ... [ask] the interviewees ... whether the particular film was obscene, the poll was relevant to an application of community standards"), with *United States v. Pryba*, 900 F.2d 748, 757 (4th Cir.1990) ("Asking a person in a telephone interview as to whether one is offended by nudity, is a far cry from showing the materials ... and then asking if they are offensive," so exclusion of the survey results was proper).

32. A classic example of selection bias is the 1936 *Literary Digest* poll. After successfully predicting the winner of every U.S. presidential election since 1916, the *Digest* used the replies from 2.4 million respondents to predict that Alf Landon would win 57% to 43%. In fact, Franklin Roosevelt won by a landslide vote of 62% to 38%. *See* FREEDMAN ET AL., *supra* note 1, at 334–35. The *Digest* was so far off, in part, because it chose names from telephone books, rosters of clubs and associations, city directories, lists of registered voters, and mail order listings. *Id.* at 335, A–20 n.6. In 1936, when only one household in four had a telephone, the people whose names appeared on such lists tended to be more affluent. Lists that overrepresented the affluent had worked well in earlier elections, when rich and poor voted

community opinion will be biased, although the magnitude of this bias may not be great.

Not all surveys use random selection. In some commercial disputes involving trademarks or advertising, the population of all potential purchasers of the products is difficult to identify. Some surveyors may resort to an easily accessible subgroup of the population, such as shoppers in a mall.[33] Such convenience samples may be biased by the interviewer's discretion in deciding whom to interview—a form of selection bias—and the refusal of some of those approached to participate—nonresponse bias.[34] Selection bias is acute when constituents write their representatives, listeners call into radio talk shows, interest groups collect information from their members,[35] or attorneys choose cases for trial.[36] Selection bias also affects data from jury-reporting services that gather information from readily available sources.

Various procedures are available to cope with selection bias. In quota sampling, the interviewer is instructed to interview so many women, so many older men, so many ethnic minorities, or the like. But quotas alone still leave too much discretion to the interviewers in selecting among the members of each category, and therefore do not solve the problem of selection bias.

Probability sampling methods, in contrast, ideally are suited to avoid selection bias. Once the conceptual population is reduced to a tangible sampling frame, the units to be measured are selected by some kind of lottery that gives each unit in the sampling frame a known, nonzero probability of being chosen. Selection according to a table of random digits or the like[37] leaves no room for selection bias. These procedures are used routinely to select individuals for jury duty[38]; they also have been used to choose "bell-

---

along similar lines, but the bias in the sampling frame proved fatal when the Great Depression made economics a salient consideration for voters. *See* Judith M. Tanur, *Samples and Surveys, in* PERSPECTIVES ON CONTEMPORARY STATISTICS 55, 57 (David C. Hoaglin & David S. Moore eds., 1992). Today, survey organizations conduct polls by telephone, but most voters have telephones, and these organizations select the numbers to call at random rather than sampling names from telephone books.

33. *E.g.*, R.J. Reynolds Tobacco Co. v. Loew's Theatres, Inc., 511 F.Supp. 867, 876 (S.D.N.Y.1980) (questioning the propriety of basing a "nationally projectable statistical percentage" on a suburban mall intercept study).

34. Nonresponse bias is discussed *infra* § 5–2.2.2.

35. *E.g.*, Pittsburgh Press Club v. United States, 579 F.2d 751, 759 (3d Cir.1978) (tax-exempt club's mail survey of its members to show little sponsorship of income-producing uses of facilities was held to be inadmissible hearsay because it "was neither objective, scientific nor impartial"), *rev'd on other grounds*, 615 F.2d 600 (3d Cir.1980).

36. *See In re* Chevron, U.S.A., Inc., 109 F.3d 1016 (5th Cir.1997). In that case, the district court decided to try 30 cases to resolve common issues or to ascertain damages in

3,000 claims arising from Chevron's allegedly improper disposal of hazardous substances. The court asked the opposing parties to select 15 cases each. Selecting 30 extreme cases, however, is quite different from drawing a random sample of 30 cases. Thus, the court of appeals wrote that although random sampling would have been acceptable, the trial court could not use the results in the 30 extreme cases to resolve issues of fact or ascertain damages in the untried cases. Id. at 1020. Those cases, it warned, were "not cases calculated to represent the group of 3,000 claimants." *Id.*

37. In simple random sampling, units are drawn at random without replacement. In particular, each unit has the same probability of being chosen for the sample. More complicated methods, such as stratified sampling and cluster sampling, have advantages in certain applications. In systematic sampling, every fifth, tenth, or hundredth (in mathematical jargon, every nth) unit in the sampling frame is selected. If the starting point is selected at random and the units are not in any special order, then this procedure is comparable to simple random sampling.

38. Before 1968, most federal districts used the "key man" system for compiling lists of eligible jurors. Individuals believed to have extensive contacts in the community would sug-

wether" cases for representative trials to resolve issues in all similar cases.[39]

§ 5–2.2.2   Of the Units Selected, Which Are Measured?

Although probability sampling ensures that, within the limits of chance, the sample will be representative of the sampling frame, the question remains as to which units of the sample actually get measured. When objects like receipts are sampled for an audit, or vegetation is sampled for a study of the ecology of a region, all the selected units can be examined. Human beings are more troublesome. Some may refuse to respond, and the survey should report the nonresponse rate. A large nonresponse rate warns of bias,[40] although a supplemental study may establish that the nonrespondents do not differ systematically from the respondents with respect to the characteristics of interest[41] or may permit the missing data to be imputed.[42]

gest names of prospective jurors, and the qualified jury wheel would be made up from those names. To reduce the risk of discrimination associated with this system, the Jury Selection and Service Act of 1968, 28 U.S.C.A. §§ 1861–1878 (1988), substituted the principle of "random selection of juror names from the voter lists of the district or division in which court is held." S. Rep. No. 891, 90th Cong., 1st Sess. 10 (1967), *reprinted in* 1968 U.S.C.C.A.N. 1792, 1793.

39.   Hilao v. Estate of Marcos, 103 F.3d 767 (9th Cir.1996); Cimino v. Raymark Indus., Inc., 751 F.Supp. 649 (E.D.Tex.1990); *cf. In re* Chevron U.S.A., Inc., 109 F.3d 1016 (5th Cir.1997) (discussed *supra* note 36). Although trials in a suitable random sample of cases can produce reasonable estimates of average damages, the propriety of precluding individual trials has been debated. *Compare* Michael J. Saks & Peter David Blanck, *Justice Improved: The Unrecognized Benefits of Aggregation and Sampling in the Trial of Mass Torts*, 44 STAN. L. REV. 815 (1992), *with Chevron*, 109 F.3d at 1021 (Jones, J., concurring); Robert G. Bone, *Statistical Adjudication: Rights, Justice, and Utility in a World of Process Scarcity*, 46 VAND. L. REV. 561 (1993).

40.   The 1936 *Literary Digest* election poll (*see supra* note 32) illustrates the danger. Only 24% of the 10 million people who received questionnaires returned them. Most of the respondents probably had strong views on the candidates, and most of them probably objected to President Roosevelt's economic program. This self-selection is likely to have biased the poll. Maurice C. Bryson, *The Literary Digest Poll: Making of a Statistical Myth*, 30 AM. STATISTICIAN 184 (1976); FREEDMAN ET AL., *supra* note 1, at 335–36.

In *United States v. Gometz*, 730 F.2d 475, 478 (7th Cir.) (en banc), the Seventh Circuit recognized that "a low rate of response to juror questionnaires could lead to the underrepresentation of a group that is entitled to be represented on the qualified jury wheel." Nev-

ertheless, the court held that under the Jury Selection and Service Act of 1968, 28 U.S.C.A. §§ 1861–1878 (1988), the clerk did not abuse his discretion by failing to take steps to increase a response rate of 30%. According to the court, "Congress wanted to make it possible for all qualified persons to serve on juries, which is different from forcing all qualified persons to be available for jury service." *Gometz*, 730 F.2d at 480. Although it might "be a good thing to follow up on persons who do not respond to a jury questionnaire," the court concluded that Congress was not concerned with anything so esoteric as nonresponse bias. *Id.* at 479, 482.

41.   Even when demographic characteristics of the sample match those of the population, however, caution still is indicated. In the 1980s, a behavioral researcher sent out 100,000 questionnaires to explore how women viewed their relationships with men. SHERE HITE, WOMEN AND LOVE: A CULTURAL REVOLUTION IN PROGRESS (1987). She amassed a huge collection of anonymous letters from thousands of women disillusioned with love and marriage, and she wrote that these responses established that the "outcry" of feminists "against the many injustices of marriage—exploitation of women financially, physically, sexually, and emotionally" is "just and accurate." *Id.* at 344. The outcry may indeed be justified, but this research does little to prove the point. About 95% of the 100,000 inquiries did not produce responses. The nonrespondents may have had less distressing experiences with men and therefore did not see the need to write autobiographical letters. Furthermore, this systematic difference would be expected within every demographic and occupational class. Therefore, the argument that the sample responses are representative because "those participating according to age, occupation, religion, and other variables known for the U.S. population at large in most cases quite closely mirrors that of the U.S. female population" is far from convincing. *Id.* at 777. In fact, the results of this nonrandom sample differ dramatically from

In short, a good survey defines an appropriate population, uses an unbiased method for selecting the sample, has a high response rate, and gathers accurate information on the sample units. When these goals are met, the sample tends to be representative of the population: the measurements within the sample describe fairly the characteristics in the population. It remains possible, however, that the sample, being less than exhaustive, is not representative; proper statistical analysis helps address the magnitude of this risk, at least for probability samples.[43] Of course, surveys may be useful even if they fail to meet all of the criteria given above; but then, additional arguments are needed to justify the inferences.

§ 5–2.3 Individual Measurements

§ 5–2.3.1 Is the Measurement Process Reliable?

There are two main aspects to the accuracy of measurements—reliability and validity. In science, "reliability" refers to reproducibility of results.[44] A reliable measuring instrument returns consistent measurements of the same quantity. A scale, for example, is reliable if it reports the same weight for the same object time and again. It may not be accurate—it may always report a weight that is too high or one that is too low—but the perfectly reliable scale always reports the same weight for the same object. Its errors, if any, are systematic; they always point in the same direction.

Reliability can be ascertained by measuring the same quantity several times. For instance, one method of DNA identification requires a laboratory to determine the lengths of fragments of DNA. By making duplicate measurements of DNA fragments, a laboratory can determine the likelihood that two measurements will differ by specified amounts.[45] Such results are needed when deciding whether an observed discrepancy between a crime sample and a suspect sample is sufficient to exclude the suspect.[46]

In many studies, descriptive information is obtained on the subjects. For statistical purposes, the information may have to be reduced to numbers, a process called "coding." The reliability of the coding process should be considered. For instance, in a study of death sentencing in Georgia, legally trained evaluators examined short summaries of cases and ranked them

---

those of polls with better response rates. *See* CHAMONT WANG, SENSE AND NONSENSE OF STATISTICAL INFERENCE: CONTROVERSY, MISUSE, AND SUBTLETY 174–76 (1993). For further criticism of this study, see David Streitfeld, *Shere Hite and the Trouble with Numbers*, 1 CHANCE 26 (1988).

42. Methods for "imputing" missing data are discussed in, *e.g.*, Tanur, *supra* note 32, at 66, and Howard Wainer, *Eelworms, Bullet Holes, and Geraldine Ferraro: Some Problems with Statistical Adjustment and Some Solutions*, 14 J. EDUC. STAT. 121 (1989) (with commentary). The easy case is one in which the response rate is so high that even if all nonrespondents had responded in a way adverse to the proponent of the survey, the substantive conclusion would be unaltered. Otherwise, imputation can be problematic.

43. *See infra* § 5–4.0.

44. Courts often use "reliable" to mean "that which can be relied on" for some purpose, such as establishing probable cause or crediting a hearsay statement when the declarant is not produced for confrontation. *Daubert v. Merrell Dow Pharms., Inc.*, 509 U.S. 579, 590 n. 9, 113 S.Ct. 2786, 125 L.Ed.2d 469 (1993), for instance, distinguishes "evidentiary reliability" from reliability in the technical sense of giving consistent results. We use "reliability" to denote the latter.

45. *See* COMMITTEE ON DNA FORENSIC SCIENCE: AN UPDATE, NATIONAL RESEARCH COUNCIL, THE EVALUATION OF FORENSIC DNA EVIDENCE 139–41 (1996).

46. *Id.*; COMMITTEE ON DNA TECHNOLOGY IN FORENSIC SCIENCE, NATIONAL RESEARCH COUNCIL, DNA TECHNOLOGY IN FORENSIC SCIENCE 61–62 (1992); *infra* Chapter 25.

according to the defendant's culpability.[47] Two different aspects of reliability are worth considering. First, the "within-observer" variability of judgments should be small—the same evaluator should rate essentially identical cases the same way. Second, the "between-observer" variability should be small—different evaluators should rate the same cases the same way.

§ 5-2.3.2   Is the Measurement Process Valid?

Reliability is necessary, but not sufficient, to ensure accuracy. In addition to reliability, "validity" is needed. A valid measuring instrument measures what it is supposed to. Thus, a polygraph measures certain physiological responses to stimuli. It may accomplish this task reliably. Nevertheless, it is not valid as a lie detector unless increases in pulse rate, blood pressure, and the like are well correlated with conscious deception. Another example involves the MMPI (Minnesota Multiphasic Personality Inventory), a pencil and paper test that, many psychologists agree, measures aspects of personality or psychological functioning. Its reliability can be quantified. But this does not make it a valid test of sexual deviancy.[48]

When an independent and reasonably accurate way of measuring the variable of interest is available, it may be used to validate the measuring system in question. Breathalyzer readings may be validated against alcohol levels found in blood samples. Employment test scores may be validated against job performance. A common measure of validity is the correlation coefficient between the criterion (job performance) and the predictor (the test score).[49]

§ 5-2.3.3   Are the Measurements Recorded Correctly?

Judging the adequacy of data collection may involve examining the process by which measurements are recorded and preserved. Are responses to interviews coded and logged correctly? Are all the responses to a survey included? If gaps or mistakes are present, do they distort the results?[50]

---

47. David C. Baldus et al., Equal Justice and the Death Penalty: A Legal and Empirical Analysis 49–50 (1990).

48. *See* People v. John W., 185 Cal.App.3d 801, 229 Cal.Rptr. 783, 785 (1986) (holding that because the use of the MMPI to diagnose sexual deviancy was not shown to be generally accepted as valid in the scientific community, a diagnosis based in part on the MMPI was inadmissible).

49. *E.g.,* Washington v. Davis, 426 U.S. 229, 252, 96 S.Ct. 2040, 48 L.Ed.2d 597 (1976); Albemarle Paper Co. v. Moody, 422 U.S. 405, 430–32, 95 S.Ct. 2362, 45 L.Ed.2d 280 (1975). As the discussion of the correlation coefficient indicates *infra* § 5-5.2, the closer the coefficient is to 1, the greater the validity. Various statistics are used to characterize the reliability of laboratory instruments, psychological tests, or human judgments. These include the standard deviation as well as the correlation coefficient. *See infra* §§ 5-3.0 & 5-5.0.

50. *See, e.g.,* McCleskey v. Kemp, 753 F.2d 877, 914–15 (11th Cir.1985) (district court was unpersuaded by a statistical analysis of capital sentencing, in part because of various imperfections in the study, including discrepancies in the data and missing data; concurring and dissenting opinion concludes that the district court's findings on missing and misrecorded data were clearly erroneous because the possible errors were not large enough to affect the overall results; for an exposition of the study and response to such criticisms, see Baldus et al., *supra* note 47), *aff'd,* 481 U.S. 279, 107 S.Ct. 1756, 95 L.Ed.2d 262 (1987); G. Heileman Brewing Co. v. Anheuser–Busch, Inc., 676 F.Supp. 1436, 1486 (E.D.Wis.1987) ("many coding errors ... affected the results of the survey"); EEOC v. Sears, Roebuck & Co., 628 F.Supp. 1264, 1304, 1305 (N.D.Ill.1986) ("[E]rrors in EEOC's mechanical coding of information from applications in its hired and non-hired samples also make EEOC's statistical analysis based on this data less reliable." The EEOC "consistently coded prior experience in such a way that less experienced women are considered to have the same experience as

§ 5–3.0   HOW HAVE THE DATA BEEN PRESENTED?

After data have been collected, they should be presented in a way that makes them intelligible. Data can be summarized with a few numbers or with graphical displays. However, the wrong summary can mislead.[1] Section 5–3.1 discusses rates or percentages, and gives some cautionary examples of misleading summaries, indicating the sorts of questions that might be considered when numerical summaries are presented in court. Percentages are often used to demonstrate statistical association, which is the topic of section 5–3.2. Section 5–3.3 considers graphical summaries of data, while sections 5–3.4 and 5–3.5 discuss some of the basic descriptive statistics that are likely to be encountered in litigation, including the mean, median and standard deviation.

§ 5–3.1   Are Rates or Percentages Properly Interpreted?

§ 5–3.1.1   Have Appropriate Benchmarks Been Provided?

Selective presentation of numerical information is like quoting someone out of context. A television commercial for the Investment Company Institute (the mutual fund trade association) said that a $10,000 investment made in 1950 in an average common stock mutual fund would have increased to $113,500 by the end of 1972. On the other hand, according to the *Wall Street Journal*, the same investment spread over all the stocks making up the New York Stock Exchange Composite Index would have grown to $151,427. Mutual funds performed worse than the stock market as a whole.[2] In this example, and in many other situations, it is helpful to look beyond a single number to some benchmark that places the isolated figure into perspective.

§ 5–3.1.2   Have the Data–Collection Procedures Changed?

Changes in the process of collecting data also can create problems of interpretation. Statistics on crime provide many examples. The number of petty larcenies reported in Chicago more than doubled between 1959 and 1960—not because of an abrupt crime wave, but because a new police commissioner introduced an improved reporting system.[3] During the 1970s, police officials in Washington, D.C., "demonstrated" the success of President Nixon's law-and-order campaign by valuing stolen goods at $49, just below the $50 threshold for inclusion in the Federal Bureau of Investigation's (FBI) Uniform Crime Reports.[4]

Changes in data-collection procedures are by no means limited to crime statistics.[5] Indeed, almost all series of numbers that cover many years are

---

more experienced men" and "has made so many general coding errors that its data base does not fairly reflect the characteristics of applicants for commission sales positions at Sears."), *aff'd*, 839 F.2d 302 (7th Cir.1988); Dalley v. Michigan Blue Cross/Blue Shield, Inc., 612 F.Supp. 1444, 1456 (E.D.Mich.1985) ("although plaintiffs show that there were some mistakes in coding, plaintiffs still fail to demonstrate that these errors were so generalized and so pervasive that the entire study is invalid.").

§ 5–3.0

1. *See generally* DAVID FREEDMAN ET AL., STATISTICS (3d ed. 1998); DARRELL HUFF, HOW TO LIE WITH STATISTICS (1954); DAVID S. MOORE, STATISTICS: CONCEPTS AND CONTROVERSIES (3d ed. 1991); HANS ZEISEL, SAY IT WITH FIGURES (6th ed. 1985).

2. MOORE, *supra* note 1, at 161.

3. *Id.* at 162.

4. JAMES P. LEVINE ET AL., CRIMINAL JUSTICE IN AMERICA: LAW IN ACTION 99 (1986).

5. For example, improved survival rates for cancer patients may result from improvements

affected by changes in definitions and collection methods. When a study includes such time series data, it is useful to inquire about changes and to look for any sudden jumps, which may signal such changes.[6]

§ 5–3.1.3   Are the Categories Appropriate?

Misleading summaries also can be produced by choice of categories for comparison. In *Philip Morris, Inc. v. Loew's Theatres, Inc.*,[7] and *R.J. Reynolds Tobacco Co. v. Loew's Theatres, Inc.*,[8] Philip Morris and R.J. Reynolds sought an injunction to stop the maker of Triumph low-tar cigarettes from running advertisements claiming that participants in a national taste test preferred Triumph to other brands. Plaintiffs alleged that claims that Triumph was a "national taste test winner" or Triumph "beats" other brands were false and misleading. An exhibit introduced by defendant contained the data shown in Table 1:[9]

Table 1

Data used by defendant to refute plaintiffs' false advertising claim

	Triumph much better than Merit	Triumph somewhat better than Merit	Triumph about the same as Merit	Triumph somewhat worse than Merit	Triumph much worse than Merit
Number	45	73	77	93	36
Percentage	14%	22%	24%	29%	11%

Only 14% + 22% = 36% of the sample preferred Triumph to Merit, while 29% + 11% = 40% preferred Merit to Triumph.[10] By selectively combining categories, however, defendant attempted to create a different impression. Since 24% found the brands about the same, and 36% preferred Triumph, defendant claimed that a clear majority (36% + 24% = 60%) found Triumph "as good or better than Merit."[11] The court correctly resisted this chicanery, finding that defendant's test results did not support the advertising claims.[12]

There was a similar distortion in claims for accuracy of a home pregnancy test.[13] The manufacturer advertised the test as 99.5% accurate under laboratory conditions. The data underlying this claim are summarized in Table 2.

in therapy. Or, the change may simply mean that cancers now are detected earlier, due to improvements in diagnostic technique, so that patients with these cancers merely appear to live longer. (Both explanations are almost certainly right, for different kinds of cancer.) *See* RICHARD DOLL & RICHARD PETO, THE CAUSES OF CANCER: QUANTITATIVE ESTIMATES OF AVOIDABLE RISKS OF CANCER IN THE UNITED STATES TODAY app. C at 1278–79 (1981).

6. MOORE, *supra* note 1, at 162.

7. 511 F.Supp. 855 (S.D.N.Y.1980).

8. 511 F.Supp. 867 (S.D.N.Y.1980).

9. 511 F. Supp. at 866.

10. *Id.* at 856.

11. *Id.* at 866.

12. *Id.* at 856–57. The statistical issues in these cases are discussed more fully in 2 JOSEPH L. GASTWIRTH, STATISTICAL REASONING IN LAW AND PUBLIC POLICY 633–39 (1988).

13. This incident is reported in Arnold Barnett, *How Numbers Can Trick You*, TECH. REV., Oct. 1994, at 38, 44–45.

Table 2
Home pregnancy test results

	Actually pregnant	Actually not pregnant
Test says pregnant	197	0
Test says not pregnant	1	2
Total	198	2

Table 2 does indicate only one error in 200 assessments, or 99.5% overall accuracy. But the table also shows that the test can make two types of errors—it can tell a pregnant woman that she is not pregnant (a false negative), and it can tell a woman who is not pregnant that she is (a false positive). The reported 99.5% accuracy rate conceals a crucial fact—the company had virtually no data with which to measure the rate of false positives.[14]

§ 5–3.1.4 How Big Is the Base of a Percentage?

Rates and percentages often provide effective summaries of data, but these statistics can be misinterpreted. A percentage makes a comparison between two numbers: one number is the base, and the other number is compared to that base. When the base is small, actual numbers may be more revealing than percentages, as demonstrated by Table 2. Media accounts in 1982 of a crime wave by the elderly give another example. The annual Uniform Crime Reports showed a near tripling of the crime rate by older people since 1964, while crimes by younger people only doubled. But people over 65 years of age account for less than 1% of all arrests. In 1980, for instance, there were only 151 arrests of the elderly for robbery out of 139,476 total robbery arrests.[15]

§ 5–3.1.5 What Comparisons Are Made?

Finally, there is the issue of which numbers to compare. Researchers sometimes choose among alternative comparisons. It may be worthwhile to ask why they chose the one they did. Would another comparison give a different view? A government agency, for example, may want to compare the amount of service now being given with that of earlier years—but what earlier year ought to be the baseline? If the first year of operation is used, a large percentage increase should be expected because of start-up problems.[16] If last year is used as the base, was it also part of the trend, or was it an unusually poor year? If the base year is not representative of other years, then the percentage may not portray the trend fairly.[17] No single question can be formulated to detect such distortions, but it may help to ask for the numbers

14. Only two women in the sample were not pregnant; the test gave correct results for both of them. Although a false-positive rate of zero is ideal, an estimate based on a sample of only two women is not.

15. MARK H. MAIER, THE DATA GAME: CONTROVERSIES IN SOCIAL SCIENCE STATISTICS 83 (1991); see also Alfred Blumstein & Jacobson Cohen, *Characterizing Criminal Careers*, 237 SCIENCE 985 (1987).

16. Cf. Michael J. Saks, *Do We Really Know Anything About the Behavior of the Tort Litigation System—And Why Not?*, 140 U. PA. L. REV. 1147, 1203 (1992) (using 1974 as the base year for computing the growth of federal product liability filings exaggerates growth because "1974 was the first year that product liability cases had their own separate listing on the cover sheets.... The count for 1974 is almost certainly an understatement....").

17. JEFFREY KATZER ET AL., EVALUATING INFORMATION: A GUIDE FOR USERS OF SOCIAL SCIENCE RESEARCH 106 (2d ed. 1982).

from which the percentages were obtained; asking about the base can also be helpful. Ultimately, however, recognizing which numbers are related to which issues requires a species of clear thinking not easily reducible to a checklist.[18]

§ 5–3.2   Is an Appropriate Measure of Association Used?

Many cases involve statistical association. Does a test for employee promotion have an exclusionary effect that depends on race or gender? Does the incidence of murder vary with the rate of executions for convicted murderers? Do consumer purchases of a product depend on the presence or absence of a product warning? This section discusses tables and percentage-based statistics that are frequently presented to answer such questions.[19]

Percentages often are used to describe the association between two variables. Suppose that a university alleged to discriminate against women in admitting students consists of only two colleges, engineering and business. The university admits 350 out of 800 male applicants; by comparison, it admits only 200 out of 600 female applicants. Such data commonly are displayed as in Table 3.[20]

Table 3
Admissions by gender

	Male	Female	Total
Admit	350	200	550
Deny	450	400	850
Total	800	600	1,400

As Table 3 indicates, 350/800 = 44% of the males are admitted, compared with only 200/600 = 33% of the females. One way to express the disparity is to subtract the two percentages: 44% – 33% = 11 percentage points. Although such subtraction is commonly seen in jury discrimination cases,[21] the difference is inevitably small when the two percentages are both close to zero. If the selection rate for males is 5% and that for females is 1%, the difference is only 4 percentage points. Yet, females have 1/5 the chance of males to be selected, and that may be of real concern.[22]

For Table 3, the selection ratio (used by the Equal Employment Opportunity Commission in its "80% rule")[23] is 33/44 = 75%, meaning that, on

18. For assistance in coping with percentages, see ZEISEL, *supra* note 1, at 1–24.

19. Correlation and regression are discussed *infra* § 5–5.0.

20. A table of this sort is called a "crosstab" or a "contingency table." Table 3 is "two-by-two" because it has two rows and two columns, not counting rows or columns containing totals.

21. *See, e.g.*, D.H. Kaye, *Statistical Evidence of Discrimination in Jury Selection, in* STATISTICAL METHODS IN DISCRIMINATION LITIGATION 13 (D. H. Kaye & Mikel Aickin eds., 1986).

22. *Cf.* United States v. Jackman, 46 F.3d 1240, 1246–47 (2d Cir.1995) (holding that the small percentage of minorities in the population makes it "inappropriate" to use an "absolute numbers" or "absolute impact" approach to measuring underrepresentation of these minorities in the list of potential jurors).

23. The EEOC generally regards any procedure that selects candidates from the least successful group at a rate less than 80% of the rate for the most successful group as having an adverse impact. EEOC Uniform Guidelines on Employee Selection Procedures, 29 C.F.R. § 1607.4(D) (1993). The rule is designed to help spot instances of substantially discriminatory practices, and the commission usually asks

average, women have 75% the chance of admission that men have.[24] However, the selection ratio has its own problems. In the last example, if the selection rates are 5% and 1%, then the exclusion rates are 95% and 99%. The corresponding ratio is 99/95 = 104%, meaning that females have, on average, 104% the risk of males of being rejected. The underlying facts are the same, of course, but this formulation sounds much less disturbing.[25]

The odds ratio is more symmetric. If 5% of male applicants are admitted, the odds on a man being admitted are 5/95 = 1/19; the odds on a woman are 1/99. The odds ratio is (1/99)/(1/19) = 19/99. The odds ratio for rejection instead of acceptance is the same, except that the order is reversed.[26] Although the odds ratio has desirable mathematical properties, its meaning may be less clear than that of the selection ratio or the simple difference.

Data showing disparate impact are generally obtained by aggregating—putting together—statistics from a variety of sources. Unless the source material is fairly homogeneous, aggregation can distort patterns in the data. We illustrate the problem with the hypothetical admission data in Table 3. Applicants can be classified not only by gender and admission but also by the college to which they applied, as in Table 4:

Table 4
Admissions by gender and college

Decision	Engineering Male	Female	Business Male	Female
Admit	300	100	50	100
Deny	300	100	150	300

The entries in Table 4 add up to the entries in Table 3; said more technically, Table 3 is obtained by aggregating the data in Table 4. Yet, there is no

employers to justify any procedures that produce selection ratios of 80% or less.

24. The analogous statistic used in epidemiology is called the relative risk. *See infra* Chapter 35. Relative risks are usually quoted as decimals rather than percentages; for instance, a selection ratio of 75% corresponds to a relative risk of 0.75. A variation on this idea is the relative difference in the proportions, which expresses the proportion by which the probability of selection is reduced. David Kairys et al., *Jury Representativeness: A Mandate for Multiple Source Lists*, 65 Cal. L. Rev. 776, 789–90 (1977); *cf.* David C. Baldus & James W.L. Cole, Statistical Proof of Discrimination § 5.1, at 530 (1980 & Supp. 1987) (listing various ratios that can be used to measure disparities). An updated version of the Baldus and Cole volume is Ramona L. Paetzold & Steven L. Wilborn, The Statistics of Discrimination: Using Statistical Evidence in Discrimination Cases (1994).

25. The Illinois Department of Employment Security tried to exploit this feature of the selection ratio in *Council 31, Am. Fed'n of State, County and Mun. Employees v. Ward,*

978 F.2d 373 (7th Cir.1992). In January 1985, the department laid off 8.6% of the blacks on its staff in comparison with 3.0% of the whites. *Id.* at 375. Recognizing that these layoffs ran afoul of the 80% rule (since 3.0/8.6 = 35%, which is far less than 80%), the department instead presented the selection ratio for retention. *Id.* at 375–76. Since black employees were retained at 91.4/97.0 = 94% of the white rate, the retention rates showed no adverse impact under the 80% rule. *Id.* at 376. When a subsequent wave of layoffs was challenged as discriminatory, the department argued "that its retention rate analysis is the right approach to this case and ... shows conclusively that the layoffs did not have a disparate impact." *Id.* at 379. The Seventh Circuit disagreed and, in reversing an order granting summary judgment to defendants on other grounds, left it to the district court on remand "to decide what method of proof is most appropriate." *Id.*

26. For women, the odds on rejection are 99 to 1; for men, 19 to 1. The ratio of these odds is 99/19. Likewise, the odds ratio for an admitted applicant being a man as opposed to a denied applicant being man is also 99/19.

association between gender and admission in either college; men and women are admitted at identical rates. Combining two colleges with no association produces a university in which gender is associated strongly with admission. The explanation for this paradox: the business college, to which most of the women applied, admits relatively few applicants; the engineering college, to which most of the men applied, is easier to get into. As this example shows, association can result from combining heterogeneous statistical material.[27]

§ 5–3.3   Does a Graph Portray Data Fairly?

Graphs are useful for revealing key characteristics of a batch of numbers, trends over time, and the relationships among variables.[28]

§ 5–3.3.1   How Are Trends Displayed?

Graphs that plot values over time are useful for seeing trends. However, the scales on the axes matter. In Figure 1, the federal debt appears to skyrocket during the Reagan and Bush administrations; in Figure 2, the federal debt appears to grow slowly.[29] The moral is simple: pay attention to the markings on the axes to determine whether the scale is appropriate.

27. Tables 3 and 4 are hypothetical, but closely patterned on a real example. *See* P.J. Bickel et al., *Sex Bias in Graduate Admissions: Data from Berkeley*, 187 SCIENCE 398 (1975); *see also* FREEDMAN ET AL., *supra* note 1, at 17–20; MOORE, *supra* note 1, at 246–47. The tables are an instance of "Simpson's Paradox." *See generally* Myra L. Samuels, *Simpson's Paradox and Related Phenomena*, 88 J. AM. STAT. ASS'N 81 (1993). Another perspective on Table 3 may be helpful. The college to which a student applies is a confounder. *See supra* § 5–2.1.1. In the present context, confounders often are called "omitted variables." For opinions discussing the legal implications of omitted variables, see cases cited, *supra* § 5–1.2 note 10 & *infra* § 5–5.4.3 note 52.

28. *See generally* WILLIAM S. CLEVELAND, THE ELEMENTS OF GRAPHING DATA (1985); DAVID S. MOORE & GEORGE P. McCABE, INTRODUCTION TO THE PRACTICE OF STATISTICS 3–20 (2d ed. 1993). Graphs showing relationships among variables are discussed *infra* § 5–5.0.

29. *See* Howard Wainer, *Graphs in the Presidential Campaign*, CHANCE, Winter 1993, at 48, 50.

Figure 1
The federal debt skyrockets under Reagan–Bush.

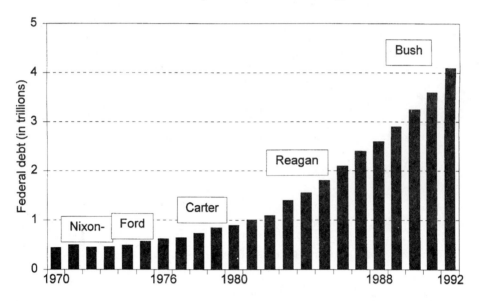

Figure 2

The federal debt grows steadily under Reagan–Bush.

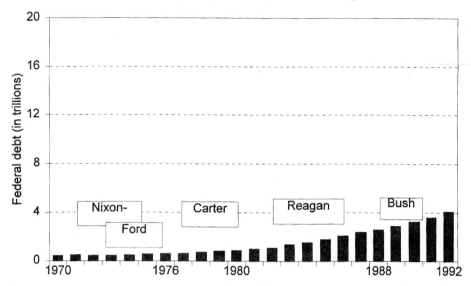

§ 5–3.3.2 How Are Distributions Displayed?

A graph commonly used to display the distribution of data is the histogram.[30] One axis denotes the numbers, and the other indicates how often those fall within specified intervals (called "bins" or "class intervals"). For example, we flipped a quarter 10 times in a row and counted the number of heads in this "batch" of 10 tosses. With 50 batches, we obtained the following counts:[31]

7 7 5 6 8	4 2 3 6 5	4 3 4 7 4	6 8 4 7 4	7 4 5 4 3
4 4 2 5 3	5 4 2 4 4	5 7 2 3 5	4 6 4 9 10	5 5 6 6 4

---

30. For small batches of numbers, a "stem-and-leaf plot" may be more convenient. For instance, a stem-and-leaf plot for 11, 12, 23, 23, 23, 23, 33, 45, 69 is given below:

```
1   1 2
2   3 3 3 3
3   3
4   5
5
6   9
```

The numbers to the left of the line are the first digits; those to the right are the second digits. Thus, the entry "2 | 3 3 3 3" stands for "23, 23, 23, 23."

31. The coin landed heads 7 times in the first 10 tosses; by coincidence, there were also 7 heads in the next 10 tosses; there were 5 heads in the third batch of 10 tosses; and so forth.

Figure 3

Histogram showing how frequently various numbers of heads appeared in 50 batches of 10 tosses of a quarter.

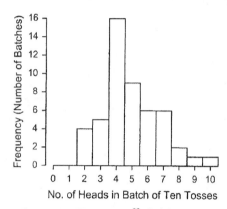

The histogram is shown in Figure 3.[32] A histogram shows how the data are distributed over the range of possible values. The spread can be made to appear larger or smaller, however, by changing the scale of the horizontal axis. Likewise, the shape can be altered somewhat by changing the size of the bins.[33] It may be worth inquiring how the analyst chose the bin widths.

§ 5–3.4 Is an Appropriate Measure Used for the Center of a Distribution?

Perhaps the most familiar descriptive statistic is the mean (or "arithmetic mean"). The mean can be found by adding up all the numbers and dividing by how many there are. By comparison, the median is defined so that half the numbers are bigger than the median, and half are smaller.[34] Yet a third statistic is the mode, which is the most common number in the data set. These statistics are different, although they are not always clearly distin-

---

32. In Figure 3, the bin width is 1. There were no 0's or 1's in the data, so the bars over 0 and 1 disappear. There is a bin from 1.5 to 2.5; the four 2's in the data fall into this bin, so the bar over the interval from 1.5 to 2.5 has height four. There is another bin from 2.5 to 3.5, which catches five 3's; the height of the corresponding bar is five. And so forth.

All the bins in Figure 3 have the same width, so this histogram is just like a bar graph. However, data are often published in tables with unequal intervals. The resulting histograms will have unequal bin widths; bar heights should be calculated so that the areas (height × width) are proportional to the frequencies. In general, a histogram differs from a bar graph in that it represents frequencies by area, not height. *See* FREEDMAN ET AL., *supra* note 1, at 31–41.

33. As the width of the bins decreases, the graph becomes more detailed. But the appearance becomes more ragged until finally the graph is effectively a plot of each datum. The

optimal bin width "depends on the subject matter and the goal of the analysis." CLEVELAND, *supra* note 28, at 125.

34. Technically, at least half the numbers are at the median or larger; at least half are at the median or smaller. When the distribution is symmetric, the mean equals the median. The values diverge, however, when the distribution is asymmetric, or skewed. The distinction between the mean and the median is critical to the interpretation of the Railroad Revitalization and Regulatory Reform Act, 49 U.S.C.A. § 11503 (1988), which forbids the taxation of railroad property at a higher rate than other commercial and industrial property. To compare the rates, tax authorities often use the mean, whereas railroads prefer the median. The choice has important financial consequences, and much litigation has resulted. *See* David A. Freedman, *The Mean Versus the Median: A Case Study in 4–R Act Litigation*, 3 J. BUS. & ECON. STAT. 1 (1985).

guished.[35] The mean takes account of all the data—it involves the total of all the numbers; however, particularly with small data sets, a few unusually large or small observations may have too much influence on the mean. The median is resistant to such outliers.

To illustrate the distinction between the mean and the median, consider a report that the "average" award in malpractice cases skyrocketed from $220,000 in 1975 to $1 million in 1985.[36] The median award almost certainly was far less than $1 million,[37] and the apparently explosive growth may result from a few very large awards. Still, if the issue is whether insurers were experiencing more costs from jury verdicts, the mean is the more appropriate statistic: The total of the awards is directly related to the mean, not to the median.[38]

§ 5–3.5   Is an Appropriate Measure of Variability Used?

The location of the center of a batch of numbers reveals nothing about the variations exhibited by these numbers.[39] Statistical measures of variability include the range, the interquartile range, and the standard deviation. The range is the difference between the largest number in the batch and the smallest. The range seems natural, and it indicates the maximum spread in

35. In ordinary language, the arithmetic mean, the median, and the mode seem to be referred to interchangeably as "the average." In statistical parlance, the average is the arithmetic mean. The distinctions are brought out by the following question: How big an error would be made if every number in a batch were replaced by the "center" of the batch? The mode minimizes the number of errors; all errors count the same, no matter what their size. Similar distributions can have very different modes, and the mode is rarely used by statisticians. The median minimizes a different measure of error—the sum of all the differences between the center and the data points; signs are not taken into account when computing this sum, so positive and negative differences are treated the same way. The mean minimizes the sum of the squared differences.

36. Kenneth Jost, *Still Warring Over Medical Malpractice: Time for Something Better*, A.B.A. J., May 1993, at 68, 70–71.

37. A study of cases in North Carolina reported an "average" (mean) award of $368,000, and a median award of only $36,000. *Id.* at 71. In *TXO Production Corp. v. Alliance Resources Corp.*, 509 U.S. 443, 113 S.Ct. 2711, 125 L.Ed.2d 366 (1993), briefs portraying the punitive damage system as being out of control reported mean punitive awards, some ten times larger than the median awards described in briefs defending the current system of punitive damages. *See* Michael Rustad & Thomas Koenig, *The Supreme Court and Junk Social Science: Selective Distortion in Amicus Briefs*, 72 N.C. L. Rev. 91, 145–47 (1993). The mean differs so dramatically from the median because the mean takes into account (indeed, is heavily influenced by) the magnitudes of the

few very large awards; the median screens these out. Of course, representative data on verdicts and awards are hard to find. For studies using a probability sample of cases, see Carol DeFrances & Marika F.X. Litras, Civil Trial Cases and Verdicts in Large Counties, 1996, Bureau of Justice Statistics Bulletin, Sept. 1999, at 1; Lea S. Gifford et al., Contract Trials and Verdicts in Large Counties, 1996, Bureau of Justice Statistics Bulletin, Apr. 2000; Marika F.X. Litras et al., Tort Trials and Verdicts in Large Counties, 1996, Bureau of Justice Statistics Bulletin, Aug. 2000. A study based on a complete set of federal cases is Marika F.X. Litras & Carol J. Frances, Federal Tort Trials and Verdicts, 1996–97, Bureau of Justice Statistics Bulletin, Feb. 1999.

38. To get the total award, just multiply the mean by the number of awards; by contrast, the total cannot be computed from the median. (The more pertinent figure for the insurance industry is not the total of jury awards, but actual claims experience including settlements; of course, even the risk of large punitive damage awards may have considerable impact.) These and related statistical issues are pursued further in, *e.g.*, Theodore Eisenberg & Thomas A. Henderson, Jr., *Inside the Quiet Revolution in Products Liability*, 39 UCLA L. Rev. 731, 764–72 (1992); Scott Harrington & Robert E. Litan, *Causes of the Liability Insurance Crisis*, 239 Science 737, 740–41 (1988); Saks, *supra* note 16, at 1147, 1248–54.

39. The numbers 1, 2, 5, 8, 9 have 5 as their mean and median. So do the numbers 5, 5, 5, 5, 5. In the first batch, the numbers vary considerably about their mean; in the second, the numbers do not vary at all.

the numbers, but it is generally the most unstable because it depends entirely on the most extreme values.[40] The interquartile range is the difference between the 25th and 75th percentiles.[41] The interquartile range contains 50% of the numbers and is resistant to changes in extreme values. The standard deviation is a sort of mean deviation from the mean.[42]

There are no hard and fast rules as to which statistic is the best. In general, the bigger these measures of spread are, the more the numbers are dispersed. Particularly in small data sets, the standard deviation can be influenced heavily by a few outlying values. To remove this influence, the mean and the standard deviation can be recomputed with the outliers discarded. Beyond this, any of the statistics can be supplemented with a figure that displays much of the data.[43]

§ 5–4.0 WHAT INFERENCES CAN BE DRAWN FROM THE DATA?

The inferences that may be drawn from a study depend on the quality of the data and the design of the study. As discussed in section 5–2, the data might not address the issue of interest, might be systematically in error, or might be difficult to interpret due to confounding. We turn now to an additional concern—random error.[1] Are patterns in the data the result of chance? Would a pattern wash out if more data were collected?

The laws of probability are central to analyzing random error. By applying these laws, the statistician can assess the likely impact of chance error,

---

40. Typically, the range increases with the size of the sample; i.e., the number of units chosen for the sample.

41. By definition, 25% of the data fall below the 25th percentile, 90% fall below the 90th percentile, and so on. The median is the 50th percentile.

42. As discussed in the Appendix, when the distribution follows the normal curve, about 68% of the data will be within one standard deviation of the mean, and about 95% will be within two standard deviations of the mean. For other distributions, the proportions of the data within specified numbers of standard deviations will be different.

Technically, the standard deviation is the square root of the variance; the variance is the mean square deviation from the mean. For instance, if the mean is 100, the datum 120 deviates from the mean by 20, and the square of 20 is $20^2 = 400$. If the variance (i.e., the mean of all the squared deviations) is 900, then the standard deviation is the square root of 900, that is,

$$\sqrt{900} = 30.$$

Among other things, taking the square root corrects for the fact that the variance is on a different scale than the measurements themselves. For example, if the measurements are of length in inches, the variance is in square inches; taking the square root changes back to inches.

To compare distributions on different scales, the coefficient of variation may be used: this statistic is the standard deviation, expressed as a percentage of the mean. For instance, consider the batch of numbers 1,4,4,7,9. The mean is $25/5 = 5$, the variance is

$$(16 + 1 + 1 + 4 + 16)/5 = 7.6,$$

and the standard deviation is

$$\sqrt{7.6} = 2.8.$$

The coefficient of variation is $2.8/5 = 56\%$.

43. For instance, the "five-number summary" lists the smallest value, the 25th percentile, the median, the 75th percentile, and the largest value. The five-number summary may be presented as a "box plot." If the five numbers were 10, 25, 40, 65 and 90, the box plot would look like the following:

There are many variations on this idea in which the boundaries of the box, or the "whiskers" extending from it, represent slightly different points in the distribution of numbers.

§ 5–4.0

1. Random error is also called sampling error, chance error, or statistical error. Econometricians use the parallel concept of random disturbance terms.

using "standard errors," "confidence intervals," "significance probabilities," "hypothesis tests," or "posterior probability distributions." The following example illustrates the ideas. An employer plans to use a standardized examination to select trainees from a pool of 5,000 male and 5,000 female applicants. This total pool of 10,000 applicants is the statistical "population." Under Title VII of the Civil Rights Act, if the proposed examination excludes a disproportionate number of women, the employer needs to show that the exam is job-related.[2]

To see whether there is disparate impact, the employer administers the exam to a sample of 50 men and 50 women drawn at random from the population of job applicants. In the sample, 29 of the men but only 19 of the women pass; the sample pass rates are therefore $29/50 = 58\%$ and $19/50 = 38\%$. The employer announces that it will use the exam anyway, and several applicants bring an action under Title VII. Disparate impact seems clear. The difference in sample pass rates is 20 percentage points: $58\% - 38\% = 20$ percentage points. The employer argues, however, that the disparity could just reflect random error. After all, only a small number of people took the test, and the sample could have included disproportionate numbers of high-scoring men and low-scoring women. Clearly, even if there were no overall difference in pass rates for male and female applicants, in some samples the men will outscore the women. More generally, a sample is unlikely to be a perfect microcosm of the population; statisticians call differences between the sample and the population, just due to the luck of the draw in choosing the sample, "random error" or "sampling error."

When assessing the impact of random error, a statistician might consider the following topics:

- *Estimation.* Plaintiffs use the difference of 20 percentage points between the sample men and women to estimate the disparity between all male and female applicants. How good is this estimate? Precision can be expressed using the "standard error" or a "confidence interval."

- *Statistical significance.* Suppose the defendant is right, and there is no disparate impact: in the population of all 5,000 male and 5,000 female applicants, pass rates are equal. How likely is it that a random sample of 50 men and 50 women will produce a disparity of 20 percentage points or more? This chance is known as a *p*-value. Statistical significance is determined by reference to the *p*-value, and hypothesis testing is the technique for computing *p*-values or determining statistical significance.[3]

- *Posterior probability.* Given the observed disparity of 20 percentage points in the sample, what is the probability that—in the population as a whole—men and women have equal pass rates? This question is of direct interest to the courts. For a subjectivist statistician, posterior probabilities

2. The seminal case is *Griggs v. Duke Power Co.*, 401 U.S. 424, 431, 91 S.Ct. 849, 28 L.Ed.2d 158 (1971). The requirements and procedures for the validation of tests can go beyond a simple showing of job relatedness. *See, e.g.*, Richard R. Reilly, *Validating Employee Selection Procedures, in* STATISTICAL METHODS IN DISCRIMINATION LITIGATION 133 (D.H. Kaye & Mikel Aickin eds., 1986); Michael Rothschild & Gregory J. Werden, *Title VII and the Use of* *Employment Tests: An Illustration of the Limits of the Judicial Process*, 11 J. LEGAL STUD. 261 (1982).

3. "Hypothesis testing" is also called "significance testing." Our treatment is somewhat informal. For details on the example, see *infra* Appendix, especially note 13 (discussing the usual test statistic for this problem).

may be computed using "Bayes' rule." Within the framework of classical statistical theory, however, such a posterior probability has no meaning.[4]

• *Applicability of statistical models.* Statistical inference—whether done with confidence intervals or significance probabilities, by objective methods or subjective—depends on the validity of statistical models for the data. If the data are collected on the basis of a probability sample or a randomized experiment, there will be statistical models that fit the situation very well, and inferences based on these models will be quite secure. Otherwise, calculations are generally based on analogy: this group of people is like a random sample, that observational study is like a randomized experiment. The fit between the statistical model and the data may then require examination: how good is the analogy?

§ 5–4.1 Estimation

§ 5–4.1.1 What Estimator Should Be Used?

An estimator is a statistic computed from sample data and used to estimate a numerical characteristic of the population. For example, we used the difference in pass rates for a sample of men and women to estimate the corresponding disparity in the population of all applicants. In our sample, the pass rates were 58% and 38%; the difference in pass rates for the whole population was estimated as 20 percentage points: 58% – 38% = 20 percentage points. In more complex problems, statisticians may have to choose among several estimators. Generally, estimators that tend to make smaller errors are preferred. However, this idea can be made precise in more than one way,[5] leaving room for judgment in selecting an estimator.

§ 5–4.1.2 What Is the Standard Error? The Confidence Interval?

An estimate based on a sample is likely to be off the mark, at least by a little, due to random error: the standard error gives the likely magnitude of this random error.[6] Whenever possible, an estimate should be accompanied by its standard error.[7] In our example, the standard error is about 10 percentage points—the estimate of 20 percentage points is likely to be off by something like 10 percentage points or so, in either direction.[8] Since the pass rates for all

---

4. This classical framework is also called "objectivist" or "frequentist," by contrast with the "subjectivist" or "Bayesian" framework. In brief, objectivist statisticians view probabilities as objective properties of the system being studied. Subjectivists view probabilities as measuring subjective degrees of belief. Section 4.2.1 explains why posterior probabilities are excluded from the classical calculus, and section 4.3 briefly discusses the subjectivist position. The procedure for computing posterior probabilities is presented *infra* Appendix. For more discussion, see David Freedman, *Some Issues in the Foundations of Statistics*, 1 FOUND. SCI. 19 (1995), *reprinted in* TOPICS IN THE FOUNDATION OF STATISTICS 19 (Bas C. van Fraasen ed., 1997).

5. Furthermore, reducing error in one context may increase error in other contexts; there may also be a trade-off between accuracy and simplicity.

6. "Standard errors" are also called "standard deviations," and courts seem to prefer the latter term, as do many authors.

7. The standard error can also be used to guage reproducibility of estimates from one random sample to another. *See infra* Appendix note 5.

8. The standard error depends on the pass rates of men and women in the sample, and the size of the sample. With larger samples, chance error will be smaller, so the standard error goes down as sample size goes up. ("Sample size" is the number of subjects in the

5,000 men and 5,000 women are unknown, we cannot say exactly how far off the estimate is going to be, but 10 percentage points gauges the likely magnitude of the error.

Confidence intervals make the idea more precise. Statisticians who say that population differences fall within plus-or-minus 1 standard error of the sample differences will be correct about 68% of the time. To write this more compactly, we can abbreviate "standard error" as "SE." A 68% confidence interval is the range

$$\text{estimate} - 1 \text{ SE to estimate} + 1 \text{ SE}$$

In our example, the 68% confidence interval goes from 10 to 30 percentage points. If a higher confidence level is wanted, the interval must be widened. The 95% confidence interval is about

$$\text{estimate} - 2 \text{ SE to estimate} + 2 \text{ SE}$$

This runs from 0 to 40 percentage points.[9] Although 95% confidence intervals are used commonly, there is nothing special about 95%. For example, a 99.7% confidence interval is about

$$\text{estimate} - 3 \text{ SE to estimate} + 3 \text{ SE}$$

This stretches from –10 to 50 percentage points.

The main point is that an estimate based on a sample will differ from the exact population value, due to random error; the standard error measures the likely size of the random error. If the standard error is small, the estimate probably is close to the truth. If the standard error is large, the estimate may be seriously wrong. Confidence intervals are a technical refinement, and "confidence" is a term of art.[10] For a given confidence level, a narrower

sample.) The Appendix gives the formula for computing the standard error of a difference in rates based on random samples. Generally, the formula for the standard error must take into account the method used to draw the sample and the nature of the estimator. Statistical expertise is needed to choose the right formula.

9. Confidence levels are usually read off the normal curve (*see infra* Appendix). Technically, the area under the normal curve between –2 and +2 is closer to 95.4% than 95.0%; thus, statisticians often use ±1.96 SEs for a 95% confidence interval. However, the normal curve only gives an approximation to the relevant chances, and the error in that approximation will often be larger than the difference between 95.4% and 95.0%. For simplicity, we use ±2 SEs for 95% confidence. Likewise, we use ±1 SE for 68% confidence, although the area under the curve between –1 and +1 is closer to 68.3%. The normal curve gives good approximations when the sample size is reasonably large; for small samples, other techniques should be used.

10. In the standard frequentist theory of statistics, one cannot make probability statements about population characteristics. *See, e.g.*, DAVID FREEDMAN ET AL., STATISTICS 383–86 (3d ed. 1998); *infra* § 5–4.2.1. Consequently, it is imprecise to suggest that "[a] 95% confi-

dence interval means that there is a 95% probability that the 'true' relative risk falls within the interval." DeLuca v. Merrell Dow Pharms., Inc., 791 F.Supp. 1042, 1046 (D.N.J.1992), *aff'd*, 6 F.3d 778 (3d Cir.1993). Because of the limited technical meaning of "confidence," it has been argued that the term is misleading and should be replaced by a more neutral one, such as "frequency coefficient," in courtroom presentations. David H. Kaye, *Is Proof of Statistical Significance Relevant?*, 61 WASH. L. REV. 1333, 1354 (1986).

Another misconception is that the confidence level gives the chance that repeated estimates fall into the confidence interval. *E.g.*, Turpin v. Merrell Dow Pharms., Inc., 959 F.2d 1349, 1353 (6th Cir.1992) ("a confidence interval of '95 percent between 0.8 and 3.10' ... means that random repetition of the study should produce, 95 percent of the time, a relative risk somewhere between 0.8 and 3.10."); United States *ex rel.* Free v. Peters, 806 F.Supp. 705, 713 n. 6 (N.D.Ill.1992) ("A 99% confidence interval, for instance, is an indication that if we repeated our measurement 100 times under identical conditions, 99 times out of 100 the point estimate derived from the repeated experimentation will fall within the initial interval estimate...."), *rev'd in part*, 12 F.3d 700

interval indicates a more precise estimate. For a given sample size, increased confidence can be attained only by widening the interval. A high confidence level alone means very little,[11] but a high confidence level for a small interval is impressive,[12] indicating that the random error in the sample estimate is low.

Standard errors and confidence intervals are derived using statistical models of the process that generated the data.[13] If the data come from a probability sample or a randomized controlled experiment,[14] the statistical model may be connected tightly to the actual data-collection process. In other situations, using the model may be tantamount to assuming that a sample of convenience is like a random sample, or that an observational study is like a randomized experiment.

Our example was based on a random sample, and that justified the statistical calculations.[15] In many contexts, the choice of an appropriate

(7th Cir.1993). However, the confidence level does not give the percentage of the time that repeated estimates fall in the interval; instead, it gives the percentage of the time that intervals from repeated samples cover the true value.

11. Statements about the confidence in a sample without any mention of the interval estimate are practically meaningless. In *Hilao v. Estate of Marcos*, 103 F.3d 767 (9th Cir. 1996), for instance, "an expert on statistics . . . testified that . . . a random sample of 137 claims would achieve 'a 95% statistical probability that the same percentage determined to be valid among the examined claims would be applicable to the totality of [9,541 facially valid] claims filed.' " *Id.* at 782. Unfortunately, there is no 95% "statistical probability" that a percentage computed from a sample will be "applicable" to a population. One can compute a confidence interval from a random sample and be 95% confident that the interval covers some parameter. That can be done for a sample of virtually any size, with larger samples giving smaller intervals. What is missing from the opinion is a discussion of the widths of the relevant intervals.

12. Conversely, a broad interval signals that random error is substantial. In *Cimino v. Raymark Industries Inc.*, 751 F.Supp. 649 (E.D.Tex.1990), the district court drew certain random samples from more than 6,000 pending asbestos cases, tried these cases, and used the results to estimate the total award to be given to all plaintiffs in the pending cases. The court then held a hearing to determine whether the samples were large enough to provide accurate estimates. The court's expert, an educational psychologist, testified that the estimates were accurate because the samples matched the population on such characteristics as race and the percentage of plaintiffs still alive. *Id.* at 664. However, the matches occurred only in the sense that population characteristics fell within very broad 99% confidence intervals computed from the samples. The court thought that matches within the 99% confidence intervals

proved more than matches within 95% intervals. *Id.* Unfortunately, this is backwards. To be correct in a few instances with a 99% confidence interval is not very impressive—by definition, such intervals are broad enough to ensure coverage 99% of the time. *Cf.* Michael J. Saks & Peter David Blanck, *Justice Improved: The Unrecognized Benefits of Aggregation and Sampling in the Trial of Mass Torts*, 44 STAN. L. REV. 815 (1992).

13. Generally, statistical models enable the analyst to compute the chances of the various possible outcomes. For instance, the model may contain parameters, that is, numerical constants describing the population from which samples were drawn. *See infra* § 5–5.0. That is the case for our example, where one parameter is the pass rate of the 5,000 male applicants, and another parameter is the pass rate of the 5,000 female applicants. As explained in the Appendix, these parameters can be used to compute the chance of getting any particular sample difference. Using a model with known parameters to find the probability of an observed outcome (or one like it) is common in cases alleging discrimination in the selection of jurors. *E.g.*, Castaneda v. Partida, 430 U.S. 482, 496, 97 S.Ct. 1272, 51 L.Ed.2d 498 (1977); D.H. Kaye, STATISTICAL EVIDENCE OF DISCRIMINATION IN JURY SELECTION, IN STATISTICAL METHODS IN DISCRIMINATION LITIGATION 13 (D.H. Kaye & Mikel Aickin eds., 1986); *cf.* Hazelwood Sch. Dist. v. United States, 433 U.S. 299, 311 n. 17, 97 S.Ct. 2736, 53 L.Ed.2d 768 (1977) (computing probabilities of selecting black teachers). But when the values of the parameters are not known, the statistician must work backwards, using the sample data to estimate the unknown population parameters. That is the kind of statistical inference described in this section.

14. *See supra* §§ 5–2.1 & 5–2.2.

15. As discussed in the Appendix, large random samples give rise to certain normally distributed statistics. Partly because the Su-

statistical model is not obvious.[16] When a model does not fit the data-collection process so well, estimates and standard errors will be less probative.[17]

Standard errors and confidence intervals generally ignore systematic errors such as selection bias or non-response bias; in other words, these biases are assumed to be negligible.[18] For example, one court—reviewing studies of whether a particular drug causes birth defects—observed that mothers of children with birth defects may be more likely to remember taking a drug during pregnancy than women with normal children.[19] This selective recall would bias comparisons between samples from the two groups of women. The standard error for the estimated difference in drug usage between the two groups ignores this bias; so does the confidence interval.[20] Likewise, the

preme Court used such a model in *Hazelwood* and *Castaneda*, courts and attorneys sometimes are skeptical of analyses that produce other types of random variables. *See, e.g.,* EEOC v. Western Elec. Co., 713 F.2d 1011 (4th Cir.1983), *discussed in* David H. Kaye, *Ruminations on Jurimetrics: Hypergeometric Confusion in the Fourth Circuit*, 26 Jurimetrics J. 215 (1986). *But see* Branion v. Gramly, 855 F.2d 1256 (7th Cir.1988) (questioning an apparently arbitrary assumption of normality), *discussed in* David H. Kaye, *Statistics for Lawyers and Law for Statistics*, 89 Mich. L. Rev. 1520 (1991) (defending the use of the normal approximation); Michael O. Finkelstein & Bruce Levin, *Reference Guide on Statistics: Non Lasciare Esperanza*, 36 Jurimetrics J. 201, 205 (1996) (review essay) ("The court was right to reject the normal distribution. . . ."). Whether a given variable is normally distributed is an empirical or statistical question, not a matter of law.

16. *See infra* § 5–5.0. For examples of legal interest, see, e.g., Mary W. Gray, *Can Statistics Tell Us What We Do Not Want to Hear?: The Case of Complex Salary Structures*, 8 Stat. Sci. 144 (1993); Arthur P. Dempster, *Employment Discrimination and Statistical Science*, 3 Stat. Sci. 149 (1988). As one statistician describes the issue:

[A] given data set can be viewed from more than one perspective, can be represented by a model in more than one way. Quite commonly, no unique model stands out as "true" or correct; justifying so strong a conclusion might require a depth of knowledge that is simply lacking. So it is not unusual for a given data set to be analyzed in several apparently reasonable ways. If conclusions are qualitatively concordant, that is regarded as grounds for placing additional trust in them. But more often, only a single model is applied, and the data are analyzed in accordance with it. . . .

Desirable features in a model include (i) tractability, (ii) parsimony, and (iii) realism. That there is some tension among these is not surprising.

Tractability. A model that is easy to understand and to explain is tractable in one sense. Computational tractability can also be

an advantage, though with cheap computing available not too much weight can be given to it.

Parsimony. Simplicity, like tractability, has a direct appeal, not wisely ignored—but not wisely over-valued either. If several models are plausible and more than one of them fits adequately with the data, then in choosing among them, one criterion is to prefer a model that is simpler than the other models.

Realism. . . . First, does the model reflect well the actual [process that generated the data]? This question is really a host of questions, some about the distributions of the random errors, others about the mathematical relations among the [variables and] parameters. The second aspect of realism is sometimes called robustness: If the model is *false* in certain respects, how badly does that affect estimates, significance test results, etc., that are based on the flawed model?

Lincoln E. Moses, *The Reasoning of Statistical Inference, in* Perspectives on Contemporary Statistics 107, 117–18 (David C. Hoaglin & David S. Moore eds., 1992).

17. It still may be helpful to consider the standard error, perhaps as a minimal estimate for statistical uncertainty in the quantity being estimated.

18. For a discussion of such systematic errors, *see supra* § 5–2.2.

19. Brock v. Merrell Dow Pharms., Inc., 874 F.2d 307, 311–12 (5th Cir.), *modified*, 884 F.2d 166 (5th Cir.1989).

20. In *Brock*, the court stated that the confidence interval took account of bias (in the form of selective recall) as well as random error. 874 F.2d at 311–12. With respect, we disagree. Even if sampling error were nonexistent—which would be the case if one could interview every woman who had a child in the period that the drug was available—selective recall would produce a difference in the percentages of reported drug exposure between mothers of children with birth defects and those with normal children. In this hypothetical situation, the standard error would vanish.

standard error does not address problems inherent in using convenience samples rather than random samples.[21]

§ 5–4.2 Significance Levels and Hypothesis Tests

§ 5–4.2.1 What Is the p-value?

In our example, 50 men and 50 women were drawn at random from 5,000 male and 5,000 female applicants. An exam was administered to this sample, and in the sample, the pass rates for the men and women were 58% and 38%, respectively. The sample difference in pass rates was 58% – 38% = 20 percentage points. The *p*-value answers the following question: If the pass rates among all 5,000 male applicants and 5,000 female applicants were identical, how probable would it be to find a discrepancy as big as or bigger than the 20 percentage point difference observed in our sample? The question is delicate, because the pass rates in the population are unknown—that is why a sample was taken in the first place.

The assertion that the pass rates in the population are the same is called the null hypothesis. The null hypothesis asserts that there is no difference between men and women in the whole population—differences in the sample are due to the luck of the draw. The *p*-value is the probability of getting data as extreme as, or more extreme than, the actual data, given that the null hypothesis is true:

$$p = \text{Probability (extreme data} \,|\, \text{null hypothesis in model)}$$

In our example, $p = 5\%$. If the null hypothesis is true, there is only a 5% chance of getting a difference in the pass rates of 20 percentage points or more.[22] The *p*-value for the observed discrepancy is 5%, or 0.05.[23]

In such cases, small *p*-values are evidence of disparate impact, while large *p*-values are evidence against disparate impact. Regrettably, multiple negatives are involved here. A statistical test is essentially an argument by contradiction. The "null hypothesis" asserts no difference in the population—that is, no disparate impact. Small *p*-values speak against the null hypothesis—there is disparate impact, because the observed difference is hard to explain by chance alone. Conversely, large *p*-values indicate that the data are compatible with the null hypothesis: the observed difference is easy to explain by chance. In this context, small *p*-values argue for the plaintiffs, while large *p*-values argue for the defense.[24]

Since *p* is calculated by assuming the null hypothesis is correct (no real difference in pass rates), the *p*-value cannot give the chance that this hypothesis is true. The *p*-value merely gives the chance of getting evidence against the null hypothesis as strong or stronger than the evidence at hand—assuming the null hypothesis to be correct. No matter how many samples are obtained, the null hypothesis is either always right or always wrong. Chance affects the

Therefore, the standard error could disclose nothing about the impact of selective recall. The same conclusion holds even in the presence of sampling error.

21. *See supra* § 5–2.2.1.

22. *See infra* Appendix.

23. Literally, 5 percent is 5 per 100, and $5/100 = 0.05$.

24. Of course, sample size must also be considered, among other factors. *See infra* § 5–4.3.

data, not the hypothesis. With the frequency interpretation of chance, there is no meaningful way to assign a numerical probability to the null hypothesis.[25]

Computing *p*-values requires statistical expertise. Many methods are available, but only some will fit the occasion. Sometimes standard errors will be part of the analysis, while other times they will not be. Sometimes a difference of 2 standard errors will imply a *p*-value of about 5%, other times it will not. In general, the *p*-value depends on the model and its parameters, the size of the sample, and the sample statistics.[26]

Because the *p*-value is affected by sample size, it does not measure the extent or importance of a difference.[27] Suppose, for instance, that the 5,000 male and 5,000 female job applicants would differ in their pass rates, but only by a single percentage point. This difference might not be enough to make a case of disparate impact, but by including enough men and women in the sample, the data could be made to have an impressively small *p*-value. This *p*-value would confirm that the 5,000 men and 5,000 women have different pass rates, but it would not show the difference is substantial.[28] In short, the *p*-value does not measure the strength or importance of an association.

§ 5–4.2.2　Is a Difference Statistically Significant?

Statistical significance is determined by comparing a *p*-value to a preestablished value, the significance level.[29] If an observed difference is in the middle of the distribution that would be expected under the null hypothesis, there is no surprise. The sample data are of the type that often would be seen when the null hypothesis is true: the difference is not significant, and the null

25. *See, e.g.*, STATISTICAL ASSESSMENTS AS EVIDENCE IN THE COURTS, NATIONAL RESEARCH COUNCIL, THE EVOLVING ROLE OF STATISTICAL ASSESSMENTS AS EVIDENCE IN THE COURTS 196–98 (Stephen E. Fienberg ed., 1989); David H. Kaye, *Statistical Significance and the Burden of Persuasion*, LAW & CONTEMP. PROBS., Autumn 1983, at 13. Some opinions suggest a contrary view. *E.g.*, Vasquez v. Hillery, 474 U.S. 254, 259 n. 3, 106 S.Ct. 617, 88 L.Ed.2d 598 (1986) ("the District Court ... ultimately accepted ... a probability of 2 in 1,000 that the phenomenon was attributable to chance."); EEOC v. Olson's Dairy Queens, Inc., 989 F.2d 165, 167 (5th Cir.1993) ("Dr. Straszheim concluded that the likelihood that [the] observed hiring patterns resulted from truly race-neutral hiring practices was less than one chance in ten thousand"); Capaci v. Katz & Besthoff, Inc., 711 F.2d 647, 652 (5th Cir.1983) ("the highest probability of unbiased hiring was 5.367×10^{-20}"). Such statements confuse the probability of the kind of outcome observed, which is computed under some model of chance, with the probability that chance is the explanation for the outcome.

In scientific notation, 10^{20} is 1 followed by 20 zeros, and 10^{-20} is the reciprocal of that number. The proverbial "one-in-a-million" is more dryly expressed as 1×10^{-6}.

26. In this context, a parameter is an unknown numerical constant that is part of the statistical model. *See supra* note 13.

27. Some opinions seem to equate small *p*-values with "gross" or "substantial" disparities. *E.g.*, Craik v. Minnesota St. Univ. Bd., 731 F.2d 465, 479 (8th Cir.1984). Other courts have emphasized the need to decide whether the underlying sample statistics reveal that a disparity is large. *E.g.*, McCleskey v. Kemp, 753 F.2d 877, 892–94 (11th Cir.1985), *aff'd*, 481 U.S. 279, 107 S.Ct. 1756, 95 L.Ed.2d 262 (1987).

28. *Cf.* Frazier v. Garrison Indep. Sch. Dist., 980 F.2d 1514, 1526 (5th Cir.1993) (rejecting claims of intentional discrimination in the use of a teacher competency examination that resulted in retention rates exceeding 95% for all groups).

29. Statisticians use the Greek letter alpha (α) to denote the significance level; α gives the chance of getting a "significant" result, assuming that the null hypothesis is true. Thus, α represents the chance of what is variously termed a "false rejection" of the null hypothesis or a "type I error" (also called a "false positive" or a "false alarm"). For example, suppose $\alpha = 5\%$. If investigators do many studies, and the null hypothesis happens to be true in each case, then about 5% of the time they would obtain significant results—and falsely reject the null hypothesis.

hypothesis cannot be rejected. On the other hand, if the sample difference is far from the expected value—according to the null hypothesis—then the sample is unusual: the difference is "significant," and the null hypothesis is rejected. In our example, the 20 percentage point difference in pass rates for the men and women in the sample, whose p-value was about 5%, might be considered significant at the 5% level. If the threshold were set lower, say at 1%, the result would not be significant.[30]

In practice, statistical analysts often use certain preset significance levels—typically 5% or 1%.[31] The 5% level is the most common in social science, and an analyst who speaks of "significant" results without specifying the threshold probably is using this figure.[32] An unexplained reference to "highly significant" results probably means that p is less than 1%.[33]

Since the term "significant" is merely a label for certain kinds of p-values, it is subject to the same limitations as are p-values themselves. Analysts may refer to a difference as "significant," meaning only that the p-value is below some threshold value. Significance depends not only on the magnitude of the effect, but also on the sample size (among other things). Thus, significant differences are evidence that something besides random error is at work, but they are not evidence that this "something" is legally or practically important. Statisticians distinguish between "statistical" and "practical" significance to make the point. When practical significance is lacking—when the size of a disparity or correlation is negligible—there is no reason to worry about statistical significance.[34]

As noted above, it is easy to mistake the p-value for the probability that there is no difference. Likewise, if results are significant at the 5% level, it is tempting to conclude that the null hypothesis has only a 5% chance of being correct.[35] This temptation should be resisted. From the frequentist perspec-

---

30. For the relationship between a test statistic and significance, see *infra* § 5–5.4.2.

31. The Supreme Court implicitly referred to this practice in *Castaneda v. Partida*, 430 U.S. 482, 496 n. 17, 97 S.Ct. 1272, 51 L.Ed.2d 498 (1977), and *Hazelwood School District v. United States*, 433 U.S. 299, 311 n. 17, 97 S.Ct. 2736, 53 L.Ed.2d 768 (1977). In these footnotes, the Court described the null hypothesis as "suspect to a social scientist" when a statistic from "large samples" falls more than "two or three standard deviations" from its expected value under the null hypothesis. Although the Court did not say so, these differences produce p-values of about 5% and 1% when the statistic is normally distributed. The Court's "standard deviation" is our "standard error."

32. Some have suggested that data not "significant" at the 5% level should be disregarded. *E.g.*, Paul Meier et al., *What Happened in* Hazelwood: *Statistics, Employment Discrimination, and the 80% Rule*, 1984 Am. B. Found. Res. J. 139, 152, *reprinted in* Statistics and the Law, 1, 13 (Morris H. DeGroot et al. eds., 1986). This view is challenged in, e.g., Kaye, *supra* note 10, at 1344 & n.56, 1345.

33. Merely labeling results as "significant" or "not significant" without providing the un-

derlying information that goes into this conclusion is of limited value. *See, e.g.*, John C. Bailar III & Frederick Mosteller, *Guidelines for Statistical Reporting in Articles for Medical Journals: Amplifications and Explanations, in* Medical Uses of Statistics 313, 316 (John C. Bailar III & Frederick Mosteller eds., 2d ed. 1992).

34. *E.g.*, Waisome v. Port Auth., 948 F.2d 1370, 1376 (2d Cir.1991) ("though the disparity was found to be statistically significant, it was of limited magnitude"); *cf.* Thornburg v. Gingles, 478 U.S. 30, 53–54, 106 S.Ct. 2752, 92 L.Ed.2d 25 (1986) (repeating the district court's explanation of why "the correlation between the race of the voter and the voter's choice of certain candidates was [not only] statistically significant," but also "so marked as to be substantively significant, in the sense that the results of the individual election would have been different depending upon whether it had been held among only the white voters or only the black voters.").

35. *E.g.*, Waisome, 948 F.2d at 1376 ("Social scientists consider a finding of two standard deviations significant, meaning there is about one chance in 20 that the explanation for a deviation could be random...."); Rivera v.

tive, statistical hypotheses are either true or false; probabilities govern the samples, not the models and hypotheses. The significance level tells us what is likely to happen when the null hypothesis is correct; it cannot tell us the probability that the hypothesis is true. Significance comes no closer to expressing the probability that the null hypothesis is true than does the underlying *p*-value.[36]

§ 5–4.3 Evaluating Hypothesis Tests

§ 5–4.3.1 What Is the Power of the Test?

When a *p*-value is high, findings are not significant, and the null hypothesis is not rejected. This could happen for at least two reasons:

1.   there is no difference in the population—the null hypothesis is true; or

2.   there is some difference in the population—the null hypothesis is false—but, by chance, the data happened to be of the kind expected under the null hypothesis.

If the "power" of a statistical study is low, the second explanation may be plausible. Power is the chance that a statistical test will declare an effect when there is an effect to declare.[37] This chance depends on the size of the effect and the size of the sample. Discerning subtle differences in the population requires large samples; even so, small samples may detect truly substantial differences.[38]

City of Wichita Falls, 665 F.2d 531, 545 n. 22 (5th Cir.1982) ("A variation of two standard deviations would indicate that the probability of the observed outcome occurring purely by chance would be approximately five out of 100; that is, it could be said with a 95% certainty that the outcome was not merely a fluke."); Vuyanich v. Republic Nat'l Bank, 505 F.Supp. 224, 272 (N.D.Tex.1980) ("[I]f a 5% level of significance is used, a sufficiently large *t*-statistic for the coefficient indicates that the chances are less than one in 20 that the true coefficient is actually zero."), *vacated*, 723 F.2d 1195 (5th Cir.1984); Sheehan v. Daily Racing Form, Inc., 104 F.3d 940, 941 (7th Cir.1997) ("An affidavit by a statistician ... states that the probability that the retentions ... are uncorrelated with age is less than 5 percent.").

36. For more discussion, see Kaye, *supra* note 10; *cf. infra* note 60.

37. More precisely, power is the probability of rejecting the null hypothesis when the alternative hypothesis is right. (On the meaning of "alternative hypothesis," see infra § 5–4.3.5.) Typically, this probability will depend on the values of unknown parameters, as well as the pre-set significance level α. Therefore, no single number gives the power of the test. One can specify particular values for the parameters and significance level, and compute the power of the test accordingly. *See infra* Appendix for an example. Power may be denoted by the Greek letter beta (β).

Accepting the null hypothesis when the alternative is true is known as a "false acceptance" of the null hypothesis or a "type II error" (also called a "false negative" or a "missed signal"). The chance of a false negative may be computed from the power, as $1-\beta$. Frequentist hypothesis testing keeps the risk of a false positive to a specified level (such as $\alpha = 5\%$) and then tries to minimize the chance of a false negative $(1-\beta)$ for that value of α. Regrettably, the notation is in some degree of flux; many authors use β to denote the chance of a false negative; then, it is β that should be minimized.

Some commentators have claimed that the cutoff for significance should be chosen to equalize the chance of a false positive and a false negative, on the ground that this criterion corresponds to the "more-probable-than-not" burden of proof. The argument is fallacious, because α and β do not give the probabilities of the null and alternative hypotheses; *see supra* § 5–4.2.2; *infra* note 167. *See* D. H. Kaye, *Hypothesis Testing in the Courtroom, in* Contributions to the Theory and Application of Statistics: A Volume in Honor of Herbert Solomon 331, 341–43 (Alan E. Gelfand ed., 1987); *see supra* § 5–4.2.1; *infra* note 58.

38. For simplicity, the numerical examples of statistical inference in this chapter presuppose large samples. Some courts have expressed uneasiness about estimates based on small samples; indeed, a few courts have re-

When a study with low power fails to show a significant effect, the results are more fairly described as inconclusive than as negative: the proof is weak because power is low.[39] On the other hand, when studies have a good chance of detecting a meaningful association, failure to obtain significance can be persuasive evidence that there is no effect to be found.[40]

§ 5–4.3.2 One- or Two-tailed Tests?

In many cases, a statistical test can done be either one-tailed or two-tailed. The second method will produce a p-value twice as big as the first method. Since small p-values are evidence against the null hypothesis, a one-tailed test seems to produce stronger evidence than a two-tailed test. However, this difference is largely illusory.[41]

fused even to consider such studies or formal statistical procedures for handling small samples. *See, e.g.*, Bunch v. Bullard, 795 F.2d 384, 395 n. 12 (5th Cir.1986) (that 12 of 15 whites and only 3 of 13 blacks passed a police promotion test created a prima facie case of disparate impact; however, "[t]he district court did not perform, nor do we attempt, the application of probability theories to a sample size as small as this" because "[a]dvanced statistical analysis may be of little help in determining the significance of such disparities"); United States v. Lansdowne Swim Club, 713 F.Supp. 785, 809–10 (E.D.Pa.1989) (collecting cases). Other courts have been much more venturesome. *E.g.*, Bazemore v. Friday, 751 F.2d 662, 673 & n. 9 (4th Cir.1984) (court of appeals applied its own *t*-test rather than the normal curve to quartile rankings in an attempt to account for a sample size of nine), *rev'd on other grounds*, 478 U.S. 385, 106 S.Ct. 3000, 92 L.Ed.2d 315 (1986).

Analyzing data from small samples may require more stringent assumptions, but there is no fundamental difference in the meaning of confidence intervals and p-values. If the assumptions underlying the statistical analysis are justified—and this can be more difficult to demonstrate with small samples—then confidence intervals and test statistics are no less trustworthy than those for large samples. Aside from the problem of choosing the correct analytical technique, the concern with small samples is not that they are beyond the ken of statistical theory, but that (i) the statistical tests involving small samples might lack power, and (ii) the underlying assumptions may be hard to validate.

39. In our example, with $\alpha = 5\%$, power to detect a difference of 10 percentage points between the male and female job applicants is only about 1/6. *See infra* Appendix. Not seeing a "significant" difference therefore provides only weak proof that the difference between men and women is smaller than 10 percentage points. We prefer estimates accompanied by standard errors to tests because the former seem to make the state of the statistical evi-

dence clearer: The estimated difference is 20 ± 10 percentage points, indicating that a difference of 10 percentage points is quite compatible with the data.

40. Some formal procedures are available to aggregate results across studies. *See In re Paoli R.R. Yard PCB Litig.*, 916 F.2d 829 (3d Cir.1990). In principle, the power of the collective results will be greater than the power of each study. *See, e.g.*, THE HANDBOOK OF RESEARCH SYNTHESIS 226–27 (Harris Cooper & Larry V. Hedges eds., 1993); LARRY V. HEDGES & INGRAM OLKIN, STATISTICAL METHODS FOR META-ANALYSIS (1985); Jerome P. Kassirer, *Clinical Trials and Meta–Analysis: What Do They Do for Us?*, 327 NEW ENG. J. MED. 273, 274 (1992) ("[C]umulative meta-analysis represents one promising approach."); NATIONAL RESEARCH COUNCIL, COMBINING INFORMATION: STATISTICAL ISSUES AND OPPORTUNITIES FOR RESEARCH (1992); Symposium, *Meta-Analysis of Observational Studies*, 140 AM. J. EPIDEMIOLOGY 771 (1994). Unfortunately, the procedures have their own limitations. *E.g.*, DIANA B. PETITTI, META-ANALYSIS, DECISION ANALYSIS, AND COST-EFFECTIVENESS ANALYSIS: METHODS FOR QUANTITATIVE SYNTHESIS IN MEDICINE (2d ed. 2000); MICHAEL OAKES, STATISTICAL INFERENCE: A COMMENTARY FOR THE SOCIAL AND BEHAVIORAL SCIENCES 157 (1986) ("a retrograde development"); John C. Bailar III, *Passive Smoking, Coronary Heart Disease, and Meta–Analysis*, 340 NEW ENG. J. MED. 958–59 (1999) ("Meta-analysis ... is widely used, but with little general understanding of its limitations and uncertainties."); John C. Bailar III, *The Promise and Problems of Meta–Analysis*, 337 NEW ENG. J. MED. 559 (1997) (editorial); David A. Katerndahl & W. Ross Lawler, *Variability in Meta–Analytic Results Concerning the Value of Cholesterol Reduction in Coronary Heart Disease: A Meta–Meta–Analysis*, 149 AM. J. EPIDEMIOLOGY 429 (1999); Charles Mann, *Meta–Analysis in the Breech*, 249 SCIENCE 476 (1990).

41. In our pass rate example, the p-value of the test is approximated by a certain area under the normal curve. The one-tailed procedure uses the "tail area" under the curve to

Some courts have expressed a preference for two-tailed tests,[42] but a rigid rule is not required if *p*-values and significance levels are used as clues rather than as mechanical rules for statistical proof. One-tailed tests make it easier to reach a threshold like 5%, but if 5% is not used as a magic line, then the choice between one tail and two is less important—as long as the choice and its effect on the *p*-value are made explicit.[43]

§ 5–4.3.3 How Many Tests Have Been Performed?

Repeated testing complicates the interpretation of significance levels. If enough comparisons are made, random error almost guarantees that some will yield "significant" findings, even when there is no real effect. Consider the problem of deciding whether a coin is biased. The probability that a fair coin will produce ten heads when tossed ten times is $(1/2)^{10} = 1/1,024$. Observing ten heads in the first ten tosses, therefore, would be strong evidence that the coin is biased. Nevertheless, if a fair coin is tossed a few thousand times, it is likely that at least one string of ten consecutive heads will appear. The test—looking for a run of ten heads—can be repeated far too often.

Such artifacts are commonplace. Since research that fails to uncover significance is not usually published, reviews of the literature may produce an unduly large number of studies finding statistical significance.[44] Even a single researcher may search for so many different relationships that a few will achieve statistical significance by mere happenstance. Almost any large data set—even pages from a table of random digits—will contain some unusual pattern that can be uncovered by a diligent search. Having detected the pattern, the analyst can perform a statistical test for it, blandly ignoring the search effort. Statistical significance is bound to follow. Ten heads in the first

---

the right of 2, giving $p = 2.5\%$ (approximately). The two-tailed procedure contemplates the area to the left of –2, as well as the area to the right of 2. Now there are two tails, and $p = 5\%$. See *infra* Appendix (figure 13); Freedman et al., *supra* note 10, at 549–52.

According to formal statistical theory, the choice between one tail or two can sometimes be made by considering the exact form of the "alternative hypothesis." *See infra* § 5–4.3.5. In our example, the null hypothesis is that pass rates are equal for men and women in the whole population of applicants. The alternative hypothesis may exclude a priori the possibility that women have a higher pass rate, and hold that more men will pass than women. This asymmetric alternative suggests a one-tailed test. On the other hand, the alternative hypothesis may simply be that pass rates for men and women in the whole population are unequal. This symmetric alternative admits the possibility that women may score higher than men, and points to a two-tailed test. *See, e.g.*, Freedman et al., *supra* note 10, at 551. Some experts think that the choice between one-tailed and two-tailed tests can often be made by considering the exact form of the null and alternative hypotheses.

42. *See, e.g.*, David C. Baldus & James W.L. Cole, Statistical Proof of Discrimination, § 9.1, at 308 n.35a (1980); The Evolving Role of Statistical Assessments as Evidence in the Courts, *supra* note 25, at 38–40 (citing EEOC v. Federal Reserve Bank, 698 F.2d 633 (4th Cir.1983), *rev'd on other grounds sub nom.* Cooper v. Federal Reserve Bank, 467 U.S. 867, 104 S.Ct. 2794, 81 L.Ed.2d 718 (1984)); Kaye, *supra* note 10, at 1358 n.113; David H. Kaye, *The Numbers Game: Statistical Inference in Discrimination Cases*, 80 Mich. L. Rev. 833 (1982) (citing Hazelwood Sch. Dist. v. United States, 433 U.S. 299, 97 S.Ct. 2736, 53 L.Ed.2d 768 (1977)). Arguments for one-tailed tests are discussed in Michael O. Finkelstein & Bruce Levin, Statistics for Lawyers 120–22 (2d ed. 2001); Richard Goldstein, *Two Types of Statistical Errors in Employment Discrimination Cases*, 26 Jurimetrics J. 32 (1985); Kaye, *supra*, at 841.

43. One-tailed tests at the 5% level are viewed as weak evidence—no weaker standard is commonly used in the technical literature.

44. *E.g.*, Stuart J. Pocock et al., *Statistical Problems in the Reporting of Clinical Trials: A Survey of Three Medical Journals*, 317 New Eng. J. Med. 426 (1987).

ten tosses means one thing; a run of ten heads somewhere along the way in a few thousand tosses of a coin means quite another.

There are statistical methods for coping with multiple looks at the data, which permit the calculation of meaningful *p*-values in certain cases.[45] However, no general solution is available, and the existing methods would be of little help in the typical case where analysts have tested and rejected a variety of regression models before arriving at the one considered the most satisfactory. In these situations, courts should not be overly impressed with claims that estimates are significant. Instead, they should be asking how analysts developed their models.[46]

§ 5–4.3.4   Tests or Interval Estimates?

Statistical significance depends on the *p*-value, and *p*-values depend on sample size. Therefore, a "significant" effect could be small. Conversely, an effect that is "not significant" could be large.[47] By inquiring into the magnitude of an effect, courts can avoid being misled by *p*-values. To focus attention where it belongs—on the actual size of an effect and the reliability of the statistical analysis—interval estimates may be valuable.[48] Seeing a plausible range of values for the quantity of interest helps describe the statistical uncertainty in the estimate.

In our example, the 95% confidence interval for the difference in the pass rates of men and women ranged from 0 to 40 percentage points. Our best estimate is that the pass rate for men is 20 percentage points higher than for women; and the difference may plausibly be as little as 0 or as much as 40 percentage points. The *p*-value does not yield this information. The confidence interval contains the information provided by a significance test—and more.[49] For instance, significance at the 5% level can be read off the 95% confidence interval.[50] In our example, zero is at the extreme edge of the 95% confidence interval, so we have "significant" evidence that the true difference in pass rates between male and female applicants is not zero. But there are values very close to zero inside the interval.

45. *See, e.g.*, Rupert G. Miller, Jr., Simultaneous Statistical Inference (2d ed. 1981).

46. *See, e.g.*, On Model Uncertainty and Its Statistical Implications: Lecture Notes in Econometric and Mathematical Systems (Theo K. Dijkstra ed., 1988); Frank T. Denton, *Data Mining As an Industry*, 67 Rev. Econ. & Stat. 124 (1985). Intuition may suggest that the more variables included in the model, the better. However, this idea often seems to be wrong. Complex models may reflect only accidental features of the data. Standard statistical tests offer little protection against this possibility when the analyst has tried a variety of models before settling on the final specification. *See* Clifford C. Clogg & Adamantious Haritou, *The Regression Method of Causal Inference and a Dilemma Confronting This Method*, *in* Causality in Crisis 83 (Vaughn R. McKim & Stephen P. Turner eds., 1997).

47. *See supra* § 5–4.2.1.

48. An interval estimate may be composed of a point estimate—like the sample mean used to estimate the population mean—together with its standard error; or the point estimate and standard error can be combined in a confidence interval.

49. Accordingly, it has been argued that courts should demand confidence intervals (whenever they can be computed) to the exclusion of explicit significance tests and *p*-values. Kaye, *supra* note 10, at 1349 n.78; *cf.* Bailar & Mosteller, *supra* note 33, at 317.

50. Instead of referring to significance at the 5% level, some writers refer to "the 95 percent confidence level that is often used by scientists to reject the possibility that chance alone accounted for the observed differences." Carnegie Comm'n on Science, Tech. & Gov't, Science and Technology in Judicial Decision Making: Creating Opportunities and Meeting Challenges 28 (1993).

On the other hand, suppose a significance test fails to reject the null hypothesis. The confidence interval may prevent the mistake of thinking there is positive proof for the null hypothesis. To illustrate, let us change our example slightly: say that 29 men and 20 women passed the test. The 95% confidence interval goes from -2 to 38 percentage points. Because a difference of zero falls within the 95% confidence interval, the null hypothesis—that the true difference is zero—cannot be rejected at the 5% level. But the interval extends to 38 percentage points, indicating that the population difference could be substantial. Lack of significance does not exclude this possibility.[51]

§ 5–4.3.5   What Are the Rival Hypotheses?

The *p*-value of a statistical test is computed on the basis of a model for the data—the null hypothesis. Usually, the test is made in order to argue for the alternative hypothesis—another model. However, on closer examination, both models may prove to be unreasonable.[52] A small *p*-value means something is going on, besides random error; the alternative hypothesis should be viewed as one possible explanation—out of many—for the data.[53]

In *Mapes Casino, Inc. v. Maryland Casualty Co.*,[54] for example, the court recognized the importance of explanations that the proponent of the statistical evidence had failed to consider. In this action to collect on an insurance policy, Mapes Casino sought to quantify the amount of its loss due to employee defalcation. The casino argued that certain employees were using an intermediary to cash in chips at other casinos. It established that over an 18–month period, the win percentage at its craps tables was 6%, compared to an expected value of 20%. The court recognized that the statistics were probative of the fact that *something* was wrong at the craps tables—the discrepancy was too big to explain as the mere product of random chance. But it was not convinced by plaintiff's alternative hypothesis. The court pointed to other possible explanations (Runyonesque activities like "skimming," "scamming," and "crossroading") that might have accounted for the discrepancy without implicating the suspect employees.[55] In short, rejection of the null hypothesis

---

51. We have used two-sided intervals, corresponding to two-tailed tests. One-sided intervals, corresponding to one-tailed tests, also are available.

52. Often, the null and alternative hypotheses are statements about possible ranges of values for parameters in a common statistical model. *See, e.g., supra* note 41. Computations of standard errors, *p*-values, and power all take place within the confines of this basic model. The statistical analysis looks at the relative plausibility for competing values of the parameters, but makes no global assessment of the reasonableness of the basic model.

53. *See, e.g.,* Paul Meier & Sandy Zabell, *Benjamin Peirce and the Howland Will*, 75 J. AM. STAT. ASS'N 497 (1980) (competing explanations in a forgery case). Outside the legal realm there are many intriguing examples of the tendency to think that a small *p*-value is definitive proof of an alternative hypothesis, even though there are other plausible explanations for the data. *See, e.g.,* FREEDMAN ET AL., *supra* note 10,

at 562–63; C. E. M. HANSEL, ESP: A SCIENTIFIC EVALUATION (1966).

In many studies, the validity of the model is secured by the procedures used to collect the data. There are formulas for standard errors and confidence intervals that hold when random samples are used. *See supra* §§ 5–4.1.2 & 5–4.2. There are statistical tests for comparing two random samples, or evaluating the results of a randomized experiment. *See supra* §§ 5–2.1 & 5–4.2.2. In such examples, the statistical procedures flow from the sampling method and the design of the study. On the other hand, if samples of convenience are used, or subjects are not randomized, the validity of the statistical procedures can be contested. *See* FREEDMAN ET AL., *supra* note 10, at 387–88, 424, 557–65.

54. 290 F.Supp. 186 (D.Nev.1968).

55. *Id.* at 193. "Skimming" consists of "taking off the top before counting the drop," "scamming" is "cheating by collusion between dealer and player," and "crossroading" in-

does not leave the proffered alternative hypothesis as the only viable explanation for the data.[56]

§ 5–4.4 Posterior Probabilities

Standard errors, *p*-values, and significance tests are common techniques for assessing random error. These procedures rely on the sample data, and are justified in terms of the "operating characteristics" of the statistical procedures.[57] However, this frequentist approach does not permit the statistician to compute the probability that a particular hypothesis is correct, given the data.[58] For instance, a frequentist may postulate that a coin is fair: it has a 50–50 chance of landing heads, and successive tosses are independent; this is viewed as an empirical statement—potentially falsifiable—about the coin. On this basis, it is easy to calculate the chance that the coin will turn up heads in the next ten tosses:[59] the answer is 1/1,024. Therefore, observing ten heads in a row brings into serious question the initial hypothesis of fairness. Rejecting the hypothesis of fairness when there are ten heads in ten tosses gives the wrong result—when the coin is fair—only one time in 1,024. That is an example of an operating characteristic of a statistical procedure.

But what of the converse probability: if a coin lands heads ten times in a row, what is the chance that it is fair?[60] To compute such converse probabilities, it is necessary to postulate initial probabilities that the coin is fair, as well as probabilities of unfairness to various degrees.[61] And that is beyond the

---

volves "professional cheaters among the players." *Id.* In plainer language, the court seems to have ruled that the casino itself might be cheating, or there could have been cheaters other than the particular employees identified in the case. At the least, plaintiff's statistical evidence did not rule out such possibilities.

56. *Compare* EEOC v. Sears, Roebuck & Co., 839 F.2d 302, 312 & n. 9, 313 (7th Cir. 1988) (EEOC's regression studies showing significant differences did not establish liability because surveys and testimony supported the rival hypothesis that women generally had less interest in commission sales positions), *with* EEOC v. General Tel. Co., 885 F.2d 575 (9th Cir.1989) (unsubstantiated rival hypothesis of "lack of interest" in "non-traditional" jobs insufficient to rebut prima facie case of gender discrimination); *cf. supra* § 5–2.1 (problem of confounding); *infra* § 5–5.4.3 note 52 (effect of omitting important variables from a regression model).

57. "Operating characteristics" are the expected value and standard error of estimators, probabilities of error for statistical tests, and related quantities.

58. *See supra* § 5–4.2.1; *infra* Appendix. Consequently, quantities such as *p*-values or confidence levels cannot be compared directly to numbers like 0.95 or 0.50 that might be thought to quantify the burden of persuasion in criminal or civil cases. *See* Kaye, *supra* note 37; D.H. Kaye, *Apples and Oranges: Confidence*

Coefficients and the Burden of Persuasion, 73 Cornell L. Rev. 54 (1987).

59. Stated slightly more formally, if the coin is fair and each outcome is independent (the hypothesis), then the probability of observing ten heads (the data) is $\Pr(\text{data}|H_0) = (1/2)^{10} = 1/1,024$, where H_0 stands for the hypothesis that the coin is fair.

60. We call this a "converse probability" because it is of the form $\Pr(H_0|\text{data})$ rather than $\Pr(\text{data}|H_0)$; an equivalent phrase, "inverse probability," also is used. The tendency to think of $\Pr(\text{data}|H_0)$ as if it were the converse probability $\Pr(H_0|\text{data})$ sometimes is called the "transposition fallacy." For instance, most United States senators are men, but very few men are senators; consequently, there is a high probability that an individual who is a senator is a man, but the probability that an individual who is a man is a senator is practically zero. For examples of the transposition fallacy in court opinions, see cases cited *supra* note 35; *see also* Committee on DNA Forensic Science: An Update, National Research Council, The Evaluation of Forensic DNA Evidence 133 (1996) (describing the fallacy in cases involving DNA identification evidence as the "prosecutor's fallacy"). The frequentist *p*-value, $\Pr(\text{data}|H_0)$, is generally not a good approximation to the Bayesian $\Pr(H_0|\text{data})$; the latter includes considerations of power and base rates.

61. *See infra* Appendix.

scope of frequentist statistics.[62]

In the Bayesian or subjectivist approach, probabilities represent subjective degrees of belief rather than objective facts. The observer's confidence in the hypothesis that a coin is fair, for example, is expressed as a number between zero and one;[63] likewise, the observer must quantify beliefs about the chance that the coin is unfair to various degrees—all in advance of seeing the data.[64] These subjective probabilities, like the probabilities governing the tosses of the coin, are set up to obey the axioms of probability theory. The probabilities for the various hypotheses about the coin, specified before data collection, are called prior probabilities.

These prior probabilities can then be updated, using "Bayes' rule," given data on how the coin actually falls.[65] In short, Bayesian statisticians can compute posterior probabilities for various hypotheses about the coin, given the data.[66] Although such posterior probabilities can pertain directly to hypothesis of legal interest, they are necessarily subjective, for they reflect not just the data but also the subjective prior probabilities—that is, the degrees of belief about the various hypotheses concerning the coin, specified prior to obtaining the data.[67]

62. In some situations, the probability of an event on which a case depends can be computed with objective methods. However, these events are measurable outcomes (like the number of heads in a series of tosses of a coin) rather than hypotheses about the process that generated the data (like the claim that the coin is fair). For example, in *United States v. Shonubi*, 895 F.Supp. 460 (E.D.N.Y.1995), *rev'd*, 103 F.3d 1085 (2d Cir.1997), a government expert estimated for sentencing purposes the total quantity of heroin that a Nigerian defendant living in New Jersey had smuggled (by swallowing heroin-filled balloons) in the course of eight trips to and from Nigeria. He applied a method known as "resampling" or "bootstrapping." Specifically, he drew 100,000 independent simple random samples of size seven from a population of weights distributed as in customs data on 117 other balloon swallowers caught in the same airport during the same time period; he discovered that for 99% of these samples, the total weight was at least 2090.2 grams. 895 F. Supp. at 504. Thus, the researcher reported that "there is a 99% chance that Shonubi carried at least 2090.2 grams of heroin on the seven [prior] trips...." *Id.* However, the Second Circuit reversed this finding for want of "specific evidence of what Shonubi had done." 103 F.3d at 1090. Although the logical basis for this "specific evidence" requirement is unclear, a difficulty with the expert's analysis is apparent. Statistical inference generally involves an extrapolation from the units sampled to the population of all units. Thus, the sample needs to be representative. In *Shonubi*, the government used a sample of weights, one for each courier on the trip at which that courier was caught. It sought to extrapolate from these data to many trips taken by a single courier—trips on which that other courier was not caught.

63. Here "confidence" has the meaning ordinarily ascribed to it rather than the technical interpretation applicable to a frequentist "confidence interval." Consequently, it can be related to the burden of persuasion. *See* Kaye, *supra* note 58.

64. For instance, let p be the unknown probability that coin lands heads: What is the chance that p exceeds 0.6? The Bayesian statistician must be prepared to answer all such questions. Bayesian procedures are sometimes defended on the ground that the beliefs of any rational observer must conform to the Bayesian rules. However, the definition of "rational" is purely formal. *See* Peter C. Fishburn, *The Axioms of Subjective Probability*, 1 STAT. SCI. 335 (1986); David Kaye, *The Laws of Probability and the Law of the Land*, 47 U. CHI. L. REV. 34 (1979).

65. *See infra* Appendix.

66. *See generally* GEORGE E.P. BOX & GEORGE C. TIAO, BAYESIAN INFERENCE IN STATISTICAL ANALYSIS (Wiley Classics Library ed., John Wiley & Sons, Inc. 1992) (1973). For applications to legal issues, see, *e.g.*, C.G.G. Aitken et al., *Estimation of Quantities of Drugs Handled and the Burden of Proof*, 160 J. ROYAL STAT. SOC'Y 333, 337–48 (1997); David H. Kaye, *DNA Evidence: Probability, Population Genetics, and the Courts*, 7 HARV. J. L. & TECH. 101 (1993).

67. In this framework, the question arises of whose beliefs to use—the statistician's or the factfinder's. *See*, *e.g.*, Michael O. Finkelstein & William B. Fairley, *A Bayesian Approach to Identification Evidence*, 83 HARV. L. REV. 489 (1970) (proposing that experts give

Such analyses have rarely been used in court,[68] and the question of their forensic value has been aired primarily in the academic literature.[69] Some statisticians favor Bayesian methods,[70] and some legal commentators have proposed their use in certain kinds of cases in certain circumstances.[71]

§ 5–5.0 CORRELATION AND REGRESSION

Regression models are often used to infer causation from association; for example, such models are frequently introduced to prove disparate treatment in discrimination cases, or to estimate damages in antitrust actions. Section 5–5.4 explains the ideas and some of the pitfalls. Sections 5–5.1 through 5–5.3 cover some preliminary material, showing how scatter diagrams, correlation coefficients, and regression lines can be used to summarize relationships between variables.

§ 5–5.1 Scatter Diagrams

The relationship between two variables can be shown in a scatter diagram.[1] Data on income and education for a sample of 350 men, age 25 to 29, residing in Texas[2] provide an example. Each person in the sample corresponds to one dot in the diagram. As indicated in Figure 4, the horizontal axis shows the person's education, and the vertical axis shows his income. Person A completed 8 years of schooling (grade school) and had an income of $19,000. Person B completed 16 years of schooling (college) and had an income of $38,000.

posterior probabilities for a wide range of prior probabilities, to allow jurors to use their own prior probabilities or just to judge the impact of the data on possible values of the prior probabilities). *But see* Laurence H. Tribe, *Trial by Mathematics: Precision and Ritual in the Legal Process*, 84 Harv. L. Rev. 1329 (1971) (arguing that efforts to describe the impact of evidence on a juror's subjective probabilities would unduly impress jurors and undermine the presumption of innocence and other legal values).

68. The exception is paternity litigation; when genetic tests are indicative of paternity, testimony as to a posterior "probability of paternity" is common. *See infra* § 19–2.5 [paternity chapter].

69. *See, e.g.*, Probability and Inference in the Law of Evidence: The Limits and Uses of Bayesianism (Peter Tillers & Eric D. Green eds., 1988); Symposium, *Decision and Inference in Litigation*, 13 Cardozo L. Rev. 253 (1991). The Bayesian framework probably has received more acceptance in explicating legal concepts such as the relevance of evidence, the nature of prejudicial evidence, probative value, and burdens of persuasion. *See, e.g.*, Richard D. Friedman, *Assessing Evidence*, 94 Mich. L. Rev. 1810 (1996) (book review); Richard O. Lempert, *Modeling Relevance*, 75 Mich. L. Rev. 1021 (1977); D.H. Kaye, *Clarifying the Burden of Persuasion: What Bayesian Decision Rules Do*

and Do Not Do, 3 Int'l J. Evidence & Proof 1 (1999).

70. *E.g.*, Donald A. Berry, *Inferences Using DNA Profiling in Forensic Identification and Paternity Cases*, 6 Stat. Sci. 175, 180 (1991); Stephen E. Fienberg & Mark J. Schervish, *The Relevance of Bayesian Inference for the Presentation of Statistical Evidence and for Legal Decisionmaking*, 66 B.U. L. Rev. 771 (1986). Nevertheless, many statisticians question the general applicability of Bayesian techniques: The results of the analysis may be substantially influenced by the prior probabilities, which in turn may be quite arbitrary. *See, e.g.*, Freedman, *supra* note 4.

71. *E.g.*, Joseph C. Bright, Jr., et al., *Statistical Sampling in Tax Audits*, 13 L. & Soc. Inquiry 305 (1988); Ira Mark Ellman & David Kaye, *Probabilities and Proof: Can HLA and Blood Group Testing Prove Paternity?*, 54 N.Y.U. L. Rev. 1131 (1979); Finkelstein & Fairley, *supra* note 67; Kaye, *supra* note 66.

§ 5–5.0

1. These diagrams are also referred to as "scatterplots" or "scattergrams."

2. These data are from a public-use file, Bureau of the Census, U.S. Dep't of Commerce, for the March 1988 Current Population Survey. Income and education (years of schooling completed) are self-reported. Income is truncated at $100,000 and education at 18 years.

Figure 4

Plotting a scatter diagram. The horizontal axis shows educational level and the vertical axis shows income.

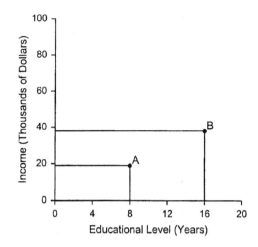

Figure 5

**Scatter diagram for income and education:
men age 25 to 29 in Texas.[3]**

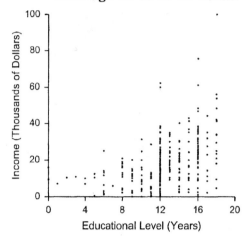

Figure 5 is the scatter diagram for the Texas data. The diagram confirms an obvious point. There is a positive association between income and education: in general, persons with a higher educational level have higher incomes. However, there are many exceptions to this rule, and the association is not as strong as one might expect.

§ 5–5.2 Correlation Coefficients

Two variables are positively correlated when their values tend to go up or down together.[4] Income and education in Figure 5 provides an example. The correlation coefficient (usually denoted by the letter r) is a single number that reflects the strength of an association. Figure 6 shows the values of r for three scatter diagrams.

---

3. Education may be compulsory, but the Current Population Survey generally finds a small percentage of respondents who report very little schooling. Such respondents will be found at the lower left corner of the scatter diagram.

4. Many statistics and displays are available to investigate association. The most common are the correlation coefficient and the scatter diagram.

Figure 6

The correlation coefficient measures the strength of linear association.

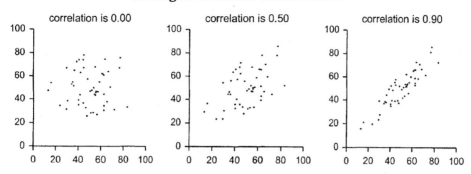

A correlation coefficient of zero indicates no linear association between the variables, while a coefficient of +1 indicates a perfect linear relationship: all the dots in the scatter diagram fall on a straight line that slopes up. The maximum value for r is +1. Sometimes, there is a negative association between two variables: large values of one tend to go with small values of the other. The age of a car and its fuel economy in miles per gallon provide an example. Negative association is indicated by negative values for r. The extreme case is an r of –1, indicating that all the points in the scatter diagram lie on a straight line which slopes down.

Moderate associations are the general rule in the social sciences; correlations larger than, say, 0.7 are quite unusual in many fields. For example, the correlation between college grades and first-year law school grades is under 0.3 at most law schools, while the correlation between LSAT scores and first-year law grades is generally about 0.4.[5] The correlation between heights of fraternal twins is about 0.5, while the correlation between heights of identical twins is about 0.95. In Figure 5, the correlation between income and education was 0.43. The correlation coefficient cannot capture all the underlying information. Several issues may arise in this regard, and we consider them in turn.

§ 5–5.2.1 Is the Association Linear?

The correlation coefficient is designed to measure linear association. Figure 7 shows a strong non-linear pattern with a correlation close to zero. When the scatter diagram reveals a strong non-linear pattern, the correlation coefficient may not be a useful summary statistic.

5. Linda F. Wightman, Predictive Validity of the LSAT: A National Summary of the 1990–1992 Correlation Studies 10 (1993); *cf.* Linda F. Wightman & David G. Muller, An Analysis of Differential Validity and Differential Prediction for Black, Mexican–American, Hispanic, and White Law School Students 11– 13 (1990). A combination of LSAT and undergraduate grade point average has a higher correlation with first-year law school grades than either item alone. The multiple correlation coefficient is typically about 0.5. Wightman, *supra*, at 10.

Figure 7

**The correlation coefficient only measures linear association.
The Scatter Diagram shows a strong nonlinear
association with a correlation coefficient close to zero.**

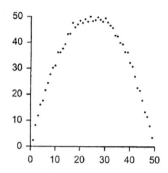

§ 5–5.2.2   Do Outliers Influence the Correlation Coefficient?

The correlation coefficient can be distorted by outliers—a few points that are far removed from the bulk of the data. The left hand panel in Figure 8 shows that one outlier (lower right hand corner) can reduce a perfect correlation to nearly nothing. Conversely, the right hand panel shows that one outlier (upper right hand corner) can raise a correlation of zero to nearly one.

Figure 8

**The correlation coefficient can be distorted by outliers.
The left hand panel shows an outlier (in the lower right
hand corner) that destroys a nearly perfect correlation. The
right hand panel shows an outlier (in the upper right hand corner)
that changes the correlation from zero to nearly one.**

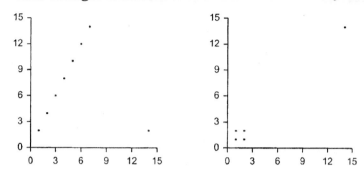

§ 5–5.2.3 Does a Confounding Variable Influence the Coefficient?

The correlation coefficient measures the association between two variables. Investigators—and the courts—are usually more interested in causation. Association is not necessarily the same as causation. As noted in section 5–2.1, the association between two variables may be driven largely by a "third variable" that has been omitted from the analysis. For an easy example, among school children, there is an association between shoe size and vocabulary. However, learning more words does not cause feet to get bigger, and swollen feet do not make children more articulate. In this case, the third variable is easy to spot—age. In more realistic examples, the driving variable may be harder to identify.

Technically, third variables are called confounders or confounding variables.[6] The basic methods of dealing with confounding variables involve controlled experiments[7] or the application, typically through a technique called "multiple regression,"[8] of "statistical controls."[9] In many examples, association really does reflect causation, but a large correlation coefficient is not enough to warrant such a conclusion. A large value of r only means that the dependent variable marches in step with the independent one—for any number of possible reasons, ranging from causation to confounding.[10]

§ 5–5.3 Regression Lines

The regression line can be used to describe a linear trend in the data. The regression line for income on education in the Texas sample is shown in

---

6. *See supra* § 5–2.1.1.

7. *See supra* § 5–2.1.2.

8. Multiple regression analysis is discussed *infra* § 5–5.4.

9. For the reasons stated *supra* § 5–2.1, efforts to control confounding in observational studies are generally less convincing than randomized controlled experiments.

10. The square of the correlation coefficient, r^2, is sometimes called the proportion of variance "explained." However, "explained" is meant in a purely technical sense, and large values of r^2 need not point to a causal explanation.

Figure 9. The height of the line estimates the average income for a given educational level. For example, the average income for people with eight years of education is estimated at $9,600, indicated by the height of the line at eight years; the average income for people with sixteen years of education is estimated at about $23,200.

Figure 10 repeats the scatter diagram for income and education (see Figure 5); the regression line is plotted too. In a general way, the line shows the average trend of income as education increases. Thus, the regression line indicates the extent to which a change in one variable (income) is associated with a change in another variable (education).

Figure 9

The regression line for income on education, and its estimates.

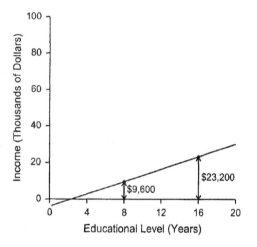

Figure 10

Scatter diagram for income and education, with the regression line indicating the trend.

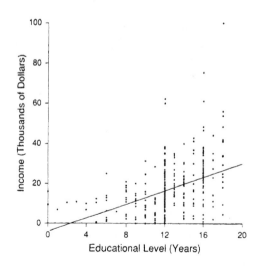

§ 5–5.3.1 What Are the Slope and Intercept?

The regression line can be described in terms of its slope and intercept.[11] In Figure 10, the slope is $1,700 per year. On average, each additional year of education is associated with an additional $1,700 of income. The intercept is– $4,000. This is an estimate of the average income for persons with zero years of education. The estimate is not a good one, for such persons are far from the center of the diagram. In general, estimates based on the regression line become less trustworthy as we move away from the bulk of the data.

The slope has the same limitations as the correlation coefficient in measuring the degree of association:[12] (i) It only measures linear relationships; (ii) it may be influenced by outliers; and (iii) it does not control for the effect of other variables. With respect to (i), the slope of $1,700 per year presents each additional year of education as having the same value, but some years of schooling surely are worth more and others less. With respect to (iii), the association between education and income graphed in Figure 10 is partly causal, but there are other factors to consider, including the family backgrounds of the people in the sample. For instance, people with college degrees probably come from richer and better educated families than those who drop out after grade school: college graduates have other advantages besides the extra education. Factors like these must have some effect on income. That is why statisticians use the qualified language of "on average" and "associated with."[13]

§ 5–5.3.2 What Is the Unit of Analysis?

If association between the characteristics of individuals is of interest, these characteristics should be measured on individuals. Sometimes the individual data are not available, but rates or averages are; correlations computed from rates or averages are termed "ecological." However, ecological correlations generally overstate the strength of an association. An example makes the point. The average income and average education can be determined for the men living in each state. The correlation coefficient for these 50 pairs of averages turns out to be 0.66. However, states do not go to school and do not earn incomes. People do. The correlation for income and education for all men in the United States is only about 0.44.[14] The correlation for state

---

11. The regression line, like any straight line, has an equation of the form $y = mx + b$. Here, m is the slope, that is, the change in y per unit change in x. The slope is the same anywhere along the line. Mathematically, that is what distinguishes straight lines from curves. The intercept b is the value of y when x is zero. The slope of a line is akin to the grade of a road; the intercept gives the starting elevation. In Figure 9, the regression line estimates an average income of $23,200 for people with 16 years of education. This may be computed from the slope and intercept as follows:

($1,700 per year) $\times$ 16 years – $4,000
$$= \$27,200 - \$4,000 =$$
$23,200.

12. In fact, the correlation coefficient is the slope of the regression line if the variables are "standardized," that is, measured in terms of standard deviations away from the mean.

13. Many investigators would use multiple regression to isolate the effects of one variable on another—for instance, the independent effect of education on income. Such efforts may run into problems. *See generally supra* § 5–2.1; *infra* § 5–5.4.

14. Correlations are computed from public-use data, Bureau of the Census, Dep't of Commerce, for the March 1993 Current Population Survey.

averages overstates the correlation for individuals—a common tendency for such ecological correlations.[15]

Ecological correlations are often used in cases claiming a dilution in the voting strength of a racial minority. In this type of voting rights case plaintiffs must prove three things: (1) the minority group constitutes a majority in at least one district of a proposed plan; (2) the minority group is politically cohesive, that is, votes fairly solidly for its preferred candidate; and (3) the majority group votes sufficiently as a bloc to defeat the minority-preferred candidate.[16] The first test is called compactness. The second and third tests deal with racially polarized voting.

Of course, the secrecy of the ballot box means that racially polarized voting cannot be directly observed.[17] Instead, plaintiffs in these voting rights cases rely on scatter diagrams and regression lines to estimate voting behavior by racial or ethnic groups. The unit of analysis is typically the precinct; hence, the technique is called "ecological regression." For each precinct, public records may suffice to determine the percentage of registrants in each racial or ethnic group, as well as the percentage of the total vote for each candidate—by voters from all demographic groups combined. The statistical issue, then, is to estimate how each demographic subgroup voted.

Figure 11 provides an example. Each point in the scatter diagram shows data for a precinct in the 1982 Democratic primary election for auditor in Lee County, South Carolina. The horizontal axis shows the percentage of registrants who are white. The vertical axis shows the "turnout rate" for the white candidate.[18] The regression line is plotted too. In this sort of diagram, the slope is often interpreted as the difference between the white turnout rate and the black turnout rate for the white candidate; the intercept would be interpreted as the black turnout rate for the white candidate.[19] However, the validity of such estimates is contested in statistical literature.[20]

---

15. The ecological correlation uses only the average figures, but within each state there is a lot of spread about the average. The ecological correlation overlooks this individual variation.

16. *See* Thornburg v. Gingles, 478 U.S. 30, 50–51, 106 S.Ct. 2752, 92 L.Ed.2d 25 (1986) ("First, the minority group must be able to demonstrate that it is sufficiently large and geographically compact to constitute a majority in a single-member district.... Second, the minority group must be able to show that it is politically cohesive.... Third, the minority must be able to demonstrate that the white majority votes sufficiently as a bloc to enable it ... usually to defeat the minority's preferred candidate.") In subsequent cases, the Court has emphasized that these factors are not sufficient to make out a violation of section 2 of the Voting Rights Act. *E.g.*, Johnson v. De Grandy, 512 U.S. 997, 1011, 114 S.Ct. 2647, 129 L.Ed.2d 775 (1994) ("Gingles ... clearly declined to hold [these factors] sufficient in combination, either in the sense that a court's examination of relevant circumstances was complete once the three factors were found to

exist, or in the sense that the three in combination necessarily and in all circumstances demonstrated dilution.").

17. Some information could be obtained from exit polls. *E.g.*, Aldasoro v. Kennerson, 922 F.Supp. 339, 344 (S.D.Cal.1995).

18. By definition, the turnout rate equals the number of votes for the candidate, divided by the number of registrants; the rate is computed separately for each precinct.

19. Figure 11 contemplates only one white candidate; more complicated techniques could be used if there were several candidates of each race. The intercept of the line is 4% and the slope is 0.52. Plaintiffs would conclude that only 4% of the black registrants voted for the white candidate, while 4% + 52% = 56% of the white registrants voted for the white candidate, which demonstrates polarization.

20. For further discussion of the problem of ecological regression in this context, see Stephen P. Klein & David A. Freedman, *Ecological Regression in Voting Rights Cases*, CHANCE, Summer 1993, at 38; BERNARD GROFMAN & CHANDLER DAVIDSON, CONTROVERSIES IN MINORITY

Figure 11

Turnout rate for the white candidate plotted against the percentage of registrants who are white. Precinct-level data, 1982 Democratic Primary for Auditor, Lee County, South Carolina.[21]

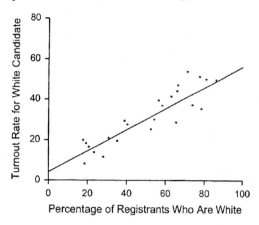

VOTING: THE VOTING RIGHTS ACT IN PERSPECTIVE (1992); D.A. Freedman et al., *Review of "A Solution to the Ecological Regression Problem,"* 93 J. AM. STAT. ASS'N 1518 (1998) (with comment, 94 J. AM. STAT. ASS'N 352, and response, 94 J. AM. STAT. ASS'N 355). The use of ecological regression increased considerably after the Supreme Court noted in *Thornburg v. Gingles,* 478 U.S. 30, 53 n. 20, 106 S.Ct. 2752, 92 L.Ed.2d 25 (1986), that "[t]he District Court found both methods [extreme case analysis and bivariate ecological regression analysis] standard in the literature for the analysis of racially polarized voting." *See, e.g.,* Teague v. Attala County, 92 F.3d 283, 285 (5th Cir. 1996) (one of "two standard methods for analyzing electoral data"); Houston v. Lafayette County, 56 F.3d 606, 612 (5th Cir.1995) (holding that district court erred in ignoring ecological regression results). Nevertheless, courts have cautioned against "overreliance on bivariate ecological regression" in light of the inherent limitations of the technique (Lewis v. Alamance County, 99 F.3d 600, 604 n. 3 (4th Cir.1996)), and some courts have found ecological regressions unconvincing. *E.g.,* Aldasoro v. Kennerson, 922 F.Supp. 339 (S.D.Cal.1995); Romero v. City of Pomona, 665 F.Supp. 853, 860 (C.D.Cal.1987), *aff'd,* 883 F.2d 1418 (9th Cir.1989); *cf.* Johnson v. Miller, 864 F.Supp. 1354, 1390 (S.D.Ga.1994) ("mind numbing and contradictory statistical data," including bivariate ecological regression, established "that some degree of vote polarization exists, but not in alarming quantities. Exact levels are un-knowable."), *aff'd,* 515 U.S. 900, 115 S.Ct. 2475, 132 L.Ed.2d 762 (1995).

Redistricting plans based predominantly on racial considerations are unconstitutional unless narrowly tailored to meet a compelling state interest. Shaw v. Reno, 509 U.S. 630, 113 S.Ct. 2816, 125 L.Ed.2d 511 (1993). Whether compliance with the Voting Rights Act can be considered a compelling interest is an open question, but efforts to sustain racially motivated redistricting on this basis have not fared well before the Supreme Court. *See* Abrams v. Johnson, 521 U.S. 74, 117 S.Ct. 1925, 138 L.Ed.2d 285 (1997); Shaw v. Hunt, 517 U.S. 899, 116 S.Ct. 1894, 135 L.Ed.2d 207 (1996); Bush v. Vera, 517 U.S. 952, 116 S.Ct. 1941, 135 L.Ed.2d 248 (1996). Of course, establishing that a district has been fashioned on racial rather than political lines can be difficult. *See* Easley v. Cromartie, 532 U.S. 234, 121 S.Ct. 1452, 149 L.Ed.2d 430 (2001) (overturning a district court's finding "that North Carolina's legislature used race as the 'predominant factor' in drawing" an oddly shaped congressional district composed largely of African–Americans was clearly erroneous, *id.* at 1455–56; because the "the legislature drew boundaries that, in general, placed more-reliably Democratic voters inside the district, while placing less-reliably Democratic voters outside the district," *id.* at 1464, it was wrong to conclude that "the legislature drew … boundaries because of race *rather than* political behavior," *id.* at 1466).

21. Data from James W. Loewen & Bernard Grofman, *Recent Developments in Methods Used in Vote Dilution Litigation,* 21 URB. LAW. 589, 591 tbl.1 (1989).

§ 5–5.4   Statistical Models

Statistical models are widely used in the social sciences and in litigation.[22] For example, the census suffers an undercount, more severe in certain places than others; if some statistical models are to be believed, the undercount can be corrected—moving seats in Congress and millions of dollars a year in entitlement funds.[23] Other models purport to lift the veil of secrecy from the ballot box, enabling the experts to determine how racial or ethnic groups have voted—a crucial step in litigation to enforce minority voting rights.[24] This section discusses the statistical logic of regression models.[25]

A regression model attempts to combine the values of certain variables (the independent variables) in order to get expected values for another variable (the dependent variable). The model can be expressed in the form of a regression equation. A simple regression equation has only one independent variable; a multiple regression equation has several independent variables. Coefficients in the equation will often be interpreted as showing the effects of changing the corresponding variables. Sometimes, this interpretation can be justified. For instance, Hooke's law describes how a spring stretches in response to the load hung from it: strain is proportional to stress.[26] There will be a number of observations on a spring. For each observation, the physicist hangs a weight on the spring, and measures its length. A statistician could apply a regression model to these data: for quite a large range of weights,[27]

$$\text{length} = a + b \times \text{weight} + \epsilon. \tag{1}$$

The error term, denoted by the Greek letter epsilon (ϵ), is needed because measured length will not be exactly equal to $a + b \times$ weight. If nothing else, measurement error must be reckoned with. We model ϵ as a draw made at random with replacement from a box of tickets. Each ticket shows a potential error, which will be realized if that ticket is drawn. The average of all the potential errors in the box is assumed to be zero. In more standard statistical terminology, the ϵ's for different observations are assumed to be "independent and identically distributed, with mean zero."[28]

In equation (1), a and b are parameters, unknown constants of nature that characterize the spring: a is the length of the spring under no load, and b is elasticity, the increase in length per unit increase in weight.[29] These

22. The frequency with which regression models are used is no guarantee that they are the best choice for a particular problem. *See, e.g.*, David W. Peterson, *Reference Guide on Multiple Regression*, 36 Jurimetrics J. 213, 214–15 (1996) (review essay). On the factors that might justify the choice of a particular model, see Lincoln E. Moses, *The Reasoning of Statistical Inference, in* Perspectives on Contemporary Statistics 107, 117–18 (David C. Hoaglin & David S. Moore eds., 1992).

23. *See supra* § 5–2.2.1.

24. *See supra* § 5–5.3.2.

25. For a more detailed treatment, see David L. Faigman, David H. Kaye, Michael J. Saks & Joseph Sanders, Modern Scientific Evidence: The Law and Science of Expert testimony, Chapter 6 (2d ed. 2002).

26. This law is named after Robert Hooke (England, 1653–1703).

27. The dependent or *response* variable in equation (1) is the length of the spring, on the left hand side of the equation. There is one independent or explanatory variable on the right hand side—weight. Since there is only one explanatory variable, equation (1) is a simple regression equation.

Hooke's law is only an approximation, although it is a very good one. With large enough weights, a quadratic term will be needed in equation (1). Moreover, beyond some point, the spring exceeds its elastic limit and snaps.

28. For some purposes, it is also necessary to assume that the errors follow the normal distribution.

29. *Cf. supra* § 5–4.1.2 note 13 & § 5–4.2.1 note 26 (defining the term "parameter").

parameters are not observable,[30] but they can be estimated by "the method of least squares."[31] In statistical notation, estimates are often denoted by hats; thus, $\hat{a}$ is the estimate for a, and $\hat{b}$ is the estimate for b.[32] Basically, the values of $\hat{a}$ and $\hat{b}$ are chosen to minimize the sum of the squared "prediction errors."[33] These errors are also called residuals: they measure the difference between the actual length and the predicted length, the latter being $\hat{a} + \hat{b} \times$ weight:[34]

$$\text{residual} = \text{actual length} - \hat{a} - \hat{b} \times \text{weight}. \qquad (2)$$

Of course, no one really imagines there to be a box of tickets hidden in the spring. However, the variability of physical measurements (under many but by no means all circumstances) does seem to be remarkably like the variability in draws from a box.[35] In short, the statistical model corresponds rather closely to the empirical phenomenon.

§ 5–5.4.1 A Social Science Example

We turn now to social science applications of the kind that might be seen in litigation. A case study would take us too far afield, but a stylized example of regression analysis used to demonstrate sex discrimination in salaries may give the idea.[36] We use a regression model to predict salaries (dollars per year) of employees in a firm from three explanatory variables: education (years of schooling completed), experience (years with the firm), and a dummy variable for gender, taking the value 1 for men and 0 for women.[37] The equation is[38]

$$\text{salary} = a + b \times \text{education} + c \times \text{experience} + d \times \text{gender} + \epsilon. \qquad (3)$$

30. It might seem that a is observable; after all, one can measure the length of the spring with no load. However, the measurement is subject to error, so one observes not a but $a + \epsilon$. *See* equation (1). The parameters a and b can be estimated, even estimated very well, but they cannot be observed directly.

31. The method was developed by Adrien-Marie Legendre (France, 1752–1833) and Carl Friedrich Gauss (Germany, 1777–1855) to fit astronomical orbits.

32. Another convention is to use Greek letters for the parameters and English letters for the estimates.

33. Given trial values for a and b, one computes residuals as in equation (2), and then the sum of the squares of these residuals. The "least squares" estimates $\hat{a}$ and $\hat{b}$ are the values of a and b that minimize this sum of squares. These least squares values can be computed from the data by a mathematical formula. They are the intercept and slope of the regression line. *See supra* § 5–5.3.1; DAVID FREEDMAN ET AL., STATISTICS 208–10 (3d ed. 1998).

34. The residual is observable, but because the estimates $\hat{a}$ and $\hat{b}$ are only approximations to the parameters a and b, the residual is only an approximation to the error term in equation (1). The term "predicted value" is used in a

specialized sense, because the actual values are available too; statisticians often refer to "fitted value" rather than "predicted value," to avoid possible misinterpretations.

35. This is Gauss' model for measurement error. *See* FREEDMAN ET AL., *supra* note 33, at 450–52.

36. For a more extended treatment of the concepts, see *infra* Chapter 6.

37. A dummy variable takes only two values (e.g., 0 and 1) and serves to identify two mutually exclusive and exhaustive categories.

38. In equation (3), the variable on the left hand side, salary, is the response variable. On the right hand side are the explanatory variables—education, experience, and the dummy variable for gender. Because there are several explanatory variables, this is a multiple regression equation rather than a simple equation; *cf. supra* note 27.

Equations like (3) are suggested, somewhat loosely, by "human capital theory." However, there remains considerable uncertainty about which variables to put into the equation, what functional form to assume, and how error terms are supposed to behave. Adding more variables is no panacea. *See* Peterson, *supra* note 22, at 214–15.

Equation (3) is a statistical model for the data, with unknown parameters a, b, c, and d; here, a is the intercept and the others are regression coefficients; ϵ is an unobservable error term. This is a formal analog of Hooke's law, shown as equation (1); the same assumptions are made about the errors. In other words, an employee's salary is determined as if by computing

$$a + b \times \text{education} + c \times \text{experience} + d \times \text{gender}, \qquad (4)$$

then adding an error drawn at random from a box of tickets. The expression (4) is the expected value for salary given the explanatory variables (education, experience, gender); the error term in equation (3) represents deviations from the expected.

The parameters in equation (3) are estimated from the data using least squares. If the estimated coefficient for the dummy variable turns out to be positive and statistically significant (by a t-test[39]), that would be taken as evidence of disparate impact: men earn more than women, even after adjusting for differences in background factors that might affect productivity. Education and experience are entered into equation (3) as statistical controls, precisely in order to claim that adjustment has been made for differences in backgrounds.

Suppose the estimated equation turns out as follows:

$$\begin{aligned} \text{predicted salary} = \ &\$7{,}100 + \$1{,}300 \times \text{education} \\ &+ \$2{,}200 \times \text{experience} + \$700 \times \text{gender}. \end{aligned} \qquad (5)$$

That is, $\hat{a} = \$7{,}100$, $\hat{b} = \$1{,}300$, and so forth. According to equation (5), every extra year of education is worth on average $\$1{,}300$; similarly, every extra year of experience is worth on average $\$2{,}200$; and, most important, the company gives men a salary premium of $\$700$ over women with the same education and experience, on average. For example, a male employee with 12 years of education (high school) and 10 years of experience would have a predicted salary of

$$\begin{aligned} \$7{,}100 + \$1{,}300 \times 12 &+ \$2{,}200 \times 10 + \$700 \times 1 \\ &= \$7{,}100 + \$15{,}600 + \$22{,}000 + \$700 = \$45{,}400. \ (6) \end{aligned}$$

A similarly situated female employee has a predicted salary of only

$$\begin{aligned} \$7{,}100 + \$1{,}300 \times 12 &+ \$2{,}200 \times 10 + \$700 \times 0 \\ &= \$7{,}100 + \$15{,}600 + \$22{,}000 + \$0 = \$44{,}700. \ (7) \end{aligned}$$

Notice the impact of the dummy variable: $\$700$ is added to equation (6), but not to equation (7).

A major step in proving discrimination is establishing that the estimated coefficient of the dummy variable—$\$700$ in our numerical illustration—is statistically significant. This depends on the statistical assumptions built into the model. For instance, each extra year of education is assumed to be worth the same (on average) at each level of experience, both for men and for women. Similarly, each extra year of experience is worth the same across all

39. *See infra* § 5–5.4.2.

levels of education, both for men and women. Furthermore, the premium paid to men does not depend systematically on education or experience. Ability, quality of education, or quality of experience are assumed not to make any systematic difference to the predictions of the model.[40]

The assumptions about the error term—that the errors are independent and identically distributed from person to person in the data set—turn out to be critical for computing *p*-values and demonstrating statistical significance. Regression modeling that does not produce statistically significant coefficients is unlikely to establish discrimination, and statistical significance cannot be established unless stylized assumptions are made about unobservable error terms.[41]

The typical regression model is based on a host of such assumptions; without them, legitimate inferences cannot be drawn from the model. With Hooke's law—equation (1), the model rests on assumptions that are relatively easy to validate experimentally. For the salary discrimination model—equation (3), validation seems more difficult.[42] Court or counsel may well inquire: What are the assumptions behind the model, and why do they apply to the case at bar? In this regard, it is important to distinguish between situations where (i) the nature of the relationship between the variables is known and regression is being used to make quantitative estimates, and (ii) where the nature of the relationship is largely unknown and regression is being used to determine the nature of the relationship—or indeed whether any relationship exists at all. The statistical basis for regression theory was developed to handle situations of the first type, with Hooke's law being an example. The basis for the second type of application is analogical, and the tightness of the analogy is a critical issue.

§ 5–5.4.2 Standard Errors, Statistics, and Statistical Significance

Statistical proof of discrimination depends on the significance of $\hat{d}$ (the estimated coefficient for gender); significance is determined by the *t*-test, using the standard error of $\hat{d}$. The standard error of $\hat{d}$ measures the likely difference between $\hat{d}$ and d, the difference being due to the action of the error term in equation (3). The *t*-statistic is $\hat{d}$ divided by its standard error. For example, in equation (5), $\hat{d} = \$700$. If the standard error of $\hat{d}$ is computed as $325, then $t = \$700/\$325 = 2.15$. This value is significant, that is, hard to explain as the mere product of random chance. Under the null hypothesis that $d = 0$, there is only about a 5% chance that the absolute value of t (denoted $|t|$) is greater than 2. A value of t larger than 2 would therefore demonstrate statistical significance.[43] On the other hand, if the standard error is $1,400, then $t = \$700/\$1,400 = 0.5$, and the discrepancy could easily result from chance. Of course, the parameter d is only a construct in a model. If the model

40. Technically, these omitted variables are assumed to be uncorrelated with the error term in the equation.

41. *See supra* § 5–4.1.2 note 16 & accompanying text.

42. Some of the material in this section is taken from David Freedman, *Some Issues in the Foundations of Statistics,* 1 Found. Sci. 19, 29–35 *reprinted in* Topics in the Foundations of Statistics 19 (Bas. C. van Fraasen ed., 1997).

43. The cutoff at 2 applies to large samples. Small samples require higher thresholds.

is wrong, the standard error, t-statistic, and significance level are rather difficult to interpret.

Even if the model is granted, there is a further issue: the 5% is a probability for the data given the model, namely, $P(|t| > 2 \mid d = 0)$. However, the 5% is often misinterpreted as $P(d = 0 \mid \text{data})$. This misinterpretation is commonplace in the social science literature, and it appears in some opinions describing expert testimony.[44] For an objectivist statistician, $P(d = 0 \mid \text{data})$ makes no sense: parameters do not exhibit chance variation. For a subjectivist statistician, $P(d = 0 \mid \text{data})$ makes good sense, but its computation via the t-test could be seriously in error, because the prior probability that $d = 0$ has not been taken into account.[45]

§ 5–5.4.3 Summary

The main ideas of regression modeling can be captured in a hypothetical exchange between a plaintiff seeking to prove salary discrimination and a company denying that allegation. Such a dialog might proceed as follows:

1. Plaintiff argues that the defendant company pays male employees more than females, which establishes prima facie case of discrimination.[46]

2. The company responds that the men are paid more because they are better educated and have more experience.

3. Plaintiff tries to refute the employer's theory by fitting a regression equation like equation (5). Even after adjusting for differences in education and experience, men earn $700 a year more than women, on average. This remaining difference in pay shows discrimination.

4. The company argues that a small difference like $700 could be the result of chance, not discrimination.

5. Plaintiff replies that the coefficient of "gender" in equation (5) is statistically significant, so chance is not a good explanation for the data.

Statistical significance is determined by reference to the observed significance level, which is usually abbreviated to p.[47] The p-value depends not only on the $700 difference in salary levels, but also on the sample size among

---

44. *See supra* § 5–4.2.

45. For an objectivist, the single vertical bar "$|$" in $P(|t| > 2 \mid d = 0)$ means "computed on the assumption that." For a subjectivist, the bar would signify a conditional probability. *See supra* § 5–4.2.1 & § 5–4.3; *infra* Appendix.

46. The conditions under which a simple disparity between two groups amounts to a prima facie case that shifts the burden of production to the defendant in Title VII and other discrimination cases have yet to be articulated clearly and comprehensively. *Compare* EEOC. v. Olson's Dairy Queens, Inc., 989 F.2d 165, 168 (5th Cir.1993) (reversing district court for failing to find a prima facie case from the EEOC's statistics on the proportion of African-Americans in defendant's workforce as compared to the proportion of food preparation and service workers in the Houston Standard Metropolitan Statistical Area), *with* Wilkins v. University of Houston, 654 F.2d 388 (5th Cir.1981) (holding that the district court correctly found that plaintiffs' proof of simple disparities in faculty salaries of men and women did not constitute a prima facie case), *vacated and remanded on other grounds*, 459 U.S. 809, 103 S.Ct. 34, 74 L.Ed.2d 47 (1982), *aff'd on remand*, 695 F.2d 134 (5th Cir.1983); *see generally* D.H. Kaye, *Statistical Evidence: How to Avoid the "Diderot Effect" of Getting Stumped*, INSIDE LITIG., Apr. 1988, at 21; Richard Lempert, *Befuddled Judges: Statistical Evidence in Title VII Cases, in* CONTROVERSIES IN CIVIL RIGHTS (Bernard Grofman ed., 2000).

47. *See supra* § 5–4.2.1.

other things.[48] The bigger the sample, other things being equal, the smaller is p—and the tighter is plaintiff's argument that the disparity cannot be explained by chance. Often, a cutoff at 5% is used; if p is less than 5%, the difference is "statistically significant."[49]

In some cases, the p-value has been interpreted as the probability that defendants are innocent of discrimination. However, such an interpretation is wrong: p merely represents the probability of getting a large test statistic, given that the model is correct and the true coefficient of "gender" is zero.[50] Therefore, even if the model is undisputed, a p-value less than 50% does not necessarily demonstrate a "preponderance of the evidence" against the null hypothesis. Indeed, a p-value less than 5% or 1% might not meet the preponderance standard.

In employment discrimination cases, and other contexts too, a wide variety of models are used. This is perhaps not surprising, for specific equations are not dictated by the science. Thus, in a strongly contested case, our dialog would be likely to continue with an exchange about which model is better. Although statistical assumptions[51] are challenged in court from time to time, arguments more commonly revolve around the choice of variables. One model may be questioned because it omits variables that should be included—for instance, skill levels or prior evaluations;[52] another model may be challenged because it includes "tainted" variables reflecting past discriminatory behavior by the firm.[53] Frequently, each side will have its own equations and its own team of experts; the court then must decide which model—if either—fits the occasion.[54]

---

48. The p-value depends on the estimated value of the coefficient and its standard error. These quantities can be computed from (i) the sample size, (ii) the means and SDs of the variables, and (iii) the correlations between pairs of variables. The computation is rather intricate.

49. *See supra* § 5–4.2.2.

50. *See supra* §§ 5–4.2 & 5–5.4.2.

51. *See generally supra* § 5–5.4.1 (discussion following equation (7)); Michael O. Finkelstein & Bruce Levin, Statistics for Lawyers 402–09 (2d ed. 2001); *infra* Chapter 6. One example of a statistical assumption is the independence from subject to subject of the error term in equation (3); another example is that the errors have mean zero and constant variance.

52. *E.g.*, Smith v. Virginia Commonwealth Univ., 84 F.3d 672 (4th Cir.1996) (dispute over omitted variables precludes summary judgment). *Compare* Bazemore v. Friday, 478 U.S. 385, 106 S.Ct. 3000, 92 L.Ed.2d 315, *on remand*, 848 F.2d 476 (4th Cir.1988), *and* Sobel v. Yeshiva Univ., 839 F.2d 18, 34 (2d Cir.1988) (failure to include variables for scholarly productivity did not vitiate plaintiffs' regression study of salary differences because "Yeshiva's experts ... [offered] no reason, in evidence or analysis, for concluding that they correlated with sex"), *with* Penk v. Oregon State Bd. of Higher Educ., 816 F.2d 458, 465 (9th Cir.1987)

("Missing parts of the plaintiffs' interpretation of the board's decision-making equation included such highly determinative quality and productivity factors as teaching quality, community and institutional service, and quality of research and scholarship ... that ... must have had a significant influence on salary and advancement decisions."); *and* Chang v. University of R. I., 606 F.Supp. 1161, 1207 (D.R.I. 1985) (plaintiff's regression not entitled to substantial weight because the analyst "excluded salient variables even though he knew of their importance").

The same issue arises, of course, with simpler statistical models, such as those used to assess the difference between two proportions. *See, e.g.*, Sheehan v. Daily Racing Form, Inc., 104 F.3d 940, 942 (7th Cir.1997) ("Completely ignored was the more than remote possibility that age was correlated with a legitimate, job-related qualification, such as familiarity with computers. Everyone knows that younger people are on average more comfortable with computers than older people are, just as older people are on average more comfortable with manual-shift cars than younger people are.").

53. Michael O. Finkelstein, *The Judicial Reception of Multiple Regression Studies in Race and Sex Discrimination Cases*, 80 Colum. L. Rev. 737 (1980).

54. *E.g.*, *Chang*, 606 F. Supp. at 1207 ("it is plain to the court that [defendant's] model comprises a better, more useful, more reliable tool than [plaintiff's] counterpart"); Presseisen v. Swarthmore College, 442 F.Supp. 593, 619 (E.D.Pa.1977) ("[E]ach side has done a superior job in challenging the other's regression analysis, but only a mediocre job in supporting their own. In essence, they have destroyed each other and the Court is, in effect, left with nothing.... Perhaps the only conclusion one can reach ... is that it is almost impossible, in the fact situation that the Court is presented with, to measure the differences in salaries between men and women by statistical analysis."), *aff'd*, 582 F.2d 1275 (3d Cir.1978).

Appendix

Probability and Statistical Inference

The mathematical theory of probability consists of theorems derived from axioms and definitions. The mathematical reasoning is not controversial, but there is some disagreement as to how the theory should be applied; that is, statisticians may differ on the proper interpretation of probabilities in specific applications. There are two main interpretations. For a subjectivist statistician, probabilities represent degrees of belief, on a scale between 0 and 1. An impossible event has probability 0, an event that is sure to happen has probability 1. For an objectivist statistician, probabilities are not beliefs; rather, they are inherent properties of an experiment. If the experiment can be repeated, then in the long run, the relative frequency of an event tends to its probability. For instance, if a fair coin is tossed, the probability of heads is 1/2; if the experiment is repeated, the coin will land heads about one-half the time. If a fair die is rolled, the probability of getting an ace (one spot) is about 1/6; if the die is rolled many times, an ace will turn up about one-sixth of the time.[1] (Objectivist statisticians are also called frequentists, while subjectivists are Bayesians, after the Reverend Thomas Bayes, England, c.1701–1761.)

Statisticians also use conditional probability, that is, the probability of one event given that another has occurred. For instance, suppose a coin is tossed twice. One event is that the coin will land HH. Another event is that at least one H will be seen. Before the coin is tossed, there are four possible, equally likely, outcomes: HH, HT, TH, TT. So the probability of HH is 1/4. However, if we know that at least one head has been obtained, then we can rule out two tails TT. In other words, given that at least one H has been obtained, the conditional probability of TT is 0, and the first three outcomes have conditional probability 1/3 each. In particular, the conditional probability of HH is 1/3. This is usually written as P(HH | at least one H) = 1/3. More generally, the probability of any event B is denoted as P(B); the conditional probability of B given A is written as P(B|A).

Two events A and B are independent if the conditional probability of B given that A occurs is equal to the conditional probability of B given that A does not occur. Statisticians often use "$\sim A$" to denote the event that A does not occur, so A and B are independent if P(B|A) = P(B|$\sim A$). If A and B are independent, then the probability that both occur is equal to the product of the probabilities:

$$\text{P}(A \text{ and } B) = \text{P}(A) \times \text{P}(B). \tag{1}$$

This is the multiplication rule (or product rule) for independent events. If the events A and B are dependent, then conditional probabilities must be used:

$$\text{P}(A \text{ and } B) = \text{P}(A) \times \text{P}(B|A). \tag{2a}$$

Appendix

1. Probabilities may be estimated from relative frequencies, but probability itself is a subtler idea. For instance, suppose a computer prints out a sequence of ten letters H and T (for heads and tails), which alternate between the two possibilities H and T as follows:

HTHTHTHTHT.

The relative frequency of heads is 5/10 or 50%, but it not at all obvious that the chance of an H at the next position is 50%.

This is the multiplication rule for dependent events. Similarly, equation (2a) implies

$$P(A \text{ and } B) = P(B \text{ and } A) = P(B) \times P(A|B). \tag{2b}$$

Bayesian statisticians assign probabilities to hypotheses as well as to events; indeed, for them, the distinction between hypotheses and events may not be a sharp one. If H_0 and H_1 are two hypotheses[2] which govern the probability of an event A, a Bayesian statistician might use the multiplication rule (2) to find that

$$P(A \text{ and } H_0) = P(H_0) \times P(A|H_0) \tag{3a}$$

and

$$P(A \text{ and } H_1) = P(H_1) \times P(A|H_1). \tag{3b}$$

Since $P(H_0|A) = P(A \text{ and } H_0)/P(A)$, while $P(A) = P(A \text{ and } H_0) + P(A \text{ and } H_1)$, the statistician would conclude that

$$P(H_0|A) = \frac{P(H_0) \times P(A|H_0)}{P(H_0) \times P(A|H_0) + P(H_1) \times P(A|H_1)} \tag{4}$$

This is a special case of Bayes' rule, which yields the conditional probability of hypothesis H_0 given that event A has occurred. For example, H_0 might be the hypothesis that blood found at the scene of a crime came from a person other than the defendant; H_1 might deny H_0 and assert that the blood came from the defendant; and A could be the event that blood from both the crime scene and the defendant is type A. Then $P(H_0)$ is the prior probability of H_0, based on subjective judgment, while $P(H_0|A)$ is the posterior probability—the prior probability updated using the data. Here, we have observed a match in type A blood, which occurs in about 42% of the population, so $P(A|H_0) = 0.42$.[3] Because the defendant has type A blood, the match probability given that the blood came from him is $P(A|H_1) = 1$. If the prior probabilities were, say, $P(H_0) = P(H_1) = 0.5$, then according to (4), the posterior probability would be

$$P(H_0|A) = \frac{0.5 \times 0.42}{0.5 \times 0.42 + 0.5 \times 1} = 0.30. \tag{5}$$

Conversely, the posterior probability that the blood is from the defendant would be

$$P(H_1|A) = 1 - P(H_0|A) = 0.70. \tag{6}$$

---

2. H_0 is read "H-sub-zero," while H_1 is "H-sub-one."

3. Not all statisticians would accept the identification of a population frequency with $P(A|H_0)$; indeed, H_0 has been translated into a hypothesis that the true donor has been randomly selected from the population, which is a major step needing justification.

Thus, the data make it more probable that the blood is the defendant's: the probability rises from the prior value of $P(H_1) = 0.50$ to the posterior value of $P(H_1|A) = 0.70$.

A frequentist statistician would not quantify the "probability" of hypotheses like H_0 and H_1. Such a statistician would merely report that if H_0 is true, then the probability of type A blood is 42%, whereas if H_1 is true, the probability is 100%. More generally, H_0 could refer to parameters in a statistical model. For example, H_0 might specify equal selection rates for a population of male and female applicants; H_1 might deny H_0 and assert that the selection rates are not equal; and A could be the event that a test statistic exceeds 2 in absolute value. A frequentist statistician would be hesitant to quantify the probability of hypotheses like H_0 and H_1. Such a statistician might just report $P(A|H_0)$ and reject H_0 if this probability fell below a figure such as 5%.

Assessing probabilities, conditional probabilities, and independence is not entirely straightforward. Inquiry into the basis for expert judgment may be useful, and casual assumptions about independence should be questioned.[4]

Technical Details on the Standard Error, the Normal Curve, and Significance Levels

This section of the Appendix describes several calculations for the pass rate example of section 4. In that example, the population consisted of all 5,000 men and 5,000 women in the applicant pool. Suppose by way of illustration that the pass rates for these men and women were 60% and 35%, respectively; so the "population difference" is 60% – 35% = 25 percentage points. We chose 50 men at random from the population, and 50 women. In our sample, the pass rate for the men was 58% and the pass rate for the women was 38%, so the sample difference was 58% – 38% = 20 percentage points. Another sample might have pass rates of 62% and 36%, for a sample difference of 62% – 36% = 26 percentage points. And so forth.

In principle, we can consider the set of all possible samples from the population, and make a list of the corresponding differences. This is a long list. Indeed, the number of distinct samples of 50 men and 50 women that can be formed is immense—nearly 5×10^{240}, or 5 followed by 240 zeros. Our sample difference was chosen at random from this list. Statistical theory enables us to make some precise statements about the list, and hence about the chances in the sampling procedure.

- The average of the list—that is, the average of the differences over the 5×10^{240} possible samples—equals the difference between the pass rates of all 5,000 men and 5,000 women. In more technical language, the expected value of the sample difference equals the population difference. Even more tersely, the sample difference is an unbiased estimate of the population difference.

---

4. For problematic assumptions of independence in litigation, see, *e.g.*, Branion v. Gramly, 855 F.2d 1256 (7th Cir.1988); People v. Collins, 68 Cal.2d 319, 66 Cal.Rptr. 497, 438 P.2d 33 (Cal. 1968); D.H. Kaye, *The Admissibility of "Probability Evidence" in Criminal Trials* (pts. 1 & 2), 26 JURIMETRICS J. 343 (1986), 27 JURIMETRICS J. 160 (1987).

• The standard deviation (SD) of the list—that is, the standard deviation of the differences over the 5×10^{240} possible samples—is equal to[5]

$$\sqrt{\frac{5,000 - 50}{5,000 - 1}} \times \sqrt{\frac{P_{\text{men}}(1 - P_{\text{men}})}{50} + \frac{P_{\text{women}}(1 - P_{\text{women}})}{50}} \tag{7}$$

In expression (7), P_{men} stands for the proportion of the 5,000 male applicants who would pass the exam, and P_{women} stands for the corresponding proportion of women. With the 60% and 35% figures we have postulated, the standard deviation of the sample differences would be 9.6 percentage points:

$$\sqrt{\frac{5,000 - 50}{5,000 - 1}} \times \sqrt{\frac{.60(1 - .60)}{50} + \frac{.35(1 - .35)}{50}} = .096 \tag{8}$$

Figure 12 shows the histogram for the sample differences.[6] The graph is drawn so the area between two values gives the relative frequency of sample differences falling in that range, among all 5×10^{240} possible samples. For instance, take the range from 20 to 30 percentage points. About half the area under the histogram falls into this range. Therefore, given our assumptions, there is about a 50% chance that for a sample of 50 men and 50 women chosen at random, the difference between the pass rates for the sample men and women will be in the range from 20 to 30 percentage points. The "central limit theorem" establishes that the histogram for the sample differences follows the normal curve, at least to a good approximation. Figure 12 shows this curve for comparison.[7] The main point is that chances for the sample difference can be approximated by areas under the normal curve.

---

5. *See, e.g.*, DAVID FREEDMAN ET AL., STATISTICS 414, 503–04 (3d ed. 1998); DAVID S. MOORE & GEORGE P. MCCABE, INTRODUCTION TO THE PRACTICE OF STATISTICS (3d ed. 2000). The standard error for the sample difference equals the standard deviation of the list of all possible sample differences, making the connection between standard error and standard deviation. If we drew two samples at random, the difference between them would be on the order of
$$\sqrt{2} \approx$$
times this standard deviation. The standard error can therefore be used to measure reproducibility of sample data. On the standard deviation, *see supra* § 5–3.5; FREEDMAN ET AL., *supra*, at 67–72.

6. The "probability histogram" in Figure 12 shows the "distribution" of the sample differences, indicating the relative likelihoods of the various ranges of possible values; likelihood

is represented by area. The lower horizontal scale shows "standard units," that is, deviations from the expected value relative to the standard error. In our example, the expected value is 25 percentage points and the standard error is 9.6 percentage points. Thus, 35 percentage points would be expressed as $(35 - 25)/9.6 = 1.04$ standard units. The vertical scale in the figures shows probability per standard unit. Probability is measured on a percentage scale, with 100% representing certainty; the maximum shown on the vertical scale in the figure is 50, i.e., 50% per standard unit. *See* FREEDMAN ET AL., *supra* note 5, at 80, 315.

7. The normal curve is the famous bell-shaped curve of statistics, whose equation is

$$y = \frac{100\%}{\sqrt{2\pi}} e^{x^2/2}$$

Figure 12

The distribution of the sample difference in pass rates when $P_{men} = 60\%$ and $P_{women} = 35\%$

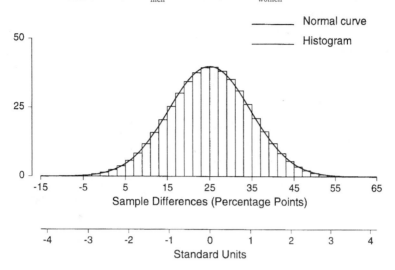

Generally, we do not know the pass rates P_{men} and P_{women} in the population. We chose 60% and 35% just by way of illustration. Statisticians would use the pass rates in the sample—58% and 38%—to estimate the pass rates in the population. Substituting the sample pass rates into expression (7) yields

$$\sqrt{\frac{5{,}000 - 50}{5{,}000 - 1}} \times \sqrt{\frac{.58(1 - .58)}{50} + \frac{.38(1 - .38)}{50}} = .097 \qquad (9)$$

That is about 10 percentage points—the standard error reported in section 4.1.2.[8]

To sum up, the histogram for the sample differences follows the normal curve, centered at the population difference. The spread is given by the standard error. That is why confidence levels can be based on the standard error, with confidence levels read off the normal curve: 68% of the area under the curve is between –1 and 1, 95% is between –2 and 2, and 99.7% is between –3 and 3, approximately.

We turn to p-values.[9] Consider the null hypothesis that the men and women in the population have the same overall pass rates. In that case, the sample differences are centered at zero, because $P_{men} - P_{women} = 0$. Since the overall pass rate in the sample is 48%, we use this value to estimate both P_{men} and P_{women} in expression (7):

---

8. There is little difference between (8) and (9)—the standard error does not depend very strongly on the pass rates.

9. *See supra* § 5–4.2.1.

$$\sqrt{\frac{5,000 - 50}{5,000 - 1}} \times \sqrt{\frac{.48(1 - .48)}{50} + \frac{.48(1 - .48)}{50}} = .099 \qquad (10)$$

Again, the standard error (SE) is about 10 percentage points. The observed difference of 20 percentage points is 20/10 = 2.0 SEs. As shown in Figure 13, differences of that magnitude or larger have about a 5% chance of occurring: about 5% of the area under the normal curve lies beyond ± 2. (In Figure 13, this tail area is shaded.) The p-value is about 5%.[10]

Figure 13

The p-value for observed difference of 20 percentage points, computed using the null hypothesis, with $P_{men} - P_{women} = 48\%$. The chance of getting a sample difference of 20 points in magnitude (or more) is about equal to the area under the normal curve beyond ± 2. That shaded area is about 5%.

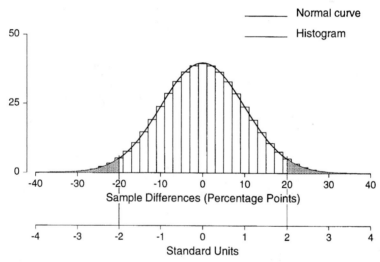

Finally, we calculate power.[11] We are making a two-tailed test at the .05 level. Instead of the null hypothesis, we assume an alternative: In the applicant pool, 55% of the men would pass, and 45% of the women. So there is a difference of 10 percentage points between the pass rates. The distribution of sample differences would now be centered at 10 percentage points (see Figure 14). Again, the sample differences follow the normal curve. The true

---

10. The p-value is the chance of getting data as extreme as, or more extreme than, the data at hand. *See supra* § 5–4.2.1. That is the chance of getting a difference of 20 percentage points or more on the right, together with the chance of getting –20 or less on the left. This chance equals the area under the histogram to the right of 19, together with the area to the left of –19. (The rectangle whose area represents the chance of getting a difference of 20 is included, and likewise for the rectangle above–20.) The area under the histogram may in turn

be approximated by the area under the normal curve beyond ± 1.9, which is 5.7%. *See, e.g.,* FREEDMAN ET AL., *supra* note 5, at 318. Keeping track of the edges of the rectangles is called the "continuity correction." *Id.* The histogram is computed assuming pass rates of 48% for the men and the women. Other values could be dealt with in a similar way. *See infra* note 13.

11. *See supra* § 5–4–3.1 note 37 (defining "power").

SE is about 10 percentage points by equation (7), and the SE estimated from the sample will be about the same. On that basis, only sample differences bigger than 20 percentage points or smaller than –20 points will be declared significant.[12] About 1/6 of the area under the normal curve in Figure 14 lies in this region.[13] Therefore, the power of the test against the specified alternative is only about 1/6. In the figure, it is the shaded area that corresponds to power.

Figure 14

Power when P_{men} = 55% and P_{women} = 45%. The chance of getting a significant difference (at the 5% level, two-tailed) is about equal to the area under the normal curve, to the right of +1 or to the left of –3. That shaded area is about 1/6. Power is about 1/6, or 17%.

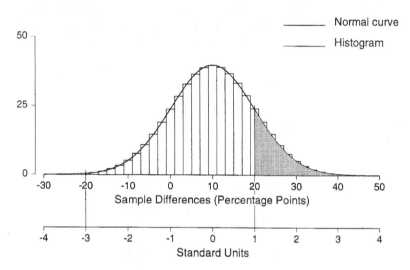

Figures 12, 13, and 14 have the same shape: the central limit theorem is at work. However, the histograms are centered differently, because the value of $P_{men} - P_{women}$ is different in all three figures. Figure 12 is centered at 25 percentage points, reflecting our illustrative values of 60% and 35% for the pass rates. Figure 13 is centered at zero, because it is drawn according to the requirements of the null hypothesis. Figure 14 is centered at 10, because the alternative hypothesis is used to determine the center, rather than the null hypothesis.

12. The null hypothesis asserts a difference of zero. In Figure 13, 20 percentage points is 2 SEs to the right of the value expected under the null hypothesis; likewise, –20 is 2 SEs to the left. However, Figure 14 takes the alternative hypothesis to be true; on that basis, the expected value is 10 instead of zero, so 20 is 1 SE to the right of the expected value, while –20 is 3 SEs to the left.

13. Let t = sample difference/SE, where the SE is estimated from the data, as in expression (10). One formal version of our test rejects the null hypothesis if $t \geq 2$. To find the power, we replace the estimated SE by the true SE, computed as in expression (7); and we replace the probability histogram by the normal curve. These approximations are quite good. The size can be approximated in a similar way, given a common value for the two population pass rates. *See supra* note 10 (taking the common value to be 0.48). Of course, more exact calculations are possible, leading to what statisticians call *Fisher's exact test*.

Appendix 1

Glossary of Terms

The following terms and definitions are adapted from a variety of sources, including Michael O. Finkelstein & Bruce Levin, Statistics for Lawyers (2d ed. 2001), and David A. Freedman et al., Statistics (3d ed. 1997).

Adjust for. See Control for.

Alpha (α). A symbol often used to denote the probability of a Type I error. See Type I error; size. Cf. Beta.

Alternative Hypothesis. A statistical hypothesis that is contrasted with the null hypothesis in a significance test. See statistical hypothesis; significance test.

Area Sample. An area sample is a probability sample in which the sampling frame is a list of geographical areas. (That is, the researchers make a list of areas, choose some at random, and interview people in the selected areas). This is a cost-effective way to draw a sample of people. See Probability Sample; Sampling Frame.

Average. See Mean.

Bayes' Rule. An investigator may start with a subjective probability (the "prior") that expresses degrees of belief about a parameter or a hypothesis. The data are collected according to some statistical model, at least in the investigator's opinion. Bayes' rule gives a procedure for combining the prior with the data to compute the "posterior" probability, which expresses the investigator's belief about the parameter or hypothesis given the data. See Appendix.

Beta (β). A symbol sometimes used to denote power, and sometimes to denote the probability of a Type II error. See Type II error; Power. Cf. Alpha.

Bias. A systematic tendency for an estimate to be too high or too low. An estimate is "unbiased" if the bias is zero. (Does not mean prejudice, partiality, or discriminatory intent.) See Non–Sampling Error. Cf. Sampling Error.

Bin. A class interval in a histogram. See Class Interval; Histogram.

Binary Variable. A variable that has only two possible values (e.g., gender). Also called a "dummy variable."

Binomial Distribution. A distribution for the number of occurrences in repeated, independent "trials" where the probabilities are fixed. For example, the number of heads in 100 tosses of a coin follows a binomial distribution. When the probability is not too close to zero or one and the number of trials is large, the binomial distribution has about the same shape as the normal distribution. See Normal Distribution; Poisson Distribution.

Blind. See Double-blind Experiment.

Bootstrapping. A procedure for estimating sampling error by constructing a simulated population on the basis of the sample, then repeatedly drawing samples from this simulated population. Also called resampling, Monte Carlo method.

Categorical Data; Categorical Variable. See Qualitative Variable. Cf. Quantitative Variable.

Central Limit Theorem. Shows that under suitable conditions, the probability histogram for a sum (or average or rate) will follow the normal curve.

Chance Error. See Random Error; Sampling Error.

Chi-squared (χ^2). The chi-squared statistic measures the distance between the data and expected values computed from a statistical model. If χ^2 is too large to explain by chance, the data contradict the model. The definition of "large" depends on the context. See Statistical Hypothesis; Significance Test.

Class Interval. The base of a rectangle in a histogram; the area of the rectangle shows the percentage of observations in the class interval. Also, Bin. See Histogram.

Cluster Sample. A type of random sample. For example, one might take households at random, then interview all people in the selected households. This is a cluster sample of people: a cluster consists of all the people in a selected household. Generally, clustering reduces the cost of interviewing. See Multi-stage Cluster Sample.

Coefficient of Determination. A statistic (more commonly known as R^2) that describes how well a regression equation fits the data. See R-squared.

Coefficient of Variation. A statistic that measures spread relative to the mean: SD/Mean, or SE/Expected Value. See Expected Value; Mean; Standard Deviation; Standard Error.

Collinearity. See Multicollinearity.

Conditional Probability. The probability that one event will occur given that another has occurred.

Confidence Coefficient. See Confidence Interval.

Confidence Interval. An estimate, expressed as a range, for a quantity in a population. If an estimate from a large sample is unbiased, a 95% "confidence interval" is the range from about two standard errors below to two standard errors above the estimate. Intervals obtained this way cover the true value about 95% of the time, and 95% is the "confidence level" or the "confidence coefficient." See Unbiased Estimator; Standard error. Cf. Bias.

Confidence Level. See Confidence Interval.

Confounding. See Confounding Variable; Observational Study.

Confounding Variable; Confounder. A variable that is correlated with the independent variables and the dependent variable. An association between the dependent and independent variables in an observational study may not be causal, but may instead be due to confounding. See Controlled Experiment; Observational Study.

Consistency; Consistent. See Consistent Estimator.

Consistent Estimator. An estimator that tends to become more and more accurate as the sample size grows. Inconsistent estimators, which do not become more accurate as the sample gets large, are seldom used by statisticians.

Content Validity. The extent to which a skills test is appropriate to its intended purpose, as evidenced by a set of questions that adequately reflect the domain being tested.

Continuous Variable. A variable that has arbitrarily fine gradations, such as a person's height. Cf. Discrete Variable.

Control for. Statisticians may "control for" the effects of confounding variables in nonexperimental data by making comparisons for smaller and more homogeneous groups of subjects, or by entering the confounders as explanatory variables in a regression model. To "adjust for" is perhaps a better phrase in the regression context, because in an observational study the confounding factors are not under experimental control; statistical adjustments are an imperfect substitute. See Regression Model.

Control Group. See Controlled Experiment.

Controlled Experiment. An experiment where the investigators determine which subjects are put into the "treatment group" and which are put into the "control group." Subjects in the treatment group are exposed by the investigators to some influence—the "treatment"; those in the control group are not so exposed. For instance, in an experiment to evaluate a new drug, subjects in the treatment group are given the drug, subjects in the control group are given some other therapy; the outcomes in the two groups are compared to see whether the new drug works.

"Randomization"—that is, randomly assigning subjects to each group—is usually the best way to assure that any observed difference between the two groups comes from the treatment rather than pre-existing differences. Of course, in many situations, a randomized controlled experiment is impractical, and investigators must then rely on observational studies. Cf. Observational Study.

Convenience Sample. A non-random sample of units, also called a "grab sample." Such samples are easy to take, but may suffer from serious bias. Mall samples are convenience samples.

Correlation Coefficient. A number between –1 and 1 that indicates the extent of the linear association between two variables. Often, the correlation coefficient is abbreviated as "r."

Covariance. A quantity that describes the statistical interrelationship of two variables. Cf. Correlation Coefficient; Standard Error; Variance.

Covariate. A variable that is related to other variables of primary interest in a study; a measured confounder; a statistical control in a regression equation.

Criterion. The variable against which an examination or other selection procedure is validated. See Predictive Validity.

Data. Observations or measurements, usually of units in a sample taken from a larger population.

Dependent Variable. See Independent Variable.

Descriptive Statistics. Like the mean or standard deviation, used to summarize data.

Differential Validity. Differences in the correlation between skills test scores and outcome measures across different subgroups of test-takers.

Discrete Variable. A variable that has only a finite number of possible values, such as the number of automobiles owned by a household. Cf. Continuous Variable.

Distribution. See Frequency Distribution; Probability Distribution; Sampling Distribution.

Disturbance Term. A synonym for "error term."

Double-blind Experiment. An experiment with human subjects in which neither the diagnosticians nor the subjects know who is in the treatment group or the control group. This is accomplished by giving a "placebo" treatment to patients in the control group. In a "single-blind" experiment, the patients do not know whether they are in treatment or control; however, the diagnosticians have this information.

Dummy Variable. A dummy variable takes only the values 0 or 1, and distinguishes one group of interest from another. See Binary Variable; Regression Model.

Econometrics. Statistical study of economic issues.

Epidemiology. Statistical study of disease or injury in human populations.

Error Term. The part of a statistical model that describes random error, i.e., the impact of chance factors unrelated to variables in the model. In econometric models, the error term is called a "disturbance term."

Estimator. A sample statistic used to estimate the value of a population parameter. For instance, the sample mean commonly is used to estimate the population mean. The term "estimator" connotes a statistical procedure, while an "estimate" connotes a particular numerical result.

Expected Value. See Random Variable.

Experiment. See Controlled Experiment; Randomized Controlled Experiment. Cf. Observational Study.

Explanatory variables. See Independent variable, Regression model.

Fisher's exact test. When comparing two sample proportions, for instance, the proportions of whites and blacks getting a promotion, an investigator may wish to test the null hypothesis that promotion does not depend on race. Fisher's exact test is one way to arrive at a p-value. The calculation is based on the hypergeometric distribution. For more details, see Michael O. Finkelstein & Bruce Levin, Statistics for Lawyers 154–56 (2d ed. 2001). See Hypergeometric Distribution; p-value; Significance Test; Statistical Hypothesis.

Fitted Value. See Residual.

Fixed Significance Level. A pre-set level, such as 5% or 1%; if the p-value of a test falls below this level, the result is deemed "statistically significant."

Also, Alpha; Size. See Significance Test. Cf. Observed Significance Level; *p*–Value.

Frequency Distribution. Shows how often specified values occur in a data set.

Gaussian Distribution. A synonym for the normal distribution. See Normal Distribution.

General Linear Model. Expresses the dependent variable as a linear combination of the independent variables plus an error term whose components may be dependent and have different variances. See Error Term; Linear Combination; Variance. Cf. Regression Model.

Grab Sample. See Convenience Sample.

Heteroscedastic. See Scatter Diagram.

Histogram. A plot showing how observed values fall within specified intervals, called "bins" or "class intervals." Generally, matters are arranged so the area under the histogram, but over a class interval, gives the frequency or relative frequency of data in that interval. With a probability histogram, the area gives the chance of observing a value that falls in the corresponding interval.

Homoscedastic. See Scatter Diagram.

Hypergeometric Distribution. Suppose a sample is drawn at random without replacement, from a finite population. How many times will items of a certain type come into the sample? The hypergeometric distribution gives the probabilities. For more details, see 1 W. Feller, An Introduction to Probability Theory and its Applications 41–42 (2d ed. 1957). Cf. Fisher's Exact Test.

Hypothesis. See Alternative Hypothesis; Null Hypothesis; One-sided Hypothesis; Significance Test; Statistical Hypothesis; Two-sided Hypothesis.

Hypothesis Test. See Significance Test.

Independence. Events are independent when the probability of one is unaffected by the occurrence or non-occurrence of the other. Cf. Conditional Probability.

Independent Variable. "Independent" variables are used in a regression model to predict the "dependent" variable. For instance, the unemployment rate has been used as the independent variable in a model for predicting the crime rate; the unemployment rate is the independent variable in this model, and the crime rate is the dependent variable. Independent variables are also called "explanatory variables." See Regression Model; cf. Dependent Variable.

Indicator Variable. See Dummy Variable.

Interval Estimate. A "confidence interval"; or, an estimate coupled with a standard error. See Confidence Interval; Standard Error. Cf. Point Estimate.

Least Squares. See Least Squares Estimator; Regression Model.

Least Squares Estimator. An estimator that is computed by minimizing the sum of the squared residuals. See Residual.

Linear Combination. To obtain a linear combination of two variables, multiply the first variable by some constant, multiply the second variable by another constant, and add the two products. For instance, $2u + 3v$ is a linear combination of u and v.

Level. The "level" of a significance test is denoted alpha. See Alpha; Fixed Significance Level; Observed Significance Level; p-value; Significance Test.

Loss Function. Statisticians may evaluate estimators according to a mathematical formula involving the "errors," i.e., differences between actual values and estimated values. The "loss" may be the total of the squared errors, or, the total of the absolute errors, etc. Loss functions seldom quantify real losses, but may be useful summary statistics, and may prompt the construction of useful statistical procedures. Cf. Risk.

Mean. The mean is one way to find the center of a batch of numbers: add up the numbers, and divide by how many there are. Weights may be employed, as in "weighted mean" or "weighted average." Also, the Average; the Expected Value of a Random Variable. See Random Variable. Cf. Median; Mode.

Median. The median is another way to find the center of a batch of numbers. The median is the 50th percentile. Half the numbers are larger, and half are smaller. (To be very precise: at least half the numbers are greater than or equal to the median; at least half the numbers are less than or equal to the median; for small data sets, the median may not be uniquely defined.) Cf. Mean; Mode; Percentile.

Meta-analysis. Attempts to combine information from all studies on a certain topic. For example, in the epidemiologic context, a meta-analysis may attempt to provide a summary odds ratio and confidence interval for the effect of a certain exposure on a certain disease.

Mode. The most commonly observed value. Cf. Mean; Median.

Model. See Probability Model; Regression Model; Statistical Model.

Multicollinearity. The existence of correlations among the "independent variables" in a regression model. Also, Collinearity. See Independent Variable; Regression Model.

Multiple Comparison. Making several statistical tests on the same data set. Multiple comparisons complicate the interpretation of a p-value. For example, if 20 divisions of a company are examined, and one division is found to have a disparity "significant" at the 0.05 level, the result is not surprising; indeed, it should be expected under the null hypothesis. Cf. p-value; Significance Test; Statistical Hypothesis.

Multiple Correlation Coefficient. A number that indicates the extent to which one variable can be predicted as a linear combination of other variables. Its magnitude is the square root of R^2. See Linear Combination; R-squared; Regression Model. Cf. Correlation Coefficient.

Multiple Regression. A regression equation that includes two or more independent variables. See Regression Model. Cf. Simple Regression.

Multivariate methods. Methods for fitting models with multiple variables, especially, multiple response variables; occasionally, multiple explanatory variables. See Regression Model.

Multi-stage Cluster Sample. A probability sample drawn in stages, usually after stratification; the last stage will involve drawing a cluster. See Cluster Sample; Probability Sample; Stratified Random Sample.

Natural Experiment. An observational study in which treatment and control groups have been formed by some natural development; however, the assignment of subjects to groups is judged akin to randomization. See Observational Study. Cf. Controlled Experiment.

Non-sampling error. A catch-all term for sources of error in a survey, other than sampling error. Non-sampling errors cause bias. One example is selection bias: the sample is drawn in way that tends to exclude certain subgroups in the population. A second example is non-response bias: people who do not respond to a survey are usually different from respondents. A final example: response bias arises, for instance, if the interviewer uses a loaded question.

Normal distribution. The density for this distribution is the famous "bell-shaped" curve. Statistical terminology notwithstanding, there need be nothing wrong with a distribution that differs from the normal. Also, Gaussian Distribution.

Null Hypothesis. For example, a hypothesis that there is no difference between two groups from which samples are drawn. Cf. Alternative Hypothesis.

Observational Study. A study in which subjects select themselves into groups; investigators then compare the outcomes for the different groups. For example, studies of smoking are generally observational. Subjects decide whether or not to smoke; the investigators compare the death rate for smokers to the death rate for non-smokers. In an observational study, the groups may differ in important ways that the investigators do not notice; controlled experiments minimize this problem. The critical distinction is that in a controlled experiment, the investigators intervene to manipulate the circumstances of the subjects; in an observational study, the investigators are passive observers. (Of course, running a good observational study is hard work, and may be quite useful.) Cf. Confounding Variable; Controlled Experiment.

Observed Significance Level. A synonym for *p*-value. See Significance Test. Cf. Fixed Significance Level.

Odds. The probability that an event will occur divided by the probability that it will not. For example, if the chance of rain tomorrow is 2/3, then the odds on rain are $(2/3)/(1/3) = 2/1$, or 2 to 1; the odds against rain are 1 to 2.

Odds Ratio. A measure of association, often used in epidemiology. For instance, if 10% of all people exposed to a chemical develop a disease, compared to 5% of people who are not exposed, then the odds of the disease in the exposed group are $10/90 = 1/9$, compared to $5/95 = 1/19$ in the unexposed group. The odds ratio is $19/9 = 2.1$. An odds ratio of 1 indicates no association. Cf. Relative Risk.

One-sided Hypothesis. Excludes the possibility that a parameter could be, e.g., less than the value asserted in the null hypothesis. A one-sided hypothesis leads to a "one-tailed" test. See Significance Test; Statistical Hypothesis; Cf. Two-sided Hypothesis.

One-tailed Test. See Significance Test.

Outlier. An observation that is far removed from the bulk of the data. Outliers may indicate faulty measurements; they may exert undue influence on summary statistics, such as the mean or the correlation coefficient.

p-value. The output of a statistical test. The probability of getting, just by chance, a test statistic as large as or larger than the observed value. Large p-values are consistent with the null hypothesis; small p-values undermine this hypothesis. However, p itself does not give the probability that the null hypothesis is true. If p is smaller than 5%, the result is said to be "statistically significant." If p is smaller than 1%, the result is "highly significant." The p-value is also called "the observed significance level." See Significance Test; Statistical Hypothesis.

Parameter. A numerical characteristic of a population or a model. See Probability Model.

Percentile. To get the percentiles of a data set, array the data from the smallest value to the largest. Take the 90th percentile by way of example: 90% of the values fall below the 90th percentile, and 10% are above. (To be very precise: at least 90% of the data are at the 90th percentile or below; at least 10% of the data are at the 90th percentile or above.) The 50th percentile is the median: 50% of the values fall below the median, and 50% are above. When the LSAT first was scored on a 10–50 scale in 1982, a score of 32 placed a test taker at the 50th percentile; a score of 40 was at the 90th percentile (approximately). Cf. Mean; Median; Quartile.

Placebo. See Double–Blind Experiment.

Point Estimate. An estimate of the value of a quantity expressed as a single number. See Estimator. Cf. Confidence Interval; Interval Estimate.

Poisson Distribution. The Poisson distribution is a limiting case of the binomial distribution, when the number of trials is large and the common probability is small. The "parameter" of the approximating Poisson distribution is the number of "trials" times the common probability, which is the "expected" number of events. When this number is large, the Poisson distribution may be approximated by a normal distribution.

Population. All the units of interest to the researcher. Also, Universe. Cf. Sample; Sampling Frame.

Posterior Probability. See Bayes' rule.

Power. The probability that a statistical test will reject the null hypothesis. To compute power, one has to fix the size of the test and specify parameter values outside the range given in the null hypothesis. A powerful test has a good chance of detecting an effect, when there is an effect to be detected. See Beta; Significance Test. Cf. Alpha; Size; P-value.

Practical significance. Substantive importance. Statistical significance does not necessarily establish practical significance. With large samples, small differences can be statistically significant. See Significance Test.

Predicted Value. See Residual.

Predictive Validity. A skills test has predictive validity to the extent that test scores are well correlated with later performance, or more generally with outcomes that the test is intended to predict.

Prior Probability. See Bayes' rule.

Probability. Chance, on a scale from 0 to 1. Impossibility is represented by 0, certainty by 1. Equivalently, chances may be quoted in percent: 100% corresponds to 1, while 5% corresponds to 0.05, and so forth.

Probability Density. Describes the probability distribution of a random variable. The chance that the random variable falls in an interval equals the area below the density and above the interval. (However, not all random variables have densities.) See Probability Distribution; Random Variable.

Probability Distribution. Gives probabilities for possible values or ranges of values of a random variable. Often, the distribution is described in terms of a density. See Probability Density.

Probability Histogram. See Histogram.

Probability Model. Relates probabilities of outcomes to parameters; also, Statistical Model. The latter connotes unknown parameters.

Probability Sample. A sample drawn from a sampling frame by some objective chance mechanism; each unit has a known probability of being sampled. Such samples minimize selection bias, but can be expensive to draw.

Psychometrics. The study of psychological measurement and testing.

Qualitative Variable; Quantitative Variable. A "qualitative" or "categorical" variable describes qualitative features of subjects in a study (e.g., marital status—never-married, married, widowed, divorced, separated). A "quantitative" variable describes numerical features of the subjects (e.g., height, weight, income). This is not a hard-and-fast distinction, because qualitative features may be given numerical codes, as in a "dummy variable." Quantitative variables may be classified as "discrete" or "continuous." Concepts like the mean and the standard deviation apply only to quantitative variables. Cf. Continuous Variable; Discrete Variable; Dummy Variable. See Variable.

Quartile. The 25th or 75th percentile. See Percentile. Cf. Median.

R-squared (R^2). Measures how well a regression equation fits the data. R^2 varies between zero (no fit) and one (perfect fit). R^2 does not measure the validity of underlying assumptions. See Regression Model. Cf. Multiple Correlation Coefficient; Standard Error of Regression.

Random Error. Sources of error that are haphazard in their effect. These are reflected in the "error term" of a statistical model. Some authors refer to "random error" as "chance error" or "sampling error." See Regression Model.

Random Variable. A variable whose possible values occur according to some probability mechanism. For example, if a pair of dice are thrown, the total number of spots is a random variable. The chance of two spots is 1/36, the chance of three spots is 2/36, and so forth; the most likely number is 7, with chance 6/36.

The "expected value" of a random variable is the weighted average of the possible values; the weights are the probabilities. In our example, the expected value is

$$\frac{1}{36} \times 2 + \frac{2}{36} \times 3 + \frac{3}{36} \times 4 + \frac{4}{36} \times 5 + \frac{6}{36} \times 7$$

$$\frac{5}{36} \times 8 + \frac{4}{36} \times 9 + \frac{3}{36} \times 10 + \frac{2}{36} \times 11 + \frac{1}{36} \times 12 = 7$$

In many problems, the weighted average is computed with respect to the density; then sums must be replaced by integrals. The expected value need not be a possible value for the random variable.

Generally, a random variable will be somewhere around its expected value, but will be off (in either direction) by something like a standard error (SE) or so. If the random variable has a more or less normal distribution, there is about a 68% chance for it to fall in the range "expected value – SE" to "expected value + SE." See Normal Curve; Standard Error.

Randomization. See Controlled Experiment; Randomized Controlled Experiment.

Randomized Controlled Experiment. A controlled experiment in which subjects are placed into the treatment and control groups at random—as if by lot, that is, by randomization. See Controlled Experiment. Cf. Observational study.

Range. The difference between the biggest and the smallest values in a batch of numbers.

Regression Coefficient. A constant in a regression equation. See Regression model.

Regression Diagnostics. Procedures intended to check whether the assumptions of a regression model are appropriate.

Regression Equation. See Regression Model.

Regression Line. The graph of a (simple) regression equation.

Regression Model. A "regression model" attempts to combine the values of certain variables (the "independent" or "explanatory" variables) in order to get expected values for another variable (the "dependent" variable). Sometimes, "regression model" refers to a probability model for the data; if no qualifications are made, the model will generally be linear, and errors will be assumed independent across observations, with common variance; the coefficients in the linear combination are called "regression coefficients"; these are parameters. At times, "regression model" refers to an equation (the "regression equation") estimated from data, typically by least squares.

For example, in a regression study of salary differences between men and women in a firm, the analyst may include a "dummy variable" for gender, as well as "statistical controls" like education and experience to adjust for productivity differences between men and women. The dummy variable would be defined as one for the men, zero for the women. Salary would be the dependent variable; education, experience, and the dummy would be the independent variables. See Least Squares; Multiple Regression; Random Error; Variance. Cf. General Linear Model.

Relative Risk. A measure of association used in epidemiology. For instance, if 10% of all people exposed to a chemical develop a disease, compared to 5% of people who are not exposed, then the disease occurs twice as frequently among the exposed people: the relative risk is 10%/5% = 2. A relative risk of one indicates no association. Cf. Odds Ratio. For more details, see A. M. Lilienfeld & D. E. Lilienfeld, Foundations of Epidemiology 209 (2d ed. 1980).

Reliability. The extent to which a measuring instrument gives the same results on repeated measurement of the same thing. Cf. Validity.

Residual. The difference between an actual and a "predicted" value. The predicted value comes typically from a regression equation, and is also called the "fitted value." See Regression Model; Independent Variable.

Risk. Expected loss. "Expected" means on average, over the various data sets that could be generated by the statistical model under examination. Usually, risk cannot be computed exactly but has to be estimated, because the parameters in the statistical model are unknown and must be estimated. See Loss Function; Random Variable.

Robust. A statistic or procedure that does not change much when data or assumptions are modified slightly.

Sample. A set of units collected for study. Cf. Population.

Sample Size. The number of units in a sample.

Sampling Distribution. The distribution of the values of a statistic, over all possible samples from a population. For example, suppose a random sample is drawn. Some values of the sample mean are more likely, others are less likely. The "sampling distribution" specifies the chance that the sample mean will fall in one interval rather than another.

Sampling Error. A sample is part of a population. When a sample is used to estimate a numerical characteristic of the population, the estimate is likely to differ from the population value, because the sample is not a perfect microcosm of the whole. If the estimate is unbiased, the difference between the estimate and the exact value is "sampling error." More generally,

$$\text{estimate} = \text{true value} + \text{bias} + \text{sampling error.}$$

Sampling error is also called "chance error" or "random error." See Standard Error. Cf. Bias; Non-sampling error.

Sampling Frame. A list of units designed to represent the entire population as completely as possible. The sample is drawn from the frame.

Scatter Diagram. A graph showing the relationship between two variables in a study. Each dot represents one subject. One variable is plotted along the horizontal axis, the other variable is plotted along the vertical axis. A scatter diagram is "homoscedastic" when the spread is more or less the same inside any vertical strip. If the spread changes from one strip to another, the diagram is "heteroscedastic." Also, scatterplot, scattergram.

Sensitivity. In clinical medicine, the probability that a test for a disease will give a positive result given that the patient has the disease. Sensitivity is analogous to the power of a statistical test. Cf. Specificity.

Sensitivity Analysis. Analyzing data in different ways to see how results depend on methods or assumptions.

Significance Level. See Fixed Significance Level; *p*-value.

Significance Test. A significance test involves formulating a statistical hypothesis and a test statistic, computing a *p*-value, and comparing *p* to some pre-established value ("alpha") to decide if the test statistic is "significant." The idea is to see whether the data conform to the predictions of the null hypothesis. Generally, a large test statistic goes with a small *p*-value; and small *p*-values would undermine the null hypothesis.

　　　For instance, suppose that a random sample of male and female employees were given a skills test and the mean scores of the men and women were different—in the sample. To judge whether the difference is due to sampling error, a statistician might consider the implications of competing hypotheses about the difference in the population. The "null hypothesis" would say that on average, in the population, men and women have the same scores: the difference observed in the data is then just due to sampling error. A "one-sided alternative hypothesis" would be that on average, in the population, men score higher than women. The "one-tailed" test would reject the null hypothesis if the sample men score substantially higher than the women—so much so that the difference is hard to explain on the basis of sampling error.

　　　In contrast, the null hypothesis could be tested against the "two-sided alternative" that on average, in the population, men score differently than women—higher or lower. The corresponding "two-tailed" test would reject the null hypothesis if the sample men score substantially higher or substantially lower than the women.

　　　The one-tailed and two-tailed tests would both be based on the same data, and use the same *t*-statistic. However, if the men in the sample score higher than the women, the one-tailed test would give a *p*-value only half as large as the two-tailed test, that is, the one-tailed test would appear to give stronger evidence against the null hypothesis. See also, Statistical Test, Hypothesis Test, Test of Significance. See *p*-value; Statistical Hypothesis; *t*-Statistic.

Significant. See *p*-value; Practical Significance; Significance Test.

Simple Random Sample. A random sample in which each unit in the sampling frame has the same chance of being sampled. One takes a unit at random (as if by lottery), sets it aside, takes another at random from what is left, and so forth.

Simple regression. A regression equation that includes only one independent variable. Cf. Multiple Regression.

Size. A synonym for alpha (α).

Specificity. In clinical medicine, the probability that a test for a disease will give a negative result given that the patient does not have the disease. Specificity is analogous to $1 - \alpha$, where α is the significance level of a statistical test. Cf. Sensitivity.

Spurious Correlation. When two variables are correlated, one is not necessarily the cause of the other. The vocabulary and shoe size of children in elementary school, for instance, are correlated—but learning more words will not make the feet grow. Such non-causal correlations are said to be "spurious." (Originally, the term seems to have been applied to the correlation between two rates with the same denominator: even if the numerators are unrelated, the common denominator will create some association.) Cf. Confounding Variable.

Standard Deviation (SD). The SD indicates how far a typical element deviates from the average. For instance, in round numbers, the average height of women age 18 and over in the United States is 5 feet 4 inches. However, few women are exactly average; most will deviate from average, at least by a little. The SD is sort of an average deviation from average. For the height distribution, the SD is 3 inches. The height of a typical woman is around 5 feet 4 inches, but is off that average value by something like 3 inches.

For distributions that follow the normal curve, about 68% of the elements are in the range "mean − SD" to "mean + SD." Thus, about 68% of women have heights in the range 5 feet 1 inch to 5 feet 7 inches. Deviations from the average that exceed three or four SDs are extremely unusual. Many authors use "standard deviation" to also mean standard error. See Standard Error.

Standard Error (SE). Indicates the likely size of the sampling error in an estimate. Many authors use the term "standard deviation" instead of standard error. Cf. Expected Value; Standard Deviation.

Standard Error of Regression. Indicates how actual values differ (in some average sense) from the fitted values in a regression model. See Regression Model; Residual. Cf. *R*-squared.

Standardization. See Standardized Variable.

Standardized Variable. Transformed to have mean zero and variance one. This involves two steps: (i) subtract the mean, (ii) divide by the standard deviation.

Statistic. A number that summarizes data. A "statistic" refers to a sample; a "parameter" or a "true value" refers to a population or a probability model.

Statistical Controls. Procedures that try to filter out the effects of confounding variables on non-experimental data, for instance, by "adjusting" through statistical procedures (like multiple regression). Variables in a multiple regression equation. See Multiple regression. Cf. Controlled Experiment. See Confounding Variable; Observational Study.

Statistical Hypothesis. Data may be governed by a probability model; "parameters" are numerical characteristics describing features of the model. Generally, a "statistical hypothesis" is a statement about the parameters in a probability model. The "null hypothesis" may assert that certain parameters have specified values or fall in specified ranges; the alternative hypothesis would specify other values or ranges. The null hypothesis is "tested" against the data with a "test statistic"; the null hypothesis may be "rejected" if there is a "statistically significant" difference between the data and the predictions of the null hypothesis.

Typically, the investigator seeks to demonstrate the alternative hypothesis; the null hypothesis would explain the findings as a result of mere chance, and the investigator uses a significance test to rule out this explanation. See Significance Test.

Statistical Model. See Probability Model.

Statistical Test. See Significance Test.

Statistical Significance. See *p*-value.

Stratified Random Sample. A type of probability sample. One divides the population up into relatively homogeneous groups called "strata," and draws a random sample separately from each stratum.

Systematic Sampling. The element of the population are numbered consecutively as 1, 2, 3.... Then, every *k*th element is chosen. If $k = 10$, for instance, the sample would consist of items, 1, 11, 21.... Sometimes the starting point is chosen at random from 1 to *k*.

t-*Statistic.* A test statistic, used to make the "*t*-test." The *t*-statistic indicates how far away an estimate is from its expected value, relative to the standard error. The expected value is computed using the null hypothesis that is being tested. Some authors refer to the *t*-statistic, others to the "*z*-statistic," especially when the sample is large. In such cases, a *t*-statistic larger than 2 or 3 in absolute value makes the null hypothesis rather unlikely—the estimate is too many standard errors away from its expected value. See Statistical Hypothesis; Significance Test; *t*-Test.

t-*Test.* A statistical test based on the *t*-statistic. Large *t*-statistics are beyond the usual range of sampling error. For example, if *t* is bigger than 2, or smaller than –2, then the estimate is "statistically significant" at the 5% level: such values of *t* are hard to explain on the basis of sampling error. The scale for *t*-statistics is tied to areas under the normal curve. For instance, a *t*-statistic of 1.5 is not very striking, because $13\% = 13/100$ of the area under the normal curve is outside the range from –1.5 to 1.5. On the other hand, $t = 3$ is remarkable: only 3/1,000 of the area lies outside the range from –3 to 3. This discussion is predicated on having a reasonably large sample; in that context, many authors refer to the "*z*-test" rather than the *t*-test.

For small samples drawn at random from a population known to be normal, the *t*-statistic follows "Student's *t*-distribution" (when the null hypothesis holds) rather than the normal curve; larger values of t are required to achieve "significance." A t-test is not appropriate for small samples drawn from a population that is not normal. See p-value; Significance Test; Statistical Hypothesis.

Test Statistic. A statistic used to judge whether data conform to the null hypothesis. The parameters of a probability model determine expected values for the data; differences between expected values and observed values are measured by a "test statistic." Such test statistics include the chi-squared statistic (χ^2) and the t-statistic. Generally, small values of the test statistic are consistent with the null hypothesis; large values lead to rejection. See p-value; Statistical Hypothesis; t-Statistic.

Time Series. A series of data collected over time, for instance, the Gross National Product of the United States from 1940 to 1990.

Treatment Group. See Controlled Experiment.

Two-sided Hypothesis. An alternative hypothesis asserting that the values of a parameter are different from—either greater than or less than—the value asserted in the null hypothesis. A two-sided alternative hypothesis suggests a two-tailed test. See Statistical Hypothesis; Significance Test. Cf. One-sided Hypothesis.

Two-tailed Test. See Significance Test.

Type I Error. A statistical test makes a "Type I error" when (i) the null hypothesis is true and (ii) the test rejects the null hypothesis, i.e., there is a false positive. For instance, a study of two groups may show some difference between samples from each group, even when there is no difference in the population. When a statistical test deems the difference to be "significant" in this situation, it makes a Type I error. See Significance Test; Statistical Hypothesis. Cf. Alpha; Type II Error.

Type II Error. A statistical test makes a "Type II error" when (i) the null hypothesis is false and (ii) the test fails to reject the null hypothesis, i.e., there is a false negative. For instance, there may not be a "significant" difference between samples from two groups when, in fact, the groups are different. See Significance Test; Statistical Hypothesis. Cf. Beta; Type I Error.

Unbiased Estimator. An estimator that is correct on average, over the possible data sets. The estimates have no systematic tendency to be high or low. Cf. Bias.

Uniform Distribution. For example, a whole number picked at random from 1 to 100 has the uniform distribution: all values are equally likely. Similarly, a uniform distribution is obtained by picking a real number at random between 0.75 and 3.25: the chance of landing in an interval is proportional to the length of the interval. "The" uniform distribution, without further qualification, is presumably on the "unit interval" (which goes from zero to one).

Validity. The extent to which an instrument measures what it is supposed to, rather than something else. The validity of a standardized test is often indicated (in part) by the correlation coefficient between the test scores and some outcome measure.

Variable. A property of units in a study, which varies from one unit to another. For example, in a study of households, household income; in a study of people, employment status (employed, unemployed, not in labor force).

Variance. The square of the standard deviation. Cf. Standard error; Covariance.

z-statistic. See *t*-Statistic.

z-test. See *t*-test.

Appendix 2

References on Statistics

General Surveys

David Freedman et al., Statistics (3d ed. 1998).

Darrell Huff, How to Lie with Statistics (1954).

Gregory A. Kimble, How to Use (and Misuse) Statistics (1978).

David S. Moore, Statistics: Concepts and Controversies (3d ed. 1991).

David S. Moore & George P. McCabe, Introduction to the Practice of Statistics (2d ed. 1993).

Michael Oakes, Statistical Inference: A Commentary for the Social and Behavioral Sciences (1986).

Perspectives on Contemporary Statistics (David G. Hoaglin & David S. Moore eds., 1992).

Statistics: A Guide to the Unknown (Judith M. Tanur et al. eds., 2d ed. 1978).

Hans Zeisel, Say It with Figures (6th ed. 1985).

Reference Works for Lawyers and Judges

David C. Baldus & James W.L. Cole, Statistical Proof of Discrimination (1980 & Supp. 1987).

David W. Barnes & John M. Conley, Statistical Evidence in Litigation: Methodology, Procedure, and Practice (1986).

James Brooks, A Lawyer's Guide to Probability and Statistics (1990).

Michael O. Finkelstein & Bruce Levin, Statistics for Lawyers (2d ed. 2001).

Ramona Paetzold & Steven L. Willborn, The Statistics of Discrimination: Using Statistical Evidence in Discrimination Cases (1994).

Panel on Statistical Assessments as Evidence in the Courts, National Research Council, The Evolving Role of Statistical Assessments as Evidence in the Courts (Stephen E. Fienberg ed., 1989).

Statistical Methods in Discrimination Litigation (David H. Kaye & Mikel Aickin eds., 1986).

Hans Zeisel & David Kaye, Prove It with Figures: Empirical Methods in Law and Litigation (1997).

General Reference

International Encyclopedia of Statistics (William H. Kruskal & Judith M. Tanur eds., (1978).

CHAPTER 6

SURVEY RESEARCH

by

Shari Seidman Diamond*

Table of Sections

* Shari Diamond, a social psychologist and attorney, is a Professor of Law and Psychology at the Northwestern University School of Law and a Senior Research Fellow at the American Bar Foundation. She has practiced intellectual property law at Sidley & Austin. She was a member of the Panel on Evaluation of DNA Forensic Evidence and the Panel on Sentencing Research for the National Academy of Sciences. Professor Diamond was President of the American Psychological Association's Division of Psychology and Law, received the APA's Distinguished Contributions to Research in Public Policy Award, and was Editor of the LAW & SOCIETY REVIEW. This chapter is an updated version of the author's contribution to the Federal Judicial Center's SCIENTIFIC EVIDENCE REFERENCE MANUAL, 2ND EDITION (2000).

Westlaw Electronic Research

See Westlaw Electronic Research Guide preceding the Summary of Contents.

---

§ 6–1.0 THE LEGAL RELEVANCE OF SURVEY RESEARCH

Surveys are used to describe or enumerate objects or the beliefs, attitudes, or behavior of persons or other social units.[1] Surveys typically are offered in legal proceedings to establish or refute claims about the characteristics of those objects, individuals, or social units. Although surveys may count or measure every member of the relevant population (e.g., all plaintiffs eligible to join in a suit, all employees currently working for a corporation, all trees in a forest), sample surveys count or measure only a portion of the objects, individuals, or social units that the survey is intended to describe.[2]

§ 6–1.0

1. Social scientists describe surveys as "conducted for the purpose of collecting data from individuals about themselves, about their households, or about other larger social units." Peter H. Rossi et al., *Sample Surveys: History, Current Practice, and Future Prospects, in* HANDBOOK OF SURVEY RESEARCH 1, 2 (Peter H. Rossi et al. eds., 1983). Used in its broader sense, however, the term survey applies to any description or enumeration, whether or not a person is the source of this information. Thus, a report on the number of trees destroyed in a forest fire might require a survey of the trees and stumps in the damaged area.

2. In J.H. Miles & Co. v. Brown, 910 F.Supp. 1138 (E.D.Va.1995), clam processors and fishing vessel owners sued the Secretary of Commerce for failing to use the unexpectedly high results from 1994 survey data on the size of the clam population to determine clam fishing quotas for 1995. The estimate of clam abundance is obtained from surveys of the amount of fishing time the research survey vessels require to collect a specified yield of

Some statistical and sampling experts apply the phrase "sample survey" only to a survey in which probability sampling techniques are used to select the sample.[3] Although probability sampling offers important advantages over nonprobability sampling,[4] experts in some fields (e.g., marketing) regularly rely on various forms of nonprobability sampling when conducting surveys. Consistent with Federal Rule of Evidence 703, courts generally have accepted such evidence.[5] Thus, in this Chapter, both the probability sample and the nonprobability sample are discussed. The strengths of probability sampling and the weaknesses of various types of nonprobability sampling are described so that the trier of fact can consider these features in deciding what weight to give to a particular sample survey.

As a method of data collection, surveys have several crucial potential advantages over less systematic approaches.[6] When properly designed, executed, and described, surveys (1) economically present the characteristics of a large group of objects or respondents and (2) permit an assessment of the extent to which the measured objects or respondents are likely to represent adequately a relevant group of objects, individuals, or social organisms.[7] All questions asked of respondents and all other measuring devices used can be examined by the court and the opposing party for objectivity, clarity, and relevance, and all answers or other measures obtained can be analyzed for completeness and consistency. To make it possible for the court and the opposing party to scrutinize the survey closely so that its relevance, objectivity, and representativeness can be evaluated, the party proposing to offer the survey as evidence should describe in detail the design and execution of the survey.

The questions listed in this Chapter are intended to assist judges in identifying, narrowing, and addressing issues bearing on the adequacy of surveys either offered as evidence or proposed as a method for developing information.[8] These questions can be (1) raised from the bench during a pretrial proceeding to determine the admissibility of the survey evidence; (2) presented to the contending experts before trial for their joint identification of disputed and undisputed issues; (3) presented to counsel with the expectation that the issues will be addressed during the examination of the experts at trial; or (4) raised in bench trials when a motion for a preliminary injunction is made to help the judge evaluate what weight, if any, the survey should be given.[9] These questions are intended to improve the utility of cross-examination by counsel, where appropriate, not to replace it.

clams in major fishing areas over a period of several weeks. *Id.* at 1144–45.

3. *E.g.*, Leslie Kish, Survey Sampling 26 (1965).

4. *See infra* § 7–3.3.

5. Fed. R. Evid. 703 recognizes facts or data "of a type reasonably relied upon by experts in the particular field. . . ."

6. This does not mean that surveys are perfect measuring devices that can be relied on to address all types of questions. For example, some respondents may not be able to predict accurately whether they would volunteer for military service if Washington, D.C., were to be bombed. Their inaccuracy may arise not because they are unwilling to answer the ques-

tion or to say they don't know, but because they believe they can predict accurately, and they are simply wrong. Thus, the availability of a "don't know" option cannot cure the inaccuracy. Although such a survey is suitable for assessing their predictions, it does not provide useful information about what their actual responses would be.

7. The ability to assess quantitatively the limits of the likely margin of error is unique to probability sample surveys.

8. *See infra* text accompanying note 28.

9. Lanham Act cases involving trademark infringement or deceptive advertising frequently require expedited hearings that request injunctive relief, so that judges may need to be

All sample surveys, whether they measure objects, individuals, or other social organisms, should address the issues concerning purpose and design (section 2.0), population definition and sampling (section 3.0), accuracy of data entry (section 6.0), and disclosure and reporting (section 7.0). Questionnaire and interview surveys raise methodological issues involving survey questions and structure (section 4.0) and confidentiality (section 7.3), and interview surveys introduce additional issues (e.g., interviewer training and qualifications) (section 5.0). The sections of this Chapter are labeled to identify immediately those topics that are relevant to the type of survey being considered. The scope of this Chapter is necessarily limited, and additional issues might arise in particular cases.

§ 6–1.1   Use of Surveys in Court

Forty years ago the question whether surveys constituted acceptable evidence still was unsettled.[10] Early doubts about the admissibility of surveys centered on their use of sampling techniques[11] and their status as hearsay evidence.[12] Federal Rule of Evidence 703 settled both matters by redirecting

more familiar with survey methodology when considering the weight to accord a survey in these cases than when presiding over cases being submitted to a jury. Even in a case being decided by a jury, however, the court must be prepared to evaluate the methodology of the survey evidence in order to rule on admissibility. *See* Daubert v. Merrell Dow Pharms., Inc., 509 U.S. 579, 589, 113 S.Ct. 2786, 125 L.Ed.2d 469 (1993).

10. Hans Zeisel, *The Uniqueness of Survey Evidence*, 45 Cornell L.Q. 322, 345 (1960).

11. In an early use of sampling, Sears, Roebuck & Co. claimed a tax refund based on sales made to individuals living outside city limits. Sears randomly sampled 33 of the 826 working days in the relevant working period, computed the proportion of sales to out-of-city individuals during those days, and projected the sample result to the entire period. The court refused to accept the estimate based on the sample. When a complete audit was made, the result was almost identical to that obtained from the sample. Sears, Roebuck & Co. v. City of Inglewood, described in R. Sprowls, *The Admissibility of Sample Data into a Court of Law: A Case History*, 4 UCLA L. Rev. 222, 226–29 (1956–57).

12. Judge Wilfred Feinberg's thoughtful analysis in *Zippo Mfg. Co. v. Rogers Imports, Inc.*, 216 F.Supp. 670, 682–83 (S.D.N.Y.1963), provides two alternative grounds for admitting opinion surveys: (1) surveys are not hearsay because they are not offered in evidence to prove the truth of the matter asserted; and (2) even if they are hearsay, they fall under one of the exceptions as a "present sense impression." In *Schering Corp. v. Pfizer Inc.*, 189 F.3d 218 (2d Cir.1999), the Second Circuit distinguished between perception surveys designed to reflect the present sense impressions of respondents and "memory" surveys designed to collect information about a past occurrence based on the recollections of the survey respondents. The court in *Schering* suggested that if a survey is offered to prove the existence of a specific idea in the public mind, then the survey does constitute hearsay evidence. As the court observed, Federal Rule of Evidence 803(3), creating "an exception to the hearsay rule for such statements [i.e., state of mind expressions] rather than excluding the statements from the definition of hearsay, makes sense only in this light." *Id.* at 230 n. 3. Two additional exceptions to the hearsay exclusion can be applied to surveys. First, surveys may constitute a hearsay exception if the survey data were collected in the normal course of a regularly conducted business activity, unless "the source of information on the method or circumstances of preparation indicate lack of trustworthiness." Fed. R. Evid. 803(6); *see also* Ortho Pharm. Corp. v. Cosprophar, Inc., 828 F.Supp. 1114, 1119–20 (S.D.N.Y.1993) (marketing surveys prepared in the course of business were properly excluded due to lack of foundation from a person who saw the original data or knew what steps were taken in preparing the report), *aff'd* 32 F.3d 690 (2d Cir.1994). In addition, if a survey shows guarantees of trustworthiness equivalent to those in other hearsay exceptions, it can be admitted if the court determines that the statement is offered as evidence of a material fact, it is more probative on the point for which it is offered than any other evidence which the proponent can procure through reasonable efforts, and admissibility serves the interests of justice. Fed. R. Evid. 807; e.g., Keith v. Volpe, 618 F.Supp. 1132 (C.D.Cal.1985). Admissibility as an exception to the hearsay exclusion thus depends on the trustworthiness of the survey.

attention to the "validity of the techniques employed."[13] The inquiry under Rule 703 focuses on whether facts or data are "of a type reasonably relied upon by experts in the particular field in forming opinions or inferences upon the subject."[14] For a survey, the question becomes, "Was the poll or survey conducted in accordance with generally accepted survey principles, and were the results used in a statistically correct way?"[15] This focus on the adequacy of the methodology used in conducting and analyzing results from a survey is also consistent with the Supreme Court's discussion of admissible scientific evidence in *Daubert v. Merrell Dow Pharmaceuticals, Inc.*[16]

Because the survey method provides an economical and systematic way to gather information about a large number of individuals or social units, surveys are used widely in business, government, and, increasingly, administrative settings and judicial proceedings. Both federal and state courts have accepted survey evidence on a variety of issues.[17] In a case involving allegations of discrimination in jury panel composition, the defense team surveyed prospective jurors to obtain age, race, education, ethnicity, and income distribution.[18] Surveys of employees or prospective employees are used to support or refute claims of employment discrimination.[19] In ruling on the admissibility of scientific claims, courts have examined surveys of scientific experts to assess the extent to which the theory or technique has received widespread acceptance.[20] Some courts have admitted surveys in obscenity cases to provide evidence about community standards.[21] Requests for a change of venue on grounds of jury pool bias often are backed by evidence from a survey of jury-eligible respondents in the area of the original venue.[22] The plaintiff in an antitrust suit conducted a survey to assess what characteristics, including price, affected consumers' preferences. The survey was offered as one way to

13. Fed. R. Evid. 703 Advisory Committee Note.

14. Fed. R. Evid. 703.

15. MANUAL FOR COMPLEX LITIGATION, SECOND, § 2.712 (1985). Survey research also is addressed in the MANUAL FOR COMPLEX LITIGATION, THIRD, § 21.493 (1995). Note, however, that experts who collect survey data, along with the professions that rely on those surveys, may differ in some of their methodological standards and principles. The required precision of sample estimates and an evaluation of the sources and magnitude of likely bias are required to distinguish methods that are acceptable from methods that are not.

16. 509 U.S. 579, 113 S.Ct. 2786, 125 L.Ed.2d 469 (1993). *See also* General Elec. Co. v. Joiner, 522 U.S. 136, 147, 118 S.Ct. 512, 139 L.Ed.2d 508 (1997).

17. Some surveys are so well accepted that they even may not be recognized as surveys. For example, some U.S. Census Bureau data are based on sample surveys. Similarly, the Standard Table of Mortality, which is accepted as proof of the average life expectancy of an individual of a particular age and gender, is based on survey data.

18. People v. Harris, 36 Cal.3d 36, 201 Cal. Rptr. 782, 679 P.2d 433 (1984).

19. EEOC v. Sears, Roebuck & Co., 628 F.Supp. 1264, 1308 (N.D.Ill.1986); Stender v. Lucky Stores, Inc., 803 F.Supp. 259, 326 (N.D.Cal.1992); Richardson v. Quik Trip Corp., 591 F.Supp. 1151, 1153 (S.D.Iowa 1984);

20. United States v. Scheffer, 523 U.S. 303, 309, 118 S.Ct. 1261, 140 L.Ed.2d 413 (1998);Meyers v. Arcudi, 947 F.Supp. 581, 588 (D.Conn.1996); United States v. Varoudakis, 1998 WL 151238 (D.Mass.1998); United States v. Orians, 9 F. Supp. 2d 1168,1174 (D.Ariz. 1998) (all cases in which courts determined, based on the inconsistent reactions revealed in several surveys, that the polygraph test has failed to achieve general acceptance in the scientific community). *See infra* § 6–1.1.1.

21. E.g., People v. Page Books, Inc., 235 Ill.App.3d 765, 175 Ill.Dec. 876, 601 N.E.2d 273, 279–80 (1992); People v. Nelson, 88 Ill. App.3d 196, 43 Ill.Dec. 476, 410 N.E.2d 476, 477–79 (1980); State v. Williams, 75 Ohio App.3d 102, 598 N.E.2d 1250, 1256–58 (1991).

22. *E.g.*, United States v. Eagle, 586 F.2d 1193, 1195 (8th Cir.1978); United States v. Tokars, 839 F.Supp. 1578,1583 (N.D.Ga.1993);

estimate damages.[23] A routine use of surveys in federal courts occurs in Lanham Act[24] cases, where the plaintiff alleges trademark infringement[25] or claims that false advertising[26] has confused or deceived consumers. The pivotal legal question in such cases virtually demands survey research because it centers on consumer perception (i.e., is the consumer likely to be confused about the source of a product, or does the advertisement imply an inaccurate message?).[27] In addition, survey methodology has been used creatively to assist federal courts in managing mass torts litigation. Faced with the prospect of conducting discovery concerning 10,000 plaintiffs, the plaintiffs and defendants in *Wilhoite v. Olin Corp.*[28] jointly drafted a discovery survey that was administered in person by neutral third parties, thus replacing interrogatories and depositions. It resulted in substantial savings in both time and cost.

§ 6–1.1.1 Surveys of Experts in the Wake of *Daubert*

Scientists who offer expert testimony at trial typically present their own opinions. These opinions may or may not be representative of the opinions of the scientific community at large. In deciding whether to admit such testimony, courts applying the *Frye* Test must determine whether the science being offered is generally accepted by the relevant scientific community. Under *Daubert* as well, a relevant factor used to decide on admissibility is the extent to which the theory or technique has received widespread acceptance. Properly conducted surveys can provide a useful way to gauge acceptance and courts have recently been offered assistance from surveys that allegedly gauge

Powell v. Superior Court, 232 Cal.App.3d 785, 283 Cal.Rptr. 777, 783 (1991).

23. Dolphin Tours, Inc. v. Pacifico Creative Service, Inc., 773 F.2d 1506, 1508 (9th Cir. 1985). *See also* Benjamin F. King, Statistics in Antitrust Litigation, in STATISTICS AND THE LAW 49 (Morris H. DeGroot et al. eds., 1986). Surveys also are used in litigation to help define relevant markets and to assess monopoly power. In United States v. E.I. Du Pont De Nemours & Co., 118 F.Supp. 41, 60 (D.Del.1953), a survey was used to develop the "market setting" for the sale of cellophane. In Mukand Ltd. v. United States, 937 F.Supp. 910 (Ct. Int'l Trade 1996), a survey of purchasers of stainless steel wire rods was conducted to support a determination of competition and fungibility between domestic and Indian wire rod. In SMS Systems Maintenance Services v. Digital Equipment, 188 F.3d 11 (1st Cir.1999), survey evidence assisted the court in determining what customers focus on in making computer system purchases.

24. Lanham Act § 43(a), 15 U.S.C.A. § 1125(a) (1946) (amended 1992).

25. *E.g.,* Union Carbide Corp. v. Ever-Ready, Inc., 531 F.2d 366 (7th Cir.); Qualitex Co. v. Jacobson Prods. Co., 21 U.S.P.Q. 1457 (C.D.Cal.1991), *aff'd* in part & *rev'd* on other grounds, 13 F.3d 1297 (9th Cir.1994), *rev'd* on other grounds, 514 U.S. 159, 115 S.Ct. 1300, 131 L.Ed.2d 248 (1995). According to Neal Miller, *Facts, Expert Facts, and Statistics: Descriptive and Experimental Research Methods*

in Litigation, 40 RUTGERS L. REV. 101, 137 (1987), trademark law has relied on the institutionalized use of statistical evidence more than any other area of the law.

26. *E.g.,* Southland Sod Farms v. Stover Seed Co., 108 F.3d 1134, 1142–43 (9th Cir. 1997); American Home Prods. Corp. v. Johnson & Johnson, 577 F.2d 160 (2d Cir.1978).

27. Courts have observed that "the court's reaction is at best not determinative and at worst irrelevant. The question in such cases is—what does the person to whom the advertisement is addressed find to be the message?" American Brands, Inc. v. R.J. Reynolds Tobacco Co., 413 F.Supp. 1352, 1357 (S.D.N.Y.1976). The wide use of surveys in recent years was foreshadowed in Triangle Publications, Inc. v. Rohrlich, 167 F.2d 969, 974 (2d Cir. 1948)(Frank, J., dissenting). Called on to determine whether a manufacturer of girdles labeled "Miss Seventeen" infringed the trademark of the magazine, *Seventeen,* Judge Frank suggested in the absence of a test of the reactions of "numerous girls and women," the trial court judge's finding as to what was likely to confuse was "nothing but a surmise, a conjecture, a guess," noting that "neither the trial judge nor any member of this court is (or resembles) a teen-age girl or the mother or sister of such a girl." *Id.* at 976.

28. No. CV–83–C–5021–NE (N.D. Ala. filed Jan. 11, 1983). The case ultimately settled before trial. *See* Francis E. McGovern & E. Allan

relevant scientific opinion. As with any scientific research, the usefulness of the information obtained from a survey depends on the quality of research design. Several critical factors have emerged that have limited the value of some of these surveys: problems in selecting the relevant population, response rates that raise questions about the representativeness of the results, and a failure to ask questions that assess opinions on the relevant issue.

Courts deciding on the admissibility of polygraph tests have considered results from several surveys of purported experts. Surveys offered as providing evidence of relevant scientific opinion have tested respondents from several populations: (1) professional polygraph examiners,[29] (2) psychophysiologists (members of the Society for Psychophysiological Research),[30] and (3) distinguished psychologists (Fellows of the Division of General Psychology of the American Psychological Association).[31] Respondents in the first group expressed substantial confidence in the scientific accuracy of polygraph testing, and those in the third group expressed substantial doubts about it. Respondents in the second group were asked the same question across three surveys that differed in other aspects of their methodology (e.g., when testing occurred and what the response rate was). Although over 60% of those questioned in two of the three surveys characterized the polygraph as a useful diagnostic tool, one of the surveys was conducted in 1982 and the more recent survey, published in 1984, achieved only a 30% response rate. The third survey, conducted in 1984, achieved a response rate of 90% and found that only 44% of respondents viewed the polygraph as a useful diagnostic tool. Based on the inconsistent reactions from several surveys, courts have determined that the polygraph has failed to achieve general acceptance in the scientific community.[32] In addition, however, courts have criticized the relevance of the population surveyed by proponents of the polygraph. For example, in *Meyers v. Arcudi* the court noted that the survey offered by proponents of the polygraph was a survey of "practitioners who estimated the accuracy of the control question technique [of polygraph testing] to be between 86% and 100%."[33] The court rejected the conclusions from this survey based on a determination that the population surveyed was not the relevant scientific community, noting that "many of them ... do not even possess advanced degrees and are not trained in the scientific method."[34]

The link between specialized expertise and self-interest poses a dilemma in defining the relevant scientific population. As the court in *United States v. Orians* recognized, "The acceptance in the scientific community depends in large part on how the relevant scientific community is defined." In rejecting

Lind, *The Discovery Survey*, 51 LAW & CONTEMP. PROBS., Autumn 1988, at 41.

29. *See* plaintiff's survey described in Meyers v. Arcudi, 947 F.Supp. 581, 588 (D.Conn. 1996).

30. Gallop Organization, *Survey of Members of the Society for Psychological Research Concerning Their Opinions of Polygraph Test Interpretation*, 13 POLYGRAPH (1984); Susan L. Amato & Charles R. Honts, *What Do Psychophysiologists Think About Polygraph Tests? A Survey of the Membership of SPR*, 31 PSYCHOPHYSIOLOGY S22 [abstract]; W.G. Iacono & D.T. Lykken, *The Validity of the Lie Detector: Two*

Surveys of Scientific Opinion, 82 J. OF APPLIED PSYCHOLOGY 426 (1997).

31. *Id.*

32. United States. v. Scheffer, 523 U.S. 303, 309, 118 S.Ct. 1261, 140 L.Ed.2d 413 (1998); Meyers v. Arcudi, 947 F.Supp. 581, 588 (D.Conn.1996); United States v. Varoudakis, 1998 WL 151238 (D.Mass.1998); United States v. Bishop, 64 F.Supp.2d 1149 (D.Utah 1999); United States v. Orians, 9 F.Supp.2d 1168, 1174 (D.Ariz.1998).

33. 947 F.Supp. 581, 588 (D.Conn.1996).

34. *Id.*

the defendants' urging that the court consider as relevant only psychophysiologists whose work is dedicated in large part to polygraph research, the court noted that *Daubert* "does not require the court to limit its inquiry to those individuals that base their livelihood on the acceptance of the relevant scientific theory. These individuals are often too close to the science and have a stake in its acceptance; i.e., their livelihood depends in part on the acceptance of the method."[35]

To be relevant to a *Frye* or *Daubert* inquiry on general acceptance, the questions asked in a survey of experts should assess opinions on the quality of the scientific theory and methodology. Thus, the fact that 60% of respondents on one survey agreed that the polygraph is "a useful diagnostic tool when considered with other available information" rather than that it is sufficiently reliable to be the sole determinant (1%), is of questionable usefulness, entitled to little weight against other available information (37%), or is of no usefulness (2%), fails to assess the relevant issue. As the court in *United States v. Cordoba* noted, because "useful" and "other available information" could have many meanings, "there is little wonder why [the response chosen by the majority of respondents] was most frequently selected."[36] Just what the appropriate question should be when assessing expert opinion on the accuracy of a measuring instrument like a polygraph is open to debate. In a survey conducted by experts opposed to the use of the polygraph in trial proceedings, survey respondents were asked whether they would advocate that courts admit into evidence the outcome of a polygraph test.[37] That question calls for more than an assessment of the accuracy of the polygraph, and thus does not assess expert opinion on the accuracy of the information provided by the test results. The survey also asked whether respondents agreed that the CQT [the control question technique, the most common form of polygraph test] is accurate at least 85% of the time in real life applications for guilty and innocent subjects.[38] Although polygraph proponents frequently claim an accuracy level of 85%, it is not clear what accuracy level would be required to justify admissibility. A better approach would be to ask survey respondents to estimate the level of accuracy they believe the test is likely to produce.[39]

Surveys of experts are no substitute for an evaluation of whether the testimony an expert witness is offering will assist the trier of fact. Nonetheless, courts can use an assessment of opinion in the relevant scientific community to aid in determining whether a particular expert is proposing to use methods that would be rejected by a representative group of experts to arrive at the opinion the expert will offer. Properly conducted surveys can provide an economical way to collect and present information on scientific consensus and dissensus.

§ 6–1.2 A Comparison of Survey Evidence and Individual Testimony

To illustrate the value of a survey, it is useful to compare the information that can be obtained from a competently done survey with the information

---

35. 9 F.Supp.2d 1168, 1173 (D.Ariz.1998).

36. 991 F.Supp. 1199 at n. 16 (1998).

37. Iacono & Lykken, *supra* note 30, at 430, Table 2.

38. *Id.*

39. At least two assessments should be made: an estimate of the accuracy for guilty subjects and an estimate of the accuracy for innocent subjects.

obtained by other means. A survey is presented by a survey expert who testifies about the responses of a substantial number of individuals who have been selected according to an explicit sampling plan and asked the same set of questions by interviewers who were not told who sponsored the survey or what answers were predicted or preferred. Although parties presumably are not obliged to present a survey conducted in anticipation of litigation by a nontestifying expert if it produced unfavorable results,[40] the court can and should scrutinize the method of respondent selection for any survey that is presented.

A party using a nonsurvey method generally identifies several witnesses who testify about their own characteristics, experiences, or impressions. While the party has no obligation to select these witnesses in any particular way or to report on how they were chosen, the party is not likely to select witnesses whose attributes conflict with the party's interests. The witnesses who testify are aware of the parties involved in the case and have discussed the case before testifying.

Although surveys are not the only means of demonstrating particular facts, presenting the testimony of an expert describing the results of a well-done survey is an efficient way to inform the trier of fact about a large and representative group of potential witnesses. In some cases, courts have described surveys as the most direct form of evidence that can be offered.[41] Indeed, several courts have drawn negative inferences from the absence of a survey, taking the position that failure to undertake a survey may strongly suggest that a properly done survey would not support the plaintiff's position.[42]

§ 6–2.0   PURPOSE AND DESIGN OF THE SURVEY

§ 6–2.1   Was the Survey Designed to Address Relevant Questions?

The report describing the results of a survey should include a statement describing the purpose or purposes of the survey. One indication that a survey offers probative evidence is that it was designed to collect information relevant to the legal controversy (e.g., to estimate damages in an antitrust suit or to assess consumer confusion in a trademark case).[1] Surveys not conducted specifically in preparation for, or in response to, litigation may

40. Loctite Corp. v. National Starch & Chem. Corp., 516 F.Supp. 190, 205 (S.D.N.Y. 1981) (distinguishing between surveys conducted in anticipation of litigation and surveys conducted for nonlitigation purposes which cannot be reproduced because of the passage of time, concluding that parties should not be compelled to introduce the former at trial, but may be required to provide the latter).

41. *E.g.,* Charles Jacquin Et Cie, Inc. v. Destileria Serralles, Inc., 921 F.2d 467, 475 (3d Cir.1990), on remand 784 F.Supp. 231 (E.D.Pa. 1992). *See also* Brunswick Corp. v. Spinit Reel Co., 832 F.2d 513, 522 (10th Cir.1987).

42. E.S. Originals, Inc. v. Stride Rite Corp., 656 F.Supp. 484, 490 (S.D.N.Y.1987); *see also* Ortho Pharm. Corp. v. Cosprophar, Inc., 32 F.3d 690, 695 (2d Cir.1994); Henri's Food Prods. Co. v. Kraft, Inc., 717 F.2d 352, 357 (7th Cir.1983); Information Clearing House, Inc. v. Find Magazine, 492 F.Supp. 147, 160 (S.D.N.Y. 1980).

§ 6–2.0

1. Note, however, that if a survey was not designed for purposes of litigation, one source of bias is less likely: the party presenting the survey is less likely to have designed and constructed the survey to prove its side of the issue in controversy.

provide important information,[2] but they frequently ask irrelevant questions[3] or select inappropriate samples of respondents for study.[4] Nonetheless, surveys do not always achieve their stated goals. Thus, the content and execution of a survey must be scrutinized even if the survey was designed to provide relevant data on the issue before the court.

§ 6–2.2 Was Participation in the Design, Administration, and Interpretation of the Survey Appropriately Controlled to Ensure the Objectivity of the Survey?

An early handbook for judges recommended that survey interviews be "conducted independently of the attorneys in the case."[5] Some courts have interpreted this to mean that any evidence of attorney participation is objectionable.[6] A better interpretation is that the attorney should have no part in carrying out the survey.[7] However, some attorney involvement in the survey design is necessary to ensure that relevant questions are directed to a relevant population.[8] The trier of fact evaluates the objectivity and relevance of the questions on the survey and the appropriateness of the definition of the population used to guide sample selection. These aspects of the survey are visible to the trier of fact and can be judged on their quality, irrespective of who suggested them. In contrast, the interviews themselves are not directly visible, and any potential bias is minimized by having interviewers and respondents blind to the purpose and sponsorship of the survey and by

2. *See, e.g.*, Wright v. Jeep Corp., 547 F.Supp. 871, 874 (E.D.Mich.1982). Indeed, as courts increasingly have been faced with scientific issues, parties have requested in a number of recent cases that the courts compel production of research data and testimony by unretained experts. The circumstances under which an unretained expert can be compelled to testify or to disclose research data and opinions, as well as the extent of disclosure that can be required when the research conducted by the expert has a bearing on the issues in the case, are the subject of considerable current debate. *See, e.g.*, Richard L. Marcus, *Discovery Along the Litigation/Science Interface*, 57 Brook. L. Rev. 381 (1991); Joe S. Cecil, *Judicially Compelled Disclosure of Research Data*, 1 Cts. Health Sci. & L. 434 (1991); *see also* Symposium, Court–Ordered Disclosure of Academic Research: A Clash of Values of Science and Law, 59 Law & Contemporary Probs., Summer 1996, at 1.

3. Loctite Corp. v. National Starch & Chem. Corp., 516 F.Supp. 190, 206 (S.D.N.Y. 1981) (marketing surveys conducted before litigation were designed to test for brand awareness, whereas the "single issue at hand ... [was] whether consumers understood the term 'Super Glue' to designate glue from a single source").

4. In *Craig v. Boren*, 429 U.S. 190, 97 S.Ct. 451, 50 L.Ed.2d 397 (1976), the state unsuccessfully attempted to use its annual roadside survey of the blood alcohol level, drinking hab-

its, and preferences of drivers to justify prohibiting the sale of 3.2% beer to males under the age of 21 and to females under the age of 18. The Court suggested that the data were biased because it was likely that the male would be driving if both the male and female occupants of the car had been drinking. As pointed out in 2 Joseph L. Gastwirth, Statistical Reasoning in Law and Public Policy: Tort Law, Evidence, and Health 527 (1988), the roadside survey would have provided more relevant data if all occupants of the cars had been included in the survey (and if the type and amount of alcohol most recently consumed had been requested so that the consumption of 3.2% beer could have been isolated).

5. Judicial Conference of the U.S., Handbook of Recommended Procedures for the Trial of Protracted Cases 75 (1960).

6. E.g., Boehringer Ingelheim G.m.b.H. v. Pharmadyne Lab., 532 F.Supp. 1040, 1058 (D.N.J.1980).

7. Upjohn Co. v. American Home Prods. Corp., No. 1–95–CV–237, 1996 U.S. Dist. LEXIS 8049, at *42 (W.D.Mich. Apr. 5, 1996) (objection that "counsel reviewed the design of the survey carries little force with this Court because [opposing party] has not identified any flaw in the survey that might be attributed to counsel's assistance").

8. J. Thomas McCarthy, McCarthy on Trademarks and Unfair Competition § 32.48(3) (3d ed. 1992).

excluding attorneys from any part in conducting interviews and tabulating results.

§ 6–2.3   Are the Experts Who Designed, Conducted, or Analyzed the Survey Appropriately Skilled and Experienced?

Experts prepared to design, conduct, and analyze a survey generally should have graduate training in psychology, sociology, political science, marketing, communication sciences, statistics, or a related discipline; that training should include courses in survey research methods, sampling, measurement, interviewing, and statistics. In some cases, professional experience in conducting and publishing survey research may provide the requisite background. In all cases, the expert must demonstrate an understanding of survey methodology, including sampling,[9] instrument design (questionnaire and interview construction), and statistical analysis.[10] Publication in peer-reviewed journals, authored books, membership in professional organizations, faculty appointments, consulting experience, and membership on scientific advisory panels for government agencies or private foundations are indications of a professional's area and level of expertise. In addition, if the survey involves highly technical subject matter (e.g., the particular preferences of electrical engineers for various pieces of electrical equipment and the bases for those preferences) or involves a special population (e.g., developmentally disabled adults with limited cognitive skills), the survey expert also should be able to demonstrate sufficient familiarity with the topic or population (or assistance from an individual on the research team with suitable expertise) to design a survey instrument that will communicate clearly with relevant respondents.

§ 6–2.4   Are the Experts Who Will Testify About Surveys Conducted by Others Appropriately Skilled and Experienced?

Parties often call on an expert to testify about a survey conducted by someone else. The secondary expert's role is to offer support for a survey commissioned by the party who calls the expert, to critique a survey presented by the opposing party, or to introduce findings or conclusions from a survey not conducted in preparation for litigation or by any of the parties to the litigation. The trial court should take into account the exact issue that the expert seeks to testify about and the nature of the expert's field of expertise.[11] The secondary expert who gives an opinion about the adequacy and interpretation of a survey not only should have general skills and experience with surveys and be familiar with all of the issues addressed in this Chapter, but also should demonstrate familiarity with the following properties of the survey being discussed: 1. the purpose of the survey; 2. the survey methodology, including a. the target population, b. the sampling design used in conducting the survey, c. the survey instrument (questionnaire or interview schedule), and d. (for interview surveys) interviewer training and instruction; 3. the

---

9. The one exception is that sampling expertise is unnecessary if the survey is administered to all members of the relevant population. *See, e.g.,* Francis E. McGovern & E. Allan Lind, *The Discovery Survey,* 51 Law & Contemp. Probs. Autumn 1988, at 41.

10. If survey expertise is being provided by several experts, a single expert may have general familiarity but not special expertise in all these areas.

11. *See* Margaret A. Berger, *Evidentiary Framework, in* Reference Manual on Scientific Evidence § IV.C (2d ed. 2000).

results, including rátes and patterns of missing data; and 4. the statistical analyses used to interpret the results.

§ 6–3.0 POPULATION DEFINITION AND SAMPLING

§ 6–3.1 Was an Appropriate Universe or Population Identified?

One of the first steps in designing a survey or in deciding whether an existing survey is relevant is to identify the target population (or universe).[1] The target population consists of all elements (i.e., objects, individuals, or other social units) whose characteristics or perceptions the survey is intended to represent. Thus, in trademark litigation, the relevant population in some disputes may include all prospective and actual purchasers of the plaintiff's goods or services and all prospective and actual purchasers of the defendant's goods or services. Similarly, the population for a discovery survey may include all potential plaintiffs or all employees who worked for Company A between two specific dates. In a community survey designed to provide evidence for a motion for a change of venue, the relevant population consists of all jury-eligible citizens in the community in which the trial is to take place.[2] The definition of the relevant population is crucial because there may be systematic differences in the responses of members of the population and nonmembers. (For example, consumers who are prospective purchasers may know more about the product category than consumers who are not considering making a purchase.)

The universe must be defined carefully. For example, a commercial for a toy or breakfast cereal may be aimed at children, who in turn influence their parents' purchases. If a survey assessing the commercial's tendency to mislead were conducted based on the universe of prospective and actual adult purchasers, it would exclude a crucial group of eligible respondents. Thus, the appropriate population in this instance would include children as well as parents.[3]

§ 6–3.2 Did the Sampling Frame Approximate the Population?

The target population consists of all the individuals or units that the researcher would like to study. The sampling frame is the source (or sources)

§ 6–3.0

1. Identification of the proper universe is recognized uniformly as a key element in the development of a survey. *See, e.g.,* JUDICIAL CONFERENCE OF THE U.S., HANDBOOK OF RECOMMENDED PROCEDURES FOR THE TRIAL OF PROTRACTED CASES 75 (1960); MANUAL FOR COMPLEX LITIGATION, THIRD § 21.493 (1995); *see also* J. THOMAS MCCARTHY ON TRADEMARKS AND UNFAIR COMPETITION § 32.166 (4th ed. 1996); COUNCIL OF AM. SURVEY RES. ORGS., CODE OF STANDARDS FOR SURVEY RESEARCH § III.B.4 (1997).

2. A second relevant population may consist of jury-eligible citizens in the community where the party would like to see the trial moved. By questioning citizens in both communities, the survey can test whether moving the trial is likely to reduce the level of animosity toward the party requesting the change of venue. *See* United States v. Haldeman, 559 F.2d 31, 140, 151, app. A, at 176–79 (D.C.Cir.1976) (court denied change of venue over the strong objection of Judge MacKinnon, who cited survey evidence that Washington, D.C., residents were substantially more likely to conclude, before trial, that the defendants were guilty), cert. denied, 431 U.S. 933, 97 S.Ct. 2641, 53 L.Ed.2d 250 (1977); *see also* People v. Venegas, 25 Cal.App.4th 1731, 31 Cal.Rptr.2d 114, 117 (Ct.App.1994) (change of venue denied because defendant failed to show that the defendant would face a less hostile jury in a different court).

3. Children and some other populations create special challenges for researchers. For example, very young children should not be asked about sponsorship or licensing, concepts that are foreign to them. Concepts, as well as wording, should be age-appropriate.

from which the sample actually is drawn. The surveyor's job generally is easier if a complete list of every eligible member of the population is available (e.g., all plaintiffs in a discovery survey), so that the sampling frame lists the identity of all members of the target population. Frequently, however, the target population includes members who are inaccessible or who cannot be identified in advance. As a result, some compromises are required in developing the sampling frame. The survey report should contain a description of the target population, a description of the survey population actually sampled, a discussion of the difference between the two populations, and an evaluation of the likely consequences of that difference.

A survey that provides information about a wholly irrelevant universe of respondents is itself irrelevant.[4] Courts are likely to exclude the survey or accord it little weight. Thus, when the plaintiff submitted the results of a survey to prove that the green color of its fishing rod had acquired a secondary meaning, the court gave the survey little weight in part because the survey solicited the views of fishing rod dealers rather than consumers.[5] More commonly, however, either the target population or the sampling frame is underinclusive or overinclusive. If either is underinclusive, the survey's value depends on the extent to which the excluded population is likely to react differently from the included population. Thus, a survey of spectators and participants at running events would be sampling a sophisticated subset of those likely to purchase running shoes. Because this subset probably would consist of the consumers most knowledgeable about the trade dress used by companies that sell running shoes, a survey based on this population would be likely to substantially overrepresent the strength of a particular design as a trademark, and the extent of that over-representation would be unknown and not susceptible to any reasonable estimation.[6]

Similarly, in a survey designed to project demand for cellular phones, the assumption that businesses would be the primary users of cellular service led surveyors to exclude potential nonbusiness users from the survey. The Federal Communications Commission (FCC) found the assumption unwarranted and concluded that the research was flawed, in part because of this underinclusive universe.[7]

4. A survey aimed at assessing how persons in the trade respond to an advertisement should be conducted on a sample of persons in the trade and not on a sample of consumers. Home Box Office v. Showtime/The Movie Channel, 665 F.Supp. 1079, 1083 (S.D.N.Y.), *aff'd* in part & vacated in part, 832 F.2d 1311 (2d Cir.1987). *But see* Lon Tai Shing Co. v. Koch & Lowy, 19 U.S.P.Q.2d 1081 (S.D.N.Y. 1991), in which the judge was willing to find likelihood of consumer confusion from a survey of lighting store salespersons questioned by a survey researcher posing as a customer. The court was persuaded that the salespersons who were misstating the source of the lamp, whether consciously or not, must have believed reasonably that the consuming public would be misled by the salespersons' inaccurate statements about the name of the company that manufactured the lamp they were selling.

5. R.L. Winston Rod Co. v. Sage Mfg. Co., 838 F.Supp. 1396 (D.Mont.1993).

6. Brooks Shoe Mfg. Co. v. Suave Shoe Corp., 533 F.Supp. 75, 80 (S.D.Fla.1981). *See also* Winning Ways, Inc. v. Holloway Sportswear, Inc., 913 F.Supp. 1454 (D.Kan.1996) (survey flawed in failing to include sporting goods customers who constituted a major portion of customers). *But see* Thomas & Betts Corp. v. Panduit Corp., 138 F.3d 277, 294–95 (7th Cir.1998) (survey of store personnel admissible because relevant market included both distributors and ultimate purchasers).

7. Gencom, Inc., 56 Rad. Reg. 2d (P & F) 1597, 1604 (1984). This position was affirmed on appeal. Gencom, Inc. v. FCC, 832 F.2d 171, 186 (D.C.Cir.1987).

In some cases, it is difficult to determine whether an underinclusive universe distorts the results of the survey and, if so, the extent and likely direction of the bias. For example, a trademark survey was designed to test the likelihood of confusing an analgesic currently on the market with a new product that was similar in appearance.[8] The plaintiff's survey included only respondents who had used the plaintiff's analgesic, and the court found that the universe should have included users of other analgesics, "so that the full range of potential customers for whom plaintiff and defendants would compete could be studied."[9] In this instance, it is unclear whether users of the plaintiff's product would be more or less likely to be confused than users of the defendant's product or users of a third analgesic.[10]

An overinclusive universe generally presents less of a problem in interpretation than does an underinclusive universe. If the survey expert can demonstrate that a sufficiently large (and representative) subset of respondents in the survey was drawn from the appropriate universe, the responses obtained from that subset can be examined, and inferences about the relevant universe can be drawn based on that subset.[11] If the relevant subset cannot be identified, however, an overbroad universe will reduce the value of the survey.[12] If the sample is drawn from an underinclusive universe, there is no way to know how the unrepresented members would have responded.[13]

§ 6–3.3 How Was the Sample Selected to Approximate the Relevant Characteristics of the Population?

Identification of a survey population must be followed by selection of a sample that accurately represents that population.[14] The use of probability sampling techniques maximizes both the representativeness of the survey results and the ability to assess the accuracy of estimates obtained from the survey.

Probability samples range from simple random samples to complex multistage sampling designs that use stratification, clustering of population elements into various groupings, or both. In simple random sampling, the most basic type of probability sampling, every element in the population has a known, equal probability of being included in the sample, and all possible samples of a given size are equally likely to be selected.[15] In all forms of

---

8. American Home Prods. Corp. v. Barr Lab., 656 F.Supp. 1058 (D.N.J.1987).

9. *Id.* at 1070.

10. *See also* Craig v. Boren, 429 U.S. 190, 97 S.Ct. 451, 50 L.Ed.2d 397 (1976).

11. This occurred in *National Football League Properties, Inc. v. Wichita Falls Sportswear, Inc.*, 532 F.Supp. 651, 657–58 (W.D.Wash.1982).

12. Schieffelin & Co. v. Jack Co. of Boca, 850 F.Supp. 232, 246 (S.D.N.Y.1994).

13. *See, e.g.*, Amstar Corp. v. Domino's Pizza, Inc., 615 F.2d 252, 263–64 (5th Cir.) (court found both plaintiff's and defendant's surveys substantially defective for a systematic failure to include parts of the relevant population).

14. Manual for Complex Litigation, Third, § 21.493 (1995). *See also* Chapters 4 and 5.

15. Systematic sampling, in which every nth unit in the population is sampled and the starting point is selected randomly, fulfills the first of these conditions. It does not fulfill the second, because no systematic sample can include elements adjacent to one another on the list of population members from which the sample is drawn. Except in very unusual situations when periodicities occur, systematic samples and simple random samples generally produce the same results. Seymour Sudman, *Applied Sampling, in* Handbook of Survey Research 145, 169 (Peter H. Rossi et al. eds., 1983).

probability sampling, each element in the relevant population has a known, nonzero probability of being included in the sample.[16]

Probability sampling offers two important advantages over other types of sampling. First, the sample can provide an unbiased estimate of the responses of all persons in the population from which the sample was drawn; that is, the results from the sample are projectable. Second, the researcher can calculate a confidence interval that describes explicitly how reliable the sample estimate of the population is likely to be. Thus, suppose a survey tested a sample of 400 dentists randomly selected from the population of all dentists licensed to practice in the United States and found that 80, or 20%, of them mistakenly believed that a new toothpaste, Goldgate, was manufactured by the makers of Colgate. A survey expert properly could compute a confidence interval around the 20% estimate obtained from this sample. If the survey were repeated a large number of times, and a 95% confidence interval was computed each time, 95% of the confidence intervals would include the actual percentage of dentists in the entire population who would believe that Goldgate was manufactured by the makers of Colgate.[17] In this example, the confidence interval, or margin of error, is the estimate (20%) plus or minus 4%, or the distance between 16% and 24%.

All sample surveys produce estimates of population values, not exact measures of those values. Strictly speaking, the margin of sampling error associated with the sample estimate assumes probability sampling. Assuming a probability sample, a confidence interval describes how stable the mean response in the sample is likely to be. The width of the confidence interval depends on three characteristics:

1. the size of the sample (the larger the sample, the narrower the interval);

2. the variability of the response being measured; and

3. the confidence level the researcher wants to have.

Traditionally, scientists adopt the 95% level of confidence, which means that if 100 samples of the same size were drawn, the confidence interval expected for at least 95 of the samples would include the true population value.[18]

Although probability sample surveys often are conducted in organizational settings and are the recommended sampling approach in academic and government publications on surveys, probability sample surveys can be expensive when in-person interviews are required, the target population is dis-

---

16. Other probability sampling techniques include (1) stratified random sampling, in which the researcher subdivides the population into mutually exclusive and exhaustive subpopulations, or strata, and then randomly selects samples from within these strata; and (2) cluster sampling, in which elements are sampled in groups or clusters, rather than on an individual basis. Martin Finkel, *Sampling Theory, in* HANDBOOK OF SURVEY RESEARCH 21, 37, 47 (Peter H. Rossi et al. eds., 1983).

17. Actually, since survey interviewers would be unable to locate some dentists and some dentists would be unwilling to participate in the survey, technically the population to which this sample would be projectable would be all dentists with current addresses who would be willing to participate in the survey if they were asked.

18. To increase the likelihood that the confidence interval contains the actual population value (e.g., from 95% to 99%), the width of the confidence interval can be expanded. An increase in the confidence interval brings an increase in the confidence level. For further discussion of confidence intervals, *see* Chapter 5.

persed widely, or qualified respondents are scarce. A majority of the consumer surveys conducted for Lanham Act litigation present results from nonprobability convenience samples.[19] They are admitted into evidence based on the argument that nonprobability sampling is used widely in marketing research and that "results of these studies are used by major American companies in making decisions of considerable consequence."[20] Nonetheless, when respondents are not selected randomly from the relevant population, the expert should be prepared to justify the method used to select respondents. Special precautions are required to reduce the likelihood of biased samples.[21] In addition, quantitative values computed from such samples (e.g., percentage of respondents indicating confusion) should be viewed as rough indicators rather than as precise quantitative estimates. Confidence intervals should not be computed.

§ 6–3.4 Was the Level of Nonresponse Sufficient to Raise Questions About the Representativeness of the Sample? If So, What Is the Evidence That Nonresponse Did Not Bias the Results of the Survey?

Even when a sample is drawn randomly from a complete list of elements in the target population, responses or measures may be obtained on only part of the selected sample. If this lack of response were distributed randomly, valid inferences about the population could be drawn from the characteristics of the available elements in the sample. The difficulty is that nonresponse often is not random, so that, for example, persons who are single typically have three times the "not at home" rate in U.S. Census Bureau surveys as do family members.[22] Efforts to increase response rates include making several attempts to contact potential respondents and providing financial incentives for participating in the survey.

One suggested formula for quantifying a tolerable level of nonresponse in a probability sample is based on the guidelines for statistical surveys issued by the former U.S. Office of Statistical Standards.[23] According to these guidelines, response rates of 90% or more are reliable and generally can be treated as random samples of the overall population. Response rates between 75% and 90% usually yield reliable results, but the researcher should conduct some check on the representativeness of the sample. Potential bias should receive greater scrutiny when the response rate drops below 75%. If the response rate drops below 50%, the survey should be regarded with significant caution as a

19. Jacob Jacoby & Amy H. Handlin, *Non-Probability Sampling Designs for Litigation Surveys,* 81 TRADEMARK REP. 169, 173 (1991). For probability surveys conducted in trademark cases, *see* National Football League Properties, Inc. v. Wichita Falls Sportswear, Inc., 532 F.Supp. 651 (W.D.Wash.1982); James Burrough, Ltd. v. Sign of Beefeater, Inc., 540 F.2d 266 (7th Cir.1976).

20. National Football League Properties, Inc. v. New Jersey Giants, Inc., 637 F.Supp. 507, 515 (D.N.J.1986). A survey of the 130 members of the Council of American Survey Research Organizations, the national trade association for commercial survey research firms

in the United States, revealed that 95% of the in-person interview studies done in 1985 took place in malls or shopping centers. Jacob Jacoby & Amy H. Handlin, *Non-Probability Sampling Designs for Litigation Surveys,* 81 TRADEMARK REP. 169, at 172–73, 176 (1991).

21. See § 6–3.5.

22. 2 JOSEPH L. GASTWIRTH, STATISTICAL REASONING IN LAW AND PUBLIC POLICY: TORT LAW, EVIDENCE, AND HEALTH 501 (1988). This volume contains a useful discussion of sampling, along with a set of examples. *Id.* at 467.

23. This standard is cited with approval by GASTWIRTH. *Id.* at 502.

basis for precise quantitative statements about the population from which the sample was drawn.[24]

Determining whether the level of nonresponse in a survey is critical generally requires an analysis of the determinants of nonresponse. For example, even a survey with a high response rate may seriously underrepresent some portions of the population, such as the unemployed or the poor. If a general population sample was used to chart changes in the proportion of the population that knows someone with the HIV virus, the survey would underestimate the population value if some groups more likely to know someone with HIV (e.g., intravenous drug users) were underrepresented in the sample. The survey expert should be prepared to provide evidence on the potential impact of nonresponse on the survey results.

In surveys that include sensitive or difficult questions, particularly surveys that are self-administered, some respondents may refuse to provide answers or may provide incomplete answers. To assess the impact of nonresponse to a particular question, the survey expert should analyze the differences between those who answered and those who did not answer. Procedures to address the problem of missing data include recontacting respondents to obtain the missing answers and using the respondent's other answers to predict the missing response.[25]

§ 6–3.5   What Procedures Were Used to Reduce the Likelihood of a Biased Sample?

If it is impractical for a survey researcher to sample randomly from the entire target population, the researcher still can apply probability sampling to some aspects of respondent selection, even in a mall intercept study, to reduce the likelihood of biased selection. For example, in many studies the target population consists of all consumers or purchasers of a product. Because it is impractical to randomly sample from that population, research is conducted in shopping malls where some members of the target population may not shop. Mall locations, however, can be sampled randomly from a list of possible mall sites. By administering the survey at several different malls, the expert can test for and report on any differences observed across sites. To the extent that similar results are obtained in different locations using different on-site interview operations, it is less likely that idiosyncrasies of sample selection or administration can account for the results.[26] Similarly, since the characteristics of persons visiting a shopping center vary by day of the week and time of day, bias in sampling can be reduced if the survey design calls for sampling time segments as well as mall locations.[27]

In mall intercept surveys, the organization that manages the on-site interview facility generally employs recruiters who approach potential survey

---

24. For thoughtful examples of judges closely scrutinizing potential sample bias when response rates were below 75%, *see* Vuyanich v. Republic Nat'l Bank, 505 F.Supp. 224 (N.D.Tex.1980); Rosado v. Wyman, 322 F.Supp. 1173 (E.D.N.Y.1970).

25. Andy B. Anderson et al., *Missing Data: A Review of the Literature, in* HANDBOOK OF SURVEY RESEARCH 415 (Peter H. Rossi et al. eds., 1983).

26. Note, however, that differences across sites may be due to genuine differences in respondents across geographic locations.

27. Seymour Sudman, *Improving the Quality of Shopping Center Sampling*, 17 J. MKTG. RES. 423 (1980).

respondents in the mall and ascertain if they are qualified and willing to participate in the survey. If a potential respondent agrees to answer the questions and meets the specified criteria, he is escorted to the facility where the survey interview takes place. If recruiters are free to approach potential respondents without controls on how an individual is to be selected for screening, shoppers who spend more time in the mall are more likely to be approached than shoppers who visit the mall only briefly. Moreover, recruiters naturally prefer to approach friendly-looking potential respondents, so that it is more likely that certain types of individuals will be selected. These potential biases in selection can be reduced by providing appropriate selection instructions and training recruiters effectively. Training that reduces the interviewer's discretion in selecting a potential respondent is likely to reduce bias in selection, as are, for example, instructions to approach every third person entering the facility through a particular door.[28]

§ 6–3.6   What Precautions Were Taken to Ensure That Only Qualified Respondents Were Included in the Survey?

In a carefully executed survey, each potential respondent is questioned or measured on the attributes that determine his or her eligibility to participate in the survey. Thus, the initial questions screen potential respondents to determine if they are within the target population of the survey (e.g., Is she at least 14 years old? Does she own a dog? Does she live within 10 miles?). The screening questions must be drafted so that they do not convey information that will influence the respondent's answers on the main survey. For example, if respondents must be prospective and recent purchasers of Sunshine orange juice in a trademark survey designed to assess consumer confusion with Sun Time orange juice, potential respondents might be asked to name the brands of orange juice they have purchased recently or expect to purchase in the next six months. They should not be asked specifically if they recently have purchased, or expect to purchase, Sunshine orange juice, because this may affect their responses on the survey either by implying who is conducting the survey or by supplying them with a brand name that otherwise would not occur to them.

The content of a screening questionnaire (or screener) can also set the context for the questions that follow. In *Pfizer, Inc. v. Astra Pharmaceutical Products, Inc.*,[29] the plaintiff claimed that the letters XL on a prescription cardiovascular medication had become distinctive of Pfizer's goods in commerce, entitling Pfizer to trademark protection. In a survey conducted to test whether physicians viewed XL as distinctive, potential respondents were asked a screening question about whether they had written prescriptions for cardiovascular medications and several other types of medications in the past year. In the interview that followed, the physicians were then asked what came to mind when they heard the letters XL. The court found that the screener "conditioned physicians to respond with the name of a product

---

28. In the end, if malls are randomly sampled and shoppers are randomly selected within malls, results from mall surveys technically can be used to generalize only to the population of mall shoppers. The ability of the mall sample to describe the likely response pattern of the broader relevant population will depend on the extent to which a substantial segment of the relevant population (1) is not found is malls and (2) would respond differently to the questions posed in the survey.

29. 858 F.Supp. 1305, 1321 (S.D.N.Y.1994).

rather than how the product functions or works, or the meaning of the acronym XL."[30]

The criteria for determining whether to include a potential respondent in the survey should be objective and clearly conveyed, preferably using written instructions addressed to those who administer the screening questions. These instructions and the completed screening questionnaire should be made available to the court and the opposing party along with the interview form for each respondent.

§ 6–4.0 SURVEY QUESTIONS AND STRUCTURE

§ 6–4.1 Were Questions on the Survey Framed to Be Clear, Precise, and Unbiased?

Although it seems obvious that questions on a survey should be clear and precise, phrasing questions to reach that goal is often difficult. Even questions that appear clear can convey unexpected meanings and ambiguities to potential respondents. For example, the question "What is the average number of days each week you have butter?" appears to be straightforward. Yet some respondents wondered whether margarine counted as butter, and when the question was revised to include the introductory phrase "not including margarine," the reported frequency of butter use dropped dramatically.[1]

When unclear questions are included in a survey, they may threaten the validity of the survey by systematically distorting responses if respondents are misled in a particular direction, or by inflating random error if respondents guess because they do not understand the question.[2] If the crucial question is sufficiently ambiguous or unclear, it may be the basis for rejecting the survey. For example, a survey was designed to assess community sentiment that would warrant a change of venue in trying a case for damages sustained when a hotel skywalk collapsed.[3] The court found that the question "Based on what you have heard, read or seen, do you believe that in the current compensatory damage trials, the defendants, such as the contractors, designers, owners, and operators of the Hyatt Hotel, should be punished?" could neither be correctly understood nor easily answered.[4] The court noted that the phrase "compensatory damages," although well-defined for attorneys, was unlikely to be meaningful for laypersons.[5]

Texts on survey research generally recommend pretests as a way to increase the likelihood that questions are clear and unambiguous,[6] and some courts have recognized the value of pretests.[7] In a pretest or pilot test,[8] the

---

30. *Id.* at 1321.

§ 6–4.0

1. Floyd J. Fowler, Jr., *How Unclear Terms Affect Survey Data*, 56 Pub. Opinion Q. 218, 225–26 (1992).

2. *Id.* at 219.

3. Firestone v. Crown Ctr. Redevelopment Corp., 693 S.W.2d 99 (Mo.1985) (en banc).

4. *Id.* at 102.

5. *Id.* at 103. When there is any question about whether some respondent will under-

stand a particular term or phrase, the term or phrase should be defined explicitly.

6. For a thorough treatment of pretesting methods, *see* Jean M. Converse & Stanley Presser, Survey Questions: Handcrafting the Standardized Questionnaire 51 (1986). *See also* Fred W. Morgan, *Judicial Standards for Survey Research: An Update and Guidelines*, 54 J. Mktg. 59, 64 (1990).

7. *E.g.*, Zippo Mfg. Co. v. Rogers Imports, Inc., 216 F.Supp. 670 (S.D.N.Y.1963).

proposed survey is administered to a small sample (usually between twenty-five and seventy-five)[9] of the same type of respondents who would be eligible to participate in the full-scale survey. The interviewers observe the respondents for any difficulties they may have with the questions and probe for the source of any such difficulties so that the questions can be rephrased if confusion or other difficulties arise. Attorneys who commission surveys for litigation sometimes are reluctant to approve pilot work or to reveal that pilot work has taken place because they are concerned that if a pretest leads to revised wording of the questions, the trier of fact may believe that the survey has been manipulated and is biased or unfair. A more appropriate reaction is to recognize that pilot work can improve the quality of a survey and to anticipate that it often results in word changes that increase clarity and correct misunderstandings. Thus, changes may indicate informed survey construction rather than flawed survey design.[10]

§ 6–4.2   Were Filter Questions Provided to Reduce Guessing?

Some survey respondents may have no opinion on an issue under investigation, either because they have never thought about it before, or because the question mistakenly assumes a familiarity with the issue. For example, survey respondents may not have noticed that the commercial they are being questioned about guaranteed the quality of the product being advertised and thus may have no opinion on the kind of guarantee it indicated. Likewise, in an employee survey, respondents may not be familiar with the parental leave policy at their company and thus may have no opinion on whether they would consider taking advantage of the parental leave policy if they became parents. The following three alternative question structures will affect how those respondents answer and how their responses are counted.

First, the survey can ask all respondents to answer the question (e.g., "Did you understand the guarantee offered by Clover to be a one-year guarantee, a sixty-day guarantee, or a thirty-day guarantee?"). Faced with a direct question, particularly one that provides response alternatives, the respondent obligingly may supply an answer even if (in this example) the respondent did not notice the guarantee (or is unfamiliar with the parental leave policy). Such answers will reflect only what the respondent can glean from the question, or they may reflect pure guessing. The imprecision introduced by this approach introduces will increase with the proportion of respondents who are unfamiliar with the topic at issue.

Second, the survey can use a quasi-filter question to reduce guessing by providing "don't know" or "no opinion" options as part of the question (e.g., "Did you understand the guarantee offered by Clover to be for more than a year, a year, or less than a year, or don't you have an opinion?").[11] By

---

8. The terms pretest and pilot test are sometimes used interchangeably. When they are distinguished, the difference is that a pretest tests the questionnaire, while a pilot test generally tests proposed collection procedures as well.

9. Jean M. Converse & STANLEY PRESSER, SURVEY QUESTIONS: HANDCRAFTING THE STANDARDIZED QUESTIONNAIRE 69 (1986). Converse and

Presser suggest that a pretest with twenty-five respondents is appropriate when the survey uses professional interviewers.

10. *See* § 6–7.2 for a discussion of obligations to disclose pilot work.

11. Norbert Schwarz & Hans–Jurgen Hippler, *Response Alternatives: The Impact of Their Choice and Presentation Order, in* MEA-

signaling to the respondent that it is appropriate not to have an opinion, the question reduces the demand for an answer and, as a result, the inclination to hazard a guess just to comply. Respondents are more likely to choose a "no opinion" option if it is mentioned explicitly by the interviewer than if it is merely accepted when the respondent spontaneously offers it as a response. The consequence of this change in format is substantial. Studies indicate that, although the relative distribution of the respondents selecting the *listed* choices are unlikely to change dramatically, presentation of an explicit "don't know" or "no opinion" alternative commonly leads to a 20%–25% increase in the proportion of respondents selecting that response.[12]

Finally, the survey can include full-filter questions, that is, questions that lay the groundwork for the substantive question by first asking the respondent if he has an opinion about the issue or happened to notice the feature that the interviewer is preparing to ask about (e.g., "Based on the commercial you just saw, do you have an opinion about how long Clover stated or implied that its guarantee lasts?"). The interviewer then asks the substantive question only of those respondents who have indicated that they have an opinion on the issue.

Which of these three approaches is used and the way it is used can affect the rate of "no opinion" responses that the substantive question will evoke.[13] Respondents are more likely to say they do not have an opinion on an issue if a full-filter is used than if a quasi-filter is used.[14] However, in maximizing respondent expressions of "no opinion," full filters may produce an underreporting of opinions. There is some evidence that full-filter questions discourage respondents who actually have opinions from offering them by conveying the implicit suggestion that respondents can avoid difficult follow-up questions by saying that they have no opinion.[15]

In general, then, a survey that uses full filters tends to provide a conservative estimate of the number of respondents holding an opinion, whereas a survey that uses neither full filters nor quasi-filters tends to overestimate the number of respondents with opinions, because some respondents offering opinions are guessing. The strategy of including a "no opinion" or "don't know" response as a quasi-filter avoids both of these extremes. Thus, rather than asking, "Based on the commercial, do you believe that the two products are made in the same way, or are they made differently?" or prefacing the question with a preliminary, "Do you have an opinion, based on the commercial, concerning the way that the two products are made?" the question could be phrased, "Based on the commercial, do you believe that the two products are made in the same way, or that they are made differently, or don't you have an opinion about the way they are made?"[16]

SUREMENT ERRORS IN SURVEYS 41, 45–46 (Paul P. Biemer et al. eds., 1991).

12. HOWARD SCHUMAN & STANLEY PRESSER, QUESTIONS AND ANSWERS IN ATTITUDE SURVEYS: EXPERIMENTS ON QUESTION FORM, WORDING AND CONTEXT 113–46 (1981).

13. Considerable research has been conducted on the effects of filters. For a review, *see* George F. Bishop et al., *Effects of Filter Questions in Public Opinion Surveys*, 47 PUB. OPINION Q. 528 (1983).

14. Norbert Schwarz & Hans–Jurgen Hippler, *Response Alternatives: The Impact of Their Choice and Presentation Order, in* MEASUREMENT ERRORS IN SURVEYS 41, 45–46 (Paul P. Biemer et al. eds., 1991).

15. *Id.* at 46.

16. The question in the example without the "no opinion" alternative was based on a question rejected by the court in Coors Brew-

§ 6–4.3   Did the Survey Use Open–Ended or Closed–Ended Questions? How Was the Choice in Each Instance Justified?

The questions that make up a survey instrument may be open-ended, closed-ended, or a combination of both. Open-ended questions require the respondent to formulate and express an answer in his own words (e.g., "What was the main point of the commercial?" "Where did you catch the fish you caught in these waters?"[17]). Closed-ended questions provide the respondent with an explicit set of responses from which to choose; the choices may be as simple as yes or no (e.g., "Is Colby College coeducational?"[18]), or as complex as a range of alternatives (e.g., "The two pain relievers have (1) the same likelihood of causing gastric ulcers; (2) about the same likelihood of causing gastric ulcers; (3) a somewhat different likelihood of causing gastric ulcers; (4) a very different likelihood of causing gastric ulcers; or (5) none of the above."[19]).

Open-ended and closed-ended questions may elicit very different responses.[20] Most responses are less likely to be volunteered by respondents who are asked an open-ended question than they are to be chosen by respondents who are presented with a closed-ended question. The response alternatives in a closed-ended question may remind respondents of options that they would not otherwise consider or which simply do not come to mind as easily.[21]

The advantage of open-ended questions is that they give the respondent fewer hints about the answer that is expected or preferred. Precoded responses on a closed-ended question, in addition to reminding respondents of options that they might not otherwise consider,[22] may direct the respondent away from or toward a particular response. For example, a commercial reported that in shampoo tests with more than 900 women, the sponsor's product

ing Co. v. Anheuser–Busch Cos., 802 F.Supp. 965, 972–73 (S.D.N.Y.1992).

17. A relevant example from Wilhoite v. Olin Corp. is described in Francis E. McGovern & E. Allan Lind, *The Discovery Survey*, Law & Contempo. Probs., Autumn 1988, at 41.

18. President & Trustees of Colby College v. Colby College–New Hampshire, 508 F.2d 804, 809 (1st Cir.1975).

19. This question is based on one asked in American Home Prods. Corp. v. Johnson & Johnson, 654 F.Supp. 568, 581 (S.D.N.Y.1987) that was found to be a leading question by the court, primarily because the choices suggested that the respondent had learned about aspirin's and ibuprofen's relative likelihood of causing gastric ulcers. In contrast, in *McNeilab, Inc. v. American Home Prods. Corp.*, 501 F.Supp. 517, 525 (S.D.N.Y.1980), the court accepted as nonleading the question: "Based only on what the commercial said, would Maximum Strength Anacin contain more pain reliever, the same amount of pain reliever, or less pain reliever than the brand you, yourself, currently use most often?"

20. Howard Schuman & Stanley Presser, *Question Wording as an Independent Variable in Survey Analysis*, 6 Soc. Methods & Res. 151 (1977); Howard Schuman & Stanley Presser, Questions and Answers in Attitude Surveys: Experiments on Question Form, Wording and Context 79–112 (1981); Converse & Presser, *supra* note 9, at 33.

21. For example, when respondents in one survey were asked, "What is the most important thing for children to learn to prepare them for life?" 62% picked "to think for themselves" from a list of five options, but only 5% spontaneously offered that answer when the question was open-ended. Schuman & Presser, *supra* note 20, at 104–07. An open-ended question presents the respondent with a free-recall task, whereas a closed-ended question is a recognition task. Recognition tasks in general reveal higher performance levels than recall tasks. Mary M. Smyth et al., Cognition in Action 25 (1987). In addition, there is evidence that respondents answering open-ended questions may be less likely to report some information that they would reveal in response to a closed-ended question when that information seems self-evident or irrelevant.

22. Schwarz & Hippler, *supra* note 14, at 43.

received higher ratings than other brands.[23] According to a competitor, the commercial deceptively implied that each woman in the test rated more than one shampoo, when in fact each woman rated only one. To test consumer impressions, a survey might have shown the commercial and asked an open-ended question: "How many different brands mentioned in the commercial did each of the 900 women try?"[24] Instead, the survey asked a closed-ended question; respondents were given the choice of "one," "two," "three," "four," or "five or more." The fact that four of the five choices in the closed-ended question provided a response that was greater than one implied that the correct answer was probably more than one.[25] Note, however, that the open-ended question also may suggest that the answer is more than one. By asking "how many different brands," the question suggests (1) that the viewer should have received some message from the commercial about the number of brands each woman tried and (2) that different brands were tried. Thus, the wording of a question, open-ended or closed-ended, can be leading, and the degree of suggestiveness of each question must be considered in evaluating the objectivity of a survey.

Closed-ended questions have some additional potential weaknesses that arise if the choices are not constructed properly. If the respondent is asked to choose one response from among several choices, the response chosen will be meaningful only if the list of choices is exhaustive, that is, if the choices cover all possible answers a respondent might give on the question. If the list of possible choices is incomplete, a respondent may be forced to choose one that does not express his or her opinion.[26] Moreover, if respondents are told explicitly that they are not limited to the choices presented, most respondents nevertheless will select an answer from among the listed choices.[27]

Although courts prefer open-ended questions on the ground that they tend to be less leading, the value of any open-ended or closed-ended question depends on the information it is intended to elicit. Open ended questions are more appropriate when the survey is attempting to gauge what comes first to a respondent's mind, but closed-ended questions are more suitable for assessing choices between well-identified options or obtaining ratings on a clear set of alternatives.

23. *See* Vidal Sassoon, Inc. v. Bristol–Myers Co., 661 F.2d 272, 273 (2d Cir.1981).

24. This was the wording of the stem of the closed-ended question in the survey discussed in *Vidal Sassoon*, 661 F.2d at 275–76.

25. Ninety-five percent of the respondents who answered the closed-ended question in the plaintiff's survey said that each woman had tried two or more brands. The open-ended question was never asked. *Vidal Sassoon*, 661 F.2d at 276. Norbert Schwarz, *Assessing Frequency Reports of Mundane Behaviors: Contributions of Cognitive Psychology to Questionnaire Construction, in* RESEARCH METHODS IN PERSONALITY AND SOCIAL PSYCHOLOGY 98 (Clyde

Hendrick & Margaret S. Clark eds., 1990), suggests that respondents often rely on the range of response alternatives as a frame of reference when they are asked for frequency judgments. *See, e.g.*, Roger Tourangeau & Tom W. Smith, *Asking Sensitive Questions: The Impact of Data Collection Mode, Question Format, and Question Context*, 60 PUB. OPINION Q. 275, 292 (1992).

26. *See, e.g.*, American Home Prods. Corp. v. Johnson & Johnson, 654 F.Supp. 568, 581 (S.D.N.Y.1987).

27. *See* Howard Schuman, *Ordinary Questions, Survey Questions, and Policy Questions*, 50 PUB. OPINION Q. 432, 435–36 (1986).

§ 6–4.4 If Probes Were Used to Clarify Ambiguous or Incomplete Answers, What Steps Were Taken to Ensure That the Probes Were Not Leading and Were Administered in a Consistent Fashion?

When questions allow respondents to express their opinions in their own words, some of the respondents may give ambiguous or incomplete answers. In such instances, interviewers may be instructed to record any answer that the respondent gives and move on to the next question, or they may be instructed to probe to obtain a more complete response or clarify the meaning of the ambiguous response. In either situation, interviewers should record verbatim both what the respondent says and what the interviewer says in the attempt to get clarification. Failure to record every part of the exchange in the order in which it occurs raises questions about the reliability of the survey, because neither the court nor the opposing party can evaluate whether the probe affected the views expressed by the respondent.

If the survey is designed to allow for probes, interviewers must be given explicit instructions on when they should probe and what they should say in probing. Standard probes used to draw out all that the respondent has to say (e.g., "Any further thoughts?" "Anything else?" "Can you explain that a little more?") are relatively innocuous and noncontroversial in content, but persistent continued requests for further responses to the same or nearly identical questions may convey the idea to the respondent that he or she has not yet produced the "right" answer.[28] Interviewers should be trained in delivering probes to maintain a professional and neutral relationship with the respondent (as they should during the rest of the interview), which minimizes any sense of passing judgment on the content of the answers offered. Moreover, interviewers should be given explicit instructions on when to probe, so that probes are administered consistently.

A more difficult type of probe to construct and deliver reliably is one that requires a substantive question tailored to the answer given by the respondent. The survey designer must provide sufficient instruction to interviewers so that they avoid giving directive probes that suggest one answer over another. Those instructions, along with all other aspects of interviewer training, should be made available for evaluation by the court and the opposing party.

§ 6–4.5 What Approach Was Used to Avoid or Measure Potential Order or Context Effects?

The order in which questions are asked on a survey and the order in which response alternatives are provided in a closed-ended question can influence the answers.[29] Thus, although asking a general question before a more specific question on the same topic is unlikely to affect the response to the specific question, reversing the order of the questions may influence

---

28. *See, e.g.,* Johnson & Johnson–Merck Consumer Pharm. Co. v. Rhone–Poulenc Rorer Pharm., Inc., 19 F.3d 125, 135 (3d Cir.1994); American Home Prods. Corp. v. Procter & Gamble Co., 871 F.Supp. 739, 748 (D.N.J. 1994).

29. *See* Schuman & Presser, *supra* note 20, at 23, 56–74; Norman M. Bradburn, *Response Effects, in* Handbook of Survey Research 289,

302 (Peter H. Rossi et al. eds., 1983). In *R.J. Reynolds Tobacco Co. v. Loew's Theatres, Inc.,* 511 F.Supp. 867, 875 (S.D.N.Y.1980), the court recognized the biased structure of a survey which disclosed the tar content of the cigarettes being compared before questioning respondents about their cigarette preferences. Not surprisingly, respondents expressed a preference for the lower tar product. *See also* E. &

responses to the general question. As a rule, then, surveys are less likely to be subject to order effects if the questions go from the general (e.g., "What do you recall being discussed in the advertisement?") to the specific (e.g., "Based on your reading of the advertisement, what companies do you think the ad is referring to when it talks about rental trucks that average five miles per gallon?").[30]

The mode of questioning can influence the form that an order effect takes. In mail surveys, respondents are more likely to select the first choice offered (a primacy effect). In telephone surveys, respondents are more likely to choose the last choice offered (a recency effect). Although these effects are typically small, no general formula is available that can adjust values to correct for order effects, because the size and even the direction of the order effects depend on the nature of the question being asked and the choices being offered. Moreover, it may be unclear which order is most appropriate. For example, if the respondent is asked to choose between two different products, and there is a tendency for respondents to choose the first product mentioned,[31] which order of presentation will produce the more accurate response?[32]

To control for order effects, the order of the questions and the order of the response choices in a survey should be rotated,[33] so that, for example, one-third of the respondents have Product A listed first, one-third of the respondents have Product B listed first, and one-third of the respondents have Product C listed first. If the three different orders[34] are distributed randomly among respondents, no response alternative will have an inflated chance of being selected because of its position, and the average of the three will provide the most appropriate estimate of response level.[35]

§ 6–4.6   If the Survey Was Designed to Test a Causal Proposition, Did the Survey Include an Appropriate Control Group or Question?

Most surveys that are designed to provide evidence of trademark infringement or deceptive advertising are not conducted to describe consumer beliefs.

J. Gallo Winery v. Pasatiempos Gallo, S.A., 905 F.Supp. 1403, 1409–10 (E.D.Cal.1994) (court recognized that earlier questions referring to playing cards, board or table games, or party supplies, such as confetti, increased the likelihood that respondents would include these items in answers to the questions that followed).

30. This question was accepted by the court in U–Haul Int'l, Inc. v. Jartran, Inc., 522 F.Supp. 1238, 1249 (D.Ariz.1981).

31. Similarly, candidates in the first position on the ballot tend to attract extra votes when the candidates are not well known. Henry M. Bain & Donald S. Hecock, Ballot Position and Voter's Choice: The Arrangement of Names on the Ballot and its Effect on the Voter (1973).

32. *See* Rust Env't & Infrastructure, Inc. v. Teunissen, 131 F.3d 1210, 1218 (7th Cir.1997) (survey did not pass muster in part because of failure to incorporate random rotation of corporate names that were the subject of a trademark dispute).

33. *See, e.g.*, In re Stouffer Foods Corp., 118 F.T.C. 746 (1994). *See also* Winning Ways, Inc. v. Holloway Sportswear, Inc., 913 F.Supp. 1454, 1465–67 (D.Kan.1996) (failure to rotate the order in which the jackets were shown to the consumers led to reduced weight for survey).

34. Actually, there are six possible orders of the three alternatives: ABC, ACB, BAC, BCA, CAB, and CBA.

35. Although rotation is desirable, many surveys are conducted with no attention to this potential bias. Since it is impossible to know in the abstract whether a particular question suffers much, little, or not at all from an order bias, lack of rotation should not preclude reliance on the answer to the question, but it should reduce the weight given to it.

Instead, they are intended to show how the trademark or content of the commercial influences respondents' perceptions or understanding of a product or commercial. Thus, the question is whether the commercial misleads the consumer into thinking that Product A is a superior pain reliever, not whether consumers hold inaccurate beliefs about the product. Yet if consumers already believe, before viewing the commercial, that Product A is a superior pain reliever, a survey that records consumers' impressions after they view the commercial may reflect those preexisting beliefs rather than impressions produced by the commercial.

Surveys that record consumer impressions have a limited ability to answer questions about the origins of those impressions. The difficulty is that the consumer's response to any question on the survey may be the result of information or misinformation from sources other than the trademark the respondent is being shown or the commercial he has just watched. In a trademark survey attempting to show secondary meaning, for example, respondents were shown a picture of the stripes used on Mennen stick deodorant and asked, "Which brand would you say uses these stripes on their package?"[36] The court recognized that the high percentage of respondents selecting "Mennen" from an array of brand names may have represented "merely a playback of brand share"[37]; that is, respondents asked to give a brand name may guess the one that is most familiar, generally the brand with the largest market share.[38]

Some surveys attempt to reduce the impact of preexisting impressions on respondents' answers by instructing respondents to focus solely on the stimulus as a basis for their answers. Thus, the survey includes a preface (e.g.,"based on the commercial you just saw") or directs the respondent's attention to the mark at issue (e.g., "these stripes on the package"). Such efforts are likely to be only partially successful. It is often difficult for respondents to identify accurately the source of their impressions.[39] The more routine the idea being examined in the survey (e.g., that the advertised pain reliever is more effective than others on the market; that the mark belongs to the brand with the largest market share), the more likely it is that the respondent's answer is influenced by preexisting impressions, by expectations about what commercials generally say (e.g., the product being advertised is better than its competitors), or by guessing, rather than by the actual content of the commercial message or trademark being evaluated.

It is possible to adjust many survey designs so that causal inferences about the effect of a trademark or an allegedly deceptive commercial become clear and unambiguous. By adding an appropriate control group, the survey expert can test directly the influence of the stimulus.[40] In the simplest version

---

36. Mennen Co. v. Gillette Co., 565 F.Supp. 648, 652 (S.D.N.Y.1983). To demonstrate secondary meaning, "the [c]ourt must determine whether the mark has been so associated in the mind of consumers with the entity that it identifies that the goods sold by that entity are distinguished by the mark or symbol from goods sold by others." *Id.* at 652.

37. *Id.*

38. *See also* Upjohn Co. v. American Home Prods. Corp., No. 1–95–CV–237, 1996 U.S.

Dist. LEXIS 8049, at *42–44 (W.D. Mich., April 5, 1996).

39. *See* Richard E. Nisbett & Timothy D. Wilson, *Telling More Than We Can Know: Verbal Reports on Mental Processes,* 84 PSY-CHOL. REV. 231 (1977).

40. *See* Shari S. Diamond, *Using Psychology to Control Law: From Deceptive Advertising to Criminal Sentencing,* 13 LAW & HUM. BEHAV. 239, 244–46 (1989); Shari S. Diamond & Linda Dimitropoulos, Deception and Puffery in Ad-

of a survey experiment, respondents are assigned randomly to one of two conditions.[41] For example, respondents assigned to the experimental condition view an allegedly deceptive commercial, and respondents assigned to the control condition either view a commercial that does not contain the allegedly deceptive material or do not view any commercial.[42] Respondents in both the experimental and control groups answer the same set of questions. The effect of the allegedly deceptive message is evaluated by comparing the responses made by the experimental group members with those of the control group members. If 40% of the respondents in the experimental group responded with the deceptive message (e.g., the advertised product has fewer calories than its competitor), whereas only 8% of the respondents in the control group gave that response, the difference between 40% and 8% (within the limits of sampling error[43]) can be attributed only to the allegedly deceptive commercial. Without the control group, it is not possible to determine how much of the 40% is due to respondents' preexisting beliefs or other background noise (e.g., respondents who misunderstand the question or misstate their responses). Both preexisting beliefs and other background noise should have produced similar response levels in the experimental and control groups. In addition, if respondents in the experimental group gave more answers suggesting deception than did members of the control group, the difference cannot be the result of a leading question, because both groups answered the same question. The ability to evaluate the effect of the wording of a particular question makes the control group design particularly useful in assessing responses to closed-ended questions,[44] which may encourage guessing or particular responses. Thus, the focus on the response level in a control group design is not on the absolute response level, but on the difference between the response level of the experimental group and that of the control group.

In designing a control group study, the expert should select a stimulus for the control group that shares as many characteristics with the experimental stimulus as possible, with the key exception of the characteristic whose influence is being assessed. A survey with an imperfect control group generally provides better information than a survey with no control group at all, but the choice of the specific control group requires some care and should influence the weight that the survey receives. For example, a control stimulus should not be less attractive than the experimental stimulus if the survey is

vertising: Behavioral Science Implication for Regulation (American Bar Found. Working Paper Series No. 9105, 1994); Jacob Jacoby & Constance Small, *Applied Marketing: The FDA Approach to Defining Misleading Advertising*, 39 J. MKTG. 65,68 (1975). For a more general discussion of the role of control groups, *see* Chapters 4 and 5.

41. Random assignment should not be confused with random selection. When respondents are assigned randomly to different treatment groups (e.g., respondents in each group watch a different commercial), the procedure ensures that within the limits of sampling error the two groups of respondents will be equivalent except for the different treatments they receive. Respondents selected for a mall intercept study, and not from a probability sample, may be assigned randomly to different

treatment groups. Random selection, in contrast, describes the method of selecting a sample of respondents in a probability sample. *See* § 7–3.3.

42. This alternative commercial could be a "tombstone" advertisement that includes only the name of the product or a more elaborate commercial that does not include the claim at issue.

43. For a discussion of sampling error, *see* Chapter 5.

44. The Federal Trade Commission has long recognized the need for some kind of control for closed-ended questions, although it has not specified the type of control that is necessary. Stouffer Foods Corp., 118 F.T.C. 746 (1994).

designed to measure how familiar the experimental stimulus is to respondents, since attractiveness may affect perceived familiarity.[45] Nor should the control stimulus share with the experimental stimulus the feature whose impact is being assessed. If, for example, the control stimulus in a case of alleged trademark infringement is itself a likely source of consumer confusion, reactions to the experimental and control stimuli may not differ because both cause respondents to express the same level of confusion.[46]

Explicit attention to the value of control groups in trademark and deceptive advertising litigation is a recent phenomenon, but it is becoming more common.[47] Database searches using "Lanham Act" and "control group" revealed twenty district court cases in which surveys with control groups were discussed. Fourteen of the district court cases appeared in the six years between in 1994 and 1999,[48] five district court cases in the seven years from 1987 to 1993,[49] and only one case before 1987.[50] Other cases, however, have described or considered surveys using control group designs without labeling the comparison group a control group.[51] Indeed, the relative absence of control

45. *See, e.g.,* Indianapolis Colts, Inc. v. Metropolitan Baltimore Football Club Ltd. Partnership, 34 F.3d 410, 415–16 (7th Cir. 1994) (The court recognized that the name "Baltimore Horses" was less attractive for a sports team than the name "Baltimore Colts."). *See also* Reed–Union Corp. v. Turtle Wax, Inc., 77 F.3d 909, 912 (7th Cir.1996) (court noted that one expert's choice of a control brand with a well-known corporate source was less appropriate than the opposing expert's choice of a control brand whose name did not indicate a specific corporate source).

46. *See, e.g.,* Western Publ'g Co. v. Publications Int'l, Ltd., 1995 WL 1684082 (N.D.Ill. 1995) (court noted that the control product was "arguably more infringing than" the defendant's product) (emphasis omitted).

47. *See, e.g.,* American Home Prods. Corp. v. Procter & Gamble Co., 871 F.Supp. 739, 749 (D.N.J.1994) (discounting survey results based on failure to control for participants' preconceived notions); ConAgra, Inc. v. Geo. A. Hormel & Co., 784 F.Supp. 700, 728 (D.Neb.1992) ("Since no control was used, the ... study, standing alone, must be significantly discounted.").

48. National Football League Properties v. ProStyle, 57 F.Supp.2d 665 (E.D.Wi.1999); Nabisco, Inc. v. PF Brands, Inc., 50 F.Supp. 2d 188 (S.D.N.Y.1999), affirmed 191 F.3d 208 (2d Cir.1999); Procter & Gamble Co. v. Colgate–Palmolive Co., 1998 WL 788802 (S.D.N.Y. Nov. 9, 1998); Mattel, Inc. v. MCA Records, Inc., 28 F.Supp.2d 1120 (C.D.Cal.1998); Westchester Media Co. L.P. v. PRL USA Holdings, H–97–3278 (S.D.Tex. July 2, 1998), final judgment H–97–3278 (S.D.Tex. Aug. 4, 1999); Time Inc. v. Peterson Publ. Co., 976 F.Supp. 263 (S.D.N.Y.1997); Adjusters Int'l, Inc. v. Public Adjusters Int'l, Inc., 1996 WL 492905 (N.D.N.Y.1996); Upjohn Co. v. American Home Products Corp., 1:95:CV:237 (W.D.Mich. Apr.

5, 1996); Copy Cop, Inc. v. Task Printing, Inc., 908 F.Supp. 37 (D.Mass.1995); Volkswagen Astiengesellschaft v. Uptown Motors, 1995 WL 605605 (S.D.N.Y.1995); Western Publishing Co. v. Publications Intl., Ltd., 1995 WL 1684082 (N.D.Ill.1995); Dogloo, Inc. v. Doskocil Mfg. Co., Inc., 893 F.Supp. 911, 35 U.S.P.Q.2d 1405 (D.Cal.1995); Reed–Union Corp. v. Turtle Wax, Inc., 869 F.Supp. 1304 (N.D.Ill.1994); Pfizer, Inc. v. Miles, Inc., 868 F.Supp. 437, 1995–1 Trade Cases ¶ 70,863 (D.Conn.1994).

49. ConAgra, Inc. v. Geo. A. Hormel & Co., 784 F.Supp. 700 (D.Neb.1992); Johnson & Johnson–Merck Consumer Pharmaceuticals Co. v. Smithkline Beecham Corp., 1991 WL 206312 (S.D.N.Y.1991); Goya Foods, Inc. v. Condal Distribs., Inc., 732 F.Supp. 453 (S.D.N.Y.1990); Strum, Ruger & Co. v. Arcadia Mach. & Tool, Inc., 10 U.S.P.Q.2d 1522, 1988 WL 391514 (C.D.Cal.1988); Frisch's Restaurant, Inc. v. Elby's Big Boy, Inc., 661 F.Supp. 971 (S.D.Ohio 1987).

50. American Basketball Ass'n v. AMF Voit, Inc., 358 F.Supp. 981 (S.D.N.Y.1973).

51. Indianapolis Colts, Inc. v. Metropolitan Baltimore Football Club, 31 U.S.P.Q.2d 1801 (S.D.Ind.1994) (district court described a survey conducted by the plaintiff's expert in which half of interviewees were shown a shirt with the name "Baltimore Colts" on it and half were shown a shirt on which the word "Horses" had been substituted for the word "Colts." The court noted that the comparison between reactions to the horse and colt versions of the shirt made it possible "to determine the impact from the use of the word 'Colts.' "). *See also* Quality Inns Int'l, Inc. v. McDonald's Corp., 695 F.Supp. 198, 218 (D.Md.1988) (survey revealed confusion between McDonald's and McSleep, but control survey revealed no confusion between McDonald's and McTavish).

groups in reported cases may reflect the fact that a survey with a control group produces less ambiguous findings, which leads to a resolution before a preliminary injunction hearing or trial occurs.[52]

Another more common use of control methodology is a control question. Rather than administering a control stimulus to a separate group of respondents, the survey asks all respondents one or more control questions along with the question about the product or service. In a trademark dispute, for example, a survey indicated that 7.2% of respondents believed that "The Mart" and "K–Mart" were owned by the same individuals. The court found no likelihood of confusion based on survey evidence that 5.7% of the respondents also thought that "The Mart" and "King's Department Store" were owned by the same source.[53]

Similarly, a standard technique used to evaluate whether a brand name is generic is to present survey respondents with a series of product or service names and ask them to indicate in each instance whether they believe the name is a brand name or a common name. By showing that 68% of respondents considered Teflon a brand name (a proportion similar to the 75% of respondents who recognized the acknowledged trademark Jell–O as a brand name, and markedly different from the 13% who thought aspirin was a brand name), the makers of Teflon retained their trademark.[54]

Every measure of opinion or belief in a survey reflects some degree of error. Control groups and control questions are the most reliable means for assessing response levels against the baseline level of error associated with a particular question.

§ 6–4.7 What Limitations Are Associated With the Mode of Data Collection Used in the Survey?

Three primary methods are used to collect survey data: (1) in-person interviews, (2) telephone surveys, and (3) mail surveys.[55] The choice of a data collection method for a survey should be justified by its strengths and weaknesses.

§ 6–4.7.1 In–Person Interviews

Although costly, in-person interviews generally are the preferred method of data collection, especially when visual materials must be shown to the respondent under controlled conditions.[56] When the questions are complex and

52. The relatively infrequent mention of control groups in surveys discussed in federal cases is not confined to Lanham Act litigation. A database search using "survey" and "control group" revealed thirty district court cases in the six years from 1994 to 1999 in which control group was used to refer to a methodological feature: the fourteen Lanham Act cases cited *supra* note 48; nine that referred to medical, physiological, or pharmacological experiments; and seven others.

53. S.S. Kresge Co. v. United Factory Outlet, Inc., 598 F.2d 694, 697 (1st Cir.1979). Note that the aggregate percentages reported here do not reveal how many of the same respondents were confused by both names, an issue that may be relevant in some situations. *See* Joseph L. Gastwirth, *Reference Guide on Survey Research*, 36 JURIMETRICS J. 181, 187–88 (1996).

54. E.I. DuPont de Nemours & Co. v. Yoshida Int'l, Inc., 393 F.Supp. 502 (E.D.N.Y. 1975).

55. Methods also may be combined, as when the telephone is used to "screen" for eligible respondents, who then are invited to participate in an in-person interview.

56. A mail survey also can include limited visual materials but cannot exercise control

the interviewers are skilled, in-person interviewing provides the opportunity to clarify or probe, the capability to implement complex skip sequences (in which the respondent's answer determines which question will be asked next), and the power to control the order in which the respondent answers the questions. As described in section 7–5.1, appropriate interviewer training is necessary if these potential benefits are to be realized. Objections to the use of in-person interviews arise primarily from their high cost or, on occasion, from evidence of inept or biased interviewers.

§ 6–4.7.2 Telephone Surveys

Telephone surveys offer a comparatively fast and low-cost alternative to in-person surveys and are particularly useful when the population is large and geographically dispersed. Telephone interviews (unless supplemented with mailed materials) can be used only when it is unnecessary to show the respondent any visual materials. Thus, an attorney may present the results of a telephone survey of jury-eligible citizens in a motion for a change of venue in order to provide evidence that community prejudice raises a reasonable suspicion of potential jury bias.[57] Similarly, potential confusion between a restaurant called McBagel's and the McDonald's fast-food chain was established in a telephone survey. Over objections from defendant McBagel's that the survey did not show respondents the defendant's print advertisements, the court found likelihood of confusion based on the survey, noting that "by soliciting audio responses[, the telephone survey] was closely related to the radio advertising involved in the case."[58] In contrast, when words are not sufficient because, for example, the survey is assessing reactions to the trade dress or packaging of a product that is alleged to promote confusion, a telephone survey alone does not offer a suitable vehicle for questioning respondents.[59]

In evaluating the sampling used in a telephone survey, the trier of fact should consider:

1. (when prospective respondents are not business personnel) whether some form of random digit dialing[60] was used instead of or to supplement telephone numbers obtained from telephone directories, because up to 65% of all residential telephone numbers in some areas may be unlisted;[61]

over when and how the respondent views them.

57. United States v. Partin, 320 F.Supp. 275 (E.D.La.1970). For a discussion of surveys used in motions for change of venue, *see* Neal Miller, *Facts, Expert Facts, and Statistics: Descriptive and Experimental Research Methods in Litigation, Part II*, 40 RUTGERS L. REV. 467, 470–74 (1988); NAT'L JURY PROJECT, JURYWORK: SYSTEMATIC TECHNIQUES (Elissa Krauss & Beth Bonora eds., 2d ed. 1983).

58. McDonald's Corp. v. McBagel's, Inc., 649 F.Supp. 1268, 1278 (S.D.N.Y.1986).

59. Thompson Medical Co. v. Pfizer, Inc., 753 F.2d 208 (2d Cir.1985); Incorporated Pub. Corp. v. Manhattan Magazine, Inc., 616 F.Supp. 370 (S.D.N.Y.1985).

60. Random digit dialing provides coverage of households with both listed and unlisted telephone numbers by generating numbers at random from the frame of all possible telephone numbers. James M. Lepkowski, *Telephone Sampling Methods in the United States*, in TELEPHONE SURVEY METHODOLOGY 81–91 (Robert M. Groves et al. eds., 1988).

61. In 1992, the percentage of households with unlisted numbers reached 65% in Las Vegas and 62% in Los Angeles. Survey Sampling, THE FRAME, March 1993. Studies comparing listed and unlisted household characteristics show some important differences. LEPKOWSKI, *supra* note 60, at 76.

2. whether the sampling procedures required the interviewer to sample within the household or business, instead of allowing the interviewer to administer the survey to any qualified individual who answered the telephone;[62] and

3. whether interviewers were required to call back at several different times of the day and on different days to increase the likelihood of contacting individuals or businesses with different schedules.

Telephone surveys that do not include these procedures may, like other nonprobability sampling approaches, be adequate for providing rough approximations. The vulnerability of the survey depends on the information being gathered. More elaborate procedures for achieving a representative sample of respondents are advisable if the survey instrument requests information that is likely to differ for individuals with listed telephone numbers and individuals with unlisted telephone numbers, or individuals rarely at home and those usually at home.

The report submitted by a survey expert who conducts a telephone survey should specify:

1. the procedures that were used to identify potential respondents;

2. the number of telephone numbers for which no contact was made; and

3. the number of contacted potential respondents who refused to participate in the survey.

Computer-assisted telephone interviewing, or CATI, is increasingly used in the administration and data entry of large-scale surveys.[63] A computer protocol may be used to generate telephone numbers and dial them as well as to guide the interviewer through the interview. The interviewer conducting a computer-assisted interview (CAI), whether by telephone or in a face-to-face setting, follows the script for the interview generated by the computer program and types in the respondent's answers as the interview proceeds. A primary advantage of CATI and other CAI procedures is that skip patterns can be built into the program so that, for example, if the respondent is asked whether she has ever been the victim of a burglary and she says yes, the computer will generate further questions about the burglary, but if she says no, the program will automatically skip the follow-up burglary questions. Interviewer errors in following the skip patterns are therefore avoided, making CAI procedures particularly valuable when the survey involves complex branching and skip patterns.[64] CAI procedures can also be used to control for order effects by having the program rotate the order in which questions or choices are presented.[65] CAI procedures, however, require additional planning

---

62. This is a consideration only if the survey is sampling individuals. If the survey is seeking information on the household, more than one individual may be able to answer questions on behalf of the household.

63. William L. Nicholls II & R.M. Groves, *The Status of Computer–Assisted Telephone Interviewing*, 2 J. OFFICIAL STAT. 93 (1986); Mary A. Spaeth, *CATI Facilities at Academic Research Organizations*, 21 SURV. RES. 11 (1990);

WILLIAM E. SARIS, COMPUTER-ASSISTED INTERVIEWING (1991).

64. Saris, *supra* note 63, at 20, 27.

65. *See, e.g.*, Intel Corp. v. Advanced Micro Devices, Inc., 756 F.Supp. 1292, 1296–97 (N.D.Cal.1991) (survey designed to test whether the term *386* as applied to a microprocessor was generic used a CATI protocol that tested reactions to five terms presented in rotated order).

to take advantage of the potential for improvements in data quality. When a CAI protocol is used in a survey presented in litigation, the party offering the survey should supply for inspection the computer program that was used to generate the interviews. Moreover, CAI procedures do not eliminate the need for close monitoring of interviews to ensure that interviewers are accurately reading the questions in the interview protocol and accurately entering the answers that the respondent is giving to those questions.

§ 6–4.7.3 Mail Surveys

In general, mail surveys tend to be substantially less costly than both in-person and telephone surveys.[66] Although response rates for mail surveys are often low, researchers have obtained 70% response rates in some general public surveys and response rates of over 90% with certain specialized populations.[67] Procedures that encourage high response rates include multiple mailings, highly personalized communications, prepaid return envelopes and incentives or gratuities, assurances of confidentiality, and first-class outgoing postage.[68]

A mail survey will not produce a high response rate unless it begins with an accurate and up-to-date list of names and addresses for the target population. Even if the sampling frame is adequate, the sample may be unrepresentative if some individuals are more likely to respond than others. For example, if a survey targets a population that includes individuals with literacy problems, these individuals will tend to be underrepresented. Open-ended questions are generally of limited value on a mail survey because they depend entirely on the respondent to answer fully and do not provide the opportunity to probe or clarify unclear answers. Similarly, if eligibility to answer some questions depends on the respondent's answers to previous questions, such skip sequences may be difficult for some respondents to follow. Finally, because respondents complete mail surveys without supervision, survey personnel are unable to prevent respondents from discussing the questions and to control the order in which respondents answer the questions. If it is crucial to have respondents answer questions in a particular order, a mail survey cannot be depended on to provide adequate data.[69]

§ 6–4.7.4 Internet Surveys

A more recent innovation in survey technology is the Internet survey in which potential respondents are contacted and their responses are collected over the Internet. Internet surveys can substantially reduce the cost of reaching potential respondents and offer some of the advantages of in-person interviews by allowing the computer to show the respondent pictures or lists

66. Don A. Dillman, *Mail and Other Self-Administered Questionnaires, in* HANDBOOK OF SURVEY RESEARCH 359, 373 (Peter H. Rossi et al. eds., 1983).

67. *Id.* at 360.

68. *See, e.g.,* Richard J. Fox et al., *Mail Survey Response Rate: A Meta–Analysis of Selected Techniques for Inducing Response,* 52 PUB. OPINION Q. 467, 482 (1988); Eleanor Singer et al., *Confidentiality Assurances and Response: A Quantitative Review of the Experi-*mental Literature, 59 PUB. OPINION Q. 66, 71 (1995); Kenneth D. Hopkins & Arlen R. Gullickson, *Response Rates in Survey Research: A Meta–Analysis of the Effects of Monetary Gratuities,* 61 J. EXPERIMENTAL EDUC. 52, 54–57, 59 (1992).

69. Don A. Dillman, *Mail and Other Self-Administered Questionnaires, in* HANDBOOK OF SURVEY RESEARCH (Peter H. Rossi et al. eds., 1983) at 359, 368–70.

of response choices in the course of asking the respondent questions. The key limitation is that the respondents accessible over the Internet must fairly represent the relevant population whose responses the survey was designed to measure. Thus, a litigant presenting the results of a web-based survey should be prepared to provide evidence on the potential bias in sampling that the web-based survey is likely to introduce. If the target population consists of computer users, the bias may be minimal. If the target population consists of owners of television sets, significant bias is likely.

§ 6–5.0 SURVEYS INVOLVING INTERVIEWERS

§ 6–5.1 Were the Interviewers Appropriately Selected and Trained?

A properly defined population or universe, a representative sample, and clear and precise questions can be depended on to produce trustworthy survey results only if "sound interview procedures were followed by competent interviewers."[1] Properly trained interviewers receive detailed instructions on everything they are to say to respondents, any stimulus materials they are to use in the survey, and how they are to complete the interview form. These instructions should be made available to the opposing party and to the trier of fact. Thus, interviewers should be told, and the interview form on which answers are recorded should indicate, which responses, if any, are to be read to the respondent. Interviewers also should be instructed to record verbatim the respondent's answers, to indicate explicitly whenever they repeat a question to the respondent, and to record any statements they make to or supplementary questions they ask the respondent.

Interviewers require training to ensure that they are able to follow directions in administering the survey questions. Some training in general interviewing techniques is required for most interviews (e.g., practice in pausing to give the respondent enough time to answer and practice in resisting invitations to express the interviewer's beliefs or opinions). Although procedures vary, one treatise recommends at least five hours of training in general interviewing skills and techniques for new interviewers.[2]

The more complicated the survey instrument is, the more training and experience the interviewers require. Thus, if the interview includes a skip pattern (where, e.g., Questions 4–6 are asked only if the respondent says yes to Question 3, and Questions 8–10 are asked only if the respondent says no to Question 3), interviewers must be trained to follow the pattern. Similarly, if the questions require specific probes to clarify ambiguous responses, interviewers must receive instruction on when to use the probes and what to say. In some surveys, the interviewer is responsible for last-stage sampling (i.e., selecting the particular respondents to be interviewed), and training is especially crucial to avoid interviewer bias in selecting respondents who are easiest to approach or easiest to find.

§ 6–5.0

1. Toys "R" Us, Inc. v. Canarsie Kiddie Shop, Inc., 559 F.Supp. 1189, 1205 (E.D.N.Y. 1983).

2. Eve Weinberg, *Data Collection: Planning and Management, in* HANDBOOK OF SURVEY RESEARCH 329, 332 (Peter H. Rossi et al. eds., 1983).

Training and instruction of interviewers should include directions on the circumstances under which interviews are to take place (e.g., question only one respondent at a time out of the hearing of any other respondent). The trustworthiness of a survey is questionable if there is evidence that some interviews were conducted in a setting in which respondents were likely to have been distracted or in which others were present and could overhear. Such evidence of careless administration of the survey was one ground used by a court to reject as inadmissible a survey that purported to demonstrate consumer confusion.[3]

Some compromises may be accepted when surveys must be conducted swiftly. In trademark and deceptive advertising cases, the plaintiff's usual request is for a preliminary injunction, because a delay means irreparable harm. Nonetheless, careful instruction and training of interviewers who administer the survey and complete disclosure of the methods used for instruction and training are crucial elements that, if compromised, seriously undermine the trustworthiness of any survey.

§ 6–5.2   What Did the Interviewers Know About the Survey and Its Sponsorship?

One way to protect the objectivity of survey administration is to avoid telling interviewers who is sponsoring the survey. Interviewers who know the identity of the survey's sponsor may affect results inadvertently by communicating to respondents their expectations or what they believe are the preferred responses of the survey's sponsor. To ensure objectivity in the administration of the survey, it is standard interview practice to conduct double-blind research whenever possible: both the interviewer and the respondent are blind to the sponsor of the survey and its purpose. Thus, the survey instrument should provide no explicit clues (e.g., a sponsor's letterhead appearing on the survey) and no implicit clues (e.g., reversing the usual order of the yes and no response boxes on the interviewer's form next to a crucial question, thereby potentially increasing the likelihood that no will be checked[4]) about the sponsorship of the survey or the expected responses.

Nonetheless, in some surveys (e.g., some government surveys), disclosure of the survey's sponsor to respondents (and thus to interviewers) is required. Such surveys call for an evaluation of the likely biases introduced by interviewer or respondent awareness of the survey's sponsorship. In evaluating the consequences of sponsorship awareness, it is important to consider (1) whether the sponsor has views and expectations that are apparent and (2) whether awareness is confined to the interviewers or involves the respondents. For example, if a survey concerning attitudes toward gun control is sponsored by the National Rifle Association, it is clear that responses opposing gun control are likely to be preferred. In contrast, if the survey on gun control attitudes is sponsored by the Department of Justice, the identity of the sponsor may not

---

3. *Toys "R" Us*, 559 F.Supp. at 1204 (some interviews apparently were conducted in a bowling alley; some interviewees waiting to be interviewed overheard the substance of the interview while they were waiting).

4. Centaur Communications, Ltd. v. A/S/M Communications, Inc., 652 F.Supp. 1105, 1111 n. 3 (S.D.N.Y.1987) (pointing out that reversing the usual order of response choices, yes or no, to no or yes may confuse interviewers as well as introduce bias).

suggest the kind of responses the sponsor expects or would find acceptable.[5] When interviewers are well trained, their awareness of sponsorship may be a less serious threat than respondents' awareness. The empirical evidence for the effects of interviewers' prior expectations on respondents' answers generally reveals modest effects when the interviewers are well trained.[6]

§ 6–5.3   What Procedures Were Used to Ensure and Determine That the Survey Was Administered to Minimize Error and Bias?

Three methods are used to ensure that the survey instrument was implemented in an unbiased fashion and according to instructions. The first, monitoring the interviews as they occur, is done most easily when telephone surveys are used. A supervisor listens to a sample of interviews for each interviewer. Field settings make monitoring more difficult, but evidence that monitoring has occurred provides an additional indication that the survey has been reliably implemented.

Second, validation of interviews occurs when a sample of respondents is recontacted to ask whether the initial interviews took place and to determine whether the respondents were qualified to participate in the survey. The standard procedure for validation is to telephone a random sample of about 10% to 15% of the respondents.[7] Some attempts to reach the respondents will be unsuccessful, and occasionally a respondent will deny that the interview took place even though it did. Because the information checked is limited to whether the interview took place and whether the respondent was qualified, this validation procedure does not determine whether the initial interview as a whole was conducted properly. Nonetheless, this standard validation technique warns interviewers that their work is being checked and can detect gross failures in the administration of the survey.

A third way to verify that the interviews were conducted properly is to compare the work done by each individual interviewer. By reviewing the interviews and individual responses recorded by each interviewer, researchers can identify any response patterns or inconsistencies for further investigation.

When a survey is conducted at the request of a party for litigation rather than in the normal course of business, a heightened standard for validation checks may be appropriate. Thus, independent validation of at least 50% of interviews by a third party rather than by the field service that conducted the interviews increases the trustworthiness of the survey results.[8]

5. *See, e.g.,* Stanley Presser et al., *Survey Sponsorship, Response Rates, and Response Effects*, 73 Soc. Sci. Q. 699, 701 (1992) (different responses to a university-sponsored telephone survey and a newspaper-sponsored survey for questions concerning attitudes toward the mayoral primary, an issue on which the newspaper had taken a position).

6. *See, e.g.,* Seymour Sudman et al., *Modest Expectations: The Effects of Interviewers' Prior Expectations on Responses*, 6 Soc. Methods & Res. 171,181 (1977).

7. *See, e.g.,* National Football League Properties, Inc. v. New Jersey Giants, Inc., 637 F.Supp. 507, 515 (D.N.J.1986); Davis v. Southern Bell Tel. & Tel. Co. 158 F.R.D. 173 (S.D.Fla.1994).

8. In *Rust Environment & Infrastructure, Inc. v. Teunissen*, 131 F.3d 1210, 1218 (7th Cir.1997), the court criticized a survey in part because it "did not comport with accepted practice for independent validation of results."

§ 6–6.0 DATA ENTRY AND GROUPING OF RESPONSES

§ 6–6.1 What Was Done to Ensure That the Data Were Recorded Accurately?

Analyzing the results of a survey requires that the data obtained on each sampled element be recorded, edited, and often coded before the results can be tabulated and processed. Procedures for data entry should include checks for completeness, checks for reliability and accuracy, and rules for resolving inconsistencies. Accurate data entry is maximized when responses are verified by duplicate entry and comparison, and when data entry personnel are unaware of the purposes of the survey.

§ 6–6.2 What Was Done to Ensure That the Grouped Data Were Classified Consistently and Accurately?

Coding of answers to open-ended questions requires a detailed set of instructions so that decision standards are clear and responses can be scored consistently and accurately. Two trained coders should independently score the same subset of responses to check for the level of consistency in classifying responses. When the criteria used to categorize verbatim responses are controversial or allegedly inappropriate, those criteria should be sufficiently clear to reveal the source of disagreements. In such cases, the verbatim responses should be available so that they can be recoded using alternative criteria.[1]

§ 6–7.0 DISCLOSURE AND REPORTING

§ 6–7.1 When Was Information About the Survey Methodology and Results Disclosed?

Objections to the definition of the relevant population, the method of selecting the sample, and the wording of questions generally are raised for the first time when the results of the survey are presented. By that time it is too late to correct methodological deficiencies that could have been addressed in the planning stages of the survey. The plaintiff in a trademark case[1] submitted a set of proposed survey questions to the trial judge, who ruled that the survey results would be admissible at trial while reserving the question of the weight the evidence would be given.[2] The court of appeals called this approach

---

§ 6–6.0

1. *See, e.g.,* Coca–Cola Co. v. Tropicana Prods., Inc., 538 F.Supp. 1091, 1094–96 (S.D.N.Y.)(plaintiff's expert stated that respondents' answers to the several open-ended questions revealed that 43% of respondents thought Tropicana was portrayed as fresh squeezed; the court's own tabulation found no more than 15% believed this was true), *rev'd* on other grounds, 690 F.2d 312 (2d Cir.1982). *See also* McNeilab, Inc. v. American Home Prods. Corp., 501 F.Supp. 517 (S.D.N.Y.1980); Rock v. Zimmerman, 959 F.2d 1237, 1253 n. 9 (3d Cir. 1992) (court found that responses on a change of venue survey incorrectly categorized respon-

dents who believes the defendant was insane as believing he was guilty); Revlon Consumer Prods. Corp. v. Jennifer Leather Broadway, Inc., 858 F.Supp. 1268, 1276 (S.D.N.Y.1994) (inconsistent scoring and subjective coding led court to find survey so unreliable that it was entitled to no weight).

§ 6–7.0

1. Union Carbide Corp. v. Ever–Ready, Inc., 392 F.Supp. 280 (N.D.Ill.1975), *rev'd,* 531 F.2d 366 (7th Cir.1976).

2. Before trial, the presiding judge was appointed to the court of appeals, so the case was tried by another district court judge.

a commendable procedure and suggested that it would have been even more desirable if the parties had "attempt[ed] in good faith to agree upon the questions to be in such a survey."[3]

The Manual for Complex Litigation, Second, recommends that parties be required, "before conducting any poll, to provide other parties with an outline of the proposed form and methodology, including the particular questions that will be asked, the introductory statements or instructions that will be given, and other controls to be used in the interrogation process."[4] The parties then are encouraged to attempt to resolve any methodological disagreements before the survey is conducted.[5] Although this passage in the second edition of the manual has been cited with apparent approval,[6] the prior agreement the manual recommends has occurred rarely and the Manual for Complex Litigation, Third, recommends, but does not advocate, requiring prior disclosure and discussion of survey plans.[7]

Rule 26 of the Federal Rules of Civil Procedure require extensive disclosure of the basis of opinions offered by testifying experts. However, these provisions may not produce disclosure of survey materials, because parties are not obligated to disclose information about nontestifying experts. Parties considering whether to commission or use a survey for litigation are not obligated to present a survey that produces unfavorable results. Prior disclosure of a proposed survey instrument places the party that ultimately would prefer not to present the survey in the position of presenting damaging results or leaving the impression that the results are not being presented because they were unfavorable. Anticipating such a situation, parties do not decide whether an expert will testify until after the results of the survey are available.

Nonetheless, courts are in a position to encourage early disclosure and discussion even if they do not lead to agreement between the parties. In *McNeilab, Inc. v. American Home Products Corp.*, Judge William C. Conner encouraged the parties to submit their survey plans for court approval to ensure their evidentiary value; the plaintiff did so and altered its research plan based on Judge Conner's recommendations.[8] Parties can anticipate that changes consistent with a judicial suggestion are likely to increase the weight given to, or at least the prospects of admissibility of, the survey.[9]

§ 6–7.2 Does the Survey Report Include Complete and Detailed Information on All Relevant Characteristics?

The completeness of the survey report is one indicator of the trustworthiness of the survey and the professionalism of the expert who is presenting the

---

3. *Union Carbide,* 531 F.2d, at 386. More recently, the Seventh Circuit recommended the filing of a motion *in limine,* asking the district court to determine the admissibility of a survey based on an examination of the survey questions and the results of a preliminary survey before the party undertakes the expense of conducting the actual survey. Piper Aircraft Corp. v. Wag–Aero, Inc., 741 F.2d 925, 929 (7th Cir.1984).

4. MANUAL FOR COMPLEX LITIGATION, SECOND, § 21.484 (1985).

5. *Id.*

6. *E.g.,* National Football League Properties, Inc. v. New Jersey Giants, Inc., 637 F.Supp. 507, 514 n. 3 (D.N.J.1986).

7. MANUAL FOR COMPLEX LITIGATION, THIRD, § 21.493 (1995).

8. McNeilab, Inc. v. American Home Prods. Corp., 848 F.2d 34, 36 (2d Cir.1988) (discussing with approval the actions of the district court).

9. Larry C. Jones, *Developing and Using Survey Evidence in Trademark Litigation*, 19 MEMPHIS ST. U. L. REV. 471, 481 (1989).

results of the survey. A survey report generally should describe in detail: 1. the purpose of the survey; 2. a definition of the target population and a description of the population that was actually sampled; 3. a description of the sample design, including the method of selecting respondents, the method of interview, the number of callbacks, respondent eligibility or screening criteria, and other pertinent information; 4. a description of the results of sample implementation, including (a) the number of potential respondents contacted, (b) the number not reached, (c) the number of refusals, (d) the number of incomplete interviews or terminations, (e) the number of noneligibles, and (f) the number of completed interviews; 5. the exact wording of the questions used, including the actual questionnaire, interviewer directions, and visual exhibits; 6. a description of any special scoring (e.g., grouping of verbatim responses into broader categories); 7. estimates of the sampling error where appropriate (i.e., in probability samples); 8. statistical tables clearly labeled and identified as to source of data, including the number of raw cases forming the base for each table, row, or column; and 9. copies of interviewer instructions, validation results, and codebooks.[10]

A description of the procedures and results of pilot testing is not included on this list. Survey professionals generally do not describe pilot testing in their reports. The Federal Rules of Civil Procedure, however, may require that a testifying expert disclose pilot work that serves as a basis for the expert's opinion. The situation is more complicated when a nontestifying expert conducts the pilot work and the testifying expert learns about the pilot testing only indirectly through the attorney's advice about the relevant issues in the case. Some commentators suggest that attorneys are obligated to disclose such pilot work.[11]

§ 6–7.3 In Surveys of Individuals, What Measures Were Taken to Protect the Identities of Individual Respondents?

The respondents questioned in a survey generally do not testify in legal proceedings and are unavailable for cross-examination. Indeed, one of the advantages of a survey is that it avoids a repetitive and unrepresentative parade of witnesses. To verify that interviews occurred with qualified respondents, standard survey practice includes validation procedures,[12] the results of which should be included in the survey report.

Conflicts may arise when an opposing party asks for survey respondents' names and addresses in order to reinterview some respondents. The party

---

10. These criteria were adapted from the COUNCIL OF AM. SURVEY RES. ORGS., CODE OF STANDARDS FOR SURVEY RESEARCH § III.B. Failure to supply this information substantially impairs a court's ability to evaluate a survey. In re Prudential Ins. Co. of Am. Sales Practices Litig., 962 F.Supp. 450, 532 (D.N.J.1997). *But see* Florida Bar v. Went for It, Inc., 515 U.S. 618, 626–28, 115 S.Ct. 2371, 132 L.Ed.2d 541 (1995), in which a majority of the Supreme Court relied on a summary of results prepared by the Florida Bar from a consumer survey purporting to show consumer objections to attorney solicitation by mail. In a strong dissent, Justice Kennedy, joined by three of his colleagues, found the survey inadequate based on

the document available to the court, pointing out that the summary included "no actual surveys, few indications of sample size or selection procedures, no explanations of methodology, and no discussion of excluded results ... no description of the statistical universe or scientific framework that permits any productive use of the information the so-called Summary of Record contains." *Id.* at 640.

11. Yvonne C. Schroeder, *Pretesting Survey Questions*, 11 AM. J. TRIAL ADVOC. 195, 197–201 (1987).

12. *See* § 6–5.3.

introducing the survey or the survey organization that conducted the research generally resists supplying such information.[13] Professional surveyors as a rule guarantee confidentiality in an effort to increase participation rates and to encourage candid responses. Because failure to extend confidentiality may bias both the willingness of potential respondents to participate in a survey and their responses, the professional standards for survey researchers generally prohibit disclosure of respondents' identities. "The use of survey results in a legal proceeding does not relieve the Survey Research Organization of its ethical obligation to maintain in confidence all Respondent-identifiable information or lessen the importance of Respondent anonymity."[14] Although no surveyor-respondent privilege currently is recognized, the need for surveys and the availability of other means to examine and ensure their trustworthiness argues for deference to legitimate claims for confidentiality in order to avoid seriously compromising the ability of surveys to produce accurate information.[15]

Copies of all questionnaires should be made available upon request so that the opposing party has an opportunity to evaluate the raw data. All identifying information, such as the respondent's name, address, and telephone number, should be removed to ensure respondent confidentiality.

13. *See, e.g.,* Alpo Petfoods, Inc. v. Ralston Purina Co., 720 F.Supp. 194 (D.D.C.1989), *aff'd* in part & vacated in part, 913 F.2d 958 (D.C.Cir.1990).

14. COUNCIL OF AM. SURVEY RES. ORGS., CODE OF STANDARDS FOR SURVEY RESEARCH § I.A.3.f. Similar provisions are contained in the By-Laws of the American Association for Public Opinion Research.

15. Litton Indus., Inc., No. 9123, 1979 FTC LEXIS 311, at *13 & n. 12 (June 19, 1979) (Order Concerning the Identification of Individual Survey–Respondents with Their Questionnaires) (citing Frederick H. Boness & John F. Cordes, Note, *The Researcher–Subject Relationship: The Need for Protection and a Model Statute,* 62 GEO. L.J. 243, 253 (1973)). *See also* Lampshire v. Procter & Gamble Co., 94 F.R.D. 58, 60 (N.D.Ga.1982) (defendant denied access to personal identifying information about women involved in studies by the Centers for Disease Control based on Fed.R.Civ.P. 26(c) giving court the authority to enter "any order which justice requires to protect a party or persons from annoyance, embarrassment, oppression, or undue burden or expense.") (citation omitted).

Appendix I

Glossary of Terms

The following terms and definitions were adapted from a variety of sources, including: Handbook of Survey Research (Peter H. Rossi et al. eds., 1983); 1 Environmental Protection Agency, Survey Management Handbook (1983); Measurement Errors in Surveys (Paul P. Biemer et al. eds., 1991); William E. Saris, Computer–Assisted Interviewing (1991); Seymour Sudman, Applied Sampling (1976).

Branching. A questionnaire structure that uses the answers to earlier questions to determine which set of additional questions should be asked (e.g., citizens who report having served as jurors on a criminal case are asked different questions about their experiences than citizens who report having served as jurors on a civil case).

CAI (computer-assisted interviewing). A method of conducting interviews in which an interviewer asks questions and records the respondent's answer by following a computer-generated protocol.

CATI (computer-assisted telephone interviewing). A method of conducting telephone interviews in which an interviewer asks questions and records the respondent's answer by following a computer-generated protocol.

Closed–Ended Question. A question that provides the respondent with a list of choices and asks the respondent to choose from among them.

Cluster Sampling. A sampling technique allowing for the selection of sample elements in groups or clusters, rather than on an individual basis; it may significantly reduce field costs and increase sampling error if elements in the same cluster are more similar to one another than are elements in different clusters.

Confidence Interval. An indication of the probable range of error associated with a sample value obtained from a probability sample. Also, margin of error.

Convenience Sample. A sample of elements selected because they were readily available.

Double–Blind Research. Research in which the respondent and the interviewer are not given information that will alert them to the anticipated or preferred pattern of response.

Error Score. The degree of measurement error in an observed score (see true score).

Full-Filter Question. A question asked of respondents to screen out those who do not have an opinion on the issue under investigation before asking them the question proper.

Mall Intercept Survey. A survey conducted in a mall or shopping center in which potential respondents are approached by a recruiter (intercepted) and invited to participate in the survey.

Multistage Sampling Design. A sampling design in which sampling takes place in several stages, beginning with larger units (e.g., cities) and then proceeding with smaller units (e.g., households or individuals within these units).

Nonprobability Sample. Any sample that does not qualify as a probability sample.

Open-Ended Question. A question that requires the respondent to formulate his or her own response.

Order Effect. A tendency of respondents to choose an item based in part on the order in which it appears in the question, questionnaire, or interview (see primacy effect, recency effect); also referred to as a context effect because the context of the question influences the way the respondent perceives and answers it.

Parameter. A summary measure of a characteristic of a population (e.g., average age, proportion of households in an area owning a computer). Statistics are estimates of parameters.

Pilot Test. A small field test replicating the field procedures planned for the full-scale survey; although the terms pilot test and pretest are sometimes used interchangeably, a pretest tests the questionnaire, whereas a pilot test generally tests proposed collection procedures as well.

Population. The totality of elements (objects, individuals, or measurements) that have some common property of interest; the target population is the collection of elements that the researcher would like to study; the survey population is the population that is actually sampled and for which data may be obtained. Also, universe.

Population Value, Population Parameter. The actual value of some characteristic in the population (e.g., the average age); the population value is estimated by taking a random sample from the population and computing the corresponding sample value.

Pretest. A small preliminary test of a survey questionnaire. See pilot test.

Primacy Effect. A tendency of respondents to choose early items from a list of choices; the opposite of a recency effect.

Probability Sample. A type of sample selected so that every element in the population has a known nonzero probability of being included in the sample; a simple random sample is a probability sample.

Probe. A follow-up question that an interviewer asks to obtain a more complete answer from a respondent (e.g., "Anything else?" "What kind of medical problem do you mean?").

Quasi–Filter Question. A question that offers a "don't know" or "no opinion" option to respondents as part of a set of response alternatives; used to screen out respondents who may not have an opinion on the issue under investigation.

Random Sample. See simple random sample.

Recency Effect. A tendency of respondents to choose later items from a list of choices; the opposite of a primacy effect.

Sample. A subset of a population or universe selected so as to yield information about the population as a whole.

Sampling Error. The estimated size of the difference between the result obtained from a sample study and the result that would be obtained by attempting a complete study of all units in the sampling frame from which the sample was selected in the same manner and with the same care.

Sampling Frame. The source or sources from which the objects, individuals, or other social units in a sample are drawn.

Secondary Meaning. A descriptive term that becomes protectable as a trademark if it signifies to the purchasing public that the product comes from a single producer or source.

Simple Random Sample. The most basic type of probability sampling; each unit in the population has an equal probability of being in the sample, and all possible samples of a given size are equally likely to be selected.

Skip Pattern, Skip Sequence. A sequence of questions in which some should not be asked (should be skipped) based on the respondent's answer to a previous question (e.g., if the respondent indicates that he does not own a car, he should not be asked what brand of car he owns).

Stratified Sampling. A sampling technique that permits the researcher to subdivide the population into mutually exclusive and exhaustive subpopulations, or strata; within these strata, separate samples are selected; results can be combined to form overall population estimates or used to report separate within-stratum estimates.

Survey Population. See Population.

Systematic Sampling. A sampling technique that consists of a random starting point and the selection of every nth member of the population; it generally produces the same results as simple random sampling.

Target Population. See Population.

Trade Dress. A distinctive and nonfunctional design of a package or product protected under state unfair competition law and the federal Lanham Act § 43(a), 15 U.S.C.A. § 1125(a) (1946) (amended 1992).

True Score. The underlying true score which is unobservable because there is always some error in measurement; the observed score = true score + error score.

Universe. See Population.

Appendix II

References on Survey Research

WILLIAM G. COCHRAN, SAMPLING TECHNIQUES (3d ed. 1977).

JEAN M. CONVERSE & STANLEY PRESSER, SURVEY QUESTIONS: HANDCRAFTING THE STANDARDIZED QUESTIONNAIRE (1986).

THOMAS D. COOK & DONALD T. CAMPBELL, QUASI-EXPERIMENTATION: DESIGN AND ANALYSIS ISSUES FOR FIELD SETTINGS (1979).

Shari S. Diamond, *Methods for the Empirical Study of Law, in* LAW AND THE SOCIAL SCIENCES (Leon Lipson & Stanton Wheeler eds., 1986).

1 FLOYD J. FOWLER, SURVEY RESEARCH METHODS (2d ed. 1984).

ROBERT M. GROVES & ROBERT L. KAHN, SURVEYS BY TELEPHONE: A NATIONAL COMPARISON WITH PERSONAL INTERVIEWS (1979).

HANDBOOK OF SURVEY RESEARCH (Peter H. Rossi et al. eds., 1983).

LESLIE KISH, SURVEY SAMPLING (1965).

MEASUREMENT ERRORS IN SURVEYS (Paul P. Biemer et al. eds., 1991).

QUESTIONS ABOUT QUESTIONS: INQUIRIES INTO THE COGNITIVE BASES OF SURVEYS (Judith M. Tanur ed., 1992).

HOWARD SCHUMAN & STANLEY PRESSER, QUESTIONS AND ANSWERS IN ATTITUDE SURVEYS: EXPERIMENTS ON QUESTION FORM, WORDING AND CONTEXT (1981).

SEYMOUR SUDMAN, APPLIED SAMPLING (1976).

SEYMOUR SUDMAN & NORMAN M. BRADBURN, RESPONSE EFFECTS IN SURVEYS: A REVIEW AND SYNTHESIS (1974).

TELEPHONE SURVEY METHODOLOGY (Robert M. Groves et al. eds., 1988).

CHAPTER 7

EPIDEMIOLOGY

Table of Sections

A. LEGAL ISSUES

Westlaw Electronic Research

See Westlaw Electronic Research Guide preceding the Summary of Contents.

A. LEGAL ISSUES

§ 7–1.0 THE LEGAL RELEVANCE OF EPIDEMIOLOGICAL RESEARCH

§ 7–1.1 Introduction

The use of epidemiological evidence in civil litigation is a recent development. Prior to the 1970s there were very few references to epidemiology in federal or state cases. The rise of epidemiology has accompanied the rise of toxic torts.[1] Toxic torts often pose aggregate questions such as whether cigarette smokers as a group suffer from higher levels of heart disease and cancer than non-smokers or whether people with silicone gel implants suffer from higher rates of auto-immune disease than people without implants. Epidemiology correlates aggregate exposure to injury. Without epidemiological evidence there would be far less information relating many exposures to injury.

Epidemiology is a two edged sword for plaintiffs alleging harm from exposure to drugs, medical devices, and toxic substances. On the one hand, this evidence sometimes provides irrefutable evidence linking many exposures to injury. For example, our knowledge of the enormous health dangers caused by tobacco consumption are largely the result of epidemiological research. On the other hand, the absence of epidemiological evidence tying an exposure to an injury sometimes acts as a barrier to recovery.

One of the earliest widespread uses of epidemiology occurred in cases alleging that the swine flu vaccine caused the plaintiff to contract Guillain–Barre syndrome.[2] Since then, the role of epidemiology has grown remarkably.[3]

---

§ 7–1.0

1. *See* Deborah R. Hensler & Mark A. Peterson, *Understanding Mass Personal Injury Litigation: A Socio–Legal Analysis*, 59 Brook. L. Rev. 961 (1993).

2. Bert Black & David E. Lilienfeld, *Epidemiologic Proof in Toxic Tort Litigation*, 52 Fordham L. Rev. 732, 772 (1984); Gerald W. Boston, *A Mass–Exposure Model of Toxic Causation: The Content of Scientific Proof and the*

Regulatory Experience, 18 Colum. J. Envtl. L. 181, 303–305 (1993); D.A. Freedman & P.B. Stark, *The Swine Flue Vaccine and Guillian–Barre Syndrome: A Case Study in Relative Risk and Specific Causation*, 64 no. 4 Law & Contemp. Prob. 49 (2001). To induce pharmaceutical companies to produce swine flu vaccines, Congress relieved them of liability. The government established a surveillance system to monitor illnesses that might be associated

Epidemiological evidence has played a central role in many mass torts,

with the vaccine. Analysis of this data indicated an association between the vaccine and Guillain–Barre Syndrome, but the period of increased risk attributable to the vaccine was limited to the first five to ten weeks following inoculation. *See* Lawrence B. Schonberger et al., *Guillain-Barre Syndrome Following Vaccination in the National Influenza Immunization Program, 1976–77*, 110 AM. J. EPIDEMIOLOGY 105 (1979). The swine flu litigation involved individuals who contracted Guillian–Barre Syndrome after a longer interval. Absent epidemiological evidence, most courts found against the plaintiff. (Because the cases were tried under the Swine Flu Vaccine Act, they were all bench trials). *See* Heyman v. United States, 506 F.Supp. 1145 (S.D.Fla.1981) (rejecting plaintiff argument that causation should be determined on an individual basis and not by reference to statistics); Cook v. United States, 545 F.Supp. 306 (N.D.Cal.1982) (rejecting plaintiff reanalysis of CDC studies that purported to show a relative risk of 3.3 in the thirteen to eighteen week period following the flu shot); Robinson v. United States, 533 F.Supp. 320 (E.D.Mich. 1982); Weldon v. United States, 744 F.Supp. 408 (N.D.N.Y.1990) (plaintiff failed to show her symptoms were those of GBS). *But see* Sulesky v. United States, 545 F.Supp. 426 (S.D.W.Va.1982) (finding that epidemiological studies do not disprove plaintiff's claim that the vaccine caused her GBS fourteen weeks later).

In a recent group of cases eerily similar to the GBS cases, plaintiffs have made claims under the National Childhood Vaccine Injury Act, 42 U.S.C.A. § 300aa–1 et seq., for injuries allegedly caused by vaccines. *See, e.g.,* Lampe v. Secretary of Health and Human Services, 219 F.3d 1357 (Fed.Cir.2000).

3. The following articles are a fair sampling of the literature on mass torts, epidemiology, and admissibility. Kenneth S. Abraham & Glen O. Robinson, *Aggregative Valuation of Mass Tort Claims*, 53 LAW & CONTEMP. PROBS. 137 (1990); Linda Bailey et al., *Reference Guide on Epidemiology*, in REFERENCE MANUAL ON SCIENTIFIC EVIDENCE (Federal Judicial Center, 1994); David Bernstein, *Out of the Fryeing Pan and Into the Fire: The Expert Witness Problem in Toxic Tort Litigation*, 10 REV. LITIG. 117 (1990); Bert Black, *A Unified Theory of Scientific Evidence*, 56 FORDHAM L. REV. 595 (1988); Bert Black et al., *Science and the Law in the Wake of* Daubert*: A New Search for Scientific Knowledge*, 72 TEX. L. REV. 715 (1994); Troyen A. Brennan, *Causal Chains and Statistical Links: The Role of Scientific Uncertainty in Hazardous–Substance Litigation*, 73 CORNELL L. REV. 469 (1988); Troyen A. Brennan, *Helping Courts With Toxic Torts: Some Proposals Regarding Alternative Methods for Presenting and Assessing Scientific Evidence in Common Law Courts*, 51 U. PITT. L. REV. 1 (1989); Ken-

neth J. Chesebro, *Taking* Daubert's *"Focus" Seriously: The Methodology/Conclusion Distinction*, 15 CARDOZO L. REV. 1745 (1994); Jean Macchhiaroli Eggen, *Toxic Torts, Causation and Scientific Evidence After* Daubert, 55 U. PITT. L. REV. 889 (1994); David L. Faigman et al., *Check Your Crystal Ball at the Courthouse Door, Please: Exploring the Past, Understanding the Present, and Worrying About the Future of Scientific Evidence*, 15 CARDOZO L. REV. 1799 (1994); Daniel A. Farber, *Toxic Causation*, 71 MINN. L. REV. 1219 (1987); *Developments in the Law, Confronting the New Challenges of Scientific Evidence*, 108 HARV. L. REV. 1481, 1490 (1995); Michael D. Green, *Expert Witnesses and Sufficiency of Evidence in Toxic Substances Litigation: The Legacy of Agent Orange and Bendectin Litigation*, 86 NW. U. L. REV. 643 (1992); Samuel R. Gross, *Expert Evidence*, 1991 WIS. L. REV. 1113 (1991); Deborah R. Hensler & Mark A. Peterson, *Understanding Mass Personal Injury Litigation: A Socio–Legal Analysis*, 59 BROOK. L. REV. 961 (1993); Edward J. Imwinkelreid, *The "Bases" of Expert Testimony: The Syllogistic Structure of Scientific Testimony*, 67 N.C. L. REV. 1(1988); Jack L. Landau & W. Hugh O'Riordan, *Of Mice and Men: The Admissibility of Animal Studies to Prove Causation in Toxic Tort Litigation*, 25 IDAHO L. REV. 521 (1988/89); Lee Loevinger, *Science as Evidence*, 35 JURIMETRICS J. 153 (1995); Leslie A. Lunney, *Protecting Juries from Themselves: Restricting the Admission of Expert Testimony in Toxic Tort Cases*, 48 SMU L. REV. 103 (1994); Paul S. Milich, *Controversial Science in the Courtroom:* Daubert *and the Law's Hubris*, 43 EMORY L.J. 913 (1994); Susan R. Poulter, Daubert *and Scientific Evidence: Assessing Evidentiary Reliability in Toxic Tort Litigation*, 1993 UTAH L. REV. 1307 (1993); Susan R. Poulter, *Science and Toxic Torts: Is There a Rational Solution to the Problem of Causation?*, 7 HIGH TECH. L.J. 189 (1992); Jon T. Powell, *How to Tell the Truth With Statistics: A New Statistical Approach to Analyzing the Bendectin Epidemiological Data in the Aftermath of* Daubert v. Merrell Dow Pharmaceuticals, 31 HOUS. L. REV. 1241 (1994); Michael Saks & Peter Blanck, *Justice Improved: The Unrecognized Benefits of Aggregation and Sampling in the Trial of Mass Torts*, 44 STAN. L. REV. 815 (1992); Joseph Sanders, *From Science to Evidence: The Testimony on Causation in the Bendectin Cases*, 46 STAN. L. REV. 1 (1993); Joseph Sanders, *Scientific Validity, Admissibility, and Mass Torts After* Daubert, 78 MINN. L. REV. 1387 (1994); Peter H. Schuck, *Multi-Culturalism Redux: Science, Law, and Politics*, 11 YALE L. & POL'Y REV. 1 (1993); Gregg L. Spyridon, *Scientific Evidence vs. "Junk Science"—Proof of Medical Causation in Toxic Tort Litigation: The Fifth Circuit "Fryes" a New Test* (Christophersen v. Allied Signal Corp.), 61 MISS. L.J. 287 (1991).

including those alleging injury due to asbestos,[4] Bendectin,[5] electro-magnetic radiation,[6] IUDs,[7] silicone implants,[8] and tobacco products,[9] to mention just a few. This type of evidence has also been introduced with respect to a wide variety of other substances, including chlorine gas,[10] benzene,[11] herbicides,[12] pesticides,[13] solvents,[14] PCBs,[15] and pharmaceuticals.[16] Epidemiological studies have been well received by courts.[17] Well conducted studies are uniformly admitted. The widespread acceptance of epidemiology is based in large part on the belief that the general techniques are valid.[18]

The rules concerning the admissibility of epidemiological evidence are best understood at two different levels: at the population level and at the individual level.[19] At the population level the questions are: a) whether, in the absence of a body of epidemiological evidence, a scientist will be allowed to testify about the existence of a relationship between an exposure and an injury, and b) whether the injuries suffered by individuals in the epidemiological research are similar enough to the type of injury suffered by the plaintiff that the epidemiological evidence is probative as to the type of harm suffered by the plaintiff. At the individual level the question is whether scientists will be allowed to testify, based on epidemiological findings, that the individual

---

4. Hendrix v. Raybestos–Manhattan, Inc., 776 F.2d 1492 (11th Cir.1985); Keene Corp. v. Hall, 96 Md.App. 644, 626 A.2d 997 (1993); Caterinicchio v. Pittsburgh Corning Corp., 127 N.J. 428, 605 A.2d 1092 (1992).

5. Turpin v. Merrell Dow Pharmaceuticals, 959 F.2d 1349 (6th Cir.1992); Richardson v. Richardson–Merrell, Inc., 857 F.2d 823 (D.C.Cir.1988).

6. Reynard v. NEC Corp., 887 F.Supp. 1500 (M.D.Fla.1995).

7. Hawkinson v. A.H. Robins Co., Inc., 595 F.Supp. 1290 (D.Colo.1984) (Dalkon Shield); Marder v. G.D. Searle & Co., 630 F.Supp. 1087 (D.Md.1986), aff'd, 814 F.2d 655 (4th Cir.1987) (Copper 7).

8. Allison v. McGhan Medical Corp., 184 F.3d 1300, 1309 (11th Cir.1999).

9. Marsee v. United States Tobacco Co., 639 F.Supp. 466 (W.D.Okla.1986).

10. Valentine v. Pioneer Chlor Alkali Co., Inc., 921 F.Supp. 666 (D.Nev.1996).

11. Mason v. Texaco, Inc., 948 F.2d 1546 (10th Cir.1991).

12. Cuevas v. E.I. DuPont de Nemours & Co., 956 F.Supp. 1306 (S.D.Miss.1997).

13. Kannankeril v. Terminix International, Inc., 128 F.3d 802, 807 (3d Cir.1997); Mascarenas v. Miles, Inc., 986 F.Supp. 582 (W.D.Mo. 1997).

14. McDaniel v. CSX Transportation, Inc., 955 S.W.2d 257 (Tenn.1997); Schudel v. General Electric Co., 120 F.3d 991 (9th Cir.1997).

15. General Electric Co. v. Joiner, 522 U.S. 136, 118 S.Ct. 512, 139 L.Ed.2d 508 (1997).

16. Merrell Dow Pharmaceuticals, Inc. v. Havner, 953 S.W.2d 706, 708 (Tex.1997) (Bendectin); Rosen v. Ciba–Geigy Corporation, 78

F.3d 316 (7th Cir.1996) (nicotine patch); Haggerty v. The Upjohn Co., 950 F.Supp. 1160 (S.D.Fla.1996) (Halcion); Lust v. Merrell Dow Pharmaceuticals, Inc., 89 F.3d 594 (9th Cir. 1996) (fertility drug).

17. "The reliability of expert testimony founded on reasoning from epidemiological data is generally a fit subject for judicial notice; epidemiology is a well-established branch of science and medicine, and epidemiological evidence has been accepted in numerous cases." DeLuca v. Merrell Dow Pharmaceuticals, Inc., 911 F.2d 941, 954 (3d Cir.1990), on remand, 791 F.Supp. 1042, cert. denied, 510 U.S. 1044, 114 S.Ct. 691, 126 L.Ed.2d 658 (1994). For a rare case critical of epidemiological data, see *Bloomquist v. Wapello County*, 500 N.W.2d 1 (Iowa 1993):

There is a risk that the difference between epidemiologist testimony and the testimony of treating doctors might be confused by the jury and experts must make numerous subjective decisions in choosing the control population, evaluating the underlying data, and interpreting the results. The best that can be said for epidemiology is that it can prove the risk but cannot prove individual causation.

Id. at 4–5.

18. Epidemiology is a methodology. The practice of epidemiology involves sampling and matching so as to minimize systematic bias and statistical analysis designed to estimate the effect of random errors on results. Epidemiology is not a theory of how a substance causes cancer, or birth defects, or autoimmune disease. These theories come from other disciplines.

19. *See* Chapter 1.

plaintiff's injury is the result of an exposure to some substance. These two levels of analysis are sometimes referred to as questions of *general causation*—does the substance in question cause harm, and *specific causation*—did the substance cause this plaintiff's injury. This legal introduction will discuss these issues in turn.[20]

§ 7–1.2 Note: The Causal Questions and the Structure of Science

Both before and after *Daubert*, courts[21] and commentators[22] divided scientific evidence into several categories. For example, Professor Giannelli divided the question of scientific validity into "(1) the validity of the underlying principle, (2) the validity of the technique applying the principle, and (3) the proper application of the technique on a particular occasion."[23] This formulation is repeated by Judge Becker in *United States v. Downing*.[24] The Supreme Court *Daubert* opinion appears to adopt the first two categories when it distinguishes between a general theory and technique.[25] Quoting Thomas,[26] Faigman, Porter and Saks distinguish between (1) "the theory or principle that provides authority for the conclusions that are drawn from the data," (2) "the general technique or procedure that produces the data," and (3) "the specific practices used to obtain the data."[27] To these categories we may add a final one, (4) the conclusions the expert draws from the theory, the general technique and its specific application.[28] Superficially, it might seem that the general causation question concerns the first two categories, theory and general technique, while the specific causation question concerns the third category, specific practices as well as the expert's conclusions. This is not the case. Both general and specific causation can involve all four levels: theory, general method, specific application of the method, and conclusions about the individual case that are drawn from the research.

§ 7–1.3 Population Level Evidence: General Causation

§ 7–1.3.1 The Role of Epidemiological Evidence in Toxic Tort Cases

[1] The Absence of Epidemiological Data

In many cases there is no epidemiological evidence indicating a consistent statistically significant relationship between exposure and injury, either be-

---

20. From time to time commentators argue that the causal element should be relaxed or even eliminated in toxic tort cases usually citing the intricate causal problems such cases sometimes pose. *See* Steve Gold, *Causation in Toxic Torts: Burdens of Proof, Standards of Persuasion, and Statistical Evidence*, 96 YALE L.J. 376 (1986); Margaret Berger, *Eliminating General Causation: Notes Towards a New Theory of Justice and Toxic Torts*, 97 COLUM. L. REV. 2117 (1997). Few courts have seen fit to retreat from requiring the plaintiff to show general causation, though some have directly or indirectly relaxed the plaintiff's burden on specific causation.

21. *See* United States v. Downing, 753 F.2d 1224, 1234 (3d Cir.1985).

22. Paul Giannelli, *The Admissibility of Novel Scientific Evidence: Frye v. United States, a Half–Century Later*, 80 COLUM. L. REV. 1197 at 1201 (1980). *See* Faigman et al., *supra* note 3, at 1800.

23. *See* Giannelli, *supra* note 22 at 1201.

24. 753 F.2d at 1234 (1985).

25. Daubert v. Merrell Dow Pharmaceuticals, Inc., 509 U.S. 579, 591–93, 113 S.Ct. 2786, 125 L.Ed.2d 469 (1993).

26. William A. Thomas, *Some Observations by a Scientist*, 115 F.R.D. 142, 144 (1986).

27. *See* Faigman et al., *supra* note 3 at 1825–1827.

28. *See supra* Chapter 1.

cause there are no epidemiological studies on the topic or because existing epidemiological studies do not indicate a consistent significant relationship.[29] Before the rise of epidemiology in litigation, courts routinely permitted experts to testify about causation without aggregate data. Thus the cancer-trauma cases (cancer allegedly caused by a physical trauma such as a blow to the breast) typically involved treating physician testimony uninformed by epidemiological evidence.[30]

With the rise of epidemiology, however, courts were forced to confront the question of whether such evidence was essential to plaintiff's case. Some courts have allowed a plaintiff's case to proceed to the jury without epidemiological data. For example, in discussing whether dermal exposure to dilute solutions of paraquat could cause pulmonary fibrosis, the court in *Ferebee v. Chevron Chemical Company* concluded, "Thus, a cause-effect relationship need not be clearly established by animal or epidemiological studies before a doctor can testify that in his opinion such a relationship exists."[31] Other courts, however, have refused to allow the plaintiff to reach the jury in the absence of epidemiological evidence supporting his causal claims. In *Brock v. Merrell Dow Pharmaceuticals, Inc.*, the court entered a j.n.o.v. against the plaintiff, declaring, "the Brocks' failure to present statistically significant epidemiological proof that Bendectin causes limb reduction defects to be fatal to their case."[32] Few courts have been as dogmatic about the need for statistically significant epidemiological evidence, but in recent years when plaintiffs have lacked supporting epidemiological studies a number of opinions have found their causal evidence either inadmissible or insufficient to support a verdict that a particular exposure caused the plaintiff's injury.[33]

29. Callahan v. Cardinal Glennon Hosp., 863 S.W.2d 852 (Mo.1993) (en banc) (allowing experts to testify whether polio vaccine will develop into polio virus if a child's immune system becomes depressed without support of epidemiological evidence. The incidence of polio is very rare and there are no definitive studies).

30. *See* National Dairy Products Corp. v. Durham, 115 Ga.App. 420, 154 S.E.2d 752 (Ga. App.1967); Daly v. Bergstedt, 267 Minn. 244, 126 N.W.2d 242 (Minn.1964); New Orleans & Northeastern R.R. Co. v. Thornton, 191 So.2d 547 (Miss.1966).

31. 736 F.2d 1529, 1535 (D.C.Cir.1984). *See also* Wells v. Ortho Pharmaceutical Corp., 788 F.2d 741, 745 (11th Cir.1986); Donaldson v. Central Illinois Public Service Co., 313 Ill. App.3d 1061, 246 Ill.Dec. 388, 730 N.E.2d 68 (Ill.App.2000).

32. 874 F.2d 307 (5th Cir.), modified, 884 F.2d 166, 167 (5th Cir.1989). *Brock* is but one of a large number of opinions concerning Bendectin that have either declared the plaintiff's expert's testimony to be inadmissible or have concluded that the plaintiff's evidence is insufficient as a matter of law to sustain a plaintiff verdict. The Bendectin litigation is discussed in MICHAEL D. GREEN, BENDECTIN AND BIRTH DEFECTS: THE CHALLENGES OF MASS TOXIC SUBSTANCES LITIGA-

TION (1996); JOSEPH SANDERS, BENDECTIN ON TRIAL: A STUDY OF MASS TORT LITIGATION (1998).

33. *See* Prescott v. United States, 858 F.Supp. 1461 (D.Nev.1994) (cancer and ionizing radiation); Porter v. Whitehall Lab., Inc., 9 F.3d 607 (7th Cir.1993) (renal failure and ibuprofen); Conde v. Velsicol Chem. Corp., 24 F.3d 809, 813–14 (6th Cir.1994) (chlordane and headache, nausea, and abdominal pain. The opinion stated that "Nineteen epidemiological studies in humans have found little evidence of long-term adverse health effects from chlordane doses hundreds of times higher than those the Condes were subjected to under a worst-case scenario."); Sorensen v. Shaklee Corp., 31 F.3d 638 (8th Cir.1994) (children's mental retardation and mother ingestion of alfalfa tablet allegedly contaminated with ethylene oxide); Chambers v. Exxon Corp., 81 F.Supp.2d 661, 665 (M.D.La.2000) (many epidemiological studies failing to show an association between benzene exposure and CML); E.I. DuPont De Nemours & Co., Inc. v. Castillo, 748 So.2d 1108, 1120 (Fla.App.2000) ("We do not conclude that epidemiological studies are a mandatory prerequisite to establish a toxic substance's teratogenicity in human beings. We do, however, conclude that where, as here, plaintiffs wish to establish a substance's teratogenicity in human beings based on animal and in vitro studies, the methodology used in the studies, including the method of extrapo-

Complete order cannot be imposed on the different positions taken by the courts as to whether the plaintiff must present epidemiological data on general causation. The two following distinctions, however, explain many apparent inconsistencies: (a) whether the case involves a mass tort or not and (b) whether there is adverse epidemiology or no epidemiological evidence at all.

Boston[34] argues that cases requiring the plaintiff to present confirming epidemiological evidence to make out a prima facie case have typically involved mass exposures.[35] Cases that have not imposed this requirement typically involve injuries that may be placed in the "sporadic accident model of tort law."[36] In the latter type of cases, where only a single plaintiff or a few plaintiffs have allegedly suffered an injury due to some exposure, an expert is frequently permitted to render an opinion as to whether the exposure caused the plaintiff's injury. Examples of such cases include, specific medical treatments,[37] nonrecurring occupational diseases that affect a limited number of individuals[38] and site-specific injuries such as the PCB contamination of the

lating from the achieved results, must be generally accepted in the relevant scientific community.").

34. *See* Boston, *supra* note 2, at 181.

35. "In mass tort cases such as Agent Orange, epidemiological studies on causation assume a role of critical importance." *In re* "Agent Orange" Liability Litigation, 611 F.Supp. 1223, 1239 (E.D.N.Y.1985).

36. *See* Boston, *supra* note 2, at 188; Green, *supra* note 3, at 680–82.

37. For example, in *Reese v. Stroh*, 74 Wash.App. 550, 874 P.2d 200, review granted, 124 Wash.2d 1018, 881 P.2d 253 (1994), plaintiff claimed that a physician's failure to treat lung disease with Prolastin, a protein replacement, allegedly enhanced the patient's injury. The appellate court, applying the *Daubert* standard, ruled that the trial court erred in excluding the testimony of a physician who could not offer statistical evidence of the effectiveness of Prolastin.

In *Callahan*, 863 S.W.2d at 863, plaintiff experts were allowed to testify that failure to properly treat an abscess three weeks after infant received live polio vaccine resulted in suppression of immune system and infant's contraction of paralytic polio. Court held causation evidence was sufficient even though experts did not base their opinion on any epidemiological studies.

In *Zuchowicz v. United States*, 140 F.3d 381 (2d Cir.1998), the plaintiff's wife died from a fatal lung condition allegedly caused by the drug Danocrine. Mrs. Zuchowicz was negligently prescribed an overdose of the drug which she took daily for over a month. She continued taking the correct dosage of the medication for another two months, when due to adverse symptoms she was advised to cease. According to the plaintiff's experts, because of the rareness of primary pulmonary hypertension and

the lack of any formal research on the effects of the drug at this dose rates, they could not point to specific research supporting their differential diagnosis that the drug caused the decedent's illness. However, they could point to studies showing other agents such as birth control pills, some appetite suppressants, and chemotherapy drugs cause this illness. In support of the conclusion to affirm the trial court's decision to admit the testimony, Judge Calabresi noted the experts were able to provide a biologically plausible reason why the drug could cause this effect. *Id.* at 387.

38. *Ferebee*, 736 F.2d at 1535 (dermal exposure to dilute solutions of paraquat allegedly causing pulmonary fibrosis); Westberry v. Gislaved Gummi, 178 F.3d 257 (4th Cir.1999) (airborne talc allegedly caused aggravation of pre-existing sinus condition); McCullock v. H.B. Fuller Co., 61 F.3d 1038 (2d Cir.1995) (glue fumes allegedly causing throat polyps); Kennedy v. Collagen Corp., 974 F.2d 1342 (9th Cir.1992) (collagen allegedly causing systemic immunological injuries); Villari v. Terminix Int'l, Inc., 692 F.Supp. 568 (E.D.Pa.1988) (termiticide potentially causing cancer); Peteet v. Dow Chem. Co., 868 F.2d 1428 (5th Cir. 1989) (herbicide allegedly caused Hodgkin's disease); Becker v. National Health Prod., Inc., 896 F.Supp. 100 (N.D.N.Y.1995) (Hot Stuff "anabolic activator" allegedly caused diverticulosis and diverticulitis); Glaser v. Thompson Medical Co., 32 F.3d 969 (6th Cir.1994) (Dexitrim allegedly caused hypertension leading to intracranial bleeding); Stewart v. F.W. Woolworth Co., 154 App.Div. 956, 139 N.Y.S. 1146 (1913) (parakeet bite allegedly caused hepatitis, plaintiff doctor allowed to testify based solely on differential diagnosis); Earl v. Cryovac, 115 Idaho 1087, 772 P.2d 725 (Idaho App. 1989) (pulmonary disease allegedly caused by exposure to fumes from plastic film used in meat packing room). The court noted "that the

Paoli railroad yard.[39]

In many of these cases there is relatively little or no epidemiological data available[40] and the courts are reluctant to burden "first plaintiffs" with the task of using epidemiology to prove general causation.[41] Most courts, however,

plaintiff's claim in a toxic tort case does not fail merely because the circumstantial evidence and the expert opinions are unsupported by animal or epidemiological studies confirming the existence of a cause-and-effect relationship." *Id.* at 733.

39. *In re* Paoli R.R. Yard PCB Litig., 35 F.3d 717, 760 (3d Cir.1994) (polychlorinated biphenyls allegedly cause a variety of injuries). *See* Heller v. Shaw, 167 F.3d 146, 155 (3d Cir.1999) (Plaintiff's respiratory illnesses were caused by volatile organic compounds emitted from new carpet installed in home. Judge Becker specifically rejected the requirement that plaintiff's expert must always cite published studies on general causation to reliably conclude that a particular object caused a particular illness.); Rubanick v. Witco Chem. Corp., 125 N.J. 421, 593 A.2d 733 (N.J.1991) (PCBs allegedly caused colon cancer); Bloomquist v. Wapello County, 500 N.W.2d 1 (Iowa 1993).

40. In *Mendes–Silva v. United States*, 980 F.2d 1482 (D.C.Cir.1993) the plaintiff claimed that her simultaneous vaccination for Yellow Fever and small pox caused encephalomyelitis. While there were epidemiological studies finding no causal relationship between the plaintiff's injury and each of the vaccines separately, there was no epidemiology supporting or rejecting the effect of simultaneous vaccinations. The plaintiff's experts relied on non-epidemiological evidence, including, Adverse Drug Reports (ADR's) submitted by physicians to argue for causation. *Id.* at 1485. The Circuit court reversed trial court summary judgment for the government following the exclusion of plaintiff's expert testimony under FRE 703. Judge Mikva relied on *Ferebee*, "a cause-effect relationship need not be clearly established by animal or epidemiological studies before a doctor can testify that, in his opinion, such a relationship exists." 736 F.2d at 1535. He distinguished this case from the rulings in *Richardson v. Richardson–Merrell, Inc.*, 857 F.2d 823 (D.C.Cir.1988) and *Ealy v. Richardson–Merrell, Inc.*, 897 F.2d 1159 (D.C.Cir.1990).

First, *Richardson* and *Ealy* do not rely on an abstract temporal argument, but rather on the existence of a longstanding series of published epidemiological studies that were irreconcilable with the plaintiffs' theory. Again, the parties agree that no such contradicting epidemiological studies exist in this case. Second, the epidemiological question in this case is on the frontier of medical science in the sense that no clear answer has been found—research ceased when the question of the combined effect of the two vaccines was rendered moot in the scientific community

by the eradication of smallpox. Thus, this case presents the same type of novel, yet properly grounded, medical conclusion that *Ferebee* held must be presented to the factfinder.

Id. at 1487. *See* Kennedy v. Collagen Corp., 974 F.2d 1342 (9th Cir.1992) (unpublished disposition) for a similar analysis.

In *Bloomquist v. Wapello*, 500 N.W.2d 1 (Iowa 1993), the plaintiffs claimed that exposure to a number of indoor air pollutants, including the insecticide Durasban, caused various injuries including respiratory problems, immune problems, brain damage, urinary incontinence, and fecal incontinence. The trial court entered a j.n.o.v. based on the failure of plaintiffs to show the pollution was the proximate cause of the injuries. The Supreme Court reversed:

If we were to require epidemiological evidence in all cases of toxic tort injury, we would automatically deny recovery to all claimants who are injured by a toxic substance that is relatively new and as to which a statistical track record has not yet been fully established. We decline to apply a per se requirement of epidemiological evidence simply because of a lack of substantial numbers of cases. The lack of similar cases, of course, would affect the weight of the plaintiffs' evidence of proximate cause.

Id. at 5.

See also Bowers v. Northern Telecom, Inc., 905 F.Supp. 1004 (N.D.Fla.1995) (design of computer keyboard allegedly caused "cumulative trauma disorders." Plaintiff's experts' testimony admissible even without epidemiological evidence. Court says no definitive epidemiological studies have been conducted.); Benedi v. McNeil–P.P.C. Incorporated, 66 F.3d 1378 (4th Cir.1995) (the trial judge did not abuse his discretion in allowing the case to go to the jury even though the plaintiff had not introduced any epidemiological evidence of the relationship between Tylenol and liver damage. Apparently, neither side introduced any epidemiology on point.); Reese v. Stroh, 74 Wash.App. 550, 874 P.2d 200 (Wash.App.1994) (no epidemiological data available).

41. Joiner v. General Elec. Co., 864 F.Supp. 1310, 1322 (N.D.Ga.1994), rev'd, Joiner v. General Electric Co., 78 F.3d 524 (11th Cir. 1996); rev'd, General Electric Co. v. Joiner, 522 U.S. 136, 118 S.Ct. 512, 139 L.Ed.2d 508 (1997); Bloomquist v. Wapello County, 500 N.W.2d 1, 5 (Iowa 1993) ("If we were to require epidemiological evidence in all cases of

will require an expert to present some evidence of general causation.[42]

On the other hand, when there is a substantial body of negative epidemiological evidence, this by itself may defeat the plaintiff's claim, either because the court rules that any other evidence the plaintiff's expert might use to show causation is inadmissible,[43] or because the evidence is insufficient to support a plaintiff verdict as a matter of law.[44] The District of Columbia

toxic tort injury, we would automatically deny recovery to all claimants who are injured by a toxic substance that is relatively new and as to which a statistical track record has not yet been fully established."); Ambrosini v. Labarraque, 101 F.3d 129 (D.C.Cir.1996); Graham v. Playtex Products, Inc., 993 F.Supp. 127 (N.D.N.Y.1998); Pick v. American Medical Systems, Inc., 958 F.Supp. 1151, 1158 (E.D.La. 1997); Globetti v. Sandoz Pharmaceuticals Corp., 111 F.Supp.2d 1174 (N.D.Ala.2000).

As epidemiological evidence develops over time, courts may change their view as to whether testimony based on other evidence is admissible. In this regard it is worth comparing *Wells v. Ortho Pharmaceutical Corp.*, 788 F.2d 741 (11th Cir.1986) with *Smith v. Ortho Pharmaceutical Corp.*, 770 F.Supp. 1561 (N.D.Ga.1991). Both involve allegations that the use of spermicide caused a birth defect. At the time of the *Wells* case there was limited epidemiological evidence and this type of claim was relatively novel. In a bench trial the court found for the plaintiff. Affirming, the 11th Circuit said,

> We recognize, as did the *Ferebee* court, that a cause-effect relationship need not be clearly established before a doctor can testify that, in his opinion, such a relationship exists. As long as the basic methodology employed to reach such a conclusion is sound, such as use of tissue samples, standard tests, and patient examination, products liability law does not preclude recovery until a "statistically significant" number of people have been injured or until science has had the "time and resources to complete sophisticated laboratory studies of the chemical."

Wells, 788 F.2d at 745.

The *Smith* court, writing five years later, noted that, "The issue of causation with respect to spermicide and birth defects has been extensively researched since the *Wells* decision." *Smith*, 770 F.Supp. at 1562–63. The court found the plaintiff's experts' testimony inadmissible under 703 because their opinion was not based on the type of data reasonably relied upon by experts in the field. *Id.* at 1681. A similar trend may be appearing in the silicone implant/ autoimmune disease litigation. *See* Chapter 40.

42. *See* David L. Faigman, David H. Kaye, Michael J. Saks & Joseph Sanders, Modern Scientific Evidence: The Law and Science of Expert Testimony, Chapter 20 (2d ed. 2002).

43. *In re* "Agent Orange", 611 F.Supp. 1223 (E.D.N.Y.1985); Lynch v. Merrell–National Laboratories, 646 F.Supp. 856 (D.Mass. 1986); Richardson v. Richardson–Merrell, Inc., 857 F.2d 823 (D.C.Cir.1988); Allison v. McGhan Med. Corp., 184 F.3d 1300, 1316 (11th Cir.1999) (noting that "case studies pale in comparison" in the face of "population-based epidemiological studies" and that the district court did not abuse its discretion by discounting expert's "reliance on case reports in the face of the overwhelming contrary epidemiological evidence presented"). *But see Longmore*, 737 F.Supp. at 1121:

> Animal studies are generally relied upon by experts determining the link between a drug and birth defects and the same is true for chemical analysis. While the Court will leave open the question of the admissibility of particular studies during the trial of this matter, the Court cannot now preclude all such studies under Rule 703.

The failure of several studies to find a statistically significant relationship between the drug Parlodel and stroke was clearly a factor in the trial judge's decision in *Hollander v. Sandoz Pharmaceuticals Corp.*, 95 F.Supp.2d 1230, 1236 (W.D.Okla.2000) to exclude plaintiff's experts' testimony based on animal studies, and case reports. *Id.* at 1238. *Hollander* is but one of a number of cases involving Parlodal, a drug given to prevent postpartum physiological lactation. As the court in *Glastetter v. Novartis Pharmaceuticals Corp.*, 107 F.Supp.2d 1015, 1044 (E.D.Mo.2000), affirmed 252 F.3d 986 (8th Cir.2001), notes "plaintiffs' experts' opinions are not based upon any epidemiological studies. In the absence of such studies, as well as the absence of any other reliable evidence supporting the plaintiffs' experts' opinions with respect to causation, the Court is unable to find that plaintiffs' experts' opinions are grounded on reliable scientific evidence." *But see* Globetti v. Sandoz Pharmaceuticals Corp., 111 F.Supp.2d 1174 (N.D.Ala.2000); Kuhn v. Sandoz Pharmaceuticals Corp., 270 Kan. 443, 14 P.3d 1170 (Kan.2000) (refusing to apply Kansas' *Frye* test to "pure opinion" testimony).

44. Brock v. Merrell Dow Pharmaceuticals, Inc., 874 F.2d 307 (5th Cir.1989), modified on reh'g, 884 F.2d 166; Turpin v. Merrell Dow Pharmaceuticals, Inc., 959 F.2d 1349 (6th Cir. 1992); *Conde*, 24 F.3d at 813–14 (6th Cir.1994).

Circuit Court distinguished *Richardson v. Richardson–Merrell* from *Ferebee* on this dimension:

> The case before us, however, is not like *Ferebee*. Indeed, we are at the other end of the spectrum, a great distance from the "frontier of current medical and epidemiological inquiry." And far from a paucity of scientific information on the oft-asserted claim of causal relationship of Bendectin and birth defects, the drug has been extensively studied and a wealth of published epidemiological data has been amassed, none of which has concluded that the drug is teratogenic. Uniquely to this case, the law now has the benefit of twenty years of scientific study, and the published results must be given their just due.[45]

A pair of more recent ethylene oxide (EtO) cases reach the same result. In *Nelson v. American Sterilizer Co.*,[46] and *Allen v. Pennsylvania Engineering Corp.*,[47] the courts ruled that when a body of epidemiological research has failed to uncover a relationship between EtO exposure and the plaintiff's ailment, the results of animal studies are inconclusive at best and fail to exhibit the level of reliability required by Rule 702.[48]

[2] The Quality and Relevance of Epidemiological Data

When epidemiological evidence does exist, the courts are confronted with the question of whether it is admissible to prove general causation. The cases addressing the admissibility of epidemiological testimony have created a complex and sometimes contradictory mosaic. The relationship between asbestos exposure and several diseases, including asbestosis, lung cancer and

---

45. *Richardson*, 857 F.2d at 831–32. *But see*, Grant v. Secretary of Dept. of HHS, 956 F.2d 1144, 1149 (Fed.Cir.1992) (This is a case under the Childhood Vaccine Act. The appellate court affirmed a special master finding that the Quadrigen variety of the DTP vaccine caused the plaintiff's injury. The Court concluded that the epidemiological studies cited by Secretary that showed no causal relationship between DTP vaccine and plaintiff's injuries were not dispositive because they examined all DTP vaccines and, therefore, could not resolve the question as to whether Quadrigen could cause the plaintiff's injury).

46. 223 Mich.App. 485, 566 N.W.2d 671, 672 (Mich.App.1997) (EtO and liver disease).

47. 102 F.3d 194, 195 (5th Cir.1996) (EtO and brain cancer).

48. The district court in *National Bank of Commerce v. Dow Chemical Co.*, 965 F.Supp. 1490, 1519 (E.D.Ark.1996), cited one epidemiological study favoring the defendant's opinion as part of the basis for granting a motion for summary judgment in a case in which the plaintiff alleged that exposure to Dursban LO had caused her birth defects. However, the court did not reach the question as to whether this study would preclude testimony based on other evidence.

The Eleventh Circuit questioned the testimony of an expert in a silicone implant case because he did not "explain why the results of these animal studies should trump more than twenty controlled epidemiological studies of breast implants in humans which have found no valid increased risk of autoimmune disease." Allison v. McGhan Medical Corp., 184 F.3d 1300, 1314 (11th Cir.1999).

The district court in *Castellow v. Chevron USA*, 97 F.Supp.2d 780, 796 (S.D.Tex.2000) rejected the plaintiff's expert's testimony in part because they were unable through toxicological evidence to overcome the epidemiological evidence which shows "that persons exposed to gasoline do not exhibit a statistically significant excess rate of AML, or even leukemias generally." *Id.* at 798.

In *Chambers v. Exxon Corp.*, 81 F.Supp.2d 661 (M.D.La.2000) the plaintiff's expert wished to testify that the plaintiffs chronic myelogenous leukemia was caused by asbestos exposure. The judge held that the testimony was inadmissible in the absence of epidemiological research that establishes a statistically significant risk of contracting CML from benzene exposure. The court noted that "there is no lack of epidemiological studies. On the contrary, experts offered by Exxon have produced a number of scientifically performed studies which demonstrate no association between exposure to benzene and development of CML." *Id.* at 665.

mesothelioma,[49] between the use of tampons and toxic shock,[50] or between the use of tobacco products and a wide range of ailments[51] are so firmly established in the epidemiological literature that they are beyond dispute. Because the techniques of epidemiological analysis are now so well accepted, a body of statistically significant and substantively important epidemiological evidence would probably suffice to prove general causation even if the plaintiff were unable to provide a good scientific theory as to how the exposure caused a given injury.[52] Unfortunately, the clear examples are outnumbered by the uncertain ones.

Some order can be brought to the cases, however, by focusing on several factors that influence admissibility. Epidemiological evidence is most clearly admissible when it is based on a number of well designed, large studies that indicate a strong and statistically significant relationship between the exact substance to which the plaintiff was exposed and the exact injury the plaintiff has suffered at a dose rate identical to that the plaintiff is known to have experienced. As each of these factors (design of studies, number of studies, strength of the relationship, statistical significance of the relationship, substance similarity, injury similarity, dose rate similarity) is removed, the value of the epidemiological research is weakened and the admissibility of the testimony becomes more problematical. Some examples indicate the nature of the issues involved.

[a] Study Design

As discussed in section 2 of this chapter, epidemiological studies vary widely in their quality. Poorly designed or poorly implemented studies may suffer from numerous threats to the validity of a conclusion about a relationship between an exposure and an injury. Such studies are an example of the improper application of a technique on a particular occasion. Occasionally, testimony based on poorly executed research is excluded on this ground alone. Such studies are the improper application of epidemiological methods. In *In re TMI Litigation Cases Consolidated II*,[53] the district court excluded the testimony of the plaintiff's epidemiological evidence based on design considerations. The expert did not select the groups to be studied, but rather data from each group were provided to him by non-epidemiologist consultants hired by plaintiffs' counsel. The court found that since the selection criteria were unknown, the error rate was potentially large.[54]

49. Peter H. Schuck, *The Worst Should Go First: Deferral Registries in Asbestos Litigation*, 15 Harv. J. L. & Pub. Pol'y 541, 545–47 (1992). *See* Cimino v. Raymark Indus., 751 F.Supp. 649, 653–55 (E.D.Tex.1990), where Judge Parker divided claimants into groups based on their worksite, trade or craft, and disease category. These groups were designed to reflect the duration and intensity of each plaintiff's exposure because the scientific evidence indicates a significant dose-response relationship between asbestos exposure and most asbestos related diseases.

50. Kehm v. Procter & Gamble Manuf. Co., 724 F.2d 613 (8th Cir.1983).

51. Robert L. Rabin, *A Sociolegal History of the Tobacco Tort Litigation*, 44 Stan. L. Rev. 853 (1992). Cipollone v. Liggett Group, Inc., 693 F.Supp. 208 (D.N.J.1988), rev'd in part, aff'd in part, 893 F.2d 541 (3d Cir.1990), rev'd in part, aff'd in part, 505 U.S. 504, 112 S.Ct. 2608, 120 L.Ed.2d 407 (1992).

52. *See* Giannelli, *supra* note 22, at 1212 (stating that "if the technique is generally accepted, then the theory must be valid although not fully understood or explainable.").

53. 922 F.Supp. 1038 (M.D.Pa.1996).

54. *Id.* at 1047–48. For example, one of the groups on which the expert performed an epidemiological analysis was a cohort of 69 wom-

The district court in the *TMI* case noted that one reason to exclude the testimony was that there was no way to know the selection criteria used to choose the groups to be studied. Absent this knowledge, the defendant would have a relatively difficult time attacking the testimony on cross.[55] A similar result was reached in *Valentine v. Pioneer Chlor Alkali Company, Inc.*[56] Plaintiff's expert, who also treated the plaintiffs, conducted an epidemiological study in which the cases were seven individuals exposed to chlorine gas (all of whom were at one time involved in the litigation and all of whom were patients referred to an environmental clinic specializing in neurotoxicology) and compared them to a control group of individuals in another town (and, therefore, unexposed to chlorine gas) matched by age, sex and educational attainment.[57] Following a useful discussion of the methodological problems with the research design, the court excluded the expert's testimony based on this study because they were not derived from acceptable scientific methodology.[58]

The preceding cases largely involve research done to further litigation. Usually, however, when the study design is known, is reasonable on its face, and is not conducted for purposes of litigation, courts will allow testimony based on the research and allow design limitations to go to the weight to be given the results.[59] In *In re Orthopedic Bone Screw Products Liability Litigation*,[60] the court reviewed several defense objections to a cohort study (selec-

en employed by the Hesteco Manufacturing Co. who were at work at the time of the accident. Ten developed cancer following the accident. This cohort had a higher incidence of cancer than a comparable group of women from the general population. *Id.* at 1046. If we imagine many groups that could have been selected instead of the Hesteco group and that each group would have a very different incidence rate and therefore a different odds ratio when compared to women from the general population, the problem with this research can be seen as one of error rate. If the incidence rate across such groups is very high, as it almost certainly would be, the error rate would also be high. Obviously, this study also is threatened by a selection bias. The court excluded the testimony on both Rule 702 and Rule 703 grounds. "Based upon the foregoing, the court will exclude the proffered testimony as scientifically unreliable pursuant to Rule 702. In addition to the study's lack of scientific reliability, the court finds, pursuant to Rule 703, that Dr. Sterling improperly relied upon data that other experts in the field would find to be unreliable." 922 F.Supp. at 1048. The Third Circuit affirmed the trial court's exclusion of this testimony, *In re* TMI Litigation, 193 F.3d 613, 708 (3d Cir.1999).

55. 922 F.Supp. at 1048.

56. 921 F.Supp. 666 (D.Nev.1996).

57. *Id.* at 676.

58. *Id.* at 677. "In summary, Dr. Kilburn's study suffers from very serious flaws. He took no steps to eliminate selection bias in the study group, he failed to identify the background rate for the observed disorders in the Henderson community, he failed to control for potential recall bias, he simply ignored the lack of reliable dosage data, he chose a tiny sample size, and he did not attempt to eliminate so-called confounding factors which might have been responsible for the incidence of neurological disorders in the subject group." *Id.*

See also DeLuca v. Merrell Dow Pharmaceuticals, Inc., 791 F.Supp. 1042 (D.N.J.1992) (the trial judge concluded that an expert's reanalysis of existing data and the use of preliminary data from a subsequently published source constituted the use of facts and data not ordinarily relied upon by experts in the field.); McKenzie v. Westinghouse Electric Co., 674 A.2d 1167, 1172 (Pa.Cmwlth.1996) (plaintiff attempted to demonstrate that a pregnant mother's exposure to trichloroethylene (TCE) and dichloroethylene (DCE) caused a fatal heart defect in her child partly on the basis of two studies he conducted on cardiac defects in Arizona. The studies were methodologically flawed and contradicted other, better designed research.); Muzzey v. Kerr–McGee Chemical Corp., 921 F.Supp. 511 (N.D.Ill.1996), the plaintiff attempted to use evidence from a cancer cluster that exposure to ionizing radiation causes polycythemia vera (PV). However, studies on survivors of the atomic bomb attack on Hiroshima and Nagasaki do not indicate any relationship. *Id.* at 517.

59. Glaser v. Thompson Medical Co., 32 F.3d 969, 975 (6th Cir.1994); Ellis v. Int'l Playtex, Inc., 745 F.2d 292, 303 (4th Cir.1984).

60. 1997 WL 230818 (E.D.Pa.1997).

tion bias, information bias, loss to follow-up, and confounding) but found that the admitted weaknesses of the study did not warrant a finding of inadmissibility.[61] Most cases that exclude testimony based on epidemiological evidence do so on grounds other than research design.

[b] Number of Studies

The number of epidemiological studies is sometimes cited as a reason for an admissibility decision. In *Allen v. Pennsylvania Engineering Corp.*,[62] the court cited a lack of positive epidemiological studies linking EtO exposure to brain cancer as a reason to exclude plaintiff's expert's testimony.[63] Similarly, in *National Bank of Commerce v. Dow Chemical Co.*,[64] the court noted there was a single study on the effects of exposure to Dursban on fetal development, and it failed to show a relationship. On the other hand, in *McDaniel v. CSX Transportation, Inc.*[65] the Tennessee Supreme Court held that the trial judge did not abuse his discretion in admitting testimony on the relationship between chronic exposure to four organic solvents and plaintiffs' brain damage. The plaintiffs' experts based their opinion on epidemiological studies done in Scandinavia in the 1970s and although later research failed to replicate these results, nevertheless they constitute a sufficient basis for the expert's opinion.[66]

[c] Substance Similarity

The Supreme Court, in its *Joiner* opinion[67] declaring that "abuse of discretion" is the appropriate standard for appellate courts to use when

61. "In sum, there is no such thing as a perfect epidemiological study. Each one has its weaknesses. The more shortcomings attendant in a particular study, the less reliable the study becomes. The court recognizes that the Cohort Study, like any cohort study, on close scrutiny, could most likely be improved. However, the court serves as the 'gatekeeper' of admissible scientific evidence and not as a scientific review board. Moreover, the Federal Rules of Evidence 'embody a strong and undeniable preference for admitting any evidence having some potential for assisting the trier of fact and for dealing with the risk of error through the adversary process.' DeLuca, 911 F.2d at 956. In this instance, the court concludes that taking all the weaknesses plaintiffs identify cumulatively into account, they do not render the Cohort Study so unreliable as to prevent it from crossing the *Paoli II* threshold for scientific reliability." *Id.* at *8.

62. 102 F.3d 194 (5th Cir.1996).

63. *Nelson v. American Sterilizer Co.*, 223 Mich.App. 485, 566 N.W.2d 671 (Mich.App. 1997), another EtO case, reached a similar result. It is important to note that there had been a good deal of epidemiological research on the adverse effects of EtO.

64. 965 F.Supp. 1490, 1519 (E.D.Ark.W.D. 1996).

65. 955 S.W.2d 257 (Tenn.1997).

66. *Id.* at 265. In *McDaniel*, the Supreme Court held that the adoption of Tennessee Rules of Evidence 702 and 703 did supersede the general acceptance test of *Frye*. Specifically, the rules require a determination as to the scientific validity or reliability of proffered evidence. The court did not expressly adopt *Daubert* but it did set forth five factors Tennessee trial courts may consider in determining reliability: (1) whether scientific evidence has been tested and the methodology with which it has been tested; (2) whether the evidence has been subjected to peer review or publication; (3) whether a potential rate of error is known; (4) whether, as formerly required by *Frye*, the evidence is generally accepted in the scientific community; and (5) whether the expert's research in the field has been conducted independent of litigation. *Id.*

Williams v. Hedican, 561 N.W.2d 817 (Iowa 1997) (any shortcomings in study showing the effectiveness of varicella-zoster immune globulin (VZIG) in destroying chicken-pox virus go to weight).

67. General Electric Co. v. Joiner, 522 U.S. 136, 118 S.Ct. 512, 139 L.Ed.2d 508 (1997).

reviewing admissibility decisions of trial courts, affirmed the trial court's exclusion of plaintiff experts in part because of the lack of substance similarity. Two of the four epidemiological studies relied upon by plaintiffs to show a causal relationship between PCB exposure and cancer in fact had involved other substances. One involved mineral oil and did not mention PCBs while the other involved workers exposed to numerous potential carcinogens, including toxic rice oil that they had ingested.[68]

In *Schudel v. General Electric Co.*,[69] the plaintiff's expert testified that the plaintiff suffered from solvent-induced toxic encephalopathy due to exposure to the solvents trichloroethane (TCA) and perchloroethylene (Perc) based on studies that involved organic solvents other than TCA or Perc.[70] Following a jury verdict for the plaintiff, the defendant appealed the trial court decision to admit this testimony. The appellate court concluded that admitting the testimony was in error, noting the plaintiff's expert agreed the mechanism of neurotoxicity from TCA and Perc had not been demonstrated.[71]

If the underlying processes are the same, however, a study does not have to examine a situation identical to that of the plaintiff to be admissible. Thus, in *Pick v. American Medical Systems*,[72] the plaintiff claimed a silicone penile implant caused auto-immune disease. Over the defendant's objection the court was prepared to admit epidemiological studies on the relationship between silicone breast implants and autoimmune disease.[73]

[d] Injury Similarity

Plaintiffs frequently allege that a substance known to cause one type of harm has caused them to suffer a different type of harm. Admissibility decisions often turn on the court's assessment of the degree of similarity between the two types of injuries.[74] For example, in *Valentine v. Pioneer Chlor Alkali Co. Inc.*,[75] plaintiffs claimed that exposure to chlorine caused damage to their brain and central nervous system. Although chlorine gas is known to be toxic and to do serious damage to an individual's pulmonary system (it is a major component of mustard gas), the court disallowed the testimony of one expert and allowed the testimony of a second only if he could point to specific research linking chlorine gas exposure to neural injuries.[76] In *Estate of*

---

68. 522 U.S. at 146.

69. 120 F.3d 991 (9th Cir.1997).

70. *Id.* at 997.

71. *Id.* at 997. *See also* Becker v. Baron Bros., 138 N.J. 145, 649 A.2d 613 (N.J.1994) (questioning whether chrysotile asbestos fibers have the capacity to produce mesotheliomas in humans).

72. 958 F.Supp. 1151 (E.D.La.1997).

73. *Id.* at 1160. The court, however, entered summary judgment because the scientific evidence was legally insufficient to prove specific causation.

74. In *Tyler v. Sterling Drug, Inc.*, 19 F.Supp.2d 1239 (N.D.Okla.1998), the court admitted epidemiological studies examining the relationship of aspirin consumption and Reyes Syndrome. This was both the same substance and the same ailment involved in the litigation.

75. 921 F.Supp. 666 (D.Nev.1996).

76. *Id.* at 677. In *Christophersen v. Allied–Signal Corp.*, 939 F.2d 1106, 1115–16 (5th Cir.1991), the appellate court (en banc) found that the trial judge was acting within his discretion when he ruled the plaintiff's expert testimony to be inadmissible. The expert wished to testify in part that epidemiological research supports a relationship between exposure to cadmium and nickel particles and small cell lung cancer and that the same exposures that are associated with carcinoma of the lung are likely to be associated with similar small-cell cancers elsewhere in the body, including the colon, the site of the plaintiff's tumor.

Mitchell v. Gencorp, Inc.,[77] the court excluded epidemiological studies showing a relationship between benzene exposure and acute meyelogenous leukemia (AML) holding that based on these studies experts could not jump to the conclusion that benzene exposure causes chronic myelogenous leukemia (CML).[78]

Again, however, a similarity requirement does not prohibit all extrapolation. Following a *Frye* analysis, the Illinois Appellate court in *Duran v. Cullinan*,[79] concluded that plaintiff experts could testify that an oral contraceptive caused the birth defects based on extrapolation from 43 epidemiological studies describing a relationship between oral contraceptives and birth defects even though none of the studies described the type of defect suffered by the plaintiff.

[e] Dosage

Dosage is often a problem for plaintiffs in cases involving exposures to chemicals in the workplace or elsewhere.[80] Sometimes, the problem is simply one of a lack of evidence. In *Allen v. Pennsylvania Engineering Corp.*,[81] the Fifth Circuit affirmed the exclusion on both Rule 702 and Rule 703 grounds of expert testimony that workplace exposure to ethylene oxide caused the plaintiff's decedent's brain cancer, in part because of the difficulty of establishing his workplace exposure. The court noted, "The experts actually knew more about Allen's exposure to EtO through his smoking a pack of cigarettes a day than they did about his occupational exposure to the chemical."[82]

It is not the case, however, that plaintiffs must have a precise measurement of their exposure in order for their experts' testimony be admissible. For example, in *Kannankeril v. Terminix International, Inc.*,[83] the Third Circuit reversed a district court decision to exclude the testimony of plaintiff's expert. The court held that the expert could rely on Terminix's application records to estimate the plaintiff's exposure.[84]

Sometimes dosages are known, or can reasonably be estimated, and the exposure experienced by the plaintiff is sufficiently below the known levels of

---

77. 968 F.Supp. 592, 600 (D.Kan.1997).

78. The court in *Chambers v. Exxon Corp.*, 81 F.Supp.2d 661, 664 (M.D.La.2000) reached the same conclusion. *See also* Austin v. Kerr–McGee Refining Corp., 25 S.W.3d 280, 290 (Tex.App.2000).

79. 286 Ill.App.3d 1005, 222 Ill.Dec. 465, 677 N.E.2d 999 (Ill.App.1997).

80. Dosage issues arise with respect to toxicological evidence as well. In *General Electric Co. v. Joiner*, 522 U.S. 136, 118 S.Ct. 512, 139 L.Ed.2d 508 (1997), the Supreme Court affirmed a trial court exclusion of expert opinion that the plaintiff's PCB exposure caused his cancer insofar as it was based on animal studies showing that infant (but not adult) mice developed cancer after exposure to PCBs. The mice had massive doses of highly concentrated PCBs injected directly into their peritoneums or stomachs. Joiner's exposure was much lower. In addition the mice contracted a different type of cancer than the plaintiff suffered from.

81. 102 F.3d 194, 198 (5th Cir.1996).

82. *Id.* at 198. *See also*, Wintz v. Northrop Corporation, 110 F.3d 508, 513 (7th Cir.1997); Valentine v. Pioneer Chlor Alkali Company, Inc., 921 F.Supp. 666, 676 (D.Nev.1996); Cuevas v. E.I. DuPont de Nemours & Co., 956 F.Supp. 1306, 1312 (S.D.Miss.1997); Savage v. Union Pacific R.R., 67 F.Supp.2d 1021 (E.D.Ark.W.D.1999); Castellow v. Chevron USA, 97 F.Supp.2d 780, 796 (S.D.Tex.2000) ("[T]here is no reliable evidence before this court on the amount of benzene, from gasoline or any other source, to which Mr. Castellow was exposed.") In some cases the plaintiff may not be able to prove that he was even exposed to the chemical in question. Mascarenas v. Miles, Inc., 986 F.Supp. 582 (W.D.Mo.1997).

83. 128 F.3d 802 (3d Cir.1997).

84. *Id.* at 808. *See also*, Sheridan v. Catering Management, Inc., 5 Neb.App. 305, 558 N.W.2d 319, 323 (Neb.App.1997).

toxicity that a court will conclude that expert opinions claiming there is a causal relationship between exposure and the plaintiff's illness are inadmissible. In *Sutera v. The Perrier Group of America*,[85] the plaintiff alleged that regular consumption of Perrier sparkling mineral water caused him to contract acute promyelocytic leukemia (APL). During the time the plaintiff consumed the product it was sufficiently contaminated with benzene that the U.S. FDA ordered a recall of some flavors produced between January 1989 and February 1990. The court concluded that the plaintiff's expert's opinion that there was a "probable causal relationship" between the plaintiff's leukemia and benzene exposure was not based on reliable scientific evidence, primarily because the plaintiff's level of exposure was far below the exposure shown to cause leukemia in epidemiological and animal studies.[86]

Dosage was also an issue in the Three Mile Island litigation. In In re TMI Litigation Consolidated Proceedings,[87] the plaintiffs' offered the testimony of a number of experts that radiation exposure caused plaintiffs' injuries that were premised on a dose in excess of 100 rems. However, the key expert witness who originally was to testify that plaintiffs' actually were exposed to this level of radiation "recanted the bulk his opinions in an unsolicited voicemail message left with counsel for Defendants."[88] Absent this testimony, the testimony of the other experts no longer fit the facts of the case and the judge granted the defendant a summary judgment on sufficiency grounds.

In asbestos litigation, courts have developed a special set of concepts to assist with problems showing level of exposure. The "frequency, regularity and proximity test"[89] has been he most widely used. Generally, this test has

---

85. 986 F.Supp. 655 (D.Mass.1997).

86. *Id.* at 662. In *In re "Agent Orange" Product Liability Litigation*, 611 F.Supp. 1223, 1238, 1241 (E.D.N.Y.1985), Judge Weinstein concluded that studies dealing with the effect of exposure to dioxin in industrial settings amounted to no more than "a scintilla of evidence," apparently because there was no evidence the plaintiffs were exposed to the very high doses involved in the industrial exposure studies.

In *Schudel v. General Electric Co.*, 120 F.3d 991, 997 (9th Cir.1997), the court concluded that studies involving long-term low chemical concentrations or short-term exposure at very high concentrations could not form the basis of an expert's opinion that short-term moderate-level exposure caused plaintiff's injury. "Extrapolation was necessary to make the studies relevant, and there was no showing that the necessary extrapolation was scientifically acceptable." *Id.*

In *Wright v. Willamette Industries, Inc.*, 91 F.3d 1105 (8th Cir.1996), the court of appeals reversed a judgment on a verdict for the plaintiff after concluding there was no valid data upon which to conclude that the plaintiffs had been exposed to a harmful dose of formaldehyde embedded in wood fiber particles. *See also* Whiting v. Boston Edison Co., 891 F.Supp. 12 (D.Mass.1995) (holding that data on the relationship between exposure to ionizing radiation and acute lymphocytic leukemia (ALL) collected from Japanese atomic bomb survivors and patients treated with x-rays for spinal arthritis cannot prove plaintiff's ALL was caused by radiation exposure because these studies involved much higher dosages and because the extrapolation model used by plaintiff's proffered witnesses does not meet *Daubert* criteria of falsifiability, peer review and general acceptance). *But see* Glaser v. Thompson Medical Co., 32 F.3d 969 (6th Cir. 1994) (concluding that evidence of effect of phenylpropanolamine, the active ingredient in Dexitrim, on hypertension at higher dose levels than taken by plaintiff was sufficient to present factual issue for jury).

87. 927 F.Supp. 834 (M.D.Pa.1996).

88. *Id.* at 863.

89. This test is generally attributed to *Lohrmann v. Pittsburgh Corning Corp.*, 782 F.2d 1156 (4th Cir.1986). The trial court in *Lohrmann* granted directed verdicts to three defendants because there was insufficient evidence the pipefitter plaintiffs came in contact with their products. The appellate court affirmed. It rejected the argument that if the plaintiff can prove that the defendant's asbestos containing product was at the workplace while the plaintiff was there, a jury question has been created as to whether the product is a proximate cause of the plaintiff's disease. In-

not been available to plaintiffs in non-asbestos cases. However, in *James v. Chevron*,[90] the plaintiff sued numerous defendants claiming that exposure to chemicals in drums sent to his employer for reconditioning caused his cancer. The appellate court reversed a summary judgment for the defendants and allowed the plaintiff to use the test to help him prove causation in a situation where the plant in which the plaintiff had worked was closed and there were no records indicating either the specific chemicals to which the plaintiff was exposed or the dosage he received.[91] The court was careful, however, to note that its decision was limited to the summary judgement decision prior to a Rule 104 hearing on the admissibility of the plaintiff's toxicological experts' testimony.[92]

[f] Strength of Relationship and Statistical Significance

In *Joiner*, the Court minimized one of the plaintiff's epidemiological studies because the relationship failed to reach statistical significance.[93] The strength of studies and whether results were statistically significant are also part of the admissibility calculus. Cases discussing these issues are reviewed below.

[g] Totality of Defects

Examining cases in terms of their discussion of a single methodological flaw helps us to understand the types of considerations that go into admissibility decisions. However, this approach suggests greater arbitrariness across cases than in fact exists. In most cases where the judge has excluded the expert's testimony, the research upon which the expert premises his opinion has more than one flaw. This is true of most of the above cases. For an example we need look no further than the *Joiner* opinion.[94] The plaintiff's expert testimony in *Joiner* involved at least three separate problems, substance similarity, injury similarity, and dose rate. More often than not, it is the combination of problems rather than any single shortcoming that leads to a decision to exclude.[95]

Multiple defects were observed by the trial judge in *Estate of Mitchell v. Gencorp, Inc.*,[96] *Valentine v. Pioneer Chlor Alkali Co. Inc.*,[97] *Schudel v. General*

stead, it concluded that "to support a reasonable inference of substantial causation from circumstantial evidence, there must be evidence of exposure to a specific product on a regular basis over some extended period of time in proximity to where the plaintiff actually worked." *Id*. at 162–63. For a more complete discussion of this issue see Chapter 38 (Asbestos).

90. 301 N.J.Super. 512, 694 A.2d 270 (App. Div.1997).

91. *Id*. at 275, 278. This result is unsurprising because, as the court notes, there has been a trend in New Jersey courts to relax the standards for determining medical causation in toxic tort litigation. *See* Landrigan v. Celotex Corp., 605 A.2d 1079 (N.J.1992).

92. *James*, 694 A.2d at 275, 281.

93. 522 U.S. at 145 (1997).

94. General Electric Co. v. Joiner, 522 U.S. 136, 118 S.Ct. 512, 139 L.Ed.2d 508 (1997).

95. It is possible, of course, for a decision to exclude to be based on a single factor. In *In re TMI Litigation Consolidated Proceedings*, 927 F.Supp. 834 (M.D.Pa.1996), dosage problems alone seem to have sufficed to grant the defendant a summary judgment on sufficiency grounds.

96. 968 F.Supp. 592, 600 (D.Kan.1997) (dosage and similarity of injury). The opinion was affirmed in *Mitchell v. Gencorp Inc.*, 165 F.3d 778 (10th Cir.1999). The appellate court noted both of these problems. *Id*. at 782.

97. 921 F.Supp. 666 (D.Nev.1996) (injury similarity, dosage, study design).

Electric Co.,[98] *Sutera v. The Perrier Group of America,*[99] *Wright v. Willamette Industries, Inc.,*[100] *National Bank of Commerce v. Associated Milk Producers, Inc.,*[101] and *Austin v. Kerr–McGee Refining Corp.*[102] It is the combination of problems that often causes the court to conclude both that the expert's methods are unreliable and that there is a lack of fit between the research and the causal question in the case.

§ 7–1.3.2   The Importance of Statistical Significance

In *Brock v. Merrell Dow Pharmaceuticals,*[103] a pre-*Daubert* case, the court found the plaintiff's evidence to be insufficient without studies demonstrating a statistically significant relationship between Bendectin exposure and relevant birth defects.[104] The case has been criticized[105] and most later cases have refused to follow *Brock's* lead.[106] Indeed, the issue of whether statistical

98. 120 F.3d 991 (9th Cir.1997) (dosage and substance similarity).

99. 986 F.Supp. 655 (D.Mass.1997) (dosage and injury similarity).

100. 91 F.3d 1105 (8th Cir.1996) (dosage and substance similarity).

101. 22 F.Supp.2d 942 (E.D.Ark.1998). Plaintiff claimed that exposure to aflatoxins in dairy products caused his laryngeal cancer. The epidemiological studies upon which he wished to rely largely involved a different and more virulent type of aflatoxin, the cancer associated with exposure were to the liver, and comparison to the plaintiff's situation was made more difficult because the plaintiff could not establish his own exposure level.

102. 25 S.W.3d 280, 292 (Tex.App.2000) (dosage and injury similarity).

103. 874 F.2d 307 (5th Cir.), modified, 884 F.2d 166, 167 (5th Cir.1989).

104. *Brock* was a sufficiency case, granting a judgment as a matter of law following a jury verdict for the plaintiff. The court did not reach the admissibility question of whether the plaintiff's expert would be permitted to make a causal argument absent any statistically significant epidemiological findings. *See also* Renaud v. Martin Marietta Corp., 749 F.Supp. 1545, 1555 (D.Colo.1990); Thomas v. Hoffman–La-Roche, Inc., 731 F.Supp. 224, 228 (N.D.Miss. 1989).

105. Green, *supra* note 3.

106. One of the clearer statements of the issues at stake is to be found in *DeLuca v. Merrell Dow Pharmaceuticals, Inc.*:

We stress at the outset that the confidence level or "significance" of a statistical analysis is but a part of a meaningful evaluation of its reliability. The results of such a study may fail to correspond to reality for a number of reasons other than "sampling error." Faulty data collection resulting from design or execution flaws, for example, can create a much greater risk of error than the sampling error.

911 F.2d 941, 955 (3d Cir.1990). The Third Circuit specifically refused to decide whether epidemiological proof is inadmissible unless the data allow one to reject the null hypothesis (no relationship between the drug and relevant birth defects) at a .05 level of statistical significance, leaving the question for the trial court on remand. *Id.* at 946–49. *See also* Berry v. CSX Transportation, Inc., 709 So.2d 552, 570 (Fla.App.1998). The trial judge in *Arnold v. Dow Chemical Co.,* 32 F.Supp.2d 584, 590 (E.D.N.Y.1999) allowed plaintiff's epidemiological expert to testify even though there were apparently no studies reporting a statistically significant relationship between TCE exposure and the plaintiff's ailment, multiple myeloma.

One case that has followed *Brock* is *Kelley v. American Heyer–Schulte Corp.,* 957 F.Supp. 873 (W.D.Tex.1997), dismissed by *Kelley v. American Heyer–Schulte,* 139 F.3d 899 (5th Cir.1998). *Kelly* is a Texas federal case and, therefore, was governed by *Brock.* In *Kelly,* the plaintiff claimed that her silicone breast implants caused her to develop Sjogren's Syndrome. The plaintiff's expert formed her opinion in part on the basis of a study that the authors reported did not achieve statistical significance at the .05 level. *Id.* at 877. The district court relied upon *Brock* to conclude that with regard to Rule 703, epidemiological studies with lower-end confidence intervals less than one are not reasonably relied upon by experts to form opinions regarding causation. *Id.* at 878. However, perhaps recognizing the minority status of the *Brock* position, the district court also held that even if *Brock* did not apply, it would be unreasonable for an epidemiologist to rely on this research because of the weakness of the relationship, the threat posed by compounding factors, and the absence of a dose-response relationship in the sense that there was no relationship between length of time of implant and incidence of disease. *Id.* at 878. The plaintiff attempted to sidestep *Brock* by offering to have the expert testify as to her reanalysis of the research substituting a one-tailed significance test for the two-tailed

significance is required for a plaintiff to reach the jury with epidemiological evidence seems to have itself become less significant in admissibility decisions.

An interesting related question is whether when considering the admissibility of an expert's opinion the court should consider the failure of the expert to provide information on statistical significance. A discussion of this question and the role of statistical significance in epidemiological data analysis can be found in *In re TMI Litigation Cases Consolidated II*.[107]

§ 6–1.3.3 Bases of Exclusion

Courts that have cited a number of different grounds for excluding expert testimony because of failure to use epidemiological evidence or because of the use of inappropriate epidemiological evidence.[108]

[1] Lack of Qualifications

Prior to *Daubert*, most courts applied a liberal standard in determining whether an expert is qualified, allowed experts from a number of disciplines to testify concerning epidemiological studies.[109] In recent years, some post-*Daubert* courts have given greater scrutiny to expert credentials and qualifications. A number of cases have rejected an expert on the basis of a lack of qualifications.[110] Representative of these is *Mancuso v. Consolidated Edison Co. of New York*.[111] There, the court concluded that an internist did not have the requisite qualifications to testify that the plaintiff's ailments were caused by exposure to polychlorinated biphenyls (PCB). The internist lacked formal training and credentials in PCB toxicology or in environmental or occupational medicine. The internist was unable to answer basic questions about PCB toxicology (e.g. what levels of PCB contamination would be dangerous to humans) and relied upon the plaintiffs' attorney to provide him with the scientific literature he relied upon to support his opinion.[112]

---

test used in the published study. *Id.* at 879. The court would have none of it, arguing that when courts speak of significance testing they are speaking of two tailed tests. The court correctly notes that by choosing a one-tailed test, "Dr. Swan assumes a priori that the data tends to show that breast implants have negative health effects on women—an assumption that the authors of the Hennekens study did not feel comfortable making when they looked at the data." 957 F.Supp. at 879.

For discussions of the role of statistical significance in cases involving scientific evidence, *see* Black, *supra* note 3; Neil B. Cohen, *Conceptualizing Proof and Calculating Probabilities: A Response to Professor Kaye*, 73 CORNELL L. REV. 78 (1987); Neil B. Cohen, *Confidence in Probability: Burdens of Persuasion in a World of Imperfect Knowledge*, 60 N.Y.U. L. REV. 385 (1985); David Kaye, *Statistical Significance and the Burden of Persuasion*, 46 LAW & CONTEMP. PROBS. 13 (1983); Charles Nesson, *Agent Orange Meets the Blue Bus: Factfinding at the Frontier of Knowledge*, 66 B.U. L. REV. 521 (1986).

107. 922 F.Supp. 1038 (M.D.Pa.1996).

108. Trial courts are obligated to assess the reliability of proffered testimony. In *Goebel v. Denver and Rio Grande Western RR. Co.*, 215 F.3d 1083 (10th Cir.2000), the court ordered a new trial because the trial court abused its discretion by failing to perform its gatekeeping function.

109. DeLuca v. Merrell Dow Pharmaceuticals, Inc., 911 F.2d 941, 953 (3d Cir.1990) (noting that pediatric pharmacologists qualified to interpret epidemiological research on Bendectin); *Rubanick*, 593 A.2d at 736 (biochemist).

110. *Wade–Greaux*, 874 F.Supp. at 1477–78; Diaz v. Johnson Matthey, Inc., 893 F.Supp. 358 (D.N.J.1995); Whiting v. Boston Edison Co., 891 F.Supp. 12 (D.Mass.1995). The *Wade–Greaux* court also noted that there was no evidence the plaintiff's expert's methodologies had been put to use outside the courtroom. 874 F.Supp. at 1479.

111. 967 F.Supp. 1437 (S.D.N.Y.1997).

112. *Id.* at 1443–45. In a subsequent proceeding the court questioned the qualifications of another plaintiff's expert offered to replace

[2] The *Daubert* Factors

The Supreme Court's *Daubert*[113] opinion listed four non-exclusive factors to consider in determining whether scientific testimony is admissible under rule 702: a) scientific validity (falsifiability), b) peer review and publication, c) error rate, and d) general acceptance.[114] A number of appellate courts have now begun to consider another factor, whether the expert's research was created for the purposes of litigation.

[a] Scientific Validity

Scientific validity is arguably the most important factor to consider when assessing the admissibility of scientific evidence under *Daubert*. It is not surprising, therefore, that courts frequently base their rulings on an assessment of the validity of the research underlying the expert's opinion.[115] Usually this analysis focuses on questions of testability or on flawed methodology. Cases citing a failure to test the expert's hypothesis include *Cuevas*,[116] *Kelly*,[117] *Estate of Mitchell*,[118] and *Grant v. Bristol–Myers Squibb*.[119] Cases citing flawed methodology as a basis for exclusion include *Valentine*,[120] *Allen*,[121] *National Bank of Commerce*,[122] *Pick*,[123] *Kennedy v. Collagen Corp.*,[124] and *Muzzey*.[125]

---

the first expert. Mancuso v. Consolidated Edison, 56 F.Supp.2d 391, 398 (S.D.N.Y.1999). Ultimately the court rejected the second expert's testimony based on flawed methodology. *Id.*

See also Sutera v. The Perrier Group of America, Inc., 986 F.Supp. 655, 667 (D.Mass. 1997) (plaintiff's expert, an oncologist and hematologist with no expertise in epidemiology, toxicology, biostatistics or risk-assessment, lacks the specific knowledge, education, training and experience to render an opinion as to whether the exposures to low levels of benzene in Perrier for a short time period caused the plaintiff's leukemia); Wintz v. Northrop Corporation, 110 F.3d 508, 512 (7th Cir.1997) (expert, a toxicologist, was not a licensed physician and lacked sufficient expertise in birth defects bromide exposure, or the specific birth defect from which the plaintiff suffered to testify that bromide exposure to the mother during her pregnancy caused the plaintiff's injury); Everett v. Georgia–Pacific Corp., 949 F.Supp. 856, 857 (S.D.Ga.1996) (expert, practicing family medicine and surgery, possesses no specialized knowledge or training in the field of toxicology); Muzzey v. Kerr–McGee Chemical Corp., 921 F.Supp. 511 (N.D.Ill.1996) (witnesses without expertise in hematology not qualified to testify whether plaintiff's exposure to radiation from refining byproduct caused her to contract the disease polycythemia vera).

113. Daubert v. Merrell Dow Pharm., Inc., 509 U.S. 579, 113 S.Ct. 2786, 125 L.Ed.2d 469 (1993).

114. *Id.* at 593–94.

115. Porter v. Whitehall Laboratories, Inc., 9 F.3d 607, 615 (7th Cir.1993); Chikovsky v. Ortho Pharmaceutical Corp., 832 F.Supp. 341, 345 (S.D.Fla.1993); Sorensen v. Shaklee Corp., 31 F.3d 638, 649 (8th Cir.1994); Casey v. Ohio Medical Products, 877 F.Supp. 1380, 1385 (N.D.Cal.1995); O'Conner v. Commonwealth Edison Co., 13 F.3d 1090, 1107 (7th Cir.1994); Bradley v. Brown, 852 F.Supp. 690, 699 (N.D.Ind.1994) (excluding expert testimony on chemical sensitivity that was "a far cry from the tested hypotheses foreseen as the basis of 'scientific knowledge' testified to under 702").

116. Cuevas v. E.I. DuPont de Nemours & Co., 956 F.Supp. 1306 (S.D.Miss.1997).

117. Kelley v. American Heyer–Schulte Corp., 957 F.Supp. 873, 875 (W.D.Tex.1997).

118. Estate of Mitchell v. Gencorp, Inc., 968 F.Supp. 592 (D.Kan.1997).

119. 97 F.Supp.2d 986, 992 (D.Ariz.2000).

120. Valentine v. Pioneer Chlor Alkali Co., Inc., 921 F.Supp. 666 (D.Nev.1996).

121. Allen v. Pennsylvania Engineering Corp., 102 F.3d 194 (5th Cir.1996).

122. National Bank of Commerce v. Dow Chemical Co., 965 F.Supp. 1490 (E.D.Ark. 1996).

123. Pick v. American Medical Systems, 958 F.Supp. 1151 (E.D.La.1997).

124. 991 F.Supp. 1185 (N.D.Cal.1997).

125. Muzzey v. Kerr–McGee Chemical Corp., 921 F.Supp. 511 (N.D.Ill.1996).

[b]   Error Rate

Error rate per se plays a limited role in cases involving toxic torts. When it does arise, it is not a determinative factor.[126]

[c]   Peer Review and Publication

A lack of peer review usually appears as a make-weight in *Daubert* analyses, and is most frequently mentioned when a party's experts have failed to publish any of their results.[127] *Valentine v. Pioneer Chlor Alkali Company, Inc.,*[128] is an exception. In *Valentine,* one of the physicians who examined the plaintiffs and who was prepared to testify that the chlorine exposure caused neural damage had not published his results nor had he conducted any pre-litigation research on the question. This weighed against admitting his testimony into evidence.[129] However, another expert in this case did publish his conclusions in a journal called the International Journal of Occupational Medicine and Toxicology. In 1995 the journal did not appear among the more than three thousand periodicals listed in the Index Medicus of the National Library of Medicine. The court concluded that "the apparent obscurity of the journal relied on by plaintiffs to legitimate Dr. Kilburn's scientific conclusions does weigh in the court's evidentiary calculus."[130]

Valentine contains a useful discussion of peer review and its proper role in a Rule 702 analysis. As the court notes, the type of editorial peer review that precedes publication in a refereed journal is not the thoroughgoing independent testing and replication of a finding that is at the heart of scientific inquiry. Rather, "editorial peer review" is a much more limited endeavor.[131] At its best, it is a check on obvious methodological flaws that threaten a study's conclusion as well as an assessment of the article's style, originality and importance.[132] By itself, neither publication nor the lack of publication should determine a result under a *Daubert* analysis.

[d]   General Acceptance (and Frye)

General acceptance is frequently cited as a basis for admitting expert testimony.[133] However, in *Daubert* jurisdictions it is rarely the primary reason

---

126. National Bank of Commerce v. Dow Chemical Co., 965 F.Supp. 1490, 1527 (E.D.Ark.1996). This is not surprising. Most epidemiological research has not lent itself to error rate calculations. Very few if any epidemiological studies are replicated in a way that would permit even a crude calculation of an error rate for a given procedure. Even when there are multiple epidemiological studies concerning a given exposure/injury relationship, e.g., Bendectin and birth defects, the studies differ along multiple dimensions, making error rate estimations difficult. Moreover, proficiency testing per se is rarely possible because we do not know the true distribution of a relationship in the population. *See* William C. Thompson, *Are Juries Competent to Evaluate Statistical Evidence?*, 52 LAW AND CONT. PROBS. 9 (Autumn 1989).

127. *See* Daubert v. Merrell Dow Pharmaceuticals, Inc., 43 F.3d 1311, 1318 (9th Cir. 1995); Cuevas v. E.I. DuPont de Nemours and Company, 956 F.Supp. 1306, 1312 (S.D.Miss. 1997); Allen v. Pennsylvania Engineering Corp., 102 F.3d 194 (5th Cir.1996); Mascarenas v. Miles, Inc., 986 F.Supp. 582, 593 (W.D.Mo. 1997).

128. 921 F.Supp. 666 (D.Nev.1996).

129. *Id.* at 673.

130. 921 F.Supp. at 670 n. 3.

131. *See* Effie J. Chan, *The "Brave New World" of* Daubert: *True Peer Review, Editorial Peer Review, and Scientific Validity*, 70 N.Y.U. L. REV. 100 (1995).

132. *Valentine,* 921 F.Supp. at 675.

133. Keene Corp. v. Hall, 96 Md.App. 644, 626 A.2d 997 (Md.App.1993) (PLM method of

for the decision. Many jurisdictions have moved toward *Daubert*.[134] In states that have not adopted *Daubert*, this remains the key factor.[135] Arguably, however, relatively few toxic tort case admissibility rulings actually turn on the difference between *Daubert* and *Frye*. *Daubert's* shadow now casts itself over state court opinions even in jurisdictions that have not formally adopted the *Daubert* test.[136] Nevertheless, there are cases where the choice might matter. For example, in *Duran v. Cullinan*,[137] following a *Frye* analysis, the Illinois Appellate court permitted plaintiff experts to testify that an oral contraceptive caused the plaintiff's birth defect based on extrapolation from 43 epidemiological studies describing a relationship between oral contraceptives and birth defects. None of the studies described the type of defect suffered by the plaintiff. Because the appellate court only conducted a *Frye* analysis to decide whether extrapolation is a generally accepted methodology, it did not reach the more difficult *Daubert* fit question, i.e., could these studies properly form the basis of an opinion as to whether this drug causes the type of defect experienced by the plaintiff. It is unclear whether the extrapolation would have passed muster under this type of *Daubert* analysis.

[e]   *Research Conducted Independent of Litigation*

Increasingly, courts consider whether research, methods, or theories

detecting asbestos fibers not generally accepted); Graham v. Playtex Products, Inc., 993 F.Supp. 127, 133 (N.D.N.Y.1998) (lack of general acceptance of conclusion not enough by itself to cause court to exclude testimony); Sutera v. The Perrier Group of America Inc., 986 F.Supp. 655, 667 (D.Mass.1997) (plaintiff's expert produced no reliable scientific evidence that plaintiff's leukemia was more likely than not caused by his drinking Perrier and his conclusion failed the general acceptance test); National Bank of Commerce v. Dow Chemical Co., 965 F.Supp. 1490 (E.D.Ark.1996); Grant v. Bristol–Myers Squibb, 97 F.Supp.2d 986, 991 (D.Ariz.2000).

134. State courts continue to grapple with the adoption of analogues to the federal rules of evidence by their state legislatures. *See* Chapter 1, § 3.0.

135. *See* Blum v. Merrell Dow Pharmaceuticals, Inc., 705 A.2d 1314 (Pa.Super.1997) (excluding plaintiff's expert opinion that Bendectin causes birth defects because their methodology and conclusions were not generally accepted). The *Blum* case poses the question whether, under the *Frye* test, the expert's conclusion is subject to the general acceptance test, or is the general acceptance test only applicable to the expert's methodology? The court in *McKenzie v. Westinghouse*, 674 A.2d 1167, 1172 (Pa.Cmwlth.1996), held that the conclusion must be generally accepted. On the other hand, reversing a lower court's finding that the expert's conclusions must be generally accepted, the court in *Berry v. CSX Transportation, Inc.* ruled that only the methodology must be generally accepted. *Berry*, 709

So.2d 552 (Fla.App.1998). Two experts may offer opposite opinions under *Frye* if both rely on the same generally accepted scientific principles and methodologies. *Id.* at 567. In another Florida case, *E.I. DuPont De Nemours & Co., Inc. v. Castillo*, 748 So.2d 1108 (Fla.App. 2000), the court found that the plaintiff's scientific evidence on the teratology of a fungicide did not satisfy *Frye*. In *Wack v. Farmland Industries, Inc.*, 744 A.2d 265 (Pa.Super.1999), the court held that an expert's opinion that plaintiff's cancer was caused by exposure to contaminates that leaked from an underground gasoline storage tank lacked the indicia of scientific reliability required under *Frye*. Similarly, in *Thomas v. West Bend Co., Inc.*, 760 A.2d 1174 (Pa.Super.2000), the court found an expert's opinion that an electrical shock suffered while plugging in a popcorn popper caused heart-related injuries was not based on a theory generally accepted by a relevant scientific community. The *Castillo* and *Wack* opinions are useful examples of the ways in which *Daubert* considerations have penetrated opinions in *Frye* jurisdictions.

Florida's rule for the admissibility of expert testimony mirrors FRE 702, but the Florida Supreme Court retained *Frye* as the test for the admissibility of expert testimony. *See* Berry v. CSX Transportation, Inc., 709 So.2d at 555. The standard of review for a *Frye* issue in Florida is de novo, not abuse of discretion. *Id.* at 557.

136. *See* Chapter 1.

137. 286 Ill.App.3d 1005, 222 Ill.Dec. 465, 677 N.E.2d 999 (Ill.App.1997).

which form the basis of an expert's testimony were generated independent of litigation.[138] As Judge Posner notes in *Braun v. Lorillard Incorporated*,[139]

> "The Supreme Court held in *Daubert v. Merrell Dow Pharmaceuticals, Inc.* that the opinion evidence of reputable scientists is admissible in evidence in a federal trial even if the particular methods they used in arriving at their opinion are not yet accepted as canonical in their branch of the scientific community. But that is only part of the holding of *Daubert*. The other part is that the district court is responsible for making sure that when scientists testify in court they adhere to the same standards of intellectual rigor that are demanded in their professional work."[140]

The Supreme Court's *Kumho Tire* opinion[141] echoes the same test. It notes that the objective of *Daubert's* gatekeeping requirement, "is to make certain that an expert, whether basing testimony upon professional studies or personal experience, employs in the courtroom the same level of intellectual rigor that characterizes the practice of an expert in the relevant field."[142]

When research is conducted independent of litigation there is a presumption that the investigator has adhered to the standards of intellectual rigor that are demanded in their professional work. Contrariwise, when the work is done in furtherance of litigation, this may count against admissibility. Courts citing this criteria include *Berry*,[143] *Cuevas*,[144] *Lust*,[145] *Muzzey*,[146] *National Bank of Commerce*,[147] *TMI*,[148] and *Valentine*.[149]

[3] Fit

The Supreme Court's incautious language in *Daubert* that "the focus, of

---

138. Daubert v. Merrell Dow Pharmaceuticals, Inc., 43 F.3d 1311, 1317 (9th Cir.1995).

One very significant fact to be considered is whether the experts are proposing to testify about matters growing naturally and directly out of research they have conducted independent of the litigation, or whether they have developed their opinions expressly for purposes of testifying. That an expert testifies for money does not necessarily cast doubt on the reliability of his testimony, as few experts appear in court merely as an eleemosynary gesture. But in determining whether proposed expert testimony amounts to good science, we may not ignore the fact that a scientist's normal workplace is the lab or the field, not the courtroom or the lawyer's office.

See Diaz v. Johnson Matthey, Inc., 893 F.Supp. 358 (D.N.J.1995).

139. 84 F.3d 230 (7th Cir.1996).

140. 84 F.3d. at 234.

141. Kumho Tire Co. Ltd. v. Carmichael, 526 U.S. 137, 119 S.Ct. 1167, 143 L.Ed.2d 238 (1999).

142. 526 U.S. at 152, 119 S.Ct. at 1176.

143. Berry v. CSX Transportation, Inc.,709 So.2d 552, 569 ("Our conclusion [to admit] is

strongly influenced by the fact that the epidemiological studies here were conducted independently of this litigation and were peer-reviewed and accepted by journals that are widely acknowledged in the scientific and medical communities.").

144. Cuevas v. E.I. DuPont de Nemours & Co., 956 F.Supp. 1306, 1312 (S.D.Miss.1997).

145. Lust v. Merrell Dow Pharmaceuticals, Inc., 89 F.3d 594, 597 (9th Cir.1996) ("Although [Dr. Alan] Done published the 1984 article prior to this litigation, he was at that time already a professional plaintiff's witness. It is not unreasonable to presume that Done's opinion on Clomid was influenced by a litigation-driven financial incentive.").

146. Muzzey v. Kerr–McGee Chemical Corp., 921 F.Supp. 511, 519 (N.D.Ill.1996) ("I also find significant the fact that none of these witnesses has done any research on this theory outside the context of this lawsuit.").

147. National Bank of Commerce v. Dow Chemical Co., 965 F.Supp. 1490, 1518 (E.D.Ark.1996).

148. *In re* TMI Litigation Cases Consolidated II, 922 F.Supp. 1038, 1054 (M.D.Pa.1996).

149. Valentine v. Pioneer Chlor Alkali Co., Inc., 921 F.Supp. 666, 670 (D.Nev.1996).

course, must be solely on principles and methodology, not on the conclusions that they generate"[150] caused a great deal of controversy in the years immediately following the decision. This is so because the court also noted that Rule 702 requires that the scientific evidence must "assist the trier of fact to understand the evidence or to determine a fact in issue." The *Daubert* court noted that "This condition goes primarily to relevance.... The consideration has been aptly described by Judge Becker as one of 'fit.' 'Fit' is not always obvious, and scientific validity for one purpose is not necessarily scientific validity for other, unrelated purposes."[151] Many "fit" analyses in the following years ultimately concluded that the evidence available to an expert does not address the particular disputed fact questions posed by the case,[152] i.e., there was no fit between the data and the conclusions the expert wished to draw. Most courts downplayed the Supreme Court's methodology-conclusion distinction. For example, in an important *Paoli* opinion following *Daubert*, Judge Becker himself said, "we think that [the distinction between principles and methods versus conclusions] has only limited practical import ... a challenge to 'fit' is very close to a challenge to the expert's ultimate conclusion about the particular case, and yet it is part of the judge's admissibility calculus under *Daubert*."[153]

In *General Electric Co. v. Joiner*,[154] the Supreme Court basically ratified Judge Becker's view. It noted that conclusions and methodology are not entirely distinct from one another. "[N]othing in either *Daubert* or the Federal Rules of Evidence requires a district court to admit opinion evidence which is connected to existing data only by the *ipse dixit* of the expert. A court may conclude that there is simply too great an analytical gap between the data and the opinion proffered. That is what the District Court did here and we hold that it did not abuse its discretion in so doing."[155]

The "fit" requirement almost always involves determining whether the expert's chain of reasoning contains an inferential gap that is too wide. The analysis has been applied to different components of an expert's chain of reasoning. For example, in *Schmaltz v. Norfolk & Western Ry. Co.*,[156] evidence that high doses of atrazine caused eye irritation in rabbits was not sufficient to allow a doctor to testify that indirect exposure could cause pulmonary or respiratory problems in humans. In this case the expert's extrapolation was across both types of scientific information, use of animal studies to show a human effect, and the conclusion of the animal study. "The analytical gap between the evidence presented and the inferences to be drawn on the ultimate issue ... is too wide in the present case."[157] Lack of fit may exist

---

150. Daubert v. Merrell Dow Pharmaceuticals, Inc., 509 U.S. 579, 113 S.Ct. 2786, 125 L.Ed.2d 469 (1993).

151. *Id.* at 589–91.

152. *In Re Paoli*, 35 F.3d 717, 743 (3d Cir.1994).

153. *In Re Paoli*, 35 F.3d 717, 746 (3d Cir.1994). One large piece of the long and tortured history of the *Paoli* litigation finally came to a conclusion with a jury verdict in favor of the defendants on all claims involving issues of exposure, causation, medical monitoring, and property damages. *In re* Paoli Railroad Yard PCB Litigation, 113 F.3d 444 (3d Cir. 1997).

154. 522 U.S. 136, 118 S.Ct. 512, 139 L.Ed.2d 508 (1997).

155. *Id.* A fit analysis may also shade into a question of scientific validity. *See* National Bank of Commerce v. Dow Chemical Co., 965 F.Supp. 1490, 1496 (E.D.Ark.1996).

156. 878 F.Supp. 1119, 1122 (N.D.Ill.1995).

157. *Id.* at 1122 (quoting Conde v. Velsicol Chem. Corp., 24 F.3d 809, 814 (6th Cir.1994)).

even when the conclusion is based on human data rather than toxicological results.[158]

Between *Daubert* and *Joiner* relatively few cases based their exclusion of expert opinion on a fit analysis. In the aftermath of *Joiner* more courts appear to be using a lack of fit as a basis for exclusion.[159]

[4] Exclusion on 703 Grounds

Prior to the Supreme Court's *Daubert* opinion, a number of courts used Rule 703 as the primary vehicle for ruling on the admissibility of expert evidence.[160] The use of Federal Rule of Evidence 703 and its state counterparts to exclude scientific evidence has declined since the *Daubert* opinion and its emphasis on Rule 702.[161] Nevertheless, some courts still use 703 as grounds for exclusion, albeit usually in conjunction with a 702 analysis. For example, the Fifth Circuit ruled in *Allen v. Pennsylvania Engineering Corp.*[162] that plaintiff's expert opinion that exposure to ethylene oxide caused brain cancer was inadmissible under both Rule 702 and Rule 703. As to Rule 703, the court noted that there was no direct evidence of the level of the plaintiff's exposure

158. In *Chikovsky,* plaintiff had to show that Retin–A caused birth defects. Absent direct evidence on point his experts presented evidence that Vitamin A causes birth defects, but the trial judge found the "analogies to research concerning Vitamin A and other Vitamin A derivatives is wanting." 832 F.Supp. at 346 (S.D. Fla.1993).

In *Cavallo,* the court concluded that "Although Dr. Monroe found support in the literature for a conclusion that exposure to similar levels of a different mixture of volatile organic compounds produce somewhat similar, short-term effects, or that exposure to higher levels of a similar substance produce different, short-term effects, he is unable to provide any scientifically valid basis to support the leap from those studies to his opinion in this case.... In other words, like the circumstances in *Chikovsky* and *Schmaltz,* there is a lack of 'fit' between the studies relied upon and the conclusion reached." Cavallo v. Star Enterprise, 892 F.Supp. 756 (E.D.Va.1995).

See also National Bank of Commerce v. Dow Chemical Co., 965 F.Supp. 1490, 1527 (E.D.Ark.1996); Lust v. Merrell Dow Pharmaceuticals, Inc., 89 F.3d 594, 598 (9th Cir.1996) ("When a scientist claims to rely on a method practiced by most scientists, yet presents conclusions that are shared by no other scientist, the district court should be wary that the method has not been faithfully applied. It is the proponent of the expert who has the burden of proving admissibility. To enforce this burden, the district court can exclude the opinion if the expert fails to identify and defend the reasons that his conclusions are anomalous.").

159. *See In re* TMI Litigation, 193 F.3d 613, 670 (3d Cir.1999) (excluding expert testimony for lack of fit.); Heller v. Shaw, 167 F.3d

146, 156 (3d Cir.1999) ("reliable methods for making a diagnosis cannot sanitize an otherwise untrustworthy conclusion."); Allison v. McGhan Medical Corp., 184 F.3d 1300, 1315–16 (11th Cir.1999) ("We find that the district court did not abuse its discretion by considering that the proffered conclusions in studies with questionable methodologies were out of sync with the conclusions in the overwhelming majority of the epidemiological studies presented to the court."); Castellow v. Chevron USA, 97 F.Supp.2d 780, 796 (S.D.Tex.2000).

160. *In re* "Agent Orange" Product Liability Litigation, 611 F.Supp. 1223, 1243 (E.D.N.Y. 1985); Richardson v. Richardson–Merrell, Inc., 857 F.2d 823 (D.C.Cir.1988); Christophersen v. Allied–Signal Corp., 939 F.2d 1106, 1110 (5th Cir.1991); Smith v. Ortho Pharmaceutical Corp., 770 F.Supp. 1561, 1581 (N.D.Ga.1991) (holding plaintiff's experts' testimony inadmissible under 703 because their opinion is not based on the type of data reasonably relied upon by experts in the field); Hayes v. Raytheon, 808 F.Supp. 1326, 1331–32 (N.D.Ill. 1992). For a discussion of the role of 703 after *Daubert,* see Edward J. Imwinkelried, *The Meaning of "Facts or Data" in Federal Rule of Evidence 703: The Significance of the Supreme Court's Decision to Rely on Federal Rule 702 in Daubert v. Merrell Dow Pharmaceuticals, Inc.,* 54 MD. L. REV. 352 (1995).

161. *Daubert* relocates much of this discussion to the Rule 702 "fit" analysis, but Justice Blackmun notes that "a judge assessing a proffer of expert scientific testimony under Rule 702 should also be mindful of other applicable rules," including Rule 703. *Daubert,* 509 U.S. at 593.

162. 102 F.3d 194 (5th Cir.1996).

to EtO. The experts relied on the affidavit of a co-worker and extrapolations based on conditions in other hospitals. The court concluded that the information on exposure "is so sadly lacking as to be mere guesswork. The experts did not rely on data concerning Allen's exposure that suffices to sustain their opinions under R. 703."[163]

[5]   Exclusion on 403 Grounds

The *Daubert* opinion saves a role for Rule 403. It quotes with approval Judge Weinstein's observation that because expert evidence can be both powerful and misleading the judge may use Rule 403 to exert greater control over experts than over lay witnesses.[164] Since *Daubert*, Rule 403 occasionally has been given as a reason for excluding expert testimony in mass tort cases.[165] For example, in *Kelley v. American Heyer–Schulte Corporation*,[166] the court did exclude an expert's reanalysis of epidemiological evidence in part on Rule 403 grounds.[167] However, here as in other areas, Rule 403 rarely if ever serves as the primary basis for exclusion. Evidence that has been excluded because of its potential for confusion or delay also has been declared to be inadmissible under Rule 702 or 703.

§ 7–1.4   Individual Level Evidence: Specific Causation

The plaintiff's burden in civil cases is to prove each element of the cause of action by a preponderance of the evidence, usually interpreted to mean proof with a degree of certainty exceeding fifty percent. The plaintiff's causal proof is in two parts: proof of general causation (does the substance in question cause any harm) and proof of specific causation (did the substance in question cause the plaintiff's injury). As discussed above, the plaintiff can meet the general causation burden with statistically significant epidemiological data, other, non-epidemiological data such as animal studies, or some combination of both. Whether the non-epidemiological data will suffice depends in large part on the quality and quantity of the epidemiological data and the nature and quality of the non-epidemiological evidence. While failure to prove general causation may foreclose the specific causation question, proof of general causation can not resolve the specific causation issue.[168]

Proof of specific causation in toxic tort cases is a troublesome problem for the courts.[169] Two aspects of the problem are worth special mention. First,

---

163. *Id.* at 199. *See also* Kelley v. American Heyer–Schulte Corp., 957 F.Supp. 873, 875 (W.D.Tex.1997).

164. *In re Paoli*, 35 F.3d at 736; *Daubert*, 509 U.S. at 595.

165. *Wade–Greaux*, 874 F.Supp. at 1485; Timblin v. Kent General Hosp., Inc., 640 A.2d 1021 (Del.1994).

166. 957 F.Supp. 873 (W.D.Tex.1997).

167. *Id.* at 881. *See In re* Paoli Railroad Yard PCB Litigation, 113 F.3d 444, 450 (3d Cir.1997) (trial court did not abuse its discretion in excluding evidence related to plaintiffs' exposure to heat-degraded PCBs and furans on Federal Rule of Evidence 403 grounds). *But see In re* TMI Litigation Cases Consolidated II, 922

F.Supp. 1038 (M.D.Pa.1996) (testimony of medical doctor, that neoplasms of alleged victims of nuclear reactor accident were caused by ionizing radiation, was not so confusing as to warrant exclusion under Federal Rule of Evidence 403).

168. *Casey*, 877 F.Supp. at 1385.

169. An interesting question arises as to whether there is a lower standard of causation in some areas and whether this should impact admissibility rulings. This issue has arisen in CERCLA cases, Kalamazoo River Study Group v. Rockwell Int'l Corp., 171 F.3d 1065 (6th Cir.1999); B.F. Goodrich v. Betkoski, 99 F.3d 505 (2d Cir.1996); Freeport–McMoran v. B–B Paint Corp., 56 F.Supp.2d 823 (E.D.Mich.

there are several interrelated questions concerning the significance of a relative risk of 2.0 or more. Second, there is the ongoing problem of the appropriate role of "differential diagnosis" in toxic tort cases.

§ 7–1.4.1 Relative Risk

A recurring question is whether a relative risk of greater than 2.0 should, by itself, be sufficient for the plaintiff to get to a jury on specific causation. The argument supporting this position is that when the relative risk is more than doubled it is more likely than not that this particular plaintiff's injury was caused by the substance in question. The argument opposing this position is in two parts: epidemiological studies frequently fail to control for confounding variables that systematically bias the true relative risk and the plaintiff may not resemble typical members of the study population.[170] Most courts that have considered the issue have concluded a plaintiff can reach a jury if she can present epidemiological studies indicating at least a doubling of the risk of injury due to exposure to a substance (relative risk of 2.0 or greater).[171]

A related question is whether the plaintiff can reach the jury when the epidemiological evidence indicates a relative risk of less than 2.0. Of course if the epidemiology fails to indicate any causal relationship, in the absence of other evidence the plaintiff's claim will fail on general causation grounds. But what if the evidence indicates a statistically significant relative risk greater than 1.0 but less than 2.0? As the Ninth Circuit noted in *Daubert*, a relative risk in this range may suggest a causal relationship, "but it actually tends to disprove legal causation, as it shows that Bendectin does not double the likelihood of birth defects."[172]

Here it is important to distinguish admissibility and sufficiency. The

1999); and in FELA cases, Claar v. Burlington Northern R.R., 29 F.3d 499 (9th Cir.1994); Savage v. Union Pacific R.R., 67 F.Supp.2d 1021 (E.D.Ark.1999). Courts have generally concluded that admissibility criteria are not relaxed in these cases.

170. D.A. Freedman & P.B. Stark, *The Swine Flue Vaccine and Guillian–Barre Syndrome: A Case Study in Relative Risk and Specific Causation*, 64 No. 4 LAW & CONTEMP. PROB. 49 (2001). All discussions concerning whether a certain relative risk is sufficient to prove specific causation presume epidemiological studies that are not biased. If a study is biased, that is, its risk estimates are influenced by factors other than the substance under investigation, then unless the direction and extent of the bias are known, any inference drawn from the research may be suspect. Under these circumstances it would not be appropriate to make a specific causation determination based solely on the epidemiological research. In *Austin v. Kerr–McGee Refining Corp.*, 25 S.W.3d 280, 292 (Tex.App.2000), the court noted:

Specific causation requires that a plaintiff show that the injured person is similar to those in the epidemiological studies, that he was exposed to the same substance, and that the exposure or dosage levels were comparable to or greater than those in the studies.

As Freedman and Stark note, when a number of studies suggest very large effects, e.g., a relative risk of 10.0, these criticisms of the 2.0 threshold lose much of their force. It is unlikely that the biases in the studies and the differences between the plaintiff and others in the research are so great that the "true" relative risk for people similar to the plaintiff falls below 2.0.

171. *In re* Joint Eastern & Southern Districts Asbestos Litig., 758 F.Supp. 199, 203 (S.D.N.Y.1991); DeLuca v. Merrell Dow Pharmaceuticals, 911 F.2d 941, 958–59 (3d Cir. 1990); *In re* "Agent Orange", 597 F.Supp. 740, 835–37 (E.D.N.Y.1984); Marder v. G.D. Searle & Co., 630 F.Supp. 1087 1092 (D.Md.1986); Landrigan v. Celotex Corp., 127 N.J. 404, 605 A.2d 1079, 1087 (1992); Merrell Dow Pharmaceuticals, Inc. v. Havner, 953 S.W.2d 706 (Tex. 1997). *But see* Lee v. A.C. & S, Co., 542 A.2d 352 (Del.Super.Ct.1987) (finding epidemiologist's opinion as to plaintiff's decedent's cause of death inadmissible).

172. *Daubert*, 43 F.3d at 1321.

Second Circuit in *In re Joint E. & S. Dist. Asbestos Litig.*,[173] concluded that the argument that an epidemiological study must show a relative risk greater than 2.0 is a sufficiency argument, not an admissibility argument. Most courts would agree that the evidence is admissible,[174] but there are dissenting opinions.[175] However, even courts that would admit the evidence might stand prepared to grant the defendant a directed verdict on sufficiency grounds.[176] A number of courts have noted that a relative risk of less than two could be combined with other information to show that it is more likely than not the alleged cause responsible for the plaintiff's injury.[177] As a practical matter, much depends on the size of the relative risk. It is easy to imagine a court allowing a case to go forward when all agree that the relative risk found in the epidemiological literature is 1.9[178] It is more difficult to imagine this outcome if the relative risk is 1.1. In the latter situation the court may very well conclude that as a matter of law the plaintiff's data are insufficient to sustain a jury verdict.[179]

173. 52 F.3d 1124, 1134 (2d Cir.1995).

174. *In re* Joint E. & S. Dist. Asbestos Litig., 52 F.3d 1124, 1134 (2d Cir.1995) (an argument that an epidemiological study must show a relative risk greater than 2.0 is a sufficiency argument not an admissibility argument). *See* Merrell Dow Pharmaceuticals, Inc. v. Havner, 953 S.W.2d 706, 718 (Tex.1997) (a relative risk of more than 2.0 is not a litmus test); McDaniel v. CSX Transportation, Inc., 955 S.W.2d 257, 263 (Tenn.1997); Pick v. American Medical Systems, 958 F.Supp. 1151, 1160 (E.D.La.1997).

175. Sanderson v. International Flavors and Fragrances, Inc., 950 F.Supp. 981, 1000 (C.D.Cal.1996); Hall v. Baxter Healthcare Corp., 947 F.Supp. 1387, 1403 (D.Or.1996).

176. For example, the court in *DeLuca v. Merrell Dow Pharmaceuticals, Inc.*, 911 F.2d 941, 958 (3d Cir.1990) said:

Hypothetically, Dr. Done may be able to testify, on the basis of adequate data and the application of reasonably reliable methodology, for example, that of women who took Bendectin and had children with birth defects, 25% of the cases of birth defects can be attributed to Bendectin exposure. This testimony would be admissible as it would be a basis from which a jury could rationally find that Bendectin could have caused Amy DeLuca's birth defects; however, it would not without more suffice to satisfy the DeLucas' burden on causation under a more likely than not standard since a fact finder could not say on the basis of this evidence alone that Amy DeLuca's birth defects were more likely than not caused by Bendectin.

If New Jersey law requires the DeLucas to show that it is more likely than not that Bendectin caused Amy DeLuca's birth defects, and they are forced to rely solely on Dr. Done's epidemiological analysis in order to avoid summary judgment, the relative risk of limb reduction defects arising from the epidemiological data Done relies upon will, at a minimum, have to exceed "2."

177. Daubert v. Merrell Dow Pharmaceuticals, Inc., 43 F.3d 1311, 1321 n. 16 (9th Cir. 1995); *Landigran*, 605 A.2d at 1087. Such data could come from a differential diagnosis, clinical data, or animal studies. Caterinicchio v. Pittsburgh Corning Corp., 127 N.J. 428, 605 A.2d 1092 (1992); *In re* Joint Eastern & Southern District Asbestos Litigation, 964 F.2d 92 (2d Cir.1992).

178. Grassis v. Johns–Manville Corp., 248 N.J.Super. 446, 591 A.2d 671 (N.J.Super.1991) (asbestos products allegedly causing colon cancer, wherein plaintiff's expert testified that asbestos was a "substantial factor"):

Defendants argue that there should be a threshold of a 2.0 correlation before an expert should be permitted to rely upon an epidemiological study. They urge that only when this figure is exceeded can it be said that the particular factor is more likely than not to have produced the particular injury. This assertion proves too much. Assuming a large group of potential plaintiffs, a causative factor of 1.99 and significant evidence eliminating other known causes, defendants' proposition would still exclude the epidemiological proof. Even though the physical problems of just under one-half of the plaintiffs (without reference to the additional causative proof) would have been statistically "caused" by the factor being studied, none could recover. Yet, if a new study raised the risk factor to 2.01, all of the plaintiffs could use the study to collect damages, although for nearly one-half of the group, the risk factor was not an actual cause of the condition. This makes little sense, scientifically or legally.

Id. at 676.

179. A related question is whether an expert should be allowed to testify based on an

§ 7–1.4.2 Differential Diagnosis

The proper role of differential diagnosis has been difficult in the post-*Daubert* environment. The Supreme Court opinion in *Kumho Tire v. Carmichael*[180] resolves any uncertainty as to whether clinical differential diagnosis testimony falls within the ambit of *Daubert*. Clearly, it does. However, courts are still confronted with difficult decisions as to when an expert's differential diagnosis testimony can survive admissibility challenges. For a full discussion of this issue, see Chapter 20.

§ 7–1.5 Conclusion

Epidemiology has grown swiftly from a bit player in the scientific evidence drama to a leading actor. Much of the current controversy surrounding scientific evidence has been occasioned by cases involving epidemiological evidence. The most difficult cases are those where there is a limited amount of epidemiological evidence. In these situations courts must examine the strengths and weaknesses of epidemiology both on its own terms and in comparison to other types of scientific evidence.

B. GENERAL CONCEPTS IN EPIDEMIOLOGY

by

Noel S.Weiss*

§ 7–2.0 GENERAL CONCEPTS OF EPIDEMIOLOGY

§ 7–2.1 Introduction

Epidemiology is the study of variations in the occurrence of illness or injury, and the reasons for those variations. The goal of epidemiologic re-

---

epidemiological analysis when the expert does not report any relative risk (or odds ratio) for the data upon which he relies. The District of Columbia Circuit concluded that he could in *Ambrosini v. Labarraque,* 101 F.3d 129 (D.C.Cir.1996). In doing so, the court made a clear distinction between admissibility and sufficiency. "That Dr. Strom's testimony alone may be insufficient for the Ambrosinis to survive summary judgment does not necessarily defeat its admissibility under the 'fitness' prong of *Daubert*. Because Dr. Strom's testimony is 'sufficiently tied' to the facts at issue, we conclude that it satisfies *Daubert's* fitness prong." *Id*. at 136. If, in fact, the epidemiology data underlying this testimony is statistically significant and shows a relative risk (or odds ratio) greater than 1.0 this seems like a reasonable conclusion. Otherwise, most courts might conclude that the testimony is inadmissible as well as insufficient to support a verdict. Contrary to the court's opinion in *Ambrisini*, predicating admissibility on some indication of the strength of the epidemiological data underlying an opinion does not seem to be an unreasonable position.

180. 526 U.S. 137, 119 S.Ct. 1167, 143 L.Ed.2d 238 (1999).

* Dr. Weiss received an M.D. degree from Stanford University School of Medicine and an M.P.H. and Dr. P.H. from the Harvard School of Public Health. In 1973, after two years at the National Center for Health Statistics, he joined the faculties of the University of Washington School of Public Health and Community Medicine and the Fred Hutchinson Cancer Research Center. He served as Chairman of the Department of Epidemiology at the University of Washington from 1984–1993. While the majority of his research has been in the area of cancer (he was awarded an Outstanding Investigator grant from the National Cancer Institute for the period 1985–1999), he has maintained an interest in and written extensively on epidemiologic methods and clinical epidemiology.

Dr. Weiss has testified in toxic tort cases on several occasions, both on behalf on plaintiffs (Dalkon Shield and subsequent infertility, aspirin use and Reye's Syndrome) and defendants (occupational asbestos exposure and cancer, oc-

search is to learn what causes disease so that preventive action can take place. To that end, epidemiologists make observations that document illness occurrence in groups of persons defined according to the presence (or levels) of one or more exposure or characteristic. They then seek to integrate these observations with laboratory results and other nonepidemiologic research in order to infer whether a causal relation exists between the exposure and illness. As an example, an epidemiologic evaluation of bicycle helmet efficacy would first determine the difference between head injury risk to cyclists who were and were not wearing a helmet when they sustained an accident. If there were a difference, its interpretation (causal versus noncausal) would take into account biomechanical studies of helmets indicating the degree to which they are able to reduce physical force to the head.

The first part of this chapter is devoted to explaining ways epidemiology can help judge which exposures have the capacity to cause illness or injury in human populations. It will describe: (1) the nature of studies that assess illness occurrence in relation to the presence of a given exposure; (2) the ways in which the relation between exposure and illness may be quantified; and then (3) the guidelines used to infer whether any difference observed in illness incidence between exposed and nonexposed groups may reflect a cause-and-effect relation. The second part of the chapter will consider how data from epidemiologic studies can be used to estimate the likelihood that an exposure with the capacity to cause an illness actually did cause the illness in a given individual.

§ 7–2.2 Assessing the Capacity of an Exposure to Cause Illness or Injury

Consider the case of the person who develops a brain tumor and who has also used a cellular phone regularly for several years prior to diagnosis. From his experience alone we can never know whether there is an actual relationship between development of the tumor and the cellular phone use, since brain tumors occur in persons who never use a cellular phone, and since people who never develop a brain tumor quite commonly use cellular phones. Based only on one person's experience we are unable to distinguish cause from coincidence.

The first step in understanding the possible role cellular phone use may play in brain tumor etiology is to determine whether brain tumor incidence is elevated in a group of people who use cellular phones. Epidemiologists employ several approaches, each of which involves a comparison of illness incidence rates in question among people who have and have not had a particular experience.

§ 7–2.3 Studies that Measure Illness Occurrence in Relation to the Presence of a Given Exposure

§ 7–2.3.1 Comparison of Rates Across Population Groups ("Correlational" or "Ecologic" Studies)

If most or all persons within a community are exposed to a particular substance—e.g., fluoridated water, or arsenical air pollution—it is necessary

cupational exposure to magnetic fields and leukemia).

The author thanks Peter Cummings, M.D., M.P.H., and Betty Ngan for their comments.

to compare their illness rates to rates in other communities that have not had the same exposure. Similarly, if the exposure varies over time within a given community, one may compare illness rates in that single community over time and attempt to correlate any changes that occur with changes in the exposure level. These approaches are of greatest use when there is a substantial degree of variation in exposure levels across communities or over time, and relatively little variation in exposure among individuals within a single community. Since data on community levels of certain exposures may already be available, as may data on death rates and the incidence of some diseases, the research may be quite inexpensive.

For example, the possible role of water fluoridation in cancer development has been readily assessed in correlational studies that have compared cancer rates in populations served by water systems of differing fluoride concentrations, since: (1) there has been substantial well-documented variation in fluoridation from community to community; and (2) mortality rates for various cancers have been monitored in many populations.[1]

However, rate comparison among entire populations only rarely constitutes a definitive evaluation of a possible etiologic relationship.[2] Even if differences in disease occurrence across communities correspond to variation in the presence or level of exposure, one must be concerned that the differences are not attributable to the exposure itself, but rather to some other exposure or characteristic that also varied across the communities. These other characteristics may not be readily measurable. Even when these "confounding" variables (i.e., those that distort the true difference related to the exposure presence) are identified and measured, the number of communities or time periods under study may be too small to permit an adequate statistical adjustment for their effects, since the analysis unit is the community as a whole and not the residents themselves.[3]

§ 7–2.3.2 Randomized Controlled Trials

When only some persons within a community have been exposed to a factor suspected of causing or protecting against a disease—for example, some people use cellular phones, others do not—it is preferable to do studies in which the experiences of individuals are assessed as opposed to assessing the entire community. Scientifically, the strongest study of this type—a randomized controlled trial—assigns participants at random to receive or not receive the exposure in question, after which all participants are monitored for the occurrence of the outcome(s) that the exposure may influence. For example, one such study sought to evaluate potential benefits of folic acid (a vitamin) taken by mothers around the time of conception on the risk of a neural tube defect (a severe malformation) in the child they were going to deliver.[4] Women who had previously given birth to a baby with this defect, and who were considering becoming pregnant again, were asked to volunteer to take a folic acid supplement or an identical looking but innocuous pill (a placebo) through

§ 7–2.0

1. *Public Health Service Report on Fluoride Benefits and Risks*, 40 Morbid. & Mortal. Wkly. Rep. 1 (1991).

2. Charles H. Hennekens & Julie E. Buring, Epidemiology in Medicine (1987).

3. *Id.* at 103–5.

4. MRC Vitamin Study Research Group, *Prevention of Neural Tube Defects: Results of the Medical Research Council Vitamin Study*, 338 Lancet 131 (1991).

the first three months of pregnancy. Half the women who agreed to participate were, at random, given folic acid pills, the other half were given placebos. The study was "double-blind," in that: a) neither the women, nor their physicians, were told whether they were taking the vitamin or the placebo, and b) evaluation of the children for a neural tube defect was done without knowledge of which pill the child's mother had been given.

Double-blind, randomized study results have the potential to be highly conclusive. First, the lack of knowledge of the intervention administered prevents intentional or unintentional bias in the measurement of the disease(s) under study. Also, study participants who receive the "exposure" being investigated (e.g., folic acid) will, on average, be identical to participants who do not receive it with regard to all *other* factors that might be important in the disease development. Thus, in the folic acid study, the finding of a 72% reduction in neural tube defects in infants whose mothers had taken folic acid ($6/593 = 1.0\%$) relative to those whose mothers had taken the placebo ($21/602 = 3.5\%$), almost certainly represents a genuine protective effect of folic acid. Because it was chance alone that dictated which mothers did and did not receive this agent, it is exceedingly unlikely that one or more confounding factors were responsible for the difference.

Unfortunately, most questions concerning ill health causes cannot readily be answered using a randomized approach. This design tends to be quite expensive, commonly requires large numbers of participants, and is prevented by ethical considerations that preclude testing many risk or protective factors scientists would like to investigate. For example, most nonsmokers of cigarettes would not be willing to participate in a research project in which a coin flip determines whether or not they will take up cigarette smoking, even to facilitate scientific rigor! Thus, often epidemiologists do not employ randomization and, instead, simply study people as they are, measuring both their experiences and subsequent health.

§ 7–2.3.3　Nonrandomized Studies

These studies are typically one of two types: follow-up (or cohort) and case-control.[5] *Follow-up*, or *cohort*, studies follow persons who do and do not have a particular exposure over time for the occurrence of one or more health outcomes. *Case-control* studies, on the other hand, compare persons who have already developed a given illness to a sample of persons who have not developed the illness in terms of the proportion who have had the exposure of interest.

Nonrandomized studies are more likely to produce a biased result (i.e., one that mis-estimates the presence or size of the association between exposure and disease) than do randomized trials. First, persons who happen to be exposed to a particular agent may not be comparable to nonexposed persons with respect to other factors that influence the occurrence of the illness in question. When interpreting results of follow-up or case-control studies, it is always necessary to ask, "Could there have been reasons that persons were exposed to the agent, reasons that themselves led to an altered

5.　HENNEKENS & BURING, *supra* note 2; JENNI-　EPIDEMIOLOGY (1996).
FER L. KELSEY ET AL., METHODS IN OBSERVATIONAL

disease risk even if the exposure had not occurred?" So, for example, when interpreting the increased risk of Reye's syndrome (a potentially fatal illness primarily involving the liver and central nervous system) in children who had taken aspirin, one must consider whether it was due to a causal relation between the two, or instead, due to the underlying reason the aspirin was given. Similarly, if men who have inhaled welding fumes are observed to have increased lung cancer risk, one must ask if this is due to the influence of the fumes per se, or to other aspects of the work environment (e.g., high levels of asbestos fibers). *If* other factors that bear on disease occurrence (reasons for a given exposure, or that tend to occur together with that exposure) can be recognized and accurately measured, their confounding (i.e., distorting) influence can be negated, thereby enabling a valid result to be obtained. This can be accomplished either by a) choosing study participants in a way that makes the exposed and non-exposed groups comparable with regard to other factors that influence the disease occurrence; or b) statistically accounting for any imbalance in those factors when analyzing the results.

Bias in non-randomized studies may also result from having imperfect information available on the actual exposures received by study participants, and occasionally by limitations on the information on health outcomes the participants sustained. These will be discussed in more detail in the following sections.

[1]   Follow-up Studies (Cohort Studies)

In cohort studies, the enumeration of persons who have sustained a given exposure (a "cohort") may take place at the beginning of the investigation, and health events are monitored forward into the future ("prospective" cohort studies). Alternatively, the exposed subjects can be identified retrospectively, after all relevant exposures and health outcomes have occurred ("retrospective" cohort studies).

Most commonly, cohort studies are based on identification of substantial numbers of people in whom a particular exposure has taken place. For example, follow-up studies have been done on the health effects of X-irradiation: (1) in Japanese cohorts identified by their residence in Hiroshima and Nagasaki during the atomic bomb detonations; (2) in X-ray treated patients identified through medical records; and (3) in persons exposed at work, such as radiologists or radiation-exposed shipyard workers.[6] Alternatively, cohort studies may be conducted in populations in which there are special resources available for follow-up for specific health outcomes. An early study of the health effects produced by cigarette smoking took place in a group of United States military veterans who held United States government life insurance policies.[7] These individuals were surveyed regarding their smoking habits and other relevant characteristics, after which life insurance claims were monitored for the occurrence of any deaths. Contemporary follow-up studies of registered nurses[8] or selected male health professionals[9] exploit the

6. John D. Boice & Charles E. Land, *Ionizing Radiation, in* CANCER EPIDEMIOLOGY AND PREVENTION (D. Schottenfeld & J.F. Fraumeni eds., 1982).

7. Harold A. Kahn, *The Dorn Study of Smoking and Mortality Among U.S. Veterans*, 1966 NAT'L CANCER INST. MONO. NO. 19.

8. K. M. Rexrode et al., *Abdominal Adiposity and Coronary Heart Disease in Women*, 280 JAMA 1843 (1998).

fact that such individuals are likely to provide reasonably valid information on illnesses developed during the follow-up period.

To determine if the illness experience of exposed individuals is atypically high or low, it is necessary to have a basis for comparison. Sometimes that basis can be found within the group under study. For example, the prostate cancer incidence in health professionals who reported having had a vasectomy on a questionnaire was compared to that in the remaining cohort members who reported no such procedure.[10]

However, it may be that all members of the particular group being studied have been exposed. For example, in follow-up studies of insulation workers, welders, electricians, etc., the occupational environment was experienced, to some extent, by every employed person. When this occurs, it is necessary to achieve a comparison by looking at illness rates in the broader population in which the study subjects reside. For some populations and some diseases, the disease rate occurrence (i.e., incidence) is available. However, the majority of cohort studies that have used population rates as a basis for comparison have had to rely on mortality rates (i.e., rates of fatal illness).

There are several advantages to being able to study both exposed and nonexposed persons whose experience can be compared directly. One advantage is the relative ease of assessing the influence of the exposure isolated from possible influence by other factors. Consider two possible studies on ovarian tumor incidence as affected by fertility drug use. "Exposed" women in each study would be those who have taken a particular fertility drug, or perhaps any one of a class of fertility drugs. Each study would monitor for ovarian tumor incidence. Comparison women in the first studies would be other infertile women identified through the same means as the exposed groups—perhaps infertility clinic records—but who were not prescribed a fertility drug. In the second study, ovarian tumor incidence in the female population as a whole would be compared to ovarian tumor incidence in females who did not use a fertility drug. The second study likely would have greater potential to produce a biased result, since almost certainly a relatively high proportion of women using fertility drugs would also be childless, which is a risk factor for developing an ovarian tumor. Other infertile women (the comparison group in the first study) would likely be childless with roughly the same frequency as fertility drug users. To the extent they were not, differences in previous childbearing between users and nonusers of these drugs could be identified in the clinic records from which the two groups had been identified, and statistical adjustments made in the analysis. These adjustments would not be possible in the second study without information on ovarian tumor rates among childless and other women in the broad population; often this information is unavailable.

The problems that arise when using the illness experience of the general population as the basis for comparison are aggravated when mortality rates must be used, because persons who have a disease from which they are likely to die in the near future will not appear in many cohorts of interest. Women with ovarian cancer, for instance, are not likely to be seeking infertility

9. Edward Giovannucci et al., *Diabetes Mellitus and Risk of Prostate Cancer,* 9 CANCER CAUSES CONTROL 3 (1998).

10. *Id.*

treatment. Men who have a debilitating or life-threatening disease are not likely to be presently employed as insulation workers, welders, or electricians. Persons with these illnesses are, of course, present in the broader populations from which mortality rates are obtained. Thus, in many cohort studies of mortality one finds that, at least in the initial period following cohort identification, there is a low death rate for diseases in exposed persons relative to that in the general population. In occupational mortality studies, this is referred to as "healthy worker" bias.[11] The presence and magnitude of this bias will depend on the criteria for entry into the cohort, and on the disease in question: it will be greatest for diseases with a relatively long duration of debility between illness onset and death. In some instances, however, the direction of the bias may be reversed, producing a spuriously elevated mortality rate, if *ill* persons are selectively included in a cohort. This could happen, for example, in a comparison of mortality in retirees from a given occupation and the population in general, if retirement occurred not only on the basis of age but also as a result of illness.

The second advantage of a cohort study that identifies and follows both exposed and nonexposed persons is that it is easier to achieve a comparable level of follow-up and to employ comparable criteria for occurrence of illness outcome. If the cohort's illness or mortality experience is to be compared to population rates, cohort follow-up will need to be relatively complete, since the population rates will generally be based on a nearly complete identification of illnesses or fatal events that have occurred. One reason little credibility could be attached to a finding of reduced risk of breast cancer in women who had undergone a breast implant in Alberta, Canada, related to potential incomplete enumeration of cancer cases in this cohort. Once identified through surgical records, names of women with implants were checked against those that appeared subsequently in the provincial cancer registry.[12] However, no provision was made for the possibility that a woman might have left the province, or changed her name. In contrast, breast cancer rates used for comparison—that of female residents of the province of Alberta—would not be subject to underascertainment from these sources. Accuracy of the provincial rates is based solely on the completeness of enumeration of breast cancer cases and the total number of women in the province during a given time period.

When outcome events are identified via registry or death records in the exposed cohort and in the comparison population, comparable diagnostic criteria generally will have been applied to the two groups. The use of comparable criteria will produce the most valid estimate of the relative impact of the exposure on the outcome being studied. This is true even when there are instances in which low sensitivity may result in the absolute rates being falsely low in both the exposed and the comparison groups. In their study of mortality from mesothelioma among North American insulation workers, Selikoff et al.[13] suspected that some men who had died from mesothelioma had been incorrectly certified as dying from another cause, since mesothelioma as

11. HARVEY CHECKOWAY ET AL., RESEARCH METHODS IN OCCUPATIONAL EPIDEMIOLOGY (1989).

12. Hans Berkel et al., *Breast Augmentation: A Risk Factor of Breast Cancer?*, 326 NEW ENG. J. MED. 1649 (1992).

13. Irving J. Selikoff et al., *Latency of Asbestos Disease Among Insulation Workers in the United States and Canada*, 46 CANCER 2736 (1980).

a diagnostic entity was not widely recognized during the follow-up period. After reviewing many medical records of insulation workers who had died, it was evident the authors' suspicion was correct. Nonetheless, when comparing mesothelioma mortality rates between the insulators and the United States male population, it was necessary to use the cause of death actually recorded, even if it was believed to be in error. Since no correction for underdiagnosis could be made for the United States population rates, applying a correction only to deaths among insulators would result in a spuriously large relative mortality from mesothelioma.

When the diagnostic criteria for a disease are not uniform across physicians, the potential exists for differentially accurate disease identification in exposed and nonexposed persons. This is particularly so when physicians are aware of a possible exposure/disease connection during the follow up period, since some may be influenced to make the diagnosis because of the exposure's presence. In such instances, it is necessary to establish firm criteria for the presence of disease that must be met irrespective of the diagnosis given. For example, the plausibility of a bona fide association between "swine" flu vaccine receipt and the Guillain–Barré syndrome (a neurologic condition whose diagnosis may be ambiguous in some cases) was strengthened when investigators observed an increased incidence in vaccine recipients even after restricting cases to those in whom the diagnosis was least in doubt.[14]

Some studies compare not the incidence, but rather the *prevalence* of illness or disability (i.e., the presence of illness or disability at a specified point in time) between persons who have and have not had a given exposure. Such studies (termed "cross-sectional" because they assess illness status at a cross-section in time with no longitudinal component) are often done to investigate possible harmful effects of the work environment, by examining employed persons with different levels of on-the-job exposure. Examples are lung function studies in pipe coverers in 1940's shipyards who were exposed to asbestos to varying degrees,[15] or studies of musculo-skeletal disorders in persons with jobs requiring repetitive or forceful hand and wrist exertion.[16] However, a cross-sectional study will not give a valid result if persons whose health has been impaired by occupational exposure(s) are no longer employed when the study is done. For example, the investigation conducted in the shipyard[17] found asbestosis prevalence was not elevated among pipe coverers who had a substantial exposure to asbestos. It is highly likely that selective retirement of men whose health was already affected by asbestos exposure led to a result that spuriously minimized the asbestosis occurrence associated with this occupation.

[2] Case Control Studies

In case-control studies, instead of comparing disease incidence in exposed and nonexposed persons, a comparison is made between the presence of prior

---

14. James Marks & T.J. Halpin, *Guillain-Barre Syndrome in Recipients of a New Jersey Influenza Vaccine*, 243 JAMA 2490 (1980).

15. W.E. Fleischer et al., *A Health Survey of Pipe Covering Operations in Constructing Naval Vessels*, 28 J. Indus. Hyg. & Toxicol. 9 (1946).

16. Barbara A. Silverstein et al., *Hand Wrist Cumulative Trauma Disorders in Industry*, 43 Brit. J. Indus. Med. 779 (1986).

17. Fleischer et al., *supra* note 15.

exposure in persons with and without a disease. At first glance, it would appear this design is ill-suited as an aid in learning about an exposure's capacity to cause an illness or injury; it seems illogical to draw inferences about the consequences of an exposure when events are not directly measured following the exposure. Nonetheless, if the disease incidence is greater in exposed than in nonexposed persons, the exposure frequency in ill persons must be higher than in well persons. As an example, consider the results from the following hypothetical study. Among 1000 persons who received a certain exposure, five became ill during a defined time period. Only one similar illness occurred during the same time period in 1000 nonexposed persons. These results could be expressed in the following table:

Table 7.1

Exposure	Ill	Well	Total
Yes	5	995	1000
No	1	999	1000

The difference in illness occurrence between exposed and nonexposed individuals necessitated there being a difference in the frequency of prior exposure in ill persons (five of six, 83.3%) and the frequency in others (995/1994, 49.9%). Furthermore, the altered risk measurement most commonly used when interpreting data from cohort studies—the relative risk—can be well estimated in most case control studies (see below).

As with other nonrandomized studies, case-control studies may be limited in their ability to distinguish a given exposure's influence in producing disease from other exposures with which it is correlated. Case-control studies have two other potential limitations that must be overcome in order to produce a valid result: selection bias and information bias.

[a] Noncomparability of Cases and Controls Chosen for Study ("Selection" Bias)

If possible, cases and controls should be drawn from the same underlying population at risk of the health outcome so that fair comparisons can be made. If such a population cannot be identified explicitly, exposure frequencies in those who are selected for study should be similar to the underlying cases and noncases in that population, or to those of a discrete subpopulation. Thus, in an ideal case-control study all persons in a defined population who develop a particular illness during a given time period would be enrolled. A sample of that defined population would serve as controls. The population could be defined either geographically or on the basis of another characteristic, such as membership in an employed group or a prepaid health care plan.

For example, in order to investigate the possibility that menopausal hormone preparations may play a role in endometrial cancer incidence, a study might enumerate cases that occurred during a specific time period among enrollees in a health care plan. Controls would be selected from female enrollees who were at risk for the disease, i.e., from those who retained their uterus. However, this same research question also can be addressed in the absence of a defined population from which controls can be selected. For example, women receiving treatment for endometrial cancer at one or more hospitals are chosen as cases, and other hospitalized women who retain their uterus are chosen as controls. The latter approach has the advantages of lower cost and accessibility of information (from patient interviews or hospital records) in a comparable setting for cases and controls. The disadvantage is that, in the absence of a defined population, there is some uncertainty when deciding which potential control subjects have the same probability of hormone use as the average woman in the hypothetical population from which the cases were derived. In the endometrial cancer example, women hospitalized for conditions whose incidence is known to be reduced by hormone use (e.g., hip fracture) would be excluded from the control group, as would women hospitalized for conditions whose incidence is increased in hormone users. This group of women is proportionately larger in the hospital population than in the general population. Unfortunately, we may be unaware that hormone use affects some conditions. Hormone use could also be related to the likelihood of hospitalization among some women who have a condition that itself is unrelated to hormones. For these reasons, small and even moderate case-control differences in the exposure frequency must be interpreted with great caution when the study is not based on cases and controls drawn from the same defined population at risk of the outcome being studied.

No matter how comparably cases and controls are defined in a given study, the degree of selection bias will increase in proportion to:

(i) The percentage of study subjects on whom information on exposure status cannot be obtained; and

(ii) Differences in the frequency or exposure level between persons on whom information is and is not available.

The opportunity for selection bias is the reason that study results of "proportional mortality" need to be interpreted with care. Such studies often are done to explore possible associations between occupational factors and mortality from various diseases, especially cancer. They compare the proportion of all deaths due to a given cause (e.g., lung cancer) among persons with a particular occupation with the corresponding proportion among all demographically similar persons who died during the same time period.[18] However, data from these studies can also be viewed from a case-control study perspective: the proportion of persons with a particular occupation in cases (e.g., persons who died from lung cancer) and in controls (all persons who died during the study period). These studies will yield a biased result to the extent that the frequency of the occupations among controls is not typical of the *living* population from which lung cancer deaths arose. This circumstance will occur if the occupational exposure in question influences mortality from other causes. For example, proportional mortality studies conducted in the past would have falsely minimized the excess lung cancer mortality among insulation workers, since the asbestos exposure sustained by these workers would have led to a sizable increased mortality from asbestosis, mesothelioma, and possibly some other conditions.[19]

[b] Inaccurate Characterization of Exposures that Occurred in Cases and Controls ("Information" Bias)

18. CHECKOWAY ET AL., *supra* note 11.   **19.** Selikoff et al., *supra* note 13.

Case-control studies try to assess the subjects' exposure status during a time period that the exposure might act to influence the occurrence of a particular disease or injury. That period will not be the same for all etiologic relationships. For example, aspirin use affects Reye's syndrome occurrence only during the few hours or days prior to the illness onset. In contrast, if aspirin use reduces colon cancer risk, such use begun at the present time would not exert a benefit for years to come.

In broad terms, three means of obtaining information on exposures occurring in cases and controls are: interviews or questionnaires, records (e.g., medical, occupational), and direct measurement made on the study subject or his environment. Each has advantages and disadvantages with regard to assessing particular exposures.[20]

The exposure status of a case or control can be assessed incorrectly because there are errors in measurement *per se*, because the exposure status has not been characterized at the relevant point(s) in time, or for both reasons. If the frequency and degree of error is similar in cases and in controls, then the size of the observed relation between exposure and disease generally will be smaller than the true one. Also, if the size of the error can be estimated—possibly by using multiple sources of measurement on a sample of the study subjects or on a different population—one can correspondingly estimate the size of the case-control difference had there been no error in measurement.[21] However, errors in exposure measurement may not occur with the same frequency, or be the same size, in cases and controls. Some interview information provided by persons with a particular illness may be more accurate than that provided by controls; other information may be less accurate. In either instance, "recall bias" would result. Laboratory values obtained from measurements on biological samples obtained from cases may reflect changes in the experience of ill or injured individuals after their diagnosis, whereas the corresponding measurements in controls would not be similarly affected. These selective differences in recall or laboratory measurement can lead either to a spuriously high or spuriously low estimate of the true case-control difference.

In some instances, the expectation of differential ascertainment of exposure between cases and an otherwise-appropriate control group has led investigators to abandon that group and choose controls from another source. For example, Daling et al.[22] wished to conduct a case-control study to determine whether anal intercourse was a risk factor for anal cancer in men. Fearing that men with anal cancer would provide a more honest answer to this sensitive question than healthy men approached at random, the investigators chose as controls men who had a cancer at another location, the colon. They opted for this control group because: a) they expected that men with colon cancer would be similarly forthcoming as men with anal cancer regarding their sexual practices; and b) there was no reason to believe that a history of anal intercourse bore any relation to the incidence of colon cancer.

20. BRUCE K. ARMSTRONG ET AL., PRINCIPLES OF EXPOSURE MEASUREMENT IN EPIDEMIOLOGY (1992).

21. *Id.*

22. Janet R. Daling et al., *Sexual Practices, Sexually Transmitted Diseases, and the Incidence of Anal Cancer*, 317 NEW ENG. J. MED. 973 (1987).

While case-control studies are confronted by barriers to validity that often are higher than those that confront other study designs, if the disease being investigated is rare, the only feasible approach may be a case-control study through which its etiologies can be sought. Experience with case-control studies over the past several decades suggests that useful information can be produced if they are well-designed and it is possible to obtain information on the exposure status of study subjects in a sensitive and relatively unbiased manner. For example, case-control studies have largely been the basis for concluding that unopposed estrogen use increases endometrial cancer risk in postmenopausal women, and that such use decreases their hip fracture risk. In response to these study results, there has been an attempt to modify ways postmenopausal hormones are administered, so as to maximize benefits and minimize adverse effects. Case-control studies also have demonstrated convincingly the association between aspirin use and Reye's syndrome,[23] highly absorbent tampon use and toxic shock syndrome,[24] and a mother's prenatal use of diethylstilbestrol and her daughter's vaginal adenocarcinoma.[25] Because Reye's syndrome, toxic shock syndrome, and vaginal adenocarcinoma are rare, cohort studies or randomized trials of these conditions either did not generate enough cases to produce a meaningful result, or were not conducted at all.

§ 7–2.4 Quantifying the Relation Between Exposure and Disease

The strength of the relation between exposure and disease or injury is most often assessed by the relative incidence ("relative risk") of disease between exposed and nonexposed persons. For example, consider the following hypothetical data summarizing a population's experience with a particular illness over a given time period:

Table 7.2

Exposed?	Ill	Well	Total
Yes	50	19,950	20,000
No	50	79,950	80,000
	100	99,900	100,000

Incidence in exposed persons = I_e = 50/20,000 = 25 per 10,000
Incidence in nonexposed persons = I_n = 50/80,000 = 6.25 per 10,000
Relative risk = I_e/I_n = 25/6.25 = 4

The disease incidence in exposed persons is four times that in nonexposed persons.

In case-control studies, generally the incidence is measured neither in exposed nor in nonexposed persons. Nonetheless, from the exposure frequency measured in cases and controls, it is usually possible to estimate the incidence rate ratio.[26] To understand how this can be done, imagine a cohort study in

23. Eugene S. Hurwitz et al., *Public Health Service Study on Reye's Syndrome and Medications: Report of the Pilot Phase*, 313 NEW ENG. J. MED. 849 (1985).

24. Seth Berkley et al., *The Relationship of Tampon Characteristics to Menstrual Toxic Shock Syndrome*, 258 JAMA 917 (1987).

25. Arthur Herbst et al., *Adenocarcinoma of the Vagina: Association of Maternal Stilbestrol Therapy with Tumor Appearance in Young Women*, 284 NEW ENG. J. MED. 878 (1971).

26. HAROLD A. KAHN & CHRISTOPHER T. SEMPOS, STATISTICAL METHODS IN EPIDEMIOLOGY (1989).

which exposed and nonexposed persons are followed for a certain time period. The table below summarizes their experience with regard to a particular disease:

Table 7.3

	Disease		
Exposed	Yes	No	
Yes	a	b	a + b
No	c	d	c + d

The relative risk (RR) = $\dfrac{a/(a + b)}{c/(c + d)}$

If the disease occurs relatively infrequently during the follow-up period in both exposed and nonexposed persons, then "a" will be small relative to "b," and "c" will be small relative to "d". Therefore:

$$RR = \frac{a/(a + b)}{c/(c + d)} \approx \frac{a/b}{c/d} = \frac{a/c}{b/d}$$

In this expression, the numerator (a/c) is the exposure odds in persons who develop disease, while the denominator (b/d) is the exposure odds in persons who do not. The ratio of the two is the relative odds, or odds ratio. The numerator can be estimated from a sample of cases, while the denominator can be estimated from a sample of non-cases. Neither estimate is influenced by the proportion of all cases and all non-cases that have been chosen to take part in the study.

Had a case-control study including 50 cases and 50 controls been done on the population described in Table 35.2, on average the following results would have been obtained:

Table 7.4

Exposed?	Cases	Controls
Yes	$a = 50 \times \dfrac{50}{100} = 25$	$b = 50 \times \dfrac{19{,}950}{99{,}900} = 10$
No	$c = 25$	$d = 40$
Total	50	50

Odds ratio = $\dfrac{a/c}{b/d} = \dfrac{25/25}{10/40} = 4.0$

The value of 4.0 is the same as was obtained for the relative risk based on the experience of the whole population.

As the illness frequency rises in the population in which the case-control study is done, the odds ratio will begin to provide a distorted impression of the relative risk.[27] Suppose that in Table 35.2, I_e actually was 5000/20,000 = 2500

27. *Id.*

per 10,000, and I_n was 5000/80,000 = 625 per 10,000 (i.e., each rate was 100 times greater than in the original table). The relative risk would still be 4, but 50 cases and 50 controls drawn from this population would be distributed as follows, on average:

Table 7.5

Exposed?	Cases	Controls
Yes	$a = 50 \times \dfrac{5000}{10000} = 25$	$b = 50 \times \dfrac{15{,}000}{90{,}000} = 8$
No	$c = 25$	$d = 42$
Total	50	50

The odds ratio would be $\dfrac{25/25}{8/42} = 5.25$

and thus give a falsely high estimate of the relative risk. Nonetheless, it is the very unusual study in which the disease incidence during the interval following exposure is as high as in this example. In most case-control studies, the odds ratio will closely approximate the relative risk.

The goal of epidemiologic research is to learn what causes disease so that preventive action can take place. Therefore, the purpose of an individual epidemiologic study is to obtain information that will improve disease occurrence prediction, either in the future in the same populations in which the study was conducted, or in other populations. The persons enrolled as subjects in each epidemiologic study can be viewed, then, as a *sample* of all potential subjects that could have been chosen, and whose experience forms a basis for a generalization to be made to other persons. It is probable that whatever altered risk (if any) associated with a given exposure observed in any given sample will not be exactly the same as that observed in a different group who might have been chosen for study. (By way of analogy, a coin flipped 10 times resulting in six "heads" wouldn't necessarily produce six "heads" if flipped an additional 10 times.) So, each epidemiologic study provides an estimate of the relative disease risk between *all* exposed and *all* nonexposed persons, i.e., a "true" relative risk estimate.

From epidemiologic study results, it is possible to enumerate a range of relative risks rates within which the true value is likely to lie. The width of this range (the "confidence interval") is dictated in part by:

(1) The number of subjects studied. As that number rises, knowledge of the true relative risk (RR) location improves, i.e., the confidence interval (CI) width decreases.

(2) The confidence one wishes to have that the range captures the true value.

While the particular confidence level is arbitrary, a common practice among researchers is to use a 95% CI. Interpreting a 95% CI for relative risk that extended, say from 2.0 to 10.0, would be as follows: Considering sampling variability alone (i.e., no bias in the study), there was a 95% likelihood that the true RR was not less than 2.0 nor more than 10.0. If one were to calculate a 90% CI, for example, it would be smaller than a 95% CI, since by choosing it one is willing to run a somewhat greater risk (i.e., 10% vs. 5%) of failing to include the true value of the relative risk in the interval. The following indicates the way in which the CI is calculated (in studies large enough so that there are at least several exposed and several nonexposed persons who developed the illness), first for relative risk calculated in a cohort study, then for an odds ratio obtained in a case-control study.

Table 7.6

Relative Risk (RR)

		General Ill	Well	Example Ill	Well
Exposed	Yes	a	b	50	19,950
	No	c	d	50	79,950

$$RR = \frac{a/a + b}{c/c + d} \qquad\qquad RR = \frac{50 / (50 + 19,950)}{50 / (50 + 79,950)} = 4.0$$

General: $\quad 95\% \text{ CI} = (RR)e \left[\pm 1.96 \sqrt{\dfrac{1 - a/(a + b)}{a} + \dfrac{1 - c/(c + d)}{c}} \right]$

Example: $\quad 95\% \text{ CI} = (4.0)e \left[\pm 1.96 \sqrt{\dfrac{1 - 50 / (20,000)}{50} + \dfrac{1 - 50 / (80,000)}{50}} \right]$

$$= (4.0) \, 2.7183^{[\pm \, 0.3917]}$$
$$= 2.70 - 5.92$$

Odds Ratio (OR)

		General Ill	Well	Example Ill	Well
Exposed	Yes	a	b	50	19,950
	No	c	d	50	79,950

$$RR = \frac{a/c}{b/d} \qquad\qquad RR = \frac{25 / 25}{10 / 40} = 4.0$$

General: $\quad 95\% \text{ CI} = (OR)e \left[\pm 1.96 \sqrt{\dfrac{1}{a} + \dfrac{1}{b} + \dfrac{1}{c} + \dfrac{1}{d}} \right]$

Example: $\quad 95\% \text{ CI} = (4.0)e \left[\pm 1.96 \sqrt{\dfrac{1}{25} + \dfrac{1}{10} + \dfrac{1}{25} + \dfrac{1}{40}} \right]$

$$= (4.0) \, 2.7183^{[\pm \, .8874]}$$
$$= 1.65 - 9.72$$

Related to the concept of a CI are:

1) The "p" value, the likelihood that any observed association could have arisen by chance in a sample of individuals given that the "null" hypothesis is true, i.e., there is no true relation between exposure and disease. Suppose, for example, that a study obtained a p value of 0.10 for a particular exposure-disease association. One would conclude that, even in the absence of no true association, there was a 10% likelihood of an association of that size or greater emerging in that number of study subjects.

2) The "power" of a proposed study to identify a specified difference in disease incidence between exposed and unexposed persons. The larger the sample of persons studied, the greater the study's power, i.e., the smaller the chance that a p value above a given threshold level would be obtained in that study when a true difference in incidence is present.[28] A study's power also is influenced by a condition's frequency (in cohort studies) or by an exposure's frequency (in case-control studies). For example, a cohort study of various illness rates in users and nonusers of oral contraceptives would have greater power to identify a 50% increased risk of a relatively common disease such as breast cancer than it would a 50% increased risk of scleroderma, a rare connective tissue disease. A scleroderma case-control study would have greater power to identify a 50% increased risk associated with the prior use of oral contraceptives (a common exposure in most populations) than a 50% increased risk associated with a prior silicone breast implant (generally a much rarer exposure).

The difference in disease incidence between exposed and nonexposed persons, I_e-I_n, is termed the "attributable risk" or "attributable rate" (AR) when a causal connection between exposure and disease has been inferred (see below). The AR quantifies the added disease risk among exposed individuals due to their exposure, and so it contributes directly to weighing favorable and unfavorable exposure consequences. For example, the decision to use postmenopausal hormone therapy does not take into consideration the relative risks of endometrial cancer, hip fracture, coronary disease, etc., associated with hormone use, but does take into consideration the corresponding attributable risks (some adverse, some beneficial).

§ 7–2.5 Guidelines for Inferring an Exposure's Capacity to Cause Illness

If exposed and nonexposed persons are found to have a different disease incidence (or, as in case-control studies, if there is a difference in the proportion of cases and controls who have been exposed), we say an *association* has been observed. The association may be due to chance, to bias, or it may reflect a causal influence of the exposure in disease production. An exposure is considered capable of causing illness or injury if, because of its presence, some individuals become ill or injured who otherwise would not have done so.

However, while statistical associations between exposures and diseases are observed, causes are not. Rather, causes are inferred, in part, from the presence of such associations. Technically, causal hypotheses are formed, and their validity is evaluated through results obtained in epidemiologic and other scientific studies. Some have suggested criteria for evaluating causal hypotheses related to disease occurrence, beginning with Hill.[29] The sets of criteria are broadly similar.[30] The one presented here considers answers to the following questions:

28. Kenneth Rothman & Sander Greenland, Modern Epidemiology (2d ed. 1998).

29. Austin B. Hill, *The Environment and Disease: Association or Causation*, 58 Proc. Roy. Soc'y Med. 295 (1965).

30. *See generally*, Kelsey et al., *supra* note

§ 7–2.5.1 Is There an Association Present Between Exposure and Disease?

The answer to this question would be sought in the aggregate of relevant studies. Depending on the number of such studies and their similarity in design, it may be desirable to pool data obtained from each in a formal way; this is called "meta-analysis."[31] At the present time, there is substantial disagreement regarding whether meta-analysis is appropriate as a means of summarizing results from multiple studies.[32]

§ 7–2.5.2 How Strong is the Association?

The greater the disparity in incidence between exposed and nonexposed persons, the less plausible are noncausal explanations for that disparity. The observation from several large studies that the incidence of and mortality from lung cancer was 10–20 times greater in cigarette smokers than in nonsmokers (i.e., a relative risk of 10–20) made it extremely unlikely that other differences between smokers and nonsmokers could have accounted for the entire association.

Clearly, the precision with which the relevant studies collectively can estimate the relative risk will influence its interpretation. However, because it is largely influenced by the study size, a "p" value cannot be considered *on its own* as an index of the strength of association. A large "p" value does not guarantee that chance is the basis for the observed association, only that it is a plausible basis. A small "p" value does not necessarily mean that the observed association is a causal one, only that chance is an unlikely explanation.

If the true relative disease risk occurrence resulting from a given exposure is close to the 1.0 null value (perhaps in the range 0.8–1.2) then there is little chance that nonrandomized epidemiological studies will be able to provide convincing evidence of a causal association. No matter how large and well done such studies may be, there will remain the possibility that bias may be the whole explanation for an association of this magnitude. However, a true relative risk presence only slightly above 1.0 associated with exposure to a particular causal agent implies that, among exposed persons who developed the disease, only a small fraction did so as a result of the exposure (see below).

§ 7–2.5.3 Is it Clear That the Illness, or a Forerunner of it, Did Not Give Rise to the Exposure?

While the temporal sequence of exposure and illness is usually unambiguous, there are instances when it is not, especially in studies of possible untoward effects of medications. For example, in studies of aspirin use in relation to Reye's syndrome, it was particularly important for cases and

5; HENNEKENS & BURING, *supra* note 2 (illustrating sets of criteria for evaluating causal hypotheses related to disease occurrence).

31. Sander Greenland, *Quantitative Methods in the Review of Epidemiologic Literature*, 9 EPIDEMIOL. REV. 1 (1987); Henry S. Sachs et al., *Meta-Analysis of Randomized Controlled Trials: An Update of the Quality and Methodol-*

ogy, in MEDICAL USES OF STATISTICS (John C. Bailar & Frederick Mosteller eds., 2d ed. 1992).

32. A. Liberati, *A Plea for a More Balanced View of Meta–Analysis and Systematic Overviews of the Effect of Health Care*, 48 J. CLIN. EPIDEMIOL. 81 (1995); Alvan R. Feinstein, *Meta-Analysis: Statistical Alchemy for the 21st Century*, 48 J. CLIN. EPIDEMIOL. 71 (1995).

controls to be comparable with regard to the presence and severity of the underlying symptoms that could lead to a child being given aspirin. Otherwise, it would be uncertain whether a case-control difference in aspirin use was due to aspirin predisposing to Reye's syndrome, or to the reverse.

§ 7–2.5.4 Which is More Credible, a Causal or a Noncausal Interpretation?

Estrogenic hormone use, unaccompanied by progestational hormones, causes endometrial cells (cells that line the uterine cavity) to proliferate. Proliferating cells of any organ are known to be those most susceptible to cancer development. Knowledge of this endocrinologic relationship supported an inference of cause and effect when an association was noted between estrogen use by menopausal women and endometrial cancer incidence.[33] In contrast, an association between propoxyphene (an analgesic) use with multiple myeloma incidence, an association largely restricted to persons who had begun using the drug within a two-year period prior to diagnosis, was interpreted as probably *not* due to a causal influence of propoxyphene.[34] This was because it was known that bone pain is present in many persons with myeloma for some time before their cancer is diagnosed, pain that plausibly could necessitate analgesic use.

The types of study that have identified the association also influence the credibility of a causal interpretation. Even an association of modest strength noted in well-done randomized trials, if that association is based on a large enough sample so that it is unlikely to be due solely to chance, argues in strong support of a causal relation. That same modest association observed in a similarly well-done cohort or case-control study generally will be less conclusive, given the relatively greater potential for bias in these nonrandomized designs. For any given set of relevant cohort or case-control studies, their ability to exclude or control for the various sources of bias will also bear on the credibility of a causal interpretation of any association found.

§ 7–2.5.5 Is the Size of the Association Between Exposure and Disease Greatest When One Might Expect It to Be?

Given the influence of the stage of development of a fetus on its susceptibility to the teratogenic effects of drugs, it might have been predicted that if *in utero* diethylstilbestrol (DES) exposure were to produce abnormal female genital development that led to vaginal adenocarcinoma, the risk would be greatest if that exposure took place during the first trimester of pregnancy. This was precisely what was observed, and so the hypothesis of a causal effect of *in utero* DES exposure was strengthened. Commonly, variation in the size of the association between exposure and disease may be predicted on the basis of the intensity of the exposure, i.e., a ''dose-response'' relationship. For example, lung cancer risk increases in relation to the number of cigarettes smoked per day. Alternatively, the association may be hypothesized to vary on the basis of exposure duration, e.g., endometrial cancer risk in relation to years of postmenopausal estrogen use. Whatever the basis, a causal

33. Lynda F. Voigt & Noel S. Weiss, *Epidemiology of Endometrial Cancer*, in ENDOMETRIAL CANCER (Earl A. Surwit & David S. Alberts eds., 1989).

34. Gary D. Friedman, *Multiple Myeloma: Relation to Propoxyphene and Other Drugs, Radiation, and Occupation*, 15 INT'L J. EPIDEMIOL. 424 (1986).

hypothesis is supported to the extent that the observed variation in the size of the association corresponds to that predicted.[35]

In order for an exposure to be judged a cause of a disease it need not have been present in every individual who develops that disease. Alcohol consumption, for example, is a well-recognized cause of motor vehicle injuries, yet many persons sustain injuries in collisions in which no participant has consumed alcohol. An agent need not be capable of acting alone to produce disease for it to be considered as a cause of that disease. A firearm in the absence of an assailant cannot cause a homicide, but if some homicides occur in the presence of a firearm that would not have occurred in its absence, firearm presence is *a* causal factor.

Since causal actions of exposures are neither observable nor provable, a subjective element is present in judging whether, for a given exposure, such an action exists. As a result, scientists may differ both in terms of interpretation of available evidence in support of criteria used to aid causal inference, and in relative weight assigned to each criteria. Nonetheless, given the goal of illness/injury prevention, there is no choice but to seek to distinguish causal from non-causal associations. We want to be able to act to minimize harmful exposures that have little or no offsetting value, e.g., cigarette smoking, or DES use during pregnancy. We want to be able to understand, and possibly control or modify, exposures that are harmful in some ways but have beneficial effects as well.

§ 7–2.6 Estimating the Likelihood That an Exposure Capable of Causing an Illness Actually Did So in a Given Exposed Individual

A particular illness can arise through more than one set of circumstances, and usually through many sets. Cigarette smoking causes some people to develop lung cancer, but occupational exposure to chloromethyl ethers (among other industrial chemicals) causes this disease as well, both in persons who have and have not smoked. Even for infectious diseases, in which the condition is defined in part on the basis of the presence of an organism, the infecting agent generally can be acquired through various means. For example, the E. coli organism that causes the hemolytic-uremic syndrome can be acquired by eating undercooked contaminated meat, but also by other means.[36] In persons exposed to an agent that is judged to be capable of causing a disease, epidemiologic studies will have measured or estimated their incidence rate of that disease (I_e). The same will have been done for persons not so exposed (I_n). The incidence rate percentage in exposed persons attributable to the exposure, as opposed to the other means of developing that disease, is

$$\frac{I_e - I_n}{I_e}$$

x 100%. This expression is known as the "attributable risk percent," or "attributable fraction."

35. Noel S. Weiss, *Inferring Causal Relationships: Elaboration of the Criterion of "Dose–Response,"* 113 Am. J. Epidemiol. 487 (1981).

36. E.A. Belongia et al., *Transmission of Escherichia Coli 0157:H7 Infection in Minnesota Child Day–Care Facilities,* 7 JAMA 883 (1993).

If, for example: a) the annual incidence of lung cancer in men with a certain level of occupational asbestos exposure were 200 per 100,000; and b) the incidence in nonexposed men were 100 per 100,000, 50 percent

$$\frac{(200 - 100)}{200}$$

$\times$ 100%, of the lung cancer rate in men with that level of exposure would be attributable to the exposure itself.

The above expression, termed the "attributable risk percent," can also be expressed as a function of the relative risk (RR), since

$$\frac{I_e - I_n}{I_e} = \frac{I_e}{I_e} - \frac{I_n}{I_e} = 1 - \frac{1}{RR} = \frac{RR - 1}{RR}$$

Therefore, even from those case-control studies in which I_e and I_n cannot be determined, it is possible to estimate the attributable risk percent from knowledge of the relative risk (itself estimated from the odds ratio).

Among the asbestos-exposed men referred to above, it would not be possible to determine which ones among them developed lung cancer because of their asbestos exposure. All that could be concluded is that half did. Therefore, for any one of the men with lung cancer, all that could be concluded is that there was a 50% chance of the disease developing as a result of that occupational exposure, and a 50% chance it developed for other reasons. Note that for any elevated relative risk short of infinity, (i.e., no other causal pathways), it is never possible to be *certain* that an ill individual who was exposed got his or her illness because of the exposure. Nonetheless, the higher the relative risk, the higher that likelihood would be. For exposures deemed to have the capacity to cause a disease, a relative risk greater than two yields an attributable risk percent of more than 50%, implying it is more likely than not the exposure contributed to the occurrence of that disease in any one of the exposed persons who developed it. For a corresponding exposure believed to convey a relative risk of less than two, an exposed person who developed the disease probably did so for another reason. (The foregoing formulation would appear to be straightforward, but Greenland has argued that it depends on "unsupported assumptions.")[37]

Since the size of the attributable risk percent is determined by the size of the relative risk, it is necessary to consider what factors may influence relative risk. Often the most important factors are characteristics of the exposure itself, such as intensity, duration, or recency. Lung cancer relative risk associated with cigarette smoking, for example, rises with the number of cigarettes smoked per day, the number of years smoked, and whether an individual has quit smoking (and if so, how long ago). Depending on an individual's cigarette smoking history, his lung cancer risk may be only slightly greater than someone who has never smoked, or it may be as much as 50 times greater. If a person with a particular smoking history is believed to have a lung cancer risk of say, 1.1 times that of a lifelong nonsmoker, and he

37. Sander Greenland, *Relation of Probability of Causation to Relative Risk and Doubling Dose. A Methodologic Error That Has* *Become a Social Problem*, 89 Am. J. Public Health 1166 (1999).

develops lung cancer, the chances that the disease arose as a result of cigarette smoking would be 9 percent. The chances it would have occurred even if he had never smoked would be 91 percent.

$$\frac{1.1 - 1}{1.1} = 9 \text{ percent.}$$

In contrast, in a long-term heavy smoker at a 40–fold increase in risk who goes on to develop lung cancer, the chances of cigarette smoking having played a causal role would be:

$$\frac{40 - 1}{40} = 97.5 \text{ percent.}$$

The relative risk size for a disease associated with one exposure also can be influenced by the presence of another exposure that acts to cause the same disease, if the means by which it does so does not involve the first exposure.[38] Data from epidemiologic studies of menopausal estrogen use in relation to endometrial cancer incidence suggests, approximately, the following pattern of results:

Table 7.7

Annual Incidence of Endometrial Cancer *

Obese	Current Estrogen user of 5 years (I_e)	Never used estrogens (I_n)	Attributable risk* $(I_e\text{-}I_n)$	Relative risk** (I_e/I_n)	Attributable risk % $\dfrac{I_e - I_n}{I_n}$
No	200	50	150	4	75%
Yes	300	150	150	2	50%

*Per 100,000 women.
**Rate in current estrogen users of 5 years duration relative to that in estrogen nonusers.

Being obese is a recognized risk factor for endometrial cancer, and from the figures provided in Table 7 obese women are seen to have a higher risk than other women whether or not they have taken estrogens. Estrogen use also increases a woman's chances of developing endometrial cancer, and by about the same amount (150 per 100,000 per year) whether she is obese or not. Thus, the *relative* contribution of estrogen use to a woman's risk differs between non–obese and obese women: the respective relative risks are 200/50 = 4 and 300/150 =2. It follows that the likelihood that current estrogen use of five years duration contributed to the occurrence of an endometrial cancer in a woman who had that exposure history also differs depending on whether she was also obese. If she were not, the likelihood that estrogen use contributed would be

$$\frac{4 - 1}{4} \times 100 = 75 \text{ percent.}$$

38. ROTHMAN & GREENLAND, *supra* note 28.

If she were obese, that likelihood would be

$$\frac{2 - 1}{2} \times 100 = 50 \text{ percent.}$$

If the second exposure acts *together* with the first to cause the disease, then the relative risk associated with the presence of the first exposure may not vary. It has been observed that the attributable lung cancer risk associated with occupational asbestos is far greater among cigarette smokers than among nonsmokers. Based on this observation, hypotheses have been put forth to explain how the two exposures could interact to produce a greater incidence of disease than either one alone. The following rates are (roughly) what have been seen in several cohort studies:

Table 7.8

Annual Incidence of Lung Cancer *

Cigarette Smoking Status	Asbestos Exposed**	Nonexposed	Attributable Risk*	Relative Risk***	Attributable Risk %
Nonsmoker	40	20	20	2	50%
Smoker	400	200	200	2	50%

*Rate per 100,000
**Occupational exposure of 100 fibers/ml × years
***Rate in asbestos-exposed persons relative to that in nonexposed persons

Despite the difference in the attributable risk size associated with asbestos exposure in nonsmokers and smokers (20 versus 200 per 100,000 per year), the relative risks are each 2.0. As a consequence, the attributable risk percent is 50% in both nonsmokers and smokers. In men with this level of occupational asbestos exposure who developed lung cancer, it would be as equally likely as not that such exposure played a causal role, and this would be equally true in nonsmokers and in smokers.

§ 35–2.7   Conclusion

Epidemiologic studies seek to uncover reasons underlying disease occurrence, but they confront potential limitations in achieving this aim. Randomization of individuals to an exposure believed to influence occurrence of one or more diseases is generally the least biased approach that can be used, but it is not practical to employ for most potential disease-causing exposures. Correlations across populations of disease rates with the prevalence of one or more exposures are usually too crude an approach to offer anything more than a suggestion of an etiologic relation. Comparisons of disease occurrence in persons exposed and not exposed to a particular agent within a population may be useful, but these studies may suffer from imprecise measurement of each study participant's exposure status, and often they have a limited ability to sort out the exposure of interest from other potential risk factors for the disease with which the exposure is correlated. As a consequence, exposures that truly produce a small relative increase in disease occurrence may not be reliably identified through epidemiologic studies.

Unfortunately, in the *absence* of epidemiologic studies we rarely have a solid basis for inferring whether there is a true hazard associated with the presence of a particular exposure. Our other sources of etiologic information—e.g., laboratory research, or impressions of health care providers—clearly have their own limitations as a means of predicting a potentially hazardous agent's impact on an actual person or group of persons. Furthermore, epidemiology now has a track record stretching back into the nineteenth century, of producing results that have led to etiologic inferences that, in turn, have led to actions that almost certainly have prevented disease. Because of epidemiologic research results, successful efforts were made to prevent pellagra through nutritional supplementation, toxic shock syndrome through avoidance of highly absorbent tampon use, Reye's syndrome through avoidance of aspirin in susceptible children, and lung cancer through cigarette smoking cessation (the latter effort has been only partially successful).

Of course, epidemiologic research quality will vary from study to study, in part based on the question being posed and on the resources available to answer it. The better the studies, and the clearer the pattern of results they produce, the more solid will be the inferences that can be drawn from this type of research.

Glossary of Terms

Unless stated otherwise, the following definitions are excerpted in whole or part from A DICTIONARY OF EPIDEMIOLOGY, (John M. Last ed., 3d ed. 1995).

Absolute Risk The observed or calculated probability of an event in a population under study, as contrasted with the relative risk.

Adjustment A summarizing procedure for a statistical measure in which the effects of differences in composition of the populations being compared have been minimized by statistical methods.

Association (Syn: correlation, [statistical] dependence, relationship) Statistical dependence between two or more events, characteristics, or other variables. An association is present if the probability of occurrence of an event of characteristic, or the quantity of a variable, depends upon the occurrence of one or more other events, the presence of one or more other characteristics, or the quantity of one or more other variables. The association between two variables is described as positive when the occurrence of higher values of a variable is associated with the occurrence of higher values of another variable. In a negative association, the occurrence of higher values of one variable is associated with lower values of the other variable. An association may be fortuitous or may be produced by various other circumstances; the presence of an association does not necessarily imply a causal relationship.

Attributable Risk Percent (attributable fraction) With a given outcome, exposure factor and population, the attributable fraction among the exposed is the proportion by which the incidence rate of the outcome among those exposed would be reduced if the exposure were eliminated. It may be estimated by the formula

$$\frac{I_e - I_n}{I_e}$$

where I_e is the incidence rate among the exposed I_n is the incidence rate among the unexposed; or the formula

$$\frac{RR - 1}{RR}$$

where RR is the relative risk.

Attributable Risk The rate of a disease or other outcome in exposed individuals that can be attributed to the exposure. This measure is derived by subtracting the rate of the outcome (usually incidence or mortality) among the unexposed from the rate among the exposed individuals.

Bias Deviation of results or inferences from the truth, or processes leading to such deviation. Any trend in the collection, analysis, interpretation, publication, or review of data that can lead to conclusions that are systematically different from the truth.

Case Control Study The observational epidemiologic study of persons with the disease (or other outcome variable) of interest and a suitable control (comparison, reference) group of persons without the disease. The relationship of an attribute to the disease is examined by comparing the diseased and nondiseased with regard to how frequently the attribute is present or, if quantitative, the levels of the attribute, in each of the groups. In short, the past history of exposure to a suspected RISK FACTOR is compared between "cases" and "controls," persons who resemble the cases in such respects as age and sex but do not have the disease or condition of interest.

Cause   (of a disease) An exposure of characteristic whose presence has led to one or more individuals developing the disease. [From Weiss, 1986]

Cohort Study   (Syn: concurrent, follow-up, incidence, longitudinal, prospective study) The analytic method of epidemiologic study in which subsets of a defined population can be identified who are, have been, or in the future may be exposed or not exposed, or exposed in difference degrees, to a factor or factors hypothesized to influence the probability of occurrence of a given disease or other outcome. The main feature of cohort study is observation of incidence rates in groups that differ in exposure levels.

Confidence Interval (CI)   The computed interval with a given probability, e.g., 95%, that the true value of a variable such as a mean, proportion, or rate in contained within the interval.

Confounding   (From the Latin *confoundere*, to mix together)

   1.   A situation in which the effects of two processes are not separated. The distortion of the apparent effect of an exposure on risk brought about by the association with other factors that can influence the outcome.

   2.   A relationship between the effects of two or more causal factors as observed in a set of data such that it is not logically possible to separate the contribution that any single causal factor has made to an effect.

   3.   A situation in which a measure of the effect of an exposure on risk is distorted because of the association of exposure with other factor(s) that influence the outcome under study.

Cross–Sectional Study   (Syn: disease frequency, prevalence study) A study that examines the relationship between diseases (or other health-related characteristics) and other variables of interest as they exist in a defined population at one particular time. The presence or absence of disease and the presence of absence of the other variables (or, if they are quantitative, their level) are determined in each member of the study population or in a representative sample at one particular time. The relationship between a variable and the disease can be examined (1) in terms of the prevalence of disease in different population subgroups defined according to the presence of absence (or level) of the variables and (2) in terms of the presence or absence (or level) of the variables in the diseased versus the nondiseased. Note that disease prevalence rather than incidence is normally recorded in a cross-sectional study. The temporal sequence of cause and effect cannot necessarily be determined in a cross-sectional study.

Ecological Study   A study in which the units of analysis are populations or groups of people, rather then individuals. An example is the study of association between median income and cancer mortality rates in administrative jurisdictions such as states and countries.

Epidemiology The study of variation in the occurrence of disease, and of the reasons for that variation. [From Weiss, 1986]

Error, Type I (Syn: alpha error) The error of rejecting a true null hypothesis, i.e., declaring that a difference exists when it does not.

Error, Type II (Syn: beta error) The error of failing to reject a false null hypothesis i.e., declaring that a difference does not exist when in fact it does.

Etiology Literally, the science of causes, causality; in common usage, cause.

Experimental Study A study in which conditions are under the direct control of the investigator. In epidemiology, a study in which a population is selected for a planned trial of a regimen whose effects are measured by comparing the outcome of the regimen in the experimental group with the outcome of another regimen in a control group. To avoid BIAS members of the experimental and control groups should be comparable except in the regimen that is offered them. Allocation of individuals to experimental or control groups is ideally by randomization. In a RANDOMIZED CONTROLLED TRIAL, individuals are randomly allocated.

Exposed In epidemiology, the exposed group (or simply, the *the exposed*) is often used to connote a group whose members have been exposed to a supposed cause of a disease or health state of interest or possess a characteristic that is a determinant of the health outcome of interest.

Exposure

   1. Proximity and/or contact with a source of a disease agent in such a manner that effective transmission of the agent or harmful effects of the agent may occur.

   2. The amount of a factor to which a group or individual was exposed; sometimes contrasted with dose, the amount that enters or interacts with the organism.

Hypothesis

   1. A supposition, arrived at from observation or reflection, that leads to refutable predictions.

   2. Any conjecture cast in a form that will allow it to be tested and refuted.

Incidence Rate The rate at which new events occur in a population. The numerator is the number of new events that occur in a defined period; the denominator is the population at risk of experiencing the event during this period, sometimes expressed as person-time. The incidence rate most often used in public health practice is calculated by the formula

$$\frac{\text{Number of new events in specified period}}{\begin{array}{l}\text{Number of persons exposed to risk}\\ \text{during this period}\end{array}} \times 10^n$$

In a DYNAMIC POPULATION, the denominator is the average size of the population, often the estimated population at the mid-period. If the period is a year, this is the annual incidence rate. This rate is an estimate of the person-time incidence rate, i.e., the rate per 10^n person-years. If the rate is low, as with many chronic diseases, it is also a good estimate of the cumulative incidence rate. In follow-up studies with no CENSORING, the incidence rate is calculated by dividing the number of new cases in a specific period by the initial size of the cohort of persons being followed; this is equivalent to the cumulative incidence rate during the period. If the number of new cases during a specified period is divided by the sum of the person-time units at risk for all persons during the period, the result is the person-time incidence rate.

Induction Period The period required for a specific cause to produce disease. More precisely, the interval from the causal action of a factor to the initiation of the disease.

Interaction

1. The interdependent operation of two or more causes of produce or prevent an effect. *Biological interaction* means the interdependent operation of two or more causes to produce, prevent, or control disease.

2. Differences in the effects of one or more factors according to the level of the remaining factor(s).

Latent Period (Syn: latency) Delay between exposure to a disease-causing agent and the appearance of manifestations of the disease.

Matching The process of making a study group and a comparison group comparable with respect to extraneous factors.

Meta-analysis The process of using statistical methods to combine the results of different studies. In the biomedical sciences, the systematic, organized and structured evaluation of a problem of interest, using information (commonly in the form of statistical tables or other data) from a number of independent studies of the problem. A frequent application has been the pooling of results from a set of randomized controlled trials, none in itself necessarily powerful enough to demonstrate statistically significant differences, but in aggregate, capable of so doing. Meta-analysis has a qualitative component, i.e., application of predetermined criteria of quality (e.g., completeness of data, absence of biases), and a quantitative component, i.e., integration of the numerical information. Statistical analysis of a collection of analyzed results, sometimes of raw data from individual studies, usually previously published peer-reviewed studies. The aim is to integrate the findings, pool the data, and identify the overall trend of results.

Misclassification The erroneous classification of an individual, a value, or an attribute into a category other than that to which it should be assigned. The probability of misclassification may be the same in all study groups (nondifferential misclassification) or may vary between groups (differential misclassification).

Morbidity Any departure, subjective or objective, from a state of physiological or psychological well-being. In this sense *sickness, illness*, and *morbid condition* are similarly defined and synonymous.

Nested Case Control Study A case control study in which cases and controls are drawn from the population in a COHORT STUDY.

Odds Ratio (Syn: cross-product ratio, relative odds) The ratio of two odds. The term *odds* is defined differently according to the situation under discussion. Consider the following notation for the distribution of a binary exposure and a disease in a population of a sample.

	Exposed	Unexposed
Disease	a	b
No disease	c	d

The *exposure-odds ratio* for a set of case control data is the ratio of the odds in favor of exposure among the cases (*a/b*) to the odds in favor of exposure among noncases (*c/d*). This reduces to *ad/bc*. With incident cases, unbiased subject selection, and a "rare" disease (say, under 2% cumulative incidence rate over the study period), *ad/bc* is an approximate estimate of the RISK RATIO.

P (Probability) Value   The probability that a test statistic would be as extreme as or more extreme than observed if the null hypotheses were true. The letter P, followed by the abbreviation n.s. (not significant) or by the symbol < (less than) and a decimal notation such as 0.01, 0.05, is a statement of the probability that the difference observed could have occurred by chance if the groups were really alike, i.e., under the null hypothesis.

Investigators may arbitrarily set their own significance levels, but in most biomedical and epidemiological work, a study result whose probability value is less than 5% ($P<0.05$) or 1% ($P < 0.01$) is considered sufficiently unlikely to have occurred by chance to justify the designation "statistically significant."

Person–Time   A measurement combining persons and time, used as denominator in person-time incidence and mortality rates. It is the sum of individual units of time that the persons in the study population have been exposed to the condition of interest.

Prevalence   The number of events, e.g., instances of a given disease or other condition, in a given population at a designated time.

Proportion   A type of ratio in which the numerator is included in the denominator.

Proportional Mortality Ratio   The proportion of observed deaths from a specified condition in a defined population, divided by the proportion of deaths expected from this condition in a standard population, expressed either on an age-specific basis or after age adjustment.

Randomized Controlled Trial (RCT)   An epidemiologic experiment in which subjects in a population are randomly allocated into groups, usually called *study* and *control* groups, to receive or not to receive an experimental preventive or therapeutic procedure, maneuver, or intervention. The results are assessed by rigorous comparison of rates of disease, death, recovery, or other appropriate outcome in the study and control groups, respectively.

Rates   A rate is a measure of the frequency of occurrence of a phenomenon. In epidemiology, demography, and vital statistics, a rate is an expression of the frequency with which an event occurs in a defined population; the use of rates rather than raw numbers is essential for comparison of experience between populations at different times, different places, or among different classes of persons.

The components of a rate are the numerator, the denominator, the specified time in which events occur, and a usually a multiplier, a power of 10, which converts the rate from an awkward fraction or decimal to a whole number:

$$\text{Rate} = \frac{\text{Number of events in specified period}}{\text{Average population during the period}} \times 10^n$$

Rate Difference (RD) The absolute difference between two rates, for example, the difference in incidence rate between a population group exposed to a causal factor and a population group not exposed to the factor.

Rate Ratio (RR) The ratio of two rates. The term is used in epidemiologic research with a precise meaning, i.e., the ratio of the rate in the exposed population to the rate in the unexposed population:

$$\text{RR} = \frac{I_e}{I_n}$$

where I_e is the incidence rate among exposed, and I_n is the incidence rate among unexposed. See also RELATIVE RISK.

Recall Bias Systematic error due to differences in accuracy or completeness of recall to memory or past events or experiences.

Relative Risk The ratio of the RISK of disease or death among the exposed to the risk among the unexposed.

Reliability The degree of stability exhibited when a measurement is repeated under identical conditions. *Reliability* refers to the degree to which the results obtained by a measurement procedure can be replicated.

Risk The probability that an event will occur, e.g., that an individual will become ill or die within a stated period of time or age. Also, a nontechnical term encompassing a variety of measures of the probability of a (generally) unfavorable outcome.

Risk Factor An aspect of personal behavior or life-style, an environmental exposure, or an inborn or inherited characteristic, which on the basis of epidemiologic evidence is known to be associated with health-related condition(s) considered important to prevent. The term risk factor is rather loosely used, with any of the following meanings:

1. An attribute or exposure that is associated with an increased probability of a specified outcome, such as the occurrence of a disease. Not necessarily a causal factor.

2. An attribute or exposure that increases the probability of occurrence of disease or other specified outcome.

3. A determinant that can be modified by intervention, thereby reducing the probability of occurrence of disease or other specified outcomes.

Selection Bias Error due to systematic differences in characteristics between those who are selected for study and those who are not.

Standardization   A set of techniques used to remove as far as possible the effect of differences in age or other confounding variables when comparing two or more populations. The common method uses weighted averaging of rates specific for age, sex, or some other potential confounding variable(s) according to some specified distribution of these variables.

Standardized Incidence Ratio   The ratio of the incident number of cases of a specified condition in the study population to the incident number that would be expected if the study population had the same incidence rate as a standard population for which the incidence rate is known; this ratio is usually expressed as a percentage.

Standardized Mortality Ratio (SMR)   The ratio of the number of deaths occurring in the study group of population to the number that would be expected to occur if the study population had the same specific rates as the standard population, multiplied by 100.

Statistical Significance   Statistical methods allow an estimate to be made of the probability of the observed or greater degree of association between independent and dependent variables under the null hypothesis. From this estimate, in a sample of given size, the statistical "significance" of a result can be stated. Usually the level of statistical significance is stated by the P VALUE.

Stratification   The process of or result of separating a sample into several subsamples according to specified criteria such as age groups, socioeconomic status, etc. The effect of confounding variables may be controlled by stratifying the analysis of results. Stratification is used not only to control for confounding effects but also as a way of detecting modifying effects. For example, lung cancer is known to be associated with smoking. To examine the possible association between urban atmospheric pollution and lung cancer, controlling for smoking, the population may be divided into strata according to smoking status. The association between air pollution and cancer can then be appraised separately within each stratum.

Synergism, Synergy   A situation in which the combined effect of two or more factors is greater than the sum of their solitary effects.

Validity, Study   The degree to which the inference drawn from a study, especially generalizations extending beyond the study sample, are warranted when account is taken of the study methods, the representativeness of the study sample, and the nature of the population from which it is drawn. Two varieties of study validity are distinguished:

     1. *Internal validitiy*: The index and comparison groups are selected and compared in such a manner that the observed differences between them on the dependent variables under study may, apart from sampling error, be attributed only to the hypothesized effect under investigation.

     2. *External validity (generalizability)*: A study is externally valid or generalizable if it can produce unbiased inferences regarding a target population (beyond the subjects in the study). This aspect of validity is only meaningful with regard to a specified external target population.

References

B.K. ARMSTRONG, E. WHITE & R. SARACCI, PRINCIPLES OF EXPOSURE MEASUREMENT IN EPIDEMIOLOGY (1992).

E.A. Belongia, M.T. Osterholm & J.T. Soler et al., *Transmission of Escherichia Coli 0157:H7 Infection in Minnesota Child Day–Care Facilities*, 7 JAMA 883 (1993).

H. Berkel, D.C. Birdsell & H. Jenkins, *Breast Augmentation: A Risk Factor of Breast Cancer?* 326 N. ENGL. J. MED. 1649 (1992).

S.F. Berkley, A.W. Hightower, C.V. Broome, et al., *The Relationship of Tampon Characteristics to Menstrual Toxic Shock Syndrome*, 258 JAMA 917 (1987).

J.D. Boice & C.E. Land, *Ionizing Radiation*, CANCER EPIDEMIOLOGY AND PREVENTION (D. Schottenfeld & J.F. Fraumeni eds., 1982).

H. CHECKOWAY, N.E. PEARCE & D.J. CRAWFORD-BROWN, RESEARCH METHODS IN OCCUPATIONAL EPIDEMIOLOGY (1989).

J.R. Daling, N.S. Weiss & T.G. Hislop et al., *Sexual Practices, Sexually Transmitted Diseases, and the Incidence of Anal Cancer*, 317 N. ENGL. J. MED 973 (1987).

A.R. Feinstein, *Meta-Analysis: Statistical Alchemy for the 21st Century*, 48 J. CLIN. EPIDEMIOL. 71 (1995).

W.E. Fleischer, F.J. Viles, R.L. Gade & P. Drinker, *A Health Survey of Pipe Covering Operations in Constructing Naval Vessels*, 28 J. IND. HYG. TOXICOL. 9 (1946).

G.D. Friedman, *Multiple Myeloma: Relation to Propoxyphene and Other Drugs, Radiation, and Occupation*, 15 INT. J. EPIDEMIOL. 424 (1986).

E. Giovannucci, A. Ascherio & E.B. Rimm et al., *A Prospective Cohort Study of Vasectomy and Prostate Cancer*, 269 JAMA 873 (1993).

E. Giovannucci, E.B. Rimm & M.J. Stampfer et al., *Diabetes Mellitus and Risk of Prostate Cancer*, 9 CANCER CAUSES CONTROL 3 (1998).

S. Greenland, *Quantitative Methods in the Review of Epidemiologic Literature*, 9 EPIDEMIOL. REV. 1 (1987).

S. Greenland, *Relation of Probability of Causation to Relative Risk and Doubling Dose. A Methodologic Error that has Become a Social Problem*, 39 AM. J. PUBLIC HEALTH 1166 (1999).

C.H. HENNEKENS & J.E. BURING, EPIDEMIOLOGY IN MEDICINE (1987).

A.L. Herbst, H. Ulfelder & D.C. Poskanzer, *Adenocarcinoma of the Vagina: Association of Maternal Stilbestrol Therapy with Tumor Appearance in Young Women*, 284 N. ENGL. J. MED. 878 (1971).

A.B. Hill, *The Environment and Disease: Association or Causation*, 58 PROC. R. SOC. MED. 295 (1965).

E.S. Hurwitz, M.J. Barrett & D. Bregman et al., *Public Health Service Study on Reye's Syndrome and Medications: Report of the Pilot Phase*, 313 N. ENGL. J. MED. 849 (1985).

H.A. Kahn, *The Dorn Study of Smoking and Mortality Among U.S. Veterans*, 19 NATIONAL CANCER INST. MONO. (1966).

H.A. KAHN & C.T. SEMPOS, STATISTICAL METHODS IN EPIDEMIOLOGY (1989).

J.L. KELSEY, A.S. WHITTEMORE, A.S. EVANS & W.D. THOMPSON, METHODS IN OBSERVATIONAL EPIDEMIOLOGY (2d ed. 1996).

A. Liberati, *A Plea for a More Balanced View of Meta–Analysis and Systematic Overviews of the Effect of Health Care*, 48 J. CLIN. EPIDEMIOL. 81 (1995).

J.S. Marks & T.J. Halpin, *Guillain-Barré Syndrome in Recipients of a New Jersey Influenza Vaccine*, 243 JAMA 2490 (1980).

MRC Vitamin Study Research Group, *Prevention of Neural Tube Defects: Results of the Medical Research Council Vitamin Study*, 338 LANCET 131 (1991).

Public Health Service Report on Fluoride Benefits and Risks, MMWR (1991); 40(RR–7):1–8.

K.M. Rexrode, V.J. Carey & C.H. Hennekens et al., *Abdominal Adiposity and Coronary Heart Disease in Women*, 280 JAMA 1843 (1998).

K.J. ROTHMAN & S. GREENLAND, MODERN EPIDEMIOLOGY (2d ed. 1998).

H.S. Sachs, J. Berrier, & D. Reitman et al., *Medical Uses of Statistics*, META-ANALYSIS OF RANDOMIZED CONTROLLED TRIALS: AN UPDATE OF THE QUALITY AND METHODOLOGY (J.C. Bailar & F. Mosteller eds., 2d ed. 1951).

I.J. Selikoff, E.C. Hammond & H. Seidman, *Latency of Asbestos Disease Among Insulation Workers in the United States and Canada*, 46 CANCER 2736–2740 (1980).

B.A. Silverstein, L.J. Fine & T.J. Armstrong, *Hand Wrist Cumulative Trauma Disorders in Industry*, 43 BRIT. J. IND. MED. 779–784 (1986).

L.F. Voigt & N.S. Weiss, *Endometrial Cancer*, EPIDEMIOLOGY OF ENDOMETRIAL CANCER (E. Surwit & D. Alberts eds. 1989).

N.S. Weiss, *Inferring Causal Relationships: Elaboration of the Criterion of "Dose–Response,"* 113 AM. J. EPIDEMIOL. 487–490 (1981).

N.S. WEISS, CLINICAL EPIDEMIOLOGY: THE STUDY OF THE OUTCOME OF ILLNESS (2d ed. 1996).

CHAPTER 8

TOXICOLOGY

Table of Sections

A. LEGAL ISSUES

Westlaw Electronic Research

See Westlaw Electronic Research Guide preceding the Summary of Contents.

A. LEGAL ISSUES

§ 8–1.0 The Legal Relevance of Toxicological Research

§ 8–1.1 Introduction

Toxicological evidence plays a central role in the regulation of drugs and assessing the risks posed by potentially dangerous substances.[1] For example, the FDA has established protocols for the testing of products on animals prior to their approval for human use.[2] With respect to environmental hazards the National Academy of Science has defined a four-fold process of risk assessment: hazard identification, dose-response estimation, exposure assessment, and risk characterization.[3] Within the regulatory arena, litigation concerning toxicological research has involved issues such as the reasonableness of regulatory agency assumptions[4] and whether the agency has followed established protocols.[5] By and large, however, the role of toxicological research in the regulatory process is well established.

The regulatory and civil litigation arenas have different goals that generate different questions about toxicological findings.[6] Within the regulatory arena the critical question is whether there might be a harmful effect in humans even though toxicological research has uncovered little by way of adverse effects in animals or other biological systems. In private litigation the crucial issue is whether a known effect in a test animal is probative of causation in humans.[7] As some courts have noted, the regulatory threshold is therefore considerably lower than required in tort claims.[8] This chapter

---

§ 8–1.0

1. *See* COMMITTEE ON RISK ASSESSMENT METHODOLOGY, NATIONAL RESEARCH COUNCIL, *ISSUES IN RISK ASSESSMENT* (1993); James P. Leape, *Quantitative Risk Assessment in Regulation of Environmental Carcinogens*, 4 HARV. ENVTL. L. REV. 86 (1980); Wendy E. Wagner, *Congress, Science, and Environmental Policy*, 1999 U. ILL. L. REV. 181 (1999).

2. *See* Advisory Committee on Protocols for Safety Evaluation: Panel on Reproduction, U.S. Food & Drug Admin., *Report on Reproduction Studies in Safety Evaluation of Food Additives and Pesticides Residues*, 16 TOXICOLOGY & APPLIED PHARMACOLOGY 264 (1970).

3. Bernard Goldstein, *Risk Assessment and the Interface Between Science and Law*, 14 COLUM. J. ENVTL. L. (1989).

4. *See e.g.* Public Citizen Health Research Group v. Tyson, 796 F.2d 1479 (D.C.Cir.1986), clarified sub nom. Public Citizen Health Research Group v. Brock, 823 F.2d 626 (D.C.Cir. 1987) (upholding the threshold model adopted by OSHA).

5. Simpson v. Young, 854 F.2d 1429 (D.C.Cir.1988) (rejecting petitioner's argument that FDA had impermissibly certified the safe-ty of a color additive because the researchers had failed to produce animal data on the maximum tolerated dose, as required by FDA protocol). *See* Wendy E. Wagner, *The Science Charade in Toxic Risk Regulation*, 95 COLUM. L. REV. 1613 (1995).

6. Steven Shavell, *Liability for Harm versus Regulation of Safety*, 13 J. LEGAL. STUD. 357 (1984). *See* Wade–Greaux v. Whitehall Lab., Inc. 874 F.Supp. 1441, 1445 (D.Virgin Islands 1994).

7. *See* Jack L. Landau & W. Hugh O'Riordan, *Of Mice and Men: The Admissibility of Animal Studies to Prove Causation in Toxic Tort Litigation*, 25 IDAHO L. REV. 521 (1988–89); Bert P. Krages II, *Rats in the Courtroom: The Admissibility of Animal Studies in Toxic Tort Cases*, 2 J. ENVTL. L. & LITIG. 229 (1987).

8. Regarding this difference, the court in *Mitchell v. Gencorp Inc.*, 165 F.3d 778, 783 n. 3 (10th Cir.1999) notes: "The methodology employed by a government agency 'results from the preventive perspective that the agencies adopt in order to reduce public exposure to harmful substances. The agencies' threshold of proof is reasonably lower than that appropriate in tort law, which traditionally makes more

focuses on toxicological evidence within the private litigation context, for it is here that most admissibility issues arise.[9]

Toxicological knowledge is derived from *in vivo* studies. These studies expose a living animal (sometimes humans) to a substance to observe the substance's effects. Knowledge is also derived from *in vitro* studies, studies that are performed in an artificial or test tube system. In addition, toxicologists frequently examine pharmacokinetic models (models depicting the absorption, distribution, metabolism or excretion of an agent in the body) and structure-activity relationships (use of information about the intrinsic physicochemical characteristics and effects of related chemicals to predict the toxicity of new chemicals) in assessing the likely effects of some exposure on individuals.

The admissibility of toxicological evidence has been contested for at least 30 years.[10] Both before and after *Daubert v. Merrell Dow Pharmaceuticals*,[11] courts have struggled with the problem of when toxicological evidence is admissible to prove a causal relationship between some substance and the plaintiff's injury.[12] It is impossible to reconcile all admissibility decisions in

particularized inquiries into cause and effect and requires a plaintiff to prove that it is more likely than not that another individual has caused him or her harm.'" (quoting Allen v. Pennsylvania Engineering Corp., 102 F.3d 194, 198 (5th Cir.1996)). With respect to the decision of the FDA to withdraw approval of Parlodel as an anti-lactation drug, the court in Glastetter v. Novartis Pharmaceuticals Corp., 107 F.Supp.2d 1015 (E.D.Mo.2000), affirmed 252 F.3d 986 (8th Cir.2001), commented that the FDA's withdrawal statement, "does not establish that the FDA had concluded that bormocriptine can cause an ICH [intreceberal hemorrhage]; instead, it indicates that in light of the limited social utility of bromocriptine in treating lactation and the reports of possible adverse effects, the drug should no longer be used for that purpose. For these reasons, the court does not believe that the FED statement alone establishes the reliability of plaintiffs' experts' causation testimony." *Id.* at 1036.

9. Toxicological issues also arise in the criminal context, most frequently with respect to laboratory tests conducted to assess things such as blood alcohol content, the presence of semen, and DNA matching. *See, e.g.,* Crouch v. State, 638 N.E.2d 861 (Ind.Ct.App.1994) (results of breath test were inadmissible since test method had not been approved by Department of Toxicology of the Indiana University School of Medicine at time test was administered). Many of these topics are discussed elsewhere in this volume. See, for example, the entries for Alcohol Testing and Drug Testing.

Coppolino v. State, 223 So.2d 68 (Fla.Dist.Ct. App.1968) is an interesting criminal case involving a very questionable admission of toxicological evidence. An anesthesiologist who worked with succinylcholine chloride, a drug that arrests respiration, was on trial for the death of his wife. An autopsy, which included a standard toxicological test, failed to show any drugs in the body. However, the state's expert toxicologist developed a new test specifically for the case and claimed that the test could and did detect abnormal amounts of the drug's components in the body. The testimony was admitted under a *Frye* test, even in the face of substantial testimony from other experts that toxicologists thought it to be impossible to detect the presence of this drug in the body. The case is discussed in *Developments in the Law, Confronting the New Challenges of Scientific Evidence*, 108 HARV. L. REV. 1490 (1995).

10. *See* Roberts v. United States, 316 F.2d 489, 493 (3d Cir.1963) (toxicologist permitted to testify that ethylene glycol mist is toxic to humans although he did not testify as to the scientific basis for this opinion).

11. 509 U.S. 579, 113 S.Ct. 2786, 125 L.Ed.2d 469 (1993).

12. The legal literature on the admissibility of expert toxicological evidence is quite large, and includes the following articles: Michael C. Anibogu, *The Future of Electromagnetic Field Litigation*, 15 PACE ENVTL. L. REV. 527 (1998); Erica Beecher–Monas, *Blinded by Science: How Judges Avoid the Science in Scientific Evidence*, 71 TEMP. L. REV. 55 (1998); Erica Beecher–Monas, *A Ray of Light for Judges Blinded by Science: Triers of Science and Intellectual Due Process*, 33 GA. L. REV. 1047 (1999); David M. Benjamin, *Elements of Causation in Toxic Tort Litigation; Science and Law Must Agree*, 14 J. LEGAL MED. 153 (1993); Bert Black, *Post–*

this area, and now that the Supreme Court has ratified the abuse of discretion standard for appellate review of trial court admissibility decisions in *General Electric v. Joiner*[13] it is inevitable that appellate courts will, from time to time, affirm opposing admissibility rulings in similar cases.[14]

Daubert Case Law: The Good, The Bad, and the Ugly, SC33 ALI–ABA 145 (1998); Gerald W. Boston, *A Mass-Exposure Model of Toxic Causation: The Content of Scientific Proof and the Regulatory Experience*, 18 COLUM. J. ENVTL. L. 181 (1993); Troyen A. Brennan, *Helping Courts with Toxic Torts: Some Proposals Regarding Alternative Methods for Presenting and Assessing Scientific Evidence in Common Law Courts*, 51 U. PITT. L. REV. 1 (1989); Troyen Brennan & Robert Carter, *Legal and Scientific Probability of Causation and Other Environmental Disease in Individuals*, 10 J. HEALTH POL. POL'Y & L. 33 (1985); Scott Brewer, *Expert Testimony and Intellectual Due Process*, 107 YALE L.J. 1535 (1998); Harvey Brown *Eight Gates For Expert Witnesses*, 36 HOUS. L. REV. 743 (1999); Harvey Brown, *Procedural Issues Under Daubert*, 36 HOUS. L. REV. 1133 (1999); Stephen D. Easton, *"Yer Outta Here!" A Framework For Analyzing the Potential Exclusion of Expert Testimony Under Federal Rules of Evidence*, 32 U. RICH. L. REV. 1 (1998); Jean Macchiaroli Eggen, *Toxic Torts, Causation, and Scientific Evidence after Daubert (Symposium: Biotechnology Law)*, 55 U. PITT. L. REV. 889 (1994); David L. Faigman, *Appellate Review of Scientific Evidence Under* Daubert *and* Joiner, 48 HASTINGS L.J. 969 (1997); Daniel A. Farber, *Toxic Causation*, 71 MINN. L. REV. 1219 (1987); Bernard D. Goldstein & Mary Sue Henifin, *Reference Guide on Toxicology, in* FEDERAL JUDICIAL CENTER, REFERENCE MANUAL ON SCIENTIFIC EVIDENCE (2D ED.) (Federal Judicial Center 2000); Suzanne Orofino Galbato, *Multiple Chemical Sensitivity: Does* Daubert v. Merrell Dow Pharmaceuticals, Inc. *Warrant Another Look at Clinical Ecology?* 48 SYRACUSE L. REV. 261 (1998); Michael Green, *Expert Witnesses and Sufficiency of Evidence in Toxic Substances Litigation: The Legacy of Agent Orange and Bendectin Litigation*, 86 NW. U. L. REV. 643 (1992); Michael D. Green, *The Road Less Well Traveled (and Seen): Contemporary Lawmaking in Products* Liability, 49 DEPAUL L. REV. 377 (1999) (toxic tort cases such as Bendectin led to the Daubert revolution); Richard Green, ET AL., *Recent Developments in Toxic Tort Law*, 35 TORT & INS. L.J. 653 (2000); Edward J. Imwinkelried, *The Admissibility of Expert Testimony in Christophersen v. Allied–Signal Corp.: The Neglected Issue of the Validity of Nonscience Reasoning by Scientific Witnesses*, 70 DENV. U. L. REV. 473 (1993); Robert C. James, *Role of Toxicology in Toxic Tort Litigation: Establishing Causation*, 61 DEF. COUNS. J. 28 (1994); Randolph N. Jonakait, *The Assessment of Expertise: Transcending Construction*, 37 SANTA CLARA L. REV. 301 (1997); Marilee Kapsa and Carl B. Meyer, *Scientific Experts: Making Their Testimony More Reliable*, 35 CAL. W. L. REV., 313 (1999); Lee Loevinger, *Science as Evidence*, 35 JURIMETRICS J. 153 (1995); Beverly W. Lubit, *The Time Has Come For Doing Science: A Call For Rigorous Application of* Daubert *Standards For the Admissibility of Expert Evidence in the Impending Silicone Breast Implant Litigation*, 42 N.Y.L. SCH. L. REV. 147 (1998); Leslie A. Lunney, *Protecting Juries from Themselves: Restricting the Admission of Expert Testimony in Toxic Tort Cases*, 48 SMU L. REV. 103 (1994); Paul S. Miller & Bert W. Rein, *Whither Daubert? Reliable Resolution of Scientifically–Based Causality Issues*, 50 RUTGERS L.REV. 563 (1998); Richard A. Nagareda, *Outrageous Fortune and the Criminalization of Mass Torts*, 96 MICH. L. REV. 1121 (1998); Wayne Roth–Nelson & Kathey Verdeal, *Risk Evidence in Toxic Torts*, 2 ENVTL. L. 405 (1996); Note, *Navigating Uncertainty: Gatekeeping in the Absence of Hard Science*, 113 HARV. L. REV. 1467 (2000) (discussing "toxic tort" and "slip-and-fall" paradigms of causation); Bruce R. Parker, *Understanding Epidemiology and Its Use in Drug and Medical Device Litigation*, 65 DEF. COUNS. J. 35 (1998); Mark R. Peterson, *Conflicts of Interest in Scientific Expert Testimony*, 40 WM. & MARY L. REV. 1313 (1999); Lawrence S. Pinsky, *The Use of Scientific Peer Review and Colloquia to Assist Judges in the Admissibility Gatekeeping Mandated by* Daubert, 34 HOUS. L. REV. 527 (1997); Susan R. Poulter, *Science and Toxic Torts: Is There a Rational Solution to the Problem of Causation?*, 7 HIGH TECH. L.J. 189 (1992); Susan R. Poulter, *Daubert and Scientific Evidence: Assessing Evidentiary Reliability in Toxic Tort Litigation*, 1993 UTAH L. REV. 1307 (1993); Mike Redmayne, *Expert Evidence and Scientific Disagreement*, 30 U.C. DAVIS L. REV. 1027 (1997); Douglas R. Richmond, *Regulating Expert Testimony*, 62 MO. L. REV. 485 (1997); Symposium, *Current Issues in Toxic Tort*, 2–FALL WIDENER L. SYMP. J. (Fall, 1997); Michael J. Saks, *The Aftermath of Daubert: An Evolving Jurisprudence of Expert Evidence*, 40 JURIMETRICS J. 229 (2000); Joseph Sanders, *From Science to Evidence: The Testimony on Causation in the Bendectin Cases*, 46 STAN. L. REV. 1 (1993).

13. 522 U.S. 136, 118 S.Ct. 512, 139 L.Ed.2d 508 (1997).

14. Compare, for example, the various outcomes in cases involving the drug Parlodel. Globetti v. Sandoz Pharmaceuticals Corp., 111 F.Supp.2d 1174 (N.D.Ala.2000) (admit) with Glastetter v. Novartis Pharm. Corp., 107 F.Supp.2d 1015, 1030 (E.D.Mo.2000), affirmed 252 F.3d 986 (8th Cir.2001), and Hollander v. Sandoz Pharmaceuticals Corp., 95 F.Supp.2d

A critical question, therefore, is whether trial courts are doing a good job in the gatekeeper role assigned them by *Daubert*.[15] In performing this task, trial and appellate courts frequently feel compelled to conduct an in-depth review of the science proffered in a case. As the Eleventh Circuit noted in *Allison v. McGhan Medical Corp.*:[16]

> While meticulous Daubert inquiries may bring judges under criticism for donning white coats and making determinations that are outside their field of expertise, the Supreme Court has obviously deemed this less objectionable than dumping a barrage of questionable scientific evidence on a jury, who would likely be even less equipped than the judge to make reliability and relevance determinations and more likely than the judge to be awestruck by the expert's mystique.[17]

As in the case with epidemiological evidence,[18] several factors seem to influence the likelihood that a court will admit toxicological evidence designed to show that some drug or substance is capable of causing harm (general causation) or that it caused harm to a particular individual (specific causation).[19] With respect to toxicological evidence, these factors include; the number of studies, the design of the studies, the strength of the relationship, the similarity between the substance in the case and the substance in the studies, the similarity between the injury in the case and the injury observed in the studies, the similarity in the dose rate found in the studies and the dose rate in the case, and whether a substantial body of epidemiological data addresses the causal question presented in the case.

A difficult problem arises in cases involving single acute exposures of a limited number of individuals to a toxic substance, such as may occur with the application of a pesticide, the installation of new carpet in a home, or benzene exposure in the workplace. Some courts have permitted experts to testify on causation even though they possess little or no data on the dose to which the plaintiffs were exposed.[20] Other courts have been less permissive in this

---

1230, 1235–38 (W.D.Okla.2000) (exclude). We should mention, however, that the judge in *Globetti* noted the injury in that case was an acute myocardial infarction whereas the injury in the other two cases was a stroke.

The problem of inconsistency across cases is one reason to have preferred the heightened scrutiny, or "hard look" standard used by the circuit court in *Joiner v. General Electric Co.*, 78 F.3d 524 (11th Cir.1996) to over overturn the trial court's refusal to admit plaintiff's expert testimony. If *Daubert* was necessary in part to reduce the likelihood of inconsistent jury verdicts, an abuse of discretion standard may simply move the problem up one level. On the other hand, a one way "hard look," that is a more searching inquiry when the admissibility decision has the effect of no-suiting the plaintiff, would put substantial pressure on trial courts to admit testimony, seriously diminishing the gatekeeper task *Daubert* assigned them.

15. Daubert v. Merrell Dow Pharm., Inc., 509 U.S. 579, 595, 113 S.Ct. 2786, 125 L.Ed.2d 469 (1993). For one assessments of their performance in this and other areas, see Paul S.

Miller & Bert W. Rein, *supra* note 12 (generally favorable review).

16. 184 F.3d 1300, 1310 (11th Cir.1999).

17. 184 F.3d at 1310 (11th Cir.1999).

18. *See* Chapter 37.

19. Although most toxicological evidence is introduced to show the relationship between some exposure and an injury, occasionally toxicologists along with other experts are asked to testify about exposure or contamination. In Berry v. Armstrong Rubber Co., 989 F.2d 822 (5th Cir.1993), plaintiffs claimed the defendant dumped waste material that left hazardous chemicals on their land and in their groundwater. The Fifth Circuit affirmed the district court's dismissal of the plaintiff's case following the exclusion of the testimony of several of its experts who were prepared to testify that the plaintiff's property was contaminated even though they had not run tests on the property itself. *Id.* at 825.

20. Arnold v. Dow Chemical Co., 32 F.Supp.2d 584, 589 (E.D.N.Y.1999); Hall v. Babcock & Wilcox, 69 F.Supp.2d 716 (W.D.Pa.

regard.[21]

These cases often involve questions of the admissibility of differential diagnosis testimony. The Supreme Court opinion in *Kumho Tire Co. v. Carmichael*,[22] resolves any uncertainty as to whether clinical differential diagnosis testimony falls within the ambit of *Daubert*. Clearly, it does. See the chapter on Clinical Medical Testimony for a discussion of these cases.

§ 8–1.2 Toxicology vs. Epidemiology

As is discussed in the epidemiology chapter, the admissibility of toxicological evidence frequently has turned in part on the quantity and quality of epidemiological evidence on point.[23] Courts routinely reject the defense claim that epidemiological evidence is required before a scientific hypothesis can be considered valid under Rule of Evidence 702.[24] However, where a substantial body of epidemiological evidence points in one direction, many courts will not permit an expert to express a contrary conclusion based on toxicological evidence.[25] The District of Columbia Circuit Court distinguished *Richardson v. Richardson–Merrell* from *Ferebee v. Chevron Chemical Company*[26] on this dimension:

> The case before us, however, is not like Ferebee. Indeed, we are at the other end of the spectrum, a great distance from the "frontier of current medical and epidemiological inquiry." And far from a paucity of scientific information on the oft-asserted claim of causal relationship of Bendectin and birth defects, the drug has been extensively studied and a wealth of published epidemiological data has been amassed, none of which has concluded that the drug is teratogenic. Uniquely to this case, the law now has the benefit of twenty years of scientific study, and the published results must be given their just due.[27]

1999); Kannankeril v. Terminix International, Inc., 128 F.3d 802 (3d Cir.1997); Louderback v. Orkin Exterminating Co., 26 F.Supp.2d 1298, 1306 (D.Kan.1998). On the other hand, the Fifth Circuit overturned the exclusion of an expert prepared to testify on the level of benzene exposure in a factory, in large part because the evidence of a very high level of exposure was very strong. Curtis v. M & S Petroleum, Inc. 174 F.3d 661 (5th Cir.1999).

21. Heller v. Shaw, 167 F.3d 146 (3d Cir. 1999); *In re* Ingram Barge Co., 187 F.R.D. 262 (M.D.La.1999).

22. 526 U.S. 137, 119 S.Ct. 1167, 143 L.Ed.2d 238 (1999).

23. In a number of cases the plaintiff's expert's opinion is based solely on a differential diagnosis, unsupported by either epidemiological or toxicological evidence. A number of these cases are discussed in the epidemiology chapter.

24. Pick v. American Medical Systems, Inc., 958 F.Supp. 1151, 1158 (E.D.La.1997).

25. The primacy of epidemiology was an important component of Judge Weinstein's ruling in *In re* Agent Orange Prod. Liab. Litig., 611 F.Supp. 1223 (E.D.N.Y.1985). The

plaintiffs' experts relied partly on animal studies which showed that Agent Orange was carcinogenic to mice and caused chloracne to developing rabbits. Judge Weinstein granted the defendants' motion for summary judgment, stating that epidemiological studies were "[t]he only useful studies having any bearing on causation [and that] all other data supplied by the parties rests on surmise and inapposite extrapolations from animal studies and industrial accidents." 611 F. Supp. at 1230. For a useful discussion of the relative value of epidemiological and toxicological evidence in proving causation see Ellen K Silbergeld, *The Role of Toxicology in Causation: A Scientific Perspective*, 1 COURTS, HEALTH, SCIENCE & THE LAW 374 (1991).

26. Ferebee v. Chevron Chem. Co., 736 F.2d 1529, 1535 (D.C.Cir.1984).

27. Richardson v. Richardson–Merrell, Inc., 857 F.2d 823, 831–32 (D.C.Cir.1988). *See also* Lynch v. Merrell–National Lab., 646 F.Supp. 856 (D.Mass.1986); Bernhardt v. Richardson–Merrell, Inc., 723 F.Supp. 1188 (N.D.Miss. 1988); Turpin v. Merrell Dow Pharmaceuticals, Inc., 736 F.Supp. 737 (E.D.Ky.1990); Lee v. Richardson–Merrell, Inc., 772 F.Supp. 1027

Likewise, in *Raynor v. Merrell Pharmaceuticals, Inc,*[28] the D.C. Circuit used a 702 analysis to conclude plaintiff's expert testimony was inadmissible and therefore defendant was entitled to a summary judgment. The court concluded that when epidemiological evidence was to the contrary it was not methodologically sound to draw inference from chemical structure, in vivo animal studies, and in vitro studies, that Bendectin causes human birth defects.[29]

A pair of more recent ethylene oxide (EtO) cases suffered a similar fate. In *Nelson v. American Sterilizer Co.,*[30] and *Allen v. Pennsylvania Engineering Corp.,*[31] the courts ruled that when a body of epidemiological research has failed to uncover a relationship between EtO exposure and the plaintiff's ailment, the results of animal studies are inconclusive at best and fail to exhibit the level of reliability required by Rule 702.[32]

When epidemiological evidence is unavailable, courts are much more likely to allow the plaintiff to proceed with only toxicological evidence.[33] For example, in *Benedi v. McNeil–P.P.C. Inc.,*[34] the Fourth Circuit held that the

(W.D.Tenn.1991) (Plaintiff's expert testimony that *in vitro* and *in vivo* studies as well as human data establish causal connection between Bendectin and birth defects could not be considered on a motion for summary judgment given overwhelming epidemiological evidence to the contrary.). *But see* Longmore v. Merrell Dow Pharmaceuticals, Inc., 737 F.Supp. 1117, 1121 (D.Idaho 1990) ("Animal studies are generally relied upon by experts determining the link between a drug and birth defects and the same is true for chemical analysis. While the Court will leave open the question of the admissibility of particular studies during the trial of this matter, the Court cannot now preclude all such studies under Rule 703.").

28. 104 F.3d 1371 (D.C.Cir.1997).

29. A similar result was reached in Conde v. Velsicol Chem. Corp., 24 F.3d 809 (6th Cir. 1994).

30. 223 Mich.App. 485, 566 N.W.2d 671, 672 (Mich.Ct.App.1997) (EtO and liver disease).

31. 102 F.3d 194, 195 (5th Cir.1996) (EtO and brain cancer).

32. The district court in *National Bank of Commerce v. Dow Chemical Co.*, 965 F.Supp. 1490, 1519 (E.D.Ark.1996), cited one epidemiological study favoring the defendant's opinion as part of the basis for granting a motion for summary judgment in a case in which the plaintiff alleged that exposure to Dursban LO had caused her birth defects. However, the court did not reach the question as to whether this study would preclude testimony based on other evidence.

The Eleventh Circuit questioned the testimony of an expert in a silicone implant case because he did not "explain why the results of these animal studies should trump more than twenty controlled epidemiological studies of breast implants in humans which have found no valid increased risk of autoimmune disease." Allison v. McGhan Medical Corp., 184 F.3d 1300, 1314 (11th Cir.1999).

The district court in *Castellow v. Chevron USA*, 97 F.Supp.2d 780, 796 (S.D.Tex.2000) rejected the plaintiff's experts' testimony in part because they were unable through toxicological evidence to overcome the epidemiological evidence which shows "that persons exposed to gasoline do not exhibit a statistically significant excess rate of AML, or even leukemias generally." *Id.* at 798.

In *Chambers v. Exxon Corp.*, 81 F.Supp.2d 661 (M.D.La.2000) the plaintiff's expert wished to testify that the plaintiffs chronic myelogenous leukemia was caused by asbestos exposure. The judge held that the testimony was inadmissible in the absence of epidemiological research that establishes a statistically significant risk of contracting CML from benzene exposure. The court note that "there is no lack of epidemiological studies. On the contrary, experts offered by Exxon have produced a number of scientifically performed studies which demonstrate no association between exposure to benzene and development of CML." *Id.* at 665.

33. Joiner v. General Elec. Co., 864 F.Supp. 1310, 1322 (N.D.Ga.1994); Bloomquist v. Wapello County, 500 N.W.2d 1, 5 (Iowa 1993) ("If we were to require epidemiological evidence in all cases of toxic tort injury, we would automatically deny recovery to all claimants who are injured by a toxic substance that is relatively new and as to which a statistical track record has not yet been fully established."); Ambrosini v. Labarraque, 101 F.3d 129 (D.C.Cir.1996); Graham v. Playtex Products, Inc., 993 F.Supp. 127 (N.D.N.Y.1998); Pick v. American Medical Systems, Inc., 958 F.Supp. 1151, 1158 (E.D.La.1997); Globetti v. Sandoz Pharmaceuticals, Corp., 111 F.Supp.2d 1174 (N.D.Ala.2000).

34. 66 F.3d 1378 (4th Cir.1995).

trial judge did not abuse his discretion in allowing the case to go to the jury even though the plaintiff had not introduced any epidemiological evidence of the relationship between Tylenol and liver damage. Apparently, neither side introduced any epidemiology on point.

§ 8–1.3 Toxicology and External Validity

Even in the absence of epidemiological evidence, courts differ in their acceptance of toxicological evidence. As we discussed in Chapter 1, causal questions are best understood at two different levels: at the population level and at the individual level.[35] At the population level the question presented to the courts is whether an expert will be allowed to testify that the proffered toxicological evidence shows any relationship between exposure and injury. At the individual level the question is whether a scientist will be allowed to testify, based on toxicological evidence, that the individual plaintiff's injury is the result of an exposure to some substance. These two levels of analysis are frequently referred to as questions of general causation—does the substance in question cause harm; and specific causation—did the substance cause this plaintiff's injury.

Toxicological evidence presents particularly complex causal questions. Even if the data do show some relationship between a substance and an "injury" in a test tube or an animal model, we still are left with the difficult task of determining whether these results have relevance for humans in general and whether they are relevant to the specific injury suffered by the plaintiff. These are questions of *external validity*. External validity involves the ability to generalize conclusions to types of persons, settings and times and to particular persons, settings and times.[36] If a study uncovers a cause and effect relationship, the researcher must determine to which settings and which categories of individuals the relationship can be generalized. A relationship observed in one circumstance may not apply in a different circumstance, i.e., it may not be externally valid. Many toxicology admissibility rulings turn on questions of external validity.[37]

§ 8–1.3.1 Structure Activity and In Vivo Studies

While all laboratory studies are vulnerable to threats to external validity, not all toxicological evidence is equal in this regard. Animal studies are generally thought to be more probative than other types of toxicological data, and, therefore, courts are more likely to exclude testimony that is based solely on *in vitro* studies or on a structure-activity analysis.[38] For example, in *Wade–*

35. *See* Chapter 1, § 1–3.3.1[2].

36. Thomas D. Cook & Donald T. Campbell, Quasi-Experimentation: Design and Analysis Issues for Field Testing 71–80 (1979).

37. *See, e.g.,* Allison v. McGhan Medical Corporation, 184 F.3d 1300, 1313–14 (11th Cir. 1999). (expert "failed to explain the correlation of the results of . . . rat studies in which the rats were directly injected with silicone to symptoms in a human patient where the inner lumen of the implants had remained intact").

38. Structure-activity evidence is sometimes admitted along with other toxicological

evidence. *See* Oxendine v. Merrell Dow Pharmaceuticals, Inc., 506 A.2d 1100 (D.C.1986).

Courts generally are unwilling to admit Drug Experience Reports (also called Adverse Drug Reports) as evidence that a product causes an alleged injury. Casey v. Ohio Medical Products, 877 F.Supp. 1380, 1385 (N.D.Cal.1995); DeLuca v. Merrell Dow Pharmaceuticals, 791 F.Supp. 1042, 1057 (D.N.J.1992); Glastetter v. Novartis Pharm. Corp., 107 F.Supp.2d 1015, 1030 (2000), affirmed 252 F.3d 986 (8th Cir. 2001), affirmed 252 F.3d 986 (8th Cir.2001) (court also questions expert structure-activity

Greaux v. Whitehall Laboratories, Inc., plaintiff's expert based her conclusion in part on chick embryo research. The court noted:

> Such chick embryo studies are an in vitro, not an in vivo, animal model, and do not replicate a mammalian, let alone a human, exposure.... At least four things happen in the exposure of a human fetus that do not occur in the chick embryo model: (i) absorption of the agent by the mother, (ii) distribution of the agent throughout the maternal and fetal systems, (iii) metabolism of the agent by the maternal system and (iv) elimination of the agent by the mother and fetus, thereby limiting the duration of the exposure. In chick embryo studies, the agent is dropped directly onto the embryo and is not subjected to maternal metabolism, is not distributed throughout the maternal and embryonic systems, and is not eliminated from the embryonic system, resulting in constant exposure until birth.[39]

Merrell Dow Pharmaceuticals, Inc. v. Havner,[40] takes the position found in many Bendectin cases that *in vitro* research by itself cannot provide a satisfactory basis for opinion about causation in the human context.[41] Recall, of course, that there was a very substantial body of negative epidemiological research on this drug. However, other cases with less well developed epidemiological evidence have also looked skeptically at testimony premised on structure-activity and *in vitro* research.[42]

However, courts are rarely confronted with pure *in vitro* cases because it is unlikely a toxicologist would conclude that a substance caused harm to an individual based solely on this type of information.[43] This situation is more

evidence. *Id.* at 1032); Hollander v. Sandoz Pharmaceuticals Corp., 95 F.Supp.2d 1230, 1235–38 (W.D.Okla.2000); Pick v. American Med. Sys., 958 F.Supp. 1151, 1161–62 (E.D.La. 1997); Wade–Greaux v. Whitehall Lab., 874 F.Supp. 1441 (D.Virgin Islands 1994). However, these reports are sometimes admitted in order to show that the defendant was on notice concerning some risk. In Benedi v. McNeil–P.P.C. Inc., 66 F.3d 1378, 1382 (4th Cir.1995), the court admitted DERs for this purpose over the defendant's 403 objection that their probative value was outweighed by their prejudicial effect.

39. 874 F.Supp. 1441, 1456–7 (D.Virgin Islands 1994) (references to transcript pages omitted).

40. 953 S.W.2d 706 (Tex.1997).

41. *Havner,* 953 S.W.2d at 729. For example, similar statements can be found in Blum v. Merrell Dow Pharmaceuticals, Inc., 705 A.2d 1314 (Pa.Super.Ct.1997); Raynor v. Merrell Pharmaceuticals, Inc., 104 F.3d 1371, 1376 (D.C.Cir.1997).

42. National Bank of Commerce v. Dow Chemical Co., 965 F.Supp. 1490, 1526–28 (E.D.Ark.1996); Rogers v. Secretary of Health and Human Services, 1999 WL 809824, at *11 (Fed.Cl.1999) ("similar pathologies" argument is insufficient).

Some courts have noted that opinions based on structure activity evidence are unreliable because of differences between the substances. Hollander v. Sandoz Pharmaceuticals Corp., 95 F.Supp.2d 1230, 1238 (W.D.Okla.2000) ("Plaintiffs have failed to demonstrate that bromocriptine and other ergots have sufficiently similar physiological effects to warrant comparison."). *See also* Revels v. Novartis Pharmaceuticals Corp., 1999 WL 644732, at *5 (Tex. App.—Austin, 1999) (rejecting as inadequate plaintiff's reliance on adverse event reports and structure activity evidence to support a causal conclusion that the drug Parlodel caused plaintiff's decedent's coronary artery vasospasm).

43. One exception is *Graham v. Playtex Products, Inc.*, 993 F.Supp. 127 (N.D.N.Y. 1998). The *Graham* court allowed plaintiff's experts to testify that all cotton tampons are less likely to cause toxic shock syndrome TSS than tampons containing rayon based solely on their *in vitro* research. The research involved placing tampons in a broth containing bacteria capable of producing the toxin most commonly associated with TSS. *Id.* at 131. Flasks containing rayon tampons produced more toxins than flasks containing cotton tampons. The court determined that the experts' methodology was valid, seemingly a reasonable conclusion. It also rejected the defendant's "fit" objection to

likely to arise when the proposed expert is a medical doctor. In these cases, courts may be presented with no more than structure-activity analysis or conclusions based on case studies, minimal tests, or a temporal relationship in which an illness follows shortly after some exposure. In this circumstance, most courts are unlikely to admit the expert's testimony.[44]

§ 8–1.3.2 Animal Studies

Animal studies also face external validity threats. Questions arise concerning their usefulness in answering causal questions about humans because the results must be extrapolated both across species and across dose rates. This fact alone has been cited as grounds for exclusion.[45] However, many

the expert's testimony. The district court refused to give much weight to this objection, arguing that what the defendant was really objecting to was the experts's conclusions, something *Daubert* said was inappropriate. *Id.* at 132. *Graham* was decided after the Supreme Court opinion in General Electric v. Joiner, 522 U.S. 136, 118 S.Ct. 512, 139 L.Ed.2d 508 (1997). The *Joiner* opinion acknowledged something noted by many appellate courts, that the line between conclusions and methods are not very distinct. *Joiner, Id.* at 518. The *Graham* court, however, refused to conclude that the *in vitro* method's failure to replicate conditions of the vaginal environment created an analytical gap sufficient to warrant exclusion. *Graham*, 993 F.Supp. at 132.

44. *See* Wintz v. Northrop Corp., 110 F.3d 508 (7th Cir.1997). The plaintiff's mother was exposed to bromide during her pregnancy and her daughter was born with a birth defect. Physician's opinion that the exposure was the cause of the defect was based primarily on elevated levels of bromide in child's system when she was approximately two weeks old. *Id.* at 513–14. The appellate court affirmed a district court decision to exclude the testimony because it was not sufficiently based on scientific methodology to be admissible. *Id.* at 514.

Cuevas v. E.I. DuPont de Nemours and Co., 956 F.Supp. 1306 (S.D.Miss.1997). Plaintiff alleged a acute exposure to herbicide containing Oust caused multiple medical problems, including neuropathy, pulmonary obstruction, and optic nerve damage. *Id.* at 1307. His treating physicians' testimony that Oust caused his problem was excluded as no more than the observation of a temporal relationship between exposure and illness. *Id.* at 1311.

Moore v. Ashland Chemical, Inc., 126 F.3d 679 (5th Cir.1997). In *Moore*, the appellant was forced to clean up a spill of solvents inside the back of a semi-truck trailer. The trial judge excluded the causation testimony of one of his experts, a specialist in pulmonary, environmental, and internal medicine, that the one-hour exposure caused the plaintiff to suffer from reactive airways dysfunction syndrome (RADS). The expert did not cite any specific in vitro or animal studies on point, but he did

eventually refer to one case study reporting a clerk exposed to Toulene for two and one-half hours who was diagnosed with RADS. *Id.* at 273. He also based his opinion on the short period of time between exposure and the onset of symptoms. *Id.* at 278.

The trial court excluded his testimony on Rule 702 grounds. 126 F.3d at 699. The Fifth Circuit reversed. It held that while *Daubert* applied to all expert evidence, the *Daubert* factors are "hard" science methods or techniques that should apply only to experts who profess to base their testimony on "hard" science knowledge. 126 F.3d at 682. These criteria should not be used to judge the admissibility of a clinical physician's expert testimony. Rather, that testimony should be judged by the principles and a methodology of the field of clinical medicine. Because the expert's proffer was so grounded, it was error to exclude it. 126 F.3d at 701.

In its en banc ruling the full circuit reversed and reinstated the district court judgment on a jury verdict for the defendant. 151 F.3d at 271. It concluded that the expert's opinion on causation was based primarily on the temporal proximity between exposure and symptoms and that it was not an abuse of discretion to conclude that reliance on this factor, was not supported by appropriate validation and was unreliable. "In sum, the district court did not abuse its discretion in finding that the 'analytical gap' between Dr. Jenkins's causation opinion and the scientific knowledge and available data advanced to support that opinion was too wide. The district court was entitled to conclude that Dr. Jenkins's causation opinion was not based on scientific knowledge that would assist the trier of fact as required by Rule 702 of the Federal Rules of Evidence." 151 F.3d at 279.

45. Wade–Greaux v. Whitehall Lab., Inc., 874 F.Supp. 1441, 1483 (D.Virgin Islands 1994) (Plaintiff alleged that primatene cold medicine taken by mother during pregnancy caused birth defect. However, there were no strong animal studies supporting this assertion.); Bell v. Swift Adhesives, Inc., 804 F.Supp. 1577,

courts are prepared to admit testimony premised on this type of research. This is especially true where there is no competing body of epidemiological evidence pointing in a single direction.[46]

When testimony based on animal studies is declared inadmissible it is usually the case that there is some problem with the research in addition to the basic external validity problems created by extrapolation across species.[47] Most frequently the problem is one of three kinds: a lack of similarity between the substance in the case and the substance in the studies,[48] a lack of similarity between the injury in the case and the injury observed in the studies,[49] or a lack of similarity in the dose rate found in the studies and the

1580 (S.D.Ga.1992) ("Nothing in the record persuades this Court to depart . . . from precedent and allow plaintiff to rely primarily upon animal studies to carry her burden on the issue of causation.").

46. When there is other evidence, animal studies are more likely to be rejected. Hall v. Baxter Healthcare Corp., 947 F.Supp. 1387 (D.Or.1996); Sutera v. The Perrier Group of America, 986 F.Supp. 655, 664 (D.Mass.1997).

47. Tyler v. Sterling Drug, Inc., 19 F.Supp.2d 1239, 1244 (N.D.Okla.1998) (animal study was "unfinished.").

48. In *Cavallo v. Star Enterprise*, 892 F.Supp. 756 (E.D.Va.1995), an expert toxicologist based his conclusion that exposure to Av Jet (aviation) fuel caused plaintiff's injury based in part on a study that measured the effect of a nearly three hour exposure to a mixture of 22 volatile organic compounds on a group of 62 individuals. None of the people in the study suffered an injury similar to that of the plaintiff. In rejecting the expert's testimony, the court commented:

> While Rule 702 does not necessarily mandate that the expert find a study linking the exact chemicals at the exact exposure levels with the exact illnesses at issue, it does require that the expert demonstrate a scientifically valid basis for projecting the findings of a study identifying a different chemical-illness relationship to the proffered causal theory. Nowhere does Dr. Monroe explain why the dose-response figures found in these studies and the ailments observed there can reliably be transferred to the case at bar.

Id. at 766.

See also McClelland v. Goodyear Tire & Rubber Co., 735 F.Supp. 172, 173 (D.Md.1990). ("Plaintiffs' attempts to hold Goodyear responsible, under product liability theories, for the total 'toxic soup' they claim existed in their workplace, without the ability to adduce competent evidence that a reasonable fact-finder could view as showing a greater than 50% chance of a causal connection between any such product and the specific injuries they allegedly suffered, must fail."); Estate of Mitchell v. Gencorp, Inc., 968 F.Supp. 592, 600 (D.Kan.1997) (plaintiff experts attempt to use

studies showing a connection between benzene exposure and worker's chronic myelogenous leukemia (CML) to suggest that toluene and xylene might cause this ailment.); Hollander v. Sandoz Pharmaceuticals Corp., 95 F.Supp.2d 1230 (W.D.Okla.2000) ("The court also rejects the plaintiffs' experts' attempt to extrapolate from animal studies to show that Parlodel causes strokes [in post-partum women]. The studies relied upon involved different drugs, did not test the systemic effect of the drug, some of the animals were anesthesitized, and the were neither pregnant nor post-partum." *Id.* at 1238).

49. In *Schmaltz v. Norfolk & Western Railway Company*, the court concluded that evidence that high doses of atrazine caused eye irritation in rabbits was not sufficient to allow a doctor to testify that indirect exposure could cause pulmonary or respiratory problems in humans. . . . "The analytical gap between the evidence presented and the inferences to be drawn on the ultimate issue . . . is too wide in the present case." 878 F.Supp. 1119, 1122 (N.D.Ill.1995) (quoting Conde v. Velsicol Chem. Corp., 24 F.3d 809, 814 (6th Cir.1994)).

In *Sorensen v. Shaklee Corporation* the plaintiffs were born mentally retarded. Their parents claimed the injuries were caused by maternal ingestion of alfalfa tablets allegedly containing ethylene oxide (EtO). The appellate court cited a substantial body of animal study evidence relating exposure to ethylene oxide (EtO) to a variety of ailments, including increased risk of cancer and adverse reproductive and teratogenic effects. Sorensen v. Shaklee, 31 F.3d 638, 649 n. 17 (8th Cir.1994). The circuit court affirmed the trial court's exclusion of plaintiff's expert testimony, justified in part by the fact that the plaintiff:

> has not found any study, even one involving animals, that shows a relationship between ingestion of ETO and mental retardation in offspring. [Dr.] Lynch's application of studies involving animals showing mutagenicity and teratogenicity from inhalation of ETO, to show that human ingestion of ETO or ECH caused mental retardation in offspring, has not been tested, has not been subjected to peer review or publication, and no evidence of its general acceptance has been offered.

dose rate in the case.[50]

Often the plaintiff's problem is exacerbated by the fact that there is little or no evidence concerning the plaintiff's level of exposure, or sometimes whether the plaintiff was in fact exposed at all to the substance under investigation.[51] Occasionally plaintiffs have attempted to sidestep difficulties

Sorensen v. Shaklee, 1993 WL 735819, *6 (S.D.Iowa 1993).

In *Viterbo v. Dow Chemical Co.*, 826 F.2d 420 (5th Cir.1987), the plaintiff claimed exposure to a herbicide lead to a variety of ailments, including depression, hypertension and allergies. His expert's opinion that the herbicide was the cause of the plaintiff's injuries was based in part on *in vivo* studies that indicated when exposed to a large amount of a chemical found in the herbicide rats developed cancers. In affirming the trial court's exclusion of the testimony, the Fifth Circuit noted:

> Here, of course, there was no evidence Viterbo had been exposed to comparable amounts, nor that his symptoms were similar in any respect. We then are left to conclude that the study, at most, is only evidence that picloram may produce some unidentified effect on humans. Such evidence is clearly not sufficient to provide a source of support for an opinion that Tordon 10K caused Viterbo's depression, nervousness, hypertension, renal failure and other ailments.

Id. at 424.

See also Boyles v. American Cyanamid Co., 796 F.Supp. 704 (E.D.N.Y.1992) (Plaintiff claimed that a 10–minute exposure to chemicals used to manufacture Malathion accidently released from a plant four miles distant caused birth defects in her unborn child. In refusing to admit the testimony of one of the plaintiff's experts, the court noted that while there was evidence that exposure to Malathion could cause a temporary disruption of nerve function, "not a single in vivo or in vitro study has ever found that such chemicals agents have a causal association with birth defects." *Id.* at 708. The court concluded that the expert's testimony was inadmissible under 703 as not based on facts, data, or methodology reasonably relied on by experts in the field. *Id.* at 709.); Goewey v. United States, 886 F.Supp. 1268 (D.S.C.1995) (Plaintiff's expert testified as to a connection between pyridines exposure and neurological disorders (chiefly Parkinson's disease). In excluding the testimony, the court noted that the plaintiff had "never manifested any Parkinson-like symptoms, and therefore, the relevancy of any pyridines-Parkinson's connection is absent in this case." *Id.* at 1282.); Cartwright v. Home Depot U.S.A., 936 F.Supp. 900 (M.D.Fla.1996) (Plaintiff's expert acknowledged he could present no epidemiological or animal studies relating latex paint and asthma, but argued that there is an effect based on the fact that a number of chemical compounds from paints are known respiratory irritants.);

Muzzey v. Kerr–McGee Chemical Corp., 921 F.Supp. 511, 515 (N.D.Ill.1996) (The plaintiff attempted to use evidence that radiation causes chronic myelogenous leukemia (CMLP) to show that exposure to radiation caused the plaintiff to suffer from polycythemia vera (PV), another myeloproliferative disease.); Lust v. Merrell Dow Pharmaceuticals, Inc., 89 F.3d 594, 596–97 (9th Cir.1996) (Animal studies showed a relationship between the fertility drug Clomid and some birth defects but not a relationship between the drug and hemifacial microsomia. The plaintiff's expert argued that some chemicals are capable of increasing the probability of all types of birth defects.); General Electric v. Joiner, 522 U.S. 136, 118 S.Ct. 512, 517, 139 L.Ed.2d 508 (1997) (mice exposed to PCB's contracted a different type of cancer than the plaintiff). In all of these cases the expert's testimony was ruled inadmissible. *But see In re* Joint Eastern & Southern District Asbestos Litigation (Maiorana), 52 F.3d 1124 (2d Cir.1995) (asbestos and colon cancer).

50. *See* Wade–Greaux v. Whitehall Lab., Inc., 874 F.Supp. 1441 (D.Virgin Islands 1994) (testimony based on study of the effect of the chemical substance on rabbits which did not take into account therapeutic human dose was inadmissible).

Nelson v. American Sterilizer, 223 Mich.App. 485, 566 N.W.2d 671 (Mich.Ct.App.1997) (The plaintiff claimed to have contracted liver disease due to chronic exposure to ethylene oxide (EtO). The court rejected expert testimony based on animal studies because they involved acute exposure. 566 N.W.2d at 675. The court also noted that while there were some adverse liver effects in mice and rats, studies involving chronic exposure of guinea pigs, rabbits and monkeys showed no ill effects. *Id.* It noted that, "None of the results demonstrate or suggest liver injury in any species as the result of chronic exposure to EtO in concentrations of 49 ppm or less." *Id.* at 676.); General Electric v. Joiner, 522 U.S. 136, 118 S.Ct. 512, 517, 139 L.Ed.2d 508 (1997) (animal studies indicated that infant (but not adult) mice developed cancer after exposure to PCBs. The mice had massive doses of highly concentrated PCBs injected directly into their peritoneums or stomachs. Joiner's exposure was much lower.).

But see Metabolife International Inc. v. Wornick, 264 F.3d 832 (9th Cir.2001). (Appellate Court reverses trial court exclusion of animal studies).

51. For example, in *Christophersen v. Allied–Signal Corporation* the court affirmed the

involved in establishing dosage by arguing a "no-threshold" theory, i.e., that any exposure to the substance in question is capable of causing plaintiff's ailment. Courts have been reluctant to absolve plaintiff's of the burden of showing dosage on the basis of this theory.[52]

The preceding criteria cannot explain every admissibility ruling, but they do help to clarify a number of seemingly contradictory rulings. Many opinions that contain broad language opposing the admissibility of all toxicological evidence have been written within the context of weak toxicological evidence supporting the expert's assertion that a substance caused the plaintiff's injury.[53]

§ 8–1.4 Mass Exposures vs. Localized Releases

One additional distinction should be mentioned. Cases involving toxicological evidence tend to fall into two broad categories: widespread mass exposure and localized releases. A typical example of the former is the Bendectin litigation, where a large number of individuals around the world claimed that the drug caused birth defects in their children.[54] An example of the latter is the litigation surrounding the Paoli Railroad Yard in Pennsylvania. There, a substantial number of individuals claim that PCBs spilled in the yard caused a variety of injuries to people working in and living around the yard.[55] Contamination cases often involve a substantial number of plaintiffs, as when it is alleged that some firm has contaminated a community's drinking

---

district court exclusion of plaintiff's experts, noting:

> If the dosage of the harmful substance and the duration of exposure to it are the types of information upon which experts reasonably rely when forming opinions on the subject, then the district court was justified in excluding Dr. Miller's opinion that is based upon critically incomplete or grossly inaccurate dosage or duration data.

939 F.2d 1106, 1114 (5th Cir.1991).

In *Wright v. Willamette Industries, Inc.*, 91 F.3d 1105, 1107 (8th Cir.1996) the plaintiff claimed injury from exposure to dust from defendant's wood fiber plant. The Eighth Circuit overturned trial court decision to admit evidence of one expert who opined that ailments were more likely than not due to exposure because "it was not based on any knowledge about what amounts of wood fibers impregnated with formaldehyde involve an appreciable risk of harms to human beings who breathe them." For a discussion of the *Wright* case, see Wade Kimmel, *Requiring Level of Exposure Showings in Toxic Tort Litigation after Wright v. Willamette: Is the Plaintiff's Burden Insurmountable?*, 52 Ark. L. Rev. (1999).

See also Cuevas v. E.I. DuPont de Nemours and Co., 956 F.Supp. 1306 (S.D.Miss.1997) (plaintiff expert cites sub-chronic or chronic studies on animals, plaintiff suffered very short

term acute expose when he was accidently sprayed with chemicals by a passing spray truck. There was no evidence on dose received by plaintiff.); Mascarenas v. Miles, Inc., 986 F.Supp. 582 (W.D.Mo.1997) (no reliable information on exposure at all to substance in question.); Savage v. Union Pacific R.R., 67 F.Supp.2d 1021, (E.D.Ark.1999) (absent supporting scientific data, plaintiff's expert's estimates of exposure are "little more than guesswork."). *Id.* at 1034.

52. Sutera v. The Perrier Group of America, 986 F.Supp. 655 (D.Mass.1997); National Bank of Commerce v. Associated Milk Producers, Inc., 22 F.Supp.2d 942 (E.D.Ark.1998).

53. *See, e.g.*, Wade–Greaux v. Whitehall Lab., Inc., 874 F.Supp. 1441, 1453 (D.Virgin Islands 1994) ("Absent consistent, repeated human epidemiological studies showing a statistically significant increased risk of particular birth defects associated with exposure to a specific agent, the community of teratologists does not conclude that the agent is a human teratogen."). All of the Bendectin cases can be understood in this way.

54. The Bendectin litigation is discussed in Michael D. Green, Bendectin and Birth Defects: The Challenges of Mass Toxic Substances Litigation. (1996); Joseph Sanders, Bendectin on Trial: A Study of Mass Tort Litigation. (1998).

55. *In re* Paoli R.R. Yard PCB Litig., 35 F.3d 717 (3d Cir.1994).

water.[56] Some contamination cases have only one or two plaintiffs.[57] Courts frequently handle these two types of cases differently because the science available in the two situations is often quite different. On the one hand, localized releases may often involve substances about which there is no substantial body of epidemiological evidence. Therefore, courts are less likely to exclude the evidence because it is not confirmed by epidemiological evidence.[58] On the other hand, localized contaminations often pose problems such as of the level of exposure and the lack of an exact animal model that make the plaintiff's causal proof more difficult.[59]

§ 8–1.5 Cases Admitting Toxicological Evidence to Prove Causation

In many cases, courts have admitted toxicological evidence offered to probe a causal connection between the plaintiff's injury and a suspect substance.[60] Courts are generally more open to toxicological evidence in situations where ethical or practical considerations impede the collection of systematic human data on the effects of exposure.

In *Ambrosini v. Labarraque,*[61] the plaintiff alleged that Bendectin and Depo–Provera, individually or in combination, caused severe birth defects including cleft palate and facial and ear malformations. The present appeal only involved the Depo–Provera claim. In overturning the lower court's ruling that the plaintiff's experts could not present testimony that Depo–Provera was a teratogen, the court differentiated between the wealth of existing epidemiological data unfavorable to the plaintiffs in Bendectin cases and the paucity of epidemiological data on the teratogenic effects of Depo–Provera. The court refused to exclude the expert's testimony that Depo–Provera is a

56. Renaud v. Martin Marietta Corp., 749 F.Supp. 1545 (D.Colo.1990); Sterling v. Velsicol Chem. Corp., 855 F.2d 1188 (6th Cir.1988).

57. Cavallo v. Star Enter., 892 F.Supp. 756 (E.D.Va.1995) (plaintiff allegedly injured by inhaling fumes from spilled jet fuel while walking across a restaurant parking lot).

58. *See e.g., Renaud,* 749 F.Supp. at 1554. In this groundwater contamination case the district court seemed to require the plaintiff to produce epidemiological evidence to prevail.

In this case, even if plaintiffs had been able to prove exposure by their direct evidence, they would have been required to submit epidemiological evidence in support of their causation contentions. Such a submission would have been necessary because this is a case where it is alleged that an entire community has been exposed to the contaminants. Under these circumstances, it is possible to perform an epidemiological study. Therefore, such evidence should have been submitted; otherwise, plaintiffs fail to meet their causation burdens.

Id. at 1554. On appeal the Tenth Circuit labeled this passage dicta and questioned whether epidemiological data would be necessary given other direct proof of exposure. *Renaud v. Martin Marietta Corp., Inc.,* 972 F.2d 304, 308 (10th Cir.1992).

59. Sorensen v. Shaklee, 31 F.3d 638 (8th Cir.1994) (plaintiffs could not prove the extent to which the particular alfalfa tablets they ingested had been contaminated with ethylene oxide); Claar v. Burlington Northern R.R. Co., 29 F.3d 499 (9th Cir.1994) (plaintiffs unable to demonstrate which workplace chemicals they were exposed to caused which injuries); Ramsey v. Consolidated Rail Corp., 111 F.Supp.2d 1030 (N.D.Ind.2000) (plaintiff's expert's models insufficiently reliable to show her wells were contaminated in the absence of test results showing contamination).

60. In *Villari v. Terminix International, Incorporated,* 692 F.Supp. 568 (E.D.Pa.1988) the district court rejected a defense motion to exclude plaintiff expert testimony based on animal studies that indicated a relationship between certain pesticides and cancer. It found the studies to be admissible under Rule 703 as the type of data experts rely on in forming opinions as to whether a substance causes cancer in humans. "While it may be true that the defendant can offer tests and experiments that do not support the findings of plaintiffs' experts, the defendant cannot deny that animal studies are routinely relied upon by the scientific community in assessing the carcinogenic effects of chemicals on human." *Id.* at 570. The court also rejected the defendant's argument that the testimony should be excluded under Rule 403 because its probative value was outweighed by its prejudicial effect. *Id.* at 572.

61. 101 F.3d 129, 138–39 (D.C.Cir.1996).

teratogen simply because no epidemiological study proves that it is.[62] The court noted that the F.D.A. mooted the issue by prohibiting the use of the drug during pregnancy because it was a teratogen (the drug's known teratogenic effects were dissimilar to the plaintiff's injuries). Thus, no epidemiological study could ever be conducted to support the plaintiff's case.[63]

Similar results were reached in *Dawsey v. Olin*[64] and *Marsee v. United States Tobacco Company*.[65] In *Dawsey*, construction workers were at a job site near the defendant's plant when the plant experienced a malfunction that released a cloud of phosgene gas. The plaintiff was taken to the hospital complaining of nausea and weakness. The court admitted the testimony of a defense toxicologist who extrapolated the effects of phosgene gas on animals to humans and concluded: "Short of intentionally exposing humans to phosgene, it would be difficult to learn any more about the effects of phosgene...."[66]

The plaintiff in *Marsee*, who was suffering from oral cancer, wished to introduce evidence regarding the carcinogenic effects of snuff and tobacco on humans. The defendant filed a motion in limine seeking to exclude the plaintiff's toxicological evidence, based on animal studies, that substances in the snuff could cause cancer in humans. The court denied the motion and entered a post-trial order expanding on its ruling. The opinion noted that animal studies had repeatedly shown the substances found in the defendant's product caused cancer in test animals and added, "Finally, the court found evidence based on experiments with animals particularly valuable and important in this litigation since such experiments with humans are impossible."[67]

Courts also cite the lack of contrary epidemiological evidence as a reason to admit toxicological evidence. The Third Circuit in In re Paoli Railroad Yard PCB Litigation,[68] reversed in part a district court opinion that had found animal studies irrelevant under Federal Rule of Evidence 402, unreliable under Rules 702 and 703, and misleading and confusing under Rule 403. The court distinguished many cases rejecting animal studies because they involved situations where epidemiological data were contrary to the proffered toxicological evidence.

> Here, where the EPA has relied on animal studies to conclude that PCBs are a probable human carcinogen, where there is reason to think that animal studies are particularly valuable because animals react similarly

62. *Id.* at 138.

63. *Id.* at 139. *See also* Pick v. American Medical Systems, Inc., 958 F.Supp. 1151, 1158 (E.D.La.1997) (Silicone implant and autoimmune disease. Note, however, the court entered a summary judgment for the defendant on sufficiency grounds.); Graham v. Playtex Products, Inc., 993 F.Supp. 127 (N.D.N.Y. 1998). The *Graham* court allowed plaintiffs experts to testify that all cotton tampons are less likely to cause toxic shock syndrome TSS than tampons containing rayon based solely on their *in vitro* research. Apparently because all cotton tampons are relatively new, there is not a body of epidemiological data concerning their relative safety. The plaintiff's experts themselves seem to concede, however, that when

such evidence does become available, it would be inappropriate to base an opinion on the *in vitro* data. *Id.* at 131.

64. 782 F.2d 1254 (5th Cir.1986).

65. 639 F.Supp. 466 (W.D.Okla.1986).

66. *Id.* at 1263.

67. *Id.* at 470. *See also* Oukrop v. Wasserburger, 755 P.2d 233 (Wyo.1988) (Defendant misprescribed medication prior to oral surgery, resulting in the plaintiff consuming pills constituting a dose 25 times greater than normal. Toxicologist allowed to testify, based on animal studies, as to the likely consequences for plaintiff's mental functioning.).

68. 35 F.3d 717 (3d Cir.1994).

to humans with respect to the chemical in question, and where the epidemiological data is inconclusive and some of it supports a finding of causation, we think that the district court abused its discretion in excluding the animal studies. Certainly, the evidence meets the relevance requirements of Rule 402 and we think, after taking a hard look, that it also meets the reliability requirement of Rules 702, 703 and 403.[69]

§ 8–1.6   Bases for Excluding Toxicological Evidence

As the preceding discussion indicates, many cases have rejected toxicological evidence offered as proof of causation in private civil litigation. Most have declared the evidence to be inadmissible, while a few have admitted the evidence but determined that it was insufficient to support a plaintiff verdict. Pre-*Daubert* courts rejecting this type of evidence frequently relied on a determination that the evidence was inadmissible under Rule 703 because it was not the type of facts or data relied upon by experts to draw causal inferences about human injuries.[70] Since *Daubert*, most cases have shifted their analysis to Rule 702.[71] In addition, there has been a small increase in the willingness of courts to exclude testimony because the expert is considered unqualified to render a causal opinion.

§ 8–1.6.1   Lack of Qualifications

Traditionally, all but the grossly unqualified experts were permitted to testify under Rule 702.[72] For example, in *Genty v. Resolution Trust Corpora-*

---

69. *Id.* at 781. *See also* Hopkins v. Dow Corning Corp., 33 F.3d 1116, 1125–26 (9th Cir.1994) (In the absence of a solid body of epidemiological evidence, toxicologist who relies on the general knowledge of silicon's deleterious effects in animal studies has satisfied *Daubert*.).

70. Until December 1, 2000 Fed. R. Evid. 703 provided:

The facts or data in the particular case upon which an expert bases an opinion or inference may be those perceived by or made known to the expert at or before the hearing. If of a type reasonably relied upon by experts in the particular field in forming opinions or inferences upon the subject, the facts or data need not be admissible in evidence.

After that date, the rule was amended to read:

The facts or data in the particular case upon which an expert bases an opinion or inference may be those perceived by or made known to the expert at or before the hearing. If of a type reasonably relied upon by experts in the particular field in forming opinions or inferences upon the subject, the facts or data need not be admissible in evidence in order for the opinion or inference to be admitted. Facts or data that are otherwise inadmissible shall not be disclosed to the jury by the proponent of the opinion or inference unless the court determines that their probative value in assisting the jury to evaluate the

expert's opinion substantially outweighs their prejudicial effect.

71. Rule 702 has also been amended. Prior to December 1, 2000 Fed. R. Evid. 702 provided:

If scientific, technical, or other specialized knowledge will assist the trier of fact to understand the evidence or to determine a fact in issue, a witness qualified as an expert by knowledge, skill, experience, training, or education, may testify thereto in the form of an opinion or otherwise.

The new rule attempts to incorporate the *Daubert* trilogy of cases into the black letter of the rule. It reads:

If scientific, technical, or other specialized knowledge will assist the trier of fact to understand the evidence or to determine a fact in issue, a witness qualified as an expert by knowledge, skill, experience, training, or education, may testify thereto in the form of an opinion or otherwise, if (1) the testimony is based upon sufficient facts or data, (2) the testimony is the product of reliable principles and methods, and (3) the witness has applied the principles and methods reliably to the facts of the case.

72. *See* Loudermill v. Dow Chem. Co., 863 F.2d 566, 569 (8th Cir.1988) ("Close scrutiny of the record shows that although Dr. Lowry's credentials are not unassailable in the specific area of the relationship between halogenated

tion,[73] a toxicologist was prepared to testify that the plaintiff's injuries could have been caused by exposure to toxic chemicals present in a landfill. The trial court excluded the plaintiff's expert because he was not a medical doctor. The Third Circuit found that this was not a proper reason.

> The language of Rule 702 [governing the admission of expert witnesses] and the accompanying advisory notes make clear that various kinds of "knowledge, skill, experience, training, or education," qualify an expert as such ... The district court's insistence on a certain kind of degree or background is inconsistent with our jurisprudence in this area.[74]

Nevertheless, it affirmed the trial court's holding because the plaintiff did not produce evidence on appeal indicating that the witness was a qualified expert. They offered "no curriculum vitae; no recitation of studies conducted or methods used; no inclusion of articles published; indeed, nothing supplementing the unadorned assertion in their brief to verify Brubaker's qualifications as an expert toxicologist."[75]

In more recent years, there seems to be a small trend toward greater scrutiny of expert credentials and qualifications in post-*Daubert* admissibility hearings. A number of recent cases have rejected an expert on the basis of a lack of qualifications. Representative of these is *Mancuso v. Consolidated Edison Co. of New York*.[76] There, the court concluded that an internist did not have the requisite qualifications to testify that the plaintiff's ailments were caused by exposure to polychlorinated biphenyls (PCB). The internist lacked formal training and credentials in PCB toxicology or in environmental or occupational medicine. The internist was unable to answer basic questions about PCB toxicology (e.g. what levels of PCB contamination would be dangerous to humans) and relied upon the plaintiffs' attorney to provide him with the scientific literature he relied upon to support his opinion.[77] Likewise, in *Summers v. Missouri Pacific Railroad System*,[78] one of the plaintiff's experts was a psychologist who examined the plaintiff and was prepared to testify only that he "was experiencing a probable dementia that was consistent with a toxic exposure."[79] The court excluded her testimony in part because, lacking expertise in medicine or toxicology, she was not qualified to render even this limited opinion as to the source of the plaintiff's ailment.[80] In

---

hydrocarbons and liver injury, the magistrate operated well within the bounds of his discretion in allowing Dr. Lowry to testify as an expert.").

73. 937 F.2d 899 (3d Cir.1991). *See* Amato v. Syntex Lab., Inc., 917 F.2d 24 (6th Cir.1990) (table).

74. 937 F.2d 899, 917 (3d Cir.1991). A similar conclusion is reached in Corrigan v. Methodist Hosp., 874 F.Supp. 657, 659 (E.D.Pa. 1995).

75. 937 F.2d 899, 917 (3d Cir.1991). *See also* Diaz v. Johnson Matthey, Inc., 893 F.Supp. 358 (D.N.J.1995):

Accordingly, the Court finds Dr. Auerbach unqualified to testify because he totally lacks experience in treating or diagnosing patients with platinum salt allergy and has at best a limited familiarity with the small amount of literature in the field which deals with the still contested issue of whether platinum salt allergy can cause long term health problems even after the patient is no longer exposed to chloroplatinate salts.

Id. at 373.

76. 967 F.Supp. 1437 (S.D.N.Y.1997).

77. *Id.* at 1443–45. In a subsequent proceeding the court also questioned the qualifications of another plaintiff's expert offered to replace the first expert. Mancuso v. Consolidated Edison, 56 F.Supp.2d 391, 398 (S.D.N.Y. 1999). Ultimately the court rejected the second expert's testimony based on flawed methodology. *Id.*

78. 132 F.3d 599 (10th Cir.1997).

79. *Id.* at 602.

80. *Id.* at 604. *See also* Sutera v. The Perrier Group of America, Inc., 986 F.Supp. 655, 667 (D.Mass.1997) (plaintiff's expert, an oncol-

Jones v. Lincoln Electric,[81] the Seventh Circuit held that the trial court abused its discretion when it admitted the testimony of defendant's expert, a metallurgist, who lacked expertise in assessing the toxicology or other health effects of manganese on the body.[82]

Genty[83] is not the only case where a court has attempted to exclude a toxicologist simply because of a lack of a medical degree. As the appellate court in *Sinkfield v. Oh*[84] noted, this is usually an error where the expert is only offering testimony as to the cause of the plaintiff's injury. In *Sinkfield*, the expert was prepared to testify that ibuprofen caused the plaintiff's miscarriage. However, in more complex situations requiring knowledge of the specific medical condition of an individual, courts are more likely to exclude testimony on this ground.[85]

§ 8–1.6.2 General Acceptance (*Frye*)

Even prior to *Daubert*, a majority of federal circuits had abandoned the *Frye* rule.[86] A lack of general acceptance did not automatically make an expert's toxicological testimony inadmissible.[87] Since *Daubert*, admissibility determinations based solely on general acceptance are to be found only in state court opinions in jurisdictions that have not abandoned the *Frye* test.

In *Donaldson v. Central Illinois Public Service Co.*,[88] an Illinois Appellate Court held that an expert's opinion that coal tar could have caused neuroblas-

ogist and hematologist with no expertise in epidemiology, toxicology, biostatistics or risk-assessment, lacks the specific knowledge, education, training and experience to render an opinion as to whether the exposures to low levels of benzene in Perrier for a short time period caused the plaintiff's leukemia); Everett v. Georgia–Pacific Corp., 949 F.Supp. 856, 857 (S.D.Ga.1996) (expert, practicing family medicine and surgery, possesses no specialized knowledge or training in the field of toxicology); Muzzey v. Kerr–McGee Chemical Corp., 921 F.Supp. 511 (N.D.Ill.1996) (witnesses without expertise in hematology not qualified to testify whether plaintiff's exposure to radiation from refining byproduct caused her to contract the disease polycythemia vera).

81. 188 F.3d 709 (7th Cir.1999).

82. *Id.* at 724. The court concluded, however, that this was harmless error. *See also* Summers v. Missouri Pacific Railroad, 897 F.Supp. 533, 540 (E.D.Okla.1995) (Court found that "the neurophysiological evaluation of Plaintiff Summers by Dr. Susan Franks, Ph.D. should be excluded because Dr. Franks, a psychologist, is not an expert in the field of medicine or toxicology."); Berry v. Armstrong Rubber Company, 989 F.2d 822, 827 (5th Cir.1993) (Court excluded the testimony of a professor of geotechnical engineering who was prepared to testify that unusual geologic conditions could allow the migration of toxic chemicals to plaintiffs' land. "The district court found that Dr. Aughenbaugh's testimony was in the area of geochemistry or hydrogeology, which require the use of models to determine the movement

of water-borne substances. Dr. Aughenbaugh had no expertise or credentials in that area and admitted that he did not know how to use such models."); Louderback v. Orkin Exterminating Co., 26 F.Supp.2d 1298, 1302 (D.Kan. 1998) (neuropsychologist not qualified to offer an opinion that plaintiff's cognitive deficits were caused by exposure to chlorpyrifos).

83. Genty v. Resolution Trust Corp., 937 F.2d 899 (3d Cir.1991).

84. 229 Ga.App. 883, 495 S.E.2d 94 (1997).

85. *See* Wintz v. Northrop Corporation, 110 F.3d 508, 512 (7th Cir.1997) (expert, a toxicologist, was not a licensed physician and lacked sufficient expertise in birth defects, bromide exposure, or the specific birth defect from which the plaintiff suffered to testify that bromide exposure to the mother during her pregnancy caused the plaintiff's injury); *In re* TMI Litigation, 193 F.3d 613, 680 (3d Cir.1999) (plant biologist unqualified to testify that residents surrounding Three Mile Island nuclear power plant were suffering from radiation-induced erythema).

86. *See* Chapter 1.

87. *See, e.g.*, Osburn v. Anchor Lab., Inc., 825 F.2d 908, 915 (5th Cir.1987) (the fact that the theory that chloramphenicol can cause leukemia without first causing aplastic anemia had not been widely accepted at the time of the trial did not preclude the testimony of plaintiff's expert).

88. 313 Ill.App.3d 1061, 246 Ill.Dec. 388, 730 N.E.2d 68 (Ill.App.Ct.2000)

tomas were admissible under Frye. The expert was permitted to "extrapolate" from data showing the substance causes other cancers to opine that it could cause neuroblastomas.[89]

The Minnesota Supreme Court used the occasion of *Goeb v. Tharaldson*[90] to hold that the state would stay with its Frye–Mack test rather than switch to Daubert. However, the Frye–Mack test has a reliability prong not altogether unlike the Daubert test and it was primarily on this basis that the court affirmed the trial judge's decision to exclude plaintiff's experts in a pesticide exposure case.[91]

In *Daubert* jurisdictions, general acceptance is rarely the primary basis of a decision. In In re TMI Litigation,[92] the plaintiff's expert's "numerical model" of dispersion of radioactive plume was rejected on general acceptance grounds. The Third Circuit noted,

> Thus, while general acceptance is not the focus of the inquiry, it is a relevant factor which may be considered. Accordingly, a court may well cast a jaundiced eye upon a technique which is not supported by any evidence of general acceptance absent other indicia of reliable methodology. Here, it is impossible to know whether the disputed model's methodology can or has been tested or whether the model has been subjected to peer review or publication. Neither can we determine its known or potential rate of error. Consequently, we can hardly conclude that the plume dispersion model Vergeiner hypothesized meets the Daubert requirement of evidentiary reliability.[93]

Most jurisdictions have moved toward *Daubert* but many states have chosen not to do so.[94]

§ 8–1.6.3 Rule 703

Prior to *Daubert* a number of courts used Rule 703 as the primary vehicle for ruling on the admissibility of toxicological expert testimony.[95] A scientific

---

89. *Id.* at 78.

90. 615 N.W.2d 800 (Minn.2000).

91. *Id.* at 815–16. For other cases relying on *Frye*, see Bass v. Florida Dep't of Law Enforcement, 627 So.2d 1321 (Fla.Dist.Ct.App. 1993); Blum v. Merrell Dow Pharmaceuticals, Inc., 705 A.2d 1314 (Pa.Super.Ct.1997); McKenzie v. Westinghouse Elec. Corp., 547 Pa. 733, 689 A.2d 237 (Pa.1997); Berry v. CSX Transp., Inc., 709 So.2d 552 (Fla.Dist.Ct.App. 1998); E.I. DuPont De Nemours & Co. v. Castillo, 748 So.2d 1108 (Fla.Dist.Ct.App.2000); Courtaulds Fibers, Inc. v. Long, 779 So.2d 198 (Ala.2000).

92. 193 F.3d 613 (3d Cir.1999).

93. *Id.* at 669. *See also* Allison v. McGhan Medical Corp., 184 F.3d 1300, 1319 (11th Cir. 1999).

94. State courts continue to grapple with the adoption of analogues to the federal rules of evidence by their state legislatures. *See* Chapter 1, § 3.0; *see also* Heather G. Hamilton, *The Movement from Frye to Daubert:*

Where Do the States Stand?, 38 Jurimetrics J.201, 209 (1998).

95. *In re* "Agent Orange" Product Liability Litigation, 611 F.Supp. 1223, 1243 (E.D.N.Y. 1985); Richardson v. Richardson–Merrell, 857 F.2d 823 (D.C.Cir.1988); Bernhardt v. Richardson–Merrell, Inc., 723 F.Supp. 1188 (N.D.Miss. 1988); Christophersen v. Allied–Signal Corp., 939 F.2d 1106, 1110 (5th Cir.1991); Boyles v. American Cyanamid Co., 796 F.Supp. 704 (E.D.N.Y.1992); Renaud v. Martin Marietta Corp., 972 F.2d 304, 308 (10th Cir.1992) ("It is unsound scientific practice to select one concentration measured at a single location and point in time and apply it to describe continuous releases of contaminants over an 11–year period."); Peteet v. Dow Chem. Co., 868 F.2d 1428, 1432 (5th Cir.) (plaintiff's toxicologist's testimony admissible because it was based on information of a type reasonably relied upon by experts in the particular field); Viterbo v. Dow Chem., 826 F.2d 420 (5th Cir.1987). For a discussion of the role of 703 after *Daubert* see Edward J. Imwinkelried, *The Meaning of*

expert's testimony was admissible only if it was based on facts or data of a "type reasonably relied on by experts in a particular field in forming opinions or inferences upon the subject."[96] Judge Weinstein used 703 to exclude expert testimony in the Agent Orange opt-out opinion.[97] Similarly, in another Agent Orange opinion, *Lilley v. Dow Chemical Company*,[98] he found the plaintiff's expert qualified under Rule 702[99] but excluded his testimony on 703 grounds.[100] *Christophersen v. Allied–Signal*,[101] another important pre-*Daubert* opinion, developed a four-fold admissibility standard that incorporated Federal Rules 702, 703, and 403 as well as *Frye*.[102] Using this test, the court held that the trial judge did not abuse his discretion in excluding expert testimony that plaintiff's exposure to nickel-cadmium fumes at the workplace caused his colon cancer.[103] *Daubert* relocates many of these issues to the Rule 702 "fit" analysis[104] and today relatively few opinions cite 703 as grounds for exclusion. When they do it is usually in conjunction with a 702 analysis. For example, the Fifth Circuit ruled in *Allen v. Pennsylvania Engineering Corp.*[105] that plaintiff's expert opinion that exposure to ethylene oxide caused brain cancer was inadmissible under both Rule 702 and Rule 703. As to Rule 703, the court noted that there was no direct evidence of the level of the plaintiff's exposure to EtO. The experts relied on the affidavit of a co-worker and extrapolations based on conditions in other hospitals. The court concluded the information on exposure "is so sadly lacking as to be mere guesswork. The experts did not rely on data concerning Allen's exposure that suffices to sustain their opinions

"Facts or Data" in Federal Rule of Evidence 703: The Significance of the Supreme Court's Decision to Rely on Federal Rule 702 in Daubert v. Merrell Dow Pharmaceuticals, Inc., 54. Md. L. Rev. 352 (1995).

96. Fed. R. Evid. 703.

97. *In re* "Agent Orange" Product Liability Litigation, 611 F.Supp. at 1223, 1243 (E.D.N.Y. 1985).

98. 611 F.Supp. 1267 (E.D.N.Y.1985).

99. "Dr. Carnow belongs to a number of professional organizations and writes for professional journals. . . . He will be considered an expert. The other elements of Rule 702 analysis—helpfulness and appropriate methodology—are equally satisfied by Dr. Carnow's testimony. His opinion is directed toward one of the most important issues in this protracted litigation—causation—and would therefore assist the trier of fact." *Id.* at 1280.

100. Dr. Carnow's resort to inappropriate studies of animals and workers exposed during industrial accidents . . . cannot redeem his unfounded opinion. The conclusions set forth in the Carnow affidavit would be excluded at trial under Rule 703 of the Federal Rules of Evidence. *Id.* at 1283.

101. 939 F.2d 1106 (5th Cir.1991).

102. (1) Whether the witness is qualified to express an expert opinion, Fed. R. Evid. 702; (2) whether the facts upon which the expert relies are the same type as are relied upon by other experts in the field, Fed. R. Evid. 703; (3)

whether in reaching his conclusion the expert used a well-founded methodology, *Frye*; and (4) assuming the expert's testimony has passed Rules 702 and 703, and the *Frye* test, whether under Fed. R. Evid. 403 the testimony's potential for unfair prejudice substantially outweighs its probative value. *Id.* at 1110.

103. *Id.* at 1115. The court found the testimony to be inadmissible under both 703 and its *Frye* test. *See* Berry v. Armstrong Rubber Co., 989 F.2d 822 (5th Cir.1993) (using the *Christophersen* test the trial court excluded expert testimony that waste dumped by defendant contaminated plaintiffs' property and water supply). *See also* Rubanick v. Witco Chem. Corp., 125 N.J. 421, 593 A.2d 733 (N.J.1991) (New Jersey adopts a test based on 702 and 703); Sterling v. Velsicol Chem. Corp. 855 F.2d 1188, 1208 (6th Cir.1988) (a four part admissibility test: qualified expert; testifying on a proper subject; which is in conformity with a generally accepted explanatory theory; and the probative value of which outweighs its prejudicial effect).

104. Recall, however, that in *Daubert* Justice Blackmun notes that "a judge assessing a proffer of expert scientific testimony under Rule 702 should also be mindful of other applicable rules" including Rule 703. Daubert v. Merrell Dow Pharmaceuticals, Inc., 509 U.S. 579, 593, 113 S.Ct. 2786, 125 L.Ed.2d 469 (1993).

105. 102 F.3d 194 (5th Cir.1996).

under R. 703.''[106] Similarly, the Third Circuit excluded the testimony of one expert in the Three Mile Island litigation because she relied on reports of patient medical condition prepared by employees of the attorneys representing plaintiffs.[107] The 2000 revisions in Rules 702 and 703 further reduce the likelihood that Rule 703 will play an important role in future admissibility rulings in the federal courts.

§ 8–1.6.4   The *Daubert* Factors

Daubert[108] listed four non-exclusive factors to consider in determining whether scientific testimony is admissible under rule 702: a) scientific validity (falsifiability), b) peer review and publication, c) error rate, and d) general acceptance.[109] A number of appellate courts have now begun to consider another factor, whether the expert's research was created for the purposes of litigation. In addition to these factors, the court in *Daubert* also instructed lower courts to assess whether whether the expert's proffered testimony "fits" the facts of the case.[110]

A strong statement for admissibility of toxicological evidence using these criteria can be found in the 1994 Third Circuit *Paoli* opinion by Judge Becker.

> Applying the Daubert factors, animal studies themselves are testable (the hypothesis that PCBs cause a particular disease can be verified or disproven in the particular animal study, in other animal studies, or in human epidemiological studies). Animal studies follow a generally accepted methodology (all of the experts who testified here accepted the methodology for the purpose of proving whether a particular chemical is harmful in animals). They have been peer reviewed (the studies referred to by experts in this case were published in peer review journals). They are used for purposes outside of litigation. Finally, although their "fit" to proof of causation in humans is in dispute, all experts acknowledge they are of some use—at least in eliminating those chemicals not likely to cause disease in humans. Given the specifics of the animal studies here, the district court should not have excluded the studies as based on unreliable data and as unhelpful.[111]

Paoli, is similar to a great many decisions in that it bases its admissibility ruling on a number of separate *Daubert* factors. For example, in *Porter v. Whitehall Laboratories, Inc.*[112] the Seventh Circuit excluded the plaintiff's experts' testimony because their theories had not been tested, because they had not been subjected to peer review nor published, and because the testimony did not "fit" the issue in the case.

Most courts would agree with the judge in *Schmaltz v. Norfolk and Western Railway Company*[113] that questions of scientific validity are at the heart of *Daubert* analyses. It is difficult to find a case that excludes toxicologi-

---

106. 102 F.3d at 199. *See also* Kelley v. American Heyer–Schulte Corp., 957 F.Supp. 873, 875 (W.D.Tex.1997).

107. *In re* TMI Litigation, 193 F.3d 613, 698 (3d Cir.1999).

108. Daubert v. Merrell Dow Pharmaceuticals, Inc., 509 U.S. 579, 113 S.Ct. 2786, 125 L.Ed.2d 469 (1993).

109. *Id.* at 2796–97.

110. *See* Margaret Berger, *Evidentiary Framework in* FEDERAL JUDICIAL CENTER, REFERENCE MANUAL OF SCIENTIFIC EVIDENCE 73 (1994).

111. *In re* Paoli Railroad Yard PCB Litigation, 35 F.3d 717, 718 (3d Cir.1994).

112. 9 F.3d 607 (7th Cir.1993).

113. 878 F.Supp. 1119, 1121 (N.D.Ill.1995).

cal evidence on *Daubert* grounds that does not cite a lack of scientific validity as its primary grounds.

Most frequently, this requirement is expressed as a failure to test a hypothesis. A typical case is *Golod v. Hoffman La Roche.*[114] There the court held that plaintiff's theory must not only be testable, but must have been tested before an expert will be allowed to testify about causation based on the theory. Plaintiff suffered eye injuries, allegedly from the use of the prescription drug Tegison taken to treat her severe recalcitrant psoriasis. Some of the plaintiffs injuries occurred some time after she ceased taking the drug. However, her expert was prepared to testify that the drug has a long "half-life" due to the fact that it is stored in the liver and in body fat and the release of metabolites from body tissues when combined with continued oral ingestion can raise concentrations to extremely toxic levels that persist after the drug is discontinued.[115] The district court refused to allow the expert to testify as to causation based on this theory. The court noted, "although Dr. Barasch's theory may be biologically plausible, it does not constitute 'scientific knowledge' within the meaning of Daubert. Instead, it is, at most, scientifically-grounded speculation: an untested and potentially untestable hypothesis."[116] Similar language can be found in numerous opinions.[117] With respect to at least one alleged ailment, multiple chemical sensitivity, courts have so routinely excluded on testability grounds that the diagnosis has nearly disappeared from the reported cases.[118]

114. 964 F.Supp. 841 (S.D.N.Y.1997).

115. *Id.* at 848.

116. *Id.* at 860. The court went on to note, "Although there may be circumstances in which a scientific hypothesis that is, practically speaking, untestable, would nevertheless be admissible, perhaps because of general acceptance in the scientific community, this is not such a case. '[T]he courtroom is not the place for scientific guesswork, even of the most inspired sort. Law lags science; it does not lead it.' Rosen v. Ciba–Geigy Corp. 78 F.3d 316, 319 (7th Cir.1996)." *Id.* at 860–861. The *Golod* court did permit the plaintiff to get to the jury based on the differential diagnosis of other experts. 964 F.Supp. at 859.

117. Allison v. McGhan Medical Corp., 184 F.3d 1300, 1321 (11th Cir.1999); Cartwright v. Home Depot U.S.A., Inc., 936 F.Supp. 900, 905 (M.D.Fla.1996); Cuevas v. E.I. DuPont de Nemours & Co., 956 F.Supp. 1306, 1311 (S.D.Miss.1997); Diaz v. Johnson Matthey, Inc., 893 F.Supp. 358 (D.N.J.1995); Edwards v. Safety–Kleen Corp., 61 F.Supp.2d 1354, 1360 (S.D.Fla.1999); Freeport–McMoran v. B–B Paint Corp., 56 F.Supp.2d 823, 833 (E.D.Mich. 1999); Frank v. State of New York, 972 F.Supp. 130, 133–35 (N.D.N.Y.1997); Greer v. Bunge Corp., 71 F.Supp.2d 592 (S.D.Miss. 1999); Goewey v. United States, 886 F.Supp. 1268, 1280–81 (D.S.C.1995); Haggerty v. Upjohn, 950 F.Supp. 1160, 1164 (S.D.Fla.1996); *In re* Ingram Barge Co., 187 F.R.D. 262, 266 (M.D.La.1999); O'Conner v. Commonwealth Edison Co., 13 F.3d 1090, 1107 (7th Cir.1994); Porter v. Whitehall Lab., Inc., 9 F.3d 607, 614 (7th Cir.1993); Ramsey v. Consolidated Rail Corp., 111 F.Supp.2d 1030, 1037 (N.D.Ind. 2000); Schmaltz v. Norfolk & Western Ry. Co., 878 F.Supp. 1119 (N.D.Ill.1995); Sorensen v. Shaklee Corp., 31 F.3d 638, 650 (8th Cir.1994); Summers v. Missouri Pacific Railroad System, 132 F.3d 599, 604 (10th Cir.1997); Wade–Greaux v. Whitehall Lab., Inc., 874 F.Supp. 1441, 1477 (D.Virgin Islands 1994) ("[E]ach of plaintiff's expert witnesses used a methodology not recognized by the relevant scientific community, and not subject to scientific verification. Therefore, each of their opinions was not helpful and must be excluded."); Wallace v. Meadow Acres Manufactured Housing, Inc., 730 N.E.2d 809, 815 (Ind.Ct.App.2000) (extrapolation of formaldehyde exposure data).

118. In *Summers v. Missouri Pacific Railroad System*, 897 F.Supp. 533 (E.D.Okla.1995), employees brought action against the railroad alleging that a two hour fifteen minute exposure to diesel fumes while "deadheading" back to Fort Worth caused them to become chemically sensitized to petrochemical compounds. Plaintiffs' primary expert witness, Dr. Alfred Johnson, was a clinical ecologist, one of a group of individuals who, "claim that various kinds of environmental insults may depress a person's immune system so that the exposed person develops a 'multiple chemical sensitivity,' that is, becomes hypersensitive to other chemicals and naturally occurring substances." 897 F.Supp. at 535. Although Dr. Johnson claimed that his diagnosis was "chemical sensi-

Sometimes courts exclude testimony on the validity prong of the *Daubert* test without directly referring to falsifiability. These courts express the validity requirement in a number of different ways, such as, the testimony was not based on scientific knowledge,[119] was not based of scientifically valid principles,[120] was not sufficiently reliable,[121] and used no reliable method.[122]

Rarely do courts refer to error rate when making admissibility decisions in the toxic tort context.[123] When they do it is nearly always included as an

tivity" and not "multiple chemical sensitivity," the court refused to recognize this distinction and found there was not reliable scientific evidence supporting the expert's conclusion that the short term exposure to diesel fumes caused the plaintiffs' conditions. *Id.* at 541. It based this conclusion in part on reports by a number of professional organizations that were critical of clinical ecology. For example, a 1986 position paper by the American Academy of Allergy and Immunology stated in part, "There are no immunological data to support the dogma of the clinical ecologists. To suggest that these patients lack suppressor T cell function has not been supported by controlled clinical studies or immunological data." *Id.* at 537. The Tenth Circuit affirmed the exclusion of the expert's testimony, 132 F.3d 599 (10th Cir.1997). The district court did not abuse its discretion in excluding the plaintiff's clinical ecologist. Even though the expert claimed his diagnosis was "chemical sensitivity" the trial court concluded that this diagnosis was in fact "multiple chemical sensitivity in part because he conducted none of the standard tests generally used to confirm whether an individual is suffering from chemical sensitivity." 132 F.3d at 604. Because the expert did not make a valid diagnosis of the generally accepted condition of chemical sensitivity, the district court did not abuse its discretion in excluding his testimony.

Multiple chemical sensitivity remains a pariah from an admissibility perspective. Not surprisingly, plaintiffs sometimes go out of their way to argue that their expert has not made a MCS diagnosis. Cavallo v. Star Enter., 892 F.Supp. 756 (E.D.Va.1995). Clinical ecology has been so strongly associated with the idea of "junk science" that once an expert is seen to be espousing multiple chemical sensitivity the prospects for admissibility are very low. Courts typically conclude that the diagnosis is not testable by any objective methods such as allergy tests, brain scans, or special blood tests and individuals said to suffer from the ailment do not exhibit a set of defined objective physical signs of abnormality. This in turn, creates the potential for a high error rate in diagnosis. Moreover, the methods of testing for MCS have not reached general acceptance in toxicology or related fields. *See* Sterling v. Velsicol Chem. Corp., 855 F.2d 1188, 1208–09 (6th Cir.1988) (opinion of clinical psychologists that chemicals in drinking water injured plaintiffs' immune

systems inadmissible); Bradley v. Brown, 42 F.3d 434 (7th Cir.1994) (affirming the district court's exclusion of expert testimony that workers who became ill due to exposure to pesticides applied at their office now suffered from MCS. The district court excluded the testimony after concluding that MCS had not been tested by the scientific method and had not been subjected to meaningful peer review. Bradley v. Brown, 852 F.Supp. 690, 698–99 (N.D.Ind.1994)); Frank v. State of New York, 972 F.Supp. 130, 133–135 (N.D.N.Y.1997). *See also* Treadwell v. Dow–United Technologies, 970 F.Supp. 974 (M.D.Ala.1997); Minner v. American Mortgage & Guaranty Co., 2000 WL 703607 (Del.Super.2000). (The court excluded expert's testimony concerning MCS as unreliable. *Id.* at *16. It concluded that MCS and "sick building syndrome" are not medically valid diagnoses. *Id.* at *18. However, expert was permitted to testify as to reactive airway dysfunction syndrome and toxic encephalopathy. *Id.* at *22–23. The *Minner* opinion contains a very useful commentary on the history of expert testimony). *But see* Elam v. Alcolac, Inc., 765 S.W.2d 42, 86 (Mo.Ct.App.1988) (clinical ecology testimony admissible).

In general, when plaintiff's expert makes a general argument that some mix of toxic substances in some unknown proportion caused plaintiff's illness, courts are likely to exclude the testimony. This is especially the case when the plaintiff suffers from a variety of relatively ill defined health problems. *See* Wynacht v. Beckman Instruments, Inc., 113 F.Supp.2d 1205 (E.D.Tenn.2000).

119. Muzzey v. Kerr–McGee Chemical Corp., 921 F.Supp. 511, 519 (N.D.Ill.1996); Treadwell v. Dow–United Technologies, 970 F.Supp. 974, 982 (M.D.Ala.1997).

120. Estate of Mitchell v. Gencorp, Inc., 968 F.Supp. 592, 601 (D.Kan.1997).

121. Goewey v. United States, 106 F.3d 390 (4th Cir.1997).

122. Sutera v. The Perrier Group of America, 986 F.Supp. 655, 667 (D.Mass.1997); Wintz v. Northrop Corporation, 110 F.3d 508, 513 (7th Cir.1997); *In re* TMI Litigation, 193 F.3d 613, 677 (3d Cir.1999).

123. There are some exceptions. *See* Wallace v. Meadow Acres Manufactured Housing, Inc., 730 N.E.2d 809, 815 (Ind.Ct.App.2000).

additional consideration.[124] Error rate discussions seem to be reserved primarily for cases involving laboratory procedures such as drug and alcohol testing.

A lack of peer review and publication is frequently cited as a reason for exclusion, albeit always as an additional factor.[125] The district court excluded the testimony of one of the plaintiff's experts on these grounds in *Goewey v. United States*.[126] The expert argued that the minor plaintiff's neurological injuries were caused by exposure to an ingredient (tri-prtho-cresyl phosphate—TOCP) in a roof sealant. Evidence of plaintiff's exposure was based on a blood test that had never previously been administered on a human. The court noted that the test had not been published or exposed to peer review and concluded that test had "no scientific credibility."[127]

The peer review and publication discussions involve two separate issues that would benefit from being kept separate. First, there is the question as to whether key parts of the expert's argument have been subjected to peer review in the sense that articles supporting the opinion can be found in the peer reviewed literature.[128] Second, there is the question as to whether this particular expert has published the argument in the peer reviewed literature. If the only shortcoming of a body of testimony is that a particular expert has not published in the area, this is an inappropriate basis for exclusion. However, most cases that exclude testimony because the witness has not published subjected his or her argument involve situations where no one else has published an article on point either.[129]

On the other hand, publication by itself does not insure admissibility. In *Allison v. McGhan Medical Corp.*,[130] the Eleventh Circuit affirmed the exclusion on fit ground of testimony, based on published animal studies, that plaintiff's injuries were caused by silicone exposure. "Publication in a peer reviewed medial journal. . . ., however, does not alone establish the necessary link required under Daubert."

In *Daubert* jurisdictions, general acceptance, like peer review, is an additional factor that is used to bolster an admissibility decision.[131] General

---

124. National Bank of Commerce v. Dow Chemical Co., 965 F.Supp. 1490, 1527 (E.D.Ark.1996); Ramsey v. Consolidated Rail Corp., 111 F.Supp.2d 1030, 1037 (N.D.Ind. 2000).

125. Schmaltz v. Norfolk & Western Ry. Co., 878 F.Supp. 1119, 1123 (N.D.Ill.1995); Goewey v. United States, 886 F.Supp. 1268, 1280–81 (D.S.C.1995); Edwards v. Safety–Kleen Corp., 61 F.Supp.2d 1354, 1360 (S.D.Fla. 1999).

126. 886 F.Supp. at 1268.

127. *Id.* at 1281. Interestingly, this expert's conclusion was criticized by another plaintiff expert who stated that the plaintiff's condition was "not consistent with exposure to TOCP 'from a neurologic point of view.' " *Id.* at 1282. Not surprisingly, this and other inconsistencies among the plaintiff experts proved to be fatal to the plaintiff's case.

128. Cartwright v. Home Depot U.S.A., Inc., 936 F.Supp. 900, 907 (M.D.Fla.1996); Cuevas v. E.I. DuPont de Nemours & Co., 956

F.Supp. 1306, 1312 (S.D.Miss.1997); Sutera v. The Perrier Group of America, 986 F.Supp. 655, 667 (D.Mass.1997).

129. Haggerty v. Upjohn, 950 F.Supp. 1160, 1163 (S.D.Fla.1996); Mascarenas v. Miles, Inc., 986 F.Supp. 582, 593 (W.D.Mo. 1997); *In re* Ingram Barge Co., 187 F.R.D. 262, 266 (M.D.La.1999).

130. 184 F.3d 1300, 1314 (11th Cir.1999).

131. Wade–Greaux v. Whitehall Lab., Inc., 874 F.Supp. 1441, 1478 (D.Virgin Islands 1994) ("I conclude that the respective methodology of each of plaintiff's expert witnesses is contrary to the generally accepted methodology employed by the relevant scientific community, and that fact weighs against the admissibility of the opinions of each of plaintiff's expert witnesses."); Cartwright v. Home Depot U.S.A., Inc., 936 F.Supp. 900, 905 (M.D.Fla. 1996); Cuevas v. E.I. DuPont de Nemours & Co., 956 F.Supp. 1306, 1312 (S.D.Miss.1997); Estate of Mitchell v. Gencorp, Inc., 968 F.Supp.

acceptance often has been given as a reason to exclude expert testimony in multiple chemical sensitivity cases.[132]

Peer review and publication as well as general acceptance are secondary indicia of scientific validity. Another such indicia, developed in *United States v. Downing*,[133] is whether the research and methods employed by the experts were created outside the context of the litigation. This "non-judicial use" criterion was cited in *Wade–Greaux v. Whitehall Laboratories, Inc.*[134] as a reason for excluding the testimony of a plaintiff expert who based her opinion in part on a rabbit and a chick embryo study she conducted for the litigation.[135]

Courts now so frequently refer to the fact that research occurred inside or outside the litigation context that it is fair to say this has become a fifth factor in *Daubert* analyses. For example, the court in *Cuevas*, noted that "none of [the expert's opinions] are an outflow of natural research done prior to being employed by the plaintiffs."[136] By itself, the fact that testimony was presented for the purposes of litigation is rarely a reason to exclude testimony. However, this fact may alter the way the court assesses the proffered testimony. As the district court in *Metabolife International, Inc. v. Wornick*,[137] noted: "Because Metabolife's experts formulated their opinions for purposes of this litigation, the Court must scrutinize closely the stated bases of those opinions."[138]

In *Daubert* the Supreme Court noted that Rule 702 requires that scientific evidence must "assist the trier of fact to understand the evidence or to determine a fact in issue." "This condition goes primarily to relevance.... The consideration has been aptly described by Judge Becker as one of 'fit.'

592, 601 (D.Kan.1997); Haggerty v. Upjohn, 950 F.Supp. 1160, 1164 (S.D.Fla.1996); Sutera v. The Perrier Group of America, 986 F.Supp. 655, 667 (D.Mass.1997).

132. As the *Summers v. Missouri Pacific Railroad System*, 132 F.3d 599, 604 (10th Cir. 1997) court noted, plaintiff's expert's tests "have been the subject of much criticism by the scientific community as not having met acceptable scientific levels of methodology and criteria, and are not designed to test for the recognized medical condition of chemical sensitivity." *See also* Frank v. State of New York, 972 F.Supp. 130, 133–135 (N.D.N.Y.1997); Treadwell v. Dow–United Technologies, 970 F.Supp. 974 (M.D.Ala.1997).

133. United States v. Downing, 753 F.2d 1224, 1238 (3d Cir.1985) ("[T]he non-judicial uses to which the scientific technique are put, may also constitute circumstantial evidence of the reliability of the technique."). *See* DeLuca v. Merrell Dow Pharmaceuticals, Inc., 791 F.Supp. 1042, 1057 (D.N.J.1992). The *Daubert* opinion encourages courts to consider additional factors germane to the issue of scientific validity. Clifton T. Hutchinson & Danny S. Ashby, *Daubert v. Merrell Dow Pharmaceuticals Inc.: Redefining the Bases for Admissibility of Expert Scientific Testimony*, 15 CARDOZO L. REV. 1875, 1909 (1994), list a number of additional factors the courts might consider, including: 1) the nature and breadth of the infer-

ence adduced, 2) the nonjudicial uses to which the scientific techniques have been put, 3) the extent to which the expert has been offered in earlier cases to support or dispute the merits of a particular scientific procedure, 4) the clarity and simplicity with which the technique can be described and its results explained, and 5) the availability of other experts to test and evaluate the technique.

134. 874 F.Supp. 1441 (D.Virgin Islands 1994).

135. "In evaluating the scientific validity or reliability of a particular methodology, it is also appropriate for a trial court to consider whether the methodology is used in a non-judicial setting. If a methodology has not been put to any non-judicial use, that weighs against admissibility. There is no evidence that any of the methodologies employed by plaintiff's expert witnesses has been put to any use outside of the courtroom." *Id.* at 1479.

136. Cuevas v. E.I. DuPont de Nemours & Co., 956 F.Supp. 1306, 1312 (S.D.Miss.1997). *See also* Estate of Mitchell v. Gencorp, 968 F.Supp. 592, 600 (D.Kan.1997); Lust v. Merrell Dow Pharmaceuticals, Inc., 89 F.3d 594, 596 (9th Cir.1996); Allison v. McGhan Medical Corp., 184 F.3d 1300, 1321 (11th Cir.1999).

137. 72 F.Supp.2d 1160 (S.D.Cal.1999).

138. *Id.* at 1168–69.

'Fit' is not always obvious, and scientific validity for one purpose is not necessarily scientific validity for other, unrelated purposes."[139] As Judge Becker noted in *Paoli*, because "fit" often involves issues of external validity, the question of "fit" is a recurring one in toxicology cases. In the *Paoli* opinion, the court set a relatively low threshold to meet the "fit" requirement.[140] Other courts set a somewhat higher threshold.[141]

Perhaps because of the Supreme Court's incautious language in *Daubert* that "the focus, of course, must be solely on principles and methodology, not on the conclusions that they generate"[142] this ground for exclusion has been used sparingly. Early courts that uses a lack of fit as a basis for exclusion downplayed the Supreme Court's methodology-conclusion distinction,[143] but many courts may have decided to sidestep the problem by ruling on other *Daubert* grounds.[144]

139. Daubert v. Merrell Dow Pharmaceuticals, 509 U.S. 579, 589–91, 113 S.Ct. 2786, 125 L.Ed.2d 469 (1993) (citing United States v. Downing, 753 F.2d 1224, 1242 (3d Cir.1985)). The fit requirement often overlaps the "scientific validity" requirement. Because of this overlap it is not always clear whether an expert's testimony is being excluded on "fit" or "validity" grounds.

140. 35 F.3d 717, 745 (3d Cir.1994) "The same standard of reliability extends to the step in the expert's analysis that 'fits' his or her conclusions to the case at hand. Once again, we emphasize that the standard is not that high. For example, in *Paoli I*, we held that testimony that PCBs cause liver cancer 'fit' the case even in the absence of plaintiffs who had liver cancer, because an expert's affidavit suggested that increased risk of liver cancer was probative of increased risk of other forms of cancer. *See Paoli I*, 916 F.2d at 858. Nonetheless, the standard is higher than bare relevance." For other liberal "fit" tests see Joiner v. General Electric Co., 78 F.3d 524 (11th Cir.1996) ("[I]t is important for trial court to keep in mind . . . the intent of Daubert to loosen the strictures of Frye and make it easier to present legitimate conflicting views of experts for the jury's consideration."); Peterson v. Sealed Air Corp., 1991 WL 66370 (N.D.Ill.1991).

141. In *Schmaltz v. Norfolk & Western Ry. Co.*, 878 F.Supp. 1119 (N.D.Ill.1995), the court concluded that evidence that high doses of atrazine caused eye irritation in rabbits were not sufficient to allow a doctor to testify that indirect exposure could cause pulmonary or respiratory problems in humans. In this case the expert's extrapolation was across both types of scientific information, use of animal studies to show a human effect, and the conclusion of the animal study. " 'The analytical gap between the evidence presented and the inferences to be drawn on the ultimate issue . . . is too wide' in the present case." Nevertheless, because the court excluded the expert's testimony, on the basis that it was not grounded in the scientific method, it did not rule on whether the testimony also failed the "fit" requirement. *Id.* at 1123.

In *Porter v. Whitehall Laboratories, Inc.*, 9 F.3d 607 (7th Cir.1993), plaintiff alleged that ingestion of ibuprofen caused his kidney failure. One of his experts opined that interstitial nephritis was the primary event causing the plaintiff's "anti-GBM RPGN." *Id.* at 609. The court noted:

> The timing of the lesions is critical to this theory; the interstitial insult must precede the glomerular reaction. The problem for the plaintiff is that Dr. Del Greco could not relate this theory to the factual situation at hand. He stated that, as to the chronology of lesions in Mr. Porter, "one has to speculate. . . ." He could not establish the factual prerequisite, that the interstitial nephritis in Mr. Porter preceded the anti-GBM RPGN, necessary to apply his theory. Consequently, with his testimony as well, there was no "fit."

Id. at 616.

142. Daubert v. Merrell Dow Pharmaceuticals, Inc., 509 U.S. 579, 595, 113 S.Ct. 2786, 125 L.Ed.2d 469 (1993).

143. For example, in an important *Paoli* opinion following *Daubert*, Judge Becker himself said "we think that [the distinction between principles and methods versus conclusions] has only limited practical import . . . a challenge to 'fit' is very close to a challenge to the expert's ultimate conclusion about the particular case, and yet it is part of the judge's admissibility calculus under Daubert." *In re Paoli*, 35 F.3d 717, 746 (3d Cir.1994).

144. Exceptions are National Bank of Commerce v. Dow Chemical Co., 965 F.Supp. 1490, 1527 (E.D.Ark.1996); Lust v. Merrell Dow Pharmaceuticals, Inc., 89 F.3d 594, 598 (9th Cir.1996). The Three Mile Island litigation opinion granting the defendant a summary judgment on sufficiency grounds involved a fit

The Supreme Court's decision in *General Electric v. Joiner*,[145] ratified Judge Becker's view along with the district court's fit analysis in *Joiner*. It noted that conclusions and methodology are not entirely distinct from one another. "[N]othing in either Daubert or the Federal Rules of Evidence requires a district court to admit opinion evidence which is connected to existing data only by the *ipse dixit* of the expert. A court may conclude that there is simply too great an analytical gap between the data and the opinion proffered. That is what the District Court did here and we hold that it did not abuse its discretion in so doing."[146] In the aftermath of *Joiner* more courts appear to be using a lack of fit as a basis for exclusion.[147]

§ 8–1.6.5 Rule 403

Courts frequently fail to reach the 403 issue, having disposed of the case on the basis of a 702 or 703 analysis.[148] Occasionally district courts will exclude expert toxicological testimony on Rule 403 grounds. However, we cannot find a case where the court did not conclude that the testimony was excludable on other grounds as well.[149] Generally, Rule 403 is not looked upon favorably as an independent ground for excluding an expert's testimony in this area.[150] When it is included as a grounds for exclusion it is generally a makeweight.

analysis. *In re* TMI Litigation Consolidated Proceedings, 927 F.Supp. 834 (M.D.Pa.1996). The plaintiff offered the testimony of a number of experts that radiation exposure caused plaintiffs' injuries that were premised on a dose in excess of 100 rems. However, the key expert witness who originally was to testify that plaintiffs' actually were exposed to this level of radiation "recanted the bulk his opinions in an unsolicited voicemail message left with counsel for Defendants." *Id.* at 863. Absent this testimony, the testimony of the other experts no longer fit the facts of the case and the judge granted the defendant a summary judgment on sufficiency grounds.

145. 522 U.S. 136, 118 S.Ct. 512, 139 L.Ed.2d 508 (1997).

146. 118 S. Ct. at 518. A fit analysis may also shade into a question of scientific validity. *See* National Bank of Commerce v. Dow Chemical Co., 965 F.Supp. 1490, 1496 (E.D.Ark. 1996).

147. *See In re* TMI Litigation, 193 F.3d 613, 670 (3d Cir.1999) (excluding expert testimony for lack of fit); Heller v. Shaw, 167 F.3d 146, 156 (3d Cir.1999) ("[R]eliable methods for making a diagnosis cannot sanitize an otherwise untrustworthy conclusion."); Edwards v. Safety–Kleen Corp., 61 F.Supp.2d 1354, 1357 (S.D.Fla.1999).

148. *See* Diaz v. Johnson Matthey, Inc., 893 F.Supp. 358, 377 (D.N.J.1995); Christophersen v. Allied–Signal Corp., 939 F.2d 1106, 1116 (5th Cir.1991).

149. *See* Wade–Greaux v. Whitehall Lab., Inc. 874 F.Supp. 1441, 1484 (D.Virgin Islands 1994) (evidence excludable on 403 grounds as well as 702 and 703 grounds); Carroll v. Litton Systems, Inc., 1990 WL 312969 (W.D.N.C. 1990) (same); *In re* "Agent Orange" Product Liability Litigation (Lilley), 611 F.Supp. 1267 (E.D.N.Y.1985) (testimony excludable on 703 and 403 grounds); *In re* "Agent Orange" Product Liability Litigation, 611 F.Supp. 1223 (E.D.N.Y.1985) (same); Kelley v. American Heyer–Schulte Corp., 957 F.Supp. 873, 881 (W.D.Tex.1997) (excludable on 7902 grounds); *In re* Paoli Railroad Yard PCB Litigation, 113 F.3d 444, 450 (3d Cir.1997) (trial court did not abuse its discretion in excluding evidence related to plaintiffs' exposure to heat-degraded PCBs and furans on Federal Rule of Evidence 403 grounds).

150. Hines v. Consolidated Rail Corp., 926 F.2d 262, 274 (3d Cir.1991) ("Furthermore, excluding evidence under Fed. R. Evid. 403 at the pretrial stage is an extreme measure.... We held that the record in Paoli failed to meet such a standard and therefore reversed the district court's exclusion of evidence under Fed. R. Evid. 403. For comparable reasons, we reverse the district court's exclusion of evidence under Fed. R. Evid. 403 in this case."); *In re* TMI Litigation Cases Consolidated II, 922 F.Supp. 1038 (M.D.Pa.1996) (testimony of medical doctor, that neoplasms of alleged victims of nuclear reactor accident were caused by ionizing radiation, was not so confusing as to warrant exclusion under Federal Rule of Evidence 403).

§ 8–1.6.6   Sufficiency

A few courts have concluded that animal studies are admissible under *Daubert* but, by themselves, are insufficient to sustain a verdict for the plaintiff. For example, in *Elkins v. Richardson–Merrell, Inc.*,[151] the Sixth Circuit considered the role played by animal studies in Bendectin lawsuits. The court held that because of the plaintiffs' reliance on *in vitro* and *in vivo* studies, their evidence was insufficient to reach a jury. The court did agree that the animal studies were admissible evidence; however, quoting *Turpin*,[152] stated: "We construe *Turpin* to treat the plaintiff's expert opinion indicating a basis of support for the plaintiffs' theories in animal studies to be admissible but 'simply inadequate . . . [to] permit a jury to conclude that Bendectin more probably than not caused birth defects.' "[153]

A similar approach was taken by the Sixth Circuit in *Conde v. Velsicol*.[154] In the face of a large number of epidemiological studies showing no adverse health effects at dose rates substantially greater than the doses the plaintiffs were exposed to, the plaintiffs' other toxicological and medical testimony was insufficient as a matter of law to permit a jury verdict that the family's exposure to chlordane caused their health problems.[155]

In *Merrell Dow Pharmaceuticals, Inc. v. Havner*,[156] the Texas Supreme Court overturned a judgment on a verdict for plaintiff. The court noted that a review of the scientific validity of testimony is appropriate in both admissibility and sufficiency determinations.[157] Sufficiency was also the basis for the court's summary judgment opinion in the Three Mile Island litigation.[158]

§ 8–1.7   Conclusion

Toxicological evidence is an important component of causal proofs in many mass tort and toxic spill cases. Not infrequently, it is the only data the plaintiff has other than the testimony of a treating physician. Cases making blanket statements that toxicological evidence is never sufficient by itself to allow the plaintiff to meet the burden of proof on the causal question are far outweighed by cases that adopt a more measured approach. For most courts, the admissibility of toxicological evidence turns on the quality of other types of data—especially epidemiological data—and the degree to which toxicological findings address the specific causal questions raised in the case.

---

151. 842 F.Supp. 996 (M.D.Tenn.1992).

152. Turpin v. Merrell Dow Pharmaceuticals, Inc., 959 F.2d 1349 (6th Cir.1992).

153. 8 F.3d at 1071.

154. 24 F.3d 809 (6th Cir.1994).

155. *Id.* at 814.

156. 953 S.W.2d 706 (Tex.1997).

157. "Indeed, the United States Supreme Court would agree that a determination of scientific reliability is appropriate in reviewing the legal sufficiency of evidence. While admissibility rather than sufficiency was the focus of the Supreme Court's decision in Daubert, that Court explained that when 'wholesale exclusion' is inappropriate and the evidence is admitted, a review of its sufficiency is not foreclosed: [I]n the event the trial court concludes

that the scintilla of evidence presented supporting a position is insufficient to allow a reasonable juror to conclude that the position more likely than not is true, the court remains free to direct a judgment . . . and likewise to grant summary judgment. 509 U.S. at 595." *Havner*, 953 S.W.2d at 713. (Tex.1997).

158. *In re* TMI Litigation Consolidated Proceedings, 927 F.Supp. 834 (M.D.Pa.1996). Wintz v. Northrop Corporation, 110 F.3d 508, 515 (7th Cir.1997) entered a summary judgment for defendant on sufficiency grounds. The plaintiff's specific causation expert was unwilling to testify with any degree of medical certainty that the plaintiff's birth defects were caused by bromine exposure.

B. SCIENTIFIC STATUS

by

Bernard D. Goldstein, M.D.* & Russellyn Carruth, J.D.**

§ 8–2.0 SCIENTIFIC INTRODUCTION

The discipline of toxicology is based primarily upon the sciences of chemistry and biology. The toxicologist must understand the basic principles of chemistry, particularly the inherent structural determinants of chemical reactivity. He or she must also understand the basic laws of biology so as to be able to infer the likely action of a chemical agent in a biological system. Straddling these two rapidly advancing scientific fields makes toxicology among the more exciting of the modern scientific disciplines. The increasing environmental concerns of the public also have focused attention on toxicology because of the insights it can provide for environmental protection.

In this Section we will focus primarily on the biological aspects of toxicology. The goal will be to describe those facets of the field that are particularly pertinent to the legal system. It will not be possible to provide a comprehensive review. We refer the reader to standard textbooks for additional information.[1]

In the twentieth century toxicology has developed on three related tracks.[2] First, forensic toxicology has continued its focus on the use of

* Bernard D. Goldstein is the Dean of the University of Pittsburgh's Graduate School of Public Health. He served as the Director of the Environmental and Occupational Health Sciences Institute, a joint program of Rutgers, The State University of New Jersey and the University of Medicine and Dentistry of New Jersey (UMDNJ)-Robert Wood Johnson Medical School from 1986–2001. He was the Chair of the Department of Environmental and Community Medicine, UMDNJ–Robert Wood Johnson Medical School from 1980–2001. He was the first Principal Investigator of the Consortium of Risk Evaluation with Stakeholder Participation (CRESP).

Dr. Goldstein earned his B.S. degree at the University of Wisconsin in 1958 and his M.D. degree at New York University School of Medicine in 1962. He is a physician, board certified in Internal Medicine and Hematology; board certified in Toxicology.

Dr. Goldstein's past activities include Member and Chairman of the NIH Toxicology Study Section and EPA's Clean Air Scientific Advisory Committee; Chair of the Institute of Medicine Committee on the Role of the Physician in Occupational and Environmental Medicine, the National Research Council Committees on Biomarkers in Environmental Health Research and Risk Assessment Methodology and the Industry Panel of the World Health Organization Commission on Health and Environment. He is a Member of the Institute of Medicine where he has chaired the Section on Public Health, Biostatistics, and Epidemiology and he has been a Member of the Institute of Medicine Committee on Environmental Justice: Research, Education, and Health Policy Needs. He is the author of over two hundred articles and book chapters related to environmental health sciences and to public policy.

** Russellyn S. Carruth is an Adjunct Professor of Law at the University of Pittsburgh School of Law, where she teaches in the environmental law clinic. She practiced law with the firm of Burr, Pease & Kurtz in Anchorage, Alaska from 1974–1995. Her practice included toxic torts litigation, which involved issues of admissibility of scientific evidence. Since retiring from private practice, she has taught environmental law at the University of Medicine and Dentistry of New Jersey, School of Public Health, where she is an Adjunct Assistant Professor. She has written and spoken on legal/scientific issues, including the admissibility of scientific evidence in litigation. She serves on the Board of the Society of Risk Analysis Section on Risk Law. She received her B.A. degree from University of California at Berkeley in 1966 and J.D. from University of California at Davis in 1974.

§ 8–2.0

1. TOXIC CHEMICALS, HEALTH, AND THE ENVIRONMENT (Lester Lave & Arthur C. Upton eds., 1987); TOXICOLOGY: THE BASIC SCIENCE OF POISONS (Curtis D. Klaassen et al. eds., 1996).

laboratory techniques as a means of determining the cause of death, particularly by poisons, and has expanded its broad support of police and the courts in developing evidence suitable for use in criminal cases, DNA fingerprinting being a recent example. Second, pharmacological toxicology has blossomed as a result of the major investment in drug development. The specter of class action tort litigation has been a spur to thorough toxicological evaluation aimed at discovering and avoiding unwanted side effects of new drugs. Toxicology is also closely intertwined with pharmacology in part because the toxicity of a chemical can also be a clue to a desired drug effect; e.g., the unwanted ability to kill cells in a specific organ may be the basis for a drug useful to treat cancer in that organ; or the toxicological effect of causing shock through dilation of blood vessels can, with appropriate manipulation of chemical structure and dose, lead to a valuable drug to treat high blood pressure.

The third form of toxicology, which we will call environmental toxicology, has antecedents as old as Ramazzini, the 17th century father of occupational medicine.[3] The field has developed rapidly in recent years as a result of the marked increase in environmental concern among the public, the development of many new occupational and general environmental laws regulating the potential for toxicity of chemical and physical agents, and the pressures of toxic tort litigation and of international trade issues. Assessment of the toxicology of chemicals present in the workplace continues to be central to environmental toxicology. We will restrict our comments to environmental toxicology as it affects human health rather than ecosystems.

There are two major differences between pharmacological toxicology and environmental toxicology. Drugs are inherently designed to have biological effects at the dose employed, while the manufacturer of a chemical consumer product, e.g., paint, usually hope for no biological activity consequent to intended use. Secondly, unwanted side effects can be justified for drugs in situations where the potential benefits to the individual outweigh the potential risk of the drug, particularly if the user is fully informed. This is almost never true for an environmental agent, for which zero toxicity is the expected norm.[4]

For these reasons drugs usually undergo a different premarketing toxicological testing process than do other chemicals in commerce. New drugs cannot be approved for use by the U.S. Food and Drug Administration until they go through a rigorous testing regime that proceeds from animal and test tube tests through carefully designed studies of efficacy and toxicity in humans. In contrast, newly introduced non-pharmaceutical chemical agents are not intended for use in humans and routine testing in humans is usually not required or performed.[5] Under the Toxic Substances Control Act, there is a required premarketing notice to the US Environmental Protection Agency

2. Michael A. Gallo, *History and Scope of Toxicology, in* Toxicology 3 (Lester Lave & Arthur C. Upton eds., 1987).

3. Michael Gallo et al., *Biomedical Aspects of Environmental Toxicology, in* Toxic Chemicals, Health, and the Environment 170, 170–204 (Lester Lave & Arthur C. Upton eds., 1987).

4. Sidney Green, *Progress of Various U.S. Regulatory Agencies in Reviewing Alternative*

Test Methods, 13 J. Toxicology Cutaneous and Ocular Toxicology 339 (1994).

5. Charles Kokoski, *Overview of FDA's Redbook Guidelines,* 32 Critical Rev. Food Sci. Nutrition 161 (1992).

(EPA). EPA may order further laboratory testing if on initial evaluation, usually done by assessing the chemical structure, there are grounds for concern. Since adverse health effects are acceptable, there is a much greater level of safety required of the environmental agents, but there is usually less human toxicological information available. There are other intended uses for chemicals that fall in the middle between the extremes of a therapeutic drug and a commercial product with no desired biological effects. For example, there are chemicals intended to kill, such as fungicides, insecticides, rodenti- cides and herbicides. For such agents the goal is to develop a chemical or a delivery system that can distinguish between the biological target and hu- mans or other desired species. Cosmetics and toiletries also fall into a somewhat different category: although intended for human use, no significant risk of side effects is considered acceptable.

The above cursory description of toxicological testing practices refers primarily to new chemicals not previously marketed. Although both the Food, Drug and Cosmetic Act and the Toxic Substances Control Act contain provi- sions allowing the evaluation of chemical compounds that were already being marketed when the laws were passed, this is usually not as thorough as for new chemicals. Thus, the decision to introduce methyl-tert butyl ether (MTBE), a compound long in commerce, in high concentrations to much of the US gasoline supply was done with far less premarketing testing than would be the case for a newly synthesized fuel additive.[6] Despite much public opposition to MTBE use, and a recognition of many unresolved uncertainties concerning its health and environmental effects, the EPA has been unwilling to obtain additional information. This reflects the political reality that more scientific information is needed to remove an existing chemical from use than it is to prevent its introduction.

Underlying all subdisciplines of toxicology is the search for understanding of the mechanisms by which exogenous chemical or physical agents interact with biological systems. Advances in the basic science of toxicology have been central to the safety assessment of chemicals, to environmental risk assess- ment and to the broad preventive approaches that are embodied in environ- mental laws. There are far too many chemicals and mixtures of chemicals, and far too many adverse health endpoints, to be able to construct a matrix in which all exogenous agents will have been tested at environmentally appropri- ate doses for all potential health consequences. Rather, through advances in the basic understanding of toxicological mechanisms an approach has been, and continues to be, developed that allows for prediction of adverse conse- quences. There is insufficient room in this chapter to discuss all of the basic principles involved, particularly as advances in toxicology are firmly rooted in the breadth of biological science. Described below are those concepts that are central to toxicology.

§ 8–2.1　Basic Principles of Toxicology

§ 8–2.1.1　The "Laws" of Toxicology

There are three basic "laws" of toxicology: 1) the dose makes the poison, i.e., everything is poisonous if the dose is high enough; 2) there is a specificity

---

6.　Bernard D. Goldstein & Serap Erdal, 　ENV'T (forthcoming 2001).
MTBE: A Policy Review, in ANN. REV. ENERGY &

of the effects of chemicals; and 3) humans are members of the animal kingdom.[7] The first law is particularly pertinent to specific causation issues while the second law is particularly pertinent to general causation issues in toxic tort cases.

[1] Law I: Dose Response Considerations

The understanding that at some dose everything is poisonous has led to a focus in toxicology on the relationship between dose and response with the presumption being that the higher the dose the greater the response.[8] Dose is defined as the exposure concentration multiplied by the time of exposure. As a simplification, two types of dose response are recognized. One is characterized as having a threshold below which no effect will be observed. For example, nitric acid can burn a hole in the skin, but there is a level of nitric acid, perhaps one drop diluted in a bathtub full of water, below which nitric acid is harmless to the skin. This threshold, or more properly the "no observed effect level", will vary depending upon the individual. For example, it will require less nitric acid to produce a painful response if the skin is broken, and less nitric acid to produce a burn in a baby's skin.[9] As a rule of thumb, all chemical and physical agents are believed to have a threshold for their effects, with the exception of those effects that are caused by a mutation.[10]

The second type of dose-response relationship is usually restricted to those agents that act through causing a specific mutagenic change in cellular genetic material that could lead to cancer, or, if occurring in reproductive cells, to change in an inherited characteristic. In such cases it has been asserted that even one molecule has some finite risk of causing the mutation. This is because a single molecule is believed to have a finite probability of itself or its metabolite altering the chemical structure of DNA so as to change the information conveyed by the genetic code and produce the specific mutation of concern. The mathematical probability of any one molecule causing such an effect is infinitesimally small, no matter how potent the compound is as a mutagen. There are many barriers that prevent a potentially mutagenic molecule from ever reaching the target cell or penetrating to the genetic material in the nucleus. Further, most alterations of DNA are either of no consequence or result in the death of the cell—and a dead cell can not be the source of cancer or of an inherited characteristic. Cells also have very potent mechanisms to repair DNA damage and to restore genetic integrity. Despite all of these and other reasons making it extremely unlikely that exposure to any one molecule of a mutagenic agent could actually cause a mutation, the risk is not zero and a threshold, by definition, does not exist. As a further simplification, it can be assumed that two molecules will have twice the risk of producing a cancer-causing mutation than one molecule, and thus

---

7. Gallo, *supra* note 3.

8. Rolf Hartung, *Dose–Response Relationships in* Toxic Substances and Human Risk: Principles of Data Interpretation 29 (Robert G. Tardiff & Joseph Rodricks eds., 1987).

9. Paul Kotin, *Dose–Response Relationships and Threshold Concepts*, 271 Annals N.Y. Acad. Sci. 22 (1976).

10. Comm. on Risk Assessment Methodology, Nat'l Research Council, Issues in Risk Assessment 34–35, 187, 198–201 (1993); Office Of Tech. Assessment, U.S. Cong., Assessment of Technologies for Determining the Cancer Risks for the Environment (1981).

there is a linear relationship between the extent of exposure and the amount of risk.

This prudent public health approach to the dose response relationship for cancer-causing agents has persisted despite much inferential evidence that for at least certain carcinogens there is a level of exposure that is without risk, i.e. below the threshold.[11] In essence, the "burden of proof" that there is a "safe" level of a compound that is believed to cause human cancer is on those who wish to use the compound in commerce. Thresholds for cancer-causing agents can and have been proven based on toxicological science, primarily through the understanding of the mechanism of action of the specific agent in question. The likelihood of a threshold is believed to be higher for those cancer-causing agents that act through mechanisms other than genotoxicity. For example, workplace exposure for many years to high levels of sulfuric acid in mists leads to cancer of the upper respiratory tract through mechanisms that appear to be related to recurrent acid inflammation of these tissues. This has led to regulation of sulfuric acid at the workplace but not to regulatory concerns about cancer causation from the far lower sulfuric acid levels in the general environment.

[2]   Law II: Specificity

The specificity of the effects of a chemical or physical agent reflects both the intrinsic physical chemistry of the agent and the many different biological processes that characterize complex organisms such as humans. Differentiation of functions among the many organs, cells and subcellular elements of our bodies has through evolution led to a marked difference in responsiveness to chemical and physical agents that is the basis for much of the organ, cellular and subcellular specificity of effects. These differentiation factors may affect absorption, distribution, metabolism or elimination of a chemical. As examples, skin is relatively impervious to caustic agents or acids that when swallowed can be fatal; radioactive iodine is preferentially distributed to the thyroid gland because of a thyroid-specific membrane pump that actively withdraws iodine from the circulation, using it to make thyroid hormone. This makes the thyroid gland the specific target for damage or for cancer as a result of the release of radioactive iodine from a nuclear incident. The liver's major role in metabolism is responsible for it being a frequent target of toxicity of compounds such as carbon tetrachloride whose metabolism results in the formation of toxic intermediates.[12] And the role of the kidney in eliminating poisons from the body makes it particularly susceptible to agents such as heavy metals, e.g. mercury and cadmium, which preferentially deposit in this organ.

[3]   Law III: Humans are Animals

There is an overwhelming biological similarity between humans and other animals, particularly mammals. With respect to the toxicological effects

11. Henry C. Pitot III & Yvonne P. Dragan, *Chemical Carcinogenesis, in* TOXICOLOGY, 201 (Curtis D. Klaassen et al. eds., 1996).

12. Mary Treinen Moslen, *Toxic Response of the Liver, in* TOXICOLOGY 403 (Curtis D. Klaassen et al. eds., 1996).

of chemicals on biological organisms, the similarities between humans and other animals are far greater than the differences. For this reason, studying the effects of toxic chemicals in laboratory animals provides valuable knowledge about the effects those same chemicals are likely to cause in humans. (This is described in more detail below in the section on Extrapolation.) The ability to predict and prevent problems due to chemicals in humans, and in animals including household pets, is almost totally dependent upon science developed through the study of the effects of toxic chemicals in laboratory animals.

§ 8–2.1.2 Life Cycle of a Chemical in the Human Body

There are four processes that describe the life cycle of an external chemical or physical agent that enter the body: absorption, distribution, metabolism and excretion.[13] These are described below.

[1] Absorption

Absorption is simply the uptake of an external agent into the body. There are three major routes of entry: by ingestion, by inhalation, and across the skin. Each portal has special anatomical and physiological features that can alter the rate of uptake and impact of exposure to a chemical or physical agent. For example, small particles of compounds such as lead and other metals are readily adsorbed into the body when inhaled but much less so when ingested. Due to the aerodynamics of the upper respiratory tract, larger particles tend to be less of a problem than smaller particles as larger particles are intercepted in the nose or upper airways and diverted through swallowing into the digestive tract where they tend to be evacuated rather than absorbed. Thus, knowledge about the impact of airborne particles on sensitive portions of the deep lung is dependent upon understanding the size characteristics as well as the inherent chemical composition of the particles.

Absorption can also be considered as the process by which external exposure is converted to an internal dose. Dose is conditioned by rate of uptake of the external contaminant. For example, children breathe more per unit body weight than do adults and are therefore more at risk than an adult when exposed to the same external concentration of an air pollutant over time. Similarly, an individual will get a larger dose of an air pollutant while exercising, and the dose of a water pollutant will be dependent on the amount ingested by that individual. The term bioavailability is often used to describe the amount of an agent that becomes available for biological effects rather than simply passing in and out of the body. Sometimes this depends upon the matrix materials enclosing the agent. For example, more than half of the dioxin was bioavailable when contaminated soil from Times Beach, Missouri, was fed to laboratory animals, while in contrast the bioavailability of dioxin in the contaminated soil of Newark, New Jersey was many hundred-fold less.[14]

---

13. Gallo et al., *supra* note 3, at 43; Karl K. Rozman & Curtis D. Klaassen, *Absorption, Distribution and Excretion of Toxicants, in* TOXICOLOGY, 91 (Curtis D. Klaassen et al. eds., 1996).

14. Thomas Umbreit et al., *Bioavailability of Dioxin in Soil From A 2, 4, 5–T Manufacturing Site*, 232 SCI. 497 (1986).

When considering absorption a key point is that an external toxicant can enter through more than one portal. For example, to calculate the uptake of a chlorinated compound of a swimmer in a pool treated with chlorine it is necessary to know not only the concentration of the compound in the water, but also to calculate the amount of water that will be ingested during swimming, the amount of chlorine that will be inhaled (based on the swimmer's inhalation rate in relation to the expected airborne concentration due to offgassing from water), and the amount that will be taken into the body across the skin.

[2] Distribution

Distribution of a chemical within the body will depend in part upon the route of absorption. For example, ingested agents absorbed in the upper gastrointestinal tract go directly to the liver, the major metabolic organ in the body, while compounds absorbed through the lungs or skin enter the blood circulation before reaching the liver. Distribution also depends upon the physicochemical status of the parent compound or its metabolites. For example, the extent of solubility in water or in fat will determine entry and storage within body compartments; ionic charge can greatly affect the ability of the compound to pass the blood-brain barrier into the central nervous system or to be distributed across other membrane barriers. Organ specific factors can have a major effect on distribution. An example cited above is the specific iodine pump which actively removes iodine from the blood into the thyroid gland.

[3] Metabolism

Understanding metabolism is central to the science of toxicology.[15] At times the term is used to indicate all four phases of absorption, distribution, metabolism and excretion. More specifically, metabolism refers to the alteration of the chemical or physical status of the exogenous agent by the body. As a simplification, metabolism can be considered as having been developed through evolution to transform unwanted exogenous agents into less toxic chemicals that are also more readily excreted—for example fat soluble agents can be changed chemically to facilitate excretion in the bile or can be made sufficiently water soluble to be released into the urine.

However, for many chemicals, metabolism converts relatively benign species into toxic agents. Many human carcinogens are classified as "indirect" carcinogens as they themselves are harmless until being transformed by metabolic processes into cancer-causing agents. A variety of reasons can be advanced for this seeming counter-evolutionary process: metabolism may detoxify the agent in terms of acute effects, but in a way that may lead to chronic toxicity; the cancer or other delayed endpoint may not be of evolutionary concern in that it will occur after the usual time of reproductive activity; and the chemical of concern may have been developed too recently to have had any evolutionary impact.

15. Andrew Parkinson, *Biotransformation*   Klaassen et al. eds., 1996). *of Xenobiotics, in* TOXICOLOGY, 113 (Curtis D.

Metabolic capacity appears to be distributed in all organs of the body, although the liver is the primary organ of metabolism for most agents. Organ specificity for toxicity is often related to specificity of metabolic processes within the organ. In recent years there have been spectacular advances in the understanding of the basic biochemical and molecular processes responsible for metabolism of foreign compounds. Various enzymes and enzyme families active in metabolism and detoxification have been identified, and the distribution of these enzymes within cells appears to be of particular importance in understanding why certain tissues are at risk from certain chemicals. Of particular interest has been the cytochrome P–450 family of metabolically active enzymes which appear to be responsible for the first phase of metabolic detoxification or activation of many different types of exogenous chemicals. This group of enzymes is particularly abundant in the liver, partially accounting for that organ's predominant role in metabolism. However, cytochrome P–450 enzymes are widely distributed through the body. Different cells and organs tending to have different patterns of cytochrome P–450 subtypes, accounting in part for the organ specificity of the toxicity of certain chemicals.

[4] Excretion

Excretion from the body can occur through a variety of different routes, primarily the gastrointestinal tract for unabsorbed agents and for compounds excreted in bile, and the urine for water soluble agents of appropriate molecular weight and ionic charge. Significant loss of volatile compounds can occur through the respiratory tract. For example, about 50 percent of an internal benzene dose is exhaled unmetabolized. Other routes of excretion include sweat and lactation, the latter unfortunately putting the infant at risk. Different compounds are excreted, metabolized or unmetabolized, at different rates. There is particular concern about chemicals that persist, or bioaccumulate, in the human body or the general environment.

§ 8–2.1.3 Organ Systems

Each organ of the body can be exposed to external chemical agents or their metabolites. Each organ has the potential to play a role in the metabolism or distribution of specific chemicals, but not all chemicals. Certain organs can store specific agents. Others metabolize them. Of importance, each organ can be the target of a specific chemical or its metabolites and the outcome can be altered based upon specific organ function. There is insufficient space in this chapter to describe how each organ responds to chemical and physical agents. Described below are three of the patterns of response that generally apply to all organs: cell death, carcinogenicity and fibrosis.

[1] Cell Death

Most cells in the body are programmed to die and be replaced by newly formed cells. The turnover time between new cell formation and death can be just a few days in the case of certain while blood cells, a few months in the case of red blood cells, or, hopefully, a lifetime in the case of certain cells in our brain. Almost all toxic agents will kill specific cells at a high enough dose. Depending upon the time period the effect can be considered acute, subacute or chronic.

Cellular repair processes and rates also differ greatly among cell types. For example the normal human bone marrow can compensate for destruction of red blood cells in the circulation by producing these cells at up to six times the normal rate, while there is little or no replacement of adult nerve cells.

These different rates of cell turnover and cell repair mean that the toxicological implications of cell death will differ greatly depending upon the cell type and organ system involved, and upon whether the toxic agent impairs cellular repair processes. For each organ there will also be different levels of redundancy and functional reserve. Thus there are differing levels of cell death that can be tolerated without an overt loss in organ function.

[2] Carcinogenicity

Carcinogenicity is the process leading to the development of human cancer. Cancer is not a single disease. The term covers a multiplicity of types of tumors, mechanisms of tumor formation and, most importantly, clinical outcome. There is about as much relation between different cancers as there is between different viral diseases, yet for some reason the government and the public are much more ready to link together all cancers in our vital statistics, or develop all-encompassing organizations such as the American Cancer Society. The term malignant tumor generally refers to those cancers that spread rapidly through the body, usually through distant metastases, while benign tumors are ones that grow slowly and locally. A slowly growing localized tumor can be fatal if it is present in a vital organ such as the brain.

Contrary to public understanding, most malignant cells appear to divide more slowly than do noncancerous cells. Unfortunately, they do not go through the normal maturation process known as cell differentiation, which eventually leads to the death of the cell. In the usual cell differentiation process, immature progenitor cells divide into two, one remaining as a progenitor cell for future cell generations while the second goes through a maturation process relevant to the function of the tissue, and then dies. Central to most cancers is an increase in the number of progenitor cells due to a failure of normal maturation. The cellular differentiation process is under complex genetic regulation that is now being unraveled by molecular biologists, including the finding of mutations in key cellular growth regulators of differentiation that underlie certain cancers.[16]

Deciding whether a specific chemical or defined chemical mixture is in fact capable of causing human cancer is often highly controversial. Because of the focus that has been placed on the possibility that chemicals cause cancer, there has been much attention to the methodology used to identify carcinogens. Decisions as to carcinogenesis potential are often made by a "weight-of-evidence" approach in which an expert panel judges the available epidemiologic and toxicological information, including mechanistic findings that are pertinent to the scientific plausibility and consistency of the observed cancer findings in laboratory animals and humans. Different classification schemes are in use by such organizations as the International Agency for Research on Cancer and the U.S. Environmental Protection Agency.[17] They tend to use

---

16. Monica Hollstein et al., *Mutations in Human Cancers*, 253 SCI. 49 (1991).

17. Guidelines for Carcinogen Risk Assessment, 51 Fed. Reg. 32,992 (1986); INT'L AGENCY

epidemiologic data to assign chemicals or defined mixtures to the classification of a known human carcinogen, and toxicological information to assign other classifications, such as possible or probable human carcinogens. However, hybrid approaches have been developed in which toxicological mechanistic information is used to supplement epidemiologic data to establish a classification of known human carcinogen.

[3]　Fibrosis: An Example of a Chronic Disease Process

Fibrosis is the laying down of fibers outside of cells. Scarring is an overtly manifest form of fibrosis. Fibrosis is a normal healing event of importance in such processes as the closure of wounds. Repetitive damage to an organ, such as occurs in an alcoholic with liver disease, leads to an increase in fibrosis that now becomes central to the disease process.

Fibrosis is a process common to chronic diseases in many organs. It results in replacement of normal cells and a loss of tissue resiliency and of intercellular communication. Examples include asbestosis of the lung and cirrhosis of the liver. Fibrosis has also been suggested to be important in the process by which silicone implants are alleged to cause disease.[18]

Fibrosis is just one example of an appropriate acute response to a toxic agent which is itself injurious when prolonged. For example, mucous production by the airways is a desirable response to inhalation of an irritant gas or particle in that it helps protect sensitive airway cells from the consequences of the irritant. Not surprisingly, there is an increase in the number of mucous secreting cells in the airway lining following an acute irritant exposure. Yet increased production of mucous is part of the pathological process leading to chronic bronchitis.

§ 8–2.1.4　Susceptibility

Basic to much toxic tort activity is that the response to the ancient human question of "Why me?" is to search for some external cause to blame. Exposure is only one determinant of environmentally caused disease—otherwise all pack-a-day cigarette smokers would get lung cancer at exactly the same age. Understanding why one individual and not another has an adverse endpoint also is of particular concern to the science of toxicology.[19] Differences in individual susceptibility are often due to differences in absorption, distribution, metabolism and excretion.

Different rates of absorption are often a reason for differences in susceptibility when exposures are similar. The higher respiratory rate of children relative to their size accounts for the all too frequent tragedy of the snowbound family car being found with the motor running, the parents uncon-

FOR RESEARCH ON CANCER (IARC), MONOGRAPH EVALUATING CARCINOGENIC RISK TO HUMANS 237 (1992).

18. Alan J. Bridges & Frank B. Vasey, *Silicone Breast Implants: History, Safety and Potential Complications*, 153 ARCH. INTERN MED. 2638 (1993); N.R. Moore et al., *Axillary Fibrosis or Recurrent Tumor; An MRI Study in Breast Cancer*, 42 CLINICAL RADIOLOGY 42 (1990).

19. *Susceptibility to Environmental Hazards*, 105 ENVTL. HEALTH PERSP. 4 (J.C. Barrett & H. Vainio eds., 1997); Philippe Grandjean, *Individual Susceptibility in Occupational and Environmental Toxicology*, 77 TOXICOLOGY LETTERS 105 (1995).

scious, but the children dead from carbon monoxide exposure.[20] Iron deficiency, which is particularly common in disadvantaged children, increases the rate of absorption of ingested lead. This is because lead and iron share a common absorption pathway in the gut and, in the absence of iron, it is more likely that lead will be absorbed. Distribution of an absorbed compound to a target organ may be altered by body acidity or hydration. It can also be affected by the presence of dietary background levels of an agent. For example, the relatively low levels of iodine in the diet of Central Ukraine and Russia led to a higher uptake into the thyroid of radioactive iodine released by the Chernobyl disaster and hence a larger radioactive dose to this organ.

Not all chemicals are metabolized at the same rate by all people. A number of factors can affect the rate of metabolism. These may genetically or environmentally determine differences in a basic enzymatic process common to the metabolism of a wide range of agents. Genetically determined processes may differ among racial and ethnic groups. For example, alcohol tends to be poorly metabolized by native Americans. Advanced modern tools of molecular toxicology and genetics are beginning to provide new insights into the causes of individual susceptibility, with potentially major implications to interpreting causality in tort suits. An example is a report of more than a seven-fold increase in benzene toxicity in workers who had both higher rates of metabolism of benzene to toxic intermediates and lower rates of detoxification of these intermediates through further metabolism. Workers who had only one of these two genetic polymorphisms had about a doubling of risk.[21]

Some metabolic processes are age or gender dependent, often due to differences in hormone levels. Environmental influences can have a major impact on altering the rate of metabolism of exogenous chemicals. This includes common dietary factors which affect the activity of specific cytochrome P–450 dependent pathways. Environmental toxins, such as alcohol, may impact these pathways leading to changes in metabolism and toxicity of another environmental agent. For example, in laboratory animals, alcohol in drinking water induces the activity of the cytochrome P–450 responsible for benzene metabolism, thereby increasing the rate of metabolism and the toxicity of benzene. Changes in susceptibility may also reflect the pattern of earlier exposure to the same chemical. For example, a chemical may induce its own metabolism so that preexposure to low levels of a chemical may protect against the acute toxicity of a higher level.

Susceptibility may also reflect differences in the response of the target organ to a compound or its metabolite. For example, asthmatics are more likely to suffer constriction of their airways when exposed to sulfur dioxide than are normal individuals. Genetic factors can be major determinants in susceptibility of specific organ systems. Inherited alterations in red blood cell structure and function are known to cause alterations in susceptibility of this cell to situations as varied as high altitude, treatment with certain drugs and infection by the malaria parasite.

20. L.M. Plunkett et al., *Differences Between Adults and Children Affecting Exposure Assessment, in* SIMILARITIES AND DIFFERENCES BETWEEN CHILDREN AND ADULTS, IMPLICATIONS FOR RISK ASSESSMENT? (Phillip Guzelian et al. eds., 1992).

21. Nathaniel Rothman et al., *Benzene Poisoning, a Risk Factor for Hematological Malignancy, Is Associated with the NQ01* [609]*C->T Mutation and Rapid Fractional Excretion of Chlorzoxazone,* 57 CANCER RES. 2839 (1997).

Susceptibility must also be considered in the context of existing organ reserve and of desired function. A given level of a lung toxin may have no more effect in terms of absolute loss of lung function in an elderly as compared to a healthy young individual—yet the impact on the elderly individual may be devastating due to the lack of any reserve. However, should the young individual be someone making a living as a professional athlete, the otherwise minimal loss in pulmonary reserve could be of great significance. Despite these many examples in which the basis for susceptibility is understood, in the overwhelming majority of instances we do not know why people suffer from diseases at specific times. The unraveling of the human genome promises to greatly expand our knowledge of the genetic basis of susceptibility. Yet this is likely to provide information only about what is necessary but not sufficient for the development of disease, the sufficiency factor being provided by complex environmental interactions.

§ 8–2.1.5 Extrapolation

In considering causation it is often necessary to extrapolate from nonhuman systems to humans or from high doses to lower doses. Accordingly, the methods used for extrapolation are an appropriate subject for consideration in assessing the basis for a toxicologist's interpretation of causation.

How to extrapolate from animals to humans is a central question in toxicology. There is a commonality to biological processes that is certainly evident among mammals in whom organ structure and function tends to be very similar across species. This allows some degree of confidence in extrapolating from other mammalian species to humans. There are of course specific cases in which substantial differences between species do occur. For example, rats do not have gall bladders, nor is the human ability to sustain higher brain function observed in any other species. These differences must be taken into account in making informed judgments about extrapolating from animals to humans.

For regulatory purposes, toxicologists have traditionally used "factors of ten" to extrapolate from findings in laboratory animals to derive a protective regulatory standard. For example, after determining the dose that causes lethality in ten percent of exposed mice, the toxicologist might decrease this concentration by a factor of ten in case humans are more sensitive than mice, another factor of ten to account for the greater variability in susceptibility of humans than laboratory mice (see below), and a further factor of ten as there are less onerous endpoints of concern than lethality. The result would be a regulatory standard one thousand fold lower than the level observed to kill 10% of exposed laboratory mice. More rigorous extrapolation techniques have generally supplanted this simplified approach, e.g. the benchmark dose, and standard setting is usually done by regulators who are not toxicologists. When there are sufficient data, such as for carbon monoxide and other primary air quality pollutants, the standard is set without recourse to factors of ten. However, the "factor of ten" approach was used in the recent Food Quality Protection Act which mandates an additional ten fold protection factor for pesticides to which children are exposed based upon evidence of increased childhood susceptibility to pesticides.[22]

22. NAT'L RESEARCH COUNCIL, PESTICIDES IN the Diets of Infants and Children (1993); ROBERT J. Scheuplein, *The FQPA: A Challenge for Sci-* *ence Policy and Pesticide Regulation*, 31 REG. TOXICOLOGY & PHARMACOLOGY 248 (2000).

The process of extrapolation puts a premium on understanding the sources of variability. In some case, variability is due to inherent limitations of measurement tools—doing seemingly identical experiments twice will rarely lead to exactly the same numerical result. Usually this limitation can be addressed by improving the measurement tool or doing more frequent measurements thereby providing greater confidence in the results. In other cases variability is due to biological differences among individuals that are not eradicable.[23] This factor is of particular importance in terms of extrapolation from animals to humans. Laboratory animals used for toxicological testing are bred to be homogenous in terms of both genetic and environmental backgrounds. Typical experimental animals are inbred strains of mice or rats who are highly similar genetically and whose environment has been controlled since birth to the extent of sharing the same animal cages, food and lighting sequences. Accordingly, far less variability is expected in the response of laboratory animals than humans to toxic agents. Traditionally, toxicologists have used a tenfold "safety factor" to account for this greater human variability when extrapolating from laboratory animals to humans.

Three issues related to extrapolating from animals to humans deserve special mention: the reason why differences among species are so prominent in the toxicological literature; the difference between qualitative and quantitative extrapolation; and the special problem of cancer assays.

Species differences in the response to toxic agents are of particular interest to toxicologists. This is because they provide the opportunity to determine the mechanism by which a toxic agent produces its adverse effects. For example, the metabolism of benzene is required for its bone marrow toxicity, but which of the complex series of metabolic pathways and intermediates is responsible for this toxicity is unknown. The fact that mice are more sensitive to benzene toxicity than are rats provides an opportunity to test which of the pathways of benzene metabolism is involved in toxicity by comparing these pathways in the two species.[24] Another example is butadiene, a common industrial chemical which at very low doses is carcinogenic to mice but not to rats. There is much interest in determining the metabolic basis for this difference and using this insight to determine whether humans are more like mice or more like rats so as to understand our risk to butadiene exposure.[25] Accordingly, toxicologists search for differences among species in metabolism or toxicity so as to isolate and establish the mechanism of toxicity, which is helpful to extrapolate from animals to humans. This search means that the toxicological literature will focus on the relatively few differences among species, rather than the overwhelmingly high number of similarities. Part of the expertise of a toxicologist is making an informed choice of which strain of animal to use in an experiment. For safety assessment purposes this usually means an animal that is most similar to humans, but this need not be

23. Adam Finkel, *Toward Less Misleading Comparisons of Uncertain Risks: The Example of Aflatoxin and Alar,* 103 ENVTL. HEALTH PERSP. 376 (1995).

24. Robert Snyder, *Recent Developments in the Understanding of Benzene Toxicity and*

Leukemogenesis, 23 DRUG & CHEMICAL TOXICOLOGY 13 (2000).

25. Parkinson, *supra* note 15.

the case when the goal is to understand the mechanism of action of the toxic agent.

Extrapolation from high to low dose also presents a number of issues. Most of our knowledge about the adverse effects of chemicals is derived from observations at higher than usual environmental doses, either in laboratory animals or in humans exposed at the workplace. Accordingly, choosing the appropriate dose-response curve is of importance. At times, animals are selectively bred for sensitivity to a chemical.[26] Justifying the choice of the dose response curve is often based upon judgments concerning the mechanism of toxicity. Extrapolation can be done with greater certainty the more information there is about toxicity at different doses. (See additional discussion of this point, infra, § 34–2.6).

The information needed for extrapolation from animals to humans is different if the question being asked has to do with qualitative rather than quantitative issues. With few exceptions, a chemical compound that can produce damage in a specific organ in one mammalian species can do so in humans, as long as the dose is sufficiently high. However, there are many reasons why the dose required for a specific level of damage will differ among species. Accordingly, findings of specific adverse endpoints in laboratory animals are very useful guides for hazard identification, but are best interpreted on the basis of known differences in human physiology and metabolism when being used for dose-response extrapolation. In recent years the use of mathematical models to depict the kinetics of the movement of toxic chemicals within a given species, often known as physiologically based pharmacokinetics, has been of great help in extrapolating from animals to humans or in exploring the reason for differences among laboratory animals. (See infra, § 34–2.6).

The statement above that animal studies are particularly reliable in identifying hazards to humans has been questioned by some scientists in the case of cancer. Their concern for the most part is based upon the hypothesis that the usual approach to performing animal cancer studies falsely identifies compounds as being carcinogens. The critics emphasize that at the usual relatively high dose employed in standard multiyear rat or mice studies there may be increased cell turnover or other unusual physiological occurrences that lead to cancer in the tested animals but that would not occur at lower doses.[27] Briefly stated, the standard approach chooses a maximum tolerated dose (MTD) based on a 90 day study, evaluating evidence of toxicity such as weight loss and animal death, which is then used in the multiyear cancer study.

The rationale supporting the use of this high dose primarily is that if usual environmental exposure levels were used in these animal studies, which rarely test more than a 100 mice or rats, it would be impossible to detect a true carcinogen that produced an increased risk of cancer of one in one

26. Richard A. Deitrich, *Selective Breeding for Ethanol Sensitivity*, in Crisp Data Base National Institutes of Health (1994).

27. Bruce N. Ames & Lois S. Gold, Too Many Rodent Carcinogens: Mitogenesis Increases Mutagenesis (1990); Philip H. Ableson, *Incorpo-*ration of a New Science into Risk Assessment, 250 Sci. 1497 (1990); John c. Bailar III et al., *One-hit Models of Carcinogenesis: Conservative or Not?*, 8 Risk Analysis 485 (1988); Jean Marx, *Animal Carcinogen Testing Challenged*, 250 Sci. 743 (1990).

hundred as that would be in the range of normal statistical variation. Yet current regulatory approaches often require protection against cancer risks as low as 1/100,000 or even 1/1,000,000. By using higher doses, and by assuming a linear dose-response curve, far fewer animals can be tested. A review of this issue by a panel of the National Academy of Sciences led to a vote in favor of retaining the MTD, although a recognition by many on the Committee of its potential pitfalls.[28]

The extrapolation processes used in regulatory toxicology tend to be conservative in that uncertainty is usually resolved in favor of prudence. This is not unreasonable, given the public health population basis of our environmental laws. But, inherent in a conservative approach to populations is the likelihood that there is an overestimate of risk to the average individual. Exceeding a numerical pollutant standard aimed at ensuring the safety of all does not necessarily mean that the exposed individual is likely to have an adverse impact. This is an important distinction when considering the use of regulatory public health standards for toxic tort cases.

§ 8–2.2 Causation in Toxicology

Consideration of the cause of an adverse endpoint by a chemical or physical agent must take all available evidence into account not just that provided by a single discipline. In toxic tort cases there are two different causation questions that may be asked of a toxicologist. The "general causation" generic question, that of whether a specific chemical or mixture is inherently capable of causing the adverse endpoint at issue, is certainly within the province of a toxicologist. The "specific causation" question—i.e. whether the putative exposure caused the adverse endpoint in a specific individual—may or may not benefit from the expertise of a toxicologist. This will depend upon whether there are questions involving exposure, dose-response, or other matters encompassed within the science of toxicology.

In establishing whether a specific agent is capable of causing a specific disease, classic toxicology has the advantage over epidemiology of being able to carefully control exposure to the compound of concern at a known dose or series of doses to a known population, usually of laboratory animals. Epidemiology has the primary advantage of being the direct study of humans in the community or in the workplace. But determination of actual exposure to a chemical presents difficulties as does providing a scientifically valid control group.

In the context of toxic tort litigation, some courts have focused solely on epidemiological evidence and eschewed toxicological evidence entirely. These courts assume that toxicological data must be unreliable because it was derived by extrapolation from animals to humans and from high to low doses. This suggests that toxicology has not been adequately explained or understood.

A qualified toxicologist should be able to explain to a court's satisfaction why toxicological data indicative (or contra-indicative) of causation are reliable. With respect to an issue of general causation, a toxicologist serving as an

---

28. NAT'L RESEARCH COUNCIL, *Use of the Maximum Tolerated Dose in Animal Bioassays for* *Carcinogenicity, in* ISSUES IN RISK ASSESSMENT 15 (1993).

expert witness should be prepared to explain why the particular strain of test animal is an appropriate model for extrapolation to humans in light of the particular chemical agent and the particular endpoint involved. This might include an explanation of the known similarities of differences between humans and the test animal in terms of the relevant organ system or metabolic processes. The toxicologist-expert witness should also be prepared to explain why the extrapolation from high dose to low dose is appropriate in the circumstances presented. This would typically include an explanation of what is known or assumed by toxicological science about the dose-response relationship for the chemical agent and the endpoint involved, including the dose-response curve and the no-observed-effect threshold, if any.

The reliance in some courts on published epidemiological evidence of 2.0 between a cause and an effect as requirement for a case to go forward is just one example of judicial over-reliance on epidemiology. Suppose there is statistically significant evidence of a 50% increase (relative risk = 1.5) in the incidence of an endpoint in a population exposed to ten times the background dose of a chemical. It would be entirely reasonable for an expert toxicologist to conclude that more than a doubling of risk occurred in an individual plaintiff who was exposed to more than 20 times the background dose, superficially making it more likely than not that the chemical caused the endpoint of concern.

The basic tool of the toxicologist is the standard scientific approach of keeping every factor constant except one, thereby relating any measured perturbation to the one variable factor, usually the dose of the chemical. Use of controls not subject to the variable is crucial to concluding that the observed change in the exposed group is causally related to the exposure. Thus a toxicologist will expose half of a group of genetically similar animal litter mates, assigned to the control or exposed groups through a random process, and will assume that the exposure condition is the cause of any differences observed between the exposed and the control. The animal can also serve as its own control, i.e., the experimenter will evaluate the same system before and after the exposure. In assessing causality, toxicologists are much more impressed with data that fulfills dose response expectations. Good toxicological studies use more than one dose and, although there are exceptions, it is difficult to accept a causal relationship if the extent of the effect is not directly related to the level of the dose.

Animal toxicology studies also provide the very valuable opportunity to obtain tissue from organs not ethically accessible from humans. *In vitro* (test tube) studies can also be of value in assessing chemicals and in providing information about cellular and subcellular mechanisms. But there are many pitfalls in attempting to extrapolate from *in vitro* systems to human exposure.[29]

There are also toxicological data derived directly from humans. Toxicological studies in humans assessing agents other than those intended for human ingestion are rarely ethically appropriate. There are exceptions. Human volunteers have been intentionally exposed under carefully controlled conditions to levels of air pollutants that are otherwise likely to be encountered on

29. *In Vitro* Methods in Toxicology (Chris K. Atterwill & C.E. Steele eds., 1987); *In Vitro* Toxicity Testing: Applications to Safety Evaluation (John M. Frazier ed., 1992).

a smoggy day. Measurement of acute changes in pulmonary function as a result of such exposure has been a very valuable approach to understanding the potential adverse effects of ozone and of other air pollutants, and has been used as a basis for setting environmental standards.

§ 8–2.3 Recognition of Expertise in Toxicology

There are a variety of mechanisms by which one establishes credentials in toxicology. As with any other scientific discipline, there is also a wide range of actual expertise among those who possess one or more of these credentials. As environmental toxicology has only recently emerged as an independent scientific discipline, it is more likely that senior toxicologists have entered the field laterally.

The oldest active organization of toxicologists is that of the Society of Toxicology (SOT), which includes individuals working for industry, government and academia. It is active as a representative of the field of toxicology on the national and international levels. Membership is not automatic. It requires evidence of involvement in the field, including scientific publications and, with rare exceptions, a doctoral degree in an appropriate field. While there are now many active doctoral degree programs in toxicology, this is a relatively new phenomenon. It is likely that the majority of SOT members have a degree in a field other than toxicology, such as pharmacology, medicine or other life sciences. SOT has a variety of subgroups organized by subspecialty (e.g., inhalation toxicology) or by geographical area. Membership in a subgroup has no additional pre-requisite except payment of additional dues, but it can be assumed to indicate evidence of particular activity or interest.

The American College of Toxicology (ACT) is a newer organization of toxicologists for which research activity in the field and payment of dues are the major criteria for membership. It does award fellowship status based upon criteria indicative of productivity and peer recognition.

The American Board of Toxicology provides a relatively rigorous examination that is usually taken by those in the field who work for government, industry or as private consultants. Academics appear to be less likely to sit for this examination as it is not of any particular value for advancement in their profession. Information about board status, including failure to pass the Board, or to be allowed to sit for the Board because of insufficient credentials, should be routinely obtained from any expert in a toxic tort case.

The rapid emergence of environmental issues as central to governmental activities has provided many opportunities for toxicologists to serve on local, national and international advisory bodies. Being asked to serve on such bodies can be taken as evidence of peer recognition for expertise. In the United States, the National Academies of Sciences have been particularly active in providing expert panels to deliberate on the scientific basis for environmental regulation or other areas in which toxicological expertise is particularly needed. The US Environmental Protection Agency (EPA) has an active Scientific Advisory Board. Some advisory bodies, such as EPA's Clean Air Scientific Advisory Committee, are established by act of Congress.

In probing an expert who has served on such advisory committees, it should be kept in mind that certain individuals are chosen because they are known to represent identifiable points of view. The National Academies of Sciences and many other bodies strive for a balance of viewpoints on their committees. Accordingly, there will often be a committee member chosen to represent industry balanced by a member chosen to represent the viewpoint of environmentalists or of labor unions. Being chosen on the basis of balance is still very much an indication of peer recognition for expertise, but it also indicates that your point of view may not be representative of the entire scientific community.

Academic toxicologists publish in a wide variety of journals often reflecting the methodology of their non-toxicologist peers, e.g. molecular biology, cell biology, or of their related disciplines, e.g., medicine, pharmacology. There are a number of very good to excellent journals that focus on toxicology. These include *Journal of Toxicology and Environmental Health; Toxicology and Applied Pharmacology; Annual Review of Pharmacology and Toxicology; Toxicological Sciences; Inhalation Toxicology; Biochemical Pharmacology; Toxicology Letters;* and *Environmental Health Perspectives.* Other journals which are frequently read by toxicologists or have a reasonably good content of toxicology articles are *Science; British Journal of Industrial Medicine; Archives of Environmental Health; Journal of Occupational Medicine; Teratogenesis, Carcinogenesis and Mutagenesis; Environmental Research; Journal of Reproductive Toxicology;* and *American Journal of Industrial Medicine.*

§ 8–2.4   The Use of Toxicology in the Safety Assessment of Chemicals

Safety assessment of chemicals is a relatively standardized approach to the testing of chemical agents for adverse biological effects. As is clear from the first law of toxicology, the dose makes the poison, all chemical agents have toxic effects at some dose levels. The question addressed in safety assessment is what specific effect at what dose. Certain standard approaches, such as determining the dose that kills half of a group of laboratory animals, have gradually gone out of favor partly due to the development of more sophisticated approaches and partly due to the pressure of animal rights activists which has led to a careful reappraisal of the use of animals in safety testing.

There are routine protocols for the battery of toxicological tests that are used in safety assessment. In many cases test procedures are being specified by government agencies. Procedural matters include the selection and handling of laboratory animals, the number of animals per cage, their diet, the statistical procedures to be used, etc. These often go under the heading of Good Laboratory Practices (GLP). Adherence to GLP in routine safety assessment is the norm and is subject to examination in litigation.[30]

Major chemical companies routinely perform toxicological tests very early in the development of new chemicals. In general, there are dozens of chemicals that are explored for possible marketing for every chemical that is developed for the market. It is in the best interest of the chemical company to screen out early in the process those chemicals that will eventually not pass

---

30. S.K. Keener & B. Kristin Hoover, *Good Laboratory Practices: A Comparison of the Regulations,* 4 J. Am. C. Toxicology 339 (1985); Paul D. Lepore, *Good Laboratory Practice Regulations for Nonclinical Laboratory Compliance: A Rededication to Effective Quality Assurance,* 5 J. Am. C. Toxicology 289 (1986); Anonymous, *Good Laboratory Practices Manual, in* Government Reports Announcements and Index 14 (1982).

the hurdle of full toxicological safety assessment. Relatively less expensive and less complex toxicological screening assays, such as the Ames bacterial assay for mutagenesis, are used early in the development of a new commercial chemical, with more expensive assays, such as two year animal assays, coming in later if warranted.

Governmental rules for information needed prior to marketing of a new chemical differ around the world. In the United States, the regulatory tools available to EPA under the Toxic Substances Control Act (TSCA) for non-pharmaceutical force a focus on structure activity relationships (SAR), the linkage of chemical structure to biological effect. Thus the manufacture supplies EPA with the chemical formula and a minimal amount of other information and it is up to EPA to require additional information, if warranted, including toxicological studies, before allowing the agent to be marketed. The legislative logic underlying TSCA clearly recognizes a need to balance the value of chemicals to society with their potential for adverse consequences.

The U.S. approach, which requires less routine toxicological information than in Europe, places much stress on understanding the relation between chemical structure and adverse effects. Historically, SAR has shown itself to be a very effective tool in certain instances, but not in others. Straight chain hydrocarbon components of gasoline have an anesthetic-like effect at high concentrations such that the effect of any particular length of the carbon chain is readily predictable from knowledge of the effect of the others. However, it is only the six carbon structure, n-hexane, which causes damage to peripheral nerves. Similarly, the anesthetic like effect of benzene and alkyl benzenes (e.g., toluene, ethylbenzene, xylenes) is also readily predictable by SAR, but only benzene produces bone marrow toxicity and acute leukemia in humans. In both cases, metabolites are responsible for the toxicity observed. Although a useful and improving technique, SAR has the pitfall of the exquisite sensitivity of certain biological processes to relatively minuscule changes in chemical structure.[31]

§ 8–2.5 Toxicological Evidence of Effects in Individual Cases

Toxicologists are asked two different questions about causation. One is the generic question of whether a chemical can cause a specific adverse event. The second is the more specific question as to whether in a particular individual the chemical exposure led to the adverse event. It is important that these two issues not be confused. The question of whether benzene causes multiple myeloma is a very different question than whether or not a specific exposure to benzene resulted to multiple myeloma in a specific case.[32] In toxic tort cases, it is not uncommon that the major part of the argument will be whether a specific chemical can have a specific adverse effect. This can obfuscate the issue of whether there was sufficient exposure to make it more likely than not that the effect was caused by the chemical in question. For the

31. Herbert Rosenkranz & G. Klopman, *Structure–Activity Relationships as Alternatives in the Study of Carcinogenesis,* in 11 ALTERNATIVE METHODS IN TOXICOLOGY AND THE LIFE SCI. 379 (Alan M. Goldberg & L.F.M. Van Zutphon eds., 1994).

32. Bernard Goldstein, *Is Exposure to Benzene a Cause of Human Multiple Myeloma?,* 609 ANNALS N.Y. ACAD. SCI. 225 (1990).

second question, an expert judgment must also take into account the extent of exposure and the specific medical findings in the individual.

§ 8–2.5.1 Exposure History

A basic tenet of environmental health risk is that without exposure there is no possibility of adverse consequences. That the dose makes the poison is central to toxicology and a toxicologist is certainly qualified to interpret dose response relationships. Further, a toxicologist should be capable of relating exposure to dose, exposure usually being considered in terms of the concentration of an agent in the external environment while dose is that which gets into the body or is present at a specific tissue location. However the extent to which the toxicologist is qualified to speak about the assessment of exposure is not always straightforward. In general, toxicologists have expertise about exposure or dose that is based primarily on biological data. For example, measurement of the level of carbon monoxide bound to human hemoglobin provides an integrated measure of carbon monoxide exposure during the previous 8–12 hours, and measurement of urinary arsenic is a good indicator of total arsenic body burden. The toxicologist should also be able to relate known external exposure levels to internal dose, for example using respiratory rate and body size to convert an airborne concentration of an agent to internal dose. However, determination of exposure to a chemical may require the assistance of industrial hygienists or experts in the relatively new field of environmental exposure assessment[33] if the environmental concentration is not known. For example, if an individual is known to use a certain amount of a solvent per day, estimating the concentration of that solvent in the air given the size of the room and air exchange rates would be beyond the expertise of the usual toxicologist.

§ 8–2.5.2 Medical Findings

In addition to a careful exploration of the extent of the exposure, three different approaches are used to assess individuals alleged to have been adversely affected by chemical or physical agents: the medical history, physical findings, and laboratory evaluation.

[1] History

The medical history is useful in assessing toxicological effects, despite there being much overlap of such effects with other medical conditions.[34] At times the reporting of symptoms can be diagnostic of the effects of a specific agent particularly when evaluating acute effects in the presence of a known exposure. However, acute exposure to many chemicals leads to a constellation of nonspecific symptoms including fatigue, headache, nausea and lightheadedness, that we all have experienced. Not only do such symptoms result from a broad variety of conditions, they are difficult to verify or to quantify beyond the patient's statement. Symptoms may be wrongly blamed on a chemical exposure or considered unimportant when in fact reflecting a significant

33. P.J. Lioy et al., *Exposure Analysis: Its Place in the 21st Century*, 8 J. EXPOSURE ANALYSIS & ENVTL. EPIDEMIOLOGY 279 (1998).

34. Arthur Frank, *The Environmental History, in* ENVIRONMENTAL MEDICINE (Stuart Brooks et al. eds., 1995).

problem. Symptoms can also be helpful as an indirect measure of dose for those chemicals for which there is good understanding of the linkage between dose and effects.

A medical history aimed at assessing causality of a human exposure to an adverse outcome will probe for other potential causes of the findings. For example, if the outcome is leukemia in an individual exposed to benzene, the history will search for other medical conditions associated with leukemia (e.g., Down's syndrome, previous treatment for Hodgkin's disease); for other external causes of leukemia (e.g., ionizing radiation); and for other sources of benzene exposure (e.g., cigarette smoke). These competing causes must be weighed in any credible assessment of the likelihood of causality. A competent, unbiased expert expressing opinions on causality will always obtain information related to significant competing causes of the same adverse endpoint.

A good medical history should also consider temporal relationships in probing for causality. Certain diseases, including many cancers, require a minimum latency period between the initial exposure and the onset of the cancer. For example, it is unreasonable to infer that a specific benzene exposure was responsible for a case of acute myelogenous leukemia that developed within a year. Even longer time periods, perhaps decades, are expected for tumors such as lung cancers to result from asbestos exposure. This is due to the fact that cancer almost always begins with a mutation in one cell and it takes many years for sufficient cancer cells to accumulate for the disease to become clinically apparent. In other situations, such as acute effects, the toxicological properties of the external agent often will determine the temporal relationship. For example, it is not unreasonable to complain of central nervous system effects, such as dizziness and nausea, from high concentrations of trichloroethylene during and immediately after an acute exposure. But as all traces of this agent are gone from the body within a few days at most, complaints of a persistent headache for many years are unreasonable. Other agents are known for delayed responses, usually because metabolism is required for toxicity to occur—for example, acute liver failure due to carbon tetrachloride. Sometimes the exposure pattern can give a clue toward assigning causality. At the workplace, Monday morning asthma is a frequently reported response consistent with the known dynamics of industrial chemicals capable of causing reactive airway disease.

The medical history should also explore whether there were other individuals in the same alleged exposure category and their reported effects, if any. The presence of others with similar exposure who either have or do not have the same medical findings can be of value in assessing causality. For example, in a crowded room into which a solvent is offgassed, it would be difficult to accept that only one individual had symptoms of dizziness or headache, unless some unique susceptibility could be demonstrated. Conversely, if almost everyone is overcome by the fumes, the causal relation to any one individual is far more likely. In issues of cancer causality occurring in large occupational cohorts, information about the overall risk of the particular cancer in the cohort can be very helpful. This would require an epidemiological study discussed in Chapter 35. It should be noted that when the cancer occurs in a small group, the subsequent finding of an additional cancer of the same type can be a point in favor of causality, while the absence of such a cancer has little meaning as the number of individuals allegedly at risk will usually be too small to carry any weight.

[2] Physical Findings

The physician's evaluation of physical findings is far less important than the medical history in all but a few instances. In comparison to issues involving trauma, few toxic tort cases will have the physical findings as central aspects of determining causation. Careful physical observation can be of value in assessing potential malingering.

[3] Laboratory Findings

Laboratory findings can be helpful in two ways. At one level they can establish a diagnosis that serves as the base for evaluating a causal effect. In certain situations the laboratory findings establish whether or not an adverse endpoint has in fact occurred. At another level they can help in assessing causality for a given diagnosis. For example, about half the individuals with newly diagnosed acute myelogenous leukemia are found to have overt blood cell chromosomal abnormalities. There is evidence that benzene causes human chromosomal abnormalities, that chromosomal abnormalities are a pathway to cancer, and that those leukemics who do have chromosomal abnormalities were more likely to have been exposed to chemicals such as benzene. Accordingly, the presence or absence of chromosomal abnormalities can be valuable in assessing the likelihood of causality in an individual with acute myelogenous leukemia who was exposed to benzene.[35]

It is often useful to obtain laboratory findings that occurred prior to the development of disease, and particularly prior to the exposure that was alleged to cause the disease. Preexisting abnormalities may turn up that obviate a causal relationship, or that indicate the presence of susceptibility thereby making the causal relationship more likely. Sometimes the extent of an exposure can be established retrospectively by demonstrating its subclinical impact as revealed in laboratory findings. For example, in a case of leukemia alleged to be due to benzene, significant exposure can be inferred by the finding of even mild degrees of blood cell abnormalities on a routine complete blood count.[36]

Finding this information may require careful questioning concerning past laboratory evaluations done as part of insurance examinations, routine preoperative or obstetrical care, preemployment examinations, and so on.

There are many limiting factors in the ability of the toxicologists to come to a conclusion in an individual toxic tort case. Very often there are two completely conflicting views presented of the extent of exposure, with the plaintiff claiming that he or she was practically swimming in the chemical and the defendant denying all but the most minuscule of exposures. The toxicologist is usually not an expert in the reconstruction of past exposure, often

35. Harvey M. Golomb et al., *Correlations of Occupation and Karyotype in Adults with Acute Non-lymphoctyic Leukemia*, 60 BLOOD 404 (1982).

36. Howard Kipen et al., *Use of Longitudinal Analysis of Peripheral Blood Counts to Validate Historical Reconstructions of Benzene Exposure*, 82 ENVTL. HEALTH PERSP. 109 (1989).

performed by an industrial hygienist or someone with that particular expertise. The toxicologist also is often limited by the non-specificity of the findings in an individual case. There are very few disorders for which there are not competing causes beyond that of chemical exposure. Mesothelioma due to asbestos is the very rare exception in which the endpoint is a sure indicator of the cause. For certain disorders there are a variety of biological markers, such as the blood lead level, which can be very valuable in establishing cause and effect relationship in a specific individual. For other disorders, the toxicologists will need to depend almost totally on the extent of exposure and the literature describing the likelihood of an adverse event for any given exposure in the context of the background incidence of the disorder.

§ 8–2.6 Risk Assessment

Toxicologists are becoming increasingly involved in the formal process of risk assessment. Risk assessment is a means to calculate the risk of an adverse event. The process was given a major impetus through a 1983 National Academy of Sciences report.[37] It is now in general use at many federal agencies, including EPA and FDA. Congressional legislation currently under consideration would require a formal risk assessment for environmental and other regulatory decisionmaking.

The risk assessment paradigm consists of four steps: 1) hazard identification, in essence based upon the specificity of toxicological effects described above; 2) dose response assessment relating the hazard to the extent of the adverse response; 3) exposure assessment, aimed at determining the extent of exposure to the toxic agent; and 4) risk characterization, which puts the other three steps together to generate a statement as to the risk.[38]

The dose response aspects of cancer risk assessment can be highly controversial, depending as they do upon the extrapolation issues described above. Making different assumptions about extrapolation from high to low doses or from animals to humans can lead to risks that differ by literally orders of magnitude.[39] In order to provide consistency and predictability to the process, EPA and other US Federal Agencies have developed guidelines that describe the specific steps to be taken in performing a risk assessment.[40] Recently, the risk characterization step has been extended to incorporate information as to the specific population at risk, the temporal frequency with which an adverse event might be expected in a given population, and to include non-health endpoints such as economic or cultural impacts.[41]

When dealing with cancer or other mutagenic endpoints, the risk characterization step has usually led to a numerical statement of risk in the form of a probability; e.g. 6.2×10^{-6}/lifetime, which translates to 6.2 chances in a

37. Nat'l Research Council, Risk Assessment in the Federal Government: Managing the Process (1983).

38. Id.

39. A. Cullen, *Measures of Compounding Conservatism in Probabilistic Risk Assessment*, 14 Risk Analysis 389 (1994); Bernard Goldstein, *Risk Assessment Methodology: Maximum Tolerated Dose and Two-stage Carcinogenesis Models*, 22 Toxicologic Pathology 194 (1994).

40. Dorothy Patton, *The NAS Paradigm as a Medium for Communication*, 14 Risk Analysis 375 (1994).

41. Bernard Goldstein, *The Who, What, When, Where, and Why of Risk Characterization*, 23 Pol'y Stud. J. 70 (1995); Edward V. Ohanian et al., *Risk Characterization: A Bridge to Informed Decision Making*, 39 Fundamental & Applied Toxicology 81 (1997).

million over a 70 year period of suffering the cancer due to a specified exposure. For non-mutagenic endpoints, such as kidney damage, risk assessment relies on variants of standard toxicological techniques to place "safety factors" on no observed effect levels (see above). There is some controversy as to what are appropriate factors to use and how to calculate these presumptively risk-free levels.

It must be emphasized that the use of such safety factors is prudent public health practice. The resultant number is most certainly not a guide to predict the level at which an individual will have an adverse effect. In fact, if safety factors are used as intended, it is very unlikely that an adverse consequence will occur in an individual whose exposure barely exceeds this regulatory number.

Societal pressure for protecting against risks as low as one adverse event per million people has been a major driving force in developing risk assessment. Accordingly, as used for regulatory purposes, risk assessment attempts to count the uncountable, i.e., it is aimed at estimating levels of risk below those that could be observed at realistic exposure concentrations using the best epidemiological or toxicological techniques available.[42] There has been substantial controversy inherent in risk extrapolation, particularly since there is concern that prudent approaches to each step in the risk assessment process compound the conservatism.[43]

In order to be predictable and comparable, risk assessment uses toxicological or epidemiological information in a consistent manner specified by guidelines. It is a regulatory tool aimed at giving guidance to decisionmakers and the public as to the potential for risk. While it is not designed to answer the question of what happened to a specific individual, it is being increasingly used by expert witnesses in toxic tort cases. This needs to be done with a full understanding that the primary goal of risk assessment is to help in population decision processes, not to assign blame in individual cases.

42. Robert C. Barnard, *Risk Assessment: The Default Conservatism Controversy*, 21 REG. TOXICOLOGY & PHARMACOLOGY 431 (1995); Bernard Goldstein, *Risk Assessment as an Indicator for Decision Making, in* RISKS, COSTS AND LIVES SAVED: GETTING BETTER RESULTS FROM REGULATION 67 (Robert W. Hahn ed., 1996).

43. Cullen, *supra* note 39; Goldstein, *supra* note 41; Y. Haimes et al., *Workshop Proceedings: When and How Can You Specify a Probability Distribution When You Don't Know Much*, 14 RISK ANALYSIS 661 (1994).

Index

References are to Sections, Segmented by Chapter

You might also consult this work's table of contents as a finding device. The table of contents lists every section included in the work and the page number where each topical section is to be found. This is most useful when you know within what chapter or for what subject heading you are searching. The summary of contents that precedes the table of contents may be similarly used.

†